1987

THE DOCUMENTARY HISTORY OF THE
RATIFICATION OF THE CONSTITUTION

VOLUME XVI

Commentaries on the Constitution
Public and Private

Volume 4

THE DOCUMENTARY HISTORY OF THE RATIFICATION OF THE CONSTITUTION

Volume XVI

Commentaries on the Constitution

Public and Private

Volume 4
1 February to 31 March 1788

Editors
JOHN P. KAMINSKI   GASPARE J. SALADINO

Associate Editor
RICHARD LEFFLER

Editorial Assistants
Charles D. Hagermann
Cynthia L. Hecht   Marybeth Carlson

MADISON
STATE HISTORICAL SOCIETY OF WISCONSIN
1 9 8 6

The Documentary History of the Ratification of the Constitution is sponsored by the National Historical Publications and Records Commission and the University of Wisconsin-Madison. Preparation of this volume was made possible by grants from the National Historical Publications and Records Commission; the Program for Editions of the National Endowment for the Humanities, an independent federal agency; the Oscar Rennebohm Foundation of Madison, Wisconsin; and from the E. Gordon Fox Fund, Madison, Wisconsin. Publication was made possible in part by a grant from the National Historical Publications and Records Commission.

Manufactured in the United States of America

LIBRARY OF CONGRESS CATALOGING IN PUBLICATION DATA [REVISED]
Main entry under title:
The Documentary history of the ratification
     of the Constitution.
          Editors for v. 16: John P. Kaminski, Gaspare J. Saladino.
          Includes indexes.
          CONTENTS: v. 1. Constitutional documents and records,
     1776–1789.–v. 2. Ratification of the Constitution by the
     States: Pennsylvania.–v. 3. Ratification of the Constitution by
     the States: Delaware, New Jersey, Georgia, Connecticut.–
     v. 13. Commentaries on the Constitution, public and private
     (1).–v. 14. Commentaries on the Constitution, public and
     private (2).–v. 15. Commentaries on the Constitution, public
     and private (3).–v. 16. Commentaries on the Constitution,
     public and private (4).
          1. United States–Constitutional history–Sources.
          I..Jensen, Merrill. II. Kaminski, John P. III. Saladino,
          Gaspare J.
     KF4502.D63   342'.73'029   75-14149
     ISBN 0-87020-245-6 (v. 1) 347.30229   AACR2

To
THE HONORABLE
WILLIAM J. BRENNAN, JR.
ASSOCIATE JUSTICE OF THE
SUPREME COURT OF THE UNITED STATES

Contents

Acknowledgments

The editing of this volume was primarily supported by grants from the National Historical Publications and Records Commission and the National Endowment for the Humanities. Substantial aid has also been received from the University of Wisconsin, The Oscar Rennebohm Foundation, and The E. Gordon Fox Fund, all in Madison. Special gratitude is owed to Mr. Frederick H. Campbell of Colorado Springs, Colorado, for his generous contributions to the project. We would also like to express our appreciation to Acting Archivist of the United States Frank G. Burke, formerly Executive Director of the NHPRC; Richard A. Jacobs, Roger A. Bruns, Mary A. Giunta, and Donald L. Singer of the NHPRC; Kathy Fuller of the NEH; and William H. Young of The Rennebohm Foundation.

The staff of the State Historical Society of Wisconsin, our primary research library and our publisher, continues to meet our many needs with a spirit of cooperation. In addition to those acknowledged in earlier volumes, we would like to thank John A. Peters and Herbert J. Tepper. The Memorial, Law, and Medical libraries of the University of Wisconsin-Madison have also been helpful, especially Arne J. Arneson of the Memorial Library and Dorothy V. Whitcomb of the Medical Library. Under the Chairmanship of Richard H. Sewell and his successor William J. Courtenay, the History Department of the University of Wisconsin-Madison has continued its support. Several colleagues on documentary histories have helped to locate documents or resolve editorial questions and have supplied useful biographical information. We thank John Catanzariti and Elizabeth M. Nuxoll of the Robert Morris Papers; Gordon DenBoer of The Documentary History of the First Federal Elections; Richard A. Ryerson and Celeste Walker of the Adams Papers; Richard K. Showman and Dennis M. Conrad of the Nathanael Greene Papers; and Dorothy Twohig of the George Washington Papers. Linda J. Pike, formerly of the Lafayette Papers, and Gail Walter assisted in translating some of the correspondence of French diplomats. Others who have provided assistance are Roland M. Baumann of the Pennsylvania Historical and Museum Commission; Ruth M. Blair of the Connecticut Historical Society; Bernard R. Crystal of Columbia University; Thomas J. Dunnings, Jr., of the New-York Historical Society; Margaret A. Fusco of the University of Chicago Library; Mary Ann Gunderson of the New Hampshire Historical

Society; Francis O. Mattson, John Rathé, and Robert Sink of the New York Public Library; Frank C. Mevers of the New Hampshire State Archives; Patricia Proscino of The Balch Institute for Ethnic Studies; Judith A. Schiff of Yale University; Saundra Taylor of The Lilly Library, Indiana University; and Lucille Wehner of The Newberry Library. Lastly, we thank the Massachusetts Historical Society, The Balch Institute for Ethnic Studies, the University of Chicago Library, and The Lilly Library for permission to publish restricted documents from their collections.

This volume is dedicated to the Honorable William J. Brennan, Jr., Associate Justice of the Supreme Court of the United States. A member of the NHPC from 1965 to 1974, Justice Brennan has served on the advisory board of the Ratification project for more than twenty years. In that time, he has encouraged the editors and has given his time and advice. The editors of this project–and historical editors in general–owe him a debt of gratitude.

Organization

The Documentary History of the Ratification of the Constitution is divided
into:

(1) *Constitutional Documents and Records, 1776–1787* (1 volume),
(2) *Ratification of the Constitution by the States* (11 volumes),
(3) *Commentaries on the Constitution: Public and Private* (4 volumes),
(4) *The Bill of Rights* (1 or 2 volumes).

Constitutional Documents and Records, 1776–1787.

This introductory volume, a companion to all of the other volumes,
traces the constitutional development of the United States during its
first twelve years. Cross-references to it appear frequently in other volumes when contemporaries refer to events and proposals from 1776 to
1787. The documents include: (1) the Declaration of Independence, (2)
the Articles of Confederation, (3) ratification of the Articles, (4) proposed amendments to the Articles, proposed grants of power to Congress, and ordinances for the Western Territory, (5) the calling of the
Constitutional Convention, (6) the appointment of Convention delegates, (7) the resolutions and draft constitutions of the Convention, (8)
the report of the Convention, and (9) the Confederation Congress and
the Constitution.

Ratification of the Constitution by the States.

The volumes are arranged in the order in which the states considered the Constitution. Although there are variations, the documents
for each state are organized into the following groups: (1) commentaries from the adjournment of the Constitutional Convention to the
meeting of the state legislature that called the state convention, (2) the
proceedings of the legislature in calling the convention, (3) commentaries from the call of the convention until its meeting, (4) the election
of convention delegates, (5) the proceedings of the convention, and (6)
post-convention documents.

Microfiche Supplements to Ratification of the Constitution by the States.

Much of the material for each state is repetitious or peripheral but
still valuable. Literal transcripts of this material are placed on
microfiche supplements. Occasionally, photographic copies of
significant manuscripts are also included.

The types of documents in the supplements are:

(1) newspaper items that repeat arguments, examples of which are printed in the state volumes,

(2) pamphlets that circulated primarily within one state and that are not printed in the state volumes or in *Commentaries*,

(3) letters that contain supplementary material about politics and social relationships,

(4) photographic copies of petitions with the names of signers,

(5) photographic copies of manuscripts such as notes of debates, and

(6) miscellaneous documents such as election certificates, attendance records, pay vouchers and other financial records, etc.

Commentaries on the Constitution: Public and Private.

This series contains newspaper items, pamphlets, and broadsides that circulated regionally or nationally. It also includes some private letters that give the writers' opinions of the Constitution in general or that report on the prospects for ratification in several states. Except for some grouped items, documents are arranged chronologically and are numbered consecutively throughout the four volumes. There are frequent cross-references between *Commentaries* and the state series.

The Bill of Rights.

The public and private debate on the Constitution continued in several states after ratification. It was centered on the issue of whether there should be amendments to the Constitution and the manner in which amendments should be proposed—by a second constitutional convention or by the new U.S. Congress. A bill of rights was proposed in the U.S. Congress on 8 June 1789. Twelve amendments were adopted on 26 September and were sent to the states on 2 October. This volume(s) will contain the documents related to the public and private debate over amendments, to the proposal of amendments by Congress, and to the ratification of the Bill of Rights by the states.

Editorial Procedures

With a few exceptions all documents are transcribed literally. Obvious slips of the pen and errors in typesetting are silently corrected. When spelling or capitalization is unclear, modern usage is followed. Superscripts and interlineated material are lowered to the line. Crossed-out words are retained when significant.

Brackets are used for editorial insertions. Conjectural readings are enclosed in brackets with a question mark. Illegible and missing words are indicated by dashes enclosed in brackets. However, when the author's intent is obvious, illegible or missing material, up to five characters in length, has been silently provided.

All headings are supplied by the editors. Headings for letters contain the names of the writer and the recipient and the place and date of writing. Headings for newspapers contain the pseudonym, if any, and the name and date of the newspaper. Headings for broadsides and pamphlets contain the pseudonym and a shortened form of the title. Full titles of broadsides and pamphlets and information on authorship are given in editorial notes. Headings for public meetings contain the place and date of the meeting.

Salutations, closings of letters, addresses, endorsements, and docketings are deleted unless they provide important information, which is then either retained in the document or placed in editorial notes.

Contemporary footnotes and marginal notes are printed after the text of the document and immediately preceding editorial footnotes. Symbols, such as stars, asterisks, and daggers have been replaced by superscripts (a), (b), (c), etc.

Many documents, particularly letters, are excerpted when they contain material that is not directly relevant to ratification. When longer excerpts or entire documents have been printed elsewhere, or are included in the microfiche supplements, this fact is noted.

Symbols

FOR MANUSCRIPTS, MANUSCRIPT DEPOSITORIES,
SHORT TITLES, AND CROSS-REFERENCES

Manuscripts

Dft	Draft
FC	File Copy
MS	Manuscript
RC	Recipient's Copy
Tr	Translation from Foreign Language

Manuscript Depositories

CSmH	Henry E. Huntington Library
CtHi	Connecticut Historical Society
CtY	Yale University
DLC	Library of Congress
DNA	National Archives
InU-Li	The Lilly Library, Indiana University
M-Ar	Archives Division, Secretary of State, Boston
MB	Boston Public Library
MH	Harvard University
MHi	Massachusetts Historical Society
MeHi	Maine Historical Society
NHi	New-York Historical Society
NN	New York Public Library
NNC	Columbia University Libraries
Nc-Ar	North Carolina Division of Archives and History
NcD	Duke University
PHi	Historical Society of Pennsylvania
PPAmP	American Philosophical Society
PPL	Library Company of Philadelphia
ViU	University of Virginia
WHi	State Historical Society of Wisconsin

Short Titles

Adams, *Defence of the Constitutions*	John Adams, *A Defence of the Constitutions of Government of the United States of America* . . . (3 vols., London, 1787–1788).
Allen, *Adams Diary*	David Grayson Allen et al., eds., *Diary of John Quincy Adams* (Cambridge, Mass., 1981–).
ASP, *Finance*, I	*American State Papers. Documents, Legislative and Executive of the Congress of the United States* . . . [1789–1815] (38 vols., Washington, D.C., 1832–1861), Class III, Finance, I.
"Belknap-Hazard Correspondence"	"The Belknap Papers," *Collections* of the Massachusetts Historical Society, 5th series, Vol. II (Boston, 1877).
Blackstone, *Commentaries*	William Blackstone, *Commentaries on the Laws of England. In Four Books* (Re-printed from the British Copy, Page for Page with the Last Edition, 5 vols., Philadelphia, 1771–1772). Originally published in London from 1765 to 1769.
Boyd	Julian P. Boyd, ed., *The Papers of Thomas Jefferson*, Volumes 1–20 (Princeton, N.J., 1950–1982).
Cooke	Jacob E. Cooke, ed., *The Federalist* (Middletown, Conn., 1961).
Evans	Charles Evans, *American Bibliography* (12 vols., Chicago, 1903–1934).
Farrand	Max Farrand, ed., *The Records of the Federal Convention* (3rd ed., 3 vols., New Haven, Conn., 1927).
Fitzpatrick	John C. Fitzpatrick, ed., *The Writings of George Washington* . . . (39 vols., Washington, D.C., 1931–1944).
Ford, *Pamphlets*	Paul Leicester Ford, ed., *Pamphlets on the Constitution of the United States, Published during Its Discussion by the People 1787–1788* (Brooklyn, N.Y., 1888).
JCC	Worthington C. Ford et al., eds., *Journals of the Continental Congress, 1774–1789* . . . (34 vols., Washington, D.C., 1904–1937).
LMCC	Edmund C. Burnett, ed., *Letters of Members of the Continental Congress* (8 vols., Washington, D.C., 1921–1936).
McRee, *Iredell*	Griffith J. McRee, ed., *Life and Correspondence of James Iredell* . . . (2 vols., New York, 1857–1858).
Montesquieu, *Spirit of Laws*	Charles, Baron de Montesquieu, *The Spirit of Laws* (Translated from the French by Thomas Nugent, 5th ed., 2 vols., London, 1773). Originally published in Geneva in 1748.

NCSR   Walter Clark, ed., *The State Records of North Carolina,* Volumes XI–XXVI (Winston and Goldsboro, N.C., 1895–1906).

PCC   Papers of the Continental Congress, 1774–1789 (Record Group 360, National Archives).

Rutland, *Madison*   Robert A. Rutland et al., eds., *The Papers of James Madison,* Volumes VIII– (Chicago, Ill., and Charlottesville, Va., 1973–).

Thorpe   Francis N. Thorpe, ed., *The Federal and State Constitutions* . . . (7 vols., Washington, D.C., 1909).

Cross-references to Volumes of
The Documentary History of the Ratification of the Constitution

CC   References to *Commentaries on the Constitution* are cited as "CC" followed by the number of the document. For example: "CC:25."

CDR   References to the first volume, titled *Constitutional Documents and Records, 1776–1787,* are cited as "CDR" followed by the page number. For example: "CDR, 325."

RCS   References to the series of volumes titled *Ratification of the Constitution by the States* are cited as "RCS" followed by the abbreviation of the state and the page number. For example: "RCS:Pa., 325."

Mfm   References to the microform supplements to the "RCS" volumes are cited as "Mfm" followed by the abbreviation of the state and the number of the document. For example: "Mfm:Pa. 25."

Calendar for the Years
1787–1788

1787

	S	M	T	W	T	F	S
JANUARY		1	2	3	4	5	6
	7	8	9	10	11	12	13
	14	15	16	17	18	19	20
	21	22	23	24	25	26	27
	28	29	30	31			

	S	M	T	W	T	F	S
FEBRUARY					1	2	3
	4	5	6	7	8	9	10
	11	12	13	14	15	16	17
	18	19	20	21	22	23	24
	25	26	27	28			

	S	M	T	W	T	F	S
MARCH					1	2	3
	4	5	6	7	8	9	10
	11	12	13	14	15	16	17
	18	19	20	21	22	23	24
	25	26	27	28	29	30	31

	S	M	T	W	T	F	S
APRIL	1	2	3	4	5	6	7
	8	9	10	11	12	13	14
	15	16	17	18	19	20	21
	22	23	24	25	26	27	28
	29	30					

	S	M	T	W	T	F	S
MAY			1	2	3	4	5
	6	7	8	9	10	11	12
	13	14	15	16	17	18	19
	20	21	22	23	24	25	26
	27	28	29	30	31		

	S	M	T	W	T	F	S
JUNE						1	2
	3	4	5	6	7	8	9
	10	11	12	13	14	15	16
	17	18	19	20	21	22	23
	24	25	26	27	28	29	30

	S	M	T	W	T	F	S
JULY	1	2	3	4	5	6	7
	8	9	10	11	12	13	14
	15	16	17	18	19	20	21
	22	23	24	25	26	27	28
	29	30	31				

	S	M	T	W	T	F	S
AUGUST				1	2	3	4
	5	6	7	8	9	10	11
	12	13	14	15	16	17	18
	19	20	21	22	23	24	25
	26	27	28	29	30	31	

	S	M	T	W	T	F	S
SEPTEMBER							1
	2	3	4	5	6	7	8
	9	10	11	12	13	14	15
	16	17	18	19	20	21	22
	23	24	25	26	27	28	29
	30						

	S	M	T	W	T	F	S
OCTOBER		1	2	3	4	5	6
	7	8	9	10	11	12	13
	14	15	16	17	18	19	20
	21	22	23	24	25	26	27
	28	29	30	31			

	S	M	T	W	T	F	S
NOVEMBER					1	2	3
	4	5	6	7	8	9	10
	11	12	13	14	15	16	17
	18	19	20	21	22	23	24
	25	26	27	28	29	30	

	S	M	T	W	T	F	S
DECEMBER							1
	2	3	4	5	6	7	8
	9	10	11	12	13	14	15
	16	17	18	19	20	21	22
	23	24	25	26	27	28	29
	30	31					

1788

	S	M	T	W	T	F	S
JANUARY			1	2	3	4	5
	6	7	8	9	10	11	12
	13	14	15	16	17	18	19
	20	21	22	23	24	25	26
	27	28	29	30	31		

	S	M	T	W	T	F	S
FEBRUARY						1	2
	3	4	5	6	7	8	9
	10	11	12	13	14	15	16
	17	18	19	20	21	22	23
	24	25	26	27	28	29	

	S	M	T	W	T	F	S
MARCH							1
	2	3	4	5	6	7	8
	9	10	11	12	13	14	15
	16	17	18	19	20	21	22
	23	24	25	26	27	28	29
	30	31					

	S	M	T	W	T	F	S
APRIL			1	2	3	4	5
	6	7	8	9	10	11	12
	13	14	15	16	17	18	19
	20	21	22	23	24	25	26
	27	28	29	30			

	S	M	T	W	T	F	S
MAY					1	2	3
	4	5	6	7	8	9	10
	11	12	13	14	15	16	17
	18	19	20	21	22	23	24
	25	26	27	28	29	30	31

	S	M	T	W	T	F	S
JUNE	1	2	3	4	5	6	7
	8	9	10	11	12	13	14
	15	16	17	18	19	20	21
	22	23	24	25	26	27	28
	29	30					

	S	M	T	W	T	F	S
JULY			1	2	3	4	5
	6	7	8	9	10	11	12
	13	14	15	16	17	18	19
	20	21	22	23	24	25	26
	27	28	29	30	31		

	S	M	T	W	T	F	S
AUGUST						1	2
	3	4	5	6	7	8	9
	10	11	12	13	14	15	16
	17	18	19	20	21	22	23
	24	25	26	27	28	29	30
	31						

	S	M	T	W	T	F	S
SEPTEMBER		1	2	3	4	5	6
	7	8	9	10	11	12	13
	14	15	16	17	18	19	20
	21	22	23	24	25	26	27
	28	29	30				

	S	M	T	W	T	F	S
OCTOBER				1	2	3	4
	5	6	7	8	9	10	11
	12	13	14	15	16	17	18
	19	20	21	22	23	24	25
	26	27	28	29	30	31	

	S	M	T	W	T	F	S
NOVEMBER							1
	2	3	4	5	6	7	8
	9	10	11	12	13	14	15
	16	17	18	19	20	21	22
	23	24	25	26	27	28	29
	30						

	S	M	T	W	T	F	S
DECEMBER		1	2	3	4	5	6
	7	8	9	10	11	12	13
	14	15	16	17	18	19	20
	21	22	23	24	25	26	27
	28	29	30	31			

American Newspapers, 1787–1788

SHORT TITLE LIST

The following short titles of selected newspapers and magazines are arranged alphabetically within each state. The full titles, the frequency of publication, the names of printers and publishers, and other information about all the newspapers of the period are contained in Clarence S. Brigham, *History and Bibliography of American Newspapers, 1690–1820* (2 vols., Worcester, Mass., 1947), and in his "*Additions and Corrections to* History and Bibliography of American Newspapers, 1690–1820," *Proceedings* of the American Antiquarian Society, LXXI, Part I (1961), 15–62. Similar data on magazines is in Frank Luther Mott, *A History of American Magazines, 1741–1850* (New York and London, 1930).

CONNECTICUT
  American Mercury, Hartford
  Connecticut Courant, Hartford
  Connecticut Gazette, New London
  Connecticut Journal, New Haven
  Fairfield Gazette
  Middlesex Gazette, Middletown
  New Haven Chronicle
  New Haven Gazette
  Norwich Packet
  Weekly Monitor, Litchfield

DELAWARE
  Delaware Courant, Wilmington
  Delaware Gazette, Wilmington

GEORGIA
  Gazette of the State of Georgia, Savannah
  Georgia State Gazette, Augusta

MARYLAND
  Maryland Chronicle, Fredericktown
  Maryland Gazette, Annapolis
  Maryland Gazette, Baltimore
  Maryland Journal, Baltimore
  Palladium of Freedom, Baltimore

MASSACHUSETTS
  American Herald, Boston
  American Recorder, Charlestown
  Berkshire Chronicle, Pittsfield
  Boston Gazette
  Continental Journal, Boston
  Cumberland Gazette, Portland, Maine
  Essex Journal, Newburyport
  Hampshire Chronicle, Springfield
  Hampshire Gazette, Northampton
  Herald of Freedom, Boston
  Independent Chronicle, Boston
  Massachusetts Centinel, Boston
  Massachusetts Gazette, Boston
  Salem Mercury
  Worcester Magazine/Massachusetts Spy

NEW HAMPSHIRE
  Freeman's Oracle, Exeter
  New Hampshire Gazette, Portsmouth
  New Hampshire Mercury, Portsmouth
  New Hampshire Recorder, Keene
  New Hampshire Spy, Portsmouth

NEW JERSEY
  Brunswick Gazette, New Brunswick
  New Jersey Journal, Elizabeth Town
  Trenton Mercury

NEW YORK
   Albany Gazette
   Albany Journal
   American Magazine, New York
   Country Journal, Poughkeepsie
   Daily Advertiser, New York
   Hudson Weekly Gazette
   Impartial Gazetteer, New York
   Independent Journal, New York
   New York Gazetteer
   New York Journal
   New York Morning Post
   New York Museum
   New York Packet
   Northern Centinel, Lansingburgh

PENNSYLVANIA
   American Museum, Philadelphia
   Carlisle Gazette
   Columbian Magazine, Philadelphia
   Evening Chronicle, Philadelphia
   Federal Gazette, Philadelphia
   Freeman's Journal, Philadelphia
   Germantauner Zeitung
   Independent Gazetteer, Philadelphia
   Lancaster Zeitung
   Pennsylvania Chronicle, York
   Pennsylvania Gazette, Philadelphia
   Pennsylvania Herald, Philadelphia
   Pennsylvania Journal, Philadelphia
   Pennsylvania Mercury, Philadelphia
   Pennsylvania Packet, Philadelphia
   Philadelphische Correspondenz
   Pittsburgh Gazette

NORTH CAROLINA
   North Carolina Gazette, Edenton
   North Carolina Gazette, New Bern
   State Gazette of North Carolina, New Bern
   Wilmington Centinel

RHODE ISLAND
   Newport Herald
   Newport Mercury
   Providence Gazette
   United States Chronicle, Providence

SOUTH CAROLINA
   Charleston Morning Post/City Gazette
   Columbian Herald, Charleston
   South Carolina Weekly Chronicle, Charleston
   State Gazette of South Carolina, Charleston

VIRGINIA
   Kentucke Gazette, Lexington
   Norfolk and Portsmouth Journal, Norfolk
   Virginia Centinel, Winchester
   Virginia Gazette, Petersburg
   Virginia Gazette, Winchester
   Virginia Gazette and Independent Chronicle, Richmond
   Virginia Gazette and Weekly Advertiser, Richmond
   Virginia Herald, Fredericksburg
   Virginia Independent Chronicle, Richmond
   Virginia Journal, Alexandria

VERMONT
   Vermont Gazette, Bennington
   Vermont Journal, Windsor

Chronology, 1786–1790

1786

21 January	Virginia calls meeting to consider granting Congress power to regulate trade.
11–14 September	Annapolis Convention.
20 September	Congress receives Annapolis Convention report recommending that states elect delegates to a convention at Philadelphia in May 1787.
11 October	Congress appoints committee to consider Annapolis Convention report.
23 November	Virginia authorizes election of delegates to Convention at Philadelphia.
23 November	New Jersey elects delegates.
4 December	Virginia elects delegates.
30 December	Pennsylvania elects delegates.

1787

6 January	North Carolina elects delegates.
17 January	New Hampshire elects delegates.
3 February	Delaware elects delegates.
10 February	Georgia elects delegates.
21 February	Congress calls Constitutional Convention.
22 February	Massachusetts authorizes election of delegates.
28 February	New York authorizes election of delegates.
3 March	Massachusetts elects delegates.
6 March	New York elects delegates.
8 March	South Carolina elects delegates.
14 March	Rhode Island refuses to elect delegates.
23 April–26 May	Maryland elects delegates.
5 May	Rhode Island again refuses to elect delegates.
14 May	Convention meets: quorum not present.
14–17 May	Connecticut elects delegates.
25 May	Convention begins with quorum of seven states.
16 June	Rhode Island again refuses to elect delegates.
27 June	New Hampshire renews election of delegates.
13 July	Congress adopts Northwest Ordinance.
6 August	Committee of Detail submits draft constitution to Convention.
12 September	Committee of Style submits draft constitution to Convention.
17 September	Constitution signed and Convention adjourns *sine die*.
20 September	Congress reads Constitution.
26–28 September	Congress debates Constitution.
28 September	Congress transmits Constitution to the states.

28–29 September	Pennsylvania calls state convention.
17 October	Connecticut calls state convention.
25 October	Massachusetts calls state convention.
26 October	Georgia calls state convention.
31 October	Virginia calls state convention.
1 November	New Jersey calls state convention.
6 November	Pennsylvania elects delegates to state convention.
10 November	Delaware calls state convention.
12 November	Connecticut elects delegates to state convention.
19 November– 7 January 1788	Massachusetts elects delegates to state convention.
20 November– 15 December	Pennsylvania Convention.
26 November	Delaware elects delegates to state convention.
27 November– 1 December	Maryland calls state convention.
27 November– 1 December	New Jersey elects delegates to state convention.
3–7 December	Delaware Convention.
4–5 December	Georgia elects delegates to state convention.
6 December	North Carolina calls state convention.
7 December	Delaware Convention ratifies Constitution, 30 to 0.
11–20 December	New Jersey Convention.
12 December	Pennsylvania Convention ratifies Constitution, 46 to 23.
14 December	New Hampshire calls state convention.
18 December	New Jersey Convention ratifies Constitution, 38 to 0.
25 December– 5 January 1788	Georgia Convention.
31 December	Georgia Convention ratifies Constitution, 26 to 0.
31 December– 12 February 1788	New Hampshire elects delegates to state convention.

1788

3–9 January	Connecticut Convention.
9 January	Connecticut Convention ratifies Constitution, 128 to 40.
9 January– 7 February	Massachusetts Convention.
19 January	South Carolina calls state convention.
1 February	New York calls state convention.
6 February	Massachusetts Convention ratifies Constitution, 187 to 168, and proposes amendments.
13–22 February	New Hampshire Convention: first session.
1 March	Rhode Island calls statewide referendum on Constitution.
3–31 March	Virginia elects delegates to state convention.
24 March	Rhode Island referendum: voters reject Constitution, 2,711 to 239.
28–29 March	North Carolina elects delegates to state convention.
7 April	Maryland elects delegates to state convention.
11–12 April	South Carolina elects delegates to state convention.
21–29 April	Maryland Convention.
26 April	Maryland Convention ratifies Constitution, 63 to 11.
29 April–3 May	New York elects delegates to state convention.

12–24 May	South Carolina Convention.
23 May	South Carolina Convention ratifies Constitution, 149 to 73, and proposes amendments.
2–27 June	Virginia Convention.
17 June–26 July	New York Convention.
18–21 June	New Hampshire Convention: second session.
21 June	New Hampshire Convention ratifies Constitution, 57 to 47, and proposes amendments.
25 June	Virginia Convention ratifies Constitution, 89 to 79, and proposes amendments.
2 July	New Hampshire ratification read in Congress; Congress appoints committee to report an act for putting the Constitution into operation.
21 July–4 August	First North Carolina Convention.
26 July	New York Convention Circular Letter calls for second constitutional convention.
26 July	New York Convention ratifies Constitution, 30 to 27, and proposes amendments.
2 August	North Carolina Convention proposes amendments and refuses to ratify until amendments are submitted to Congress and to a second constitutional convention.
13 September	Congress sets dates for election of President and meeting of new government under the Constitution.
20 November	Virginia requests Congress under the Constitution to call a second constitutional convention.
30 November	North Carolina calls second state convention.

1789

21–22 August	North Carolina elects delegates to second state convention.
25 September	Congress adopts twelve amendments to Constitution to be submitted to the states.
16–23 November	Second North Carolina Convention.
21 November	Second North Carolina Convention ratifies Constitution, 194 to 77, and proposes amendments.

1790

17 January	Rhode Island calls state convention.
8 February	Rhode Island elects delegates to state convention.
1–6 March	Rhode Island Convention: first session.
24–29 May	Rhode Island Convention: second session.
29 May	Rhode Island Convention ratifies Constitution, 34 to 32, and proposes amendments.

Commentaries on the Constitution
Public and Private

491. James Madison to George Washington
New York, 1 February[1]

The Eastern Mail which arrived yesterday brought me a letter from Mr. King[2] of which a copy follows. "Our prospects are gloomy, but hope is not entirely extinguished. Gerry has not returned to the Convention, and I think will not again be invited.[3] We are now thinking of amendments to be submitted not as a condition of our assent & ratification, but as the opinion of the Convention subjoined to their ratification. This scheme may gain a few members but the issue is doubtful."

In this case as in the last[4] Mr. King's information is accompanied with letters from other persons on the spot which dwell more on the favorable side of the prospect. His anxiety on the subject may give a greater activity to his fears than to his hopes; and he would naturally lean to the cautious side. These circumstances encourage me to put as favorable a construction on his letter as it will bear.

A vessel is arrived here from Charlestown which brings letters that speak with confidence of an adoption of the fœdl Government in that State; and make it very probable that Georgia had actually adopted it. Some letters on the subject from N. Carolina speak a very equivocal language as to the prospect there.

The French Packet arrived yesterday. As she has been out since early in November little news can be expected by her. I have not yet got my letters if there be any for me and I have heard the contents of no others.

1. RC, Washington Papers, DLC.
2. Madison copied the entire letter dated 23 January that he had received from Rufus King, who was serving as a Newburyport delegate to the Massachusetts Convention.
3. Upon invitation, Elbridge Gerry attended the Massachusetts Convention where he almost came to blows with Francis Dana, a Cambridge delegate and fellow townsman. King described the incident in a letter to Madison dated 20 January (Rutland, *Madison*, X, 400–1).
4. Madison probably refers to King's letter of 20 January (note 3 above).

492. Publius: The Federalist 48
New York Packet, 1 February

This essay, written by James Madison, was reprinted in the New York *Independent Journal*, 2 February, and the New York *Daily Advertiser*, 4 February. It is number 48 in the M'Lean edition and number 47 in the newspapers.
For the authorship, circulation, and impact of *The Federalist*, see CC:201, 639.

The FŒDERALIST, No. 47.
To the People of the State of New-York.

It was shewn in the last paper,[1] that the political apothegm there examined, does not require that the legislative, executive and judiciary departments should be wholly unconnected with each other. I shall undertake in the next place, to shew that unless these departments be so far connected and blended, as to give to each a constitutional controul over the others, the degree of separation which the maxim requires as essential to a free government, can never in practice, be duly maintained.

It is agreed on all sides, that the powers properly belonging to one of the departments, ought not to be directly and compleatly administered by either of the other departments. It is equally evident, that neither of them ought to possess directly or indirectly, an overruling influence over the others in the administration of their respective powers. It will not be denied, that power is of an encroaching nature, and that it ought to be effectually restrained from passing the limits assigned to it. After discriminating therefore in theory, the several classes of power, as they may in their nature be legislative, executive, or judiciary; the next and most difficult task, is to provide some practical security for each against the invasion of the others. What this security ought to be, is the great problem to be solved.

Will it be sufficient to mark with precision the boundaries of these departments in the Constitution of the government, and to trust to these parchment barriers against the encroaching spirit of power? This is the security which appears to have been principally relied on by the compilers of most of the American Constitutions. But experience assures us, that the efficacy of the provision has been greatly over-rated; and that some more adequate defence is indispensibly necessary for the more feeble, against the more powerful members of the government. The legislative department is every where extending the sphere of its activity, and drawing all power into its impetuous vortex.

The founders of our republics have so much merit for the wisdom which they have displayed, that no task can be less pleasing than that of pointing out the errors into which they have fallen. A respect for truth however obliges us to remark, that they seem never for a moment to have turned their eyes from the danger to liberty from the overgrown and all-grasping prerogative of an hereditary magistrate, supported and fortified by an hereditary branch of the legislative authority. They seem never to have recollected the danger from legislative usurpations; which by assembling all power in the same hands, must lead to the same tyranny as is threatened by executive usurpations.

In a government, where numerous and extensive prerogatives are placed in the hands of a hereditary monarch, the executive department is very justly regarded as the source of danger, and watched with all the jealousy which a zeal for liberty ought to inspire. In a democracy, where a multitude of people exercise in person the legislative functions, and are continually exposed by their incapacity for regular deliberation and concerted measures, to the ambitious intrigues of their executive magistrates, tyranny may well be apprehended on some favorable emergency, to start up in the same quarter. But in a representative republic, where the executive magistracy is carefully limited both in the extent and the duration of its power; and where the legislative power is exercised by an assembly, which is inspired by a supposed influence over the people with an intripid confidence in its own strength; which is sufficiently numerous to feel all the passions which actuate a multitude; yet not so numerous as to be incapable of pursuing the objects of its passions, by means which reason prescribes; it is against the enterprising ambition of this department, that the people ought to indulge all their jealousy and exhaust all their precautions.

The legislative department derives a superiority in our governments from other circumstances. Its constitutional powers being at once more extensive and less susceptible of precise limits, it can with the greater facility, mask under complicated and indirect measures, the encroachments which it makes on the co-ordinate departments. It is not unfrequently a question of real nicety in legislative bodies, whether the operation of a particular measure, will, or will not extend beyond the legislative sphere. On the other side, the executive power being restrained within a narrower compass, and being more simple in its nature; and the judiciary being described by land marks, still less uncertain, projects of usurpation by either of these departments, would immediately betray and defeat themselves. Nor is this all: As the legislative department alone has access to the pockets of the people, and has in some Constitutions full discretion, and in all, a prevailing influence over the pecuniary rewards of those who fill the other departments, a dependence is thus created in the latter, which gives still greater facility to encroachments of the former.

I have appealed to our own experience for the truth of what I advance on this subject. Were it necessary to verify this experience by particular proofs, they might be multiplied without end. I might find a witness in every citizen who has shared in, or been attentive to, the course of public administrations.[2] I might collect vouchers in abundance from the records and archieves of every State in the Union. But as a more concise and at the same time, equally satisfactory evidence, I will refer to the example of two States, attested by two unexceptionable authorities.

The first example is that of Virginia, a State which, as we have seen, has expressly declared in its Constitution, that the three great departments ought not to be intermixed.[3] The authority in support of it is Mr. Jefferson, who, besides his other advantages for remarking the operation of the government, was himself the chief magistrate of it.[4] In order to convey fully the ideas with which his experience had impressed him on this subject, it will be necessary to quote a passage of some length from his very interesting "Notes on the State of Virginia." (P. 195.)[5] "All the powers of government, legislative, executive and judiciary, result to the legislative body. The concentrating these in the same hands is precisely the definition of despotic government. It will be no alleviation that these powers will be exercised by a plurality of hands, and not by a single one, 173 despots would surely be as oppressive as one. Let those who doubt it turn their eyes on the republic of Venice. As little will it avail us that they are chosen by ourselves. An *elective despotism*, was not the government we fought for; but one which should not only be founded on free principles, but in which the powers of government should be so divided and balanced among several bodies of magistracy, as that no one could transcend their legal limits, without being effectually checked and restrained by the others. For this reason that Convention which passed the ordinance of government, laid its foundation on this basis, that the legislative, executive and judiciary departments should be separate and distinct, so that no person should exercise the powers of more than one of them at the same time. *But no barrier was provided between these several powers.* The judiciary and executive members were left dependent on the legislative for their subsistence in office, and some of them for their continuance in it. If therefore the Legislature assumes executive and judiciary powers, no opposition is likely to be made; nor if made can it be effectual; because in that case, they may put their proceeding into the form of an act of Assembly, which will render them obligatory on the other branches. They have accordingly *in many* instances *decided rights* which should have been left to *judiciary controversy*; and *the direction of the executive, during the whole time of their session, is becoming habitual and familiar.*"

The other State which I shall take for an example, is Pennsylvania; and the other authority the council of censors which assembled in the years 1783 and 1784. A part of the duty of this body, as marked out by the Constitution was, "to enquire whether the Constitution had been preserved inviolate in every part; and whether the legislative and executive branches of government had performed their duty as guardians of the people, or assumed to themselves, or exercised other or greater powers than they are entitled to by the Constitution."[6] In the execution of this trust, the council were necessarily led to a comparison, of both the legislative and executive proceedings, with the constitutional powers of these departments; and from the facts enumerated, and to the truth of most of which, both sides in the council subscribed, it appears that the Constitution had been flagrantly violated by the Legislature in a variety of important instances.

A great number of laws had been passed violating without any apparent necessity, the rule requiring that all bills of a public nature, shall be previously printed for the consideration of the people; altho' this is one of the precautions chiefly relied on by the Constitution, against improper acts of the Legislature.

The constitutional trial by jury had been violated; and powers assumed, which had not been delegated by the Constitution.

Executive powers had been usurped.

The salaries of the Judges, which the Constitution expressly requires to be fixed, had been occasionally varied; and cases belonging to the judiciary department, frequently drawn within legislative cognizance and determination.

Those who wish to see the several particulars falling under each of these heads, may consult the Journals of the council which are in print. Some of them, it will be found may be imputable to peculiar circumstances connected with the war: But the greater part of them may be considered as the spontanious shoots of an ill constituted government.

It appears also, that the executive department had not been innocent of frequent breaches of the Constitution. There are three observations however, which ought to be made on this head. *First.* A great proportion of the instances, were either immediately produced by the necessities of the war, or recommended by Congress or the Commander in Chief. *Secondly.* in most of the other instances, they conformed either to the declared or the known sentiments of the legislative department. *Thirdly.* The executive department of Pennsylvania is distinguished from that of the other States, by the number of members composing it.[7] In this respect it has as much affinity to a legislative assembly, as to an executive council. And being at once exempt from the restraint of an individual responsibility for the acts of the body, and deriving confidence from mutual example and joint influence; unauthorized measures would of course be more freely hazarded, than where the executive department is administered by a single hand or by a few hands.

The conclusion which I am warranted in drawing from these observations is, that a mere demarkation on parchment of the constitutional limits of the several departments, is not a sufficient guard against those encroachments which lead to a tyrannical concentration of all the powers of government in the same hands.

1. See *The Federalist* 47, New York *Independent Journal*, 30 January (CC:486).

2. This sentence was omitted in the M'Lean edition.

3. The constitution of 1776 stated: "The legislative, executive, and judiciary department, shall be separate and distinct . . ." (Thorpe, VII, 3815). This section was previously quoted in *The Federalist* 47 (CC:486).

4. Jefferson was governor of Virginia from 1779 to 1781.

5. Jefferson first wrote his *Notes on the State of Virginia* in 1781 and revised them over the next three years. In May 1785 an English-language edition of the *Notes* was published in France, and in early 1787 a French-language version appeared. In the summer of 1787 John Stockdale, a London printer, published another edition that was apparently used by "Publius." (See pages 195–96 of the Stockdale edition.) The first American printing occurred in Philadelphia in 1788 (Evans 21176). All of the italics in the quoted passage, except the words "elective despotism," were inserted by "Publius."

6. Thorpe, V, 3091. The constitution of 1776 provided that the Council of Censors, consisting of two delegates from each city and county, meet every seven years. The Council met from November 1783 through January 1784, recessed to June 1784, and adjourned in September. See the *Journal of the Council of Censors* . . . (Philadelphia, 1783) (Evans 18093). For various addresses and reports, see Evans 18677, 18692–94, 18715.

7. The Supreme Executive Council, elected by the freemen, was composed of a member from the city of Philadephia and from each county. The president and vice president of the Council were chosen annually by joint ballot of the General Assembly and Council from among the members of the Council (Thorpe, VI, 3086–87).

493. Luther Martin: Genuine Information X
Baltimore Maryland Gazette, 1 February[1]

Mr. MARTIN'S *Information to the House of Assembly, continued.*

By the *third article,* the judicial power of the United States is vested in *one supreme court,* and in such *inferior courts,* as the Congress may from time to time ordain and establish.–These courts, and *these only,* will have a right to decide upon the laws of the United States, and all questions arising upon their construction, and in a judicial manner to carry those laws into execution; to which the courts both superior and inferior of the respective States and their judges and other magistrates are rendered incompetent.– To the courts of the general government are also *confined* all cases in law or equity, arising under the proposed constitution, and treaties made under the authority of the United States–all cases affecting ambassadors, other public ministers and consuls–all cases of admiralty and maritime jurisdiction–all controversies to which the United States are a party–all controversies between two or more States–between a State and citizens of another State–between citizens of the same State claiming lands under grants of different States, and between a State or the citizens thereof, and foreign States, citizens, or subjects.–Whether therefore, any *laws* or *regulations* of the *Congress,* or any *acts* of *its president* or *other officers* are *contrary to,* or not *warranted by* the constitution, rests *only* with the judges, who are *appointed* by Congress to *determine*; by whose determinations *every State* must be *bound.*–Should any question arise between a foreign consul and any of the citizens of the United States, however remote from the seat of empire, it is to be heard before the judiciary of the general government, and in the *first* instance to be heard in the supreme court, however inconvenient to the parties, and however trifling the subject of dispute.

Should the mariners of an American or foreign vessel, while in any American port, have occasion to sue for their wages, or in any other instance a controversy belonging to the admiralty jurisdiction should take place between them and their masters or owners, it is in the courts of the general government the suit must be instituted–and either party may carry it by appeal to its supreme court–the injury to commerce and the oppression to individuals which may thence arise need not be enlarged upon.– Should a citizen of Virginia, Pennsylvania, or any other of the United States be indebted to, or have debts due from, a citizen of this State, or any other claim be subsisting on one side or the other, in consequence of commercial or other transactions, it is only in the courts of Congress that either can apply for redress. The case is the same should any claims subsist between citizens of this State and foreigners, merchants, mariners and others, whether of a commercial or of any other nature, they must be prosecuted in the same courts; and though in the first instance they may be brought in the inferior, yet an appeal may be made to the supreme judiciary, even from the remotest State in the union.

The inquiry concerning, and trial of every offence against, and breach of the laws of Congress are also *confined* to its courts–the same courts also have the *sole* right to inquire concerning and try every offence, from the lowest to the highest, committed by the citizens of any other State, or of a foreign nation, against the laws of this State within its territory–and in *all these cases* the decision may be ultimately brought before the supreme tribunal, since the *appellate jurisdiction* extends to *criminal* as well as to civil cases.

And in all those cases where the general government has jurisdiction in civil questions, the proposed constitution *not only* makes *no provision for the trial by jury* in the *first* instance, but by its appellate jurisdiction *absolutely takes away that inestimable priviledge*, since it expressly declares the supreme court shall have appellate jurisdiction both as to law and *fact*.–Should, therefore, a jury be adopted in the *inferior* court, it would only be a *needless expence*, since on an appeal the *determination* of that *jury even on questions of fact*, however honest and upright, is to be of *no possible effect*–the supreme court is to take up *all questions of fact*–to *examine the evidence relative* thereto–to *decide upon* them in the *same manner* as if they had *never been tried by a jury*–Nor is *trial by jury secured in criminal cases;* it is true, that in the first instance, in the inferior court the trial is to be by jury, in this and in this only, is the difference between criminal and civil cases; but, Sir, the *appellate jurisdiction extends*, as I have observed, to cases *criminal* as well as to civil, and on the *appeal* the *court* is to *decide not only* on the law but on the *fact*, if, therefore, *even* in *criminal* cases the general government is not satisfied with the verdict of the jury, its officer may remove the prosecution to the supreme court, and *there* the *verdict of the jury is to be of no effect*, but the *judges of this court* are to *decide upon the fact* as well as the law, the *same as in civil cases.*

Thus, Sir, *jury trials*, which have ever been the *boast* of the English constitution, which have been by our several *State constitutions* so *cautiously secured* to us,–*jury trials* which have so long been considered the *surest barrier* against *arbitrary power*, and the *palladium* of *liberty*,–with the *loss of which* the *loss* of our *freedom* may be dated, are *taken away* by the proposed form of government, not *only* in a *great variety* of questions between *individual* and *individual*, but in *every case* whether *civil* or *criminal* arising *under the laws of* the United States or the *execution* of those laws.–It is *taken away* in *those very cases* where of *all others* it is *most essential for our liberty*, to have it *sacredly guarded* and *preserved*–in *every case* whether *civil* or *criminal*, between *government* and *its officers* on the one part and the *subject or citizen* on the other.–Nor was this the effect of inattention, nor did it arise from any real difficulty in establishing and securing jury trials by the proposed constitution, if the convention had wished so to do–But the *same reason* influenced *here* as in the case of the establishment of inferior courts;–as they could not trust *State judges*, so would they not confide in *State juries*.–They alledged that the general government and the State governments would always be at variance–that the citizens of the different States would enter into the views and interests of their respective States, and therefore ought not to be trusted in determining causes in which the general government was any way interested, without giving the general government an opportunity, if it disapproved the verdict of the jury, to appeal, and to have the *facts examined* into *again* and *decided upon* by *its own judges*, on whom it was thought a reliance might be had by the general government, they being appointed under its authority.

Thus, Sir, in consequence of this *appellate jurisdiction* and its *extension to facts* as well as to law, every *arbitrary act* of the general government, and every *oppression* of all those *variety of officers* appointed under its authority for the *collection* of *taxes, duties, impost, excise*, and other *purposes*, must be *submitted* to by the *individual*, or must be *opposed* with *little prospect* of *success* and *almost a certain prospect* of *ruin*, at least in those cases where the *middle* and *common class* of citizens are interested–Since to *avoid* that *oppression*, or to *obtain redress*, the application must be made to one of the courts of the United States–by good fortune should this application be in the *first* instance attended with success, and should damages be recovered equivalent to the injury sustained, an *appeal* lies to the *supreme court*, in which case the citizen must at once give up his cause, or he must attend to it at the distance of perhaps more than a thousand miles from the place of his residence, and must take measures to procure before that court on the appeal all the evidence necessary to support his action, which even if ultimately prosperous must be attended with a *loss of time*, a *neglect of business*, and an *expence* which will be *greater* than the *original grievance*, and *to which* men in *moderate* circumstances would be *utterly unequal*.

By the *third* section of this article it is declared that treason against the United States, shall consist in levying war against them, or in adhering to their enemies giving them aid or comfort.

By the *principles* of the American revolution, *arbitrary power may* and *ought* to be resisted even by *arms* if necessary–The time may come when it shall be the *duty* of a *State*, in order to preserve itself from the oppression of the general government, to have recourse to the sword–In which case the proposed form of government declares that the *State* and every of *its citizens* who *act under its authority* are guilty of a direct act of treason–reducing by this provision the different States to this alternative that they must *tamely* and *passively yield to despotism* or *their citizens* must *oppose it* at the *hazard* of the *halter* if unsuccessful–and reducing the citizens of the State which shall take arms to a situation in which they must be *exposed to punishment*, let them *act as they will*, since if they *obey* the authority of their *State government*, they will be *guilty of treason against* the *United States*–if they *join* the *general government* they will be *guilty of treason* against *their own State*.

To save the citizens of the respective States from this disagreeable dilemma, and to secure them from being punishable as *traitors* to the *United States* when *acting* expressly in *obedience* to the *authority of their own State*, I wished to have obtained as an amendment to the third section of this article the following clause: "Provided that no act or acts done by *one* or *more of the States* against the United States, or by *any citizen* of any *one* of the United States *under the authority* of *one* or *more of the said States*, shall be deemed *treason* or *punished as such;* but in case of war being levied by one or more of the States against the United States the conduct of each party towards the other, and their adherents respectively, shall be regulated by the *laws of war* and of *nations*."[2]

But this provision was not adopted, being too much opposed to the great object of many of the leading members of the convention, which was by all means to *leave the States* at the *mercy* of the *general government*, since they could not succeed in their *immediate* and *entire* abolition.

(To be continued.)

1. Reprinted: *Pennsylvania Packet*, 8 February; Philadelphia *Independent Gazetteer*, 15 February; *New York Journal*, 17, 18, 19 March; Boston *American Herald*, 10, 18 April (except for the last three paragraphs). For the impact of the *Genuine Information*, see CC:389.

2. No other record of Martin's amendment has been found. For the debate on the treason clause on 20 August, see Farrand, II, 345–50.

494. Gaspard Joseph Amand Ducher to Comte de la Luzerne Wilmington, N.C., 2 February[1]

The Convention for the examination of the new Constitution will not take place in this state until next july in south Carolina in *may*, in virginia in *june*, in maryland in *april*. georgia was the first of the five southern states which has adopted the new constitution; attacked by savages, it was in its interest to appear federally inclined in order to obtain help from the present union: But if georgia preceded the other southern states in adopting of the new Constitution, it can hardly be expected from an eagerness to *execute* it. by my no. 2.[2] I had the honor to send you, My Lord, a study of the new constitution, permit me to add the following Reflections to it.

The Framers of the new constitution divided the *legislative Body* into two chambers, one of which would be for the *people*, the other for the *States*, the different *legislatures* of which they wanted to preserve and nevertheless establish *a single* general government. these two houses one of which represents *13 States* and the other *two million 573 thousand* citizens proportionally to their number in *each* of the 13. states,[3] are to Balance one another; will this not result in much inconvenience because of the opposition of its two chambers? but the plan for a general government that would literally abolish the 13. sovereignties would not be admissible at the present time.

The necessity of circumstances also dictated the Clause in the new constitution that states that the Representation in the second house will be proportional to the number of inhabitants in each state by counting in it 3. fifths of the slaves and that the *direct* taxes Required by the new Congress will be proportional to the number of Representatives in the second house, which will be *one* for 30 thousand inhabitants 3 fifths of negroes counted.

there are in the five southern states *520 thousand negroes* for whom the Representation and the taxes will be equal to the taxes and the Representation of 312 thousand Whites in the 8 other states. by article 8 of the present Confederation the taxes were to be Borne by the states in proportion to the value of lands and Buildings;[4] this Method of taxation by Congress has been Recognized as impractical and the new constitution calculates the wealth of a state only by the *work* of its inhabitants: will not *five* negroes who work *the entire year* in the southern states give more territorial wealth, than 3. Whites whose work is halted by the winter during at least 4. months of the year? but the negroes are themselves a *Commodity* that the new constitution declares must be subjected to a tax of about 5 percent of its value, 10 piastres per head.

The southern states by the new constitution will be subject to fewer *direct* taxes; they would pay more if the contributions were proportional to the extent and to the fertility of the land: the increase of negroes will increase the proportion of taxes, the number of Representatives in Congress and their influence in the general government; but the new congress in *20. years will be able to prohibit the importation of* negroes: at that time will it not be in the interest of the 8. northern states to prohibit the introduction of negroes into the southern states? these 8. states will have the majority in the two houses.

there will not be any *export* duties on articles *exported* from the united states; but *imports* from Europe, africa and the two indies, into the five southern states where there are more luxuries and fewer manufactures than in the north, exceed the imports from the same places into the 8. other states in which the population is above that of the southern states, by 208 thousand inhabitants because the census made by the new constitution excluded two fifths of the 520 thousand negroes. the southern states will thus pay *more* in *import* duties collected totally for the benefit of the new Congress and these five states, unless the population is increased considerably by the importation of negroes permitted for 20 years, as well as Whites emigrating from the northern states, will have but *10.* votes against *16* in the 1st. house of the new Congress and *29* against *36.* in the second. The interest of the 8. northern states will thus be preferred in the 2. houses by a majority of *6* or *7.* whereas by the old confederation, all important issues, peace, war, loans, expenditures, . . . were able to be determined only by *9.* states,[5] *9* votes against *13*, which required a more general desire, the welfare of *more parts* of the union.

Will not the commercial interest of the five southern states be sacrificed to that of the 8 other states? by my nos. 3, 8 and 20 from portsmouth, I explained that the purpose of the annapolis Congress was to Consider the *Relative* state of the Commerce of the 13. Republics and to what point a uniform System in their commercial laws was necessary for the continuation of their union, that the Navigation acts of the states of Newhampshire and massachusetts had been suspended because the other states did not wish to proclaim similar ones, designed to punish england for its strictness against american Commerce,[6] that the annapolis congress having Recognized that the general Commercial interest of the 13 united states required the Reform of some of the articles of the present Confederation, a convention was to take place at philadelphia, that a uniform commercial Bill would make the new englanders the principal navigators of the Continent, that it was difficult to apportion the votes, the contributions, to take away from Each state in matters of Commerce custom duties, rebates, and bounties, to Give a new congress more energy without destroying the sovereignty of the 13. states, that england would plot against all uniform Commercial regulations in the 13. states because its flag and its commodities were not submitted to the same Restrictions that the flag and goods of the united states were in the english possessions, &c.

The Circumstances explained, My Lord, in the 3. Nos. from portsmouth were perceived as a lost Cause, it is said, by the delegates of the southern states at the philadelphia convention. it is claimed here that the new constitution is all to the advantage of the northern states which would always have the Majority in the new congress. the southern delegates were not able to obtain a resolve that a navigation *act* could be Made only by *two thirds* of the two houses.[7] all the workers employed in Shipbuilding, all the sailors, all the merchants of the northern states will build, navigate carry the Commerce for the southern states some of which by tonnage duties and Rebates import duties aided the private Construction and Manufacture in these states. The Builders and navigators of the northern states, independent of the large coastal trade that they carry from one state to another, tie the Commerce of the five southern states to that of the west indies; I have seen at savannah, charleston, here New-england Built and owned Ships Loading up for our islands and I had seen the same Ships at portsmouth Boston and newport Returning from our islands after having exchanged their Return cargoes from the islands in one of the five southern states; it is especially during winter that the new-englanders make these double voyages: they also come here to Load for Europe and the greater antilles.

The exportation of the commodities of the five southern states employs a number of Ships whose Tonnage is about *200 thousand tons*; there are not, small coastal vessels excepted, 25 thousand tons of ships Built and owned in the southern states, all the rest belong to the 8. other states or to *foreigners*. according to the new constitution, there will no longer be, for americans, duties from one port to another, nor preference for one state over another, the entry and exit of american Ships, will be free unconstrained and equal for all the states; they will not fail to proclaim a navigation act against *foreigners*, english and others, which will subject them to tonnage duties and to formalities and duties calculated to increase the Shipbuilding navigation and commerce of the United States; But since the peace these foreigners, the english especially, have flocked to the ports of the *southern states*: there they carried off the Rice, tobacco, indigo, Wood, naval stores, ginseng, pelts.–while the Strictness of england made itself felt in the 8. northern states, by the non-admission of the american flag into the english islands, prohibitive duties on fish oil in england, and the prohibition of american salted meat and fish, even in the Case of importation made on english Ships.[8] if a Navigation act excludes these foreigners from the five southern states, by a tonnage duty or other preference for the Ships of the united states, the *markets and the prices of the commodities of the southern states will diminish*; it is this fear that sets the virginia and North Carolina planters especially, against the new Constitution and which led them not to Convene their Conventions to examine it until next june and july, thus to delay as long as possible, the moment to adhere to the new government or to Reject it. it is also the Fear of seeing the diminishing exportation of southern commodities that had prevented these states from acquiescing to the Navigation acts Passed at portsmouth and Boston in 1785. it is not enough that the 8. northern states are able to furnish the Ships necessary for the exportation of southern commodities, it must give the foreigners and the english reason to close their ports to the principal commodities of the southern states, Rice, tobacco &c.

plausible Reasons to lessen these worries are not lacking; as soon as england, it is said, sees the 13. states Well united, disposed to Reply to it with a Navigation act, it will conclude a treaty of Commerce with them that will open the english islands to the american flag, it is added that if the 8. northern states must have some commercial advantages over the five southern states, for Shipbuilding, freight and the introduction into the southern states of certain commodities and manufactures of the northern states, the five southern states have Richness of soil Rice, tobacco, indigo, that it is in the interest of all *to become a Maritime power* so that in case of invasion of the southern states where the country is flat and contains half negroes, help can be brought, *by sea* from portsmouth to Savannah, that a navy is necessary for their defense, that this navy will Make the 13. united states Respectable to foreign powers, especially those who have possessions in the west indies, that the 8. northern states consented to give Those of the south a Representation for their negroes who are not good to defend the country, that if uniformity of Commercial Regulations should not accord some advantage to the northern states, they would not have any reason to Preserve the Union with those of the south and that the Latter are too weak not to be divided *by powerful Creditors*.

It is thus, My Lord, that the new Constitution is discussed; the delegates from north Carolina are not to be appointed before the end of next march to assemble in july, each party promises itself Success at that time.

The opposition Against its *Execution* Will Be stronger still.

1. RC (Tr), Correspondance Politique, États-Unis, Supplement, Vol. IV, ff. 324–27, Archives du Ministère des Affaires Étrangères, Paris, France. This dispatch was docketed "No 6." Ducher was French vice consul at Portsmouth, N.H., 1785–87, and at Wilmington, N.C., 1787–88. The Comte de la Luzerne (1741–1791) was minister plenipotentiary to the United States, 1779–84, and Minister of Marine and Colonies, 1787–90.

2. Dispatch number 2, dated 25 October 1787, has not been located.

3. This estimate of population was taken from a speech that Charles Cotesworth Pinckney, a former Constitutional Convention delegate, delivered before the South Carolina House of Representatives on 17 January during a debate over calling a state convention. Pinckney's speech was published in the Charleston *City Gazette* on 24 January. The population estimate only was printed in the New York *Daily Advertiser* on 5 February and was reprinted more than twenty-five times. (See Appendix I.)

4. For Article VIII of the Articles of Confederation, see CDR, 89. In April 1783 Congress recommended an amendment that would have changed the method of sharing expenses from the value of land and buildings to population (CDR, 148–50). Eleven states adopted the amendment.

5. See CDR, 92. Ellipses in the original.

6. On 23 June 1785 New Hampshire and Massachusetts passed similar navigation acts limiting trade with Great Britain. The acts were suspended in June and July 1786, respectively, because the other states had not adopted similar acts.

7. The report of the Committee of Detail (6 August) required that "No navigation act shall be passed without the assent of two thirds of the members present in each House." On 29 August this provision was stricken from the report as part of the compromise which prohibited Congress from interfering with the importation of slaves until 1808. George Mason of Virginia unsuccessfully moved to get the provision on navigation acts restored on 15 September (Farrand, II, 183, 449–53, 631. See also Mason's objections to the Constitution, CC:138, 276.).

8. In May 1783 a British order-in-council allowed the importation of oil and other unmanufactured goods from America into Great Britain in American vessels on payment of colonial duties. In July 1783 an order-in-council listed a large number of American products that could be imported into the British West Indies but only "by British subjects in British built Ships, owned by His Majesty's Subjects, and navigated according to Law." Specifically excluded from this list were cured meats, fish, and dairy

products–all important exports of the Northern States. In December 1783 another order-in-council removed oil from the list, thereby subjecting oil to a prohibitive duty.

495. Publius: The Federalist 49
New York Independent Journal, 2 February

The authorship of essays 49–58 and 62–63 is uncertain but most scholars believe
that James Madison, not Alexander Hamilton, wrote all of them. Hamilton himself never claimed that he wrote number 49. Consequently, it is attributed to James
Madison. The essay was reprinted in the *New York Packet*, 5 February, and the
New York *Daily Advertiser*, 6 February. It is number 49 in the M'Lean edition and
number 48 in the newspapers.

For a general discussion of the authorship, circulation, and impact of *The Federalist*, see CC:201, 639; and for the disputed authorship of this essay, see Cooke,
xix–xxx, 633, and Rutland, *Madison*, X, 261–63.

The FŒDERALIST. No. XLVIII.
To the People of the State of New-York.

The author of the "Notes on the state of Virginia," quoted in the last
paper,[1] has subjoined to that valuable work, the draught of a constitution
which had been prepared in order to be laid before a convention expected
to be called in 1783 by the legislature, for the establishment of a constitution for that commonwealth. The plan, like every thing from the same
pen, marks a turn of thinking original, comprehensive and accurate; and
is the more worthy of attention, as it equally displays a fervent attachment
to republican government, and an enlightened view of the dangerous propensities against which it ought to be guarded. One of the precautions
which he proposes, and on which he appears ultimately to rely as a palladium to the weaker departments of power, against the invasions of the
stronger, is perhaps altogether his own, and as it immediately relates to
the subject of our present enquiry, ought not to be overlooked.

His proposition is, "that whenever any two of the three branches of
government shall concur in opinion, each by the voices of two thirds of
their whole number, that a convention is necessary for altering the constitution or *correcting breaches of it*, a convention shall be called for the purpose."[2]

As the people are the only legitimate fountain of power, and it is from
them that the constitutional charter, under which the several branches of
government hold their power, is derived; it seems strictly consonant to the
republican theory, to recur to the same original authority, not only whenever it may be necessary to enlarge, diminish, or new-model the powers of
government; but also whenever any one of the departments may commit
encroachments on the chartered authorities of the others. The several departments being perfectly co-ordinate by the terms of their common commission, neither of them, it is evident, can pretend to an exclusive or
superior right of settling the boundaries between their respective powers;
and how are the encroachments of the stronger to be prevented, or the
wrongs of the weaker to be redressed, without an appeal to the people

themselves; who, as the grantors of the commission, can alone declare its true meaning and enforce its observance?

There is certainly great force in this reasoning, and it must be allowed to prove, that a constitutional road to the decision of the people, ought to be marked out, and kept open, for certain great and extraordinary occasions. But there appear to be insuperable objections against the proposed recurrence to the people, as a provision in all cases for keeping the several departments of power within their constitutional limits.

In the first place, the provision does not reach the case of a combination of two of the departments against a third. If the legislative authority, which possesses so many means of operating on the motives of the other departments, should be able to gain to its interest either of the others, or even one third of its members, the remaining department could derive no advantage from this remedial provision. I do not dwell however on this objection, because it may be thought to lie rather against the modification of the principle, than against the principle itself.

In the next place, it may be considered as an objection inherent in the principle, that as every appeal to the people would carry an implication of some defect in the government, frequent appeals would in great measure deprive the government of that veneration, which time bestows on every thing, and without which perhaps the wisest and freest governments would not possess the requisite stability. If it be true that all governments rest on opinion, it is no less true that the strength of opinion in each individual, and its practical influence on his conduct, depend much on the number which he supposes to have entertained the same opinion. The reason of man, like man himself is timid and cautious, when left alone; and acquires firmness and confidence, in proportion to the number with which it is associated. When the examples, which fortify opinion, are *antient* as well as *numerous*, they are known to have a double effect. In a nation of philosophers, this consideration ought to be disregarded. A reverence for the laws, would be sufficiently inculcated by the voice of an enlightened reason. But a nation of philosophers is as little to be expected as the philosophical race of kings wished for by Plato. And in every other nation, the most rational government will not find it a superfluous advantage, to have the prejudices of the community on its side.

The danger of disturbing the public tranquility by interesting too strongly the public passions, is a still more serious objection against a frequent reference of constitutional questions, to the decision of the whole society. Notwithstanding the success which has attended the revisions of our established forms of government, and which does so much honour to the virtue and intelligence of the people of America, it must be confessed, that the experiments are of too ticklish a nature to be unnecessarily multiplied. We are to recollect that all the existing constitutions were formed in the midst of a danger which repressed the passions most unfriendly to order and concord; of an enthusiastic confidence of the people in their patriotic leaders, which stifled the ordinary diversity of opinions on great national questions; of a universal ardor for new and opposite forms, produced by a universal resentment and indignation against the antient government; and whilst no spirit of party, connected with the changes to be made, or the abuses to be reformed, could mingle its leven in the operation. The future situations in which we must expect to be usually placed, do not present any equivalent security against the danger which is apprehended.

But the greatest objection of all is, that the decisions which would probably result from such appeals, would not answer the purpose of maintaining the constitutional equilibrium of the government. We have seen that the tendency of republican governments is to an aggrandizement of the legislative, at the expence of the other departments.[3] The appeals to the people therefore would usually be made by the executive and judiciary departments. But whether made by one side or the other, would each side enjoy equal advantages on the trial? Let us view their different situations. The members of the executive and judiciary departments, are few in number, and can be personally known to a small part only of the people. The latter by the mode of their appointment, as well as, by the nature and permanency of it, are too far removed from the people to share much in their prepossessions. The former are generally the objects of jealousy: And their administration is always liable to be discoloured and rendered unpopular. The members of the legislative department, on the other hand, are numerous. They are distributed and dwell among the people at large. Their connections of blood, of friendship and of acquaintance, embrace a great proportion of the most influencial part of the society. The nature of their public trust implies a personal influence among the people, and that they are more immediately the confidential guardians of the rights and liberties of the people. With these advantages, it can hardly be supposed that the adverse party would have an equal chance for a favorable issue.

But the legislative party would not only be able to plead their cause most successfully with the people. They would probably be constituted themselves the judges. The same influence which had gained them an election into the legislature, would gain them a seat in the convention. If this should not be the case with all, it would probably be the case with many, and pretty certainly with those leading characters, on whom every thing depends in such bodies. The convention in short would be composed chiefly of men, who had been, who actually were, or who expected to be, members of the department whose conduct was arraigned. They would consequently be parties to the very question to be decided by them.

It might however sometimes happen, that appeals would be made under circumstances less adverse to the executive and judiciary departments. The usurpations of the legislature might be so flagrant and so sudden, as to admit of no specious colouring. A strong party among themselves might take side with the other branches. The executive power might be in the hands of a peculiar favorite of the people. In such a posture of things, the public decision might be less swayed by prepossessions in favor of the legislative party. But still it could never be expected to turn on the true merits of the question. It would inevitably be connected with the spirit of pre-existing parties, or of parties springing out of the question itself. It would be connected with persons of distinguished character and extensive influence in the community. It would be pronounced by the very men who had been agents in, or opponents of the measures, to which the decision would relate. The *passions* therefore not *the reason*, of the public, would sit in judgment. But it is the reason of the public alone that ought to controul and regulate the government. The passions ought to be controuled and regulated by the government.

We found in the last paper[4] that mere declarations in the written constitution, are not sufficient to restrain the several departments within their legal limits. It appears in this, that occasional appeals to the people would be neither a proper nor an effectual provision, for that purpose. How far the provisions of a different nature contained in the plan above quoted, might be adequate, I do not examine. Some of them are unquestionably founded on sound political principles, and all of them are framed with singular ingenuity and precision.

1. See CC:492.
2. Thomas Jefferson, *Notes on the State of Virginia* (London, 1787), 376. The italics were supplied by "Publius."
3. See CC:492.
4. *Ibid.*

496. John Jay to George Washington
New York, 3 February (excerpt)[1]

. . . our Legislature has agreed to call a Convention–the opponents to the proposed Constitution are nevertheless numerous & indefatigable; but as the Ballance of abilities and Property is against them, it is reasonable to expect that they will lose ground as the People become better informed: I am therefore inclined to think that the Constitution will be adopted in this State; especially if our Eastern neighbours should generally come into the measure. our accounts, or rather Calculations from Massachusets are favorable, but not decisive.

Your favor of the 20th. ulto.[2] was delivered to me this morning. The Letters which accompanied it shall be conveyed by the most early & proper opportunities that may offer. are you apprized that all American Letters, and indeed most others, which pass thro' the french Post office are opened! so is the fact–while in that Country I never recd. a single one from the office that did not bear marks of Inspection.

The Influence of Massachusets on the one Hand, and of Virginia on the other, renders their Conduct on the present occasion, very interesting–I am happy that we have as yet no Reason to despair of either.–Connecticut has acceded, and the Gazettes tell us that Georgia has done the same. a few Months more will decide all Questions respecting the adoption of the proposed Constitution. I sincerely wish it may take Place, tho' less from an Idea that it will fully realize the sanguine Expectations of many of·its Friends, than because it establishes some great Points, and smooths the Way for a System more adequate to our national objects. Its Reputation & Success will I think greatly depend on the manner in which it may at first be organized and administred–but on this head we have no Reason to despond.

Mrs. Jay's Health which was a little deranged by her too kind attendance on me while sick, is again pretty well established. For my Part I have much Reason to be thankful, for altho a constant pain in my left Side continues to give me some, but no great Trouble, yet I am happy that my long and severe Illness has left me nothing more to complain of[3]–We are both obliged by your kind attention, & assure you & Mrs. Washington of our best wishes–

1. RC, Washington Papers, DLC.
2. See Fitzpatrick, XXIX, 389–90. Washington had given Jay his opinion that the Constitution would be ratified. Acting on a previous offer from Jay, Washington enclosed letters to be forwarded to Europe.
3. In mid-November, Jay's illness temporarily ended his contributions to *The Federalist* (CC:201).

497. William Robinson, Jr., to John Langdon
Philadelphia, 4 February (excerpt)[1]

My dear Friend
　　. . . Our Eyes are now turned towards the East to view the Motions of Massachusetts–you by this Time may possibly know the Event of the Proceedings of their Convention–The Dissention existing in that State is well known here; their Example will be interesting & should they reject the New Constitution, who can tell the Consequences? Should they adopt it I doubt not but the States will be regularly connected from N Scotia to the Chesapeake forming nine bounding each other–But Sir turn the Reverse–If Massachusetts rejects–what will be the Conduct of N Hampshire, R Iland & N York?–N York stands wavering & that State is important–the Decision in Boston will fix them–Let us but Suppose Massachusetts & New York reject, what will Virginia do? In that Case they also will probably reject & No. Carolina will follow them–then how shall we stand[?] N Hampshire, R Island, Connecticut, N Jersey, Pensylva., Delaware, Maryland, S Carolina & Georgia–these indeed would make nine, but I think no one would pronounce they could form an Empire seperated by Massachusetts, N York, Virga. & No. Carolina–on the contrary should all

adopt from N Hampshire to Maryland inclusive, with S Carolina & Georgia, any testy Humour of Virginia would avail them Little as the nine northernmost States would alone form a strong, compact Empire & with the aid of the two most Southern, would induce Virginia & N Carolina to concur–May Heaven inspire American Bosoms with Patriotism, for if we are not now wise, in vain has our blood been spilt. Again may the Furies rage & Civil Discord raise again her Crest with Horrors unknown before–Heaven avert the Evil! . . .

1. RC, Langdon/Elwyn Papers, New Hampshire Historical Society. Robinson, a merchant, represented Philadelphia County in the Pennsylvania Assembly from 1785 to 1789, and in the state constitutional convention in 1789 and 1790.

498. Civis: To the Citizens of South Carolina
Charleston Columbian Herald, 4 February

On 19 January the South Carolina House of Representatives adopted a resolution calling a state convention to consider the Constitution. Rawlins Lowndes, a member of the House of Representatives from the Charleston parishes of St. Philip and St. Michael, believed that the Constitution would give unfair commercial advantages to New England. He also objected to the excessive powers of the Senate and the President, and to the power of Congress to prohibit the slave trade after 1808.

David Ramsay, who represented the same parishes, charged that Lowndes had "an illiberal jealousy of New: England men" and did not have "one foederal idea in his head." Lowndes's "opposition has poisoned the minds of some" (to Benjamin Lincoln, 29 January, CC:482). "To obviate" Lowndes's arguments, Ramsay wrote an essay, signed "Civis," extolling the virtues of the Constitution and the benefits of the Union. Drafted "in a few hours," the essay was written "in a summary way & in a plain stile for the benefit of common people" (to Benjamin Lincoln, 31 March, Lincoln Papers, MHi).

"Civis" was published in the Charleston *Columbian Herald* on 4 February, and as a twelve-page pamphlet by the printer of the *Herald*. The same plates were used for the texts of both printings. According to Ramsay, copies of the pamphlet–entitled *An Address to the Freemen of South-Carolina, on the Subject of the Fœderal Constitution, Proposed by the Convention, which Met in Philadelphia, May 1787* (Evans 21414)–were distributed to members of the South Carolina legislature. On 23 and 27 February, the New York *Independent Journal* reprinted the *Columbian Herald's* version of "Civis" at the request of "A Constant Reader."

Ramsay sent copies of the pamphlet to Benjamin Lincoln in Massachusetts, and to Benjamin Rush in Philadelphia, describing it to Rush as "merely a local answer to local objections & not worth sending so far" (to Rush, 17 February, Rush Papers, PPL). Nevertheless, Rush had the pamphlet reprinted in the *Pennsylvania Mercury* on 3 April with this statement: "Said to be written by Dr. RAMSAY." (John Vaughan of Philadelphia sent a copy of this issue of the *Mercury* to John Dickinson in Delaware, pointing to the "address of D Ramsay to the Carolinians" [6 April, Dickinson Papers, PPL].) The pamphlet version, with Ramsay identified as the author, was also reprinted in the Fredericksburg *Virginia Herald*, 17 April (supplement); *Maryland Journal*, 25 April; *Virginia Centinel*, 30 April; and in the May issue of the Philadelphia *American Museum*.

Friends, Countrymen, and Fellow Citizens, You have at this time a new federal constitution proposed for your consideration. The great importance of the subject demands your most serious attention. To assist you in forming a right judgment on this matter, it will be proper to consider,

1st. It is the manifest interest of these states to be united. Eternal wars among ourselves would most probably be the consequence of disunion. Our local weakness particularly proves it to be for the advantage of South-Carolina to strengthen the federal government; for we are inadequate to secure ourselves from more powerful neighbours.

2d. If the thirteen states are to be united in reality, as well as in name, the obvious principle of the union should be, that the Congress or general government, should have power to regulate all general concerns. In a state of nature, each man is free and may do what he pleases; but in society, every individual must sacrifice a part of his natural rights; the minority must yield to the majority, and the collective interest must controul particular interests. When thirteen persons constitute a family, each should forego every thing that is injurious to the other twelve. When several families constitute a parish, or county, each may adopt any regulations it pleases with regard to its domestic affairs, but must be abridged of that liberty in other cases, where the good of the whole is concerned.

When several parishes, counties or districts form a state, the separate interests of each must yield to the collective interest of the whole. When thirteen states combine in one government, the same principles must be observed. These relinquishments of natural rights, are not real sacrifices: each person, county or state, gains more than it loses, for it only gives up a right of injuring others, and obtains in return aid and strength to secure itself in the peaceable enjoyment of all remaining rights. If then we are to be an united people, and the obvious ground of union must be, that all continental concerns should be managed by Congress–let us by these principles examine the new constitution. Look over the 8th section, which enumerates the powers of Congress, and point out one that is not essential on the before recited principles of union. The first is a power to lay and collect taxes, duties, imposts and excises, to pay the debts, and provide for the common defence and general welfare of the United States.

When you authorised Congress to borrow money, and to contract debts for carrying on the late war, you could not intend to abridge them of the means of paying their engagements, made on your account. You may observe, that their future power is confined to provide for the *common defence* and *general welfare* of the United States. If they apply money to any other purposes, they exceed their powers. The people of the United States who pay, are to be judges how far their money is properly applied. It would be tedious to go over all the powers of Congress, but it would be easy to shew that they all may be referred to this single principle, "that the general concerns of the union ought to be managed by the general government." The opposers of the constitution, cannot shew a single power delegated to Congress, that could be spared consistently with the welfare of the whole, nor a single one taken from the states, but such as can be more advantageously lodged in the general government, than in that of the separate states.

For instance–the states cannot emit money; this is not intended to prevent the emission of paper money, but only of state paper money. Is not this an advantage? To have thirteen paper currencies in thirteen states is embarrassing to commerce, and eminently so to travellers. It is obviously our interest, either to have no paper, or such as will circulate from Georgia to New-Hampshire. Take another instance–the Congress are authorised to provide and maintain a navy–Our sea coast in its whole extent needs the protection thereof; but if this was to be done by the states, they who build ships, would be more secure than they who do not. Again, if the local legislatures might build ships of war at pleasure, the Eastern would have a manifest superiority over the Southern states. Observe how much better this business is referred to the regulations of Congress. A common navy, paid out of the common treasury, and to be disposed of by the united voice of a majority for the common defence of the weaker as well as of the stronger states, is promised, and will result from the federal constitution. Suffer not yourselves to be imposed on by declamation. Ask the man who objects to the powers of Congress two questions. Is it not necessary that the supposed dangerous power be lodged somewhere? and secondly, where can it be lodged consistently with the general good, so well as in the general government? Decide for yourselves on these obvious principles of union.

It has been objected, that the eastern states have an advantage in their representation in Congress. Let us examine this objection–the four eastern states send seventeen members to the house of representatives, but Georgia, South-Carolina, North-Carolina and Virginia, send twenty-three. The six northern states send twenty-seven, the six southern thirty. In both cases we have a superiority;–but, say the objectors, add Pennsylvania to the northern states, and there is a majority against us. It is obvious to reply, add Pennsylvania to the Southern states, and they have a majority. The objection amounts to no more than that seven are more than six. It must be known to many of you, that the Southern states, from their vast extent of uncultivated country, are daily receiving new settlers; but in New-England their country is so small, and their land so poor, that their inhabitants are constantly emigrating. As the rule of representation in Congress is to vary with the number of inhabitants, our influence in the general government will be constantly increasing. In fifty years, it is probable that the Southern states will have a great ascendency over the Eastern. It has been said that thirty-five men, not elected by yourselves, may make laws to bind you. This objection, if it has any force, tends to the destruction of your state government. By our constitution, sixty-nine make a quorum, of course, thirty-five members may make a law to bind all the people of

South-Carolina.–Charleston, and any one of the neighbouring parishes send collectively thirty-six members; it is therefore possible, in the absence of all others, that three of the lower parishes might legislate for the whole country. Would this be a valid objection against your own constitution? It certainly would not–neither is it against the proposed federal plan. Learn from it this useful lesson–insist on the constant attendance of your members, both in the state assembly, and Continental Congress: your representation in the latter, is as numerous in a relative proportion with the other states as it ought to be. You have a thirteenth part in both houses; and you are not, on principles of equality, entitled to more.

It has been objected, that the president, and two-thirds of the senate, though not of your election, may make treaties binding on this state. Ask these objectors–do you wish to have any treaties? They will say yes.–Ask then who can be more properly trusted with the power of making them, than they to whom the convention have referred it? Can the state legislatures? They would consult their local interests–Can the Continental House of Representatives? When sixty-five men can keep a secret, they may. Observe the cautious guards which are placed around your interests. Neither the senate nor president can make treaties by their separate authority.–They must both concur.–This is more in your favor than the footing on which you now stand. The delegates in Congress of nine states, without your consent can not bind you;–by the new constitution there must be two thirds of the members present, and also the president, in whose election you have a vote. Two thirds are to the whole nearly as nine to thirteen. If you are not wanting to yourselves by neglecting to keep up the states compliment of senators, your situation with regard to preventing the controul of your local interests by the Northern states, will be better under the proposed constitution than now it is under the existing confederation.

It has been said, we will have a navigation act, and be restricted to American bottoms, and that high freight will be the consequence. We certainly ought to have a navigation act, and we assuredly ought to give a preference, though not a monopoly, to our own shipping.

If this state is invaded by a maritime force, to whom can we apply for immediate aid?–To Virginia and North-Carolina? Before they can march by land to our assistance, the country may be over run. The Eastern states, abounding in men and in ships, can sooner relieve us, than our next door neighbours. It is therefore not only our duty, but our interest, to encourage their shipping. They have sufficient resources on a few months notice, to furnish tonnage enough to carry off all your exports; and they can afford, and doubtless will undertake to be your carriers on as easy terms as you now pay for freight in foreign bottoms.

On this subject, let us consider what we have gained, & also what they have lost by the revolution. We have gained a free trade with all the world, and consequently a higher price for our commodities, it may be said, and so have they; but they who reply in this manner, ought to know, that there is an amazing difference in our favor: their country affords no valuable exports, and of course the privilege of a free trade is to them of little value, while our staple commodity commands a higher price than was usual before the war. We have also gained an exemption from quit rents, to which the eastern states were not subjected. Connecticut and Rhode-Island were nearly as free before the revolution as since. They had no royal governor or councils to control them, or to legislate for them. Massachusetts and New-Hampshire were much nearer independence in their late constitutions than we were. The eastern states, by the revolution, have been deprived of a market for their fish, of their carrying-trade, their ship building, and almost of every thing but their liberties.

As the war has turned out so much in our favor, and so much against them, ought we to begrudge them the carrying of our produce, especially when it is considered, that by encouraging their shipping, we increase the means of our own defence. Let us examine also the federal constitution, by the principle of reciprocal concession. We have laid a foundation for a navigation act.–This will be a general good; but particularly so to our northern brethren. On the other hand, they have agreed to change the federal rule of paying the continental debt, according to the value of land as laid down in the confederation, for a new principle of apportionment, to be founded on the numbers of inhabitants in the several states respectively. This is an immense concession in our favor. Their land is poor; our's rich; their numbers great; our's small; labour with them is done by white men, for whom they pay an equal share; while five of our negroes only count as equal to three of their whites. This will make a difference of many thousands of pounds in settling our continental accounts. It is farther objected, that they have stipulated for a right to prohibit the importation of negroes after 21 years. On this subject observe, as they are bound to protect us from domestic violence, they think we ought not to increase our exposure to that evil, by an unlimited importation of slaves. Though Congress may forbid the importation of negroes after 21 years, it does not follow that they will. On the other hand, it is probable that they will not. The more rice we make, the more business will be for their shipping: their interest will therefore coincide with our's. Besides, we have other sources of supply–the importations of the ensuing 20 years, added to the natural increase of those we already have, and the influx from our northern neighbours, who are desirous of getting rid of their slaves, will afford a sufficient number for cultivating all the lands in this state.

Let us suppose the union to be dissolved by the rejection of the new constitution, what would be our case? The United States owe several millions of dollars to France, Spain, and Holland. If an efficient government is not adopted, which will provide for the payment of our debt, especially of that which is due to foreigners–who will be the losers? Most certainly the southern states. Our exports, as being the most valuable, would be the first objects of capture on the high seas; or descents would be made on our defenceless coasts, till the creditors of the United States had paid themselves at the expence of this weaker part of the union. Let us also compare the present confederation, with the proposed constitution. The former can neither protect us at home, nor gain us respect abroad: it cannot secure the payment of our debts, nor command the resources of our country, in case of danger. Without money, without a navy, or the means of even supporting an army of our own citizens in the field, we lie at the mercy of every invader; our sea port towns may be laid under contribution, and our country ravaged.

By the new constitution, you will be protected with the force of the union, against domestic violence and foreign invasion. You will have a navy to defend your coasts.–The respectable figure you will make among the nations, will so far command the attention of foreign powers, that it is probable you will soon obtain such commercial treaties, as will open to your vessels the West-India islands, and give life to your expiring commerce.

In a country like our's, abounding with free men all of one rank, where property is equally diffused, where estates are held in fee simple, the press free, and the means of information common; tyranny cannot readily find admission under any form of government; but its admission is next to impossible, under one where the people are the source of all power, and elect either mediately by their representatives, or immediately by themselves the whole of their rulers.

Examine the new constitution with candor and liberality. Indulge no narrow prejudices to the disadvantage of your brethren of the other states; consider the people of all the thirteen states, as a band of brethren, speaking the same language, professing the same religion, inhabiting one undivided country, and designed by heaven to be one people. Consent that what regards all the states should be managed by that body which represents all of them; be on your guard against the misrepresentations of men who are involved in debt;[1] such may wish to see the constitution rejected, because of the following clause "no state shall emit bills of credit, make any thing but gold and silver coin, a tender in payment of debts, pass any *expost facto* law, or law impairing the obligation of contracts." This will doubtless bear hard on debtors who wish to defraud their creditors, but it will be of real service to the honest part of the community. Examine well the characters & circumstances of men who are averse to the new constitution. Perhaps you will find that the above recited clause is the real ground of the opposition of some of them, though they may artfully cover it with a splendid profession of zeal for state privileges and general liberty.

On the whole, if the proposed constitution is not calculated to better your country, and to secure to you the blessings for which you have so successfully contended, reject it: but if it is an improvement on the present confederation, and contains within itself the principles of farther improvement suited to future circumstances, join the mighty current of federalism, and give it your hearty support. You were among the first states that formed an independent constitution;[2] be not among the last in accepting and ratifying the proposed plan of federal government; it is your sheet anchor; and without it, independence may prove a curse.

1. On 29 January Ramsay had written: "I fear the numerous class of debtors more than any other" (to Benjamin Lincoln, CC:482).

2. On 26 March 1776 the South Carolina Provincial Congress adopted a provisional constitution. On 19 March 1778 the state legislature replaced this constitution with another one.

499. George Washington to James Madison
Mount Vernon, 5 February[1]

I am indebted to you for several of your favors, and thank you for their enclosures.[2]–The rumours of War between France and England have subsided; and the poor Patriots of Holland, it seems, are left to fight their own Battles or negotiate–in neither case with any great prospect of Advantage–They must have been deceived, or their conduct has been divided, precipant, & weak:–the former, with some blunders, have, I conceive, been the causes of their misfortunes.[3]–

I am sorry to find by yours,[4] and other accts. from Massachusetts,[5] that the decision of its Convention (at the time of their dates) remained problematical.–A rejection of the New form by that State will envigorate the opposition, not only in New York, but in all those which are to follow;–at the same time that it will afford materials for the Minority in such as have adopted it to blow the Trumpet of discord more loudly.–The acceptance by a *bare*[6] majority, tho' preferable to rejection, is also to be depricated.

It is scarcely possible to form any decided opinion of the *general* sentiment of the people of this State, on this important subject.–Many have asked me with anxious sollicitude, if you did not mean to get into the Convention; conceiving it of indispensable necessity.[7]–Colo. Mason, who returned home only yesterday, has offered himself, I am told, for the County of Stafford;[8] and his friends add, he can be elected not only there, but for Prince William & Fauquier also.–The truth of this I know not.–I rarely go from home–and my visitors who for the most part are travellers and strangers, have not the best information.

At the time you suggested for my consideration, the expediency of a communication of my sentiments on the proposed Constitution, to any corrispondent I might have in Massachusetts, it did not occur to me that Genl Lincoln & myself frequently interchanged letters[9]–much less did I expect that a hasty, and indigested extract of one which I had written–intermixed with a variety of other matter to Colo. Chas. Carter, in answer

to a letter I had received from him respecting Wolf dogs–Wolves–Sheep–
experiments in Farming &ca &ca. &ca.[10]–was then in the press, and would
bring these sentiments to public view by means of the extensive circulation
I find that extract has had.–Altho' I never have concealed, and am perfectly regardless who becomes acquainted with my sentiments on the proposed Constitution, yet nevertheless, as no care had been taken to dress
the ideas, nor any reasons assigned in support of my opinion, I felt myself
hurt by the publication; and informed my friend the Colonel of it.–In
answer, he has fully exculpated himself from the *intention*, but his zeal in
the cause prompted him to distributt copies, under a prohibition (which
was disregarded) that they should not go to the press.–As you have seen
the rude, or crude extract (as you may please to term it), I will add no
more on the Subject[11]

Perceiving that the Fœderalist, under the signature of Publius, is about
to be re-published, I would thank you for forwarding to me three or four
Copies; one of which to be neatly bound, and inform me of the cost.[12]–

Altho' we have not had many, or deep Snows since the commencement
of them, yet we have had a very severe Winter; and if the cold of this day
is proportionably keen with you, a warm room, & a good fire will be found
no bad, or uncomfortable antidote to it.[13]–

1. RC, Special Collections, Signers of the Declaration of Independence, Amherst
College Library, Amherst, Mass. Washington's letterbook copy (Washington Papers,
DLC) differs in paragraphing, punctuation, spelling, capitalization, and italics. For
significant differences between the two versions, see notes 3, 6, 10, and 13 below.

2. Since Washington had written to Madison on 10 January, he had probably received four letters–dated 14, 20, 25, and 28 January–from him. (See CC:446, 464, and
Rutland, *Madison*, X, 357–59, 419–20, 437–38.) Enclosed in Madison's letter of 14
January were several newspapers, including the New York *Daily Advertiser* of 14 January. For the enclosures in Madison's letters of 25 and 28 January, see note 4.

3. In the letterbook copy, the two preceding sentences read: "They must have been
deceived, or their conduct has been weak and precipitate, and absurd.–The former
however I believe is the truth."

4. In his letters of 25 and 28 January, Madison quoted in full letters that he had
received from Massachusetts Convention delegate Rufus King dated 16 and 20 January, respectively.

5. Delegate Benjamin Lincoln had written Washington on 20 and 27 January describing events in the Massachusetts Convention and enclosing newspaper reports of
the debates. On 14 January Henry Knox wrote Washington that the Convention would
adopt the Constitution but that it was "questionable whether it will be by a large majority." (These three letters are in the Washington Papers at the Library of Congress.)

6. The italics here and in the paragraph immediately below are not in the letterbook
copy.

7. Madison represented Orange County in the Virginia Convention in June 1788.

8. George Mason represented Stafford County in the Virginia Convention.

9. See Madison to Washington, 20 December (CC:359); Washington to Madison, 10
January (Rutland, *Madison*, X, 358); and "George Washington on the Ratification of
the Constitution by Massachusetts" (CC:638).

10. In the letterbook copy, "&ca &ca. &ca." reads: "and the lord knows what else."

11. For the documents relating to this incident and its impact, see CC:386.

12. The publication of a book edition of *The Federalist* had been announced on 2 January (CC:406) and on 22 March it was offered for sale (CC:639-A). Two days later John Jay, one of the authors, sent Washington a copy (Washington Papers, DLC). There is no record that Washington received any copies from Madison who had left New York City early in March.

13. In the letterbook copy, this paragraph reads: "Altho' we have not had many, or deep snows yet we have since the commencemt. of it, had a very severe, winter; and if this day, with you, is as much keener than we now feel it, as the difference of lattitude ought to make it you will feel a comfortable fire no bad antidote against cold fingers and Toes."

500. Publius: The Federalist 50
New York Packet, 5 February

James Madison and Alexander Hamilton both claimed authorship of this essay but internal evidence suggests that it was written by Madison. The essay was reprinted in the New York *Independent Journal*, 6 February, and the New York *Daily Advertiser*, 9 February. It is number 50 in the M'Lean edition and number 49 in the newspapers.

For a general discussion of the authorship, circulation, and impact of *The Federalist*, see CC:201, 639; and for the disputed authorship of this essay, see Cooke, xix-xxx, 633–634, and Rutland, *Madison*, X, 261–63.

The FŒDERALIST, No. 49

To the People of the State of New-York.

It may be contended perhaps, that instead of *occasional* appeals to the people, which are liable to the objections urged against them, *periodical* appeals are the proper and adequate means *of preventing and correcting infractions of the Constitution.*

It will be attended to, that in the examination of these expedients, I confine myself to their aptitude for *enforcing* the Constitution by keeping the several departments of power within their due bounds, without particularly considering them, as provisions for *altering* the Constitution itself. In the first view, appeals to the people at fixed periods, appear to be nearly as ineligible, as appeals on particular occasions as they emerge. If the periods be separated by short intervals, the measures to be reviewed and rectified, will have been of recent date, and will be connected with all the circumstances which tend to viciate and pervert the result of occasional revisions. If the periods be distant from each other, the same remark will be applicable to all recent measures, and in proportion as the remoteness of the others may favor a dispassionate review of them, this advantage is inseparable from inconveniencies which seem to counterbalance it. In the first place, a distant prospect of public censure would be a very feeble restraint on power from those excesses, to which it might be urged by the force of present motives. Is it to be imagined, that a legislative assembly, consisting of a hundred or two hundred members, eagerly bent on some favorite object, and breaking through the restraints of the Constitution in pursuit of it, would be arrested in their career, by considerations drawn from a censorial revision of their conduct at the future distance of ten, fifteen or twenty years? In the next place, the abuses would often have compleated their mischievous effects, before the remedial provision would be applied. And in the last place, where this might not be the case, they would be of long standing, would have taken deep root, and would not easily be extirpated.

The scheme of revising the Constitution in order to correct recent breaches of it, as well as for other purposes, has been actually tried in one of the States. One of the objects of the council of censors, which met in Pennsylvania, in 1783 and 1784, was, as we have seen, to enquire "whether the Constitution had been violated, and whether the legislative and executive departments had encroached on each other."[1] This important and novel experiment in politics, merits in several points of view, very particular attention. In some of them it may perhaps, as a single experiment, made under circumstances somewhat peculiar, be thought to be not absolutely conclusive. But as applied to the case under consideration, it involves some facts which I venture to remark, as a compleat and satisfactory illustration of the reasoning which I have employed.

First. It appears from the names of the gentlemen, who composed the council, that some at least of its most active and leading members, had also been active and leading characters in the parties which pre-existed in the State.

Secondly. It appears that the same active and leading members of the council, had been active and influential members of the legislative and executive branches, within the period to be reviewed; and even patrons or opponents of the very measures to be thus brought to the test of the Constitution. Two of the members had been Vice-Presidents of the State, and several others, members of the executive council, within the seven preceding years. One of them had been Speaker, and a number of others distinguished members of the legislative assembly, within the same period.[2]

Thirdly. Every page of their proceedings witnesses the effect of all these circumstances on the temper of their deliberations. Throughout the continuance of the council, it was split into two fixed and violent parties. The fact is acknowledged and lamented by themselves. Had this not been the case, the face of their proceedings exhibit a proof equally satisfactory. In all questions, however unimportant in themselves, or unconnected with each other, the same names, stand invariably contrasted on the opposite columns. Every unbiassed observer, may infer without danger of mistake, and at the same time, without meaning to reflect on either party, or any individuals of either party, that unfortunately *passion*, not *reason*, must have presided over their decisions. When men exercise their reason cooly and freely, on a variety of distinct questions, they inevitably fall into different opinions, on some of them. When they are governed by a common passion, their opinions if they are so to be called, will be the same.

Fourthly. It is at least problematical, whether the decisions of this body, do not, in several instances, misconstrue the limits prescribed for the legislative and executive departments, instead of reducing and limiting them within their constitutional places.

Fifthly. I have never understood that the decisions of the council on constitutional questions, whether rightly or erroneously formed, have had any effect in varying the practice founded on legislative constructions. It even appears, if I mistake not, that in one instance, the cotemporary Legislature denied the constructions of the council, and actually prevailed in the contest.

This censorial body therefore, proves at the same time, by its researches, the existence of the disease; and by its example, the inefficacy of the remedy.

This conclusion cannot be invalidated by alledging that the State in which the experiment was made, was at that crisis, and had been for a long time before, violently heated and distracted by the rage of party. Is it to be presumed, that at any future septennial epoch, the same State will be free from parties? Is it to be presumed that any other State, at the same or any other given period, will be exempt from them? Such an event ought to be neither presumed nor desired; because an extinction of parties necessarily implies either a universal alarm for the public safety, or an absolute extinction of liberty.

Were the precaution taken of excluding from the assemblies elected by the people to revise the preceding administration of the government, all persons who should have been concerned in the government within the given period, the difficulties would not be obviated. The important task would probably devolve on men, who with inferior capacities, would in other respects, be little better qualified. Although they might not have been personally concerned in the administration, and therefore not immediately agents in the measures to be examined; they would probably have been involved in the parties connected with these measures, and have been elected under their auspices.

1. See CC:492, note 6.
2. The Council of Censors included former vice presidents of the Supreme Executive Council George Bryan and Joseph Potter; former members of the Supreme Executive Council James Edgar, Joseph Hart, Richard M'Allister, James M'Lene, John McDowell, and James Read; and former speakers of the Assembly James M'Lene and Frederick A. Muhlenberg. A total of fourteen former assemblymen served on the Council of Censors.

501. Centinel XIV
Philadelphia Independent Gazetteer, 5 February[1]

TO THE PEOPLE OF PENNSYLVANIA.

Fellow-Citizens, I am happy to find the comment that I have made upon the nature and tendency of the new constitution, and my suspicions of the principles and designs of its authors, are fully confirmed by the evidence of the Honorable LUTHER MARTIN, Esquire, late deputy in the general convention. He has laid open the conclave, exposed the dark scene within, developed the mystery of the proceedings, and illustrated the machinations of ambition. His public spirit has drawn upon him the rage of the conspirators, for daring to remove the veil of secrecy, and announcing to the public the meditated, gilded mischief: all their powers are exerting for his destruction; the mint of calumny is assiduously engaged in coining scandal to blacken his character, and thereby to invalidate his testimony;[2] but this illustrious patriot will rise superior to all their low arts, and be the better confirmed in the good opinion and esteem of his fellow-citizens, upon whose gratitude he has an additional claim by standing forth their champion at a crisis when most men would have shrunk from such a duty. Mr. Martin has appealed to general Washington for the truth of what he has advanced,[3] and undaunted by the threats of his and his country's enemies, is nobly persevering in the cause of liberty and mankind. I would earnestly recommend it to all well meaning persons to read his communication, as the most satisfactory and certain method of forming a just opinion on the present momentous question, particularly the three or four last continuances, as they go more upon the general principles and tendency of the new constitution. I have in former numbers alluded to some passages in this publication;[4] I shall in this number quote some few others, referring to the work itself for a more lengthy detail. The following paragraphs[5] are extracted from the continuances republished in the Independent Gazetteer of the 25th January, and the Pennsylvania Packet of the 1st February instant, viz.

"By the eighth section of this article, Congress is to have power to lay and collect taxes, duties, imposts, and excises.–When we met in convention after our adjournment, to receive the report of the committee of detail, the members of that committee were requested to inform us what powers were meant to be vested in Congress by the word duties in this section, since the word imposts extended to duties on goods imported, and by another part of the system no duties on exports were to be laid.–In answer to this inquiry we were informed, that it was meant to give the general government the power of laying stamp duties on paper, parchment and vellum. We then proposed to have the power inserted in express words, lest disputes hereafter might arise on the subject, and that the meaning might be understood by all who were to be affected by it; but to this it was objected, because it was said that the word stamp would probably sound odiously in the ears of many of the inhabitants, and be a cause of objection. By the power of imposing stamp duties the Congress will

have a right to declare that no wills, deeds, or other instruments of writing, shall be good and valid, without being stamped–that without being
reduced to writing and being stamped, no bargain, sale, transfer of property, or contract of any kind or nature whatsoever shall be binding; and
also that no exemplifications of records, depositions, or probates of any
kind shall be received in evidence, unless they have the same solemnity–
They may likewise oblige all proceedings of a judicial nature to be stamped
to give them effect–those stamp duties may be imposed to any amount
they please, and under the pretence of securing the collection of these
duties, and to prevent the laws which imposed them from being evaded,
the Congress may bring the decision of all questions relating to the conveyance, disposition and rights of property and every question relating to
contracts between man and man into the courts of the general government.–Their inferior courts in the first instance and the superior court by
appeal. By the power to lay and collect imposts, they may impose duties
on any or every article of commerce imported into these states to what
amount they please. By the power to lay excises, a power very odious in
its nature, since it authorises officers to go into your houses, your kitchens,
your cellars, and to examine into your private concerns; the Congress may
impose duties on every article of use or consumption, on the food that we
eat–on the liquors we drink–on the cloaths we wear–on the glass which
enlighten our houses–or the hearths necessary for our warmth and comfort. By the power to lay and collect taxes, they may proceed to direct
taxation on every individual either by a capitation tax on their heads, or
an assessment on their property. By this part of the section, therefore, the
government has a power to lay what duties they please on goods imported–
to lay what duties they please afterwards on whatever we use or consume–
to impose stamp duties to what amount they please, and in whatever cases
they please–afterwards to impose on the people direct taxes, by capitation
tax, or by assessment, to what amount they choose, and thus to sluice
them at every vein as long as they have a drop of blood, without any
controul, limitation or restraint–while all the officers for collecting these
taxes, stamp duties, imposts and excises, are to be appointed by the general government, under its direction, not accountable to the states; nor is
there even a security that they shall be citizens of the respective states, in
which they are to exercise their offices; at the same time the construction
of every law imposing any and all these taxes and duties, and directing the
collection of them, and every question arising thereon, and on the conduct
of the officers appointed to execute these laws, and to collect these taxes
and duties so various in their kinds, are taken away from the courts of
justice of the different states, and confined to the courts of the general

government, there to be heard and determined by judges holding their offices under the appointment, not of the states, but of the general government.

"Many of the members, and myself in the number, thought that the states were much better judges of the circumstances of their citizens, and what sum of money could be collected from them by direct taxation, and of the manner in which it could be raised, with the greatest ease and convenience to their citizens, than the general government could be; and that the general government ought not in any case to have the power of laying direct taxes, but in that of the delinquency of a state. Agreeable to this sentiment, I brought in a proposition on which a vote of the convention was taken. The proposition was as follows: 'And wherever the legislature of the United States shall find it necessary that revenue should be raised by direct taxation, having apportioned the same by the above rule, requisitions shall be made of the respective states to pay into the continental treasury their respective quotas within a time in the said requisition to be specified, and in case of any of the states failing to comply with such requisition, then and then only, to have power to devise and pass acts directing the mode and authorising the collection of the same.' Had this proposition been acceded to, the dangerous and oppressive power in the general government of imposing direct taxes on the inhabitants, which it now enjoys in all cases, would have been only vested in it in case of the non-compliance of a state, as a punishment for its delinquency, and would have ceased that moment that the state complied with the requisition–But the proposition was rejected by a majority, consistent with their aim and desire of encreasing the power of the general government as far as possible, and destroying the powers and influence of the states–And though there is a provision that all duties, imposts and excises shall be uniform, that is, to be laid to the same amount on the same articles in each state, yet this will not prevent Congress from having it in their power to cause them to fall very unequal and much heavier on some states than on others, because these duties may be laid on articles but little or not at all used in some states, and of absolute necessity for the use and consumption of others, in which case the first would pay little or no part of the revenue arising therefrom, while the whole or nearly the whole of it would be paid by the last, to wit, the states which use and consume the articles on which the imposts and excises are laid."

Another extract,[6] viz.

"But even this provision apparently for the security of the state governments, inadequate as it is, is entirely left at the mercy of the general government, for by the fourth section of the first article, it is expressly provided, that the congress shall have a power to make and alter all regulations concerning the time and manner of holding elections for senators; a provision expressly looking forward to, and I have no doubt designed for the utter extinction and abolition of all state governments; nor will this I believe be doubted by any person, when I inform you that some of the warm advocates and patrons of the system in convention, strenuously opposed the choice of the senators by the state legislatures, insisting that the state governments ought not to be introduced in any manner so as to be component parts of, or instruments for carrying into execution the general government–Nay, so far were the friends of the system from pretending that they meant it or considered it as a federal system, that on the question being proposed, 'that a union of the states, merely federal, ought to be the sole object of the exercise of the powers vested in the convention;' it was negatived by a majority of the members, and it was resolved, 'that a national government ought to be formed;' afterwards the word 'national' was struck out by them, because they thought the word might tend to alarm–and although now, they who advocate the system, pretend to call themselves federalists; in convention the distinction was just the reverse–those who opposed the system, were there considered and stiled the federal party, those who advocated it, the antifederal.

"Viewing it as a national not a federal government, as calculated and designed not to protect and preserve, but to abolish and annihilate the state governments, it was opposed for the following reasons:–It was said that this continent was much too extensive for one national government, which should have sufficient power and energy to pervade and hold in obedience and subjection all its parts, consistent with the enjoyment and preservation of liberty–That the genius and habits of the people of America were opposed to such a government–That during their connexion with Great-Britain they had been accustomed to have all their concerns transacted within a narrow circle, their colonial districts–They had been accustomed to have their seats of government near them, to which they might have access, without much inconvenience when their business should require it–That at this time we find if a county is rather large, the people complain of the inconvenience, and clamour for a division of their county, or for a removal of the place where their courts are held, so as to render it more central and convenient–That in those states, the territory of which is extensive, as soon as the population encreases remote from the seat of government, the inhabitants are urgent for a removal of the seat of their government, or to be erected into a new state–As a proof of this, the inhabitants of the western parts of Virginia and North Carolina, of Vermont and the province of Main, were instances, even the inhabitants of the western parts of Pennsylvania, who it was said already seriously look forward to the time when they shall either be erected into a new state, or have their seat of government removed to the Susquehanna. If the inhabitants of the different states consider it as a grievance to attend a county court or the seat of their own government, when a little inconvenient, can it be supposed they would ever submit to have a national government established, the seat of which, would be more than a thousand miles removed from some of them? It was insisted that governments of a republican nature, are those best calculated to preserve the freedom and happiness of the citizen–That governments of this kind, are only calculated for a territory but small in its extent–That the only method by which an extensive continent like America could be connected and united together consistent with the principles of freedom, must be by having a number of strong and energetic state governments for securing and protecting the rights of the individuals forming those governments, and for regulating all their concerns; and a strong energetic federal government over those states for the protection and preservation, and for regulating the common concerns of the states.–It was further insisted, that even if it was possible to effect a total abolition of the state governments at this time, and to establish one general government over the people of America, it could not long subsist, but in a little time would again be broken into a variety of governments of a smaller extent, similar in some manner to the present situation of this continent; the principal difference in all probability would be that the governments, so established, being effected by some violent convulsion, might not be formed on principles so favorable to liberty as those of our present state governments–That this ought to be an important consideration to such of the states who had excellent governments, which was the case with Maryland and most others, whatever it might be to persons who disapproving of their particular state government, would be willing to hazard every thing to overturn and destroy it.–These reasons, Sir, influenced me to vote against two branches in the legislature, and against every part of the system which was repugnant to the principles of a federal government–Nor was there a single argument urged, or reason assigned, which to my mind was satisfactory, to prove that a good government on federal principles was unattainable, the whole of their arguments only proving, what none of us controverted, that our federal government as originally formed was defective and wanted amendment–However, a majority of the convention hastily and inconsiderately, without condescending to make a fair trial, in their great wisdom, decided that a kind of government which a Montesquieu and a Price have declared the best calculated of any to preserve internal liberty, and to enjoy external strength and security, and the only one by which a large continent can be connected and united consistent with the principles of liberty was totally impracticable, and they acted accordingly."

After such information, what are we to think of the declarations of Mr. Wilson, who assured our state convention, that it was neither the intention of the authors of the new constitution, nor its tendency to establish a consolidated or national government, founded upon the destruction of the state governments, that such could not have been the design of the general convention he said was certain, because the testimony of experience, the opinions of the most celebrated writers, and the nature of the case demonstrated in the clearest manner, that so extensive a territory as these United States includes, could not be governed by any other mode than a confederacy of republics consistent with the principles of freedom, and that their own conviction was, that nothing short of the supremacy of despotism could connect and bind together this country under ONE GOVERN-MENT?[7] Has any one a doubt now remaining of the guilt of the conspirators!

The O—rs of the P–t O—ce, fearful of the consequences of their conduct, are taking measures to invalidate the charge made against them.[8] As this is a matter of the highest importance to the public, it will be necessary to state the charge and the evidence. In two of my former numbers,[9] I asserted that the patriotic newspapers of this city and that of New-York miscarried in their passage, whilst the vehicles of despotism, meaning those newspapers in favor of the new constitution, passed as usual; and it was particularly asserted that the patriotic essays of Brutus, Cincinnatus, Cato, &c. published at New-York,[10] were withheld during the greatest part of the time that our state convention sat; and in a late number,[11] I further asserted that since the late arrangement at the P–t O—ce, scarcely a newspaper was suffered to pass by the usual conveyance, and for the truth of this last charge I appealed to the printers; however I understand this last is not denied or controverted. When the dependence of the printers on the P–t O—ce is considered, the injury they may sustain by incurring the displeasure of these of—rs, and when to this is added that of the complexion of the printers in respect to the new constitution, that most of them are zealous in promoting its advancement, it can scarcely be expected that they would volunteer it against the P–t O—rs, or refuse their names to a certificate exculpating the of—rs; accordingly we find that most of the printers have signed a certificate that the newspapers arrived as usual prior to the first of January, when the new arrangement took place; however, the printer of the Freeman's Journal when applied to, had the spirit to refuse his name to the establishment of a falsehood, and upon being called upon to specify the missing papers, particularly during the sitting of the state convention, he pointed out and offered to give a list of a considerable number, instancing no less than seven successive Greenleaf's patriotic New-York papers, besides others occasionally with-held from him; Colonel Oswald was out of town when his family was applied to, or I have no doubt he would have observed a similar conduct. But there is a fact that will invalidate any certificate that can be procured on this occasion,[12] and is alone demonstrative of the suppression of the patriotic newspapers. The opponents to the new constitution in this state were anxious to avail themselves of the well-written essays of the New-York patriots, such as Brutus, Cincinnatus, Cato, &c. and with that view were attentive to have them republished here as soon as they came to hand, and especially during the sitting of our state convention, when they would have been the most useful to the cause of liberty by operating on the members of that convention; a recurrence to the free papers of this city at that period, well shew a great chasm in these republications, owing to the miscarriage of Greenleaf's New-York papers; agreeable to my assertions it will appear, that for the greatest part of the time that our state convention sat, scarcely any of the numbers of Brutus, Cincinnatus, Cato, &c. were republished in this city; the fifth number of Cincinnatus[13] that contained very material information about the finances of the union, which strikes at some of the principal arguments in favor of the new constitution, which was published at New-York the 29th November, was not republished here until the 15th December following, two or three days after the convention rose, and so of most of the other numbers of this and the other signatures; so great was the desire of the opponents here to republish them, that the fourth number of Cincinnatus[14] was republished so lately as in Mr. Bailey's last paper, which with other missing numbers were procured by private hands from New-York, and in two or three instances, irregular numbers were republished. The new arrangement at the P–t O—ce, novel in its nature, and peculiarly injurious by the suppression of information at this great crisis of public affairs, is a circumstance highly presumptive of the truth of the other charge.

1. Reprinted: Philadelphia *Freeman's Journal*, 6 February; *New York Journal*, 13, 15 February; Boston *American Herald*, 3, 6, 10 March.

2. For Federalist reaction to Martin's *Genuine Information*, see CC:389.

3. Such an appeal has not been located in the *Genuine Information*, although Washington was mentioned in the first installment on 28 December (CC:389). In mid-April the *Genuine Information* was published as a pamphlet by Eleazer Oswald of the *Independent Gazetteer*. It includes a letter by Martin, dated 30 March, which states that "...I can, with confidence, appeal to a *Washington*, a *Franklin*, and other respectable members of the convention, for the veracity of my information" (Evans 21220).

4. See "Centinel" XI–XII, *Independent Gazetteer*, 16, 23 January (CC:453, 470).

5. See *Genuine Information* VI, Baltimore *Maryland Gazette*, 15 January (CC:451).
6. See *Genuine Information* IV, *ibid.*, 8 January (CC:425).
7. See James Wilson's 24 November speech (RCS:Pa., 339–63; and CC:289).
8. See note 12 (below) and "Officers of the Post Office," *New York Journal*, 23 January (Appendix II).
9. See "Centinel" IX and XI, 8 and 16 January (Appendix II).
10. For general discussions of these writers, see CC:103, 178, 222.
11. See "Centinel" XIII, 30 January (Appendix II).
12. Ebenezer Hazard obtained the signatures of the Philadelphia printers, including that of Eleazer Oswald's foreman, on a certificate verifying "that during the time the *Centinel* said the papers were withheld (while the Pennsylvania Convention were sitting) they were received as regularly as at other times" (Hazard to Jeremy Belknap, 10 May, Appendix II). On 14 February "Detector" charged that "Centinel's" evidence was "quite as novel as the new arrangement he complains of. . . . It may here be observed, that his memory begins to fail; for, he appears to have forgotten that in the former number ["Centinel" XIII] he roundly asserted that all the printers were free except one, and now he seems to find but one firm-spirited fellow among them" (*Pennsylvania Mercury*, Mfm:Pa. 431).
13. "Cincinnatus" V was printed in the *New York Journal* on 29 November (CC:307) and reprinted in the *Independent Gazetteer* on 15 December.
14. "Cincinnatus" IV was printed in the *New York Journal* on 22 November and reprinted in the *Freeman's Journal* on 30 January with a statement about the delay (CC:287).

502. Luther Martin: Genuine Information XI
Baltimore Maryland Gazette, 5 February[1]

Mr. MARTIN's *Information to The House of Assembly, continued.*

By the third section of the fourth article, no new State shall be formed or erected within the jurisdiction of any other State, without the consent of the legislature of such State.

There are a number of States which are so circumstanced with respect to themselves and to the other States, that every principle of justice and sound policy, require their dismemberment or division into smaller States.–Massachusetts is divided into two districts, totally separated from each other by the State of New-Hampshire,–on the northeast side of which lies the provinces of Main and Sagadohock, more extensive in point of territory, but less populous than old Massachusetts, which lies on the other side of New-Hampshire.–No person can cast their eye on the map of that State but they must in a moment admit, that every argument drawn from convenience, interest, and justice require that the provinces of Main and Sagadohock should be erected into a new State, and that they should not be compelled to remain connected with old Massachusetts under all the inconveniences of their situation.

The State of Georgia is larger in extent than the whole island of Great-Britain, extending from its sea coast to the Missisippi, a distance of eight hundred miles or more; its breadth for the most part, about three hundred miles.–The States of North-Carolina and Virginia in the same manner reach from the sea coast unto the Missisippi.

The hardship, the inconvenience, and the injustice of compelling the inhabitants of those States who may dwell on the western side of the mountains and along the Ohio and Missisippi rivers to remain connected with the inhabitants of those States respectively, on the atlantic side of the mountains, and subject to the same State governments, would be such as would in my opinion, justify even recourse to arms to free themselves from and to shake off so ignominious a yoke.

This representation was made in convention, and it was further urged that the territory of these States were too large, and that the inhabitants thereof would be too much disconnected for a *republican government* to extend to them its benefits, *which* is only suited to a small and compact territory–That a regard also for the peace and safety of the union, ought to excite a desire that those States should become in time divided into separate States, since when their population should become proportioned in any degree to their territory, they would from their strength and power become *dangerous members* of a *federal* government.–It was further said that if the general government was not by its constitution to interfere, the inconvenience would soon remedy itself, for that as the population increased in those States, their legislatures would be obliged to consent to the erection of new States to avoid the evils of a civil war, but as by the proposed constitution the general government is obliged to protect each State against domestic violence, and consequently will be obliged to assist in suppressing such commotions and insurrections as may take place from the struggle to have new States erected, the general government ought to have a power to decide upon the propriety and necessity of establishing or erecting a new State even without the approbation of the legislature of such States, within whose jurisdiction the new State should be erected, and for this purpose I submitted to the convention the following proposition–"That on the application of the inhabitants of any district of territory within the limits of any of the States, it shall be lawful for the legislature of the United States, if they shall under all circumstances think it reasonable, to erect the same into a new State, and admit it into the union *without the consent* of the State of which the said district may be a part."[2] And it was said that we surely might trust the general government with *this power* with *more propriety* than with *many others* with which they were proposed to be entrusted–and that as the general government was bound to suppress all insurrections and commotions which might arise on this subject, it ought to be in the power of the general government to decide upon it, and not in the power of the legislature of a single State by obstinately and unreasonably opposing the erection of a new State to prevent its taking effect, and thereby extremely to *oppress* that part of its citizens which live remote from, and inconvenient to, the seat of its government, and even to involve the union in war to support its injustice and oppression.–But, upon the vote being taken, Georgia, South-Carolina, North-Carolina, Virginia, Pennsylvania and Massachusetts, were in the *negative*.–New-Hampshire, Connecticut, Jersey, Delaware and Maryland, were in the *affirmative*.–New York was absent.[3]

That it was inconsistent with the rights of free and independent States, to have their territory dismembered without their consent, was the principal argument used by the opponents of this proposition.–The truth of the objection we readily admitted, but at the same time, insisted that it was not *more inconsistent* with the rights of free and independent States than *that inequality of suffrage* and *power* which the *large States* had *extorted* from *the others;* and that if the *smaller States* yielded up *their rights* in *that instance, they* were *entitled* to demand from the States of extensive territory a *surrender* of their rights in *this instance;* and in a particular manner, as it was *equally necessary* for the true interest and happiness of the *citizens* of *their own States*, as of *the union*.–But, Sir, although when the large States demanded *undue* and *improper* sacrifices to be made to their *pride* and *ambition*, they treated the rights of free States with more contempt than ever a British parliament treated the rights of her colonial establishments, yet when a *reasonable* and *necessary sacrifice* was asked *from them* they spurned the idea with ineffable disdain. They *then perfectly understood* the *full value* and the *sacred obligation* of *State rights*, and at the least attempt to infringe them *where they were concerned*, they were tremblingly alive and agonized at every pore.

When we reflect how *obstinately* those States contended for that *unjust superiority* of power in the government, which they have *in part* obtained, and for the establishment of this superiority by the constitution.–When we reflect that they appeared willing to hazard the existence of the union rather than not to succeed in their unjust attempt–That should their legislatures consent to the erection of new States within their jurisdiction, it would be an immediate sacrifice of that power, to obtain which they appeared disposed to sacrifice every other consideration.

When we further reflect that they *now* have a *motive* for desiring to preserve their territory entire and unbroken, which they *never had before–the gratification* of *their ambition in possessing and exercising superior power over their sister States*–and that this constitution is to give them the *means* to *effect* this desire *of which* they were *formerly destitute–the whole force of the United States pledged to them for restraining intestine commotions*, and *preserving to them the obedience and subjection of their citizens*, even in the *extremest part of their terri-*

tory;-I say, Sir, when we consider these things it would be too absurd and improbable to deserve a serious answer, should any person suggest that *these States* mean ever *to give their consent* to the *erection of new States within their territory.*-Some of them it is true, have been for some time past *amusing* their inhabitants in those districts that wished to be erected into new States, but should this constitution be adopted, *armed with a sword and halter* to compel their obedience and subjection, they will no longer act with indecision;-and the State of Maryland may, and probably will be called upon to assist with her wealth and her blood in subduing the inhabitants of Franklin, Kentucky, Vermont, and the provinces of Main and Sagadohock, and in compelling them to continue in subjection to the States which respectively claim jurisdiction over them.

Let it not be forgotten at the same time, that a great part of the territory of these large and extensive States, which they now hold in possession, and over which they now claim and exercise jurisdiction, were crown lands, unlocated and unsettled when the American revolution took place-Lands which were *acquired* by the *common blood and treasure*, and which *ought* to have been the *common stock*, and for the *common benefit* of the Union.-Let it be remembered that the State of Maryland was so deeply sensible of the injustice that these lands should be held by particular States for their own emolument, even at a time when *no superiority* of *authority or power* was *annexed to extensive territory*, that in the *midst of the late war* and all the *dangers* which *threatened* us, *it* withheld for a long time its assent to the articles of confederation for that reason, and when it ratified those articles it entered a *solemn protest* against what it considered so *flagrant injustice;*[4]-But, Sir, the question is not *now* whether those States shall hold that territory unjustly to themselves, but whether by *that act of injustice* they shall *have superiority of power and influence over the other States*, and *have a constitutional right* to *domineer* and *lord it* over them-Nay, more, whether we will *agree* to a *form of government* by which we *pledge* to *those States* the *whole force of the union* to *preserve* to them that *extensive territory entire* and *unbroken*, and with *our blood and wealth to assist them*, whenever they please to demand it, to *preserve the inhabitants thereof under their subjection*, for the *purpose* of *increasing their superiority over us*-of *gratifying their unjust ambition*-in a word, for the *purpose* of *giving ourselves masters*, and of *rivetting our chains!*

(*To be continued.*)

1. Reprinted: *Pennsylvania Packet*, 12 February; Philadelphia *Independent Gazetteer*, 21 February; *New York Journal*, 7 April.

2. Martin's resolution, as recorded in the Convention Journal and James Madison's notes for 30 August, reads differently: "The Legislature of the United States shall have power to erect new States within as well as without the territory claimed by the several States or either of them and admit the same into the Union: Provided that nothing in

this Constitution shall be construed to affect the claim of the United States to vacant lands ceded to them by the late treaty of Peace" (Farrand, II, 457–58, 464). For the evolution of this clause of the Constitution from the time that it appeared in the report of the Committee of Detail on 6 August, see CDR, 268–69, 282–83, 295.

3. Martin's resolution was defeated eight states to three; New Jersey, Delaware, and Maryland voted for it (Farrand, II, 458, 464).

4. For Maryland's position on western lands and its ratification of the Articles of Confederation in 1781, see CDR, 55–57, 97–100, 135–37.

503. Publius: The Federalist 51
New York Independent Journal, 6 February

James Madison and Alexander Hamilton both claimed authorship of this essay but internal evidence suggests that it was written by Madison. This essay was reprinted in the *New York Packet*, 8 February, and the New York *Daily Advertiser*, 11 February. It was the last number printed in the *Advertiser*. The essay is number 51 in the M'Lean edition and number 50 in the newspapers.

For a general discussion of the authorship, circulation, and impact of *The Federalist*, see CC:201, 639; and for the disputed authorship of this essay, see Cooke, xix–xxx, 634, and Rutland, *Madison*, X, 261–63.

The FŒDERALIST. No. L.
To the People of the State of New-York.

To what expedient then shall we finally resort for maintaining in practice the necessary partition of power among the several departments, as laid down in the constitution? The only answer that can be given is, that as all these exterior provisions are found to be inadequate, the defect must be supplied, by so contriving the interior structure of the government, as that its several constituent parts may, by their mutual relations, be the means of keeping each other in their proper places. Without presuming to undertake a full developement of this important idea, I will hazard a few general observations, which may perhaps place it in a clearer light, and enable us to form a more correct judgment of the principles and structure of the government planned by the convention.

In order to lay a due foundation for that separate and distinct exercise of the different powers of government, which to a certain extent, is admitted on all hands to be essential to the preservation of liberty, it is evident that each department should have a will of its own; and consequently should be so constituted, that the members of each should have as little agency as possible in the appointment of the members of the others. Were this principle rigorously adhered to, it would require that all the appointments for the supreme executive, legislative, and judiciary magistracies, should be drawn from the same fountain of authority, the people, through channels, having no communication whatever with one another. Perhaps such a plan of constructing the several departments would be less difficult in practice than it may in contemplation appear. Some difficulties however, and some additional expence, would attend the execution of it. Some deviations therefore from the principle must be admitted. In the constitution of the judiciary department in particular, it might be inexpedient to insist rigorously on the principle; first, because peculiar qualifications being essential in the members, the primary consideration ought to be to select that mode of choice, which best secures these qualifications; secondly, because the permanent tenure by which the appointments are held in that department, must soon destroy all sense of dependence on the authority conferring them.

It is equally evident that the members of each department should be as little dependent as possible on those of the others, for the emoluments annexed to their offices. Were the executive magistrate, or the judges, not independent of the legislature in this particular, their independence in every other would be merely nominal.

But the great security against a gradual concentration of the several powers in the same department, consists in giving to those who administer each department, the necessary constitutional means, and personal motives, to resist encroachments of the others. The provision for defence must in this, as in all other cases, be made commensurate to the danger of attack. Ambition must be made to counteract ambition. The interest of the man must be connected with the constitutional rights of the place. It may be a reflection on human nature, that such devices should be necessary to controul the abuses of government. But what is government itself but the greatest of all reflections on human nature? If men were angels, no government would be necessary. If angels were to govern men, neither external nor internal controuls on government would be necessary. In framing a government which is to be administered by men over men, the great difficulty lies in this: You must first enable the government to controul the governed; and in the next place, oblige it to controul itself. A dependence on the people is no doubt the primary controul on the government; but experience has taught mankind the necessity of auxiliary precautions.

This policy of supplying by opposite and rival interests, the defect of better motives, might be traced through the whole system of human affairs, private as well as public. We see it particularly displayed in all the subordinate distributions of power; where the constant aim is to divide and arrange the several offices in such a manner as that each may be a check on the other; that the private interest of every individual, may be a centinel over the public rights. These inventions of prudence cannot be less requisite in the distribution of the supreme powers of the state.

But it is not possible to give to each department an equal power of self defence. In republican government the legislative authority, necessarily, predominates. The remedy for this inconveniency is, to divide the legislature into different branches; and to render them by different modes of election, and different principles of action, as little connected with each other, as the nature of their common functions, and their common dependence on the society, will admit. It may even be necessary to guard against dangerous encroachments by still further precautions. As the weight of the legislative authority requires that it should be thus divided, the weakness of the executive may require, on the other hand, that it should be fortified. An absolute negative, on the legislature, appears at first view to be the natural defence with which the executive magistrate should be armed. But perhaps it would be neither altogether safe, nor alone sufficient. On ordinary occasions, it might not be exerted with the requisite firmness; and on extraordinary occasions, it might be perfidiously abused. May not this defect of an absolute negative be supplied, by some qualified connection between this weaker department, and the weaker branch of the stronger department, by which the latter may be led to support the constitutional rights of the former, without being too much detached from the rights of its own department?

If the principles on which these observations are founded be just, as I persuade myself they are, and they be applied as a criterion, to the several state constitutions, and to the federal constitution, it will be found, that if the latter does not perfectly correspond with them, the former are infinitely less able to bear such a test.

There are moreover two considerations particularly applicable to the federal system of America, which place that system in a very interesting point of view.

First. In a single republic, all the power surrendered by the people, is submitted to the administration of a single government; and usurpations are guarded against by a division of the government into distinct and separate departments. In the compound republic of America, the power surrendered by the people, is first divided between two distinct governments, and then the portion allotted to each, subdivided among distinct and separate departments. Hence a double security arises to the rights of the people. The different governments will controul each other; at the same time that each will be controuled by itself.

Second. It is of great importance in a republic, not only to guard the society against the oppression of its rulers; but to guard one part of the society against the injustice of the other part. Different interests necessarily exist in different classes of citizens. If a majority be united by a common interest, the rights of the minority will be insecure. There are but two methods of providing against this evil: The one by creating a will in the community independent of the majority, that is, of the society itself; the other by comprehending in the society so many separate descriptions of citizens, as will render an unjust combination of a majority of the whole, very improbable, if not impracticable. The first method prevails in all governments possessing an hereditary or self appointed authority. This at best is but a precarious security; because a power independent of the society may as well espouse the unjust views of the major, as the rightful interests, of the minor party, and may possibly be turned against both parties. The second method will be exemplified in the federal republic of the United States. Whilst all authority in it will be derived from and dependent on the society, the society itself will be broken into so many parts, interests and classes of citizens, that the rights of individuals or of the minority, will be in little danger from interested combinations of the majority. In a free government, the security for civil rights must be the same as that for religious rights. It consists in the one case in the multiplicity of interests, and in the other, in the multiplicity of sects. The degree of security in both cases will depend on the number of interests and sects; and this may be presumed to depend on the extent of country and number of people comprehended under the same government. This view of the subject must particularly recommend a proper federal system to all the sincere and considerate friends of republican government: Since it shews that in exact proportion as the territory of the union may be formed into more circumscribed confederacies or states, oppressive combinations of a majority will be facilitated, the best security under the republican form, for the rights of every class of citizens, will be diminished; and consequently, the stability and independence of some member of the government, the only other security, must be proportionally increased. Justice is the end of government. It is the end of civil society. It ever has been, and ever will be pursued, untill it be obtained, or untill liberty be lost in the pursuit. In a society under the forms of which the stronger faction can readily unite and oppress the weaker, anarchy may as truly be said to reign, as in a state of nature where the weaker individual is not secured against the violence of the stronger: And as in the latter state even the stronger individuals are prompted by the uncertainty of their condition, to submit to a government which may protect the weak as well as themselves: So in the former state, will the more powerful factions or parties be gradually induced by a like motive, to wish for a government which will protect all parties, the weaker as well as the more powerful. It can be little doubted, that if the state of Rhode Island was separated from the confederacy, and left to itself, the insecurity of rights under the popular form of government within such narrow limits, would be displayed by such reiterated oppressions of factious majorities, that some power altogether independent of the people would soon be called for by the voice of the very factions whose misrule had proved the necessity of it. In the extended republic of the United States, and among the great variety of interests, parties and sects which it embraces, a coalition of a majority of the whole society could seldom take place on any other principles than those of justice and the general good; and there being thus less danger to a minor from the will of the major party, there must be less pretext also, to provide for the security of the former, by introducing into the government a will not dependent on the latter; or in other words, a will independent of the society itself. It is no less certain than it is important, notwithstanding the contrary opinions which have been entertained, that the larger the society, provided it lie within a practicable sphere, the more duly capable it will be of self government. And happily for the *republican cause*, the practicable sphere may be carried to a very great extent, by a judicious modification and mixture of the *federal principle*.

504. A.B.: The Raising
Pennsylvania Gazette, 6 February

"A.B." is Francis Hopkinson's poetic extension of his essay "The New Roof," which was first printed in the *Pennsylvania Packet* on 29 December (CC:395). By 26 March "A.B." was reprinted fifteen times: N.H. (2), Mass. (3), R.I. (1), Conn. (2), N.Y. (2), Pa. (1), Md. (1), Va. (2), S.C. (1). In the reprintings by the *Massachusetts Gazette*, 29 February, and the *Massachusetts Centinel*, 1 March, the poem was preceded by a cartoon of six upright pillars each labeled for a state that had ratified the Constitution. A seventh pillar, New Hampshire, was in the process of being raised, and a caption read: "It WILL yet rise." A few months elapsed before "A.B." was reprinted three more times: Philadelphia *American Museum*, July issue; *Gazette of the State of Georgia*, 14 August; and Philadelphia *Federal Gazette*, 1 January 1789. The *American Museum* and *Federal Gazette* identified Hopkinson as the author. Lastly, "A.B." appeared in *The Miscellaneous Essays and Occasional Writings of Francis Hopkinson, Esq.* (3 vols., Philadelphia, 1792), II, 320–22 (Evans 24407).

THE RAISING:
A NEW SONG FOR FEDERAL MECHANICS.

I.

Come muster, my Lads, your mechanical Tools,
Your Saws and your Axes, your Hammers and Rules;
Bring your Mallets and Planes, your Level and Line,
And Plenty of Pins of American Pine;
    For our Roof we will raise, and our Song still shall be–
    A Government firm, and our Citizens free.

II.

Come, up with *the Plates*, lay them firm on the Wall,
Like the People at large, they're the Ground-work of all;
Examine them well, and see that they're sound,
Let no rotten Parts in our Building be found;
    For our Roof we will raise, and our Song still shall be–
    Our Government firm, and our Citizens free.

III.

Now hand up *the Girders*, lay each in his Place,
Between them *the Joists* must divide all the Space;
Like Assembly-men, *these* should lye level along,
Like *Girders*, our Senate prove loyal and strong;
    For our Roof we will raise, and our Song still shall be–
    A Government firm, over Citizens free.

IV.

The Rafters now frame–your *King-Posts* and *Braces*,
And drive your Pins home, to keep all in their Places;
Let Wisdom and Strength in the Fabric combine,
And your Pins be all made of American Pine;
    For our Roof we will raise, and our Song still shall be–
    A Government firm, over Citizens free.

V.

Our *King-Posts* are Judges–how upright they stand,
Supporting the *Braces*, the Laws of the Land–
The Laws of the Land, which divide Right from Wrong,
And strengthen the Weak, by weak'ning the Strong;
    For our Roof we will raise, and our Song still shall be–
    Laws equal and just, for a People that's free.

VI.

Up! Up with the Rafters–each Frame is a State!
How nobly they rise! their Span, too, how great!
From the North to the South, o'er the Whole they extend,
And rest on the Walls, while the Walls they defend!
    For our Roof we will raise, and our Song still shall be–
    Combined in Strength, yet as Citizens free.

VII.

Now enter the *Purlins*, and drive your Pins through,
And see that your Joints are drawn home, and all true;
The *Purlins* will bind all the Rafters together,
The Strength of the Whole shall defy Wind and Weather;
    For our Roof we will raise, and our Song still shall be–
    United as States, but as Citizens free.

VIII.

Come, raise up the Turret–our Glory and Pride–
In the Centre it stands, o'er the Whole to preside;
The Sons of *Columbia* shall view with Delight
It's Pillars, and Arches, and Towering Height;
    Our Roof is now rais'd, and our Song still shall be–
    A Fœderal Head, o'er a People still free.

IX.

Huzza! my brave Boys, our Work is complete,
The World shall admire *Columbia*'s fair Seat;
It's Strength against Tempest and Time shall be Proof,
And Thousands shall come to dwell under our ROOF.
    Whilst we drain the deep Bowl, our Toast still shall be–
    Our Government firm, and our Citizens free.

505. A Freeman III
Pennsylvania Gazette, 6 February

In this third and last installment of his "Freeman" essays, Tench Coxe continued to demonstrate that the Constitution did not create a consolidated government or annihilate the state governments. Coxe's determination to pursue these themes was apparently reinforced by *The Federalist* 45–46, copies of which James Madison, who had received "A Freeman" I, had sent him from New York City on 30 January (CC:485. See *The Federalist* 45–46, New York *Independent Journal*, 26 January, and *New York Packet*, 29 January, CC:478, 483.). Madison had recommended "that if any hints are contained" in the two essays "they may be pursued in your enquiry." On 6 February Coxe responded that the essays "are very valuable papers" and that he would "retouch" the theme of "Consolidation" (Rutland, *Madison*, X, 473. For an idea that Coxe apparently took from *The Federalist* 45, see note 5 below.). Coxe returned to the issue of consolidation in "A Pennsylvanian" III, where he again praised *The Federalist* 45–46 for demonstrating that the central government, under the Constitution, "cannot possibly absorb the state governments." He also praised "A Freeman" I–III for illustrating *"the indefeasible powers of the separate states"* (*Pennsylvania Gazette*, 20 February, Mfm:Pa. 439).

On 6 February Coxe sent "A Freeman" III to James Madison and Mathew Carey, asking the latter to insert it in his Philadelphia *American Museum* (Rutland, *Madison*, X, 473; and Coxe Papers, Series II, Correspondence and General Papers, PHi). Coxe also forwarded the essay to Thomas Hartley of York, Pa., and he encouraged Jacob Broome of Wilmington, Del., to have it printed in Delaware (Hartley to Coxe, 15 February, and Broome to Coxe, 25 February, *ibid.*; and Coxe to Broom, 9 February, Coxe Papers, Series I, Volumes and Printed Material, PHi). "A Freeman" III was reprinted in the *Pennsylvania Packet*, 7 February; the *Philadelphische Correspondenz*, 26 February; and probably in the no longer extant issue of the *Delaware Gazette*, 20 February. Mathew Carey also printed the essay, under Coxe's name, in the April issue of the *American Museum*.

For more on the authorship, circulation, and impact of "A Freeman," see CC:472.

To the MINORITY of the CONVENTION of *Pennsylvania*.

Gentlemen, In my former letters[1] I endeavoured to point out certain provisions of the new Constitution, and several circumstances that must result from the proposed frame of government and the state constitutions, which might demonstrate, that there is no ground to apprehend a consolidation of the states, that shall join in the depending confederacy, into one government.

An observation of the honorable Mr. Wilson's has been adduced, among other arguments, to prove, that despotism would follow such a general government. I believe with him and with you that such would be the consequence of *a single national constitution, in which all the objects of society and government were so compleatly provided for, as to place the several states in the union on the footing of counties of the empire.*[2]–But permit me to ask you, gentlemen, will such be the condition of the states? Where is the county that can independently train its own militia, appoint its civil and militia officers, establish *a peculiar system* of penal laws, issue criminal process *in its own name*, erect corporations, *impose direct taxes*, excises and duties, hold lands in its own right, *commence war* on any emergency, *regulate descents*, prescribe *the qualifications* of electors, alter its constitution or *the principles* of its government, divide itself into separate and *independent parts*, join itself to another state, issue writs for elections, and regulate the same, enact inspection laws, *erect courts*, appoint judges, *commission* all its officers, create new offices, sell and give away its lands, *erect fortifications*, and, in short where is the county in the union, or in the world, that can exercise in any instance *independent legislative, executive or judicial powers?*

Those three gentlemen[3] who with-held their names from the act of the fœderal convention could not have apprehended the annihilation of the state governments, while that house was sitting, or they would, under the influence of such a fear, certainly have pressed for a bill of rights. It appears they did not think one so necessary, as to concert a single motion to obtain it:[4] A conclusive proof, in my mind, that they saw no symptoms of a design to consolidate in the framers of the plan, and that they had no apprehensions of the kind themselves.

The construction of the senate affords an absolute certainty, that the states will not lose their present share of separate powers. No state is to lose its voice therein without *its own consent.* Governor Randolph justly observes, that the force of the constitution of any state can only be lessened *by the absolute grant of its own citizens.* Whatever therefore is now possessed will remain, unless transferred by new grants. The state legislatures too being the immediate representatives and guardians of their *respective* constituents, and being the powerful creators of the senators, it cannot be apprehended, either that they will give away their own powers, or that they will chuse men who are unfriendly to them; nor is it at all probable that a senator would hazard the displeasure of the people, or the vengeance of so potent a body as a state legislature, by sacrificing their interests or powers. Rather may it be expected, that his interest and connexions in the state will too partially attach him to it, to the injury of national objects; or that he may neglect general concerns, from a desire to please a legislature or a people, who will be to him *the source of honors, emolument and power.*

So *independent* will the state governments remain, that their laws may, and in some instances will, be *severer* than those of the union. Treason against the United States, for instance, cannot be attended with confiscation and corruption of blood; but by the existing laws of all the states, *the unoffending families* of attainted persons, stripped of all hereditary rights, and condemned to the bitter portion of extreme poverty, are left without their friend and parent, to meet the trials of the world alone: an awful monument of *the sovereign and avenging power* of their native state. Let the Representative or Senator who may meditate the annihilation of the government of his state duly consider this, before it be too late.

You apprehend the power of Congress to lay direct taxes will tend to produce consolidation. But the several states possess that power also, and by an *early*, wise and faithful exercise of it, can always supercede the use of it by Congress. For example; if ten thousand pounds were apportioned to Pennsylvania, to make up the interest on our foreign debts by the end of 1788, a tax for which would be laid in July, our legislature might proceed in the most easy and expeditious way to raise the money, against the time when the fœderal government must necessarily proceed, and by paying our quota into the fœderal treasury would fulfil the requisitions of the law. A fœderal government, that shall possess the least degree of policy or virtue, would never attempt to interfere with such honest, wise and effectual arrangements of any state.[5] It cannot be reasonably feared that a fœderal legislature, chosen by *the equal voices* of all our citizens, *the poor, as well as the rich*, will ever wrest from the hands of the people and states, who respectively appoint them, powers so wisely placed and so honestly applied.

The check of the Senate on the appointment of officers will exceedingly favor the preservation of the state governments. Let us suppose an expedition on foot, which requires a number of general officers, whom a President might be inclined to appoint from the state to which he belongs, or for which several persons are nominated, that are too partially attached to the fœderal government, or desirous of lessening the powers of the separate states. *The Senate can reject them all*, and independently give their reasons to the people and the legislatures. That they will often do so, we cannot doubt, when we remember *where their private interests, affections and connexions lie*, to whom they will owe *their seats*–to whom they must look for *future favors* of the same kind.

The lordship of the soil is one of the most valuable and powerful appendages of sovereignty–This remains *in full perfection* with every state. From them must grants flow, to them must be paid *the annual acknowledgment*, whether it be a mere compliance with form in the rendering of a pepper corn, or *a solid revenue* in the payment of a quit-rent. To them also, as original and rightful proprietaries and *lords of the soil*, will the estates of extinct families revert.

Independent revenues and resources are indubitable proofs of *sovereignty*. The states will possess many of those which now exist, and which may hereafter be created. Taxes on state offices, fees for grants of lands, and various licences, tolls on rivers, canals, and roads not being post-roads, rents of public buildings, escheats, the mighty fund of quit-rents, and sales of lands; these and many others are (exclusively of Congress) within the power of the several states, besides their having access, in common with the fœderal government, to every source of revenue, but the duties on foreign merchandize and ships.

IMPEACHMENTS within the several states will afford them opportunities of exerting the most dignified and aweful powers of sovereignty. The people of every state, by their constitutional representatives, may impeach the public officer, however great or daring, that shall presume to violate their exclusive rights, or offend against the peace and dignity of their commonwealth, and may punish him, on conviction, by fine, imprisonment or death, without any possible interference of Congress.

But, Gentlemen, the subject is inexhaustible. Every section in the fœderal constitution, as we peruse it, affords new ideas opposed to consolidation: Every moment's reflexion, on the operation and tendency of the proposed government, adds to their number. I will not therefore trespass longer on your time. I will rest the matter on your own good sense and candor, confidently trusting that the removal of your apprehensions on this important point will render the new Constitution more agreeable to you. Thinking, as you did, consolidation was intended and would take place, and that it must produce a despotism, you would have been criminal in assenting to the plan proposed; but I will hope that the consideration of this point which we have taken together, will remove your fears, and open the door to comfortable hopes, rather than to apprehensions, from the great measure now waiting the Fiat of the people of the United States.

1. For numbers I–II, which were printed on 23 and 30 January, see CC:472, 488.

2. See James Wilson's speech of 24 November to the Pennsylvania Convention (RCS:Pa., 339–63; and CC:289).

3. Elbridge Gerry, George Mason, and Edmund Randolph.

4. On 12 September Elbridge Gerry moved and George Mason seconded a proposal that the Constitutional Convention appoint a committee to draft a bill of rights. The motion was defeated unanimously (CC:75).

5. This uncommon Federalist position on the use of the requisition system in collecting federal revenue from the states under the Constitution was probably borrowed by Tench Coxe from James Madison's *The Federalist* 45, which Madison had sent to Coxe on 30 January. (See CC:478, note 1.)

506. An Old Whig VIII
Philadelphia Independent Gazetteer, 6 February[1]

MR. PRINTER, It is the fate of political controversies to begin with argument and end with abuse: And hence we find, in many instances, that a subject which for a time, has engaged the most earnest attention of the people, is at length quitted with horror and disgust. The question, however, concerning the total adoption of the plan of government, proposed by the late federal convention, is too important for good men to suffer themselves to be diverted from giving it a full consideration by the bouncing of squibs or the whizzing of political firebrands. I therefore persuade myself that a few candid observations on this subject will yet be heard with attention.

The real question is this;–Whether the people of this country ought to adopt the proposed constitution in its present form, without limitation or alteration, or whether we ought to insist upon amendments being made previous to its adoption.

Most men seem to agree that amendments ought to be made in the proposed plan in some stage of the business; and all seem agreed that an efficient form of continental government ought to be established. Shall we then first adopt the constitution and afterwards amend it; or shall we first amend it and afterwards adopt it? Let us for a moment consider the propriety of adopting it first, and trusting to its being afterwards amended. These necessary amendments, after the constitution is adopted, can only be made in one or two ways;–either by our future rulers in the continental legislature by their own act–or in the way provided for in the fifth article, by a convention to be called for proposing amendments, whenever two-thirds of both houses shall deem it necessary, or whenever the legislatures of two-thirds of the states shall make application for that purpose, such amendments afterwards to be valid if ratified by the legislatures of three-fourths of the states, or by conventions in three-fourths thereof, if Congress should think proper to call them. This latter mode is so intricate, that an attempt to investigate it is like endeavouring to trace the windings of a labyrinth, and I have therefore observed that people willingly turn aside from the subject, as confused and disgusting. Some former observations on this article I found were very little attended to: However I will attempt once more to find a clue to its mazes, after I shall first have considered that more inviting ground of expectation to which most of those who assume the name of federalists turn their eyes with so much confidence.

First then, the general expectation seems to be that our future rulers will rectify all that is amiss. If a bill of rights is wanting, they will frame a bill of rights. If too much power is vested in them, they will not abuse it; nay, they will divest themselves of it. The very first thing they will do, will be to establish the liberties of the people by good and wholesome ordinances, on so solid a foundation as to baffle all future encroachments from themselves or their sucessors. Much good no doubt might be done in this way; if Congress should possess the most virtuous inclinations, yet there are some things which it will not be in their power to rectify. For instance; *the appellate jurisdiction both as to law and fact*, which is given to the supreme court of the continent, and which annihilates the trial by jury in all civil causes, the Congress can only modify:–They cannot extinguish this power, so destructive to the principles of real liberty. It would not by any means be extravagant to say, that a new continental convention ought to be called, if it were only for the sake of preserving that sacred palladium–THE INESTIMABLE RIGHT OF TRIAL BY JURY.–But even if we were to delude ourselves so far as to believe that it would be entirely in the power of the future legislature to set every thing right, to build up our liberties against all invasions, and to protect us from every political calamity, still we ought not to repose all our liberty and all our happiness in the virtue of our future rulers. I speak not with reference to any particular set of men. I pretend not to know who will be our rulers one year hence. In the state of Pennsylvania I have seen the administration of our constitution in the hands of its bitterest enemies, during near one half of its existence; and I shall not be at all surprized to find that if the new continental government shall be set a-going, that the jockies who at present have vaulted into the saddle; should be the first to be thrown into the dirt and trampled upon; nor, on the other hand, that some of those who are foremost in contending for a permanent security to the rights of the people, should be in the first rank of oppressors. These things have frequently happened; and the only safe way of reasoning on political subjects is, to consider men, abstractly as men, with like passions and infirmities throughout the world, in every age, and every country; and to believe that the same guards and checks against arbitrary power, which were necessary two thousand years ago, are equally necessary at present, and will be so two thousand years hence. Idolatry is the parent of errors in politics as well as religion;–and an implicit confidence in our rulers now, will be abused as much as implicit confidence in priests ever was in the days of superstition. I know well that instances of political moderation may be found, and a tyrant has before now descended from the plenitude of power, satiated with dominion, or worn out with care; but there is not one instance on record in all history of a number of men voluntarily abandoning the powers of an aristocracy. Look at the Decemviri, look at the thirty tyrants of Athens, look at all the lordly aristocracies that ever existed, and shew me one instance–such an instance cannot be shewn. Nay farther, a single monarch has many times used his power with moderation; but a number of men combined in an aristocracy, never knew what moderation meant. They are all struggling to be most powerful, all aiming to enrich themselves and provide for their friends, and all of them plundering the people. And shall we foolishly, after so many thousand examples, trust to the virtue and moderation of our future rulers, to divest themselves of those powers which may be abused to our prejudice, and are no way useful to our protection? Not to insist upon Swift's ludicrous tale of Jack's hanging himself at the instigation of Humphry Hocus, on the promise of being cut down before he should be dead, and when he had hanged himself, of being left to kick his heels in the air, the moral of which, by the bye, is strictly founded in human nature;[2]–let us attend to a more serious fable.–"A man, says Æsop, coming into a wood, begged the trees to grant him the favor of a handle to his axe. The whole forest consented; upon which he provided himself with a strong handle; which he had no sooner done, than he began to fell the trees without number, then the trees, though too late, repented of their weakness, and an universal groan was heard throughout the forest. At length, when the man came to cut down the tree which had furnished him with the handle, the trunk fell to the ground uttering these words: Fool that I was! I have been the cause of my own destruction."[3] If we perish in America, we shall have no better comfort than the same mortifying reflection, that we have been the cause of our own destruction.

I have said that many of the liberties which, by the proposed constitution, are to be surrendered up into the hands of our rulers, will be of no use towards the protection of the people; and a little reflection will convince us, that it is certainly the case. If, indeed, government were really strengthened by such surrender, if the body of the people were made more secure, or more happy by the means, we ought to make the sacrifice. An individual ought to submit to be tossed about, imprisoned and treated injuriously, if the good of his country should require it; and every individual in the community ought to strip himself of some convenience for the sake of the public good.

I know it is an error not uncommon to believe, that a government is the more powerful in proportion as it is more tyrannical; but this is not the case: so far from it, that it has always been found, that free countries have been able to exert powers far superior to those in which a more absolute government prevailed. For instance, a senate which is master of its own elections, without any or with very little dependence on the people, would not be able to exert as much force as a senate which is freely elected by the people; because the chearful support which would be yielded in the latter case, would far exceed that which could be exacted by the mere force of authority. Again; how could the stripping people of the right of trial by jury conduce to the strength of the state? Do we find the government in England at all weakened by the people retaining the right of trial by jury? Far from it. Yet these things which merely tend to oppress the people, without conducing at all to the strength of the state, are the last which aristocratic rulers would consent to restore to the people; because they encrease the personal power and importance of the rulers. Judges, unincumbered by juries, have been ever found much better friends to government than to the people. Such judges will always be more desireable than juries to a self-created senate, upon the same principle that a large standing army, and the entire command of the militia and of the purse, is ever desireable to those who wish to enslave the people, and upon the same principle that a bill of rights is their aversion.

In like manner, if we should trace the several branches of the proposed constitution, which are obnoxious to the liberties of the people, we shall find them to consist of such articles as are rather fitted to encrease the powers of the rulers, than the strength of the nation. Union is the great source of strength to a nation, not vassalage. To an aristocractic government vassalage is the great object even at the expence of union among the people. We ought not, therefore, by any means to rely upon the virtue of our future rulers for a reformation of those things which at present are amiss in the proposed constitution. The president and senate will ever be grasping at more and more power until they are completely masters of the people, and the president at last master of all.

Let us then turn to the article in the proposed constitution, which provides for the making alterations at some future period; and let us figure to ourselves the time when two-thirds of both houses of Congress shall think it necessary to call a convention, or two-thirds of the legislatures of the individual states shall apply for the calling of a convention, and when a continental convention shall agree upon amendments, and when the legislatures of three-fourths of the states, or three-fourths of the conventions to be called in the several states, if Congress shall prefer that mode of proceeding, shall ratify such amendments; and again, after all these strainings, and filtrings, and refinings, of the hopes and expectations of the people through the channels of power, when the amendments so asked for, proposed, digested, twistificated, altered, and at last ratified, will be of any essential importance. For my part I would full as soon sit down and take my chance of winning an important privilege to the people, by the casting the dice 'till I could throw sixes an hundred times in succession.–There is no doubt but the thing has been purposely contrived to make alterations extremely difficult; and so it certainly ought to be if the proposed constitution were a good one. I do not therefore so much blame the late federal convention for making their constitution very difficult of alteration, as I insist upon it as an argument in favor of making our amendments beforehand. A machine which cannot be taken to pieces after it is once set a-going, ought to be very well finished at first.

Yet this is not all the difficulty. Inveterate power is at all times very hard to be controuled. Habits, connexions, dependence, and a thousand circumstances in course of time, rivet the chains of slavery 'till we grow either callous to their galling, or too feeble to shake them off, or too listless to resist. Ask the beaten Turk to resume his liberty, or the tired horse to resume his pristine freedom.–As well might you ask the galled sons of America, a few years hence, to assert the native rights of men, if the proposed constitution be once fixed upon us. It will be extremely difficult to change it for the better even in the beginning; but in a little time it will become utterly impossible.

A little prudence, a little patience, and a little serious reflection, would lead us to concur in calling a new convention, to revise the constitution proposed to us. That convention, I have no doubt, if fully, freely, and deliberately chosen, would concur in some essential amendments; and we might yet be a united and a happy people.

1. This essay, mistakenly given the number seven, was not reprinted. "An Old Whig" VII was published on 28 November (CC:301). For the authorship of "An Old Whig," see CC:157.

2. The character "Jack," popularized by Jonathan Swift, represented the Protestant Dissenters, especially Calvinists; "Humphrey Hocus" was Whig leader the Duke of Marlborough. See Alan W. Bower and Robert A. Erickson, eds., *John Arbuthnot: The History of John Bull* (Oxford, England, 1976), "An Appendix to John Bull Still in His Senses: or, Law is a Bottomless-Pit," chapter III, 84–87. "An Appendix," first printed in London in 1712, was a satire on the Dissenters and the Whigs for the roles they played in the passage of the Occasional Conformity Act of 1711.

3. See Benjamin Cole, ed., *Select Tales and Fables with Prudential Maxims in Prose and Verse* (2 vols. in 1, London, 1746), I, Fable XXX.

507. Philadelphiensis IX
Philadelphia Freeman's Journal, 6 February[1]

Instamus tamen immemores, cœcique furore,
Et monstrum infelix sacrata sistimus arce.   Virg.
TRANSLATION.
Thus we, by madness blinded and o'ercome,
Lodge the dire monster in the sacred dome.[2]   ·

My Fellow-Citizens, Before *martial law* is declared to be the supreme law of the land, and your character of free citizens be changed to that of the subjects of a *military king,* which are necessary consequences of the adoption of the proposed constitution, let me admonish you in the name of *sacred liberty,* to make a solemn pause. Permit a freeman to address you, and to solicit your attention to a cause wherein yourselves and your posterity are concerned. The sun never shone upon a more important one: It is the cause of freedom–of a whole continent–of yourselves and of your fellow men.

Men who have so gloriously asserted the rights of human nature, and overcome tyranny, one ought reasonably to suppose could not have their spirits so much broken as peaceably to submit to it a few years afterwards. By the declaration of peace, wherein Britain acknowledged the independence and sovereignty of the United States, the people of America became citizens of the freest country under heaven. But under the proposed plan of government the least fragment of liberty cannot exist.

The writers against the proposed constitution are denominated, by the *aristocratics, incendiaries,* and enemies to America, men whose writings tend to involve this devoted country in anarchy, and in all the horrors of a civil war. Now, in reply to this charge; let me ask the friends of this government, Is that man an *incendiary* who advocates the unalienable rights of the people? Is he an enemy to America who endeavors to protect the *oppressed* from the *oppressor;* who opposes a conspiracy against the liberties of his country, concerted by a few *tyrants,* whose views are to lord it over the rest of their fellow citizens, to trample the poorer part of the people under their feet, that they may be rendered their servants and slaves? If such a writer is an incendiary, and an enemy to America, then I glory in the character. A conspiracy against the freedom of America, both deep and dangerous, has been formed by an infernal junto of demagogues. Our thirteen free commonwealths are to be consolidated into one *despotic monarchy.* Is not this a position obvious? Its evidence is intuitive; and the address and dissent of the minority of the convention of Pennsylvania[3] add such strength to its illustration, that no man of common sense can refuse his assent. But why need I attempt to prove a point, that that honest man and firm patriot, Mr. MARTIN, says the monarchy men of the federal convention declared was their intention.[4]

Who can deny but the *president general* will be a *king* to all intents and purposes, and one of the most dangerous kind too; a king elected to command a standing army? Thus our laws are to be administered by this *tyrant*; for the whole, or at least the most important part of the executive department is put in his hands.

A quorum of 65 representatives, and of 26 senators, with a *king* at their head, are to possess powers, that extend to the *lives*, the *liberties*, and *property* of every citizen of America. This novel system of government, were it possible to establish it, would be a compound of *monarchy* and *aristocracy*, the most accursed that ever the world witnessed. About 50 (these being a quorum) of the *well born*, and a *military king*, with a *standing army* devoted to his will, are to have an uncontrouled power over our lives, our liberties, and property, in all cases whatsoever. Is he an incendiary who abhors the thought of such a government, who declares it his opinion, that none but a sycophant or a slave could submit to it? I think not; and there is no power under heaven that could cause me to change my opinion; which has the joint evidences of reason and experience for its foundation.

There is not a tincture of democracy in the proposed constitution, except the nominal elections of the president general and the illustrious Congress be supposed to have some colour of that nature; but this is a mere deception, invented to gull the people into its adoption. Its framers were well aware that some appearance of election ought to be observed, especially in regard to the first Congress; for without such an appearance there was not the smallest probability of their having it organized and set in operation. But let the wheels of this government be once cleverly set in motion, and I'll answer for it, that the people shall not be much troubled with future elections, especially in choosing their *king*, the *standing army* will do that business for them.

The thoughts of a military officer possessing such powers, as the proposed constitution vests in the president general, are sufficient to excite in the mind of a freeman the most alarming apprehensions; and ought to rouse him to oppose it at *all events*. Every freeman of America ought to hold up this idea to himself, *that he has no superior but God and the laws*. But this tyrant will be so much his superior, that he can at any time he thinks proper, order him out in the militia to exercise, and to march when and where he pleases. His officers can wantonly inflict the most disgraceful punishment on a peaceable citizen, under pretence of disobedience, or the smallest neglect of militia duty.

Among the substantial objections to the great powers of the president, that of his *negative* upon the laws, is one of the most inconsiderable, indeed it is more a sound than any thing else; For, if he be a bold enterprising fellow, there is little fear of his ever having to exercise it. The two branches of the legislature, will be at his service; no law contrary to his sentiments, however salutary in its operation, dare be mentioned by them. As a body, and as individuals, they will be his sycophants and flatterers. But, if on the contrary he should not be a man of spirit, a thing very improbable, as none but an ambitious man, well versed in the ways of men, could have the address to be raised to that elevated station; if, however, I say, he should not be a man of an enterprising spirit, in that case he will be a *minion* of the aristocratics, doing according to their will and pleasure, and confirming every law they may think proper to make, without any regard to their public utility.

Every idea of such unlimited powers being lodged in so small a number of the *well born*, elevated so far above the rest of their fellow citizens, and supported by a *king* with a *standing army* at his disposal, ought to cause the blood of a free citizen to boil with indignation: the very mentioning of it shocks my whole frame. I abhor the thought from my soul: And I flatter myself that the people of this continent will not suffer such a government to be placed over them. Indeed it astonishes me, that the conspirators who framed it, had not the most dreadful apprehensions of their personal safety, from the just resentment of the freemen of an insulted country.

To such lengths have these bold conspirators carried their scheme of despotism, that your most sacred rights and privileges are surrendered at discretion. When government thinks proper, under the pretence of writing a libel, *&c.* it may imprison, inflict the most cruel and unusual punishment, seize property, carry on prosecutions, *&c.* and the unfortunate citizen has no *magna charta*, no *bill of rights*, to protect him; nay, the prosecution may be carried on in such a manner that even a *jury* will not be allowed him. Where is that *base slave* who would not appeal to the *ultima ratio*, before he submits to this government?

If the despots persist in pushing it on, let them answer the consequences; they may fall a sacrifice to their own obstinacy; for liberty will triumph over every obstacle, even were a *standing army* opposed to it.

To preserve the peace of the country, every patriot should exert himself at this awful crisis, and use his influence to have another federal convention called as soon as possible; either to amend the old articles of confederation, or to frame a constitution on revolution principles, that may secure the freedom of America to the remotest time.[5]

If the State of Massachusetts should reject the proposed constitution, of which there is a strong probability, what a contemptible figure must its advocates make, who, after it made its appearance from the *dark conclave*, affirmed that there was but *five men* opposed to it in the United States.[6] The convention of that state was chosen in the moment of blind enthusiasm, and yet we find it so much divided that the issue is doubtful. The sentiments of the people are changing every day, and were that convention to be elected now, I doubt not but four fifths would be against it. In the back counties of Pennsylvania, where the *well born* have no influence, the opposition is said to have become so powerful that a person would be in danger of losing his life, if he ventured to speak a word in its favor.

The conspirators saw clearly, that such a system of government could never be established over freemen, except they were taken by surprize; and hence they hurried matters forward with that view; in short, the people were made to believe, that they were all *dead men*, if they did not adopt it immediately. Even still they are endeavoring to hold up the idea of anarchy being the consequence of rejection: But he must have very weak intellects indeed, and little acquainted with the spirit of freemen, to whom it is not obvious that adoption will produce anarchy and ruin.

No evil can result from calling another general convention, but much good would be the consequence. The distresses of America are not of that nature to be healed all of a sudden; some of them indeed have arisen from the defects in the general government; but there are others of a different kind, that must be removed by time, and by the prudence of the people at large.

Ye patriots! ye lovers of peace, of liberty, and of your fellow men! Ye are called upon at this solemn juncture, to stand forth and save your country; before the breach is too wide, and while the parties may still be reconciled to each other; before anarchy stalks through the land; and before the sword of civil discord is unsheathed. For the sake of every thing that is great and good, and as you shall answer for it at the great tribunal, use your influence to procure another general convention with all possible speed, as the only way left to preserve the union of America, and to save your fellow citizens from misery and destruction.

1. On the same day the Philadelphia *Independent Gazetteer* announced that the essay would appear, as it did, in its issue of 7 February. See also note 5 below.

2. A reference to the Trojan horse being brought into the city of Troy. See C. Day Lewis, trans., *The Aeneid of Virgil* (New York, 1952), 38 (Book II, lines 244–45). For a satirical response to "Philadelphiensis'" use of the Trojan horse allusion, see "Philadelphiensis," No. X, *Pennsylvania Mercury*, 9 February (Mfm:Pa. 417).

3. For the "Dissent," see *Pennsylvania Packet*, 18 December (CC:353).

4. *Genuine Information* II, Baltimore *Maryland Gazette*, 1 January (CC:401).

5. This paragraph was reprinted in the *Maryland Journal*, 12 February, and Winchester *Virginia Gazette*, 7 March.

6. A satirical Federalist letter, said to be written by Daniel Shays to the Antifederal junto of Philadelphia, asserted that the opposition to the Constitution in Pennsylvania was composed of "five gentlemen" (*Independent Gazetteer*, 25 September, CC:94).

508. Massachusetts Convention: Amendments to the Constitution
Boston, 6 February

On 9 January the Massachusetts Convention met in Boston. Because of the state's prominence, Federalists believed that the rejection of the Constitution by Massachusetts "will be fatal to the Plan" (John Brown to James Breckinridge, 28 January, CC:480). In particular, they believed that Massachusetts would have a significant impact on two of its neighbors–New Hampshire and New York. On 9 January Convention delegate Christopher Gore wrote that, if Massachusetts ratified the Constitution, "there is a very great probability, that New Hampshire will add one State to the affirmative" (to Jeremiah Wadsworth, RCS:Conn., 603). John Langdon of Portsmouth, who had been elected a delegate to the New Hamp-

shire Convention scheduled to convene on 13 February, attended the Massachu-
setts Convention for several days and said "that If Massachustts adopted the
Constitution, N. Hampshire would not be one week in Session" (Caleb Gibbs to
George Washington, 9 February, Washington Papers, DLC). Writing from New
York City, Virginia delegate to Congress James Madison declared that "The de-
cision of Massts. in either way, will decide the voice of this State" (to Edmund
Randolph, 20 January, Rutland, *Madison*, X, 398). Samuel Blachley Webb, a
New York City commercial agent, worried that should Massachusetts "reject it we
are ruined, on them depends every thing, every Fedral Man in this City looks up"
to Massachusetts "for our political salvation" (to Joseph Barrell, 13 January,
CC:444). And Philip Schuyler, a leader of New York's Federalists, wrote that "If
that event takes place there, I believe we shall have little contest here" (to Stephen
Van Rensselaer, 8 February, Schuyler Papers, DLC).

During the first three weeks of the Massachusetts Convention, people on both
sides claimed they had a majority. Antifederalists estimated they had a majority of
anywhere from forty to eighty-four delegates; while Federalists placed their majority or plurality at between twenty and thirty. Some Federalists, however, believed
they were in the minority. Henry Knox reflected that "on the opening of the conventions a majority were prejudiced against" the Constitution (to George Washington, 10 February, Washington Papers, DLC). On 16 January Convention
delegate Nathaniel Gorham stated that "numbers are at present against us"; while
on the same day Dwight Foster, a Brookfield, Mass., lawyer visiting in Boston,
declared that "a very great Proportion of Antifederalism prevails" (Gorham to
Henry Knox, Knox Papers, MHi; and Foster to Rebecca Foster, Dwight Foster
Papers, MWA). On 20 January Rufus King, another Convention delegate, told
James Madison that "The Opponents affirm to each other that they have an unalterable majority on their side; the Friends doubt the strength of their Adversaries
but are not entirely confident of their own" (Rutland, *Madison*, X, 400). Three
days later King wrote Madison that "Our prospects are gloomy, but hope is not
entirely extinguished. ... We are now thinking of amendments to be submitted not
as a condition of our assent & Ratification, but as the opinion of the Convention
subjoined to their Ratification–This scheme may gain a few members, but the issue
is doubtful" (23 January, *ibid.*, 411. See also CC:491.). On 25 January Boston
clergyman Jeremy Belknap indicated that the Constitution was gaining "many
converts" (to Ebenezer Hazard, Belknap Papers, MHi).

The willingness of Federalists to affix amendments to the state's ratification of
the Constitution was a significant departure from their previous position of opposing all amendments–a position adamantly adhered to by Federalists throughout
America. The list of recommended amendments, which would accompany the
Massachusetts form of ratification, would be submitted to the other states and to
the first Congress under the Constitution. Federalists hoped that such a proposal
would persuade moderate Antifederalists to vote in favor of ratification. Such hope
was expressed by Nathaniel Gorham who wrote James Madison on 27 January
that "we shall loose the question–unless we can take of[f] some of the opposition
by amendments–I do not mean those to be made the condition of the ratification–
but recommendatory only–upon this plan I flatter myself we may possibly get a
majority of 12 or 15–& not more" (Rutland, *Madison*, X, 436).

On 26 January Federalists were both pleased and disturbed to see an article
signed "Hampden" in the *Massachusetts Centinel*, believed to have been written by
Boston Antifederalist James Sullivan. "Hampden" recommended seven amendments to the Constitution and stated that the Convention should ratify the Constitution on the condition that the new Congress should take into consideration, as its
first order of business, all of the amendments proposed by the state conventions. If
seven state conventions had agreed to any amendment, that amendment should

become part of the Constitution immediately. After reading "Hampden," Convention delegate Benjamin Lincoln dismissed the idea that the Constitution would ever "be adopted on any conditions. It will pass absolutely or be rejected." It was possible, however, that the Convention might recommend some amendments (to George Washington, 27 January, Washington Papers, DLC). Rufus King wrote Henry Knox that Antifederalists gave "Hampden" "some Countenance–I mention the Circumstance rather to shew that our Opponents are not too confident of their Numbers, since hitherto they have reprobated the Suggestion of amendments and insisted among their Party on a total Rejection of the Constitution" (27 January, Knox Papers, MHi).

There was one more important element in the Federalist strategy–Governor John Hancock–the president of the Massachusetts Convention who had not yet attended any meetings. Several days before the Convention met on 9 January, it was reported that Hancock was "laid up *with the Gout*," a perennial ailment which he seemed to suffer during politically troublesome times. Nevertheless, he was elected president of the Convention, and Supreme Court Chief Justice William Cushing was elected vice president so "that he might officiate, in the absence of the President." Federalist delegate Christopher Gore explained that this procedure was followed so that "we might have the advantage of the former's name,–whether capable of attending or not" (Rufus King to Jeremiah Wadsworth, 6 January, Wadsworth Papers, CtHi; Gore to Wadsworth, 9 January, RCS:Conn., 603; and Gore to George Thatcher, 9 January, William F. Goodwin, ed., "The Thatcher Papers," *The Historical Magazine*, 2nd ser., VI [1869], 263). On 20 January Rufus King reported that he had seen Hancock "several Times . . . in his Chamber–he is not yet able to attend the Convention, but I hope he will improve in his Health as soon as a majority shews itself on either side of the convention" (to Horatio Gates, Emmet Collection, NN). A week later William Cranch, a young Boston lawyer, noted that "Our Governor the President, has not yet been able to attend. It is supposed by some people that he has not declared his opinion upon the subject yet because, he wishes first to know, on which side the majority will be. but now he begins to favour the Constitution because he hears that the majority is like to be upon that side. If he should come out fully in favour of it, it is the general opinion that his popularity will draw a large majority in its train" (to John Quincy Adams, 22, 27 January, Adams Family Papers, MHi). Federalists believed that, if the popular governor presented their amendments to the Convention, the amendments would be more readily accepted by the delegates. Jeremy Belknap thought that "coming from him they would be better recd. than from any other Person" (to Ebenezer Hazard, 3 February, Belknap Papers, MHi).

Even though the Convention was moving toward ratification, Governor Hancock still needed other inducements to attend. In exchange for his presenting the Federalist amendments, Federalists agreed to support him for reelection in the next gubernatorial election. (Many Federalists had opposed Hancock's election as governor in 1787 and were expected to continue their opposition in 1788.) Federalists also told Hancock that they would support him for president of the United States if Virginia rejected the Constitution, thereby rendering Washington ineligible for the position. Newspapers reported that Federalists had agreed to support Hancock for vice president. (See "John Hancock and the Constitution," 3 January–4 February, CC:Vol. 3, pp. 562–64.)

On 30 January Governor Hancock attended the Convention for the first time, but he did not speak. Federalist leaders were meeting in caucus and the list of amendments had not been completed. The next morning the Convention finished discussing the Constitution by paragraphs, and Theophilus Parsons, one of the Federalist leaders, moved "*that this Convention do assent to and ratify this Constitution.*" Delegate William Heath, a more moderate Federalist, in a seemingly well-orchestrated script, acknowledged "that many gentlemen appear opposed to the system," but he stressed the need to ratify the Constitution in order to preserve the Union. Heath suggested that the Convention "ratify the Constitution, and instruct our first Members to Congress, to exert their utmost endeavours to have such checks, and guards provided as appears to be necessary in some of the paragraphs of the Constitution, and communicate what we may judge proper, to our sister States, and request their concurrence...." When Heath sat down, Hancock rose and, acknowledging the "impropriety" of the president "entering into the deliberations," announced that, with the permission of the Convention, he would "hazard a proposition" in the afternoon that would "remove the objections of some gentlemen" (*Massachusetts Centinel*, 20 February).

When the Convention reassembled at 3:00 P.M., "The house was uncommonly crouded." Many of the spectators "were so anxious on this occasion, to obtain good places in the *Gallery*, that hundreds continued there the whole of the adjournment, and sent home & had their *dinners* brought to them" (Henry Jackson to Henry Knox, 3 February, Knox Papers, MHi). "The most profound silence was observed" while Hancock delivered his address to the Convention. Hancock believed that the new Constitution, if adopted, would "extend its good influences to every part of the United States, and advance the prosperity of the whole world." Therefore he proposed "some general amendments" to the Constitution which he hoped would "remove the doubts, and quiet the apprehensions" of the delegates (*Massachusetts Centinel*, 2, 20 February).

After Hancock submitted his amendments, Antifederalist Samuel Adams admitted to the Convention that he had doubts about the Constitution, but that the proposed amendments "will have a tendency to remove such doubts, and to conciliate the minds of the Convention, and people without doors." Adams believed that the Union was of permanent importance in helping the people "to withstand the common enemy, and to preserve their valuable rights and liberties." Accordingly, "The only difficulty on gentlemen's minds is, whether it is best to accept this Constitution on conditional amendments, or to rely on amendments in future, as the Constitution provides." Adams preferred Hancock's amendments because they would influence the states that had not yet ratified. Should this "be the case, the necessary amendments would be introduced more early, and more safely." Adams then moved that the amendments be considered (*Massachusetts Centinel*, 20 February).

Some Antifederalists were elated by their opponents' admission that the Constitution needed amending. "'You have told us of the Perfections of the Constitution,'" they said, "'now you acknowledge defects & want amendments *yourselves*.'" Federalists answered: "'We are quite willing to take it as it is trusting to amendments hereafter, but, to accomodate some Gentln. of a delicate mind propose them now & think there is a better chance of success, because those States who have not yet adopted the Plan may follow our Example & instruct their Representatives in the same manner'" (Jeremy Belknap to Ebenezer Hazard, 3 February, Belknap Papers, MHi).

On 2 February Hancock's "conciliatory proposition," as it was called, was submitted to a committee consisting of members from each county represented in the Convention. The next day Convention delegate Nathaniel Gorham, who had earlier alluded to an Antifederalist majority, asserted that, when the final vote was taken to ratify the Constitution, the vote would be 185 to 160 or more in favor of it (to Henry Knox, 3 February, Knox Papers, MHi). The committee altered Hancock's original amendments and on 4 February reported back to the Convention. Fifteen members agreed to the report, seven opposed, one abstained, and one was absent. The next day Antifederalists moved that the Convention adjourn to a later date, but this motion was defeated by ninety-nine votes, 214 to 115. In the after-

noon of 6 February, the Convention voted 187 to 168 to ratify the Constitution
with the recommendatory amendments. Whereupon, several leading Antifederalists, who said that they had been given a fair hearing, told the Convention that
they would support the Constitution. The next day they were joined by other
Antifederalists.

Governor Hancock's role was critical in getting some Antifederalists to change
their votes so that the Convention was able to ratify the Constitution with a small
majority. Caleb Gibbs of Boston asserted that "many of our ablest politicians say
that if he [Hancock] had not been well enough to have come out & appeared in the
Convention, it was more than probable the *important* question would have been
lost" (to George Washington, 9 February, Washington Papers, DLC). Jeremy
Belknap declared that, if Hancock had not acted in "midwifing the ... amendments into ye World," the entire Federalist "exertion" would have been "in vain"
(to Ebenezer Hazard, 10 February, Belknap Papers, MHi). And Jeremiah Hill of
Biddeford, Maine, looked upon Hancock's amendments as "a compleat finesse"
(to George Thatcher, 14 February, Chamberlain Collection, Thatcher Papers,
MB).

Massachusetts Antifederalists and Federalists had mixed feelings about their
state's ratification of the Constitution with recommendatory amendments. William
Widgery, a leading Antifederalist spokesman who had made a conciliatory speech
on 6 February, believed that Hancock's proposed amendments "furnished many
with Excuseces to their Constituants" for voting to ratify the Constitution (to
George Thatcher, 8 February, C.P. Greenough Papers, MHi). Federalist Secretary of State John Avery thought that the amendments "greatly tended to reconcile
all parties and dissipated many Evils from the Minds of many" (to George
Thatcher, 13 February, Chamberlain Collection, Thatcher Papers, MB). In mid-
March moderate Antifederalist Nathan Dane, a delegate to Congress, agreed that
both parties considered "the question as settled" after the Convention ratified the
Constitution with recommendatory amendments, but, that after the adjournment
of the New Hampshire Convention and some bad news from Virginia and North
Carolina, the ratification of the Constitution became "much more doubtful–and all
parties here [New York] consider the great question far from being dicided" (to
Samuel Holten, 15 March, CC:618). Two months later Dane described the Massachusetts ratification as "by far the wisest & best that had been made on the
Subject" (to Samuel Adams, 10 May, Samuel Adams Papers, NN). Federalist
Samuel A. Otis, another delegate to Congress, believed that the Massachusetts
"plan" of ratification would facilitate ratification in New York and Virginia which
would both adopt upon that "plan" (to Benjamin Lincoln, 8 May, J.S.H. Fogg
Autograph Collection, MeHi).

Out-of-state Federalists initially were uncertain about the recommendatory
amendments annexed to the Massachusetts form of ratification. James Madison
wrote George Washington that "The amendments are a blemish, but are in the
least offensive form" (15 February, Rutland, *Madison*, X, 510). To Thomas Jefferson, Madison wrote that "The amendments as recommended by the Convention
were as I am well informed not so much calculated for the minority in the Convention, on whom they had little effect, as for the people of the State" (19 February,
CC:541). George Washington thought that "The decision of Massachusetts would
have been more influential had the Majority been greater, and the ratification
unaccompanied by the recommendatory Act.–As it stands however, the blow is
severely felt by antifederalists in the equivocal States" (to John Jay, 3 March, John
Jay-Iselin Collection, NNC).

In time, however, Federalists became more appreciative of the Convention's
innovative plan of ratification. Philadelphia merchant Walter Stewart believed that
Pennsylvania Antifederalists "have abated much in their warmth since they see

Massachusets have come into it. And they at last say they think Amendments may possibly be made" (to William Irvine, 20 February, RCS:Pa., 715); while Philadelphia Assemblyman Thomas FitzSimons suspected that Massachusetts' ratification would derail the petition campaign to undo Pennsylvania's ratification (to William Irvine, 22 February, RCS:Pa., 716). Virginia Federalist Edward Carrington declared that, if Massachusetts had rejected the Constitution, "I am certain there would not have been the most remote chance for its adoption in Virginia" (to Henry Knox, 13 March, Knox Papers, MHi). Virginian William Short, Thomas Jefferson's private secretary in Paris, thought that Massachusetts had set a "wise & prudent example" that Virginia would follow–"surely nothing can be more wise" (to Thomas Lee Shippen, 31 May, Shippen Papers, DLC; and to William Stephens Smith, 27 May, Gilpin Papers [William Short Letters], PHi). After analyzing Massachusetts' ratification, Thomas Jefferson changed his mind about the best procedure to follow in ratifying the Constitution: "my first wish was that 9 states would adopt it in order to ensure what was good in it, & that the others might, by holding off, produce the necessary amendments. but the plan of Massachusetts is far preferable, and will I hope be followed by those who are yet to decide" (to Edward Carrington, 27 May, Boyd, XIII, 208-9). Virginian George Nicholas saw only one safe compromise–a ratification "on the plan of the Massachusetts convention" (to James Madison, 5 April, CC:663). And by April, even James Madison had accepted the concept of recommendatory amendments. "I shall be extremely happy to see a coalition among all the real fœderalists. Recommendatory alterations are the only ground that occurs to me." "The plan of Massts. is unquestionably the Ultimatum of the fœderalists" (to Edmund Randolph, 10 April; and to George Nicholas, 8 April, CC:673, 667).

In New York, Federalists tried to turn the Massachusetts amendments to their own advantage during the campaign to elect delegates to the state convention. In mid-April the Albany Federal Committee expressed the hope that the New York Convention might adopt the first, third, and eighth amendments proposed by the Massachusetts Convention. The committee also complimented the Massachusetts Convention for having "led the way in recommending amendments, which will be considered as standing instructions to the Representatives until Congress in their wisdom, meet the wishes of their constituents" (An Impartial Address, to the Citizens of the City and County of Albany: or, The 35 Anti-Federal Objections Refuted, by the Federal Committee, of the City of Albany, 9-10, 17-18, 20, 22-23, 25 [Evans 21167]). On 28 April a New York City election handbill, signed "Many Federalists," stated that "We are for adopting the constitution; but still we wish that they, who compose the convention, may propose amendments, after the manner of Massachusetts" (Evans 21501). In Dutchess County, "A Friend to Good Government" dismissed the Massachusetts amendments as "trivial," declaring that "the spirits" of the amendments "are already contained in the Constitution" (Poughkeepsie Country Journal, 15 April).

Antifederalists also had mixed feelings about the recommendatory amendments. In a letter allegedly written by George Bryan of Philadelphia, the Massachusetts amendments were viewed as having broken "the sanctity of the new Constitution," even though they were admittedly "superficial" (CC:647). An Antifederalist satirist, posing as a Philadelphia Federalist merchant, declared that the amendments were "but a decent way of rejecting" the Constitution (Carlisle Gazette, 27 February, Mfm:Pa. 453); while a Philadelphia Antifederalist, writing on the "real state of the proposed constitution in the United States," asserted that more than three-quarters of the people of Massachusetts "warmly opposed" the Constitution and "even the friends of it themselves would not dare to adopt it without considerable amendment" (Philadelphia Independent Gazetteer, 7 March, CC:603).

Other Antifederalists, however, wondered why people would be willing to ratify a defective constitution and amend it later. Such a policy seemed "utterly absurd" to George Mason who could "not think any Man of Sense candid in proposing it" (to Thomas Jefferson, 26 May, Boyd, XIII, 206). Richard Henry Lee asked his friend Samuel Adams why the Massachusetts Convention would "submit to a system requiring such amendments, and trust to creatures of our own creation, for the correcting of evils in it that threaten the destruction of those ends for which the system was formed?" (28 April, CC:714). "A Plebeian" (Melancton Smith) advised New Yorkers to "place confidence" in men who favored adopting the Constitution with conditional amendments while distrusting "those who urge the adoption of a bad constitution, under the delusive expectation of making amendments after it is acceded to" (*An Address to the People of the State of New-York...*, CC:689). "Philadelphiensis" X bitterly denounced Governor John Hancock for proposing amendments which "will be another source of mischief; the people cannot be so ignorant as to be deceived by so pitiful a manœuvre. Here is a positive acknowledgement made by one of its advocates, who hopes to be appointed the *little king* if not the *big one*, that it is objectionable; and his amendments are introduced as a blind; the weighty ones are untouched: not a whimper of the extraordinary powers of the *President-general*, the *standing army, the liberty of the press, &c.* No, no! if these *glorious parts* be lopped off, what would become of the monarchy-men? And respecting *internal taxation*, is not his amendment a disgrace to himself, and an insult to the understanding of the people? Mr. Hancock knows, or ought to know at least, that the liberties of the citizens of America are not to be trifled with: his schemes are too flimsey not to be seen through" (CC:547).

On 10 April the Albany Antifederal Committee, in a handbill for the elections to the state convention and legislature, attacked Federalists who "endeavor to prevail on the people, *first* to adopt it [the Constitution], and *afterwards* (like Massachusetts) *trust to a recommendation for future amendments.*" The committee asked: "Would it be prudent or safe for the people to surrender their dearest rights and liberties, *to the discretionary disposal of their future rulers? First* to make a *surrender* and *afterwards* ask for terms of *capitulation.*" The committee viewed the Constitution as "dangerous to the rights and liberties of the people, and which, if adopted without previous amendments will, in our opinion, terminate in slavery" (Evans 45215). On 2 May "Spectator," writing in the *New York Journal*, asserted that the new Congress under the Constitution had to adopt amendments, such as those proposed by the Massachusetts Convention, or it "will find it very difficult, and perhaps impossible, to put the new government in execution." If amendments were not obtained, the government would, in twenty years, be "as arbitrary and despotick as that of the republic of Venice."

The recommendatory amendments were analyzed by both Antifederalists and Federalists, and some were praised, others were criticized. In New York, "A Plebeian" pointed to the Massachusetts amendments as evidence that Antifederalists throughout America wanted similar amendments to the Constitution–"they object to indefinite powers in the legislature–to the power of laying direct taxes–to the authority of regulating elections–to the extent of the judicial powers, both as it respects the inferior courts and the appellate jurisdiction–to the smallness of the representation, &c." (CC:689). Richard Henry Lee wrote that "The Massachusetts amendments are good, as far as they go. The first, third, and fourth amendments are well contrived to keep in existence the state sovereignties; and the first particularly proper for securing liberty from the abuse of construction, which the new plan most amply admits of." Lee, however, objected to the second amendment and believed that the seventh, limiting the jurisdiction of the federal judiciary, should extend its limitations to cases involving foreigners. He also decried the failure to sever "the impolitic combination of president and senate" and the failure to "sufficiently" attend to the freedom of the press (to Samuel Adams, 28 April, CC:714; and to George Mason, 7 May, Richard H. Lee, *Memoir of the Life of*

Richard Henry Lee, and His Correspondence ... [2 vols., Philadelphia, 1825], II, 90).
Thomas Jefferson still believed that a bill of rights was necessary and that Massachusetts' first amendment limiting the new federal government only to delegated
powers "will in some degree answer this end, but not so well." Jefferson, however,
was worried that the first amendment would "do too much in some instances & too
little in others. it will cripple the federal government in some cases where it ought
to be free, and not restrain it in some others where restraint would be right" (to
Edward Carrington, 27 May, Boyd, XIII, 208). Antoine de la Forest, French vice
consul in New York, predicted that the first amendment would encourage "continual quarrels." The Confederation Congress, though strapped with a similar limitation, "proceeded according to the *implicit* sense," and had it not done so, "it
would have been stopped at each step." Forest also saw the danger in the fourth
amendment that would reimpose the requisition system on delinquent states. "This
clause complicates the machine of Government and at a critical moment would
show the United States to lack something essential; Twelve years' experience proved
how much the slow route of requisitions set back the Service" (to the Comte de la
Luzerne, 18 February, CC:536).

Virginia Governor Edmund Randolph attacked the proposed amendments as "a
paltry snare." "Some of the amts. are inadmissible, others pointed against the
Negro states, and others milk & water. The first is among the rocks on which the
old conf[ederatio]n. has split; the 2d. is aimed against the So. Ss [Southern States]–
the 3d. provides vs. no real danger; the first part of the 4th. is as the 3d. and
moreover destroys an essential idea of a national govt.; the 5th. tho' a new and
juster theory now prevails, ought to be left to the occasional wisdom of congress;
the 6th. sounds an unnecessary alarm; the 7th. strikes not at all the most exceptionable points of the jurisdiction; the 8th. I conceive is not true in supposing even at
common law a trial of fact to be best *on all occasions* by a jury; and the 9th. can have
been designed only to make out a number of am[endmen]ts equal to the no. of
states, who may give birth to the govt. In short H—k. proposes them not in the
form of objections, but *to remove fears*" (to James Madison, 29 February, Rutland,
Madison, X, 542–43). Madison replied: "I view the amendments of Massachusetts
pretty nearly in the same light that you do. ... I do not see that the 2d. amendment, if I understand its scope, can be more exceptionable to the S. Sts. than the
others. I take it to mean that the number of Reps. shall be limited to 200, who will
be apportioned from time to time according to a census; not that the apportionment first made when the Reps. amount to that number shall be perpetual. The
9th. amendment I have understood was made a very serious point of by S. Adams"
(10 April, CC:673).

Without the recommendatory amendments, it is unlikely that the Massachusetts
Convention would have ratified the Constitution, or that the required nine states
would have adopted the Constitution. Edward Carrington believed that "The de-
cision of Massachusetts is perhaps the most important event that ever took place in
America, as upon her in all probability depended the fate of the Constitution" (to
Henry Knox, 13 March, Knox Papers, MHi).

The following is the form of the ratification of the constitution for the United States,
by the Convention of this Commonwealth.[1]

COMMONWEALTH of MASSACHUSETTS.

In convention of the delegates of the people of the commonwealth of
Massachusetts, Feb. 6, 1788.

The convention having impartially discussed, and fully considered, the
constitution for the United States of America, reported to Congress, by
the convention of delegates from the United States, of America, and sub-

mitted to us, by a resolution of the General Court of the said commonwealth, passed the twenty fifth day of October last past; and acknowledging with grateful hearts the goodness of the Supreme Ruler of the universe, in affording the people of the United States, in the course of his Providence, an opportunity, deliberately and peaceably, without fraud or surprise, of entering into an explicit and solemn compact with each other, by assenting to and ratifying a new constitution, in order to form a more perfect union, establish justice, insure domestick tranquillity, provide for the common defence, promote the general welfare, and secure the blessings of liberty to themselves, and their posterity–DO, in the name and in behalf of the people of the commonwealth of Massachusetts, ASSENT to and RATIFY the said *constitution, for the United States of America.*

And as it is the opinion of this convention, that certain amendments and alterations in the said constitution, would remove the fears, and quiet the apprehensions of many of the good people of this commonwealth, and more effectually guard against an undue administration of the federal government, the convention do therefore recommend, that the following alterations and provisions be introduced into the said constitution:

First. That it be explicitly declared, that all powers, not expressly delegated by the aforesaid constitution, are reserved to the several states, to be by them exercised.

Secondly. That there shall be one representative to every thirty thousand persons, according to the census mentioned in the constitution, until the whole number of the representatives amounts to two hundred.

Thirdly. That Congress do not exercise the powers vested in them by the 4th sect. of the 1st art. but in cases when a state neglect or refuse to make regulations therein mentioned, or shall make regulations subversive of the rights of the people, to a free and equal representation in Congress, agreeably to the constitution.

Fourthly, That Congress do not lay direct taxes, but when the monies arising from the impost and excise are insufficient for the publick exigencies; nor then, until Congress shall have first made a requisition upon the states, to assess, levy and pay their respective proportions of such requisition, agreeably to the census fixed in the said constitution, in such way and manner as the legislature of the state shall think best,–and in such case, if any state shall neglect or refuse to pay its proportion, pursuant to such requisition, then Congress may assess and levy such states proportion, together with interest thereon, at the rate of six per cent. per annum, from the time of payment prescribed in such requisition.

Fifthly. That Congress erect no company of merchants with exclusive advantages of commerce.

Sixthly. That no person shall be tried for any crime by which he may incur an infamous punishment, or loss of life, until he be first indicted by a grand jury, except in such cases as may arise in the government and regulation of the land and naval forces.

Seventhly. The supreme judicial federal court shall have no jurisdiction of causes between citizens of different states, unless the matter in dispute, whether it concerns the reality or personality, be of the value of three thousand dollars, at the least: Nor shall the federal judicial powers extend to any actions between citizens of different states where the matter in dispute, whether it concerns the reality or personality, is not of the value of fifteen hundred dollars, at the least.

Eighthly. In civil actions, between citizens of different states, every issue of fact, arising in actions at common law, shall be tried by a jury, if the parties, or either of them, request it.

Ninthly. Congress shall, at no time, consent, that any person, holding an office of trust or profit, under the United States, shall accept of a title of nobility, or any other title or office, from any king, prince, or foreign state.

And the Convention do, in the name and in behalf of the people of this commonwealth, enjoin it upon their representatives in Congress, at all times, until the alterations and provisions aforesaid have been considered, agreeably to the fifth article of the said constitution, to exert all their influence, and use all reasonable and legal methods to obtain a ratification of the said alterations and provisions in such manner as is provided in the said article.

And that the United States in Congress assembled may have due notice of the assent and ratification of the said constitution by this Convention–It is

RESOLVED, That the assent and ratification aforesaid be engrossed on parchment, together with the recommendation and injunction aforesaid, and with this resolution; and that his excellency JOHN HANCOCK, esquire, president, and the honourable WILLIAM CUSHING, esquire, vice-president, of this Convention, transmit the same, countersigned by the secretary of the Convention, under their hands and seals, to the United States in Congress assembled.

(Signed) JOHN HANCOCK, President,
WILLIAM CUSHING, Vice-President.

(Countersigned)
GEORGE RICHARDS MINOT, Sec'y.

1. The transcription is taken from the *Massachusetts Gazette*, 8 February, which varies only in capitalization and punctuation from the manuscript versions retained by Massachusetts and sent to Congress and to the other states on 8 and 16 February, respectively. The recommendatory amendments were reprinted in the February issues of the Philadelphia *American Museum* and New York *American Magazine* and in twenty-four newspapers by 19 April: Vt. (1), N.H. (1), Mass. (6), R.I. (4), Conn. (1), N.Y. (2), Pa. (5), Md. (3), S.C. (1). Hancock's unamended proposition was printed in the *Massachusetts Centinel* on 2 February and was reprinted in thirty-two newspapers by 28 February: N.H. (1), Mass. (8), R.I. (3), Conn. (5), N.Y. (5), N.J. (1), Pa. (6), Md. (1), Va. (2).

509. George Washington to the Marquis de Lafayette
Mount Vernon, 7 February[1]

You know it always gives me the sincerest pleasure to hear from you, my dear Marquis, and therefore I need only say that your two kind letters of the 9th & 15th. of Octo. so replete with personal affection and confidential intelligence, afforded me inexpressible satisfaction. I shall myself be happy in forming an acquaintance and cul[t]ivating a friendship with the new Minister Plenipotentiary of France,[2] whom you have commended as "a sensible & honest man"–these are qualities too rare & too precious not to merit on[e]'s particular esteem–You may be persuaded he will be well received by the Congress of the United States, because they will not only be influenced in their conduct by his individual merits, but also by their affection for the nation of whose Sovereign he is the Representative.–For it is an undoubted fact, that the People of America entertain a greateful remembrance of past services as well as a favourable disposition for commercial and friendly connections with your Nation.–

You appear to be, as might be expected from a real friend to this Country, anxiously concerned about its present political situation. So far as I am able I shall be happy in gratifying that friendly solicitude. As to my sentiments with respect to the merits of the new Constitution, I will disclose them without reserve (although by passing through the Post offices they should become known to all the world) for, in truth, I have nothing to conceal on that subject. It appears to me, then, little short of a miracle, that the Delegates from so many different States (which States you know are also different from each other in their manners, circumstances and prejudices) should unite in forming a system of national Government, so little liable to well founded objections. Nor am I yet such an enthusiastic, partial or undiscriminating admirer of it, as not to perceive it is tinctured with some real (though not radical) defects. The limits of a letter would not suffer me to go fully into an examination of them; nor would the discussion be entertaining or profitable, I therefore forbear to touch upon it. With regard to the two great points (the pivots on which the whole machine must move) my Creed is simply:–

1st.–That the general Government is not invested with more Powers than are indispensably necessary to perform the functions of a good Government; and, con[se]quently, that no objection ought to be made against the quantity of Power delegated to it:

2ly.–That these Powers (as the appointment of all Rulers will forever arise from, and, at short stated intervals, recur to the free suffrage of the People) are so distributed among the Legislative, Executive, and Judicial Branches, into which the general Government is arranged, that it can never be in danger of degenerating into a monarchy, an Oligarchy, an Aristocracy, or any other despotic or oppressive form; so long as there shall remain any virtue in the body of the People.–

I would not be understood my dear Marquis to speak of consequences which may be produced, in the revolution of ages, by corruption of morals, profligacy of manners, and listlessness for the preservation of the natural and unalienable rights of mankind; nor of the successful usurpations that may be established at such an unpropitious juncture, upon the ruins of liberty, however providently guarded and secured, as these are contingencies against which no human prudence can effectually provide. It will at least be a recommendation to the proposed Constitution that it is provided with more checks and barriers against the introduction of Tyranny, & those of a nature less liable to be surmounted, than any Government hitherto instituted among mortals, hath possessed. we are not to expect perfection in this world: but mankind, in modern times, have apparently made some progress in the science of Government.–Should that which is now offered to the People of America, be found on experiment less perfect than it can be made–a Constitutional door is left open for its amelisration [sic]. Some respectable characters have wished that the States, after having pointed out whatever alterations and amendments may be judged necessary, would appoint another federal Co[n]vention to modify it upon those documents. For myself I have wondered that sensible men should not see the impracticability of the scheme. The members would go fortified with such Instructions that nothing but discordant ideas could prevail. Had I but slightly suspected (at the time when the late Convention was in session) that another Convention would not be likely to agree upon a better form of Government, I should now be confirmed in the fixed belief that they would not be able to agree upon any System whatever:–So many, I may add, such contradictory, and, in my opinion, unfounded objections have been urged against the System in contemplation; many of which would operate equally against every efficient Government that might be proposed. I will only add, as a farther opinion founded on the maturest deliberation, that there is no alternative–no hope of alteration–no intermediate resting place–between the adoption of this and a recurrence to an unqualified state of Anarchy, with all its deplorable consequences.–

Since I had the pleasure of writing to you last, no material alteration in the political State of affairs has taken place to change the prospect of the Constitution's being adopted by nine States or more. Pennsylvania, Delaware, Jersey and Connecticut have already done it. It is also said Georgia has acceded.–Massachusetts, which is perhaps thought to be rather more doubtful than when I last addressed you, is now in Convention.[3]

A spirit of emigration to the western Country is very predominant. Congress have sold, in the year past, a pretty large quantity of lands on the Ohio, for public Securities, and thereby diminished the domestic debt considerably. Many of your Military acquaintances such as the Generals Parsons, Varnum and Putnam, the Colos. Tupper Sprout and Sherman,[4] with many more, propose settling there. From such beginnings much may be expected.

The storm of war between England and your Nation, it seems, is dissipated. I hope and trust the political affairs in France are taking a favorable turn. If the Ottomans wod. suffer themselves to be precipitated into a war, they must abide the consequences. Some Politicians speculate on a triple Alliance between the two Imperial Courts & Versailles.

I think it was rather fortunate, than otherwise, that the incaution of an Ambassador and the rascality of a Rhinegrave prevented you from attempting to prop a falling fabric.–

It gives me great pleasure to learn the present ministry of France are friendly to America; and that Mr Jefferson & yourself have a prospect of accomplishing measures which will mutually benefit and improve the commercial intercourse between the two Nations.

1. FC, Washington Papers, DLC.
2. On 24 January the Comte de Moustier, the new French minister plenipotentiary to the United States, wrote Washington from New York City. He enclosed Lafayette's letters of 9 and 15 October 1787 which had been entrusted to him by Lafayette (Washington Papers, DLC). The letter of the 15th introduced Moustier to Washington. On 7 February Washington replied to Moustier (Fitzpatrick, XXIX, 407–8). Lafayette's letters of 9 and 15 October are in Louis Gottschalk and Shirley A. Bill, eds., *The Letters of Lafayette to Washington, 1777–1799* (2nd ed., Philadelphia, 1976), 326–32, 332–33.
3. On 10 January Washington had written Lafayette that New England, with the exception of Rhode Island, "will cheerfully and fully accept" the Constitution (CC:435).
4. Samuel Holden Parsons, James M. Varnum, Rufus Putnam, Benjamin Tupper, Ebenezer Sproat, and Isaac Sherman were former Continental Army officers and all but Sherman were members of the Ohio Company. In October 1787 Parsons and Varnum were appointed judges of the Northwest Territory by Congress.

510. Brutus XII
New York Journal, 7 February[1]

In my last,[2] I shewed, that the judicial power of the United States under the first clause of the second section of article eight, would be authorized to explain the constitution, not only according to its letter, but according to its spirit and intention; and having this power, they would strongly incline to give it such a construction as to extend the powers of the general government, as much as possible, to the diminution, and finally to the destruction, of that of the respective states.

I shall now proceed to shew how this power will operate in its exercise to effect these purposes. In order to perceive the extent of its influence, I shall consider,

First. How it will tend to extend the legislative authority.

Second. In what manner it will increase the jurisdiction of the courts, and

Third. The way in which it will diminish, and destroy, both the legislative and judicial authority of the United States.

First. Let us enquire how the judicial power will effect an extension of the legislative authority.

Perhaps the judicial power will not be able, by direct and positive decrees, ever to direct the legislature, because it is not easy to conceive how a question can be brought before them in a course of legal discussion, in which they can give a decision, declaring, that the legislature have certain powers which they have not exercised, and which, in consequence of the determination of the judges, they will be bound to exercise. But it is easy to see, that in their adjudications they may establish certain principles, which being received by the legislature, will enlarge the sphere of their power beyond all bounds.

It is to be observed, that the supreme court has the power, in the last resort, to determine all questions that may arise in the course of legal discussion, on the meaning and construction of the constitution. This power they will hold under the constitution, and independent of the legislature. The latter can no more deprive the former of this right, than either of them, or both of them together, can take from the president, with the advice of the senate, the power of making treaties, or appointing ambassadors.

In determining these questions, the court must and will assume certain principles, from which they will reason, in forming their decisions. These principles, whatever they may be, when they become fixed, by a course of decisions, will be adopted by the legislature, and will be the rule by which they will explain their own powers. This appears evident from this consideration, that if the legislature pass laws, which, in the judgment of the court, they are not authorised to do by the constitution, the court will not take notice of them; for it will not be denied, that the constitution is the highest or supreme law. And the courts are vested with the supreme and uncontroulable power, to determine, in all cases that come before them, what the constitution means; they cannot, therefore, execute a law, which, in their judgment, opposes the constitution, unless we can suppose they can make a superior law give way to an inferior. The legislature, therefore, will not go over the limits by which the courts may adjudge they are confined. And there is little room to doubt but that they will come up to those bounds, as often as occasion and opportunity may offer, and they may judge it proper to do it. For as on the one hand, they will not readily pass laws which they know the courts will not execute, so on the other, we may be sure they will not scruple to pass such as they know they will give effect, as often as they may judge it proper.

From these observations it appears, that the judgment of the judicial, on the constitution, will become the rule to guide the legislature in their construction of their powers.

What the principles are, which the courts will adopt, it is impossible for us to say; but taking up the powers as I have explained them in my last number, which they will possess under this clause, it is not difficult to see, that they may, and probably will, be very liberal ones.

We have seen, that they will be authorized to give the constitution a construction according to its spirit and reason, and not to confine themselves to its letter.

To discover the spirit of the constitution, it is of the first importance to attend to the principal ends and designs it has in view. These are expressed in the preamble, in the following words, viz. "We, the people of the United States, in order to form a more perfect union, establish justice, insure domestic tranquility, provide for the common defence, promote the general welfare, and secure the blessings of liberty to ourselves and our posterity, do ordain and establish this constitution," &c. If the end of the government is to be learned from these words, which are clearly designed to declare it, it is obvious it has in view every object which is embraced by any government. The preservation of internal peace–the due administration of justice–and to provide for the defence of the community, seems to include all the objects of government; but if they do not, they are certainly comprehended in the words, "to provide for the general welfare." If it be further considered, that this constitution, if it is ratified, will not be a compact entered into by states, in their corporate capacities, but an agreement of the people of the United States, as one great body politic, no doubt can remain, but that the great end of the constitution, if it is to be collected from the preamble, in which its end is declared, is to constitute a government which is to extend to every case for which any government is instituted, whether external or internal. The courts, therefore, will establish this as a principle in expounding the constitution, and will give every part of it such an explanation, as will give latitude to every department under it, to take cognizance of every matter, not only that affects the general and national concerns of the union, but also of such as relate to the administration of private justice, and to regulating the internal and local affairs of the different parts.

Such a rule of exposition is not only consistent with the general spirit of the preamble, but it will stand confirmed by considering more minutely the different clauses of it.

The first object declared to be in view is, "To form a perfect union." It is to be observed, it is not an union of states or bodies corporate; had this been the case the existence of the state governments, might have been secured. But it is a union of the people of the United States considered as one body, who are to ratify this constitution, if it is adopted. Now to make a union of this kind perfect, it is necessary to abolish all inferior governments, and to give the general one compleat legislative, executive and judicial powers to every purpose. The courts therefore will establish it as a rule in explaining the constitution. To give it such a construction as will best tend to perfect the union or take from the state governments every power of either making or executing laws. The second object is "to establish justice." This must include not only the idea of instituting the rule of justice, or of making laws which shall be the measure or rule of right, but also of providing for the application of this rule or of administering justice under it. And under this the courts will in their decisions extend the power of the government to all cases they possibly can, or otherwise they will be restricted in doing what appears to be the intent of the constitution they should do, to wit, pass laws and provide for the execution of them, for the general distribution of justice between man and man. Another end declared is "to insure domestic tranquility." This comprehends a provision against all private breaches of the peace, as well as against all public commotions or general insurrections; and to attain the object of this clause fully, the government must exercise the power of passing laws on these subjects, as well as of appointing magistrates with authority to execute them. And the courts will adopt these ideas in their expositions. I might proceed to the other clause, in the preamble, and it would appear by a consideration of all of them separately, as it does by taking them together, that if the spirit of this system is to be known from its declared end and design in the preamble, its spirit is to subvert and abolish all the powers of the state government, and to embrace every object to which any government extends.

As it sets out in the preamble with this declared intention, so it proceeds in the different parts with the same idea. Any person, who will peruse the 8th section with attention, in which most of the powers are enumerated, will perceive that they either expressly or by implication extend to almost every thing about which any legislative power can be employed. But if this equitable mode of construction is applied to this part of the constitution; nothing can stand before it.

This will certainly give the first clause in that article a construction which I confess I think the most natural and grammatical one, to authorise the Congress to do any thing which in their judgment will tend to provide for the general welfare, and this amounts to the same thing as general and unlimited powers of legislation in all cases.

(To be continued.)

1. This essay was not reprinted. The conclusion of "Brutus" XII was published in the *New York Journal* on 14 February (CC:530). For the authorship and impact of "Brutus," see CC:178.
2. See "Brutus" XI, *New York Journal*, 31 January (CC:489).

511. Advertisement for Thomas Lloyd's Debates of the Pennsylvania Convention, 7 February

Thomas Lloyd (1756–1827) was born in London and educated by English Jesuits in Flanders and Bruges, Belgium. He emigrated to St. Mary's County, Md., in 1771, and served in the Maryland militia from 1776 to 1779. In 1779 he superintended the printing of the Journals of Congress, and the next year he was appointed clerk to the Treasurer of the United States. He settled in Philadelphia in 1783, and four years later, he advertised as a teacher of shorthand. In September 1787 Lloyd began taking notes of the debates in the Pennsylvania Assembly, and by the end of the next year he had published four volumes of the *Proceedings and Debates of the General Assembly of Pennsylvania* (Evans 20631-32, 21370-71).

On 23 November 1787 Thomas Lloyd petitioned to become assistant secretary of the Pennsylvania Convention, but consideration of his request was indefinitely postponed on the motion of two leading Antifederalists and no assistant secretary was ever appointed (RCS:Pa., 329). However, Lloyd began taking notes of the debates with the idea of publication in mind. In April 1788 Lloyd also took notes of the debates in the Maryland Convention. He never published these debates, although he advertised that he would print them if 600 copies were subscribed (Baltimore *Maryland Gazette*, 6 June). Lloyd attended the first federal Congress in New York in 1789, took notes of the debates in the House of Representatives, and published *The Congressional Register* until 1790 (Evans 22203-4, 22973-75). (See Marion Tinling, "Thomas Lloyd's Reports of the First Federal Congress," *William and Mary Quarterly*, 3rd series, XVIII [1961], 519-45; and Martin I.J. Griffin, "Thomas Lloyd...," *The American Catholic Historical Researches*, VII [1890], 17-32.)

Thomas Lloyd was not the only person to take notes of debates in the Pennsylvania Convention, with a view toward publication. On 28 November 1787 a pamphlet edition was published of Alexander J. Dallas' notes of James Wilson's speech of 24 November–the first day of substantial Convention debates (Evans 20889; and CC:289). On 1 December Dallas, editor of the *Pennsylvania Herald*, began publishing his shorthand notes of the Convention debates in the *Herald*, beginning with the notes for 27 November. (Dallas continued publishing full accounts of the debates until 5 January, after which he was fired by the publisher. Before his firing, Dallas had published full debates for 27 and 28 November and 12 December and part of the debates for 30 November.)

On 3 December Lloyd placed an advertisement in the Philadelphia *Independent Gazetteer*: "Now in the Press, and will with all possible expedition be published in one Volume, Octavo, Debates of the Convention of the State of Pennsylvania ... accurately taken in Short Hand, by Thomas Lloyd." Subscriptions would be received by Lloyd and his printer, Joseph James. The price would depend on the length of the debates, but it was "intended to be at the rate of one dollar per 100 pages." The advertisement also included Lloyd's denial that his shorthand notes had been used in the pamphlet edition of Wilson's speech and his pledge that he would publish the speech "without mutilation or misrepresentation" (Mfm:Pa. 252). The advertisement was printed in Pennsylvania, Maryland, and New York until early February.

In general, people believed that Lloyd intended to publish all of the debates, or at least all of the principal speeches, both Federalist and Antifederalist. On 29 November Philadelphia Antifederalist William Shippen, Jr., wrote his son Thomas Lee Shippen in Paris that "Lloyd is taking down the debates in short hand & you shall have them as soon as published" (RCS:Pa., 424. See also Samuel Vaughan, Jr., to James Bowdoin, 30 November, RSC:Pa., 263.). Two weeks later Shippen told his son that the Convention had just ratified the Constitution and that Lloyd would "publish the whole debates as soon as possible. They will be a treat to you & Mr. Jefferson" (12 December, RCS:Pa., 602). Commenting on the Convention debates, Francis Hopkinson wrote Jefferson on 14 December that "the true Principles of Government were never upon any Occasion more fully & ably developed." Hopkinson believed that "the principal Speeches have been taken in short hand & will soon be published. I shall take Care to secure you a Copy" (Mfm:Pa. 262). Lloyd himself led people to believe that the debates would be complete. Lloyd attacked Alexander J. Dallas' account of Benjamin Rush's 12 December speech, calling it "a gross misrepresentation" and promising to give his readers "a short account of the substance of it, and hereafter shall in my printed volume of debates give you every word of it" (CC:357; RCS:Pa., 592-96; and *Pennsylvania Gazette*, 19

December). On 20 December the Northampton County delegates to the Pennsylvania Convention reported to a county meeting that it was unnecessary to enter into a detailed discussion of the Constitution because "The debates at large we have reason to expect will be published, wherein those, whose inclination may lead them to it, will find a detail of all the arguments made use of either for or against the adoption of the constitution" (*Pennsylvania Gazette*, 2 January 1788, RCS:Pa., 646–48). On 25 December the Reverend Charles Nisbet of Carlisle, Pa., wrote the Earl of Buchan that in the Pennsylvania Convention there were only three Antifederalist speakers "and these ignorant & illiterate Men, who had their Speeches made for them by two or three ostensible Characters without Doors. They will all be printed, & sent abroad, being already taken down in short hand" (CC:374).

At about this time, unknown to Nisbet, Convention delegate Timothy Pickering discovered that Thomas Lloyd had decided to publish initially only a partial edition of the debates, consisting of Federalist speeches. Pickering, in the first paragraph of a draft of a long letter, dated 24 December, wrote that the publication of the debates had been delayed because of their great length. At the end of the draft, which was probably completed on a later date, Pickering wrote (and crossed out) that he had just learned that Wilson's speeches were to "be published by themselves & therefore appear sooner than I before expected" (to Charles Tillinghast, CC:288–C. See also Tillinghast to Hugh Hughes, 27–28 January, CC:479, in which he wrote that he received Pickering's letter "a few days ago.").

Tench Coxe of Philadelphia obtained sixty pages of Lloyd's debates about three weeks before their publication and sent these pages to James Madison in New York on 16 January 1788. Coxe asked Madison to send them to Rufus King for use in the Massachusetts Convention. On 27 January Coxe told Madison that "There were some pages more struck off, which I have obtained," and he asked Madison to send these to King as well, which was done (see Coxe to Madison, 16 and 27 January, Rutland, *Madison*, X, 375, 435; Madison to Coxe, 20 and 30 January, *ibid.*, 444–45, XII, 480–81; and King to Coxe, 6 February, Coxe Papers, Series II, General Correspondence and Papers, PHi).

Even before Lloyd's shorthand notes appeared in print, Antifederalists attacked his version of the Convention debates. Late in January "Centinel" pointed to the "suppression" of Dallas' account of the debates, which he considered "a faithful representation," and called Lloyd's version "a spurious publication" (*Independent Gazetteer*, 23 and 30 January, CC:470, 487. For a rejoinder, see "G.R.," *ibid.*, 31 January, Mfm:Pa. 393.). "Peep Junior" supported "Centinel" and claimed that "Centinel" "has the *best intelligence*, that he has the whole history of the writing, manufacturing, fabricating, dressing, transcribing, printing, moulding, coining and casting anew, and reprinting of this spurious work." "Peep Junior" promised that all of this would be revealed to the public. Based on his experience with Lloyd's Assembly *Debates*, "Peep Junior" believed that Lloyd was a "party implement. As to abilities *he can write short-hand*, and can make shift in *his own language*, to take down *the ideas of others*; which are afterwards altered, dressed or undressed by, and at the pleasure of his benefactors" (*Independent Gazetteer*, 5 February, Mfm:Pa. 399).

On 30 January an advertisement in the *Pennsylvania Packet* announced that the first volume of the Convention debates would be published on Monday, 4 February, and that it would contain the speeches of James Wilson and Thomas McKean, both Federalists. On 5 February the *Pennsylvania Herald* declared that the debates would be published in "a few days" by Thomas Seddon. Two days later the *Pennsylvania Mercury* announced that the first volume was published. The price was set at eleven shillings and three pence but only three shillings and nine pence to subscribers of Lloyd's Assembly *Debates*. Within a week, however, the *Pennsylvania Mercury* advertised that the price had been lowered to five shillings and three pence for non-subscribers to Lloyd's Assembly *Debates*.

The volume was entitled *Debates of the Convention, of the State of Pennsylvania, on the Constitution, Proposed for the Government of the United States. In Two Volumes. Vol. I. Taken Accurately in Short-Hand, by Thomas Lloyd*. It was subtitled *The Speeches of Thomas M'Kean & James Wilson, Esquires, In Which They Have Unfolded the Principles of Free Government, Demonstrated the Superior Advantages of the Constitution, and Answered Every Objection Hitherto Suggested* (Evans 21365). A statement by the prothonotary of the City and County of Philadelphia certified that the volume had been entered in his office on 29 December 1787. The volume was inscribed "To the Society for Political Enquiries in the City of Philadelphia ... as a Mark of the High Esteem Entertained, both of the Advantages of that *New Institution* and of the Characters Who Compose It, by the Society's Most Obedient and Very Humble Servant, Thomas Lloyd." The Society was founded in February 1787 for the "mutual improvement in the knowledge of government and the advancement of political science." Benjamin Franklin was president and George Clymer and William Bingham were vice presidents. Included among the forty-two members were Francis Hopkinson, Timothy Pickering, and Benjamin Rush.

The 150-page volume consists of the Constitution and accompanying resolutions of the Constitutional Convention (CC:76); the minutes of the Pennsylvania Convention for 20, 21, 22, 23, and 24 November; Wilson's speeches on 24, 28, 30 November, and 1, 3, 4, 7, and 11 December; McKean's motion of 24 November and his statement concerning it; and McKean's speech of 10 December. Contrary to Lloyd's promises, Benjamin Rush's 12 December speech was not included, nor were any speeches by Antifederalists. The volume contained a two-page index and an errata.

According to the advertisement in the *Pennsylvania Mercury* of 7 February 1788, the *Debates* was available from the principal booksellers in Pennsylvania, New York City, Baltimore, Richmond, and elsewhere throughout the United States. By mid-April advertisements for its sale also appeared in Newport, Lancaster, Annapolis, and Charleston. In March James Madison carried a complimentary copy from James Wilson to George Washington. By July other copies were obtained by or sent to such prominent individuals as Stephen Van Rensselaer in New York; John Dickinson in Delaware; William Tilghman in Maryland; Bushrod Washington in Virginia; William R. Davie in North Carolina; and Thomas Jefferson in France.

Thomas Lloyd's account with his publisher, Thomas Seddon, indicates that 266 copies of the *Debates* were sold–a smaller quantity than Lloyd had expected. One disappointing market was North Carolina. Lloyd shipped fifty copies to Newbern, but in June 1789 forty-nine were returned. Lloyd also sent "several volumes" to John Debrett of London, publisher of the *Parliamentary Register*, and "750 Vols. in sheets" to Joshua Johnson, also in London, but a London edition by Debrett was not printed until 1792. (See "Mr. Thomas Lloyd in Acct. with Thos. Seddon Co.," [14 February 1788–15 December 1789]; Lloyd to Debrett, 7 December 1789; Lloyd to Johnson, 7 December, Lloyd Papers, PPAmP; and Griffin, "Thomas Lloyd," 24.)

The response to the publication of the *Debates* was mixed. On 27 February an Antifederalist satirist, addressing James Wilson, noted that "I was glad to find you had stopped the publication of the debates of your convention; and that you had suited *your own* so well *to the tune*; you was very right to hold back the second volume containing the speeches of the minority, as perhaps the real ones might come out. But I was sorry you *could not silence* the press entirely..." (CC:570). A reviewer in the New York *American Magazine*, probably editor Noah Webster, called Lloyd's *Debates* "a very useful publication, and calculated to diffuse a true knowledge of the principles of government in general, and particularly of the New Federal Constitution." (This sentence was quoted in advertisements for the *Debates* in the Baltimore *Maryland Gazette*, 2 May, and *Virginia Independent Chronicle*, 14 May.) The reviewer in the *American Magazine* could not, however, understand why "the compiler suppressed the speeches of the most able men on the opposite party? Are they to appear in the second volume? and if so, will they not be mis-placed. It is presumed that the principles of the Constitution, like those of the Christian religion will bear the severest scrutiny; and that its cause will even gain strength by discussion. The omission of the anti-federal arguments as stated by the opposition, may give uneasiness to some warm friends to the Constitution. On this subject however it is necessary to suspend our opinion, till the appearance of the second volume" (March, Mfm:Pa. 592). Others also anticipated a second volume. On 11 April New York delegate to Congress Leonard Gansevoort sent Stephen Van Rensselaer leather-bound copies of the *Debates* and the first volume of *The Federalist* and promised that "when the 2d. Volumes are published one of each will be bound in like Manner & forwarded" (Miscellaneous Manuscripts, NHi). But when Philadelphian John Vaughan sent the *Debates* to John Dickinson on 6 April he told him "the Second will not appear thro' the inattention of the Editor" (Dickinson Papers, PPL). On 20 May an "Anecdote" in the *Maryland Journal* speculated that "If Mr. Lloyd should publish the arguments of the opposition in that [the Pennsylvania] convention, it will probably be *after* the decision by all the conventions." On 21 July, shortly after the adjournment of the Virginia Convention, Antifederalist delegate George Mason wrote his son John that the Convention debates "are not Yet published; nor is there any Cause to expect that they will be authentic; the Short Hand Man who took them down, being a *federal* Partizan, they will probably be garbled, in some such Partial Manner as the Debates of the Pensylvania Convention have been by Lloyd" (21 July, Robert A. Rutland, ed., *The Papers of George Mason, 1725–1792* [3 vols., Chapel Hill, N.C., 1970], III, 1126).

The records of the Pennsylvania Convention are printed in RCS:Pa., 322–616, and Mfm:Pa. 237, 239, 263–65, 266.

Pennsylvania Mercury, 7 February

THIS DAY IS PUBLISHED,
on an entire new American Type and good Paper,
(Price 11s 3d in boards)
The FIRST VOLUME of the
DEBATES OF THE CONVENTION
Of the STATE of PENNSYLVANIA,
On the CONSTITUTION proposed for the GOVERN-
MENT of the UNITED STATES.
Taken accurately in Short hand by THOMAS LLOYD.
Containing–

The Speeches of Thomas M'Kean and James Wilson, Esqrs. In which they have *unfolded* the principles of *Free Governments*; *demonstrated* the superior advantages *of this Constitution*, and *answered every Objection* hitherto suggested.

Philadelphia, SOLD by T. SEDDON, in Market-street, and the principal booksellers in Pennsylvania–At New-York, by Messrs. BERRY and ROGERS, Messrs. S. and J. LOUDON, Mr. HODGE–At Baltimore, by Mr. CLARKE–At Richmond, by Mr. A. DAVIS, and by the principal booksellers in the United States.

∴ Subscribers to the Debates of the General Assembly will be furnished with one copy each, on application to the Editor, for 3s. 9d. He is happy to embrace this opportunity of returning the patrons of that undertaking his most grateful acknowledgments.

February 6, 1788.

512. James Madison to George Washington
New York, 8 February[1]

The prospect in Massts. seems to brighten, if I view in the true light the following representation of it. "This day, (Jany. 30) for the first our President Mr. Handcock took his seat in Convention, and we shall probably terminate our business on saturday or tuesday next. I cannot predict the issue, but our hopes are increasing. If Mr. Hancock does not disappoint our present expectations, our wishes will be gratified."[2] Several reflections are suggested by this paragraph which countenance a favorable inference from it. I hope from the rapid advance towards a conclusion of the business, that even the project of recommendatory alterations has been dispensed with.

The form of the ratification of Georgia is contained in one of the papers herewith inclosed.[3] Every information from S. Carolina continues to be favorable. I have seen a letter from N. Carolina of pretty late date which admits that a very formidable opposition exists, but leans towards a fœderal result in that State. As far as I can discover, the state of the question in N. Carolina, is pretty analogous to that in Virginia. The body of the people are better disposed than some of a superior order. The Resolutions of New York for calling a Convention appear by the paper to have passed by a majority of two only in the House of Assembly.[4] I am told this proceeded in some degree from an injudicious form in which the business was conducted; and which threw some of the fœderalists into the opposition.

I am just informed by a gentleman who has seen another letter from Boston of the same date with mine, that the plan of recommendatory alterations has not been abandoned, but that they will be put into a harmless form, and will be the means of saving the Constitution from all risk in Massts.[5]

1. RC, Washington Papers, DLC.
2. See Rufus King to Madison, 30 January (Rutland, *Madison*, X, 445. See also CC:508.).
3. The Georgia form of ratification was reprinted in four New York City newspapers from 5 to 8 February.
4. On 4 February the *New York Journal* reported that a resolution calling a state convention had been passed by "a majority of TWO" in the House of Assembly.
5. On 30 January Nathaniel Gorham, a delegate to the Massachusetts Convention, wrote Secretary at War Henry Knox in New York that "We almost got through the discussion in paragraphs.–we cannot gain the question without some recommendatory amendments–with them I presume we shall have a small majority–they are preparing

and will be ready for tomorrow. we shall then there present them–if a proper pause offers–we are now in Caucas–& King who is with us–cant write–but makes his compliments to you" (Knox Papers, MHi. See also CC:508.).

513. Comte de Moustier to Comte de Montmorin
New York, 8 February (excerpt)[1]

The packet boat whose departure from this city was established by the arrêt of Council on the 25th of January, having not yet even arrived at this time, I made use of this delay to acquire some preliminary knowledge of the present situation in this country. In spite of the advantage that I had in gathering an endless amount of interesting and instructive information from the correspondence of M. le Chev. de la Luzerne, M. de Marbois and M. Otto,[2] affairs present so many different aspects here and are subject to such singular and rapid variations, that it is difficult to form a perfectly accurate understanding of them, if one wants to include them all. The more distant one is, the more difficult it is to judge them well, in the same way I had occasion to be convinced of that in comparing my opinion of these people while I was in Europe to that which I am beginning to form since I am examining them in their country, only in which it seems to me one can know them well. I will not hurry to form a judgment on a subject as complicated as that of pronouncing on the present situation and the future fate of these States, as well as on their true interests and the ties that they might have with European powers and particularly with France.

The Congress had not even assembled by the time I arrived. As soon as there was a quorum of States represented, to form a Congress,[3] they were urged to name a President. The choice fell on M. Griffin, Delegate from Virginia. It is thought that this haste was caused by the arrival of the King's Minister, for whom Congress wanted to prepare itself to give an audience; until now it has only been composed of seven States. The Delegates of the others are in no hurry at all to arrive. The State of Rhodeisland has not even named one.[4] The indifference of the members who compose or ought to compose this Assembly causes much slowness in the expedition of affairs.

The Congress which owed its importance and its consideration to the circumstances that made united Americans feel the necessity for an extended and active power, lost the little that it had held, as soon as it was perceived that it had no means at all to exercise the rights that the confederation seemed to have assured it. Also this Assembly can no longer be regarded as anything but the shadow of a Sovereign power. It can deliberate and prescribe but cannot in the least compel obedience. Its insufficiency is generally recognized throughout the entire united States. In spite of the opinion of people who believe that these States are not exposed to the influence of disturbances that could agitate and trouble European powers, one would have been soon convinced, that the same weakness that renders Congress insufficient for governing at home renders it equally incapable of taking any effective measures abroad, if the wisdom and firmness of the King had not averted the war that seemed on the verge of breaking out between France and England. In the present situation Congress cannot at all be useful to the allies of the united States and is not in any position to harm their enemies. Without a navy, troops, fortifications, without coercive force to keep them in good order, it cannot prevent the most important posts from falling to the power of the first occupier.

Without examining here if the schism or consolidation of these States suits the European powers and which would suit one or the other the most, I think that it is impossible for the present form of Government to stand. Opinions are not in the least divided on the necessity of establishing another one. The diversity of interests creates a great diversity in the ideas that different parties form about the kind of government that would be most suitable to adopt. You have been informed, My Lord, by M. Otto of all that has happened to bring about this revolution. I do not doubt that his reports have seemed very satisfactory to You and have aroused Your full attention. The Constitution proposed by the general Convention of Philadelphia has already been accepted by five States in the following order; Delaware, Pennsylvania, Jersey, Georgia, Connecticut. The States of Newhampshire, Carolina, Virginia, Maryland and Newyork have fixed the time of their individual conventions to examine the Constitution according to the request of Congress. Massachusetts is presently deliberating.[5] The first appearances there were against its adoption; it seems now that its supporters will carry it. The decision of that State is infinitely important because it seems that it should influence the determination of Newhampshire and Rhodeisland and probably that of some other States. Consequently it should determine the fate of the new Constitution, since nine states are sufficient for its adoption.

It is possible, My Lord, that the revolution will be completed by the time You receive this Dispatch. The European powers are no longer in a position, either to foster, or to hinder the adoption of the new Constitution. What it seems ought to be occupying them now is regulating their political conduct toward an event that would procure for the united States the strength and vigor of a solid and powerful Government through the union of several opposing powers into a single body, which would be the source and distributor of power. It can be presumed that England awaits the moment of decision on this present crisis in order to take a definite stand with regard to the united States. Without having a representative here, she has maintained so many partisans and she takes care to maintain so many Emissaries, that she can give all the attention to the movements of these States that her interests require without giving that appearance. . . .

1. RC (Tr), Correspondance Politique, États-Unis, Vol. 33, ff. 16–21, Archives du Ministère des Affaires Étrangères, Paris, France. In September 1787 the Comte de

Moustier (1751–1817) was appointed minister plenipotentiary to the United States succeeding the Comte de la Luzerne who had ended his stay in America in 1784. Moustier arrived in New York City on 18 January 1788 and presented his credentials to Congress on 26 February. He remained in America until October 1789.

2. The Comte de la Luzerne was minister plenipotentiary to the United States from 1779 to 1784. François Barbé de Marbois was chargé d'affaires from 1780 to 1785 and was succeeded by Louis-Guillaume Otto.

3. Congress attained a quorum on 21 January.

4. Rhode Island had elected two delegates to Congress on 2 May 1787.

5. On 15 February Moustier wrote Montmorin that "The adoption of the new Constitution of the Government of the United States made on the 9. of this month by the State of Massachusetts will probably provide all the support necessary for the general establishment of this Constitution. The number of States that have ratified it are six. Newhampshire, which should decide this week, will probably be the seventh. Consequently, it is expected that one of the most important revolutions on this Continent is on the eve of being consummated. It is no longer on the probability of the disunion or the consolidation of the American Confederation that the European Powers should exercise their political speculations. This consolidation can be regarded as effective, consequently, from now on we must think about the conduct we should observe toward the United States which will take on a completely different existence from that which they had until now" (Tr, Correspondance Politique, États-Unis, Vol. 33, f. 43, Archives du Ministère des Affaires Étrangères, Paris, France).

514. Publius: The Federalist 52
New York Packet, 8 February

The authorship of this essay was claimed by both James Madison and Alexander Hamilton, but it is generally attributed to Madison. This essay was reprinted in the New York *Independent Journal* on 9 February. It is number 52 in the M'Lean edition and number 51 in the newspapers.

For a general discussion of the authorship, circulation, and impact of *The Federalist*, see CC:201, 639; and for the disputed authorship of this essay, see Cooke, xix–xxx, 634–35, and Rutland, *Madison*, X, 261–63.

The FŒDERALIST, No. 51.

To the People of the State of New-York.

From the more general enquiries pursued in the four last papers,[1] I pass on to a more particular examination of the several parts of the government. I shall begin with the House of Representatives.

The first view to be taken of this part of the government, relates to the qualifications of the electors and the elected. Those of the former are to be the same with those of the electors of the most numerous branch of the State Legislatures. The definition of the right of suffrage is very justly regarded as a fundamental article of republican government. It was incumbent on the Convention therefore to define and establish this right, in the Constitution. To have left it open for the occasional regulation of the Congress, would have been improper for the reason just mentioned. To have submitted it to the legislative discretion of the States, would have been improper for the same reason; and for the additional reason, that it would have rendered too dependent on the State Governments, that branch of the Fœderal Government, which ought to be dependent on the people alone. To have reduced the different qualifications in the different States, to one uniform rule, would probably have been as dissatisfactory to some of the States, as it would have been difficult to the Convention. The provision made by the Convention appears therefore, to be the best that lay within their option. It must be satisfactory to every State; because it is conformable to the standard already established, or which may be established by the State itself. It will be safe to the United States; because, being fixed by the State Constitutions, it is not alterable by the State Governments, and it cannot be feared that the people of the States will alter this part of their Constitutions, in such a manner as to abridge the rights secured to them by the Fœderal Constitution.

The qualifications of the elected being less carefully and properly defined by the State Constitutions, and being at the same time more susceptible of uniformity, have been very properly considered and regulated by the Convention. A representative of the United States must be of the age of twenty-five years; must have been seven years a citizen of the United States, must at the time of his election, be an inhabitant of the State he is to represent, and during the time of his service must be in no office under the United States. Under these reasonable limitations, the door of this part of the Fœderal Government, is open to merit of every description, whether native or adoptive, whether young or old, and without regard to poverty or wealth, or to any particular profession of religious faith.

The term for which the Representatives are to be elected, falls under a second view which may be taken of this branch. In order to decide on the propriety of this article, two questions must be considered; first, whether biennial elections will, in this case, be safe; secondly, whether they be necessary or useful.

First. As it is essential to liberty that the government in general, should have a common interest with the people; so it is particularly essential that the branch of it under consideration, should have an immediate dependence on, & an intimate sympathy with the people. Frequent elections are unquestionably the only policy by which this dependence and sympathy can be effectually secured. But what particular degree of frequency may be absolutely necessary for the purpose, does not appear to be susceptible of any precise calculation; and must depend on a variety of circumstances with which it may be connected. Let us consult experience, the guide that ought always to be followed, whenever it can be found.

The scheme of representation, as a substitute for a meeting of the citizens in person, being at most but very imperfectly known to ancient polity; it is in more modern times only, that we are to expect instructive examples. And even here, in order to avoid a research too vague and diffusive, it will be proper to confine ourselves to the few examples which are best known, and which bear the greatest analogy to our particular case. The first to which this character ought to be applied, is the House of

Commons in Great Britain. The history of this branch of the English Constitution, anterior to the date of Magna Charta, is too obscure to yield instruction. The very existence of it has been made a question among political antiquaries. The earliest records of subsequent date prove, that Parliaments were to *sit* only, every year; not that they were to be *elected* every year. And even these annual sessions were left so much at the discretion of the monarch, that under various pretexts, very long and dangerous intermissions, were often contrived by royal ambition. To remedy this grievance, it was provided by a statute in the reign of Charles the second, that the intermissions should not be protracted beyond a period of three years. On the accession of Wil. III. when a revolution took place in the government, the subject was still more seriously resumed, and it was declared to be among the fundamental rights of the people, that Parliaments ought to be held *frequently*. By another statute which passed a few years later in the same reign, the term "frequently" which had alluded to the triennial period settled in the time of Charles II. is reduced to a precise meaning, it being expressly enacted that a new parliament shall be called within three years after the determination of the former. The last change from three to seven years is well known to have been introduced pretty early in the present century, under an alarm for the Hanoverian succession.[2] From these facts it appears, that the greatest frequency of elections which has been deemed necessary in that kingdom, for binding the representatives to their constituents, does not exceed a triennial return of them. And if we may argue from the degree of liberty retained even under septennial elections, and all the other vicious ingredients in the parliamentary constitution, we cannot doubt that a reduction of the period from seven to three years, with the other necessary reforms, would so far extend the influence of the people over their representatives, as to satisfy us, that biennial elections under the fœderal system, cannot possibly be dangerous to the requisite dependence of the house of representatives on their constituents.

Elections in Ireland till of late were regulated entirely by the discretion of the crown, and were seldom repeated except on the accession of a new Prince, or some other contingent event. The parliament which commenced with George II. was continued throughout his whole reign, a period of about thirty-five years. The only dependence of the representatives on the people consisted, in the right of the latter to supply occasional vacancies, by the election of new members, and in the chance of some event which might produce a general new election. The ability also of the Irish parliament, to maintain the rights of their constituents, so far as the disposition might exist, was extremely shackled by the controul of the crown over the subjects of their deliberation. Of late these shackles, if I mistake not, have been broken; and octennial parliaments have besides been established.[3] What effect may be produced by this partial reform, must be left to further experience. The example of Ireland, from this view of it, can throw but little light on the subject. As far as we can draw any conclusion from it, it must be, that if the people of that country have been able, under all these disadvantages, to retain any liberty whatever, the advantage of biennial elections would secure to them every degree of liberty which might depend on a due connection between their representatives and themselves.

Let us bring our enquiries nearer home. The example of these States when British colonies claims particular attention; at the same time that it is so well known, as to require little to be said on it. The principle of representation, in one branch of the Legislature at least, was established in all of them. But the periods of election were different. They varied from one to seven years. Have we any reason to infer from the spirit and conduct of the representatives of the people, prior to the revolution, that biennial elections would have been dangerous to the public liberties? The spirit which every where displayed itself at the commencement of the struggle; and which vanquished the obstacles to independence, is the best of proofs that a sufficient portion of liberty had been every where enjoyed to inspire both a sense of its worth, and a zeal for its proper enlargement. This remark holds good as well with regard to the then colonies, whose elections were least frequent, as to those whose elections were most frequent. Virginia was the colony which stood first in resisting the parliamentary usurpations of Great-Britain: it was the first also in espousing by public act, the resolution of independence. In Virginia nevertheless, if I have not been misinformed, elections under the former government were septennial. This particular example is brought into view, not as a proof of any peculiar merit, for the priority in those instances, was probably accidental; and still less of any advantage in *septennial* elections, for when compared with a greater frequency they are inadmissible: but merely as a proof, and I conceive it to be a very substantial proof, that the liberties of the people can be in no danger from *biennial* elections.

The conclusion resulting from these examples will be not a little strengthened by recollecting three circumstances. The first is that the Fœderal Legislature will possess a part only of that supreme legislative authority which is vested completely in the British parliament, and which with a few exceptions was exercised by the colonial Assemblies and the Irish Legislature. It is a received and well founded maxim, that, where no other circumstances affect the case, the greater the power is, the shorter ought to be its duration; and, conversely, the smaller the power, the more safely may its duration be protracted. In the second place, it has, on another occasion, been shewn that the Fœderal Legislature will not only be restrained by its dependence on the people as other legislative bodies are; but that it will be moreover watched and controuled by the several collateral Legislatures, which other legislative bodies are not. And in the third place, no comparison can be made between the means that will be possessed by the more permanent branches of the Fœderal Government for seducing, if they should be disposed to seduce, the House of Representatives from their duty to the people; and the means of influence over the popular branch, possessed by the other branches of the governments above cited. With less power therefore to abuse, the Fœderal Representatives, can be less tempted on one side, and will be doubly watched on the other.

1. *The Federalist* 48–51 (CC:492, 495, 500, 503).

2. In 1664 Parliament enacted the Triennial Act providing for "the assembling and holding of parliaments once in three years at the least." The Declaration of Rights of 1689 declared that parliaments should be "held frequently," and in 1694 Parliament passed another Triennial Act stipulating "that from henceforth a parliament shall be holden once in three years at the least." The Septennial Act of 1716 stated that parliaments "shall . . . have continuance for seven years and no longer."

3. In 1768 the Irish Parliament provided that general elections be held every eight years. Before the passage of this Octennial Act, Irish parliaments did not dissolve regularly, and general elections could be required only upon the death of the British monarch (J.C. Beckett, *The Making of Modern Ireland, 1603–1923* [New York, 1973], 162, 200–1).

515. Philadelphia Independent Gazetteer, 8 February[1]

Extract of a letter from the Eastern Shore of Maryland, to a gentleman in this city, dated Jan. 29, 1788.

"We are all in an uproar in Maryland; the federal agents, have taken the alarm, since the substance of the honorable Mr. Martin's examination before the Assembly, appeared in Mr. Hayes's papers.[2] This gentleman at the instance of a great number of his constituents, was called upon to declare his objections in the public prints, to the new federal government, in order to enable them to form some opinion of the merits or demerits, ascribed to it, as well by its numerous advocates, as opposers. I should be glad to have your ideas, whether Mr. Martin, as one of the delegates to the late Convention, had acted a becoming part, by complying with the requisition of his constituents, and that in a matter of such infinite importance to the present, if not to future generations. If Mr. Martin refused the reiterated applications made to him on this occasion, they might naturally suppose that his objections were ill grounded and futile; or otherwise, that he sacrificed the public welfare to some private and interested considerations, highly incompatible with the dignity of a delegate to the honorable General Convention of the United States. The *federal hacks* here say, that he was not justifiable in holding any opinion that militated against their measures; because influence and the power of making proselytes is on their side; ergo, right or wrong, the current of faction must bear down all that comes before it; and a fig for the feeble efforts of the *low born* peasantry, who ought not to be allowed even the privilege of a groan, whilst they wear the galling fetters of the great, unless in the silent and solitary shade of wretchedness, and obscurity.

"The federal hacks assert, that whoever dares to utter a syllable in disapprobation of their cause, is from that instant, to be publicly charged as inimical to his country; and as they have the advantage of every press, from New Hampshire, to Georgia, to circulate their calumnies, the unfortunate objects of their rancour, in that extent of country, can only resort to two or three,[3] at most, who have spirit and independence enough to publish in vindication of these devoted victims to power and tyranny. This circumstance accounts fully for the unanimity that prevails throughout the whole continent, in adopting the new federal government, for wherever there is a printing press, there you will find some federal hacks, or company of hacks, who claim an absolute dominion over *Mr. Type*, as if unlimited monarchy had already been established in this wretched country. The *Post-Offices*[4] are also under the influence of these sons of power, so much so that a paper printed at New-York cannot find its way to Philadelphia, Baltimore, or any of the other states; neither can the papers of the Southward proceed an inch farther than the office they are put in at, unless they should happen to contain the most fulsome elogiums, on Franky's *New Roof*,[5] which is to accommodate him and all the *Office-hunters* on the continent. The *minority* whom I shall call every man in the community, from whom a fair, open and candid enquiry is withheld, either by direct or indirect means, and who have no views of lucrative offices under the federal government; I say, sir, that the minority, these real disinterested patriots should assiduously exhort each other, to exert every nerve for the good of their country and posterity; and not suffer *one tenth* part of their fellow subjects, with the help of their expecting, gaping minions, to enslave all the rest. But these salutary admonitions, I fear, cannot impede the evil in its rapid progress, unless the federal *bandage* can be removed from the people's eyes. For it is the peculiar property of the bandage to keep every thing from their sight, which would enable them to judge for themselves, especially at this critical important juncture.

"It is plain to see, that those who have had the art to blindfold them, will have the *constitutional legal* privilege of judging for them forever after, with respect to *life, liberty* and *property*: These being trifling matters not worthy the people's consideration, and of course, not fit to be entrusted to them, who neither know their value, nor use. When these rights and privileges get into other hands, their meaning will be fully explained, not by *precept*, but most assuredly by *woeful example*; and those who helped to cut the rod, should never in prudence or justice, complain of the smart it may create."

1. Reprinted: *New York Morning Post*, 12 February; *New York Journal*, 22 February; Boston *American Herald*, 10 March. The *Journal* and *Herald* deleted the *Gazetteer's* italics.

2. By 29 January nine of the twelve installments of Luther Martin's *Genuine Information* were printed in the Baltimore *Maryland Gazette*. For the *Genuine Information*, see CC:389.

3. Perhaps a reference to Eleazer Oswald of the *Independent Gazetteer*; Thomas Green-leaf of the *New York Journal*; and Edward E. Powars of the *American Herald*–all of whom published this item.

4. For the post office and the circulation of newspapers, see Appendix II.

5. See Francis Hopkinson's "The New Roof," *Pennsylvania Packet*, 29 December (CC:395).

516. Luther Martin: Genuine Information XII
Baltimore Maryland Gazette, 8 February[1]

Mr. Martin's *Information to the House of Assembly, concluded.*

The part of the system, which provides that *no religious test* shall ever be required as a qualification to any office or public trust under the United States, was adopted by a very great majority of the convention, and with-out much debate,[2]–however, there were some members *so unfashionable* as to think that a *belief of the existence of a Deity*, and of a *state of future rewards and punishments* would be some security for the good conduct of our rulers, and that in a Christian country it would be at *least decent* to hold out some distinction between the professors of Christianity and downright infidelity or paganism.

The seventh article declares, that the ratification of *nine States* shall be sufficient for the establishment of this constitution between the States rati-fying the same.

It was attempted to obtain a resolve that if seven States, whose votes in the first branch should amount to a majority of the representation in that branch, concured in the adoption of the system, it should be sufficient, and this attempt was supported on the principle, that a majority ought to govern the minority;[3]–but to this it was objected that although it was true, after a constitution and form of government is agreed on, in every act done under and consistent with that constitution and form of government, the act of the majority, unless otherwise agreed in the constitution, should bind the minority, yet it was directly the *reverse* in *originally forming* a consti-tution, or *dissolving it*–That in originally forming a constitution, it was necessary that *every individual* should agree to it to become bound thereby–and that when *once adopted* it could not be *dissolved* by consent, unless with the consent of *every individual* who was *party* to the original agreement–That in forming our original federal government *every member* of that govern-ment, that is each State, expressly consented to it;–that it is a *part* of the *compact* made and entered into in the *most solemn* manner, that there should be no *dissolution* or *alteration* of that federal government without the consent of *every State*, the members of, and parties to the original compact; that therefore *no alteration* could be made by the consent of a *part* of the States, or by the consent of the *inhabitants* of a *part of the States*, which could either *release* the States so consenting from the obligation they are under to the other States, or which could in any manner become *obligatory* upon those States that should not ratify such alterations.–Satisfied of the *truth* of these positions, and not holding ourselves at liberty to *violate* the *compact*, which this State had *solemnly entered into* with the others, by *altering* it in a *different* manner from that which by the same compact is provided and stipulated, a number of the members and among those the *delegation* of *this State* opposed the ratification of this system in *any other manner* than by the *unanimous consent* and agreement of *all the States*.

By our original articles of confederation any alterations proposed are in the first place to be *approved* by Congress.–Accordingly as the resolutions were originally adopted by the convention, and as they were reported by the committee of detail, it was proposed that this system should be laid before Congress *for their approbation*;–but, Sir, the warm advocates of this system fearing it would not meet with the approbation of Congress, and determined, even though Congress and the respective State legislatures should disapprove the same, to force it upon them, if possible, through the intervention of the people at large moved to strike the words "for their approbation" and succeeded in their motion; to which, it being directly in violation of the mode prescribed by the articles of confederation for the alteration of our federal government, a part of the convention, and myself in the number, thought it a duty to give a decided negative.[4]

Agreeable to the articles of confederation entered into in the most *solemn* manner, and for the *observance* of which the States *pledged* themselves to each other, and called upon the *Supreme Being* as a *witness* and *avenger* between them, *no alterations* are to be made in those articles unless after they are approved by Congress, they are agreed to and ratified by the *legislature* of *every* State; but by the resolve of the convention this constitution is not to be ratified by the legislatures of the respective States, but is to be submitted to conventions chosen by the people, and if ratified by them is to be binding.

This resolve was opposed among others by the delegation of Maryland;–your delegates were of opinion that as the form of government proposed was, if adopted, most essentially to *alter* the *constitution* of *this State*, and as our constitution had pointed out a mode by which, and by which *only*, alterations were to be made therein, a convention of the people could not be called to agree to and ratify the said form of government without a *direct violation* of our constitution, which it is the duty of every individual in this State to protect and support;–in this opinion all your delegates who were attending were unanimous–I, Sir, opposed it also upon a more extensive ground–as being directly *contrary* to the mode of altering our federal government *established* in our original compact, and as such being a *direct violation* of the mutual faith plighted by the States to each other, I gave it my negative.[5]

I also was of opinion that the States considered as States, in their political capacity, are the members of a federal government–That the States in their political capacity, or as sovereignties, are entitled, and *only entitled* originally to agree upon the form of, and submit themselves to, a federal government, and afterwards by mutual consent to dissolve or to alter it– That every thing which relates to the formation, the dissolution or the alteration of a *federal* government over States equally free, sovereign and independent is the *peculiar* province of the *States* in their *sovereign* or *political* capacity, in the same manner as what relates to forming alliances or treaties of peace, amity or commerce, and that the people at large in their individual capacity, have no more right to interfere in the one case than in the other–That according to these principles we originally acted in forming our confederation; it was the States as States, by their representatives in Congress, that formed the articles of confederation;–it was the States as States, by their legislatures, ratified those articles, and it was there established and provided that the States as States, that as by their legislatures, should agree to any alterations that should hereafter be proposed in the federal government, before they should be binding–and any alterations agreed to in any other manner cannot release the States from the obligation they are under to each other by virtue of the original articles of confederation.–The people of the different States never made any objection to the manner the articles of confederation were formed or ratified, or to the mode by which alterations were to be made in that government–with the rights of their respective States they wished not to interfere–Nor do I believe the people in their individual capacity would ever have expected or desired to have been appealed to on the present occasion, in violation of the rights of their respective States, if the favourers of the proposed constitution, imagining they had a better chance of forcing it to be adopted by a *hasty* appeal to the people at large, who could not be so good judges of the dangerous consequences, had not insisted upon this mode–Nor do these positions in the least interfere with the principle, that all power originates from the people, because when once the people have *exercised their power* in *establishing* and *forming* themselves into a *State government*, it never *devolves back* to them, nor have they a *right* to *resume* or *again to exercise that power* until such events take place as will amount to a *dissolution* of their *State government*:–And it is an established principle that a dissolution or alteration of a *federal* government doth not dissolve the *State* governments which compose it.–It was also my opinion that upon *principles of sound policy*, the agreement or disagreement to the proposed system ought to have been by the State legislatures, in which case, let the event have been what it would, there would have been but little prospect of the *public peace* being *disturbed* thereby–Whereas the attempt to force down this system, although Congress and the respective State legislatures should disapprove, by appealing to the people, and to procure its establishment in a manner totally unconstitutional, has a tendency to set the *State governments* and their *subjects* at *variance* with each other–to *lessen* the *obligations* of *government*–to *weaken* the *bands of society*–to introduce *anarchy* and *confusion*–and to *light* the *torch of discord and civil war* throughout this continent.–All these considerations weighed with me most forcibly against giving my assent to the mode by which it is resolved this system is to be ratified, and were urged by me in opposition to the measure.[6]

I have now, Sir, in discharge of the duty I owe to this house, given such information as hath occured to me, which I consider most material for them to know; and you will easily perceive from this detail that a great portion of that time, which ought to have been devoted calmly and impartially to consider what alterations in our federal government would be most likely to procure and preserve the happiness of the union, was employed in a *violent struggle* on the one side to obtain *all power* and *dominion* in their own hands, and on the other to prevent it–and that the *aggrandizement* of particular States and particular individuals appears to have been much more the object sought after than the welfare of our country.

The interest of this State, not confined merely to itself, abstracted from all others, but considered relatively; and as far as was consistent with the common interest of the other States, I thought it my duty to pursue according to the best opinion I could form of it.

When I took my seat in the convention, I found them attempting to bring forward a system, which I was sure never had entered into the contemplation of those I had the honour to represent, and which upon the fullest consideration, I considered not only injurious to the interest and the rights of this State, but also incompatible with the political happiness and freedom of the States in general; from that time until my business compelled me to leave the convention, I gave it every possible opposition in every stage of its progression.–I opposed the system there with the same explicit frankness with which I have here given you a history of our proceedings, and an account of my own conduct, which in a particular manner I consider you as having a right to know–While there, I endeavoured to act as became a free man, and the delegate of a free State. Should my conduct obtain the approbation of those who appointed me, I will not deny it would afford me satisfaction; but to me that approbation was at most no more than a *secondary* consideration–my *first* was to *deserve* it;–left to myself to act according to the best of my discretion, my conduct should have been the same, had I been even sure your censure would have been my only reward, since I hold it sacredly my duty to dash the cup of poison, if possible, from the hand of a State or an individual, however anxious the one or the other might be to swallow it.

Indulge me, Sir, in a single observation further. There are persons who endeavour to hold up the idea that this system is only opposed by the officers of government–I, Sir, am in that predicament.–I have the honor to hold an appointment in this State.[7] Had it been considered any objection, I presume I should not have been appointed to the convention–If it could have any effect on my mind, it would only be that of warming my heart with gratitude, and rendering me more anxious to promote the true interest of that State which has conferred upon me the obligation, and to heighten my guilt had I joined in sacrificing its essential rights–But, Sir, it would be well to remember, that this system is not calculated to *diminish* the *number* or the *value* of *offices*–on the contrary, if adopted, it will be productive of an enormous increase in their number–many of them will be also of great honour and emolument. Whether, Sir, in this variety of appointments and in the scramble for them, I might not have as good a prospect to advantage myself as many others is not for me to say–but this, Sir, I can say with truth, that so far was I from being influenced in my conduct by interest, or the consideration of office, that I would cheerfully resign the appointment I now hold–I would bind myself never to accept another either under the general government or that of my own State–I would do more, Sir, so destructive do I consider the present system to the happiness of my country, I would cheerfully sacrifice that share of property with which Heaven has blessed a life of industry,–I would reduce myself to indigence and poverty; and those who are dearer to me than my own existence I would entrust to the care and protection of that Providence who hath so kindly protected myself, if on *those terms only* I could procure my country to reject those chains which are forged for it.

1. Reprinted: *Pennsylvania Packet*, 19 February; Philadelphia *Independent Gazetteer*, 25 February; *New York Journal*, 3, 7 April; Boston *American Herald*, 8 May (only the first five paragraphs). For the impact of the *Genuine Information*, see CC:389.

After reading this last installment of the *Genuine Information*, a Baltimore "gentleman" noted that "The conclusion of Martin's information to the House of Assembly, has convinced all his former friends, who have any sense, that he is an artful hypocrite. Even Mr. Goddard, hitherto against the new constitution, is now, by the force of the arguments published in his own paper, become highly and truly federal" (*Pennsylvania Mercury*, 26 February, Appendix I). Another Federalist criticized Martin for his insistence that the Constitutional Convention should have asked the state legislatures, not the state conventions, to ratify the Constitution. He could not understand how Martin could complain that the Constitution was to be "*forced* upon us through the medium of the people" (*ibid.*, 28 February, Appendix I).

2. On 30 August the Constitutional Convention adopted this clause unanimously. The only recorded opposition to it was made by Roger Sherman who "thought it unnecessary, the prevailing liberality being a sufficient security agst. such tests" (Farrand, II, 468).

3. On 31 August James Madison made this motion, thus providing that ratification "would require the concurrence of a majority of both the States and people" (*ibid.*, 475).

4. On 31 August Gouverneur Morris and Charles Pinckney moved to strike out the words "for their approbation," and the motion was adopted eight states to three, with Maryland in the minority (*ibid.*, 478).

5. On 20 June Martin attacked the ratification of the Constitution by state conventions. According to Maryland delegate James McHenry, on 7 August the state's delegation (excepting Martin who had gone to New York) agreed to oppose ratification by state conventions. On 31 August Martin "insisted on a reference to the State Legislatures. He urged the danger of commotions from a resort to the people & to the first principles in which the Governments might be on one side & the people on the other."

On this day Maryland voted, with a minority of delegations, for striking out the phrase requiring ratification by state conventions. Martin and his fellow Maryland delegates then tried to have the Convention agree to ratification by all thirteen states; only Maryland supported this motion (Farrand, I, 340-41; II, 209, 211-12, 475-79).

6. Martin stated this position on 20 and 27 June and on 31 August. He believed that the central government was "meant merely to preserve the State Governts: not to govern individuals..." (Farrand, I, 340-41, 437; II, 476). See also note 5 above.

7. Martin was state attorney general.

517. John Craighead to John Nicholson
Rocky Spring, Pa., 9 February[1]

Gratefully acknowledge your many favours. Particularly tha[n]k you for the copy of the View of the proposed constitution, which you sent me inclosed soon after it was printed.[2] And your friendly letter by Majr. M'Calmont.[3] & feel myself much obliged by the care you took to transact the business I troubled you with relative to my Nephew's land.

Cannot see how my being in favour of, or opposed to, the proposed constitution should affect my character, unless as a Patriot, for I am no politician. But being persuaded of your sincere friendship, shall give you all ye satisfaction in my power.–You have been wrong informed, Sir, when told that I was a great advocate for ye proposed continental government. This I could not be unless in the *first particular*, because I understand so little about civil governmts. Have never been strenuous on either side. But in the present case have been more undecided, than in any other, that I was called to judge in, since the revolution.

Must acknowledge that after having read all that I could see, both for & against the proposed plan, I know not what would be best to be done in the present crisis. I dread the rejection of it, lest another convention would propose something worse (which perhaps you think impossible) or rather, lest they should agree upon nothing at all, after the minds of many have been so much heated & agitated. I am not without my fears of it's adoption without amendments. Think ye greatest difficulty arises from the conduct of the federal convention, after the constitution was framed. Had they adjourned, to meet at some proper period of time, apprehend they would have met most of the material objections, & brought ye now contending parties to an amicable agreement.

You may, Sir, without hesitation contradict the report of my exhorting the people, from ye pulpit, to accept the federal government. Never spoke of it in the pulpit but once, & that purely with a view to excite the people to attend the *then* ensuing election, to vote for men of approved abilities & integrity to represent them, at such a critical period.[4] Then I had only once slightly glanced the proposed plan, by piece-meal & apprehended by the information given me, (for had not got the public Newspapers of the preceding week) that the assembly had been unanimous & regular in their procedure[5] & happened to let slip, that their conduct was laudable in doing wt. they did, designing thereby to lead the people to acquiesce in what I apprehended to be regularly done; for I am not ready to find fault with ye conduct of the assembly without apparent cause, & had not then discovered [all?] ye imperfections in this plan which I have since seen, much less all th[ose?] alledged by some to attend it.–Sincerely des[ire?] to see it amended, if adopted. But whether it be safe [to?] attempt it now in our disunited, mouldering state or immediately or as soon as possible after adoption of the general plan, in the mode pointed out by ye convention, I leave to politicians to determine.

That ye supreme ruler of ye Universe may direct the States in general to adopt such measures as shall tend to hand down liberty civil & religious to ye latest posterity, & yt you & yours may partake of her blessings is ye sincere desire of, Sir, Your sincere friend & huml. Servt

1. RC, Nicholson Papers, Pennsylvania Historical and Museum Commission, Harrisburg. The letter was carried to Philadelphia by James M'Calmont (see note 3 below). It was endorsed: "Recd Feby 1788." Craighead (1742–1799), a Princeton College graduate, was pastor of the Rocky Spring Presbyterian church in Franklin County, Pa.

2. Nicholson's Antifederalist pamphlet–*A View of the Proposed Constitution of the United States*...–was published in Philadelphia in mid-October (CC:172; RCS:Pa., 207–8, 256–57; and Mfm:Pa. 141).

3. James M'Calmont (1737–1809), a Franklin County assemblyman, was one of the two seceding assemblymen forcibly returned to the Pennsylvania Assembly on 29 September so that the Assembly would have a quorum to vote on the resolutions calling a state convention.

4. A reference either to the state Assembly election on 9 October or the state Convention election on 6 November.

5. Craighead is evidently referring to the Assembly's adoption on 29 September of the resolutions calling a state convention. (See CC:546, note 4.)

518. Reverend James Madison to James Madison
Williamsburg, Va., 9 February[1]

I should, my dear Friend, have acknowledged ye Favr of your last,[2] long before this, had my Answer been as little delayed, as the Satisfaction reced. from it, was sincere: but as I always write to you, rather to get your Observations upon political Subjects, than for ye Sake of communicating my own, I have been unwilling to impose that Burthen too frequently upon you. Your Answer, tended greatly to satisfy some of my Doubts–whilst those valuable Papers (ye Federalist) wch. are generally attributed to you, have well nigh worked a Conversion. Whoever may be ye Author of them, they are certainly well written, as far at least as I have seen them, & well calculated to promote ye great Object in View. They must be read with ~~great~~ much Pleasure & Advantage by every one who wishes to examine ye Subject with Candour.

But I fear, a Question of some Importance still remains, even admitting that ye Govt. proposed, would, if adopted & *conformed* to, be productive of ye Advantages expected.–~~or be ye best for ye Am[erica]n States~~ Is it, in

reality practicable?-You will say, Nothing but Experience can solve such
a Question; and that, if it be ye best, it should at all Events be tried-I
agree with you-But we may still reflect upon ye Consequences which will
probably attend the Adoption of it. It's Execution, or it's Operation requires Sacrifices, wch. I ~~fear~~ suspect our State Legislatures, & that of
Virga. in particular, will never be willing to make. For when has ye Legislature of this State failed evincing, as ye Oppy. presented itself, Principles directly the reverse of those wch. ye proposed Govt. requires. It's
Conduct during ye last Session, with Respect to ye Treaty, (notwithstanding ye plain & sensible Address from Congress upon that Subject, & notwithstanding ye Impropriety of an Interference must occur, one wd think,
to every Man of common Sense, I do not say to those ye least versed in
the Laws of Nations)-too plainly shews a Degre of antifederal Spirit, wch.
will not easily be assimilated to ye new Govt.[3] Other Instances of ye same
Nature might easily be given as Proofs of ye real Existence of this Spirit.
The Love of Power is too great, ye supposed Importance of an independent Legislator is too flattering to most, to admit of ye least voluntary
Diminution.-Nor is it improbable, but that ye same Spirit exists in most
of ye other States, because it originates from Principles common to
Am[erica]ns. Viz. ye highest Idea of ye independent Sovereignty of their
own States-& at ye same Time, ye Desire of enjoying all the Advantages
of Govt. at ye least possible Expence to Natural Liberty.-Whether ye new
Govt. can, in it's Operation, controul suffly. this Spirit, you are the best
Judge. But that no Govt. can be durable wch. is not perfectly conformable
to ye Genius of ye People, unless it be supported by Force, is plain, and
whether this under Consideration will not meet with such Opposition from
ye Reaction or Jealousy of ye State Legislatures, & from the Parties it will
have to struggle with, in its very Infancy-as to render it impracticable, or
of short Duration-is perhaps a Problem not unworthy of ~~solution~~ the Attention of a Philosopher. The Imperium in imperio will be the fruitful
Source of a thousand jarring Principles, wch. will make ye new Machine,
notwithstanding all ye Oil you can give it, to go heavily along.

Whether Virga. will adopt ye Plan, ~~unless in~~ if she be not in some
Measure compelled by ye previous Adoption of ye other States, is considered as questionable, especially unless there be tack'd to it, some Clause
of Amendment. How ye Majority may be-is hard or impossible to determine. The opposite Parties however, greatly to their Credit, have hitherto
observed ye Line of candid Discussion. None of those acrimonious Principles have yet appeared wch. generally agitate a People, when Questions of
such Importance create Divisions.-It is hoped by all, that you will be in ye
Convention.-The Atty Gen. will represent this Town.[4]

We did not receive ye Packet you were so kind as to forward till about a
Fortnight past-but it came at last, safe thro' ye Hands of ye Govr.

1. RC, Madison Papers, DLC.

2. James Madison's letter, in which he responded to his cousin's undated letter (CC:118–B, c. 1 October), has not been located.

3. On 21 March 1787 Congress asked the states to repeal all laws "repugnant" to the Treaty of Peace of 1783. On 17 November the Virginia House of Delegates passed a resolution repealing all Virginia acts repugnant to the peace treaty, to have effect only after the other states adopted similar measures. This resolution was embodied in a bill and debated on 3 December, when the House adopted an amendment suspending the act of repeal until Great Britain evacuated its military posts in the Northwest Territory and compensated Virginians for the loss of slaves confiscated during the war (JCC, XXXII, 124–25, 177–84; and Rutland, *Madison*, X, 136n, 257n, 292n).

4. James Innes (1754–1798) had been state attorney general since November 1786. In June 1788 he represented Williamsburg in the state Convention, where he voted to ratify the Constitution.

519. Publius: The Federalist 53
New York Independent Journal, 9 February

The authorship of this essay has been attributed to James Madison and Alexander Hamilton. Hamilton himself attributed authorship to Madison. This essay was reprinted in the *New York Packet*, 12 February. It is number 53 in the M'Lean edition and number 52 in the newspapers.

For a general discussion of the authorship, circulation, and impact of *The Federalist*, see CC:201, 639; and for the disputed authorship of this essay, see Cooke, xix–xxx, 635, and Rutland, *Madison*, X, 261–63.

The FŒDERALIST. No. LII.
To the People of the State of New-York.

I shall here perhaps be reminded of a current observation, "that where annual elections end, tyranny begins." If it be true as has often been remarked, that sayings which become proverbial, are generally founded in reason, it is not less true that when once established, they are often applied to cases to which the reason of them does not extend. I need not look for a proof beyond the case before us. What is the reason on which this proverbial observation is founded? No man will subject himself to the ridicule of pretending that any natural connection subsists between the sun or the seasons, and the period within which human virtue can bear the temptations of power. Happily for mankind, liberty is not in this respect confined to any single point of time; but lies within extremes, which afford sufficient latitude for all the variations which may be required by the various situations and circumstances of civil society. The election of magistrates might be, if it were found expedient, as in some instances it actually has been, daily, weekly, or monthly, as well as annual; and if circumstances may require a deviation from the rule on one side, why not also on the other side. Turning our attention to the periods established among ourselves, for the election of the most numerous branches of the state legislatures, we find them by no means coinciding any more in this instance, than in the elections of other civil magistrates. In Connecticut and Rhode-Island, the periods are half-yearly. In the other states, South-Carolina excepted, they are annual. In South-Carolina, they are biennial; as is proposed in the federal government. Here is a difference, as four to one, between the longest and shortest periods; and yet it would be not easy to shew that Connecticut or Rhode-Island is better governed, or enjoys a greater share of rational liberty than South-Carolina; or that either the one or the other of these states are distinguished in these respects, and by these causes, from the states whose elections are different from both.

In searching for the grounds of this doctrine, I can discover but one, and that is wholly inapplicable to our case. The important distinction so well understood in America between a constitution established by the people, and unalterable by the government; and a law established by the government, and alterable by the government, seems to have been little understood and less observed in any other country. Wherever the supreme power of legislation has resided, has been supposed to reside also, a full power to change the form of the government. Even in Great-Britain, where the principles of political and civil liberty have been most discussed; and where we hear most of the rights of the constitution, it is maintained that the authority of the parliament is transcendent and uncontroulable, as well with regard to the constitution, as the ordinary objects of legislative provision. They have accordingly, in several instances, actually changed, by legislative acts, some of the most fundamental articles of the government. They have in particular, on several occasions, changed the periods of election; and on the last occasion, not only introduced septennial, in place of triennial, elections; but by the same act continued themselves in place four years beyond the term for which they were elected by the people.[1] An attention to these dangerous practices has produced a very natural alarm in the votaries of free government, of which frequency of elections is the corner stone; and has led them to seek for some security to liberty against the danger to which it is exposed. Where no constitution paramount to the government, either existed or could be obtained, no constitutional security similar to that established in the United States, was to be attempted. Some other security therefore was to be sought for; and what better security would the case admit, than that of selecting and appealing to some simple and familiar portion of time, as a standard for measuring the danger of innovations, for fixing the national sentiment, and for uniting the patriotic exertions. The most simple and familiar portion of time, applicable to the subject, was that of a year; and hence the doctrine has been inculcated by a laudable zeal to erect some barrier against the gradual innovations of an unlimited government, that the advance towards tyranny was to be calculated by the distance of departure from the fixed point of annual elections. But what necessity can there be of applying this expedient to a government, limited as the federal government will be, by the authority of a paramount constitution? Or who will pretend that the liberties of the people of America will not be more secure under biennial elections, unalterably fixed by such a constitution, than those of any other nation would be, where elections were annual or even more frequent, but subject to alterations by the ordinary power of the government?

The second question stated is, whether biennial elections be necessary or useful? The propriety of answering this question in the affirmative will appear from several very obvious considerations.

No man can be a competent legislator who does not add to an upright intention and a sound judgment, a certain degree of knowledge of the subjects on which he is to legislate. A part of this knowledge may be acquired by means of information which lie within the compass of men in private as well as public stations. Another part can only be attained, or at least thoroughly attained, by actual experience in the station which requires the use of it. The period of service ought therefore in all such cases to bear some proportion to the extent of practical knowledge, requisite to the due performance of the service. The period of legislative service established in most of the states for the more numerous branch is, as we have seen, one year. The question then may be put into this simple form; does the period of two years bear no greater proportion to the knowledge requisite for federal legislation, than one year does to the knowledge requisite for state legislation? The very statement of the question in this form, suggests the answer that ought to be given to it.

In a single state the requisite knowledge, relates to the existing laws which are uniform throughout the state, and with which all the citizens are more or less conversant; and to the general affairs of the state, which lie within a small compass, are not very diversified, and occupy much of the attention and conversation of every class of people. The great theatre of the United States presents a very different scene. The laws are so far from being uniform, that they vary in every state; whilst the public affairs of the union are spread throughout a very extensive region, and are extremely diversified by the local affairs connected with them, and can with difficulty be correctly learnt in any other place, than in the central councils, to which a knowledge of them will be brought by the representatives of every part of the empire. Yet some knowledge of the affairs, and even of the laws of all the states, ought to be possessed by the members from each of the states. How can foreign trade be properly regulated by uniform laws, without some acquaintance with the commerce: the ports, the usages, and the regulations, of the different states. How can the trade between the different states be duly regulated without some knowledge of their relative situations in these and other points? How can taxes be judiciously imposed, and effectually collected, if they be not accommodated to the different laws and local circumstances relating to these objects in the different states? How can uniform regulations for the militia be duly provided without a similar knowledge of many[2] internal circumstances by which the states are distinguished from each other? These are the principal objects of federal legislation, and suggest most forceably, the extensive information which the representatives ought to acquire. The other inferior objects will require a proportional degree of information with regard to them.

It is true that all these difficulties will by degrees be very much diminished. The most laborious task will be the proper inauguration of the government, and the primeval formation of a federal code. Improvements on the first draught will every year become both easier and fewer. Past transactions of the government will be a ready and accurate source of information to new members. The affairs of the union will become more and more objects of curiosity and conversation among the citizens at large. And the increased intercourse among those of different states will contribute not a little to diffuse a mutual knowledge of their affairs, as this again will contribute to a general assimilation of their manners and laws. But with all these abatements the business of federal legislation must continue so far to exceed both in novelty and difficulty, the legislative business of a single state as to justify the longer period of service assigned to those who are to transact it.

A branch of knowledge which belongs to the acquirements of a federal representative, and which has not been mentioned, is that of foreign affairs. In regulating our own commerce he ought to be not only acquainted with the treaties between the United States and other nations, but also with the commercial policy and laws of other nations. He ought not be altogether ignorant of the law of nations, for that as far [as] it is a proper object of municipal legislation is submitted to the federal government. And although the house of representatives is not immediately to participate in foreign negotiations and arrangements, yet from the necessary connection between the several branches of public affairs, those particular branches will frequently deserve attention in the ordinary course of legislation, and will sometimes demand particular legislative sanction and co-operation. Some portion of this knowledge may no doubt be acquired in a man's closet; but some of it also can only be derived from the public sources of information; and all of it will be acquired to best effect by a practical attention to the subject during the period of actual service in the legislature.

There are other considerations of less importance perhaps, but which are not unworthy of notice. The distance which many of the representatives will be obliged to travel, and the arrangements renderd necessary by that circumstance, might be much more serious objections with fit men to this service if limited to a single year than if extended to two years. No argument can be drawn on this subject from the case of the delegates to the existing Congress. They are elected annually it is true; but their re-election is considered by the legislative assemblies almost as a matter of course. The election of the representatives by the people would not be governed by the same principle.

A few of the members, as happens in all such assemblies, will possess superior talents, will by frequent re-elections. become members of long standing; will be thoroughly masters of the public business, and perhaps not unwilling to avail themselves of those advantages. The greater the proportion of new members, and the less the information of the bulk of the members, the more apt will they be to fall into the snares that may be laid for them. This remark is no less applicable to the relation which will subsist between the house of representatives and the senate.

It is an inconveniency mingled with the advantages of our frequent elections, even in single states where they are large and hold but one legislative session in the year, that spurious elections cannot be investigated and annulled in time for the decision to have its due effect. If a return can be obtained, no matter by what unlawful means, the irregular member, who takes his seat of course, is sure of holding it a sufficient time, to answer his purposes. Hence a very pernicious encouragement is given to the use of unlawful means for obtaining irregular returns. Were elections for the federal legislature to be annual, this practice might become a very serious abuse, particularly in the more distant states. Each house is, as it necessarily must be, the judge of the elections, qualifications and returns of its members, and whatever improvements may be suggested by experience for simplifying and accelerating the process in disputed cases. So great a portion of a year would unavoidably elapse, before an illegitimate member could be dispossessed of his seat, that the prospect of such an event, would be little check to unfair and illicit means of obtaining a seat.

All these considerations taken together warrant us in affirming that biennial elections will be as useful to the affairs of the public, as we have seen that they will be safe to the liberties of the people.

1. See CC:514, note 2.
2. Changed to "some" in the M'Lean edition.

520. Edward Carrington to Henry Knox
Manchester, Va., 10 February[1]

Since my last I have made a circuit through two or three of the Southern Counties and arrived here last ev'ning[2]–the State of the ice is such as to render the passage of the River unsafe–a Canoe with difficulty makes its way through the falls by which means I to day, got my letters from the Post Office–amongst them I am favored with yours of the 18th. ult. and thank you sincerely for it. The event in Connecticut is in perfect conformity with the expectations I had formed, but the appearances in Massachusetts, as communicated by Mr. Madison & yourself[3] alarm me exceedingly–The doctrine of Amendment has gained such strong ground in Virginia, that I am pretty confident a direct adoption, is not to be expected, should less than Nine States have adopted when the convention goes into session. Ideas however of the necessity of preserving the Union are so prevailent that Mr. Henry will draw but few after him in an attempt to dictate to that Number–Massachusetts is one of the Nine to be calculated on by the month of June, her Assent is therefore important in point of Numbers, with a view to the adoption here, but, joined with Virginia it would be in her power to suspend the operation of the constitution longer than the state of our affairs will admit, indeed it might, probably, be practicable, for two such important states, to frustrate the measure altogether–I am the more alarmed for the event in Massachusetts when I reflect on the Numbers in the Convention–so great a body must be made up of many weak Men, who are subjects of artifice and Management, which will be addressed to their passions and prejudices.

My situation here is in the Midst of Mr. Henries influence, and I find he has pretty well prepared the people for being his blind followers–his demagogues are loud in their clamours against the Constitution, professing a determination to reject unless amendments can be had even at the hazard of standing alone–I cannot learn that he has ever specified the amendments he would have, and therefore, it is fairly to be concluded, his views are a dismemberment of the Union[4]–I have not seen him, but shall shortly pay him a visit.

without consulting the extent of my influence, or the hazards of facing the Torrent, I have thought it my duty to make an unequivocal declaration of my sentiments in the Counties with which I am immediately connected,[5] and shall endeavour to fix the minds of the people upon the preservation of the Union as the first object, and to bring them as much farther as I can–it may, at least, be in my power to bring them into instructions which will oblige their Members to separate from Mr. Henry at the point of Nine States having adopted. It is interesting that the elections should be turned upon Men of real discernments–weak Men may go into the convention friends to the Measure, and afterwards be drawn into the opposition by Management.

Appearances in N. York are that the Senate will refuse even to call a Convention–this might have been, from the first, expected in a State whose measures have for a Number of years been Uniformly against the federal Interests–the letter of the dissenting Members in the federal Convention is in perfect uniformity with the purpose of their Mission, and gives me no concern[6]–upon Massachusetts my views are altogether turned in the Eastern quarter.

The most certain Test of truth, that I can conceive, is consistency amongst Numbers who affect to take the same ground–on the other hand discordancy is as certain a Test of error, and I never knew so much of this as now exists amongst the opponents of the Constitution–if Reason & Common Sense could have fair play in the different conventions, this circumstance would certainly be an incontrovertible argument in Support of a Measure which was, unanimously, voted by a large and respectable Assembly

I shall do myself the pleasure to communicate to you the intelligence which events in this quarter may afford and will thank [you] for what may occur in your quarter.

1. RC, Knox Papers, MHi. Carrington dated this letter from "Manchester (opposite Richmond)." On the same day he also wrote a letter to James Madison with more detail on Virginia politics (Rutland, *Madison*, X, 493-95).

2. Carrington had written Knox on 12 January from Fredericksburg after having passed through Virginia's Northern Neck, where he had found many opponents to the Constitution. He was much concerned about the Southern counties: "My Accounts from the southern parts of the State are alarming–so many of the influential characters Unite there on the wrong side, that the people must be misled for want of the necessary information–I am unhappily placed in the midst of this influence–so far as my efforts will go to counteract it, they shall be exerted, but it will be hard to stem the Torrent [of] folly which must, by this time, be created under such a combination" (Knox Papers, MHi). In his letter of 10 February to Madison (note 1 above), Carrington identified the "two or three of the Southern Counties" as Cumberland, Powhatan, and Chesterfield.

3. Madison's letters of 11, 15, and 25 January, and Knox's letter of 18 January have not been located. For examples of Madison's pessimism about Massachusetts, see Rutland, *Madison*, X, 398, 399, 433, 445.

4. For more on Patrick Henry's alleged support for separate confederacies, see CC:276-D, note 4.

5. The Carrington family was especially prominent in the upper Southside counties of Cumberland and Powhatan.

6. See the letter from Robert Yates and John Lansing, Jr., to Governor George Clinton, 21 December 1787, published on 14 January in the New York *Daily Advertiser* and *New York Journal* (CC:447).

521. Phineas Miller to Samuel Ward, Jr.
Wethersfield, Conn., 10 February (excerpt)[1]

. . . Will the little sketch of politics which popular reports and news papers brings to my knowledge afford you any pleasure? Perhaps your distance may render trifles important.–I will suppose it.–

The new Constitution you will know, is at present the principle object of public attention–It was much agitated before your departure–Five States have now sign'd their accession, and the convention of Massachusetts on which the fate of at least the present form of Constitution seems much to depend, are now sitting–No accounts we have hitherto received will give us authority to form a conjecture about the majority–The parties seem very equally divided–From the genius and perseverance however of Mr King and several other gentlemen of abilities & popularity the hopes of our politi[ci]ans are flattered–Rhode-Island begins to come to her senses– The idea of calling a convention begins to be agitated and will probably from fear or necessity soon take place.–Pensylvania was the first State in the adoption. The majority was (I think) 26 & the minority 19.–The parties debated, and acted, with zeal and spirit. The minority once withdrew and were some of them almost or quite compel'd to resume their seats– Since the adoption, they have entered a protest which is said to be violent as the resentment of its authors[2]–In Delaware and New Jersey it is said there was not a dissenting voice–Georgia has decided, but we are uninform'd of particulars–The debates in this State continued about a week & ended in the conviction of almost the whole convention, some of whom almost made acknowlegement of their error but from obstinacy voted in the negative–the decision was taken on the 9th of Jany with a majority of 128 to 41 and applauded with a chearful, universal clap, from a pretty numerous collection of spectators.–The Assembly of New York are now sitting and will probably recommend the calling a convention but at such a distant period as will give the opposition an opportunity to discover the prevailing sentiments of the rest of the union–A favourable circumstance is, that Gov. Clinton (tho' known to be against it) has not dared openly to avow his sentiments–Colo. Hambleton & others are as indefatigable in their endeavors to gain the desirable majority, as Colo. Lamb and his party are in the opposition–Upon the whole our prospects are favorable and the opinions of our best politicians concur that if even the present form of constitution should fail of success, the necessities of the times will at last effect a cement of that union which has been long wished for with so much anxiety–

Georgia is still embarass'd with the indian war; the southern frontiers of the State have been ravagd by incursions of the Savages, to within thirty miles of Savannah–But the measures which are now taken by the legislature, aim at entirely driving them from the Settlements, and probably will soon render the inhabitants secure from their attacks.–

Mrs. Greene has lately received letters from Capt. Littlefield,[3] who informs of the health of her friends, and that her property is in as good a condition as was expected except Cumberland Island which is in the heart of the Indian war–The crops of the Plantations, are equal to those in the vicinity, tho' from an uncommon drought are inferior to general expectations.

The Settlement on the Ohio is still a popular topic The adventurers proceed with enthusiasm; and if the same spirit should continue we may soon expect to [see] the face of that country materially altered. . . .

1. RC (incomplete), Ward Papers, Rhode Island Historical Society. Because this letter is a fragment, neither the names of the writer nor the recipient appear. The handwriting and internal evidence suggest that the writer was Phineas Miller (1764–1803), a native of Middletown, Conn., who had been graduated from Yale College in 1785. In the autumn of that year Miller became the tutor to the children of General Nathanael Greene, a hero of the Revolution, and moved with the family to its Mulberry Grove plantation, fourteen miles north of Savannah, Ga. After General Greene died in June 1786, his widow Catherine (1755–1814) made Miller the plantation manager. In the summer of 1787 Mrs. Greene and Miller journeyed to Connecticut so that Mrs. Greene could confer with Jeremiah Wadsworth, a Hartford merchant and co-executor of General Greene's estate. In 1796 Miller married Mrs. Greene.

The recipient of the letter was Samuel Ward, Jr. (1756–1832), a Warwick, R.I., merchant who had left for China late in December 1787 as a supercargo on the ship *George Washington*. During the Revolution Ward served as a captain under General

Greene during the siege of Boston, and he left the service as a lieutenant colonel. Ward was married to Mrs. Greene's sister Phebe.

2. Miller apparently confused two incidents. On 29 September two of the nineteen seceding members of the Pennsylvania Assembly were forcibly returned to the house so that there would be a quorum to adopt the resolutions calling a state convention. Three days later the seceding assemblymen published a criticism of the Constitution and the actions of the majority of the Assembly (CC:125). On 12 December the Pennsylvania Convention adopted the Constitution by a vote of 46 to 23; and six days later twenty-one members of the minority published the "Dissent of the Minority of the Pennsylvania Convention" (CC:353).

3. William Littlefield (1753–1814), a brother of Catherine Greene, had been managing her Georgia plantation since 1 December 1787 while she and Phineas Miller were in Connecticut.

522. Richard Morris to James Maury
Green Springs, Va., 11 February (excerpt)[1]

· · · Whenever you can find time pray tell me how you like your present prospects, what are like to be your profits for be assured nothing could give greater pleasure than your telling me they were flattering–

Your business I think will continue to grow better every year in this quarter, if the evil genius of America does not plunge us into new difficulties. The times are in my opinion as critical just now as I have ever seen them. The government of the United [States] was found to be inadequate to the purpose, & it was universally agreed throughout the continent that amendments to the articles of confederation were absolutely necessary; accordingly delegates were appointed to meet at Philadelphia in last [May] (except Rhode Island) for this purpose–After deliberating upon this subject for months they determined it would be best to frame a constitution for the Government of the U S which they have published, & offered to the people at large for acceptance or rejection. There are great divisions on this subject among our wisest people, & of course among the subordinate ranks–The good & honest people were very generally in favour of it, but we have so many rascals that I am very fearfull it will be rejected. Pensylvania, Jersey & Delaware Connecticut, Georgia, Massachusetts & some say N. Hampshire have acceded to it & it generally [is] believed 9 states will approve of it. ~~Supposing it would be amusing to you I have sent a copy of the consitution itself with sundry publications for & against~~

Our assembly were sitting at the time of its appearance, & Henry was among the first opposers. His influence has occasioned many of the Assembly men to declare against it; they have carried his objections & prejudices with them to their counties where they have spread them so generally that I fear the consequence.

I was, during this hard weather, to see your old friend Ths. Lewis.[2] He is, you may be sure, a strong advocate for the Constitution, & if you could but transfer yourself across the Atlantic with a wish, you might spend a few hours agreeably with the Old man in hearing him abuse the anti-constitutionalists. . . .

1. FC, Morris Papers, ViU. Morris (c. 1736–1821), a planter-merchant, represented Louisa County in the Virginia House of Delegates from June to December 1788. Maury (1746–1840), a former Fredericksburg, Va., merchant, moved to Liverpool, England, in 1786, and became a leading importer of tobacco. Morris acted as a merchant-factor for Maury and sent him some of his own tobacco as well. Maury was American consul at Liverpool from 1790 to 1830.

2. Thomas Lewis (1718–1790), a planter, represented Rockingham County in the Virginia Convention, where he voted to ratify the Constitution in June 1788.

523. Charleston City Gazette, 11 February[1]

Extract of a letter from Wilmington, North Carolina, February 2.

"I am just arrived at this place, on my return to the northward, having spent more than a year past in travelling through those parts of the United States bounding on the Ohio and Missisippi. The situation and soil of those territories, in general, are extremely flattering, but the immense population that has already taken place in these parts has really astonished me. The face of these countries is every day visibly improving; forests as old as the creation are hourly falling before the ax of the hardy emigrant from the old states; elegant farms in abundance are already settled along the banks of some of the deepest and most beautiful rivers that America can boast of; and, in short, every circumstance seems to point out that country as the future seat of a great and powerful empire of confederated republics. The people are universally well disposed towards the states on the atlantic, and even those that have been born there mention them as the parent country, with a degree of fondness that I could not well account for. They cannot hear, with patience, of the Spaniards claiming or demanding an exclusive right to the navigation of the Missisippi[2]–and any man that should attempt to recommend a cession of that nature upon any consideration whatever, would, if amongst them, be made to repent dearly for his temerity. What is of very great consequence too, is, that these countries abound with *lead mines* as well as *salt petre*; and I speak within bounds when I say there is timber in sufficient quantities to build a thousand navies, without going a mile from the banks of the rivers–It must give pain to a reflective mind when it considers that such oceans of blood have been repeatedly spilt in Europe, often for the sake of some miserable and insignificant spot of territory, when such a noble and extensive region as that of which I am speaking, has been so long neglected, as if hardly worth the attention of a civilized race of men.–God grant that we may speedily establish a free and energetic government upon the broad basis of republican equality, which may take the western territories under its wing, and assist them in repelling any insults that may be offered by the jealous and avaricious devotees on the other side of the Missisippi, or those insolent intruders, who, contrary to the faith of treaties, still possess our posts to the northward."

1. Reprints by 24 April (10): Conn. (4), N.Y. (2), N.J. (1), Pa. (2), Md. (1).
2. For the controversy over the navigation of the Mississippi River, see CC:46, 270.

524. Publius: The Federalist 54
New York Packet, 12 February

The authorship of this essay has been attributed to James Madison and Alexander Hamilton. Internal evidence suggests that Madison was the author. This essay was reprinted in the New York *Independent Journal* on 13 February. It is number 54 in the M'Lean edition and number 53 in the newspapers.

For a general discussion of the authorship, circulation, and impact of *The Federalist*, see CC:201, 639; and for the disputed authorship of this essay, see Cooke, xix–xxx, 635–36, and Rutland, *Madison*, X, 261–63.

The FŒDERALIST, No. 53.
To the People of the State of New-York.

The next view which I shall take of the House of Representatives, relates to the apportionment of its members to the several States, which is to be determined by the same rule with that of direct taxes.

It is not contended that the number of people in each State ought not to be the standard for regulating the proportion of those who are to represent the people of each State. The establishment of the same rule for the apportionment of taxes, will probably be as little contested; though the rule itself in this case, is by no means founded on the same principle. In the former case, the rule is understood to refer to the personal rights of the people, with which it has a natural and universal connection. In the latter, it has reference to the proportion of wealth, of which it is in no case a precise measure, and in ordinary cases a very unfit one. But notwithstanding the imperfection of the rule as applied to the relative wealth and contributions of the States, it is evidently the least exceptionable among the practicable rules; and had too recently obtained the general sanction of America, not to have found a ready preference with the Convention.[1]

All this is admitted, it will perhaps be said: But does it follow from an admission of numbers for the measure of representation, or of slaves combined with free citizens, as a ratio of taxation, that slaves ought to be included in the numerical rule of representation? Slaves are considered as property, not as persons. They ought therefore to be comprehended in estimates of taxation which are founded on property, and to be excluded from representation which is regulated by a census of persons. This is the objection, as I understand it, stated in its full force. I shall be equally candid in stating the reasoning which may be offered on the opposite side.

We subscribe to the doctrine, might one of our southern brethren observe, that representation relates more immediately to persons, and taxation more immediately to property, and we join in the application of this distinction to the case of our slaves. But we must deny the fact that slaves are considered merely as property, and in no respect whatever as persons. The true state of the case is, that they partake of both these qualities; being considered by our laws, in some respects, as persons, and in other respects, as property. In being compelled to labor not for himself, but for a master; in being vendible by one master to another master; and in being subject at all times to be restrained in his liberty, and chastised in his body, by the capricious will of another, the slave may appear to be degraded from the human rank, and classed with those irrational animals, which fall under the legal denomination of property. In being protected on the other hand in his life & in his limbs, against the violence of all others, even the master of his labor and his liberty; and in being punishable himself for all violence committed against others; the slave is no less evidently regarded by the law as a member of the society; not as a part of the irrational creation; as a moral person, not as a mere article of property. The Fœderal Constitution therefore, decides with great propriety on the case of our slaves, when it views them in the mixt character of persons and of property. This is in fact their true character. It is the character bestowed on them by the laws under which they live; and it will not be denied that these are the proper criterion; because it is only under the pretext that the laws have transformed the negroes into subjects of property, that a place is disputed them in the computation of numbers; and it is admitted that if the laws were to restore the rights which have been taken away, the negroes could no longer be refused an equal share of representation with the other inhabitants.

This question may be placed in another light. It is agreed on all sides, that numbers are the best scale of wealth and taxation, as they are the only proper scale of representation. Would the Convention have been impartial or consistent, if they had rejected the slaves from the list of inhabitants when the shares of representation were to be calculated; and inserted them on the lists when the tariff of contributions was to be adjusted? Could it be reasonably expected that the southern States would concur in a system which considered their slaves in some degree as men, when burdens were to be imposed, but refused to consider them in the same light when advantages were to be conferred? Might not some surprize also be expressed that those who reproach the southern States with the barbarous policy of considering as property a part of their human brethren, should themselves contend that the government to which all the States are to be parties, ought to consider this unfortunate race more compleatly in the unnatural light of property, than the very laws of which they complain!

It may be replied perhaps that slaves are not included in the estimate of representatives in any of the States possessing them. They neither vote themselves, nor increase the votes of their masters. Upon what principle then ought they to be taken into the fœderal estimate of representation? In rejecting them altogether, the Constitution would in this respect have followed the very laws which have been appealed to, as the proper guide.

This objection is repelled by a single observation. It is a fundamental principle of the proposed Constitution, that as the aggregate number of representatives allotted to the several States, is to be determined by a fœderal rule founded on the aggregate number of inhabitants, so the right of choosing this allotted number in each State is to be exercised by such part of the inhabitants, as the State itself may designate. The qualifications on which the right of suffrage depend, are not perhaps the same in any two States. In some of the States the difference is very material. In every State, a certain proportion of inhabitants are deprived of this right by the Constitution of the State, who will be included in the census by which the Fœderal Constitution apportions the representatives. In this point of view, the southern States might retort the complaint, by insisting, that the principle laid down by the Convention required that no regard should be had to the policy of particular States towards their own inhabitants; and consequently, that the slaves as inhabitants should have been admitted into the census according to their full number, in like manner with other inhabitants, who by the policy of other States, are not admitted to all the rights of citizens. A rigorous adherence however to this principle is waved by those who would be gainers by it. All that they ask is, that equal moderation be shewn on the other side. Let the case of the slaves be considered as it is in truth a peculiar one. Let the compromising expedient of the Constitution be mutually adopted, which regards them as inhabitants, but as debased by servitude below the equal level of free inhabitants, which regards the *slave* as divested of two fifths of the *man*.

After all may not another ground be taken on which this article of the Constitution, will admit of a still more ready defence. We have hitherto proceeded on the idea that representation related to persons only, and not at all to property. But is it a just idea? Government is instituted no less for protection of the property, than of the persons of individuals. The one as well as the other, therefore may be considered as represented by those who are charged with the government. Upon this principle it is, that in several of the States, and particularly in the State of New-York, one branch of the government is intended more especially to be the guardian of property, and is accordingly elected by that part of the society which is most interested in this object of government. In the Fœderal Constitution, this policy does not prevail. The rights of property are committed into the same hands with the personal rights. Some attention ought therefore to be paid to property in the choice of those hands.

For another reason the votes allowed in the Fœderal Legislature to the people of each State, ought to bear some proportion to the comparative wealth of the States. States have not like individuals, an influence over each other arising from superior advantages of fortune. If the law allows an opulent citizen but a single vote in the choice of his representative, the respect and consequence which he derives from his fortunate situation, very frequently guide the votes of others to the objects of his choice; and through this imperceptible channel the rights of property are conveyed into the public representation. A State possesses no such influence over other States. It is not probable that the richest State in the confederacy will ever influence the choice of a single representative in any other State. Nor will the representatives of the larger and richer States, possess any other advantage in the Fœderal Legislature over the representatives of other States, than what may result from their superior number alone; as far therefore as their superior wealth and weight may justly entitle them to any advantage, it ought to be secured to them by a superior share of representation. The new Constitution is in this respect materially different from the existing confederation, as well as from that of the United Netherlands, and other similar confederacies. In each of the latter the efficacy of the fœderal resolutions depends on the subsequent and voluntary resolutions of the States composing the Union. Hence the States, though possessing an equal vote in the public councils, have an unequal influence, corresponding with the unequal importance of these subsequent and voluntary resolutions. Under the proposed Constitution, the fœderal acts will take effect without the necessary intervention of the individual States. They will depend merely on the majority of votes in the Fœderal Legislature, and consequently each vote whether proceeding from a larger or a smaller State, or a State more or less wealthy or powerful, will have an equal weight and efficacy; in the same manner as the votes individually given in a State Legislature, by the representatives of unequal counties or other districts, have each a precise equality of value and effect; or if there be any difference in the case, it proceeds from the difference in the personal character of the individual representative, rather than from any regard to the extent of the district from which he comes.

Such is the reasoning which an advocate for the southern interests might employ on this subject: And although it may appear to be a little strained in some points, yet on the whole, I must confess, that it fully reconciles me to the scale of representation, which the Convention have established.

In one respect the establishment of a common measure for representation and taxation will have a very salutary effect. As the accuracy of the census to be obtained by the Congress, will necessarily depend in a considerable degree on the disposition, if not the co-operation of the States, it is of great importance that the States should feel as little bias as possible to swell or to reduce the amount of their numbers. Were their share of representation alone to be governed by this rule they would have an interest in exaggerating their inhabitants. Were the rule to decide their share of taxation alone, a contrary temptation would prevail. By extending the rule to both objects, the States will have opposite interests, which will controul and ballance each other; and produce the requisite impartiality.

1. A reference to the proposed amendment to the Articles of Confederation that would have changed the method of apportioning expenses of government from a system

based on land values to one based on population, including slaves who were to count as three-fifths of a free person (CDR, 148–50). This proposed amendment had been ratified by eleven states (only New Hampshire and Rhode Island had not yet adopted the amendment).

525. Publius: The Federalist 55
New York Independent Journal, 13 February

The authorship of this essay was claimed by both James Madison and Alexander Hamilton, but it is generally attributed to Madison. The essay was reprinted in the *New York Packet* on 15 February. It is number 55 in the M'Lean edition and number 54 in the newspapers.

For a general discussion of the authorship, circulation, and impact of *The Federalist*, see CC:201, 639; and for the disputed authorship of this essay, see Cooke, xix–xxx, 636–37, and Rutland, *Madison*, X, 261–63.

The FŒDERALIST. No. LIV.
To the People of the State of New-York.

The number of which the House of Representatives is to consist, forms another, and a very interesting point of view under which this branch of the federal legislature may be contemplated. Scarce any article indeed in the whole constitution seems to be rendered more worthy of attention, by the weight of character and the apparent force of argument, with which it has been assailed. The charges exhibited against it are, first, that so small a number of representatives will be an unsafe depository of the public interests; secondly, that they will not possess a proper knowledge of the local circumstances of their numerous constituents; thirdly, that they will be taken from that class of citizens which will sympathize least with the feelings of the mass of the people, and be most likely to aim at a permanent elevation of the few on the depression of the many; fourthly, that defective as the number will be in the first instance, it will be more and more disproportionate, by the increase of the people, and the obstacles which will prevent a correspondent increase of the representatives.

In general it may be remarked on this subject, that no political problem is less susceptible of a precise solution, than that which relates to the number most convenient for a representative legislature: Nor is there any point on which the policy of the several states is more at variance; whether we compare their legislative assemblies directly with each other, or consider the proportions which they respectively bear to the number of their constituents. Passing over the difference between the smallest and largest states, as Delaware, whose most numerous branch consists of twenty-one representatives, and Massachusetts, where it amounts to between three and four hundred; a very considerable difference is observable among states nearly equal in population. The number of representatives in Pennsylvania is not more than one-fifth of that in the state last mentioned. New-York, whose population is to that of South-Carolina as six to five, has little more than one third of the number of representatives. As great a disparity prevails between the states of Georgia and Delaware, or Rhode-

Island. In Pennsylvania the representatives do not bear a greater proportion to their constituents than of one for every four or five thousand. In Rhode-Island, they bear a proportion of at least one for every thousand. And according to the constitution of Georgia, the proportion may be carried to one for every ten electors; and must unavoidably far exceed the proportion in any of the other States.

Another general remark to be made is, that the ratio between the representatives and the people, ought not to be the same where the latter are very numerous, as where they are very few. Were the representatives in Virginia to be regulated by the standard in Rhode-Island, they would at this time amount to between four and five hundred; and twenty or thirty years hence, to a thousand. On the other hand, the ratio of Pennsylvania, if applied to the state of Delaware, would reduce the Representative assembly of the latter to seven or eight members. Nothing can be more fallacious than to found our political calculations on arithmetical principles. Sixty or seventy men, may be more properly trusted with a given degree of power than six or seven. But it does not follow, that six or seven hundred would be proportionally a better depository. And if we carry on the supposition to six or seven thousand, the whole reasoning ought to be reversed. The truth is, that in all cases a certain number at least seems to be necessary to secure the benefits of free consultation and discussion, and to guard against too easy a combination for improper purposes: As on the other hand, the number ought at most to be kept within a certain limit, in order to avoid the confusion and intemperance of a multitude. In all very numerous assemblies, of whatever characters composed, passion never fails to wrest the sceptre from reason. Had every Athenian citizen been a Socrates; every Athenian assembly would still have been a mob.

It is necessary also to recollect here the observations which were applied to the case of biennial elections.[1] For the same reason that the limited powers of the Congress and the controul of the state legislatures, justify less frequent elections than the public safety might otherwise require; the members of the Congress need be less numerous than if they possessed the whole power of legislation, and were under no other than the ordinary restraints of other legislative bodies.

With these general ideas in our minds, let us weigh the objections which have been stated against the number of members proposed for the House of Representatives. It is said in the first place, that so small a number cannot be safely trusted with so much power.

The number of which this branch of the legislature is to consist at the outset of the government, will be sixty five. Within three years a census is to be taken, when the number may be augmented to one for every thirty thousand inhabitants; and within every successive period of ten years, the census is to be renewed, and augmentations may continue to be made under the above limitation. It will not be thought an extravagant conjecture, that the first census, will, at the rate of one for every thirty thousand raise the number of representatives to at least one hundred. Estimating the negroes in the proportion of three fifths, it can scarcely be doubted that the population of the United States will by that time, if it does not already, amount to three millions. At the expiration of twenty five years, according to the computed rate of increase, the number of representatives will amount to two hundred; and of fifty years, to four hundred. This is a number which I presume will put an end to all fears arising from the smallness of the body. I take for granted here what I shall in answering the fourth objection hereafter shew, that the number of representatives will be augmented from time to time in the manner provided by the constitution. On a contrary supposition, I should admit the objection to have very great weight indeed.

The true question to be decided then is whether the smallness of the number, as a temporary regulation, be dangerous to the public liberty: Whether sixty five members for a few years, and a hundred or two hundred for a few more, be a safe depositary for a limited and well guarded power of legislating for the United States? I must own that I could not give a negative answer to this question, without first obliterating every impression which I have received with regard to the present genius of the people of America, the spirit, which actuates the state legislatures, and the principles which are incorporated with the political character of every class of citizens. I am unable to conceive that the people of America in their present temper, or under any circumstances which can speedily happen, will chuse, and every second year repeat the choice of sixty five or an hundred men, who would be disposed to form and pursue a scheme of tyranny or treachery. I am unable to conceive that the state legislatures which must feel so many motives to watch, and which possess so many means of counteracting the federal legislature, would fail either to detect or to defeat a conspiracy of the latter against the liberties of their common constituents. I am equally unable to conceive that there are at this time, or can be in any short time, in the United States any sixty five or an hundred men capable of recommending themselves to the choice of the people at large, who would either desire or dare within the short space of two years, to betray the solemn trust committed to them. What change of circumstances time and a fuller population of our country may produce, requires a prophetic spirit to declare, which makes no part of my pretensions. But judging from the circumstances now before us, and from the probable state of them within a moderate period of time, I must pronounce that the liberties of America can not be unsafe in the number of hands proposed by the federal constitution.

From what quarter can the danger proceed? Are we afraid of foreign gold? If foreign gold could so easily corrupt our federal rulers, and enable them to ensnare and betray their constituents, how has it happened that we are at this time a free and independent nation? The Congress which conducted us through the revolution were a less numerous body than their successors will be; they were not chosen by nor responsible to their fellow citizens at large; though appointed from year to year, and recallable at pleasure, they were generally continued for three years; and prior to the ratification of the federal articles, for a still longer term; they held their consultations always under the veil of secrecy; they had the sole transaction of our affairs with foreign nations; through the whole course of the war, they had the fate of their country more in their hands, than it is to be hoped will ever be the case with our future representatives; and from the greatness of the prize at stake and the eagerness of the party which lost it, it may well be supposed, that the use of other means than force would not have been scrupled: yet we know by happy experience that the public trust was not betrayed; nor has the purity of our public councils in this particular ever suffered even from the whispers of calumny.

Is the danger apprehended from the other branches of the federal government? But where are the means to be found by the President or the Senate, or both? Their emoluments of office it is to be presumed will not, and without a previous corruption of the house of representatives cannot, more than suffice for very different purposes: Their private fortunes, as they must all be American citizens, cannot possibly be sources of danger. The only means then which they can possess, will be in the dispensation of appointments. Is it here that suspicion rests her charge? Sometimes we are told that this fund of corruption is to be exhausted by the President in subduing the virtue of the Senate. Now the fidelity of the other house is to be the victim. The improbability of such a mercenary and perfidious combination of the several members of government standing on as different foundations as republican principles will well admit, and at the same time accountable to the society over which they are placed, ought alone to quiet this apprehension. But fortunately the constitution has provided a still further safeguard. The members of the Congress are rendered ineligible to any civil offices that may be created or of which the emoluments may be increased, during the term of their election. No offices therefore can be dealt out to the existing members, but such as may become vacant by ordinary casualties; and to suppose that these would be sufficient to purchase the guardians of the people, selected by the people themselves, is to renounce every rule by which events ought to be calculated, and to substitute an indiscriminate and unbounded jealousy, with which all reasoning must be vain. The sincere friends of liberty who give themselves up to the extravagancies of this passion are not aware of the injury they do their own cause. As there is a degree of depravity in mankind which requires a certain degree of circumspection and distrust: So there are other qualities in human nature, which justify a certain portion of esteem and confidence. Republican government presupposes the existence of these qualities in a higher degree than any other form. Were the pictures which have been drawn by the political jealousy of some among us, faithful likenesses of the human character, the inference would be that there is not sufficient virtue among men for self government; and that nothing less than the chains of despotism can restrain them from destroying and devouring one another.

1. See *The Federalist* 52, CC:514.

526. A Citizen of the United States
Pennsylvania Gazette, 13 February[1]

A correspondent, under the signature of *A Citizen of the United States*, says–"It is curious to observe the difference and the contrariety of the objections made against the new constitution. His Excellency Governor Randolph urges the equality of suffrage in the senate as his principal objection–Mr. Martin of Maryland inveighs with great bitterness against the inequality of suffrage in the house of representatives–Mr. Mason appears much mortified that his constitutional council was not incorporated in the plan–Mr. Gerry complains that the rights of election are not properly secured, nor an adequate provision for the representation of the people–Mr. Lansing and Mr. Yates remonstrate against any system that has the most feeble trait of a consolidated Government–Mr. R. H. Lee and other gentlemen of the southern states object that commercial regulations will be under the undue controul of the eastern states–the inhabitants of the latter complain of the unequal burthen of an impost, of which the southern states must pay but very little from the nature of their population–In the middle states the clamor of opposition has been from the want of a bill of rights–Besides these, the commercial states object to parting with their commercial revenues; while the non-importing states complain of being tributary to the others.–Notwithstanding these various objections, all who urge them acknowledge the merit of the new system in other points, and frequently in those parts opposed by others. Does not all this tend to produce the most decided conviction of the difficulties that were encountered by the late fœderal convention, and the spirit of conciliation manifested in the plan they have proposed? Does it not equally demonstrate the utter impossibility of another general convention, chosen by a people so agitated, and so divided, agreeing upon any general system? And is it not doubtful, that, after such experience, characters of eminence and ability could be found to undertake the task? As such then must be the conclusion of every thinking man, he must deprecate the wretch with execrations of tenfold horror, who should dare to suggest means of violence to reconcile such jarring opinions, and to endeavor to involve this peaceful country in the horrors of intestine war."

1. Reprints by 6 April (9): N.H. (1), Mass. (3), Conn. (1), N.Y. (3), Md. (1). Five newspapers, beginning with the Boston *American Herald*, 25 February, reprinted this item without the pseudonym. For the Antifederalists' objections mentioned in this es-

say, see Edmund Randolph (CC:385), Luther Martin (CC:401, 414, 425), George Mason (CC:276), Elbridge Gerry (CC:227-A), Robert Yates and John Lansing, Jr. (CC:447), and Richard Henry Lee (CC:325).

527. Joseph Jones to James Madison
Richmond, 14 February (excerpt)[1]

... Your two last favors I have received that of the 25th. since my arrival here and am much obliged to you for the communications they contain. S. Adams's silence as to the N. plan of Government, if not calculated to secure him a seat in the Convention, proceeded very probably from his desire of discovering the temper of the people in General before he took a decided part[2]-this with the admission of Gerry to a seat in the Convention when not a member and the great number that compose the Body are unfavourable circumstances, and authorise a conjecture that the new system will not be adopted by Massts.[3]-Should that State give it a negative and not proceed to offer some amendments and propose another convention, I fear it will produce disagreeable consequences, as it will not only confirm N. York in her opposition but will contribute greatly to strengthen the opposition in the States that are yet to consider the measure. If nine States assent before Virga. meets in convention her course I think will be to adopt the plan, protesting or de[c]laring her disapprobation of those parts she does not approve or if not agreed to by nine she will in that case propose amendments and another general Convention-H—y[4] will I think use all his influence to reject at all events, but am satisfied those who are for it as it stands, and those who wish some alterations in it before its adoption if circumstances authorise the attempt, will be greatly the majority-what change may be produced shod. Mass. reject cannot well be foreseen; I think however in that event Virga. will propose amendments, and another Convention, and I trust such will be the conduct of Mass. rather than hazard the loss of the System, and the mischevous consequences that may result from disagreement and delay. I congratulate my friend Griffin on his being placed in the Chair[5] to whom Be pleased to present my best wishes. R-d—h R. H. L. M—n. have been assailed in our papers. The inclosed will if you have not seen them exhibit some specimens, and serve to amuse you.[6]

1. RC, Madison Papers, DLC. Printed: Rutland, *Madison*, X, 509-10.
2. For Samuel Adams's position on the Constitution and his role as a delegate to the Massachusetts Convention, see CC:388, 424, 508.
3. For Elbridge Gerry's admission to the Massachusetts Convention in order to answer questions put to him, see CC:Vol. 3, Appendix I, *Massachusetts Gazette*, 15 January, note 4.
4. Patrick Henry.
5. Cyrus Griffin had been appointed President of Congress on 22 January.
6. Jones probably sent four issues of the Richmond *Virginia Independent Chronicle* containing "Valerius" on Richard Henry Lee (23 January); "Civis Rusticus" on George Mason (30 January); "Philanthropos" (Tench Coxe) on Gerry, Mason, and Edmund

Randolph (6 February); and "A Plain Dealer" (Spencer Roane) on Randolph (13 February).

528. Silas Lee to George Thatcher
Biddeford, Maine, 14 February[1]

As antifederal as you may think me, I can sincerely congratulate you on the adoption of the N. Constitution in this Commonwealth–It has ever been, as it now is, my opinion, that that is the safest of the Alternatives–Notwithstanding I have great doubts whether the Liberties of the people are not exceedingly e[n]dangered by it–and the Idea of an amendment, together with the further consideration that something Must immediately be done, & that this Country can scarcely be in a worse situation, are far the greatest arguments in my mind to Justify its ratification. From what you have heretofore wrote me, I have been led to think that you saw no imperfection at all, in the plan, & that you espoused its adoption, not with the violence & implacability of a partizan, who condemns every man to the stake, or halter, that is not of his colour; that I knew was impossible, but rather, with the *resolute warmth* of an honest Man, who was *possitive that he was right*–and I confess to you that I feel not a little flattered to find from your last letter, that my Sentiments have not been wholly opposed to yours–& that you seem to think it wants amendments–which I hope will immediately be taken into Consideration–But I hope the precedent of the late federal Convention will not be followed by the next that may be appointed; viz instead of revising or amending this in certain parts, which may be found inconvenient, they will not with one Stroke wipe the whole away, as was the fate of the old Confederation, & propose a new one; but on the contrary provide a remedy for the inconveniencies felt, without interfering with or altering the advantages already experienced–But, altho you say, that "it will ever be as easy to alter & amend, as it can be to form another, if not more so," you seem to think, by what follows, that every General Convention will propose a plan of their own–notwithstanding, I suppose you must mean, their commission impowers them only to amend–This I have ever understood was the fact in the late federal convention But altho compossd of the first characters in the Continent I, by no means, think it the *less unwarrantable* on that account–when Officers throw aside their commissions, or Servants their orders, then the liberties of the people depend entirely upon the humour of the one, & the property of the Master on the uncertain conduct of the other, which may be good or bad as the disposition of the agent may happen to be–& then indeed all Laws or rules are wholly aflut[.] But as to the Constitution, it is established in this State & I doubt not but it will soon be through out the whole–I shall therefore find no more fault with it, but rather examine & enquire into it for the sake of information–hoping that it will prove to be not only the best in the world, but also that the people will be perfectly happy under it–In a former letter I mentioned Mr Wilson–I believe I was wrong then, in part at least.[2] At another time I may explain myself–I differ so far from the opinions of your friends with you, respecting the Opposition in this State, that on the contrary, I am surprised at the struggle that was made–I think Most of the Opposers have done honour to their places, both by the ingenuity of some of their arguments, & the liberality of their Conduct after the decission. . . .

1. Printed: William F. Goodwin, ed., "The Thatcher Papers," *The Historical Magazine*, 2nd series, VI (1869), 338–39. This is the entire excerpt published by Goodwin.

2. In his letter of 23 January Lee wrote: "Sixthly, whether this constitution will not finally consolidate the States–or rather totally annihilate the State governments?–Mr Willson if I mistake not, averd. that the Congress could not exist without the State legislatures–with deference to that great Man's better Judgment, I differ far from him–I think that Congress have not only the power of Judging of their own Elections, but also the *Sovereign Right of Regulating* them at any time–If so, should all the States refuse to take any steps towards the choice of Senators & representatives, Congress may provide for their Election" (Chamberlain Collection, Thatcher Papers, MB). For James Wilson's speech of 6 October, see CC:134.

529 A–B. Popular Support for the Constitition in the Ratifying States, 14, 26 February

529-A. New Haven Gazette, 14 February[1]

Of the CONVENTIONS which have ratified the Federal CONSTITUTION, That of

Massachusetts contained	355 Members.	168 Nays.
Pennsylvania	69	23
Delaware	22[2]	
New-Jersey	39[3]	
Connecticut	168	40
Georgia	33[4]	
	686	231

From hence it appears that nearly Two-Thirds of Six States, which contain 1,187,000 taxable and representible Inhabitants,[5] have adopted the Federal Constitution.

529-B. A Real Patriot
   Pennsylvania Mercury, 26 February[6]

Mr. HUMPHREYS, The federal constitution has been ratified·by six states, (which are all that have yet considered it) with a degree of unanimity which, at once, demonstrates the excellence of this plan of government, and the wisdom of its adopters. In three of the states it passed without even *one* dissenting voice; and in *one only* did the minority exceed one third. An erroneous calculation has appeared, in some of the newspapers, by which it would seem that upwards of one third of the six states, which have adopted the constitution, are opposed to it; this mistake was occasioned by computing the yeas and nays in the different conventions, as if an equal representation had taken place in all the states; but this is not the case; for the minority in the convention of Massachusetts, alone, was more numerous than the four conventions of Pennsylvania, New-Jersey, Delaware, and Georgia, because of the large number of delegates chosen in that state.

The following mode of calculation, I flatter myself, will appear unexceptionably just.

	No. of taxable inhabitants.	No. of del. in conven.	Nays.	Prop. of antifed. inhab.
New-Jersey,	130,000[7]	39	00	
Delaware,	37,000	22	00	
Georgia,	90,000	33	00	
Pennsylvania,	360,000	69	23	120,000
Connecticut,	202,000	168	40	48,095
Massachusets,	360,000	355	168	170,366
	1179,000			338,461

Hence it appears that, in these six states, nearly five sevenths of the people were in favour of the constitution, and if to these we add absent members, whom it is reasonable to suppose federal, and members, in the several minorities, who have since acquiesced, and are now zealous in support of this system, I have no doubt, that at least six sevenths of the people are, at this moment, friends to the proposed plan.

That so near an approach to unanimity should prevail in adopting this constitution, is truly an event hitherto unparallelled, a phenomenon in politics–and recommends it to the freemen of America, who have yet to decide upon it, more warmly than the eloquence of a Cicero, the fire of a Demosthenes, and the wisdom of a Solon, combined in every one of its advocates, could possibly do.

I sincerely congratulate the citizens of America upon the fair prospect which now presents itself to their view; and promises a long reign of virtue, happiness, and glory, as the result of a constitution which is the real *vox populi* so often ardently desired by mankind, in vain, and now, for the first time, discovered by the patriotic sages of America.

February 25th, 1788.

1. Reprints by 20 March (22): N.H. (2), Mass. (7), R.I. (2), Conn. (2), N.Y. (2), N.J. (2), Pa. (4), S.C. (1). When this item was reprinted in the *Maryland Journal* on 6 May, Maryland was added to the list of ratifying states. The number of delegates was increased to 760, the number of nays to 242, and the number of "taxable and representable Inhabitants" to 1,467,000. The *Journal's* version was reprinted eleven times by 28 May: Mass. (2), N.Y. (4), Pa. (3), Va. (2). Four of the eleven newspapers had reprinted the earlier account.

2. The Delaware Convention consisted of 30 delegates, all of whom voted to ratify the Constitution.

3. One delegate to the New Jersey Convention did not attend. The Convention voted 38 to 0 to ratify the Constitution.

4. Georgia ratified the Constitution unanimously but only 26 of the Convention's 33 delegates voted.

5. This figure was obtained from population estimates used by the Constitutional Convention to apportion representation among the states in the first federal Congress. These estimates were incorporated by Charles Cotesworth Pinckney into a speech he delivered on 17 January during the debate in the South Carolina House of Representatives on calling a state convention to ratify the Constitution. Pinckney's speech was printed in the Charleston *City Gazette* on 24 January. The population estimates alone were printed in the New York *Daily Advertiser* on 5 February and were widely reprinted (Appendix I).

6. Reprinted: New York *Daily Advertiser*, 6 March; *Massachusetts Centinel*, 15 March; Providence *United States Chronicle*, 27 March.

7. The population estimate for New Jersey used by the Constitutional Convention was 138,000. About half of the newspapers that reprinted the population figures used the incorrect figure of 130,000 (see Appendix I, New York *Daily Advertiser*, 5 February).

530. Brutus XII
New York Journal, 14 February[1]

(Continued from last Thursday's paper.)

This same manner of explaining the constitution, will fix a meaning, and a very important one too, to the 12th clause of the same section, which authorises the Congress to make all laws which shall be proper and necessary for carrying into effect the foregoing powers, &c. A voluminous writer in favor of this system, has taken great pains to convince the public, that this clause means nothing: for that the same powers expressed in this, are implied in other parts of the constitution.[2] Perhaps it is so, but still this will undoubtedly be an excellent auxilliary to assist the courts to discover the spirit and reason of the constitution, and when applied to any and every of the other clauses granting power, will operate powerfully in extracting the spirit from them.

I might instance a number of clauses in the constitution, which, if explained in an *equitable* manner, would extend the powers of the government to every case, and reduce the state legislatures to nothing; but, I should draw out my remarks to an undue length, and I presume enough has been said to shew, that the courts have sufficient ground in the exercise of this power, to determine, that the legislature have no bounds set to them by this constitution, by any supposed right the legislatures of the respective states may have, to regulate any of their local concerns.

I proceed, 2d, To inquire, in what manner this power will increase the jurisdiction of the courts.

I would here observe, that the judicial power extends, expressly, to all civil cases that may arise save such as arise between citizens of the same state, with this exception to those of that description, that the judicial of the United States have cognizance of cases between citizens of the same state, claiming lands under grants of different states. Nothing more, therefore, is necessary to give the courts of law, under this constitution, complete jurisdiction of all civil causes, but to comprehend cases between citizens of the same state not included in the foregoing exception.

I presume there will be no difficulty in accomplishing this. Nothing more is necessary than to set forth, in the process, that the party who brings the suit is a citizen of a different state from the one against whom the suit is brought, & there can be little doubt but that the court will take cognizance of the matter, & if they do, who is to restrain them? Indeed, I will freely confess, that it is my decided opinion, that the courts ought to take cognizance of such causes, under the powers of the constitution. For one of the great ends of the constitution is, "to establish justice." This supposes that this cannot be done under the existing governments of the states; and there is certainly as good reason why individuals, living in the same state, should have justice, as those who live in different states. Moreover, the constitution expressly declares, that "the citizens of each state shall be entitled to all the privileges and immunities of citizens in the several states." It will therefore be no fiction, for a citizen of one state to set forth, in a suit, that he is a citizen of another; for he that is entitled to all the privileges and immunities of a country, is a citizen of that country. And in truth, the citizen of one state will, under this constitution, be a citizen of every state.

But supposing that the party, who alledges that he is a citizen of another state, has recourse to fiction in bringing in his suit, it is well known, that the courts have high authority to plead, to justify them in suffering actions to be brought before them by such fictions. In my last number[3] I stated, that the court of exchequer tried all causes in virtue of such a fiction. The court of king's bench, in England, extended their jurisdiction in the same way. Originally, this court held pleas, in civil cases, only of trespasses and other injuries alledged to be committed *vi et armis*. They might likewise, says Blackstone,[4] upon the division of the *aula regia*, have originally held pleas of any other civil action whatsoever (except in real actions which are now very seldom in use) provided the defendant was an officer of the court, or in the custody of the marshall or prison-keeper of this court, for breach of the peace, &c. In process of time, by a fiction, this court began to hold pleas of any personal action whatsoever; it being surmised, that the defendant has been arrested for a supposed trespass that "he has never committed, and being thus in the custody of the marshall of the court, the plaintiff is at liberty to proceed against him, for any other personal injury: which surmise of being in the marshall's custody, the defendant is not at liberty to dispute." By a much less fiction, may the pleas of the courts of the United States extend to cases between citizens of the same state. I shall add no more on this head, but proceed briefly to remark, in what way this power will diminish and destroy both the legislative and judicial authority of the states.

It is obvious that these courts will have authority to decide upon the validity of the laws of any of the states, in all cases where they come in question before them. Where the constitution gives the general government exclusive jurisdiction, they will adjudge all laws made by the states, in such cases, void *ab initio*. Where the constitution gives them concurrent jurisdiction, the laws of the United States must prevail, because they are the supreme law. In such cases, therefore, the laws of the state legislatures must be repealed, restricted, or so construed, as to give full effect to the laws of the union on the same subject. From these remarks it is easy to see, that in proportion as the general government acquires power and jurisdiction, by the liberal construction which the judges may give the constitution, will those of the states lose its rights, until they become so trifling and unimportant, as not to be worth having. I am much mistaken, if this system will not operate to effect this with as much celerity, as those who have the administration of it will think prudent to suffer it. The remaining objections to the judicial power shall be considered in a future paper.

1. This essay, continued from the *New York Journal* of 7 February (CC:510), was not reprinted. For the authorship and impact of "Brutus," see CC:178.

2. See *The Federalist* 33 and 44, New York *Independent Journal*, 2 January, and *New York Packet*, 25 January (CC:405, 476).

3. See "Brutus" XI, 31 January (CC:489).

4. *Commentaries*, Book III, chapter IV, 42.

531. Tench Coxe to James Madison
Philadelphia, 15 February[1]

If you thought it worth attention to publish N. 1. of the Pennsylvanian perhaps No. 2, enclosed may also be properly inserted in the same paper. The first was in Hall & Sellers's of 6th. sent before.[2]

I wish to believe the accot. of the 11th from New York informing of the Adoption by Massachussets on 5th instant[3]–but we wait for the Numbers, the form, the more perfect Certainty. To Morrow I trust will bring it.

Will you take the trouble of mentioning to the hon. Mr. Contee from Maryland that Judge Hanson sent me a large pacquet of Pamphlets for him which I sent on yesterday.[4] Mr. Hanson writes me there is no doubt in Maryland, and tho [he] considers the Opposition in Virga. as very powerful, he says he is well grounded in assuring me of its final Success there.

I am gratified by the Unanimity of Georgia, and by the unanimous Vote of thanks by the Senate of S. Carolina.[5]

I have two letters from gentlemen of very opposite characters, and very differently situated in London, who assure me, one that the Constitution is approved by all the warmest friends of America in England,[6] the other that [it] is in his opinion & all he has conversed with most likely to retrieve the lost Reputation of this Country.[7] Those things are of little really consequence, opposite letters & opinions would have been used to its prejudice here.–I shall therefore furnish some extracts to our printers–

I am very troublesome to you, but I can never be so again because I believe Nothing will ever happen again that will furnish so great an Apology-

1. RC, Madison Papers, DLC. Coxe initially dated his letter 25 February on both the first and last pages. On the last page, however, he struck over the date changing it to 15 February. Internal evidence indicates that the letter was written on the 15th rather than the 25th.

2. "A Pennsylvanian" I–IV were printed in the *Pennsylvania Gazette* on 6, 13, 20, and 27 February (Mfm:Pa. 408, 430, 439, 459). Coxe had sent the first number to Madison in New York City on 6 February (Rutland, *Madison*, X, 473). Neither the first nor the second essay was reprinted in New York City.

3. On 13 and 14 February the *Pennsylvania Packet* and *Pennsylvania Mercury*, respectively, published an extract of a letter from a New York gentleman, dated 11 February, stating that the Massachusetts Convention had ratified the Constitution. On 18 February the *Mercury* printed the form of ratification and the vote on ratification; while the *Packet* reported that the state Convention had ratified by a majority of nineteen.

4. Coxe refers to Judge Alexander Contee Hanson's Federalist pamphlet "Aristides," *Remarks on the Proposed Plan of a Federal Government...*, published on 31 January (CC:490). Judge Hanson's uncle, Benjamin Contee, was serving as a Maryland delegate to Congress in New York City.

5. Between 11 and 13 February, four Philadelphia newspapers reprinted a resolution of the South Carolina Senate, dated 14 January, stating that the thanks of the house be given to the state's delegates to the Constitutional Convention "for their great attention to, and faithful discharge of the duties of their appointment."

6. On 14 November and 4 December John Brown Cutting, a young American who had just completed his legal studies in England, wrote to Coxe from London that "Every *learned*, and *good* and great man here who is a well-wisher to our country–applauds the fœderal constitution–and only fears the people will be *misled*, & not adopt it" (CC:Vol. 2, Appendix II). Excerpts from this letter were printed in the *Pennsylvania Packet*, 18 February, and were widely reprinted ("Accounts from England," 18 February–22 March, Appendix I).

7. On 13 November Andrew Allen, a Loyalist who had been a Pennsylvania delegate to Congress in 1775 and 1776, wrote from his London home that if the new government under the Constitution were "properly regulated & fixed, the People of America may if they *are wise* undoubtedly become a much happier & more respectable Community than they have been since the dissolution of their Connexion with G[reat Britain]. They will have it in their Power to retrieve their Character as a People which has brought upon them the Dislike & Contempt of Europe..." (Tench Coxe Papers, Series II, Correspondence and General Papers, PHi).

532. From George Nicholas
Charlottesville, Va., 16 February[1]

The great importance of a proper decision on the subject of the new constitution as proposed to us by the federal convention renders it the duty of every good citizen to give to his countrymen all the information in his power. Under this impression we shall take the liberty of stating to you our ideas respecting some particular parts of the constitution which have been represented to the people as most faulty. and to assure you that the other objections appear to me to be equally [void?] of foundation as those which I now observe on.

The first objection that is made is that by this constitution the Congress will have lodged in their hands an unlimited and absolute power.

This is by no means true, because as they will have no power unless that constitution is agreed to, so if it is adopted they can have no greater or other powers than what are expressly given to them in that constitution: thus you find that the constitution points out what particular acts of power they may exercise which would have been totally unnecessary if they had a general power to do whatever they pleased. Neither does that part of the constitution which says "this constitution and the laws of the united states which shall be made [in] pursuance thereof shall be the supreme law of the land" in any manner give them this unlimited power, because this only declares those laws binding which are made in pursuance of or in conformity to the particular powers given by the constitution and was only intended to prevent the different states from passing laws which should might defeat the measures of Congress in such things as they have an express power given to them to manage for the good of the whole.

The next objection is that this government will entirely destroy the state governments.

We have already shewn you that Congress will have no powers but what are expressly given to them, and it will follow as a natural consequence that all the powers which are now vested in the state legislatures will after the adoption of this government still belong to them, except such as are by that government specially given to Congress and such as the state legislatures are expressly forbid to exercise, such as the power to make ex post facto laws, to pass bills of attainder and tender laws and it must give every reflecting mind pleasure to find them prohibited from exercising those dreadful engines of iniquity and tyranny (in all other cases the authority of the state governments will be the same as at present).

The next objection is that by this new constitution there is to be a standing army always kept up in America. The constitution says no such thing; it is only declared there that "the Congress shall have power to raise and support armies": this is a power which must be lodged somewhere in every government and could be lodged here no where so properly as in the *Congress our general head*: but it by no means follows that because they have a power to raise and support armies, that they shall always keep an army on foot. There will be less occasion to keep a standing army in America so long as the different states continue united than in any other country in the world; because she is so far removed from all other powers that there will be but little danger of her being attacked without having sufficient previous notice; but if the Congress had been altogether forbid to keep an army on foot except in case of actual invasion, then although they had the most certain information that an attack was intended on them they could not provide for their defence until the attack was actually made and then perhaps it might be too late. This proves that it was necessary to give them a discretionary power to raise troops when they judged it necessary: but that power is given under such checks that no danger is to be apprehended from it, because an army never can be kept together without money and Congress are forbid to vote any money for that use for a longer term than two years, and when you recollect that at that same period the people at large will be called upon to choose new representatives you will readily see that by changing the men they may always prevent an appropriation of money for that purpose from being renewed and then [the?] army will fall of course. But these same persons by another objection they make "that power to call on the militia is also given to Congress" must defeat their own argument. Because if Congress are neither to have power to raise troops or to call on the militia the natural consequence must be that America must be left totally defenceless, which I suppose is such a situation that no friend to his country would wish to see her placed in. By giving Congress a discretionary power to raise troops or call forth the militia the consequence will be that in times of peace and tranquillity neither will be employed; that on any sudden occasion the militia will be called forth and kept in the field until regular troops can be raised if the occasion continues long enough to make it necessary: and thus by giving them both these powers under the check contained in the constitution America will enjoy the safety which can be derived from a standing force without being burdened by the expence or running the hazard generally attendant on such establishments. Let it be remembered too that Congress now have power to raise armies witht. these checks.

The next objection is to the federal courts and the powers given to those courts.

That such courts were necessary must strike every man; in disputes between different independent states unless a tribunal had been established by the general government for the determining of such disputes they must have appealed to the sword for a decision; so in cases between citizens of different states, and between foreigners and citizens, if the decision had been left to the court of an individual state the jealousies which would have been caused by the decisions of these tribunals might ultimately have ended in the same things but where these disputes are determined by a court established by the general government and unconnected with any particular state there can be no room for jealousies or fraud on either side. Between citizens of the same state these courts have no jurisdiction but in one instance and that is "where they claim lands under grants of different states": and I assert to you in the most positive manner that this is the only instance where one citizen can carry another before any of the federal courts and in the cases of disputes between citizens of different states, and between foreigners and citizens the constitution directs that there shall be inferior tribunals established for the convenience of the people and that these suits shall never be carried before the supreme court but by way of appeal.

The next objection is that if this government is adopted the property that we have in slaves may be lost or injured So far is this from being true that we can venture to say that the new government will be the best security that we can have for retaining that property. Congress could pass no act which would injure that property but in one of three ways either

1st. by passing an act of emancipation: or

2dly. by permitting the other states to harbour the fugitives

or 3dly. by imposing such taxes on them as would oblige the owners to discharge them.

They could not pass an act for their emancipation because both Congress and the different state legislatures are forbid to pass *ex post facto* laws and therefore if the new government should take place neither Congress or a state legislature could pass an act to deprive any man or set of men of property which they hold under the general laws of the land. And therefore if this government had taken place prior to the last session of our assembly they could not have passed a law for the emancipation of Robt. Mooreman's Negroes.[2] Neither could Congress secondly injure you by permitting them to be harboured and protected in the other states for by an express clause in the constitution all slaves escaping from one state into another shall be delivered up. Nor could they in the third instance injure you by the mode of imposing the taxes. A poll tax is the only tax they could impose which could affect our slaves and the constitution is so guarded in that respect that we can receive no injury by that means. It is expressly declared that no capitation or poll tax shall be imposed except in proportion to the enumeration therein directed which is that we should be charged with only three fifths of the number of our slaves. It never could be the interest therefore of the states which have no slaves to impose a poll tax. Because in case of a poll tax if Massachussets had one thousand white inhabitants, and Virginia also one thousand inhabitants but one half of them white and the other half black; Massachussets would be obliged to pay Congress for her whole number whereas Virginia would pay for only eight hundred. Thus by this constitution this part of our property is much better secured and the possessors of it less liable to oppressive taxes than even under our state government.

The next objection is to the power given them to levy direct taxes.

Here we refer you to the Governor's reasoning on that subject in the seventh and eigth pages of his letter[3] with these additional observations: that the taxes that are now imposed by the state are for the use of both the continent and the state and therefore if Congress have the power given them of imposing direct taxes the state taxes must be lessoned as much as the continental taxes shall amount to. If you now pay six shillings tax to the sheriff, three shillings of it are applied to the use of the state and three to the use of Congress; if the new government takes place you would pay only six shillings in the whole, three shillings to the sheriff and three shillings to the continental collector. By the return made from the continental treasurer to the last assembly it appears that two states in the union have not [so far?] paid [the?] [---] one shilling, seven other states have paid very little, and the remainder has been paid by the remaining four states of which Virginia is one. If you wish then that the present unequal burden which is imposed on us should be divided amongst all the states you cannot object to giving Congress the power to levy direct taxes the [collection?] that by the impost Congress would probably raise as much money as would be necessary for the common purposes [....]

The next objection is that the states and Congress both are prohibited from laying any higher duty on exports than will be sufficient to support the inspections.

This so far from being an objection is with us a strong argument in favor of the new government. The only export from this state which has ever been or can be taxed is tobacco; last year there was a tax of sixteen shillings a hogshead paid on it six shillings has been taken off but there still remains a tax of ten shillings a hogshead which will be continued unless the new government shall take place. This tax of ten shillings after supporting the inspections will carry into the treasury about twenty thousand pounds a year which sum the tobacco makers in this state pay over and above what the other citizens pay for they pay the same taxes on their property that the others pay, and have this deduction made by the merchants from the purchase value of their tobacco.

The last objection that we shall take notice of (for the bounds of a letter will prevent me from going as far as I could wish) is that so much power is given to Congress by this new government that our liberties will be endangered.

If we supposed this true we should be amongst the last persons in America who would advocate this measure; but we can truly say that we are well convinced there is no such [danger?]. Will you believe after all that you have heard on this subject that if the new government takes place Congress and the legislature of this state will together have no greater power and will be entrusted with no greater authority than Congress and the legislature now have; and that the only difference will be that of the powers which are now vested in them if the new government takes place. Congress will have a greater share and the legislature of the state less than they now respectively enjoy and yet you may rely on it this [is] a true state of the case. Do you not see then that it is no more than a dispute about who shall have the power that we have already parted with, and that as no greater powers are asked for from the bulk of the people it is to their interest to divide what they have already given in a way that will be more to their advantage than it stands at present. The bulk of the people will be as free as they are now, and may expect much greater advantages than they at present enjoy for the sacrafice they make to obtain a government;

and I know no person who will be injured but the great men in each of the states. We also assert to you as a fact that if the new government shall take place the bulk of the people of Virginia will part with no more power than they have done already, and that Congress and the legislature of the state will together have no greater power or authority than the present Congress and the legislature of the state now possess: and the only difference will be that of the powers already parted with by the people, under the new government Congress will have a greater share and the legislature of the state less than they now respectively enjoy. Thus the bulk of the people will be greatly benefited because without their parting with any greater share of their natural rights and privileges they will live under a government which will be much better calculated to secure their welfare and prosperity than the one under which they now live. and you may find that it is only a dispute about who shall have the power already given away by the people and that the great men in the different states will be the only sufferers by the change.

But suppose there are some imperfections in the government that is offered are we never to have one until such as is perfect can be obtained. All human works are imperfect and we may reasonably suppose that one in which the interests of thirteen states were to be considered may be so too; but the way to know that certainly is to put it to the proof; if it contains errors it also has in itself the seeds of reformation by which those errors may be rectified For the constitution expressly declares that whenever the legislatures of two thirds of the several states shall make application to Congress for that purpose they shall call a convention for proposing amendments which when ratified by three fourths of the states shall become part of this constitution. We are convinced that we can get no better government at this time and that we must adopt the one now offered or submit to see America disunited and a prey to foreign and domestic tyranny. It confirms us in this opinion when we find that the man upon earth whose judgment as well as integrity we have the greatest deference for entertains the same sentiments; Genl. Washington in a letter to Mr Charles Carter speaks thus upon this subject:

here insert his letter.[4]

We have thus delivered you our opinion very freely on the necessity of adopting the government now offered, and of [the] weakness of the objections that are made to it; in both these [we] may be mistaken but if we are they are the errors of the head and not of the heart.

If you consider these observations as worthy of notice you will oblige us by communicating them to your neighbours.

With the most fervent prayers that the divine giver supreme dispenser of every good and perfect gift may inspire our countrymen with a knowledge of what will best tend to promote their lasting welfare and happiness.

We are Sir, Yr. friends and hum: servts.

1. FC, Reuben T. Durrett Collection, George Nicholas, Department of Special Collections, University of Chicago Library. This manuscript in the handwriting of George Nicholas appears to be a draft of a letter that went through at least one revision. It is addressed to "Sir" and the closing in the first draft reads "I am Sir, Yr. friend and hum: servt." In revising the draft, Nicholas changed all of the pronouns "I" to "we" and the closing to "We are Sir, Yr. friends and hum: servts." Thus, this manuscript became, at least outwardly, the product of multiple authorship. It is also possible that the manuscript was a draft for a newspaper essay or for a speech to be given at the Albemarle County election for delegates to the Virginia Convention. That Nicholas may have intended that the manuscript be published in a newspaper is suggested by the request: "If you consider these observations as worthy of notice you will oblige us by communicating them to your neighbours." Parts of this manuscript are similar to sections of "The State Soldier" IV, *Virginia Independent Chronicle*, 19 March.

George Nicholas (1754?-1799), a Charlottesville lawyer-planter and a former officer in the Continental Army, represented Albemarle County in the Virginia House of Delegates. On 13 March Nicholas and his brother Wilson Cary Nicholas (1761-1820) were elected to represent Albemarle in the state Convention, and in June both voted to ratify the Constitution.

2. In his last will and testament, dated 2 September 1778, Charles Moorman of Louisa County provided for the emancipation of his slaves. Four years later the Virginia legislature passed a manumission law allowing slaveowners to free their slaves. In December 1787, the legislature passed an act confirming "the freedom of certain negroes late the property of Charles Moorman, deceased" (William Waller Hening, ed., *The Statutes at Large; Being a Collection of All the Laws of Virginia...* [13 vols., Richmond, 1809-1823], XI, 39-40; XII, 613-16).

3. See Governor Edmund Randolph's 10 October letter to the Virginia House of Delegates which was published around 27 December (CC:385, pp. 126-27).

4. For Washington's letter to Carter, 14 December, see CC:386-A.

533. Publius: The Federalist 56
New York Independent Journal, 16 February

The authorship of this essay was claimed by both James Madison and Alexander Hamilton, but it is generally attributed to Madison. The essay was reprinted in the *New York Packet* on 19 February. Four days earlier the *Packet* had announced that it would not reprint the essay until its next issue of the 19th. The essay is number 56 in the M'Lean edition and number 55 in the newspapers.

For a general discussion of the authorship, circulation, and impact of *The Federalist*, see CC:201, 639; and for the disputed authorship of this essay, see Cooke, xix-xxx, 637-41, and Rutland, *Madison*, X, 261-63.

The FŒDERALIST. No. LV.
To the People of the State of New-York.

The *second* charge against the House of Representatives is, that it will be too small to possess a due knowledge of the interests of its constituents.

As this objection evidently proceeds from a comparison of the proposed number of representatives, with the great extent of the United States, the number of their inhabitants, and the diversity of their interests, without taking into view at the same time the circumstances which will distinguish the Congress from other legislative bodies, the best answer that can be given to it, will be a brief explanation of these peculiarities.

It is a sound and important principle that the representative ought to be acquainted with the interests and circumstances of his constituents. But this principle can extend no farther than to those circumstances and interests, to which the authority and care of the representative relate. An ignorance of a variety of minute and particular objects, which do not lie within the compass of legislation, is consistent with every attribute necessary to a due performance of the legislative trust. In determining the extent of information required in the exercise of a particular authority, recourse then must be had to the objects within the purview of that authority.

What are to be the objects of federal legislation? Those which are of most importance, and which seem most to require local knowledge, are commerce, taxation, and the militia.

A proper regulation of commerce requires much information, as has been elsewhere remarked;[1] but as far as this information relates to the laws and local situation of each individual state, a very few representatives would be very sufficient vehicles of it to the federal councils.

Taxation will consist, in great measure, of duties which will be involved in the regulation of commerce. So far the preceeding remark is applicable to this object. As far as it may consist of internal collections, a more diffusive knowledge of the circumstances of the state may be necessary. But will not this also be possessed in sufficient degree by a very few intelligent men diffusively elected within the state. Divide the largest state into ten or twelve districts, and it will be found that there will be no peculiar local interest in either, which will not be within the knowledge of the representative of the district. Besides this source of information, the laws of the state framed by representatives from every part of it, will be almost of themselves a sufficient guide. In every state there have been made, and must continue to be made, regulations on this subject, which will in many cases leave little more to be done by the federal legislature, than to review the different laws, and reduce them into one general act. A skilful individual in his closet, with all the local codes before him, might compile a law on some subjects of taxation for the whole union, without any aid from oral information; and it may be expected, that whenever internal taxes may be necessary, and particularly in cases requiring uniformity throughout the states, the more simple objects will be preferred. To be fully sensible of the facility which will be given to this branch of federal legislation, by the assistance of the state codes, we need only suppose for a moment, that this or any other state were divided into a number of parts, each having and exercising within itself a power of local legislation. Is it not evident that a degree of local information and preparatory labour would be found in the several volumes of their proceedings, which would very much shorten the labours of the general legislature, and render a much smaller number of members sufficient for it? The federal councils will derive great advantage from another circumstance. The representatives of each state will not only bring with them a considerable knowledge of its laws, and a local knowledge of their respective districts; but will probably in all cases have been members, and may even at the very time be members of the state legislature, where all the local information and interests of the state are assembled, and from whence they may easily be conveyed by a very few hands into the legislature of the United States.

The observations made on the subject of taxation apply with greater force to the case of the militia. For however different the rules of discipline may be in different states; They are the same throughout each particular state; and depend on circumstances which can differ but little in different parts of the same state.[2]

The attentive reader will discern that the reasoning here used to prove the sufficiency of a moderate number of representatives, does not in any respect contradict what was urged on another occasion with regard to the extensive information which the representatives ought to possess, and the time that might be necessary for acquiring it.[3] This information, so far as it may relate to local objects, is rendered necessary and difficult, not by a difference of laws and local circumstances within a single state; but of those among different states. Taking each state by itself, its laws are the same, and its interests but little diversified. A few men therefore will possess all the knowledge requisite for a proper representation of them. Were the interests and affairs of each individual state, perfectly simple and uniform, a knowledge of them in one part would involve a knowledge of them in every other, and the whole state might be competently represented, by a single member taken from any part of it. On a comparison of the different states together, we find a great dissimilarity in their laws, and in many other circumstances connected with the objects of federal legislation, with all of which the federal representatives ought to have some acquaintance. Whilst a few representatives therefore from each state may bring with them a due knowledge of their own state, every representative will have much information to acquire concerning all the other states. The changes of time, as was formerly remarked,[4] on the comparative situation of the different states, will have an assimilating effect. The effect of time on the internal affairs of the states taken singly, will be just the contrary. At present some of the states are little more than a society of husbandmen. Few of them have made much progress in those branches of industry, which give a variety and complexity to the affairs of a nation. These however will in all of them be the fruits of a more advanced population; and will require on the part of each state a fuller representation. The foresight of the Convention has accordingly taken care that the progress of population may be accompanied with a proper increase of the representative branch of the government.

The experience of Great Britain which presents to mankind so many political lessons, both of the monitory and exemplary kind, and which has been frequently consulted in the course of these enquiries, corroborates the result of the reflections which we have just made. The number of inhabitants in the two kingdoms of England and Scotland, cannot be stated at less than eight millions. The representatives of these eight millions in the House of Commons, amount to five hundred fifty eight. Of this number one ninth are elected by three hundred and sixty four persons, and one half by five thousand seven hundred and twenty three persons.[a] It cannot be supposed that the half thus elected, and who do not even reside among the people at large, can add any thing either to the security of the people against the government; or to the knowledge of their circumstances and interests, in the legislative councils. On the contrary it is notorious that they are more frequently the representatives and instruments of the executive magistrate, than the guardians and advocates of the popular rights. They might therefore with great propriety be considered as something more than a mere deduction from the real representatives of the nation. We will however consider them, in this light alone, and will not extend the deduction, to a considerable number of others, who do not reside among their constituents, are very faintly connected with them, and have very little particular knowledge of their affairs. With all these concessions two hundred and seventy nine persons only will be the depository of the safety, interest and happiness of eight millions; that is to say: There will be one representative only to maintain the rights and explain the situation *of twenty eight thousand six hundred and seventy* constituents, in an assembly exposed to the whole force of executive influence, and extending its authority to every object of legislation within a nation whose affairs are in the highest degree diversified and complicated. Yet it is very certain not only that a valuable portion of freedom has been preserved under all these circumstances, but that the defects in the British code are chargeable in a very small proportion, on the ignorance of the legislature concerning the circumstances of the people. Allowing to this case the weight which is due to it: And comparing it with that of the House of Representatives as above explained, it seems to give the fullest assurance that a representative for every *thirty thousand inhabitants* will render the latter both a safe and competent guardian of the interests which will be confided to it.

(a) Burgh's polit. disquis.[5]

1. See *The Federalist* 53 (CC:519).
2. This paragraph was replaced in the M'Lean edition with the following paragraph: "With regard to the regulation of the militia, there are scarcely any circumstances in reference to which local knowledge can be said to be necessary. The general face of the country, whether mountainous or level, most fit for the operations of infantry or cavalry, is almost the only consideration of this nature that can occur. The art of war teaches general principles of organization, movement, and discipline, which apply universally."
3. See note 1.
4. See note 1.

5. James Burgh, *Political Disquisitions: or, An Enquiry into Public Errors, Defects, and Abuses*... (3 vols., London, 1774–1775), I, 45, 48.

534. Spurious Centinel XV
Pennsylvania Mercury, 16 February

In the first four months of the ratification debate, the *Pennsylvania Mercury* contained few original essays–Federalist publisher Daniel Humphreys primarily reprinted items from other newspapers. In late January, however, Humphreys began filling the *Mercury* with original essays supporting the Constitution. Antifederalists believed that this change of policy occurred at the instigation and with the assistance of Benjamin Rush who had advocated the ratification of the Constitution in essays, public meetings, and the Pennsylvania Convention. Whether or not Rush was connected with the *Mercury* cannot be determined with certainty, but the hardhitting articles in the *Mercury* reflected his vigor and style.

One of the more popular items to appear in the *Pennsylvania Mercury* was a satirical essay entitled "Centinel" XV, which was published on 16 February, eleven days after the publication of "Centinel" XIV (CC:501). On 19 February Antifederalist printer Eleazer Oswald of the Philadelphia *Independent Gazetteer* announced that, despite a request of some of his customers, he would not reprint the spurious "Centinel" XV even though he had previously printed the first fourteen "Centinel" essays. He had "no doubt" that the article was "*spurious.*" Oswald also attacked "Galen" (i.e., Benjamin Rush), who "in order to *save his bacon,* [had] become the *humble* copyist of Mr. *D. Humphreys*" (Mfm:Pa. 436. For Oswald's subsequent attacks upon the *Pennsylvania Mercury*, see *Independent Gazetteer*, 12 March, note 6, Appendix II.). Writing for the *Pennsylvania Mercury* on 21 February, "A Friend to Real Liberty of the Press" chided Oswald, who, despite his professed "impartiality," refused to reprint the "views of the enemies to the new constitution." "A Friend..." continued that "...however he [Oswald] may affect to despise being 'a copyist' from other papers, assure him, that his 'bacon' and his impartiality are equally regarded by those who have the real good of their country at heart..." (Mfm:Pa. 443). Signing himself "*Friend to real Liberty of the Press,*" Oswald countered by calling his adversary "some poor tool or *tiffany*" who wrote "*trash.*" Oswald expressed contempt for "the *abortions* of his distempered *brain*," and promised that he would not be "diverted from the strict line of our duty." Evidently making a reference to his own notoriety and propensity for duelling, Oswald wrote that "we do not *affect* to carry our 'arguments on the point of the sword' ... *fairplay* shall ever command a full share of our regards" (*Independent Gazetteer*, 22 February, Mfm:Pa. 447).

Federalists were delighted with the spurious "Centinel." "One of Your Constant Readers" rejoiced that the piece "hit the mark," and he thought that the satirist had "taken Mr. Centinel as nearly on his own ground as any thing I have seen written yet on the subject, and would wish to see it inserted in every paper in the city." He also believed that "Centinel" was "a shame to the whole union, but more especially to Pennsylvania" (*Pennsylvania Mercury*, 21 February, Mfm:Pa. 446). "Thomas Noodle" satirically reported that his neighbor "Goosecap" believed that "the XVth Centinel was the most alarming number of them all–that it brought all the horrors of the new constitution into one point of view–into a kind of focus–that it brought them 'home to mens bosoms and business'–to their very *feelings,* and that it proved beyond a doubt, that we should have no more peace under it [the Constitution] than a toad under a harrow" (*ibid.*, 28 February, Mfm:Pa. 465).

The spurious "Centinel" XV was reprinted, in whole or in part, sixteen times by 14 June: N.H. (1), Mass. (3), R.I. (2), Conn. (4), N.Y. (1), Pa. (1), Md. (1), Va. (2), S.C. (1). Neither the *Pennsylvania Mercury* nor eleven of these sixteen news-

papers had printed any of the fourteen numbers of the real "Centinel." The real
"Centinel" XV (CC:556), printed in the *Independent Gazetteer*, 22 February, made
no mention of its bogus counterpart.

Friends, Countrymen, and Fellow-citizens! You have fought, you have bled,
and you have conquered.–You have established your independence, and
you ought to be free–But, behold! a set of aristocrats, demagogues, conspirators, and tyrants, have arisen up, and say you shall be governed–Is
this to be endured by freemen,–men, who have lain in the open air, exposed to cold and hunger,–men who have worn out their health and constitutions in marches and counter-marches from one end of the continent
to the other; and after they have attained the noble prize, for which they
contended, are they to sit down tamely and be governed? Of what service
is a man's liberty to him, unless he can do as he pleases? And what man
can do as he pleases, who lives under a government?–The very end of
government is to bind men down to certain rules and duties; therefore, 'tis
only fit for slaves and vassals.–Every freeman ought to govern himself,
and then he will be governed most to his own mind.

Thus, my friends, you see all government is tyrannical and oppressive.
In the next place it is insulting: It is as much as to tell us, we know not
how to take care of ourselves, and therefore should submit to be directed
by others, who are appointed as guardians over so many wards. Now, of
what use can our reason be to us, if after we have come (or ought to have
come) to years of discretion, we are still to be led, guided, and bandied
about by those who pretend to know better than we?–And, who pray are
those who are to be thus led, guided, and bandied about? Why, the people!–Strange! that three millions of people should be led, guided, and bandied about by ninety or an hundred aristocratical, demagogical, tyrannical
conspirators!–Would it not be more according to order, propriety, and the
nature of things, that the ninety or an hundred conspirators should be led,
guided, and bandied about by the three millions of people.

In the third place, all government is expensive; for these ninety or an
hundred conspirators will not govern us for nothing, they must be paid for
it.–Think on that, my countrymen, we must not only be governed, be
insulted by being governed, but we must pay these demagogues for coming from all parts of the continent, to lay their heads together how to
govern us most effectually–for this, we must pay them mileage, pay them
wages, fill their purses, supply their tables to keep them in idleness to riot
on the fat of the land, to plot, contrive, and juggle us into good order and
government. Now all this money might be saved to the public, by each
man governing himself, and doing as he pleased, which by nature he has
a right to do.

Oh my countrymen! my bowels yearn with affliction, when I think to
what a pass we are likely to come–When I think, after all we have done
and suffered for dear liberty, we must still be kept in order, and gov-

erned.–I had hoped, after our glorious struggle, this country would be an asylum for all those noble, untamed spirits, who were desirous of flying from all law, gospel, and government.–But alas! after all I have said and written, after all the inventions I have racked my brain for, and horrible descriptions I have laid before you, you are still unroused, and I have made no impression on any, except a few of those choice spirits at Carlisle.[1]–And how have these been treated by the conspirators and federalists–they have been called insurgents, rioters, and British deserters–true, many of them were deserters, and to their credit be it spoken,–they deserted from king and country, friends and relations, wives and children, to come here and be free–they expected we were to be a free people, and they have come among us to live at large, and do as they please–Think then how disappointed they must be, and how peculiarly hard their case is, either to stay here and be governed, or to return and be hanged.

Rouse then, my friends, my countrymen, my fellow-citizens!–Rouse, ye Shayites, Dayites, and Shattuckites![2]–Ye insurgents, rioters, and deserters!–Ye tories, refugees, and antifœderalists!–Rouse, and kick up a dust before it is too late!–Be not such a parcel of stupid, dunder-headed, blunder-headed, muddle-headed, puddle-headed blockheads–Such a tribe of snivelling, drivelling, sneaking, slinking, moping, poking, mumping, pitiful, pimping, pettifogging, poltrons,–such a set of nincumpoops, ninny-hammers, mushrooms, jackasses, jackanapeses, jackadandies, goosecaps, tom-noodles, yahooes, shitepokes, and p–ssab–ds–Rouse!–awaken!–rub your eyes!–Do not you see the aristocrats, monocrats, demagogues, pedagogues, gogmagogs, brobdingnags, conspirators, and fœderal hobgoblins, are preparing to govern you, to enslave you, enthral you, and bemaul you.–If you submit to them, they will rob you of your liberties–they will tie you hand and foot,–they will play hob with you, play the dickens with you, and play the d–v–l with you–they will put halters round your necks, and hold your noses to the grindstone–they will purge you and bleed you, glister you and blister you, drench you and vomit you–they will tread on your toes, break your shins, dock your tails, draw your teeth, tear your hair and scratch out your eyes,–they will pull your noses, lug your ears, punch you in the guts, and kick you in the breech—ZOUNDS! will nothing rouse you!

1. For an Antifederalist-provoked riot in Carlisle that broke up a Federalist celebration of Pennsylvania's ratification of the Constitution, see Philadelphia *Independent Gazetteer*, 4 March (Appendix I).

2. Daniel Shays, Luke Day, and Job Shattuck were leaders of Shays's Rebellion in Massachusetts in 1786-87.

535. Benjamin Franklin to Louis-Guillaume Le Veillard
Philadelphia, 17 February (excerpt)[1]

. . . I sent you with my last a copy of the new constitution proposed for the United States by the late general convention. I sent one also to our excellent friend the Duke de la Rochefoucauld.[2] I attended the business of the convention faithfully for four months. Enclosed you have the last speech I made in it.[3] Six States have already adopted the constitution, and there is now little doubt of its being accepted by a sufficient number to carry it into execution, if not immediately by the whole. It has however met with great opposition in some States, for we are at present a nation of politicians. And though there is a general dread of giving too much *power* to our *governors*, I think we are more in danger from too little obedience in the *governed*.

We shall, as you suppose, have imposts on trade, and custom-houses, not because other nations have them, but because we cannot at present do without them. We want to discharge our public debt occasioned by the late war. Direct taxes are not so easily levied on the scantily settled inhabitants of our wide extended country; and what is paid in the price of merchandize is less felt by the consumer, and less the cause of complaint. When we are out of debt we may leave our trade free, for our ordinary charges of government will not be great.

Where there is a free government, and the people make their own laws by their representatives, I see no injustice in their obliging one another to take their own paper money. It is no more so than compelling a man by law to take his own note. But it is unjust to pay strangers with such money against their will. The making of paper money with such a sanction is however a folly, since although you may by law oblige a citizen to take it for his goods, you cannot fix his prices; and his liberty of rating them as he pleases, which is the same thing as setting what value he pleases on your money, defeats your sanction.

I have been concerned to hear of the troubles in the internal government of the country I love; and hope some good may come out of them; and that they may end without mischief. . . .

1. Printed: William Temple Franklin, ed., *Memoirs of the Life and Writings of Benjamin Franklin...* (3 vols., London, 1817–1818), II, 107–9. Franklin and Le Veillard (1733–1794), a physician and the owner-manager of mineral baths at Passy, France, had been close friends since early 1777, shortly after Franklin had arrived in France as one of the American commissioners authorized to establish friendly relations with France and to negotiate a treaty of commerce.

2. Franklin and Louis-Alexandre, duc de La Roche-Guyon et de La Rochefoucauld D'Enville (1743–1792), had met in 1769 but did not become friends until 1777. Franklin sent him a copy of the Constitution on 14 October 1787, stating that "You have an undoubted Right to the Communication of every Thing that regards the American Constitutions of Government" (Franklin Papers, DLC).

3. For Franklin's speech of 17 September, see CC:77.

536. Antoine de la Forest to Comte de la Luzerne
New York, 18 February[1]

I received your letters of the 19th. and 27th. of last October which you did me the honor of writing to me. The one that you sent to M. Rolland to order his return to france I had forwarded to Brest.

The details that I had the honor of writing you, My Lord, on the result of the federal assembly [Constitutional Convention] and the measures taken in consequence in the different States of the union, will have reached you successively. All the legislatures, except that of Rhode island, have now called the special assemblies of the people of their respective States. The one in New-Hampshire began on the 13th of this month, New york's will take place on the 17th of June, Maryland's on the 21st of april, Virginia's on the 26th of May, North Carolina's on the 21st of July and South Carolina's on the 3rd of March.[2] Those in Georgia, Delaware, New jersey, Pennsylvania, Connecticut and Massachusetts have already ratified the proposed Constitution. There was almost a unanimous Vote in the assemblies of the first three States. That of [Delaware] especially displayed a remarkable approbation. The Constitution there had been read, accepted and ratified in three hours, without their having the slightest debate on the merit of the question. Those of Connecticut and Massachusetts discussed all the parts of the Government for a long time and as warmly as that of Pennsylvania. The majority was almost three-quarters of the assembly of Connecticut and before breaking up the members of the minority expressed their intention of recommending the Acquiescence of their Constituents. There were very serious alarms over the side that the Massachusetts assembly would take. Of 355 representatives, there were among them [several?] who had taken part in the [farmers'?] rebellion in 1786.[3] The refusal to ratify the new plan of Government on the part of such an important State could have entailed the ruin of the edifice. But it was finally adopted on the 6th of this month by a majority of only 19 [votes?]. To calm men's minds it was found necessary to add to the act of ratification *the recommendation* to make some changes and some additions to the Constitution. The recommendation fortunately is not conditional; it simply carries an injunction to the future representatives of the State in the new Government to make all their efforts to obtain the recommended points in the manner pointed out by the 5th. article of the constitution.[4] Two of these points, My Lord, essentially attack the proposed plan. It is demanded that it be explicitly declared that all the powers that are not *expressly* delegated to the federal body are reserved to the members of the union. Such a clause would furnish reason for continual quarrels; it is found in the old act of confederation[5] and experience has proven that if Congress had not proceeded according to the *implicit* sense, it would have been stopped at each step. In addition it is demanded that Congress be able to levy *direct Taxes* only when the revenues from import duties and the excise are insufficient for the public needs; It is even desired that in this last case Congress first try to *requisition* the States to go forward only insofar as they neglect to furnish their quota. This clause complicates the machine of Government and at a critical moment would show the United States to lack something essential; Twelve years' experience proved how much the slow route of requisitions set back the Service. The other changes or additions are less important, My Lord, and perhaps it is even good that the republicans have such a Jealous caution on all that could affect their liberty, without major [damage?] to public affairs. If four [more?] States ratify the new Government without demanding changes, as five of them have already done, those desired by Massachusetts will probably not even be taken into [consideration?]. But its example is important and it could be followed by the assemblies which are to meet. Never have the intrigues of the opposition to the new Government been so strong. [They?] have circulated their publications in all the corners of [the country?]. It attacks the character of all the deputies who signed the Constitution. Even General Washington, against whom no paper contained an unpleasant aspersion for Twelve years, is accused of having had personal designs.[6] The Delegate from the State of Maryland who did not sign the new plan [with?] his Colleagues, in some way [described?] it to the legislature of his State as a Plot of some Aristocrats.[7] But one must consider these clamors as the last efforts of a party that becomes weaker Every Day. The hopes of federalists are now well founded.

1. RC (Tr), Affaires Étrangères, Correspondance Consulaires, BI 910, New York, ff. 19–20, Archives Nationales, Paris, France. Endorsed as received on 29 March. Some of the words are lost in the gutter.

2. South Carolina's convention was scheduled to convene on 12 May. See the Boston *Independent Chronicle*, 7 February, note 2 (Appendix I).

3. Shays's Rebellion.

4. For the amendments proposed by the Massachusetts Convention, see CC:508.

5. Article II (CDR, 86).

6. Forest possibly refers to "Centinel" XI, Philadelphia *Independent Gazetteer*, 16 January (CC:453), or "An American," Boston *American Herald*, 28 January (CC:386–F). "A Citizen of Philadelphia" (Pelatiah Webster?) defended Washington against "Centinel's" charges (*Pennsylvania Gazette*, 23 January, RCS:Pa., 658–59). "Centinel" XI and "An American" were reprinted in the *New York Journal* on 21 January and 12 February, respectively; while "A Citizen of Philadelphia" was reprinted in the *New York Morning Post* on 30 January.

7. See Luther Martin's *Genuine Information* (CC:389).

537. Cyrus Griffin to Thomas FitzSimons
New York, 18 February (excerpt)[1]

· · · The proposed constitution now stands upon a firm basis; The ratification of Massachusets will carry it triumphantly throughout. N. Ham. will presently adopt it–Maryland and South-Carolina by large majorities in convenient time; N. York, Virginia, and N. Carolina must find their concurrence indispensably necessary; and even Rhode Island in all probability will soon be deliberating.

Colonel R. H. Lee and mr. John Page, men of Influence in Virginia, are relinquishing their opposition; but what to us is very extraordinary and unexpected, we are told that mr. George Mason has declared himself so great an enemy to the constitution that he will heartily join mr. Henry and others in promoting a southern Confederacy[2]–alas! how inconstant is the mind of man.

all the European Information of a public nature has been communicated in the news-papers.

I beg leave to recommend the enclosed letter to your friendly attention.

1. RC, Gratz Collection, PHi. Griffin (1748–1810), a Lancaster County, Va., lawyer, was a delegate to Congress from 1778 to 1780 and 1787 to 1788. He served as President of Congress from 22 January to 15 November 1788. Griffin was also a member of Congress' Court of Appeals in Cases of Capture from 1780 to 1787 and judge of the U.S. District Court of Virginia from 1789 to 1810. FitzSimons (1741–1811), a Philadelphia merchant, was a delegate to Congress from 1782 to 1783, a Pennsylvania assemblyman from 1786 to 1788, and a delegate to the Constitutional Convention, where he signed the Constitution. He served in the U.S. House of Representatives from 1789 to 1795.

2. For Patrick Henry's alleged support of a Southern confederacy, see CC:276, note 4.

538. Collin McGregor to Neil Jamieson
New York, 18 February (excerpts)[1]

I have now the pleasure of acknowledg. receipt of your much Esteemed favor of 14 Octr P Mr Pollock which came to hand the 3d inst.–Your other favors of 7 Novr. & 5 Decr. P Packet of [those?] months came to hand only the 11th. & 12th. inst.–These several letters are now before me, and I shall endeavour to make a reply. . . .

I do most heartily approve of your writing a Complimentary letter to Colo Hamilton.–He is a worthy Character and has Considerable Interest in this State, which I am clear will every day increase.–His unshaken integrity & Conspicuous Abilities will soon place him at the head of Affairs, And as you have so much property in this State, keeping or renewing friendship with a person of this distinction I think is of much Consequence to your Interest. . . .

With respect to the Certification–these being blinded with the Political State of the Country leads me into a wide labyrinth.–The New Constitution as framed by the late Convention is now adopted & Ratified by Six States.–Massachusetts, on whom many eyes were fixed, gave their assent about ten days ago, and as their Neighbours of Connecticut have done the same, it is Supposed that it will have much influence on the Characters who are Antifœderal in this State; because it is endless to persist when so powerful a portion of the Continent have acceded–The example therefore of our Eastern Councils make it Almost a Certainty that the Constitution will be Adopted throughout, and the only fear we now have of serious opposition is from the State of Virginia, where there are many respectable & powerful Men strenuously against the Constitution.–Genl Washington however with a Strong party are clear for its adoption, and all his influence will be exerted to bring it about.–South & N. Carolina we have no doubt of, and as for Georgia that State has already, Come into the Measure.–

Having thus given you the situation of the New Constitution, I am now led to mention that its progress has had & will Continue to have an influence on Securities.–Final settlements have in particular taken a start, and are now 3/6 paper money.–My opinion is that when they get to abt 4/ or 4/6 it will be better to part with them than trust to uncertainties, for even should the New Constitution be finally adopted, it will be a long time ere the finances of the Country will be in such Condition as to effect a redemption of the Public Securities.–

With respect to the Securities of this State they are every day mending, And it is with no small degree of pleasure that I inform you of my havg recd. the other day £213..11..8 Currcy as one fourth part of the Interest on the Certificates, which with what I formerly recd. goes great way towards refunding the original purchase.–The Treasurer has made up his Accounts & they have been made public, as well as an Accot. of the State Debt.–from these vouchers the Public Creditors have great hopes, and it is thought that the present Legislature will do something further towards the extinction of the Debt.–

I shall as soon as I can make out an exact List of the securities I hold & send you the same agreeable to Your request.–In the meantime I think that I have abt. £7000 of Bankers Notes for Principal which have Interest thereon from 31 Decr 1784; also abt. £850 of Bankers Notes for Interest deducting therefrom the one fourth which I recd. as above £213..11..8d.– Besides these, the final settlements in Company with P. Hart; amount whereof you already know.

You may rest assured I will pay close attention to the manœuvres of the Legislature, and endeavor to make the most of the securities I can. . . .

I think that New York is a place where a field is open to any industrious person, and should the N Government take effect the value of this Spot will be enhanced & property become secure.–However of this matter I will again give you my sentiments more Clearly & at large. . . .

1. FC, Collin McGregor Letterbook, 1787–1788, NN. The name of the addressee does not appear but it was apparently Neil Jamieson. Because McGregor did not have time to copy this letter, he kept it until 4 March, when he sent it to Jamieson as an enclosure in another letter (CC:590). On 2 April McGregor forwarded duplicates of his letters of 18 February and 4 March to Jamieson. McGregor (d. 1801), a native of Scotland who came to America in 1781, was a New York City merchant and a speculator in land and securities. Jamieson, also a native of Scotland, came to America in 1760 as a member of a Scottish mercantile firm and settled in Norfolk, Va., where he became a wealthy merchant. A Loyalist, he fled to New York in 1776 and remained there until April 1785. In 1788 Jamieson was a London merchant, and McGregor was serving as his American business agent.

539. William Fleming to Thomas Madison
Belmont, Botetourt County, Va., 19 February[1]

Your favour of Jany 2d is before me. A trip to G. Jones[2] & diffrent affairs, since prevented me from acknowleging the receipt sooner–In this County, we have few Polititians, nor do the People seem to concern them-selves much about the New fœderal Constitution. on the day of Election I suppose they will choose those of the Candidates, they can best confide in. Who will offer I know not. should the Voters choose me for one,[3] I will serve them as I look on it to be my duty, and the last [years?] service I can render my Country, should I be rejected, it will give me no umbrage, it will be a pleasure to see members of superior abilities, and equal willing-ness, ready to serve the County–You desire me to write you my thoughts on the Constitution, and hint that I am against it. On my receiving a Copy of the Plan when first published to that before I had seen any thing pro or Con, on the Subject, I declared that poor Democracy was at the last gasp, Aristocracy was establishing, which I feard would end in Tyrannical Regality. this declaration has unjustly, perhaps stamp'd me with many, an Ante Confœdralist, I most heartily agree with you that the Union of the American states ought to be consolidated, and this force, power & energy of the Confederation be brought to point. this would give us weight with foreign Nations, and make us respectable in the political Scale of Europe, on the Contrary an independant Sovereignty in each state, will directly & immediatly produce sciens of blood amongst ourselves, & make us an easy prey to the first powerfull foreign invader, but can not the last inconvenience & the former advantage be obtained without depriving the Citizens of their priveleges? I think it may.–let me say it without the im-putation of vanity, that I was pleased the letter from Mr Lee[4] contained many of my private objections before I had seen it. I therefore refer you to that and at present shall only remove one objection you make in yours. Viz the Influence the President may have in Council the Members of his own choosing. May not this be obviated by the Members of the Privy Council being chosen by the Legislators of the diffrent States, from the above you will, see that I am for the Constitution with such amendments as will secure the liberty of the Subject, for of all Governments an Oligar-chy is the worst, and power once parted with can never be reclaimed with-out bloodshed–I am in the same situation with respect to having the public prints that you are, I have not seen a paper since I came up from the River, and even in the small circle of Botetourt, the communication is interrupted from the Inhabitants at the Courthouse innoculating for the small pox. Your Unckle Lewis and Jones,[5] are strongly for the Confœderation as new modeled. Mr Lewis I believe will offer for Rock-ingham, I have received a letter from the General[6] on this subject which I will answer by this conveyance (which I expect will be by Mr G Nelson), and as The Tomahawk is burried between you, & the Tree of Peace

planted, and in a fair way to flourish Green & Strong, You will see it–
What occasion for an excuse for the length of Your letter? the longer the
better, it supplies a tete a tete conversation. I am well pleased to hear, you
have got a sufficiency of good water, for the making of Salt, and likely to
shorten the process.–In your old habitation which looks like a deserted
place, I found a small decanter with Sixteen ounces of Quicksilver as it
was standing open to every one and would certainly be lost, last week I
took it home for which I am accountable to you.–

1. RC, Draper Manuscripts, Virginia Papers, WHi. Belmont was Fleming's plantation. The letter was addressed to "Thomas Madison-Esqr./Saltworks/Washington Cty."
In the left corner of the address page, Fleming wrote "*Recommended to/Mr Waltons care/to
forward/* P Favour/Mr Tanhersly."
2. Gabriel Jones. See note 5 below.
3. In March Fleming was elected to represent Botetourt County in the state Convention, where, in June 1788, he voted to ratify the Constitution.
4. For Richard Henry Lee to Governor Edmund Randolph, 16 October, first published on 6 December, see CC:325.
5. Thomas Lewis and Gabriel Jones represented Rockingham County in the Virginia
Convention, where both voted to ratify the Constitution.
6. Probably a reference to General William Russell's letter to Fleming, dated 25
January (CC:475).

540. Henry Knox to Jean-Baptiste Gouvion
New York, 19 February[1]

With great pleasure my dear Gouvion I acknowledge the receipt of
you[r] favour of the 5th of Nov last with the enclosures–The speeches mark
with great force the dignity of the human mind in France–I rejoice that
liberty expands itself with manner that reflects honor on the Age–

Our attention has been exceedingly occupied by the affairs of Europe
during some months past–It would seem by the declarations and counter-
declarations &c that the storm which was collecting has been dissipated by
the voice of Reason–The inveterate English rejoice as if they had gained
some important victory–I hope the issue will prove otherwise–

The patriots of this Country have been laboring to establish a better
system of government than the confederation–we were becoming litterally
a rope of sand–a Union in name only without substance or strength–You
have seen the system–It might probably have been formed with greater
consistency in the closet of a Philosophic–but a better could not be obtained by a free compromise–We shall try it–six states has received it and
a seventh will follow in a few days. probably it will be received by all the
states in the course of the present Year

I write to the Marquis[2] for an authenticate List of the french officers
who served in the american army entitled to become members of the Cincinnati–I want this list to ground the diplomas upon—push him on the
subject–his busy mind otherwise may overlook it

1. RC, Miscellaneous Letters, MeHi. Endorsed: *"Private."* Jean-Baptiste Gouvion (1747–1792), a French military engineer, was a lieutenant colonel in the Continental Army's corps of engineers during the Revolution, and in November 1781 he was promoted to brevet colonel by Congress. He returned to France after the war with the rank of lieutenant colonel in the French army, and in December 1787 he was promoted to the rank of Mestre de Camp.

2. Lafayette.

541. James Madison to Thomas Jefferson
New York, 19 February (excerpts)[1]

By the Count de Moustier I received your favour of the 8th. of October.[2] . . .

The public here continues to be much agitated by the proposed fœderal Constitution and to be attentive to little else. At the date of my last Delaware Pennsylvania and New Jersey had adopted it. It has been since adopted by Connecticut, Georgia, and Massachussetts. In the first the minority consisted of 40 against 127. In Georgia the adoption was unanimous. In Massachussetts the conflict was tedious and the event extremely doubtful. On the final question the vote stood 187 against 168; a majority of 19 only being in favor of the Constitution. The prevailing party comprized however all the men of abilities, of property, and of influence. In the opposite multitude there was not a single character capable of uniting their wills or directing their measures. It was made up partly of deputies from the province of Maine who apprehended difficulties from the New Government to their scheme of separation, partly of men who had espoused the disaffection of Shay's; and partly of ignorant and jealous men, who had been taught or had fancied that the Convention at Philada. had entered into a conspiracy against the liberties of the people at large, in order to erect an aristocracy for the rich the *well-born*, and the men of Education. They had no plan whatever. They looked no farther than to put a negative on the Constitution and return home. The amendments as recommended by the Convention were as I am well informed not so much calculated for the minority in the Convention, on whom they had little effect, as for the people of the State. You will find the amendments in the Newspapers which are sent from the office of foreign affairs. It appears from a variety of circumstances that disappointment had produced no asperity in the minority, and that they will probably not only acquiesce in the event, but endeavour to reconcile their constituents to it. This was the public declaration of several who were called the leaders of the party. The minority of Connecticut behaved with equal moderation. That of Pennsylvania has been extremely intemperate and continues to use a very bold and menacing language. Had the decision in Massachussetts been adverse to the Constitution, it is not improbable that some very violent measures would have followed in that State. The cause of the inflamation however is much more in their State factions, than in the system proposed by the

Convention. New Hampshire is now deliberating on the Constitution. It is generally understood that an adoption is a matter of certainty. South Carolina & Maryland have fixed on April or May for their Conventions. The former it is currently said will be one of the ratifying States. Mr. *Chace* and a few others will raise a considerable opposition in the latter. But the weight of personal influence is on the side of the Constitution, and the present expectation is that the opposition will be outnumbered by a great majority. This State is much divided in its sentiment. Its Convention is to be held in June. The decision of Massts. will give the turn in favor of the Constitution unless an idea should prevail or the fact should appear, that the voice of the State is opposed to the result of its Convention. North Carolina has put off her Convention till July.[3] The State is much divided it is said. The temper of Virginia, as far as I can learn, has undergone but little change of late. At first there was an enthusiasm for the Constitution. The tide next took a sudden and strong turn in the opposite direction. The influence and exertions of Mr. Henry, and Col. Mason and some others will account for this. Subsequent information again represented the Constitution as regaining in some degree its lost ground. The people at large have been uniformly said to be more friendly to the Constitution than the Assembly. But it is probable that the dispersion of the latter will have a considerable influence on the opinions of the former. The previous adoption of nine States ~~will have~~ must have a very persuasive effect on the minds of the opposition, though I am told that a very bold language is held by Mr. H—y and some of his partizans. Great stress is laid on the self-sufficiency of that State, and the prospect of external props is alluded to.

Congress have done no business of consequence yet, nor is it probable that much more of any sort will precede the event of the great question before the public. . . .

1. RC, Madison Papers, DLC. Printed: Rutland, *Madison*, X, 518–21; and Boyd, XII, 607–10.

2. Writing in code at the end of his letter, Jefferson confided that "De Moustier is remarkably communicative. With adroitness he may be pumped of anything. His openness is from character not from affectation. An intimacy with him will on this account be politically valuable" (Rutland, *Madison*, X, 187–88; and Boyd, XII, 218–19).

3. At a later date, Madison placed an asterisk here and wrote at the bottom of the page: "see letter from Col: Davie to J.M." He was probably referring to William R. Davie's letter of 10 June 1789 in which Davie considered the prospects for ratification in North Carolina (Madison Papers, DLC).

542. Publius: The Federalist 57
New York Packet, 19 February

The authorship of this essay was claimed by both James Madison and Alexander Hamilton, but it is generally attributed to Madison. The essay was reprinted in the New York *Independent Journal* on 20 February. It is number 57 in the M'Lean edition and number 56 in the newspapers.

For a general discussion of the authorship, circulation, and impact of *The Federalist*, see CC:201, 639; and for the disputed authorship of this essay, see Cooke, xix–xxx, 641–42, and Rutland, *Madison*, X, 261–63.

The FŒDERALIST, No. 56.
To the People of the State of New-York.

The *third* charge against the House of Representatives is, that it will be taken from that class of citizens which will have least sympathy with the mass of the people, and be most likely to aim at an ambitious sacrifice of the many to the aggrandizement of the few.

Of all the objections which have been framed against the Fœderal Constitution, this is perhaps the most extraordinary. Whilst the objection itself is levelled against a pretended oligarchy, the principle of it strikes at the very root of republican government.

The aim of every political Constitution is or ought to be first to obtain for rulers, men who possess most wisdom to discern, and most virtue to pursue the common good of the society; and in the next place, to take the most effectual precautions for keeping them virtuous, whilst they continue to hold their public trust. The elective mode of obtaining rulers is the characteristic policy of republican government. The means relied on in this form of government for preventing their degeneracy are numerous and various. The most effectual one is such a limitation of the term of appointments, as will maintain a proper responsibility to the people.

Let me now ask what circumstance there is in the Constitution of the House of Representatives, that violates the principles of republican government; or favors the elevation of the few on the ruins of the many? Let me ask whether every circumstance is not, on the contrary, strictly conformable to these principles; and scrupulously impartial to the rights and pretensions of every class and description of citizens?

Who are to be the electors of the Fœderal Representatives? Not the rich more than the poor; not the learned more than the ignorant; not the haughty heirs of distinguished names, more than the humble sons of obscure and unpropitious fortune. The electors are to be the great body of the people of the United States. They are to be the same who exercise the right in every State of electing the correspondent branch of the Legislature of the State.

Who are to be the objects of popular choice? Every citizen whose merit may recommend him to the esteem and confidence of his country. No qualification of wealth, of birth, of religious faith, or of civil profession, is permitted to fetter the judgment or disappoint the inclination of the people.

If we consider the situation of the men on whom the free suffrages of their fellow citizens may confer the representative trust, we shall find it involving every security which can be devised or desired for their fidelity to their constituents.

In the first place, as they will have been distinguished by the preference of their fellow citizens, we are to presume, that in general, they will be somewhat distinguished also, by those qualities which entitle them to it, and which promise a sincere and scrupulous regard to the nature of their engagements.

In the second place, they will enter into the public service under circumstances which cannot fail to produce a temporary affection at least to their constituents. There is in every breast a sensibility to marks of honor, of favor, of esteem, and of confidence, which, apart from all considerations of interest, is some pledge for grateful and benevolent returns. Ingratitude is a common topic of declamation against human nature; and it must be confessed, that instances of it are but too frequent and flagrant both in public and in private life. But the universal and extreme indignation which it inspires, is itself a proof of the energy and prevalence of the contrary sentiment.

In the third place, these ties which bind the representative to his constituents are strengthened by motives of a more selfish nature. His pride and vanity attach him to a form of government which favors his pretensions, and gives him a share in its honors and distinctions. Whatever hopes or projects might be entertained by a few aspiring characters, it must generally happen that a great proportion of the men deriving their advancement from their influence with the people, would have more to hope from a preservation of the favor, than from innovations in the government subversive of the authority of the people.

All these securities however would be found very insufficient without the restraint of frequent elections. Hence, in the fourth place, the House of Representatives is so constituted as to support in the members an habitual recollection of their dependence on the people. Before the sentiments impressed on their minds by the mode of their elevation, can be effaced by the exercise of power, they will be compelled to anticipate the moment when their power is to cease, when their exercise of it is to be reviewed, and when they must descend to the level from which they were raised; there for ever to remain, unless a faithful discharge of their trust shall have established their title to a renewal of it.

I will add as a fifth circumstance in the situation of the House of Representatives, restraining them from oppressive measures, that they can make no law which will not have its full operation on themselves and their friends, as well as on the great mass of the society. This has always been deemed one of the strongest bonds by which human policy can connect the rulers and the people together. It creates between them that communion of interests and sympathy of sentiments of which few governments have furnished examples; but without which every government degenerates into tyranny. If it be asked what is to restrain the House of Representatives from making legal discriminations in favor of themselves and a particular class of the society? I answer, the genius of the whole system, the nature of just and constitutional laws, and above all the vigilent and manly spirit which actuates the people of America, a spirit which nourishes freedom, and in return is nourished by it.

If this spirit shall ever be so far debased as to tolerate a law not obligatory on the Legislature as well as on the people, the people will be prepared to tolerate any thing but liberty.

Such will be the relation between the House of Representatives and their constituents. Duty, gratitude, interest, ambition itself, are the chords by which they will be bound to fidelity and sympathy with the great mass of the people. It is possible that these may all be insufficient to controul the caprice and wickedness of man. But are they not all that government will admit, and that human prudence can devise? Are they not the genuine and the characteristic means by which Republican Government provides for the liberty and happiness of the people? Are they not the identical means on which every State Government in the Union, relies for the attainment of these important ends? What then are we to understand by the objection which this paper has combated? What are we to say to the men who profess the most flaming zeal for Republican Government, yet boldly impeach the fundamental principle of it; who pretend to be champions for the right and the capacity of the people to chuse their own rulers, yet maintain that they will prefer those only who will immediately and infallibly betray the trust committed to them?

Were the objection to be read by one who had not seen the mode prescribed by the Constitution for the choice of representatives, he could suppose nothing less than that some unreasonable qualification of property was annexed to the right of suffrage; or that the right of eligibility was limited to persons of particular families or fortunes; or at least that the mode prescribed by the State Constitutions was in some respect or other very grossly departed from. We have seen how far such a supposition would err as to the two first points.[1] Nor would it in fact be less erroneous as to the last. The only difference discoverable between the two cases, is, that each representative of the United States will be elected by five or six thousand citizens; whilst in the individual States the election of a representative is left to about as many hundred. Will it be pretended that this difference is sufficient to justify an attachment to the State Governments and an abhorrence to the Fœderal Government? If this be the point on which the objection turns, it deserves to be examined.

Is it supported by *reason*? This cannot be said, without maintaining that five or six thousand citizens are less capable of chusing a fit representative, or more liable to be corrupted by an unfit one, than five or six hundred. Reason, on the contrary assures us, that as in so great a number, a fit representative would be most likely to be found, so the choice would be less likely to be diverted from him, by the intrigues of the ambitious, or the bribes of the rich.

Is the *consequence* from this doctrine admissible? If we say that five or six hundred citizens are as many as can jointly exercise their right of suffrage, must we not deprive the people of the immediate choice of their public servants in every instance where the administration of the government does not require as many of them as will amount to one for that number of citizens?

Is the doctrine warranted by *facts*? It was shewn in the last paper,[2] that the real representation in the British House of Commons very little exceeds the proportion of one for every thirty thousand inhabitants. Besides a variety of powerful causes, not existing here, and which favor in that country, the pretensions of rank and wealth, no person is eligible as a representative of a county, unless he possess real estate of the clear value of six hundred pounds sterling per year; nor of a city or borough, unless he possess a like estate of half that annual value. To this qualification on the part of the county representatives, is added another on the part of the county electors, which restrains the right of suffrage to persons having a freehold estate of the annual value of more than twenty pounds sterling according to the present rate of money. Notwithstanding these unfavorable circumstances, and notwithstanding some very unequal laws in the British code, it cannot be said that the representatives of the nation have elevated the few on the ruins of the many.

But we need not resort to foreign experience on this subject. Our own is explicit and decisive. The districts in New-Hampshire in which the Senators are chosen immediately by the people are nearly as large as will be necessary for her representatives in the Congress. Those of Massachusetts are larger, than will be necessary for that purpose. And those of New-York still more so. In the last State the members of Assembly, for the cities and counties of New-York and Albany, are elected by very nearly as many voters, as will be entitled to a representative in the Congress, calculating on the number of sixty-five representatives only. It makes no difference that in these senatorial districts and counties, a number of representatives are voted for by each elector at the same time. If the same electors, at the same time are capable of choosing four or five representatives, they cannot be incapable of choosing one. Pennsylvania is an additional example. Some of her counties which elect her State representatives, are almost as large as her districts will be by which her Fœderal Representatives will be elected. The city of Philadelphia is supposed to contain between fifty and sixty thousand souls. It will therefore form nearly two districts for the choice of Fœderal Representatives. It forms however but one county, in which every elector votes for each of its representatives in the State Legislature. And what may appear to be still more directly to our purpose, the whole city actually elects a *single member* for the executive council. This is the case in all the other counties of the State.

Are not these facts the most satisfactory proofs of the fallacy which has been employed against the branch of the Fœderal Government under consideration? Has it appeared on trial that the Senators of New-Hampshire, Massachusetts, and New-York; or the Executive Council of Pennsylvania; or the members of the Assembly in the two last States, have betrayed any peculiar disposition to sacrifice the many to the few; or are in any respect less worthy of their places than the representatives and magistrates appointed in other States, by very small divisions of the people?

But there are cases of a stronger complexion than any which I have yet quoted. One branch of the Legislature of Connecticut is so constituted that each member of it is elected by the whole State.[3] So is the Governor of that State, of Massachusetts, and of this State, and the President of New-Hampshire. I leave every man to decide whether the result of any one of these experiments can be said to countenance a suspicion that a diffusive mode of chusing representatives of the people tends to elevate traitors, and to undermine the public liberty.

1. See *The Federalist* 52 (CC:514).
2. See *The Federalist* 56 (CC:533).
3. The twelve assistants in the state Council were elected at large.

543. John Armstrong, Sr., to George Washington
Carlisle, Pa., 20 February[1]

As a Citizen of the united States, I always consider my Self your debtor, and the annual tribute of a short letter, the smallest remittance we can well conceive. It is perhaps more than a year past since I took the liberty of telling you, that however attatched to retirement & rural life, you must suffer a little more interruption to domestick enjoyments & give some more attention to the suffrages of yr. countrymen in publick employ. this you see Sir, has proved true, and the same object & same motives induce me to think, that one other tour of this kind of duty will fall to your Lot.

Old as I am, I rejoice at the high probability and therefore, near prospect of a general adoption of the Federal Constitution; this hope leads us on to the use of that System, in which the Federal voice of Pennsylvania stands ready to announce your Excellency the first President ~~general~~ of the union.–of this there need be little hesitation amongst the Citizens, but not so with you; persuaded as I am, it will cost you much anxious thought– nevertheless if the call of God, is manifested to you in a plenary or unanimous call of the people, I hope that will obviate every objection; if not for the whole term of four years, at least for half that time if health admit: considering as you will, that we were not made for our Selves, therefore must not live to our Selves. my sole reason for these early hints, is that by a divine blessing you may be made instrumental of giving a wise & useful *Example to successors* in more things than what may be merely essential to the office; I had like to be so imprudent as to mention a few, but am checked, not by modesty alone, but by former demonstration that you will have in full view, all I mean and much more.–the more dissipated customs of the age, prompted by elevation of Rank, National dignity & other inflated ideas, will but too probably contrast themselves, to National Economy, real dignity, & private virtue too; this battle you will have in your own breast, it must principally be fought with yourself, an opponent harder to be overcome & more ready to give the foil, than any in all creation except One–but resistance on behalf of the publick & of the Church of God, is worthy of double praise: nor is any man who has these as his motive, likely to fight this battle alone–*the wise medium* an indulgent providence will direct, tho' no precise & invariable rule is admisable in the case.

The proposed Federal Constitution is well approved of this way by the more candid & better informed part of the people, some of whom are even surprized at the propriety of the first draught, all things considered; but look up for some amendments or alterations in the way prescribed in the Constitution itself, when experience & time shall point out the expedience of the measure–these perhaps will be of two kinds, some truly salutary, others in the way of explanation, merely to please. We have in this State had the most sanguine & unreasonable Opposition of any I have yet heard of, and hope that none other of the Union will follow the insidious example, and had it not been assiduously contrasted might have proved very injurious to the union and peace of this country; nor has this evil & demented Spirit yet subsided–you cannot have read the Centinel in his numerous & baneful productions, the Old Whig–and the reasons of dissent exhibited by the minority of our Convention–without discovering the treasonable & delusive views of the junto, from whom our Confusions proceed, a sordid & contemptible junto too, but they have their emissaries & interpreters over a great part of the State, whereby they have allarmed the fears & deranged the common sense of the otherwise Sober & orderly Citizens, beyond any thing you can well conceive. this wild & destructive Spirit appears to abate, but we are Sorry that yr. State has postponed their decision to so late a day–the Suspence of that large State, keeps our Opposition in countenance–some of whom, (men of some note too) have lately declared that if Virginia, do not adopt, they entertain no doubt, but that the Maelcontents of the two States, will prevent the Execution of the proposed Federal plan! this is very rediculouse, yet very disagreeable, nor much to be doubted, but that some of the Western people talk together in this stile. The Struggle we hear of in the Convention of Massachusets, must principally be owing to the redundancy of their numbers, of whom like our Selves, too many must be unacquainted with the Science & principles of Government–Old Sam: Adams amazes me more than any other individuel, because I cannot conceive what can induce one of his years to overlook the immediate necessity of at least begining to make a reform– Mr. R–Lees letter[2] too, tho' wrote with decency, contains more of the air, than the Substance of the Statesman; and in which he has fallen below himself. The Federalist *Publius*, in my Opinion deserves much of his

Country–at first from his sage manner, I took the auther to have been Mr. Jay, but it's now said he is not–that these Nos. are wrote by a small junto, of whos names none are gone out, but that of Coll. Hamilton. be the Authur who may, he has great merit & his papers may be of farther use, than a present inducement to embrace the new System–

I hope Dr. Nisbets discourse on Litterature & address to the Students of this College has met your approbation–he is a good man, a great Scholar, a kind of moving library, with as little vanity or parade on the whole, as any man I ever Saw–yet I am afraid thro' the weakness of our funds, that we must Lose him, as unable to pay his Salary with the various other expences. this College was precipitately undertaken, and the present scarcity of money not sufficiently foreseen, deters many from sending their children abroad tho' the College & boarding which includes Washing makes but 32£ a year. If our New Congress should think of a Federal University, Dr. Nisbet would be the man to lay the foundation of it, but this appears to be at some distance.

Coll. Blain[3] informed me of yr. request that he should give you a Call before he left the City in order to carry a line to me, this he forgot, and knowing your embarrassed situation & the impediments of the City, I charge him only in the account–this letter please to accept in the ruff, as I cannot well copy–therefore cannot correct, tho' sensible of the need.

1. RC, Washington Papers, DLC.
2. For Richard Henry Lee to Governor Edmund Randolph, 16 October, first published on 6 December, see CC:325.
3. Colonel Ephraim Blaine (1741–1808) of Carlisle, a former commissary general of purchases for the Continental Army, was a large merchant and landowner.

544. St. John de Crevecoeur to William Short
New York, 20 February[1]

I have received your Kind Letter of the 9th Octr., and thank you very sincerely for all the Details it contains; Things begins here to wear a better aspect; the turbulent & tumultuous behaviour of the Minority of Pensilvania, *State convention*, had alarmed many People, but the adoption of the new Constitution by Massachusetts gives it such a weight as will in all probability cause it to be universally adopted; next week we expect to hear the glad tidings from New Hampshire; the Legislature of this State has by a majority of only three in the lower house, & of only two in the upper one, appointed a Convention, which is to be held next June; I flatter myself that the State at large, is more strongly Federalists than the Members of both Houses; if the Tide turns here in favor of the new Constitution down goes the Idol of the People, that tool of Popularity of which you have often heard me speak, our Governors I mean; already has Georgia accepted the new form, we have good news from S. Carolina. Virginia is the only state in which the parties pro. & con. seem to run very high; but as the Convention of that State, is to sit very late, I don't doubt but the general example will carry every thing before it;–Mr. P: Henry is in my eyes a very guilty man, for I abhor all Antifederalists & cannot help considering them as people who want to sacrifice the glory, the Prosperity of this Country to their selfish, or rather hellish views; such is I believe Messrs. Lee,[2] Henry & Co.–not so the good Mr. Randolph; his Letter against the Constitution is the best thing that has appeared in favor of it.[3]

Your Letter I carried myself to the Post Office, & found there but one for you, which went by the way of London on the 21st of last December. Mr. Bedlow[4] is so much my friend that you may rely on your Letters being particularly taken care of; how happy I shall be whenever I can inform you, that all the states are come into the new measures: Next week we shall have seven States. Thank you for your Kind notice of my two Boys, God grant they may turn out well. My best respects to Mr. Jefferson & to you, my Dear Sir, my most Sincere friendship & regard

1. RC, Short Papers, DLC. Endorsed: "(Crevecoeur. 29th. March)."
2. Richard Henry Lee.
3. For Edmund Randolph's letter of 10 October to the Virginia House of Delegates, published around 27 December, see CC:385.
4. William Bedlow was postmaster of New York City.

545. Harry Innes to John Brown
Danville, Ky., 20 February[1]

I returned late last evening from Fayette & found Mr. Lacasagne[2] here on his way to Philadelphia. I have snatched up my pen to let you know that I am not altogether thoughtless of you; this letter should be more full but the bearer sets out early this morning & I am obliged to curtail it. I wrote you via Richmond very fully on the subject of your business & what I thought the Court would probably do at the March Term. I have nothing to add on that head but to assure you that everything in my power shall be done for the benefit of yours and your clients interest.

The subject of the Federal Constitution begins to engross the attention of the people & I am endeavoring to bring about a convention on that important subject big with the fate of Kentucky & the Western Country. The objections which have been generally made to the eastward are of a general nature and appear to affect the general interest of United America; they are of too much importance to be looked over. I need not repeat them here as they have often appeared in the Public Print, but my Dr. Sir. the adoption of that Constitution would be the destruction of our young & flourishing country which I shall endeavor to point out concisely to you, viz: All commercial regulations "are to be vested in the General Congress". Our interests and the interests of the Eastern states are so diametrically opposite to each other that there cannot be a ray of hope left to the Western Country to suppose that when once that interest clashes we shall have justice done us. There is no such idea as justice in a Political society when the interests of 59/60 are to be injured thereby and that this will be the case as soon as we have the liberty of exportation, is self evident. Is there an article that the Eastern States can export except Fish oil & rice that we shall not abound in. I say not one. So long therefore as Congress hath this sole power & a majority have the right of deciding on those grand questions we cannot expect to enjoy the navigation of the Mississippi,[3] but another evil equally great will arise from the same point. If ever we are a great and happy people, it must arise from our industry and attention to manufactories. This desirable end can never be brought about so long as the state Legislatures have the power of prohibiting imports, can we suppose that Congress will indulge us with a partial import when we must otherwise procure all our resources from the Eastward, the consequence of which is that we will be impoverished and the Eastern States will draw all our wealth and emigration will totally cease.

The most particular objection is the power of the Judiciary if our separation takes place, there will probably arise disputes between the Citizens of New Jersey, Pennsylvania, Delaware, Maryland, Virginia, & North Carolina and the Citizens of Kentucky; it is hardly to be supposed that each of the Citizens of these States as may have disputes with the Citizens of Kentucky will sue in Kentucky we shall be drawn away to the Federal Court and the Citizens from Kentucky away from their local habitations will nine times out of ten fall a sacrifice to their contests.

there are with me three insurmountable objections to the New Constitution. I wish to see a convention of the people on the subject & to remonstrate against it through the convention of Virginia & if that cannot be done, at least to address. Our local situation must justify any measures which may be adopted upon this occasion, certain that if the Constitution is adopted by us that we shall be the mere vassals of the Congress and the consequences to me are horrible and dreadful.

I would write more, but am obliged to conclude but before I lay down my pen must observe that the Indians continue hostile. 25 horses were taken in the latter end of January when the earth was covered 5 inches of snow. Will Congress do anything for us. Let us hear from you as soon as possible. Mr. Lacasagne will stay some time in Philadelphia & hath promised me to inform you of his lodgings, & to undertake to forward any letter you may send to his care. Mr. Al Parker of Lexington[4] will leave Philadelphia the beginning of April. We have had a most severe winter, which is not ended. I know of no changes among your acquaintances here. We are all well.

1. Typescript, Innes Papers, DLC. Innes (1752–1816) was attorney general for the Kentucky District from 1784 to 1789 and was U.S. district judge for Kentucky from 1789 until his death. Innes and Brown were charter members of "The Political Club of Danville," ardent supporters of Kentucky statehood, and members of various Kentucky statehood conventions.

2. Michael Laccasagne represented Jefferson County in the January 1787 Kentucky statehood convention.

3. For the dispute over the navigation of the Mississippi River, see CC:46, 270.

4. Alexander Parker was one of eight surveyors appointed by Congress pursuant to the Land Ordinance of May 1785 (CDR, 156–63).

546. Publius: The Federalist 58
New York Independent Journal, 20 February

The authorship of this essay was claimed by James Madison and Alexander Hamilton, but it is generally attributed to Madison. This essay was reprinted in the *New York Packet* on 22 February. It is number 58 in the M'Lean edition and number 57 in the newspapers.

For a general discussion of the authorship, circulation, and impact of *The Federalist*, see CC:201, 639; and for the disputed authorship of this essay, see Cooke, xix–xxx, 642–43, and Rutland, *Madison*, X, 261–63.

The FŒDERALIST. No. LVII.
To the People of the State of New-York.

The remaining charge against the House of Representatives which I am to examine, is grounded on a supposition that the number of members will not be augmented from time to time, as the progress of population may demand.

It has been admitted that this objection, if well supported, would have great weight.[1] The following observations will shew that like most other objections against the constitution, it can only proceed from a partial view of the subject; or from a jealousy which discolours and disfigures every object which is beheld.

1. Those who urge the objection seem not to have recollected that the federal constitution will not suffer by a comparison with the state constitutions, in the security provided for a gradual augmentation of the number of representatives. The number which is to prevail in the first instance is declared to be temporary. Its duration is limited to the short term of three years.

Within every successive term of ten years, a census of inhabitants is to be repeated. The unequivocal objects of these regulations are, first, to readjust from time to time the apportionment of representatives to the number of inhabitants; under the single exception that each state shall have one representative at least: Secondly, to augment the number of representatives at the same periods; under the sole limitation, that the whole number shall not exceed one for every thirty thousand inhabitants. If we review the constitutions of the several states, we shall find that some of them contain no determinate regulations on this subject; that others correspond pretty much on this point with the federal constitution; and that the most effectual security in any of them is resolvable into a mere directory provision.

2. As far as experience has taken place on this subject, a gradual increase of representatives under the state constitutions, has at least kept

pace with that of the constituents; and it appears that the former have been as ready to concur in such measures, as the latter have been to call for them.

3. There is a peculiarity in the federal constitution which ensures a watchful attention in a majority both of the people and of their representatives, to a constitutional augmentation of the latter. The peculiarity lies in this, that one branch of the legislature is a representation of citizens; the other of the states: in the former consequently the larger states will have most weight; in the latter, the advantage will be in favour of the smaller states. From this circumstance it may with certainty be inferred, that the larger states will be strenuous advocates for increasing the number and weight of that part of the legislature in which their influence predominates. And it so happens that four only of the largest, will have a majority of the whole votes in the house of representatives. Should the representatives or people therefore of the smaller states oppose at any time a reasonable addition of members, a coalition of a very few states will be sufficient to overrule the opposition; a coalition, which notwithstanding the rivalship and local prejudices which might prevent it on ordinary occasions, would not fail to take place, when not merely prompted upon by common interest, but justified by equity and the principles of the constitution.

It may [be] alledged, perhaps, that the senate would be prompted by like motives to an adverse coalition; and as their concurrence would be indispensable, the just and constitutional views of the other branch might be defeated. This is the difficulty which has probably created the most serious apprehensions in the jealous[2] friends of a numerous representation. Fortunately it is among the difficulties which, existing only in appearance, vanish on a close and accurate inspection. The following reflections will, if I mistake not, be admitted to be conclusive and satisfactory on this point.

Notwithstanding the equal authority which will subsist between the two houses on all legislative subjects, except the originating of money bills, it cannot be doubted that the house composed of the greater number of members, when supported by the more powerful states, and speaking the known and determined sense of a majority of the people, will have no small advantage in a question depending on the comparative firmness of the two houses.

This advantage must be increased by the consciousness felt by the same side, of being supported in its demands, by right, by reason, and by the constitution; and the consciousness on the opposite side, of contending against the force of all these solemn considerations.

It is farther to be considered that in the gradation between the smallest and largest states, there are several which, though most likely in general to arrange themselves among the former, are too little removed in extent and population from the latter, to second an opposition to their just and legitimate pretensions. Hence it is by no means certain that a majority of votes, even in the senate, would be unfriendly to proper augmentations in the number of representatives.

It will not be looking too far to add, that the senators from all the new states may be gained over to the just views of the house of representatives, by an expedient too obvious to be overlooked. As these states will for a great length of time advance in population with peculiar rapidity, they will be interested in frequent reapportionments of the representatives to the number of inhabitants. The large states therefore, who will prevail in the house of representatives, will have nothing to do, but to make reapportionments and augmentations mutually conditions of each other; and the senators from all the most growing states will be bound to contend for the latter, by the interest which their states will feel in the former.

These considerations seem to afford ample security on this subject; and ought alone to satisfy all the doubts and fears which have been indulged with regard to it. Admitting however that, they should all be insufficient to subdue the unjust policy of the smaller states, or their predominant influence in the councils of the senate; a constitutional and infallible resource, still remains with the larger states, by which they will be able at all times to accomplish their just purposes. The house of representatives can not only refuse, but they alone can propose the supplies requisite for the support of government. They in a word hold the purse; that powerful instrument by which we behold in the history of the British constitution, an infant and humble representation of the people, gradually enlarging the sphere of its activity and importance, and finally reducing, as far as it seems to have wished, all the overgrown prerogatives of the other branches of the government. This power over the purse, may in fact be regarded as the most compleat and effectual weapon with which any constitution can arm the immediate representatives of the people, for obtaining a redress of every grievance, and for carrying into effect every just and salutary measure.

But will not the house of representatives be as much interested as the senate in maintaining the government in its proper functions, and will they not therefore be unwilling to stake its existence or its reputation on the pliancy of the senate? Or[3] if such a trial of firmness between the two branches were hazarded, would not the one be as likely first to yield as the other? These questions will create no difficulty with those who reflect, that in all cases the smaller the number and the more permanent and conspicuous the station of men in power, the stronger must be the interest which they will individually feel in whatever concerns the government. Those who represent the dignity of their country in the eyes of other nations, will be particularly sensible to every prospect of public danger, or of a dishonorable stagnation in public affairs. To those causes we are to ascribe the continual triumph of the British house of commons over the other branches of the government, whenever the engine of a money bill has been employed. An absolute inflexibility on the side of the latter, although it could not have failed to involve every department of the state in the general confusion, has neither been apprehended nor experienced. The utmost degree of firmness that can be displayed by the federal senate or president will not be more than equal to a resistance in which they will be supported by constitutional and patriotic principles.

In this review of the constitution of the house of representatives, I have passed over the circumstance of economy which in the present state of affairs might have had some effect in lessening the temporary number of representatives; and a disregard of which would probably have been as rich a theme of declamation against the constitution as has been furnished by the smallness of the number proposed. I omit also any remarks on the difficulty which might be found, under present circumstances, in engaging in the federal service, a large number of such characters as the people will probably elect. One observation however I must be permitted, to add, on this subject, as claiming in my judgment a very serious attention. It is, that in all legislative assemblies, the greater the number composing them may be, the fewer will be the men who will in fact direct their proceedings. In the first place, the more numerous any assembly may be, of whatever characters composed, the greater is known to be the ascendancy of passion over reason. In the next place, the larger the number, the greater will be the proportion of members of limited information and of weak capacities. Now it is precisely on characters of this description that the eloquence and address of the few are known to act with all their force. In the antient republics, where the whole body of the people assembled in person, a single orator, or an artful statesman, was generally seen to rule with as compleat a sway, as if a sceptre had been placed in his single hands. On the same principle the more multitudinous a representative assembly may be rendered, the more it will partake of the infirmities incident to collective meetings of the people. Ignorance will be the dupe of cunning; and passion the slave of sophistry and declamation. The people can never err more than in supposing that by multiplying their representatives, beyond a certain limit, they strengthen the barrier against the government of a few. Experience will forever admonish them that on the contrary, *after securing a sufficient number for the purposes of safety, of local information, and of diffusive sympathy with the whole society*, they will counteract their own views by every addition to their representatives. The countenance of the government may become more democratic; but the soul that animates it will be more oligarchic. The machine will be enlarged, but the fewer and often, the more secret will be the springs by which its motions are directed.

As connected with the objection against the number of representatives, may properly be here noticed, that which has been suggested against the number made competent for legislative business. It has been said that more than a majority ought to have been required for a quorum, and in particular cases, if not in all, more than a majority of a quorum for a decision. That some advantages might have resulted from such a precaution, cannot be denied. It might have been an additional shield to some particular interests, and another obstacle generally to hasty and partial measures. But these considerations are outweighed by the inconveniencies in the opposite scale. In all cases where justice or the general good might require new laws to be passed, or active measures to be pursued, the fundamental principle of free government would be reversed. It would be no longer the majority that would rule; the power would be transferred to the minority. Were the defensive privilege limited to particular cases, an interested minority might take advantage of it to skreen themselves from equitable sacrifices to the general weal, or in particular emergencies to extort unreasonable indulgences. Lastly, it would facilitate and foster the baneful practice of secessions; a practice which has shewn itself even in states where a majority only is required; a practice subversive of all the principles of order and regular government; a practice which leads more directly to public convulsions, and the ruin of popular governments, than any other which has yet been displayed among us.

1. See *The Federalist* 55 (CC:525).
2. Changed to "zealous" in the 1818 edition of *The Federalist*.
3. Changed to "for" in the M'Lean edition.

547. Philadelphiensis X
Philadelphia Freeman's Journal, 20 February[1]

My Fellow-Citizens, If stupid irony, falsehood, scurrility, and abusive language, be sufficient to silence a writer in the cause of freedom, my sentiments must have been suppressed long ago; but that old saying, that *nothing cuts like the truth*, has encouraged me to address you once more. Probably this essay may be more obnoxious to the friends of the proposed plan of government than any of my former publications; and if so, the above saying is farther confirmed. A freeman must have a *little soul* indeed, whose attention can be diverted from its proper object, by the schemes practised by the friends of unlimited dominion. His own happiness, as being connected with the happiness of his fellow-men, ought to be his chiefest good. The *divine founder* of our religion and his beatified followers had no aim but this, and they pursued it with a zeal consistent with its excellence.

If the proposed plan be a good one upon the whole, why should its friends endeavour to prevent investigating its merits or defects? Why should they hurry it on us before we have even read it? Does not this look suspicious like? Is it not a proof that it is the works of darkness, and cannot bear the light? Why should they summon a Convention in Pennsylvania, before the tenth part of the people had time to judge for themselves, or to know whether it was a free or a tyrannical system of government? Why employ bullies to drag some members of the Assembly per force to the House to make a quorum, in order to call a Convention?[2] The answers of these interrogatives are obvious, and the conclusions deduced from them will in time have their proper effect.

The principles of its framers are now clearly understood; the proceedings of the *dark conclave* have undergone an *ordeal* in Maryland, that exhibits the monarchy-men in convention as a set of the basest conspirators that ever disgraced a free country.[3] At the time that these men were plotting the ruin of their country, and forming a system of national cruelty unequalled in the annals of time, the unsuspecting freemen of America were blessing them, were praying for them in their private families, and in their public churches, and looking up to them for relief; they even called the federal convention an *august body, the most excellent assembly of men that ever appeared in the world.*

The *President-general*, who is to be our *king* after this government is established, is vested with powers exceeding those of the most *despotic monarch* we know of in modern times. What a handsome return have these men made to the people of America for their confidence! Through the misconduct of these bold conspirators we have lost the most glorious opportunity that any country ever had to establish a free system of government. America under one purely democratical, would be rendered the happiest and most powerful nation in the universe; but under the proposed one, composed of an *elective king* and a standing army, officered by his sycophants, the starvelings of the Cincinnati, and an aristocratical Congress of the *well-born*, an iota of happiness, freedom or national strength cannot exist. What a pitiful figure will these ungrateful men make in history; who, for the hopes of obtaining some lucrative employment, or of receiving a little more homage from the rest of their fellow creatures, framed a system of oppression that must involve in its consequences the misery of their own offspring? There is but one rational way remaining to prevent themselves from being eye witnesses of a dreadful scene, and that is for them to cease immediately every operation that respects the establishing of this plan of government; and then all parties will join heartily in calling another federal convention, and the peace of the country will be preserved.

One of the members of the virtuous minority of the convention of Massachusetts openly declared in that assembly, that pushing on this accursed system would produce a *civil war*:[4] the freemen of New-England, the best soldiers on the continent, have had their eyes opened, and begin to see through the conspiracy; that sacred palladium of liberty, *the freedom of the press*, has dispelled the cloud, and cleared their understandings. In that state, through the influence of the tyrants of Boston, very little information has reached the people;[5] the *press*, generally speaking, was devoted to the *well-born* and their tools; yet out of near 400 members, of which that convention consisted, only a majority of 19 could be procured, notwithstanding every possible method of overawing, threatening and *bribing* was practised.[6]

I conceive that carrying it by so small a majority, is little better than a rejection; in fact it may prove worse, for the breach is only widened so much the more by it, and truly it was wide enough before. The freemen of Massachusetts will never cowardly surrender their sacred rights and liberties into the hands of one man, or any body of men whatever. They know what freedom is, and they will support it at the risque of their lives and fortunes. Their courage, fortitude, and atchievments in the late war have rendered their character, as friends to liberty, immortal.

The amendments proposed by the president will be another source of mischief; the people cannot be so ignorant as to be deceived by so pitiful a manœuvre. Here is a positive acknowledgement made by one of its advocates, who hopes to be appointed the *little king* if not the *big one*, that it is objectionable; and his amendments are introduced as a blind; the weighty ones are untouched: not a whimper of the extraordinary powers of the *President-general*, the *standing army, the liberty of the press, &c.*[7] No, no! if these *glorious parts* be lopped off, what would become of the monarchy-men? And respecting *internal taxation*,[8] is not his amendment a disgrace to himself, and an insult to the understanding of the people? Mr. Hancock knows, or ought to know at least, that the liberties of the citizens of America are not to be trifled with: his schemes are too flimsey not to be seen through.

The allegiance of freemen to government will ever be a consequence of protection; the Congress of America withdrew their allegiance from the king of Great-Britain when he changed his protection into acts of cruelty; and on the same account the citizens of these United States will not chearfully bear allegiance to the new government; which, instead of protecting them in their sacred rights and privileges, will be a system of tyranny and oppression. The unlimited powers of the new Congress in respect to taxation, are abundantly sufficient to alarm the people. While the state assemblies retained the right of *internal taxation*, the country farmers could not be burdened beyond their abilities; these men being the true representatives of the people, would never attempt to levy an oppressive tax; their own feelings and interests being congenial with those of their constituents, their consent must be withheld when a measure was proposed subversive of public good.

That the new Congress will not be the immediate representatives of the people, that their number is too small, their powers too great, their accountability to the people not properly secured, and above all the *executive* dangerously placed in the hands of one man, who is really a *king*, have been fully illustrated by many able writers, and ably proved in the conventions of this state and Massachusetts by worthy patriots whose names will be revered as long as time shall remain. Upon the whole, my fellow citizens, if the great characters, who are said to advocate this system of government, wish to act consistently, the greatest proof they can give of their love for their country, is to join the rest of their fellow citizens in endeavouring to call another federal convention.

1. Reprinted: Philadelphia *Independent Gazetteer*, 21 February.

2. See CC:546, note 4.

3. See Luther Martin, *Genuine Information* II, Baltimore *Maryland Gazette*, 1 January (CC:401).

4. Perhaps a reference to a speech made by General Samuel Thompson of Topsham, Maine, one of the most ardent Antifederalists in the Massachusetts Convention. He voted against ratification of the Constitution on 6 February. On 21 January Thompson warned: "Don't let us be in a hurry. ... Let us wait to see what our sister States will do. What shall we suffer, if we adjourn the consideration of it [the Constitution], for five or six months?–It is better to do this, than adopt it so hastily. Take care we don't disunite the State.–By uniting we stand, by dividing we fall." This speech was first published in the *Massachusetts Centinel* on 30 January, and reprinted in Philadelphia in the *Pennsylvania Packet* on 15 February.

5. For example, Antifederalists charged that the "Dissent of the Minority of the Pennsylvania Convention" had not been printed in Boston while the Massachusetts Convention was in session (CC:353).

6. On 21 January the *Boston Gazette* published this item which was reprinted in six Philadelphia newspapers by 19 February: "*Bribery and Corruption!!!* The most diabolical plan is on foot to corrupt the Members of the Convention who oppose the adoption of the New Constitution.–Large sums of money have been brought from a neighbouring State for that purpose, contributed by the wealthy;–if so, is it not probable there may be collections for the same accursed purpose nearer home?"

7. On 31 January Governor John Hancock, president of the Massachusetts Convention, who it was rumored would be President or Vice President of the United States under the new Constitution, presented to the state Convention an act of ratification that included nine recommendatory amendments. The amendments and Hancock's speech were written by some of the Convention's Federalist leaders who promised not to oppose Hancock's reelection in the upcoming gubernatorial election. (See CC:508 and CC:Vol. 3, Appendix I, "John Hancock and the Constitution," 3 January-4 February.)

8. For the text of this amendment, see CC:508.

548. Marcus I
Norfolk and Portsmouth Journal, 20 February

"Marcus," a response to George Mason's objections to the Constitution (CC:276), was written by James Iredell (1751-1799), a resident of Edenton and one of the leading lawyers in North Carolina. Born in England, he went to Edenton, N.C., in 1768 as a customs official. Iredell studied law with Samuel Johnston, whose sister he married in 1773. He was a state judge in 1777 and 1778, attorney general from 1779 to 1781, and a member of the Council of State in 1788. In 1787 the state Assembly authorized him to compile and revise the state's laws, a task he completed in 1791 (Evans 23641). Throughout the 1780s, Iredell, Johnston, Archibald Maclaine, and several others opposed the issuance of paper money, the banishment of Loyalists and confiscation and sale of their property, and the refusal of the state to honor the provisions of the Treaty of Peace concerning debts owed to British citizens and Loyalists.

Iredell was an ardent supporter of the Constitution. In November 1787 Iredell had written the resolutions of the Chowan and Edenton meeting and the presentment of the Edenton grand jury (see CC:560 and McRee, II, 180-83). In July

1789 he described some of the feelings that motivated his writings on the Constitution, including "Marcus": "My Zeal I fear far outran my discretion, for I was fully convinced in my own mind that the fate of America depended on the adoption of the Constitution in that particular period, and I had long been ashamed of the disgraceful light in which we appeared, not only to every other Country in the world, but even to ourselves" (to Baron de Poellnitz, 25 July 1789, Iredell Papers, NcD). In all likelihood, this feeling led him to accept his only elective office–delegate to the Hillsborough Convention–where, along with Maclaine and Governor Johnston, he led the Federalist forces in their unsuccessful attempt to ratify the Constitution in July and August 1788. Iredell was an associate justice of the U.S. Supreme Court from 1790 until his death.

George Mason's objections to the Constitution, based on his criticisms in the Constitutional Convention, were originally published in the *Massachusetts Centinel* and *Virginia Journal* in mid-November (CC:276). They were widely reprinted in newspapers, in a magazine, in two pamphlet anthologies, and as a broadside. The *Massachusetts Centinel* version, which had a wider circulation and was used by "Marcus," omitted Mason's objection to the constitutional provision allowing a simple majority of Congress to enact commercial legislation. The omission was noted in some newspapers, but "Marcus" never mentioned or answered this objection.

On 13 February John M'Lean, printer of the weekly *Norfolk and Portsmouth Journal*, received Iredell's manuscript. Two days later M'Lean received "some material omissions respecting it." These omissions were "strictly attended to and inserted in their proper place." The manuscript, dated "*January* 1788," was accompanied by "an half Joe for four Books of the Federalist" and for a subsidy for printing the manuscript. (The New York City firm of John and Archibald M'Lean published *The Federalist*. An advertisement in the *Norfolk and Portsmouth Journal*, published in January, announced that the printer was taking subscriptions for *The Federalist* at a cost of one dollar. A "half Joe" was equal to eight dollars. Thus, Iredell paid M'Lean four dollars for *The Federalist* and four dollars to publish "Marcus.") M'Lean informed Iredell that the length of the manuscript would force him to omit some advertising, and that he was publishing "Marcus" in preference to "Several other political pieces [that] have been sent for Appearance in my next, but defective of Marcus' Merit and Argument...." Because of these factors, M'Lean had "no doubt" that Iredell would make further payments to compensate him for "the Attention and pecuniary disadvantages" of publication (M'Lean to Iredell, 15 February, Iredell Papers, NcD).

M'Lean published the first of five unnumbered installments of "Marcus" in the *Norfolk and Portsmouth Journal* on 20 February; the subsequent installments appeared on 27 February, 5, 12, and 19 March (CC:571, 596, 616, 630). The essay was reprinted in at least one North Carolina newspaper, but no copies are extant (see Iredell to Baron de Poellnitz, [15 April?], Charles E. Johnson Collection, Nc-Ar). The essay, without the author's preface, was reprinted as a pamphlet by Hodge and Wills of Newbern. On 27 March the printers advertised the sale of the pamphlet for two-and-a-half shillings in their newspaper, the *State Gazette of North Carolina*. (Earlier advertisements might have appeared in no-longer-extant issues.) The twelve-page pamphlet, also containing "Publicola" by Archibald Maclaine (CC:633, 648), is entitled: *Answers to Mr. Mason's Objections to the New Constitution Recommended by the Late Convention at Philadelphia. By Marcus. To Which Is Added, An Address to the Freemen of North-Carolina. By Publicola* (Evans 45276). There are no significant differences between the newspaper and pamphlet versions. A copy of the pamphlet at Harvard University (Evans 45276) is annotated and corrected by James Iredell. Significant annotations have been footnoted.

David Witherspoon, a Newbern lawyer, praised the essay in a letter to Iredell on 3 April: "I have read with very great pleasure your answers to Mr. Masons

objections, and surely every man who reads them & on whom Mr. Masons observations or indeed the arguments of those in opposition in general have had any
effect, must be convinced that the objections to the constitution are without foundation. ... Your publication has been made, I believe very correctly by Mr. Hodge
I was sorry that my business called me out of town while it was in hand You were
very soon known to be the author by what means I do not know" (Iredell Papers,
NcD).

MR. M'LEAN, *I beg the favour of you to publish in your paper, the following
Answers to Mr. Mason's Objections to the New Constitution. Each objection is
inserted in his own words (as taken from a printed newspaper) before the answer given
to it, so that the merits of both will be fairly before the Public. –Nothing can be more
easy than the business of objecting, and as mankind are generally much more apt to
find fault than to approve its success is commonly proportionable; but I trust the good
sense of America, at this awful period, will exert itself to judge coolly and impartially,
especially as the dissenting gentlemen appear to differ as much from each other as from
the respectable majority who have recommended the New Constitution to the public. –I
am Sir, your very humble servant,*

The AUTHOR.

Answers to Mr. Mason's *Objections* to the New Constitution, Recommended by the late Convention at Philadelphia.

Ist. Objection.

"There is no declaration of rights, and the laws of the general government being paramount to the laws and constitutions of the several States,
the declarations of rights in the separate States are no security; nor are the
people secured even in the enjoyment of the benefit of the common law,
which stands here upon no other foundation than its having been adopted
by the respective acts forming the constitutions of the several States."

Answer.

1. *As to the want of a Declaration of Rights.*
The introduction of these in England, from which the idea was originally taken, was in consequence of usurpations of the Crown, contrary, as
was conceived, to the principles of their government. But there, no original constitution is to be found, and the only meaning of a declaration of
rights in that country is, that in certain particulars specified, the Crown
had no authority to act. Could this have been necessary, had there been a
Constitution in being, by which it could have been clearly discerned
whether the Crown had such authority or not? Had the people by a solemn
instrument delegated particular powers to the Crown at the formation of
their government, surely the Crown which in that case could claim under
that instrument only, could not have contended for more power than was
conveyed by it. So it is in regard to the new Constitution here: The future
government which may be formed under that authority, certainly cannot
act beyond the warrant of that authority. As well might they attempt to
impose a King upon America, as go one step in any other respect beyond

the terms of their institution. The question then only is, whether more power will be vested in the future government than is necessary for the general purposes of the Union. This may occasion a ground of dispute—but after expressly defining the powers that are to be exercised, to say that they shall exercise no other powers (either by a general or particular enumeration) would seem to me both nugatory and ridiculous. As well might a Judge when he condemns a man to be hanged, give strong injunctions to the Sheriff that he should not be beheaded.[a]

2. As to the common law, it is difficult to know what is meant by that part of the objection. So far as the people are now entitled to the benefit of the common law, they certainly will have a right to enjoy it under the new constitution, till altered by the general Legislature, which even in this point has some cardinal limits assigned to it. What are most acts of Assembly but a deviation in some degree from the principles of the common law? The people are expressly secured (contrary to Mr. Mason's wishes) against *ex post facto* laws, so that the tenure of any property at any time held under the principles of the common law, cannot be altered by any act of the future general legislature. The principles of the common law, as they now apply, must surely always hereafter apply, except in those particulars in which express authority is given by this Constitution; in no other particular can the Congress have authority to change it, and I believe it cannot be shewn that any one power of this kind given is unnecessarily given, or that the power would answer its proper purpose if the Legislature was restricted from any innovations on the principles of the common law, which would not in all cases suit the vast variety of incidents that might arise out of it.

IId. Objection.

"In the House of Representatives there is not the substance but the shadow only of representation, which can never produce proper information in the Legislature, or inspire confidence in the people; the laws will therefore be generally made by men little concerned in, and unacquainted with, their effects and consequences."

Answer.

This is a mere matter of calculation. It is said the weight of this objection was in a great measure removed by altering the number of 40000 to 30000 constituents. To shew the discontented nature of man, some have objected to the number of representatives as being too large. I leave to every man's judgment whether the number is not sufficiently respectable, and whether if that number be sufficient it would have been right, in the very infancy of this government, to burthen the people with a great additional expence to answer no good purpose.[b]

IIId. Objection.

"The Senate have the power of altering all money bills, and of originating appropriations of money, and the salaries of the officers of their own appointment, in conjunction with the President of the United States; although they are not the Representatives of the people, or amenable to them. These, with their other great powers (*viz.* their powers in the appointment of ambassadors and all public officers, in making treaties, and in trying all impeachments), their influence upon and connection with the Supreme Executive from these causes; their duration of office, and their being a constant existent body almost continually sitting, joined with their being one complete branch of the Legislature, will destroy any balance in the government, and enable them to accomplish what usurpations they please upon the rights and liberties of the people."

Answer.

This objection respecting the dangerous power of the Senate, is of that kind which may give rise to a great deal of gloomy prediction, without any solid foundation. An imagination indulging itself in chimerical fears, upon the disappointment of a favourite plan may point out danger arising from any system of government whatever, even if Angels were to have the administration of it; since I presume, none but the Supreme Being himself is altogether perfect, and of course every other species of beings may abuse any delegated portion of power. This sort of visionary scepticism therefore will lead us to this alternative, either to have no government at all, or to form the best system we can, making allowance for human imperfection. In my opinion, the fears as to the power of the Senate are altogether groundless, as to any probability of their being either able or willing to do any important mischief. My reasons are–

1. Because tho' they are not immediately to represent the people, yet they are to represent the Representatives of the people, who are annually chosen, and it is therefore probable, the most popular, or confidential persons in each State, will be elected members of the Senate.

2. Because one third of the Senate are to be chosen as often as the immediate Representatives of the people, and as the President can act in no case from which any great danger can be apprehended without the concurrence of two-thirds, let us think ever so ill of the designs of the President, and the danger of a combination of power among a standing body generally associated with him, unless we suppose every one of them to be base and infamous (a supposition, thank God, bad as human nature is, not within the verge of the slightest probability), we have reason to believe that the one third newly introduced every second year, will bring with them from the immediate body of the people a sufficient portion of patriotism and independence to check any exorbitant designs of the rest.

3. Because in their legislative capacity they can do nothing without the concurrence of the House of Representatives, and we need look no further than England for a clear proof of the amazing consequence which Representatives of the people bear in a free government. There the King (who is hereditary, and therefore not so immediately interested, according to nar-

row views of interest which commonly govern Kings, to consult the welfare of his people) has the appointment to almost every office in the government, many of which are of high dignity and great pecuniary value; has the creation of as many Peers as he pleases, is not restricted from bestowing places on the members of both Houses of Parliament, and has a direct negative on all bills, besides the power of dissolving the Parliament at his pleasure. In theory would not any one say this power was enormous enough to destroy any balance in the Constitution? Yet what does the history of that country tell us?–That so great is the natural power of the House of Commons (tho' a very imperfect representation of the people, and a large proportion of them actually purchasing their seats), that ever since the Revolution the Crown has continually aimed to corrupt them by the disposal of places and pensions; that without their hearty concurrence it found all the wheels of government perpetually clogged; and, that notwithstanding this, in great critical emergencies, the members have broke through the trammels of power and interest, and, by speaking the sense of the people (tho' so imperfectly representing them) either forced an alteration of measures, or made it necessary for the Crown to dissolve them. If their power under these circumstances, is so great, what would it be if their Representation was perfect and their members could hold no appointments, and at the same time had a security for their seats? The danger of a destruction of the balance would be perhaps on the popular side, notwithstanding the hereditary tenure and weighty prerogatives of the Crown, and the permanent station and great wealth and consequence of the Lords. Our Representatives therefore, being an adequate and fair representation of the people, and they being expressly excluded from the possession of any places, and not holding their existence upon any precarious tenure must have vast influence; and considering that in every popular government the danger of faction is often very serious and alarming, if such a danger could not be checked in its instant operation by some other power more independent of the immediate passions of the people, and capable therefore of thinking with more coolness, the government might be destroyed by a momentary impulse of passion, which the very members who indulged it might for ever afterwards in vain deplore. The institution of the Senate seems well calculated to answer this salutary purpose. Excluded as they are from places themselves, they appear to be as much above the danger of personal temptation as they can be. They have no permanent interest as a body to detach them from the general welfare, since six years is the utmost period of their existence, unless their respective legislatures are sufficiently pleased with their conduct to re-elect them. This power of re-election is itself a great check upon abuse, because if they have ambition to continue members of the Senate, they can only gratify this ambition by acting agreeably to the opinion of their constituents. The House of Representatives, as immediately representing the people, are to originate all money bills. This I think extremely right, and it is certainly a very capital acquisition to the popular Representative. But what harm can arise from the Senate, who are nearly a popular Representative also, proposing amendments when those amendments must be concurred with by the original proposers? The wisdom of the Senate may sometimes point out amendments, the propriety of which the other House may be very sensible of, though they had not occurred to themselves. There is no great danger of any body of men suffering by too eager an adoption of any amendment proposed to any system of their own. The probability is stronger of their being too tenacious of their original opinion, however erroneous, than of their profiting by the wise information of any other persons whatever. Human nature is so constituted, and therefore I think we may safely confide in the admission of a free intercourse of opinion on the detail of business, as well as to taxation as to other points. Our House of Representatives surely could not have such reason to dread the power of a Senate circumstanced as ours must be, as the House of Commons in England the permanent authority of the Peers, and therefore a jealousy which may be well grounded in the one case, would be entirely ill directed in the other. For similar reasons, I dread not any power of originating appropriations of money as mentioned in the objection. While the concurrence of the other House must be had, and as that must necessarily be the most weighty in the government, I think no danger is to be apprehended. The Senate has no such authority as to awe or influence the House of Representatives, and it will be as necessary for one as for the other that proper active measures should be pursued. And in regard to appropriations of money, occasions for such appropriations may, on account of their concurrence with the executive power, occur to the Senate, which would not to the House of Representatives; and therefore if the Senate were precluded from laying any such proposals before the House of Representatives, the government might be embarrassed, and it ought ever to be remembered, that in our views of distant and chimerical dangers we ought not to hazard our very existence as a people, by proposing such restrictions as may prevent the exertion of any necessary power.–The power of the Senate in the appointment of Ambassadors, &c. is designed as a check upon the President.–They must be appointed in some manner. If the appointment was by the President alone, or by the President and a Privy Council (Mr. Mason's favourite plan), an objection to such a system would have appeared much more plausible. It would have been said that this was approaching too much towards Monarchical power, and if this new Privy Council had been like all I have ever heard of it would have afforded little security against an abuse of power in the President. It ought to be shewn by reason and probability (not bold assertion) how this concurrence of power with the President can make the Senate so dangerous. It is as good an argument to say that it will not, as that it will.[c] The power of making treaties is so important, that it would have been highly dangerous to vest it in the Executive alone, and would have been the subject of much greater clamour. From the nature of the thing, it could not be vested in the popular Representative. It must therefore have been provided for, with the Senate's concurrence, or the concurrence of a Privy Council (a thing which I believe nobody has been mad enough to propose), or the power, the greatest Monarchical power that can be exercised, must have been vested in a manner that would have excited universal indignation, in the President alone. As to the power of trying impeachments, let Mr. Mason shew where this power could more properly have been placed. It is a necessary power in every free government, since even the Judges of the Supreme Court of Judicature themselves may require a trial, and other public officers might have too much influence before an ordinary and common Court. And what probability is there that such a Court acting in so solemn a manner, should abuse its power (especially as it is wisely provided that their sentences shall extend only to removal from office and incapacitation) more than any other Court? The argument as to the possible abuse of power, as I have before suggested, will reach all delegation of power whatever, since all power may be abused where fallible beings are to execute it; but we must take as much caution as we can, being careful at the same time not to be too wise to do any thing at all. The bold assertions at the end of this objection are mere declamation, and till some reason is assigned for them, I shall take the liberty to rely upon the reasons I have stated above, as affording a belief that the popular Representative must for ever be the most weighty in this government, and of course that apprehensions of danger from such a Senate are altogether ill founded.

(To be continued.)

(*a*) It appears to me a very just remark of Mr. Wilson in his celebrated speech,[1] that a Bill of Rights would have been dangerous, as implying that without such a reservation the Congress would have authority in the cases enumerated, so that if any had been omitted (and who would undertake to recite all the state and individual rights not relinquished by the new Constitution?) they might have been considered at the mercy of the general Legislature.

(*b*) I have understood it was considered at the Convention, that the proportion of one Representative to 30,000 Constituents, would produce at the very first nearly the number that would be satisfactory to Mr. Mason. So that I presume this reason was wrote before the material alteration was made from 40,000 to 30,000, which is said to have taken place the very last day, just before the signature.[2]

(*c*) It seems, by the letter which has been published of Mr. Elseworth and Mr. Sherman,[3] as if one reason of giving a share in these appointments to the Senate was, that persons in what are called the lesser States might have an equal chance for such appointments, in proportion to their merit, with those in the larger, an advantage that could only be expected from a body in which the States were equally represented.

1. For James Wilson's speech on 6 October, see CC:134.

2. For the change from 40,000 to 30,000, which took place on 17 September after the Constitution had been engrossed and read in the Convention, see "George Washington in the Constitutional Convention," CC:233. Mason first wrote out his objections on the back of his copy of the Committee of Style report. The Committee had reported on 12 September. On 7 October Mason sent a manuscript copy of his objections to Washington and added a footnote at the end of this objection, which was printed in the *Massachusetts Centinel* version of his objections and paraphrased in the *Virginia Journal* version: "This Objection has been in some Degree lessened by an Amendment, often before refused, and at last made by an Erasure, after the Engrossment upon Parchment, of the word *forty*, and inserting *thirty*, in the 3d. Clause of the 2d. Section of the 1st. Article" (CC:138-B).

3. In their 26 September letter transmitting the Constitution to the governor of Connecticut, Constitutional Convention delegates Roger Sherman and Oliver Ellsworth wrote: "The equal representation of the states in the senate, and the voice of that branch in the appointment to offices, will secure the rights of the lesser as well as the greater states." The letter was printed on 25 October and widely reprinted (CC:192).

549. James Madison to Edmund Pendleton
New York, 21 February[1]

The receipt of your favor of the 29th Ult.[2] which did not come to hand till a few days ago was rendered particularly agreeable to me by the prospect it gives of a thorough reestablishment of your health. I indulge the reflection and the hope that it denotes a remaining energy in the Constitution, which will long defend it against the gradual waste of time.

Your representation of the politics of the State coincides with the information from every other quarter. Great fluctuations and divisions of opinion, naturally result in Virginia from the causes which you describe; but they are not the less ominous on that account. I have for some time been persuaded that the question on which the proposed Constitution must turn, is the simple one whether the Union shall or shall not be continued. There is in my opinion no middle ground to be taken. The opposition with some has disunion assuredly for its object; and with all for its real tendency. Events have demonstrated that no coalition can ever take place in favor of a new plan among the adversaries to the proposed one. The grounds of objection among the non-signing members of the Convention are by no means the same. The disapproving members who were absent but who have since published their objections differ irreconcileably from each of them. The writers against the Constitution are as little agreed with one another; and the principles which have been disclosed by the several minorities where the Constitution has not been unanimously adopted, are as heterogeneous as can be imagined. That of Massachussetts, as far as I can learn was averse to any Government that deserved the name, and it is certain looked no farther than to reject the Constitution in toto and return home in triumph. Out of the vast number which composed it there was scarce a man of respectability, and not a single one capable of leading the formidable band.[3] The men of abilities, of property, of character, with every judge, lawyer of eminence, and the Clergy of all Sects, were with scarce an exception deserving notice, as unanimous in that State as the same description of characters are divided and opposed to one another in Virginia. This contrast does not arise from circumstances of local interest, but from causes which will in my opinion produce much regret hereafter in the Opponents in Virginia, if they should succeed in their opposition.– N. Hampshire is now in Convention. It is expected that the result will be in favor of the Constitution. R. Island takes no notice of the matter. N. York is much divided. The weight of abilities and of property is on the side of the Constitution. She must go with the Eastern States let the direction be what it may. By a vessel just from Charlestown we understand that opposition will be made there. Mr. Lowndes is the leader of it.[4]

A *British* packet brings a picture of affairs in France which indicates some approaching events in that Kingdom which may almost amount to a revolution in the form of its Government. The authority is in itself suspicious; but it coincides with a variety of proofs that the spirit of liberty has made a progress which must lead to some remarkable conclusion of the scene. The Dutch patriots seem to have been the victims partly of their own folly, and partly of something amiss in their friends. The present state of that Confederacy is or ought to be a very emphatic lessen to the U. States. The want of Union and an capable Government is the source of all their calamities; and particularly of that dependence on foreign powers, which is as dishonorable to their character as it is destructive of their tranquility.

1. RC, Madison Papers, DLC.

2. This letter has not been located. A list of letters found in the Madison Miscellany at the Library of Congress, probably kept by Peter Force, reveals that Pendleton wrote a two-page letter to Madison from his home in Edmundsbury on 29 January. The summary reads: "The reception of the proposed Constitution by the Virginia Assembly. The feeling among the middle and lower classes. Mr. Pendleton favors it, but is open to conviction after hearing all that can be said. The importance of Mr. Madisons presence. The feeling in other southern States. Taxes lessened. The District Court Bill" (Rutland, *Madison*, X, 444n).

3. This sentence was enclosed in parentheses at a later date, probably by William C. Rives who published an edition of Madison's papers in 1865 (*ibid.*, xxiii, 533). The sentence was omitted from the Rives edition.

4. For Rawlins Lowndes's opposition to the Constitution in the South Carolina House of Representatives, see David Ramsay to Benjamin Lincoln, 29 January (CC:482).

550. Gouverneur Morris to James LaCaze
Williamsburg, Va., 21 February (excerpt)[1]

. . . I come now to Politics in which during the last Summer I had a greater Share than I expected ever to have had again when last I quitted the public Theatre.[2] . . .

To come then at last to our poor Politics in this obscure Corner[.] You will long ere this have seen the Constitution proposed for the United States. I intended to have sent you a Copy immediately after the formation but have no good Opportunity and it was not worth while to make you pay the Packet postage[.] This Paper has been the Subject of infinite Investigation Disputation and Declamation. While some have boasted it as a Work from Heaven others have given it a less righteous origin and charged it to the old great Devil. Medio tutissimus ibis I have many Reasons to believe that it was the Work of plain honest Men and such I think it will appear. Faulty it must be for what is perfect? But if adopted Experience will I think shew that its Faults are just the Reverse of what are supposed. As Yet this Paper is but a dead Letter. Pensilvania Delaware New Jersey Connecticutt and Georgia have adopted it. We wait impatiently the Result of their Deliberations in Massachusetts. Should that State also adopt it which I hope and beleive there will then be little Doubt of a general Acquiescence but otherwise it may be a tedious and Difficult Business. Should it however take Effect the Affairs of this Country will put on a much better Aspect than they have yet worn and America will soon be as much respected abroad as she has for some Time past been disregarded.

1. FC, Gouverneur Morris Collection, NNC. The letter is signed "G.M." and endorsed "Dr[aft] Letter 21 feby. 1788 to/James LaCaze." The first four pages of this eight-page letter are missing. The letter was written from Virginia, where Gouverneur and Robert Morris had been since November 1787 (CC:255). On Sunday, 17 February, the Morrises were in Portsmouth, from which place Robert Morris wrote his wife, informing her that he and Gouverneur Morris planned to go to Williamsburg and Richmond at "the latter end of this Week" (to Mary Morris, Robert Morris Collection, CSmH). On 24 March William Finnie of Williamsburg wrote that the Morrises had spent six weeks in Williamsburg (to Horatio Gates, Gates Mss, NN.).

During the Revolution James LaCaze and a partner established a Philadelphia branch of Mercy and LaCaze and Fils of Cadiz. LaCaze became a friend of Gouverneur Morris and had business dealings with both Morrises from at least 1783 to 1790. On page 5 of his letter to LaCaze, Gouverneur Morris wrote that, due to a temporary cash flow problem, Robert Morris was unable to pay his debts to LaCaze, who was now based in France with his own company.

This letter fragment was one of many letters published by Jared Sparks in his three-volume edition of *The Life of Gouverneur Morris*... (Boston, 1832), I, 290–91. As was his practice, Sparks deleted words, phrases, and sentences; altered punctuation; and even substituted one word for another.

2. Morris, an active member of the Constitutional Convention from May to September 1787, had resigned as the Confederation's Assistant Superintendent of Finance in 1785.

551. Brutus XIII
New York Journal, 21 February[1]

Having in the two preceding numbers,[2] examined the nature and tendency of the judicial power, as it respects the explanation of the constitution, I now proceed to the consideration of the other matters, of which it has cognizance.–The next paragraph extends its authority, to all cases, in law and equity, arising under the laws of the United States. This power, as I understand it, is a proper one. The proper province of the judicial power, in any government, is, as I conceive, to declare what is the law of the land. To explain and enforce those laws, which the supreme power or legislature may pass; but not to declare what the powers of the legislature are. I suppose the cases in equity, under the laws, must be so construed, as to give the supreme court not only a legal, but equitable jurisdiction of cases which may be brought before them, or in other words, so, as to give them, not only the powers which are now exercised by our courts of law, but those also, which are now exercised by our court of chancery. If this be the meaning, I have no other objection to the power, than what arises from the undue extension of the legislative power. For, I conceive that the judicial power should be commensurate with the legislative. Or, in other words, the supreme court should have authority to determine questions arising under the laws of the union.

The next paragraph which gives a power to decide in law and equity, on all cases arising under treaties, is unintelligible to me. I can readily comprehend what is meant by deciding a case under a treaty. For as treaties will be the law of the land, every person who have rights or privileges secured by treaty, will have aid of the courts of law, in recovering them. But I do not understand, what is meant by equity arising under a treaty. I presume every right which can be claimed under a treaty, must be claimed by virtue of some article or clause contained in it, which gives the right in plain and obvious words; or at least, I conceive, that the rules for explaining treaties, are so well ascertained, that there is no need of having recourse to an equitable construction. If under this power, the courts are to explain treaties, according to what they conceive are their spirit, which is nothing less than a power to give them whatever extension they may judge proper, it is a dangerous and improper power. The cases affecting ambassadors, public ministers, and consuls–of admiralty and maritime jurisdiction; controversies to which the United States are a party, and controversies between states, it is proper should be under the cognizance of the courts of the union, because none but the general government, can, or ought to pass laws on their subjects. But, I conceive the clause which extends the power of the judicial to controversies arising between a state and citizens of another state, improper in itself, and will, in its exercise, prove most pernicious and destructive.

It is improper, because it subjects a state to answer in a court of law, to the suit of an individual. This is humiliating and degrading to a government, and, what I believe, the supreme authority of no state ever submitted to.

The states are now subject to no such actions. All contracts entered into by individuals with states, were made upon the faith and credit of the states, and the individuals never had in contemplation any compulsory mode of obliging the government to fulfil its engagements.

The evil consequences that will flow from the exercise of this power, will best appear by tracing it in its operation. The constitution does not direct the mode in which an individual shall commence a suit against a state or the manner in which the judgement of the court shall be carried into execution, but it gives the legislature full power to pass all laws which shall be proper and necessary for the purpose. And they certainly must make provision for these purposes, or otherwise the power of the judicial will be nugatory. For, to what purpose will the power of a judicial be, if they have no mode, in which they can call the parties before them? Or of what use will it be, to call the parties to answer, if after they have given judgment, there is no authority to execute the judgment? We must, therefore, conclude, that the legislature will pass laws which will be effectual in this head. An individual of one state will then have a legal remedy against a state for any demand he may have against a state to which he does not belong. Every state in the union is largely indebted to individuals. For the payment of these debts they have given notes payable to the bearer. At least this is the case in this state. Whenever a citizen of another state becomes possessed of one of these notes, he may commence an action in the supreme court of the general government; and I cannot see any way in which he can be prevented from recovering. It is easy to see, that when this once happens, the notes of the state will pass rapidly from the hands of citizens of the state to those of other states.

And when the citizens of other states possess them, they may bring suits against the state for them, and by this means, judgments and executions may be obtained against the state for the whole amount of the state debt. It is certain the state, with the utmost exertions it can make, will not be able to discharge the debt she owes, under a considerable number of years, perhaps with the best management, it will require twenty or thirty years to discharge it. This new system will protract the time in which the ability of the state will enable them to pay off their debt, because all the funds of the state will be transferred to the general government, except those which arise from internal taxes.

The situation of the states will be deplorable. By this system, they will surrender to the general government, all the means of raising money, and at the same time, will subject themselves to suits at law, for the recovery of the debts they have contracted in effecting the revolution.

The debts of the individual states will amount to a sum, exceeding the domestic debt of the United States; these will be left upon them, with power in the judicial of the general government, to enforce their payment, while the general government will possess an exclusive command of the most productive funds, from which the states can derive money, and a command of every other source of revenue paramount to the authority of any state.

It may be said that the apprehension that the judicial power will operate in this manner is merely visionary, for that the legislature will never pass laws that will work these effects. Or if they were disposed to do it, they cannot provide for levying an execution on a state, for where will the officer find property whereon to levy?

To this I would reply, if this is a power which will not or cannot be executed, it was useless and unwise to grant it to the judicial. For what purpose is a power given which it is imprudent or impossible to exercise? If it be improper for a government to exercise a power, it is improper they should be vested with it. And it is unwise to authorise a government to do what they cannot effect.

As to the idea that the legislature cannot provide for levying an execution on a state, I believe it is not well founded. I presume the last paragraph of the 8th section of article 1, gives the Congress express power to pass any laws they may judge proper and necessary for carrying into execution the power vested in the judicial department. And they must exercise this power, or otherwise the courts of justice will not be able to carry into effect the authorities with which they are invested. For the constitution does not direct the mode in which the courts are to proceed, to bring parties before them, to try causes, or to carry the judgment of the courts into execution. Unless they are pointed out by law, how are they to proceed, in any of the cases of which they have cognizance? They have the same authority to establish regulations in respect to these matters, where a state is a party, as where an individual is a party. The only difficulty is, on whom shall process be served, when a state is a party, and how shall execution be levied. With regard to the first, the way is easy, either the executive or legislative of the state may be notified, and upon proof being made of the service of the notice, the court may proceed to a hearing of the cause. Execution may be levied on any property of the state, either real or personal. The treasury may be seized by the officers of the general government, or any lands the property of the state, may be made subject to seizure and sale to satisfy any judgment against it. Whether the estate of any individual citizen may not be made answerable for the discharge of judgments against the state, may be worth consideration. In some corporations this is the case.

If the power of the judicial under this clause will extend to the cases above stated, it will, if executed, produce the utmost confusion, and in its progress, will crush the states beneath its weight. And if it does not extend to these cases, I confess myself utterly at a loss to give it any meaning. For if the citizen of one state, possessed of a written obligation, given in pursuance of a solemn act of the legislature, acknowledging a debt due to the bearer, and promising to pay it, cannot recover in the supreme court, I can conceive of no case in which they can recover. And it appears to me ridiculous to provide for obtaining judgment against a state, without giving the means of levying execution.

1. This essay was not reprinted. On Thursday, 14 February, the *New York Journal* announced that the publication of "Brutus" XIII was "unavoidably postponed to next Thursday."

2. "Brutus" XI–XII, 31 January, 7, 14 February (CC:489, 510, 530).

552. A Yankee
Pennsylvania Mercury, 21 February

"A Yankee" responds to verse in the Philadelphia *Independent Gazetteer*, 19 February, that followed a report that the Massachusetts Convention had ratified the Constitution:

> "In consequence of which the Boston folks had a GRAND Procession–
> There they went up, up, up,
> And there they went down, down, downy,
> There they went backwards and forwards,
> And poop for *Boston* towny!

> "This *grand intelligence* reached Philadelphia, on Saturday evening last, when the bells of Christ Church were rung–
> Here they rung, rung, rung,
> And here they bobb'd about, abouty.
> Here were *doubles* and *majors* and *bobs*,
> And heigh for *'delphia* city!"

In March Francis Hopkinson of Philadelphia satirized this verse in an unpublished piece entitled "Literary Intelligence Extraordinary" in which he charged that the author was a professor at the University of Pennsylvania, a "Dr D-." Hopkinson's biographer believed that "Dr D-" was Dr. George Duffield (1732–1790), pastor of Philadelphia's Third Presbyterian Church (George Everett Hastings, *The Life and Works of Francis Hopkinson* [Chicago, 1926], 402–4). Duffield, however, was not a member of the University faculty at this time.

The verse was reprinted in six newspapers, all of which also reprinted "A Yankee": N.H. (2), Mass. (3), N.Y. (1). "A Yankee" was reprinted thirty-one times by 21 April: Vt. (2), N.H. (2), Mass. (6), R.I. (3), Conn. (5), N.Y. (2), N.J. (1), Pa. (1), Md. (1), Va. (4), S.C. (2), Ga. (2). Only eight newspapers printed "A Yankee's" introductory statement: Mass. (3), Conn. (2), N.Y. (1), Md. (1), S.C. (1). "A Yankee" was also reprinted by John Reid of New York in *Four Excellent New Songs, Called Yankee Doodle...* (Evans 45260).

Mr. Humphreys, The Independent Gazetteer has been long famous for its Attic salt; and it now lays a claim to Parnassian wit. I am sorry, however, that an Hibernian muse should be invoked to give an account of the proceedings at Boston; for, however meritorious Dean Swift's "O my kitten, my kitten, my deary,"[1] may be, yet *Yankee doodle* seems best adapted to this country, and you know we ought to encourage our own *spiritu* as well as *manu* factures. So please to accept the following from

A YANKEE.

The 'Vention did in Boston meet,
But State-house could not hold 'em,
So then they went to Fed'ral-street,
And there the truth was told 'em–
Yankee doodle, keep it up!
Yankee doodle, dandy,
Mind the music and the step,
And with the girls be handy.

They ev'ry morning went to prayer,
And then began disputing,
'Till opposition silenc'd were,
By arguments refuting.
Yankee doodle, keep it up! &c.

Then 'squire Hancock like a man,
Who dearly loves the nation,
By a concil'atry plan,
Prevented much vexation.[2]
Yankee doodle, &c.

He made a *woundy* fed'ral speech,
With sense and elocution;
And then the 'Vention did beseech
T' adopt the Constitution.
Yankee doodle, &c.

The question being outright put,
(Each voter independent)
The Fed'ralists agreed t' adopt,
And then propose amendment.
Yankee doodle, &c.

The other party seeing then
The people were against 'em,
Agreed like honest, faithful men,
To mix in peace amongst 'em.
Yankee doodle, &c.

The Boston folks are *deucid* lads,
And always full of notions;
The boys, the girls, their mams and dads,
Were fill'd with joy's commotions.
Yankee doodle, &c.

So straightway they procession made,[3]
Lord! how *nation* fine, Sir!
For ev'ry man of ev'ry trade
Went with his tools–to dine, Sir.
Yankee doodle, &c.

JOHN FOSTER WILLIAMS[4] in a ship,
Join'd in the social band, Sir,
And made the lasses dance and skip,
To see him sail on land, Sir.
Yankee doodle, &c.

Oh then a *whapping* feast begun,
And all hands went to eating;
They drank their toasts, shook hands and sung,
Huzza! for 'Vention meeting.
Yankee doodle, &c.

Now Politicians of all kinds,
Who are not yet decided;
May see how Yankees speak their minds;
And yet are not divided.
Yankee doodle, &c.

Then from this 'sample let 'em cease,
Inflammatory writing,
For FREEDOM, HAPPINESS, and PEACE,
Is better far than fighting.
Yankee doodle, &c.

So here I end my fed'ral song,
Compos'd of thirteen verses,
May agriculture flourish long,
And commerce fill our purses!
Yankee doodle, keep it up!
Yankee doodle, dandy,
Mind the music and the step,
And with the girls be handy.

1. The quoted material is part of an anonymous eighteenth century nursery rhyme wrongfully ascribed to Jonathan Swift. The rhyme reads: "O my kitten, a kitten,/And O my kitten, my deary;/Such a sweet pap as this,/There is not far nor neary:/There we go up, up, up–/Here we go down, down, down–/Here we go backwards and forwards–/And here we go round, round, round" (C. Lovat Fraser, ed., *Nurse Lovechild's Legacy, Being a Mighty Fine Collection of the Most Noble, Memorable and Veracious Nursery Rhymes...* [London, 1922], 35).

2. For Governor John Hancock's conciliatory plan, see CC:508 and CC:547, note 7.

3. For a description of the Boston procession on 8 February, see *Massachusetts Centinel*, 9 February.

4. During the Revolution, John Foster Williams (1743–1814) commanded several Massachusetts vessels and privateers, taking many prizes. In the procession, Williams was "Commander" of "The Ship FEDERAL CONSTITUTION," "Manned by thirteen seamen and marines." In 1790 Williams was made captain of the revenue cutter *Massachusetts* by President Washington and retained that position until his death.

553. The New Litany
Virginia Herald, 21 February[1]

Spare us, good Lord.

From all evil and mischievous members of the state legislature, from the sin of ingratitude, from the power of ex post facto laws, and from everlasting damnation.

Good Lord, deliver us.

From such laws as do discriminate in favour of sheriffs and others who are in arrears for taxes; from all pompous and inaccurate statements of the public debt, and from such statements as may tend to sooth and flatter the people into a willingness to remain in their present state, rather than to adopt the new government,

Good Lord deliver us.

From state chicanery, government speculation, and from all the uncharitableness concomitant therewith.

Good Lord deliver us.

From intestine war; from the assemblies of such clubs as are gathered to oppose the new constitution; and from the rage of those who burn with choler, as knowing their consequence will be lessened by the adoption thereof:

We beseech thee to hear us, good Lord.

That it may please thee to keep and strengthen in the true knowledge of thy ways, thy servants WASHINGTON, RANDOLPH, and MADISON, and all that are put in authority under them, and to enable them to be instrumental in promoting such wise government as may best tend to the peace and happiness of all thy people,

We beseech thee to hear us, good Lord.

That it may please thee to incline the hearts of thy people to adopt the new Fœderal Constitution; to endow the president thereof, the vice-president, senators and house of representatives, with grace, wisdom and understanding, to make and execute such laws as will best tend to secure to thy people the blessings of liberty, peace and concord, in those states, and that they may so far retrieve their lost credit, that they no longer be a reproach and hissing amongst the nations of the earth.

We beseech thee to hear us, good Lord.

That it may please thee to shield us from the rage of malicious and disappointed men, and to strengthen us in the principles of the Fœderal Constitution, so as to enable us to triumph over all the enemies thereof, that so hereafter we may attain to a government which will have such energy and stability as will be adequate to the exigencies of the union.

We beseech thee to hear us, good Lord.

That it may please thee to save from anarchy all thy people.

1. "The New Litany" was published in the *Pennsylvania Journal* on 1 March under the heading–"From the VIRGINIA HERALD." The Fredericksburg *Virginia Herald* was printed on 7, 14, 21, and 28 February, but none of these issues is extant. "The New Litany" is placed under 21 February because the *Pennsylvania Journal*, in its issue of 1 March, published an item from Richmond, Va., dated 19 February. "The New Litany" was reprinted fifteen more times by 19 July: Vt. (2), N.H. (1), Mass. (2), Conn. (2), N.Y. (1), Pa. (1), Va. (2), N.C. (1), S.C. (2), Ga. (1).

554 A–B. The Adjournment of the New Hampshire Convention Exeter, 22 February

Throughout America, it was generally believed that the New Hampshire Convention would ratify the Constitution with little opposition. After the Massachusetts Convention ratified the Constitution on 6 February, New Hampshire's acceptance of the Constitution seemed even more certain because everyone expected it to follow the lead of its powerful and influential neighbor. On 15 February James Madison in New York wrote that "The Convention of N Hampshire is now sitting. There seems to be no question that the issue there will add a *seventh* pillar, as the phrase now is, to the fœderal Temple" (to George Washington, Rutland, *Madison*, X, 510). Five days later the Federalist *Massachusetts Centinel*, even though it was known that there was opposition to the Constitution in the New Hampshire Convention, predicted "that the New Hampshire Pillar will ... be added as another supporter of the FEDERAL SUPERSTRUCTURE" (Appendix I).

As the Convention neared, however, some New Hampshire Federalists began having misgivings. On 11 February state President John Sullivan, who had been elected to represent Durham in the state Convention, believed that prospects for New Hampshire's ratification were "not so favorable as I expected" (to Henry Knox, J.S.H. Fogg Autograph Collection, MeHi). When the Convention met in Exeter on 13 February, Sullivan's fears were soon realized–a majority of the delegates opposed the Constitution. Estimates placed Federalist strength at between 30 and 48 of the 108 delegates in attendance. A number of Federalist delegates lamented that "the only thing that can be done to prevent its rejection is to have an adjournment of the Convention" (Jeremiah Libbey to Jeremy Belknap, 19 February, Belknap Papers, MHi). Adjournment was the only Federalist recourse because many towns had instructed their delegates to vote against the Constitution. According to delegate John Langdon of Portsmouth, these instructed delegates felt bound to vote against ratification, even though some of them (estimates ranged from about 7 to 30 delegates) had become supporters of the Constitution (to Rufus King, 23 February, CC:554–A). Others believed that the delegates who were also state legislators were afraid of "incurring the displeasure of their constituents" who might vote them out of office in the upcoming elections in March (*New Hampshire Spy*, 23 February, extra; and John Vaughan to John Dickinson, 9 March, Dickinson Papers, PPL). The delegates hoped that they could get their constituents to change their instructions. Therefore, on 22 February John Langdon moved that the Convention "adjourn to some future day." The Convention voted 56 to 51 to adjourn and to meet in Concord on 18 June (*New Hampshire Spy*, 23 February, extra). Antifederalist John Quincy Adams of Massachusetts, an observer of the debates, wrote in his diary that the motion "was the offspring of the fears of the federal party; and was faintly opposed by the other faction, who appeared to be equally fearful of the event; though more confident of their numbers" (22 February, Allen, *Adams Diary*, 366).

Americans everywhere wondered what effect New Hampshire's adjournment would have on the prospects for ratification of the Constitution. Federalists tried to put the best possible light on the adjournment and predicted publicly that the Convention would ratify the Constitution when it reconvened in June. Antifederalists emphasized that the adjournment was the first public rejection of the Constitution. For instance, the *New York Journal*, 3 March, reported that the adjournment "alone, prevented a rejection of the system; and there is no great probability, that, in June, it will have a greater number of friends than it now has." (See also *New York Morning Post*, 3 March, Appendix I.)

Some observers thought that the adjournment to the inland town of Concord benefited Antifederalists. A letter dated 12 March and allegedly written by Pennsylvania Antifederalist George Bryan declared that the move "100 miles farther inland ... bodes no good to the *fœderal* party, as they falsely call themselves" (CC:647). A satirical letter from James de Caledonia (James Wilson) to James Bowdoin expressed the same idea: "But I find the country members have carried the convention farther back in the country at least 100 miles, to a place called *Concord*. How, in the name of wonder, could you suffer this to take place..." (Philadelphia *Freeman's Journal*, 12 March, Mfm:Pa. 512. See also *ibid.*, CC:614.). When Federalist Nicholas Gilman, a New Hampshire delegate to Congress, heard that the Convention would reconvene in Concord he lamented that "the field assigned for the scene of action is so much in favor of the adverse party" (to John Sullivan, 22 March, CC:637). Federalist Samuel A. Otis, a Massachusetts delegate to Congress, worried that the Convention's "adjournment into the Wilderness augurs ill" (to Benjamin Lincoln, 8 May, J.S.H. Fogg Autograph Collection, MeHi).

Concord was chosen, not to benefit Antifederalists, but because the legislature was scheduled to convene there on 4 June. The choice of Concord would be convenient for those Convention delegates who also served in the legislature. The legislature met on 4 June and adjourned on 18 June–the opening day of the second session of the Convention.

On 24 February news of the adjournment reached Boston, where several prominent Federalists expressed their disappointment but predicted that New Hampshire would ratify in June (William Heath Diary, and Henry Jackson to Henry Knox, Knox Papers, MHi; and Caleb Gibbs to George Washington, and Benjamin Lincoln to Washington, Washington Papers, DLC). The next day the Antifederalist Boston *American Herald* reported that the New Hampshire Convention had voted against ratification of the Constitution and, that after reconsidering the question, it had voted to adjourn (see note 3 below). On the 26th the *Herald's* erroneous report was refuted by a correspondent in the *Massachusetts Gazette*: "Please to inform a certain anti-federal editor, that his intelligence from New-Hampshire is groundless.–His forwardness for publishing reports unfavourable to the adopting the federal constitution, is well known.–Your correspondent assures the publick, that the decisive question, respecting the adopting the federal constitution, was not voted upon. The only vote that was taken was for an adjournment–which was carried–yeas 57, nays 48." The next day the *Massachusetts Centinel* (CC:554–B) published a lengthy, widely reprinted refutation of the *Herald's* report.

Despite their public optimism, Federalists privately worried about the effect the adjournment might have on the states that had not ratified the Constitution. Maryland's Convention was scheduled to meet on 21 April, South Carolina's on 12 May, Virginia's and New York's on 2 and 17 June, respectively, and North Carolina's on 21 July. Rhode Island had not even called a convention. George Washington noted that the adjournment in New Hampshire would "possibly" make "Rhode Island more backward than she otherwise would have been, if *all* the New

England States had *finally* decided in favor of the measure" (to Henry Knox, 30 March, Fitzpatrick, XXIX, 450). James Madison wrote that the adjournment was "no small check to the progress of the business" and that the "mischief elsewhere will in the meantime be of a serious nature" (to Edmund Randolph, and to George Washington, 3 March, CC:587, and Rutland, *Madison*, X, 555). Nicholas Gilman agreed: "much is to be apprehended from this unfortunate check to the tide of our political prosperity. ... This unfortunate affair will at least give a temporary spring to the opposition and I fear its effects in other States; though I cannot doubt the final ratification in ours, if proper measures are adopted, to counteract the nefarious designs of the enemys to our Country" (to John Langdon, 6 March, Dreer Collection, PHi). Two weeks later Gilman's worst fears seemed to be realized, as he declared that "Those that have not been in the way of seeing and hearing can hardly imagine what pernicious effects our Convention business has produced in a number of the States." After Massachusetts ratified the Constitution, Gilman continued, Antifederalists "began to make excuses and change sides in all Quarters," but after New Hampshire's adjournment "they augmented their forces took possession of their old ground and seem determined to maintain it at all hazards" (to John Sullivan, 22 March, CC:637). Paine Wingate, Gilman's colleague in Congress, wrote that "the ill impression on the minds of people by the adjournment is more extensive & mischievous than you would imagine. It is complained of as far as Virginia, & believed that if New Hampshire had adopted, there would not have been one dissenting state. Whereas, there is now some danger that the whole plan will miscarry" (to Samuel Lane, 12 April, Wingate Papers, MH). And Antoine de la Forest, the French vice consul in New York, reported that New Hampshire's adjournment was "a dangerous setback" that "had the most unfortunate effect on the people of the States of New york, Maryland Virginia and the two Carolinas. The opposition there has taken on new strength; *antifederalists* have stolen more easily into all the state conventions" (to Comte de la Luzerne, 15 April, CC:681).

Federalists were especially concerned about New York and Virginia–two large states where the opposition to the Constitution was particularly strong. In New York City, the news of New Hampshire's adjournment caused the price of public securities to fall in early March (Collin McGregor to Neil Jamieson, 4 March, CC:590). Samuel Blachley Webb, a New York City commercial agent, lamented "O New Hampshire, you have (perhaps unintentionally) done us much injury.– Anti-federalists lift their heads." Confederation Secretary at War Henry Knox reported from New York City that Antifederalists had been given "new life and Spirits" while the "ardor" of Federalists had been "damped." Rufus King wrote that "the spirit of Federalism" had been checked in the state of New York. Similar reports came from Thomas Tillotson in Dutchess County, N.Y., who noted that New Hampshire's adjournment "has revived the drooping spirits of the Opposition" (Webb to Joseph Barrell, 9 March, in Worthington Chauncey Ford, ed., *Correspondence and Journals of Samuel Blachley Webb* [3 vols., New York, 1893–1894], III, 97; Knox to John Sullivan, 9 April, CC:669; King to Tench Coxe, 18 March, CC:623; and Tillotson to Robert R. Livingston, 31 March, Livingston Papers, NHi). And Richard Stockton, a Princeton, N.J., lawyer, described the adjournment as "a most unlucky accident." Stockton had been "informed by a Gentleman who may be depended on that the antifederal junto in N York had agreed to give up all opposition if Hampshire adopted" the Constitution (to Benjamin Rush, 14 April, Rush Papers, PPL).

Virginia Federalists were particularly alarmed by the adjournment because news of the "untoward event" arrived in the state while elections (3–31 March) were being held for the Virginia Convention. George Washington believed that all Antifederalist efforts in Virginia "would have proved entirely unavailing" if New Hampshire had ratified the Constitution. The news gave Virginia Antifederalists the "opportunity" to demonstrate that the Constitution was not "so generally approved of in other States as they [Virginians] had been taught to believe." Antifederalists also maintained that if Virginia rejected the Constitution, "all those [state conventions] which are to follow will do the same; & consequently, the Constitution cannot obtain, as there will be only eight States in favor of the measure" (to Henry Knox, 30 March, and to John Langdon, 2 April, Fitzpatrick, XXIX, 449, 452–53). Even some Federalists believed that the New Hampshire adjournment might destroy the Constitution's chances of ratification. Virginian Cyrus Griffin, president of Congress, worried that "nine states will not have agreed to the System before Virginia shall be assembled; this will make her in fact the preponderating state of the union; and being so placed I fear the consequences" (to Thomas FitzSimons, 3 March, Gratz Collection, PHi).

The first test of the impact of New Hampshire's adjournment would be in Maryland whose Convention was scheduled to convene on 21 April. Rufus King expressed the concern of most Federalists when he stated on 16 April that "we are not so confident of Maryland as we once were of New Hampshire" (to John Langdon, CC:686). On 20 April George Washington wrote Thomas Johnson of Maryland "that an adjournment, (if attempted), of your Convention to a later period than the decision of the question in this State, will be tantamount to the rejection of the Constitution." Such an act "would have the worst tendency imaginable; for indecision there wld. have considerable influence upon South Carolina, the only other State which is to precede Virginia, and submits the question almost wholly to the determination of the latter. The *pride* of the State is already touched upon this string, & will be strained much higher if there is an opening for it" (Fitzpatrick, XXIX, 463).

Washington was not alone in his fear that the Maryland and South Carolina conventions might not ratify the Constitution, thereby endangering the prospects for ratification by the Virginia Convention. Early in April, Federalist George Nicholas of Charlottesville, Va., had urged James Madison to write his friends in Maryland and South Carolina asking them to resist attempts to adjourn their state conventions. Madison replied that he would "cheerfully execute" Nicholas' request in order to avert "the mischievous influence here [Virginia] of such examples as N. Hampshire has set" (Nicholas to Madison, 5 April, and Madison to Nicholas, 8 April, CC:663, 667).

Federalist fears about adjournment in Maryland were apparently well-founded. On 20 April, the day before the Maryland Convention met, Baltimore delegate James McHenry wrote Washington that "Our opposition intend to push for an adjournment under the pretext of a conference with yours respecting amendments. As I look upon such a step to amount to a rejection in both States I shall do every thing in my power to prevent it" (Washington Papers, DLC).

Despite such fears, some Maryland and South Carolina Federalists believed that those states would ratify the Constitution. Dr. Philip Thomas of Frederick, Md., thought that Maryland would ratify "by a pretty large majority" even though the opponents of the Constitution "have begun to pluck up their crests since the conflict happened in the Convention of N. Hampshire & the nefarious 'doings' in Rhode Island" (to Horatio Gates, 21 March, Gates Mss., NN). Judge Alexander Contee Hanson, a Maryland Convention delegate from Annapolis, asserted that "The fatal supineness of the federalists in New-Hampshire will occasion much trouble, altho', upon the whole, I do not believe what has happened there will injure the cause. Whilst it gives spirits to scoundrels and demagogues, it rouses the friends to order and good government, and I trust, that, in no other state, will they be deceived by the apparent quiet submission of the former" (to Tench Coxe, 27 March, Coxe Papers, Series II, Correspondence and General Papers, PHi. A lengthy extract of Hanson's letter, including the material quoted here, was edited by Coxe and printed in the *Pennsylvania Gazette*, 9 April, and was widely circulated.). David Ramsay of Charleston, S.C., wrote that "I am more anxious since the adjournment of New Hampshire convention. ... I counted on the support of New: Hampshire & am since doubly anxious for the vote of our State to be in favor of it. I still have a great preponderance of hope & only fear a delay in the business" (to Benjamin Lincoln, 31 March, Lincoln Papers, MHi).

Some Federalists were worried that New Hampshire's adjournment might even have a negative effect on Pennsylvania–a state which had already ratified the Constitution. James Madison thought that the opposition in New York "will take new spirits" and "That in Pena. will probably be equally encouraged" (to Edmund Randolph, 3 March, CC:587). Virginia delegate to Congress John Brown feared that the adjournment "will be productive of bad consequences as it will give fresh spirits & Confidence to the Malcontents who were begining to dispair & relax in their opposition–Altho Pensilva. had adopted it yet there is a very powerful party opposed who are growing very tumultuous having been exasperated by the intemperate Zeal of the friends to the Plan" (to James Breckinridge, 17 March, CC:621). This "very powerful party" had launched a petition campaign to overthrow Pennsylvania's ratification of the Constitution and had gathered more than 6,000 signatures (RCS:Pa., 709–25).

On 26 March the Federalist *Pennsylvania Gazette* printed a letter allegedly written by Antifederalist leader George Bryan of Philadelphia, stating that Antifederalists considered New Hampshire's adjournment "as fatal to the business. So do its advocates here, and they are in the dumps, and some of the members of the General Convention are apologising for their conduct. Before this news came, the party was up in the skies, as their behaviour seemed to express" (CC:647). The next week "A Pennsylvanian" asked Bryan if he "*conscientiously*" believed that Philadelphia Federalists considered the adjournment "*fatal* to the business" (*Pennsylvania Gazette*, 2 April, Mfm:Pa. 600).

The adjournment of the New Hampshire Convention had less impact than was anticipated. The petition campaign in Pennsylvania to overthrow the state's ratification of the Constitution was unsuccessful, as the state legislature tabled the petitions and adjourned at the end of March. The Maryland and South Carolina conventions ratified the Constitution by overwhelming majorities on 26 April and 23 May, respectively, becoming the seventh and eighth states to ratify. In mid-May Jeremiah Libbey, the postmaster of Portsmouth, N.H., wrote that "several" Antifederalists in the New Hampshire Convention "are said to be quite alterd from Antifederal to Federal" (to Jeremy Belknap, 12 May, Belknap Papers, MHi). On 21 June the reconvened New Hampshire Convention ratified the Constitution by a vote of 57 to 47–the ninth state to ratify.

554-A. John Langdon to Rufus King
Portsmouth, 23 February[1]

I am sorry to inform you that our Convention adjourned yesterday (to meet again in June next), without compleating the important business of adopting the Constitution. contrary to the expectation of almost ev'ry man of reflection at our first meeting a majority appeared against the plan a great part of whom had positive Instructions to Vote against it. however after spending ten days in the arguments a number of opponents came to me, and said, they were convinced and should be very unhappy to Vote against the Constitution, which they (however absurd) must do, in case the question was called for. I therefore moved for the adjournment which was carried though much opposed by the other side. This question determined a majority in favor of the Constitution had it not been for their Instructions. This shews the fatality of the times.

554-B. *Massachusetts Centinel, 27 February*[2]

NEW-HAMPSHIRE CONVENTION.

In order to give time to those Delegates in the Convention of New-Hampshire, who were instructed to vote against the Constitution, to return home, and get their instructions taken off, that hon. body, on Friday last, adjourned, to meet at Concord, in that State, on the third Wednesday in June next. No other question was taken. This being the truth, to endeavour by the publication of a contrary report, as was the case in the Herald of Monday last,[3] wickedly to deceive the publick, argues a depravity of mind, which, until the days of antifederalism, was unknown in the world; and instead of calling forth the sympathy of the publick, for the misfortune of erroneous judgment, will induce them to wish, and to endeavour, that the sphere of circulation of the paper thus employed, narrow as it is, may yet be contracted.

⟨No one circumstance attending the discussion of the proposed Federal Constitution, has demonstrated its superiour excellence and perfection more than the measure of adjournment, adopted by the Convention of New-Hampshire, last week, if we consider the situation of affairs there respecting it.–Almost the whole of that State is inland, and a great part of it remote from the regular channels of information–by far the greater part of the people had not seen it, and received their information of it from factious demagogues and popularity-seekers, who had rode through the back parts of the State, inflaming and prejudicing the people's minds against it. While under this infatuation, they chose delegates to meet in Convention, and bound them by INSTRUCTIONS to vote against it–and no delegate would have consented to have acted under such instructions, unless his sentiments on the subject, were in unison with those of his constituents.[4]–This being the case, on the meeting of the Convention, a majority (all of whom were from the remote parts of the State) were found opposed to the adoption of the Constitution.–It was, however discussed for several days, and such lights thrown on the subject–and so many objections obviated, as induced many, thus instructed, and who had considered the Constitution as dangerous, to change their sentiments.–But these considering their instructions *sacred*, could not, on conviction, vote for it–and their *consciences* forbade their voting against it.–What was now the alternative? Either to reject the Constitution, (which they certainly would have done, had their opinions of it continued the same,) or for those thus convinced, (who with those originally in favour of it, made a considerable majority) to return home to their constituents–acquaint them of the conviction that had arisen in their minds, and of the arguments which produced it–and to prevail on them to annul the instructions, which bound them to act contrary to their opinions. The latter was thought the most proper–and, therefore, the Convention adjourned to a distant day, to give time for the circulation in every part of the State, of the information and arguments, which had thus proved convincing to the members of the Convention–and as the Conventions of several of the States are not to meet until June, no delay it was thought would arise from adjourning to the third Wednesday of that month,⟩ which was agreed to by a considerable majority.–From this statement–we may venture to assert, that the cause of federalism, in New-Hampshire, will not suffer a diminution–and that their Pillar of the Federal Edifice, THOUGH IT NOW RESTETH, WILL MOST ASSUREDLY RISE.

1. RC, King Papers, NHi.
2. Reprinted ten times by 14 March: Mass. (1), N.Y. (3), N.J. (1), Pa. (4), Md. (1). This report was preceded by a cartoon entitled "The GLORIOUS FABRICK" which contained six pillars, each labeled for a state that had already ratified the Constitution. New Hampshire's pillar was resting on a brace, and a caption read "It WILL yet rise." The cartoon was not reprinted. The text in angle brackets was reprinted in the Boston *Independent Chronicle* on 28 February. The *Chronicle's* excerpt was reprinted within a week once in Massachusetts and five times in Connecticut. Excerpts or summaries of the *Centinel's* account appeared in five newspapers by 2 April: Mass. (1), R.I. (1), Md. (1), Va. (2).
3. The Boston *American Herald*, 25 February, reported that: "The Convention of the State of New-Hampshire, on FRIDAY last, brought on the decisive Question respecting the New Constitution–yeas 51–nays 54.—This Question being reconsidered, it was then moved for an Adjournment, and was carried, yeas 53, nays 52, to meet again on the THIRD Tuesday in JUNE next." The *Herald's* account was reprinted nine times by 26 March: Mass. (1), R.I. (2), Conn. (1), N.Y. (2), Pa. (1), Md. (1), Va. (1). It was also summarized in the *Salem Mercury* on 26 February.
4. On 28 February John Langdon wrote Washington that "just at the moment of choice for members of our convention (in one of our principal counties) took place, a report was circulated by a few designing men who wished for confusion, that Massachusetts Convention who had just met, were against the plan would certainly refuse it, the liberties of the people were in danger, and that the great men (as they call them) were forming a plan for themselves to-gether with a thousand other absurdities, which frightened the people almost out of what *little* senses they had. This induced them to choose not only such men as were against the plan but to instruct them positively against receiving it" (Washington Papers, DLC. See also Extract of a letter from Exeter, N.H., 22 February, *New York Journal*, 3 March, Appendix I.).

555. Publius: The Federalist 59
New York Packet, 22 February

This essay, written by Alexander Hamilton, was reprinted in the New York *Independent Journal* on 23 February. It is number 59 in the M'Lean edition and number 58 in the newspapers.

For a general discussion of the authorship, circulation, and impact of *The Federalist*, see CC:201, 639.

The FŒDERALIST, No. 58.
To the People of the State of New-York.

The natural order of the subject leads us to consider in this place, that provision of the Constitution which authorises the national Legislature to regulate in the last resort the election of its own members. It is in these words–"The *times, places* and *manner* of holding elections for Senators and Representatives, shall be prescribed in each State by the Legislature thereof; but the Congress may at any time by law, make or alter *such regulations* except as to the *places* of choosing senators.[(a)]" This provision has not only been declaimed against by those who condemn the Constitution in the gross; but it has been censured by those, who have objected with less latitude and greater moderation; and in one instance, it has been thought exceptionable by a gentleman who has declared himself the advocate of every other part of the system.[1]

I am greatly mistaken, notwithstanding, if there be any article in the whole plan more completely defensible than this–Its propriety rests upon the evidence of this plain proposition, that *every government ought to contain in itself the means of its own preservation*. Every just reasoner will at first sight, approve an adherence to this rule, in the work of the Convention; and will disapprove every deviation from it, which may not appear to have been dictated by the necessity of incorporating into the work some particular ingredient, with which a rigid conformity to the rule was incompatible. Even in this case, though he may acquiesce in the necessity; yet he will not cease to regard and to regret[2] a departure from so fundamental a principle, as a portion of imperfection in the system which may prove the seed of future weakness and perhaps anarchy.

It will not be alledged that an election law could have been framed and inserted into the Constitution, which would have been always[3] applicable to every probable change in the situation of the country; and it will therefore not be denied that a discretionary power over elections ought to exist somewhere. It will, I presume, be as readily conceded, that there were only three ways, in which this power could have been reasonably modified and disposed, that it must either have been lodged wholly in the National Legislature, or wholly in the State Legislatures, or primarily in the latter, and ultimately in the former. The last mode has with reason been preferred by the Convention. They have submitted the regulation of elections for the Fœderal Government in the first instance to the local administrations; which in ordinary cases, and when no improper views prevail, may be both more convenient and more satisfactory; but they have reserved to the national authority a right to interpose, whenever extraordinary circumstances might render that interposition necessary to its safety.

Nothing can be more evident, than that an exclusive power of regulating elections for the National Government, in the hands of the State Legislatures, would leave the existence of the Union entirely at their mercy. They could at any moment annihilate it, by neglecting to provide for the choice of persons to administer its affairs. It is to little purpose to say that a neglect or omission of this kind, would not be likely to take place. The constitutional possibility of the thing, without an equivalent for the risk, is an unanswerable objection. Nor has any satisfactory reason been yet assigned for incurring that risk. The extravagant surmises of a distempered jealousy can never be dignified with that character. If we are in a humour to presume abuses of power, it is as fair to presume them on the part of the State Governments, as on the part of the General Government. And as it is more consonant to the rules of a just theory to intrust the Union with the care of its own existence, than to transfer that care to any other hands; if abuses of power are to be hazarded, on the one side, or on the other, it is more rational to hazard them where the power would naturally be placed, than where it would unnaturally be placed.

Suppose an article had been introduced into the Constitution, empowering the United States to regulate the elections for the particular States, would any man have hesitated to condemn it, both as an unwarrantable transposition of power, and as a premeditated engine for the destruction of the State governments? The violation of principle in this case would have required no comment; and to an unbiassed observer, it will not be less apparent in the project of subjecting the existence of the National Government, in a similar respect to the pleasure of the State governments. An impartial view of the matter cannot fail to result in a conviction, that each, as far as possible, ought to depend on itself for its own preservation.

As an objection to this position, it may be remarked, that the Constitution of the national Senate, would involve in its full extent the danger which it is suggested might flow from an exclusive power in the State Legislatures to regulate the fœderal elections. It may be alledged, that by declining the appointment of Senators, they might at any time give a fatal blow to the Union; and from this, it may be inferred, that as its existence would be thus rendered dependent upon them in so essential a point, there can be no objection to entrusting them with it, in the particular case under consideration. The interest of each State, it may be added, to maintain its representation in the national councils, would be a complete security against an abuse of the trust.

This argument though specious, will not upon examination be found solid. It is certainly true, that the State Legislatures, by forbearing the appointment of Senators, may destroy the National Government. But it will not follow, that because they have the power to do this in one instance, they ought to have it in every other. There are cases in which the pernicious tendency of such a power may be far more decisive, without any motive, equally cogent with that which must have regulated the conduct of the Convention, in respect to the construction of the Senate, to recommend their admission into the system. So far as that construction may expose the Union to the possibility of injury from the State Legislatures, it is an evil; but it is an evil, which could not have been avoided without excluding the States, in their political capacities, wholly from a place in the organization of the National Government. If this had been done, it

would doubtless have been interpreted into an entire dereliction of the
fœderal principle; and would certainly have deprived the State governments of that absolute safe-guard, which they will enjoy under this provision. But however wise it may have been, to have submitted in this
instance to an inconvenience, for the attainment of a necessary advantage,
or a greater good, no inference can be drawn from thence to favor an
accumulation of the evil, where no necessity urges, nor any greater good
invites.

It may easily be discerned also, that the National Government would
run a much greater risk from a power in the State Legislatures over the
elections of its House of Representatives, than from their power of appointing the members of its Senate. The Senators are to be chosen for the
period of six years; there is to be a rotation, by which the seats of a third
part of them are to be vacated, and replenished every two years; and no
State is to be entitled to more than two Senators: A quorum of the body is
to consist of sixteen members. The joint result of these circumstances would
be, that a temporary combination of a few States, to intermit the appointment of Senators, could neither annul the existence nor impair the activity
of the body: And it is not from a general or permanent combination of the
States, that we can have any thing to fear. The first might proceed from
sinister designs in the leading members of a few of the State Legislatures;
the last would suppose a fixed and rooted disaffection in the great body of
the people; which will either never exist at all, or will in all probability
proceed from an experience of the inaptitude of the General Government
to the advancement of their happiness; in which event no good citizen
could desire its continuance.

But with regard to the Fœderal House of Representatives, there is intended to be a general election of members once in two years. If the State
Legislatures were to be invested with an exclusive power of regulating
these elections, every period of making them would be a delicate crisis in
the national situation; which might issue in a dissolution of the Union, if
the leaders of a few of the most important States should have entered into
a previous conspiracy to prevent an election.

I shall not deny that there is a degree of weight in the observation, that
the interest of each State to be represented in the fœderal councils will be
a security against the abuse of a power over its elections in the hands of
the State Legislatures. But the security will not be considered as complete,
by those who attend to the force of an obvious distinction between the
interest of the people in the public felicity, and the interest of their local
rulers in the power and consequence of their offices. The people of America may be warmly attached to the government of the Union at times,
when the particular rulers of particular States, stimulated by the natural
rivalship of power and by the hopes of personal aggrandisement, and supported by a strong faction in each of those States, may be in a very oppo-

site temper. This diversity of sentiment, between a majority of the people, and the individuals who have the greatest credit in their councils, is exemplified in some of the States, at the present moment, on the present question. The scheme of separate confederacies, which will always multiply the chances of ambition, will be a never failing bait to all such influential characters in the State administrations as are capable of preferring their own emolument and advancement to the public weal; with so effectual a weapon in their hands as the exclusive power of regulating elections for the National Government a combination of a few such men, in a few of the most considerable States, where the temptation will always be the strongest, might accomplish the destruction of the Union, by seizing the opportunity of some casual dissatisfaction among the people (and which perhaps they may themselves have excited) to discontinue the choice of members for the Fœderal House of Representatives. It ought never to be forgotten, that a firm Union of this country, under an efficient government, will probably be an encreasing object of jealousy to more than one nation of Europe; and that enterprises to subvert it will sometimes originate in the intrigues of foreign powers, and will seldom fail to be patronised and abetted by some of them. Its preservation therefore ought in no case, that can be avoided, to be committed to the guardianship of any but those, whose situation will uniformly beget an immediate interest in the faithful and vigilant performance of the trust.

(a) 1 Clause, 4 Sect. of the 1st Art.

1. "A Citizen of America" (Noah Webster) objected to Congress' power over the election of its own members: "I see no occasion for any power in Congress to interfere with the choice of their own body ... [it] gives *needless* and *dangerous* powers" (*Examination into the Leading Principles of the Federal Constitution...*, 17 October, CC:173; and Mfm:Pa. 142, pp. 26, 49–50).
2. "And to regret" was deleted in the M'Lean edition.
3. "Always" was deleted in the M'Lean edition.

556. Centinel XV
Philadelphia Independent Gazetteer, 22 February[1]

TO THE PEOPLE OF PENNSYLVANIA.

Fellow-Citizens, There are few of the maxims or opinions we hold, that are the result of our own investigation or observation, and even those we adopt from others are seldom on a conviction of their truth or propriety, but from the facination of example and the influence of what is or appears to be the general sentiment. The science of government being the most abstruse and unobvious of all others, mankind are more liable to be imposed upon by the artful and designing in systems and regulations of government, than on any other subject: hence a jealousy of innovation confirmed by uniform experience prevails in most communities; this reluc-

tance to change, has been found to be the greatest security of free governments, and the principal bulwark of liberty; for the aspiring and ever-
restless spirit of ambition would otherwise, by her deceptive wiles and
ensnaring glosses, triumph over the freest and most enlightened people. It
is the peculiar misfortune of the people of these United States, at this awful
crisis of public affairs, to have lost this useful, this absolutely necessary
jealousy of innovation in government, and thereby to lie at the mercy and
be exposed to all the artifices of ambition, without this usual shield to
protect them from imposition. The conspirators, well aware of their advantage, have seized the favorable moment, and by the most unparalleled
arts of deception, have obtained the sanction of the conventions of several
states to the most tyrannic system of government ever projected.

The magic of great names, the delusion of falsehood, the suppression of
information, precipitation and fraud have been the instruments of this
partial success, the pillars whereon the structure of tyranny has been so far
raised. Those influential vehicles, the newspapers with few exceptions, have
been devoted to the cause of despotism, and by the subserviency of the
P— O—, the usefulness of the patriotic newspapers has been confined to
the places of their publication,[2] whilst falsehood and deception have had
universal circulation, without the opportunity of refutation. The feigned
unanimity of one part of America, has been represented to produce the
acquiescence of another, and so mutually to impose upon the whole by the
force of example.

The adoption of the new constitution by the convention of the state of
Massachusetts, by a majority of nineteen out of near four hundred members, and that too qualified by a number of propositions of amendment,
cannot afford the conspirators much cause for triumph, and especially
when all the circumstances under which it has been obtained, are considered. The late alarming disorders which distracted that state,[3] and even
threatened subversion of all order and government, and were with difficulty suppressed, occasioned the greatest consternation among all men of
property and rank: in this disposition even the most high toned and arbitrary government became desirable as a security against licentiousness and
agrarian laws; consequently the new constitution was embraced with eagerness by men of these descriptions, who, in every community, form a
powerful interest, and added to the conspirators, office-hunters, &c. &c.
made a formidable and numerous party in favor of the new constitution.
The elections of the members of convention were moreover made in the
first moments of blind enthusiasm, when every artifice was practised to
prejudice the people against all those who had the enlightened patriotism
to oppose this system of tyranny: thus was almost every man of real ability, who was in opposition, excluded from a seat in the convention; consequently the contest was very unequal; well-meaning, though uninformed
men, were opposed to great learning, eloquence and sophistry in the shape

of lawyers, doctors and divines, who were capable and seemed disposed to delude by deceptive glosses and specious reasoning; indeed, from the specimens we have seen of the discussion on this occasion, every enlightened patriot must regret that the cause of liberty has been so weakly, although jealously[4] advocated, that its champions were so little illuminated. In addition to these numerous advantages in the convention, the friends of the new constitution had the weight and influence of the town of Boston to second their endeavors, and yet, notwithstanding all this, were near losing the question, although delusively qualified. Is this any evidence of the excellency of the new constitution? Certainly not. Nor can it have any influence in inducing the remaining states to accede. They will examine and judge for themselves, and from their wisdom in taking due time for deliberation, I have no doubt will prove the salvation of the liberties of the United States.

Philadelphia, February 20th, 1788.

1. Reprinted: *New York Journal*, 26 February; Philadelphia *Freeman's Journal*, 27 February; *Albany Journal*, 3 March; *Carlisle Gazette*, 19 March. For a spurious "Centinel" XV and its impact, see CC:534.

2. For the post office and its alleged suppression of newspapers, see Appendix II.

3. Shays's Rebellion.

4. In an errata published in the *Gazetteer* on 26 February, this word was changed to "zealously." The reprints in the *Freeman's Journal* and the *Carlisle Gazette* made this change.

557. John Adams on the Constitution
New York Journal, 23 February

The third volume of John Adams's *Defence of the Constitutions* was published in London in January 1788. Like the two preceding volumes, it was made up of letters written by Adams to his son-in-law William Stephens Smith, secretary in the American legation in London. Adams described this volume as "the boldest & freest [of the three] and most likely to be unpopular"; while his wife Abigail asserted that her husband's "sentiments" on the Constitution "will be very unpopular in our Country, but time and experience will bring them into fashion" (John Adams to Benjamin Rush, 2 December 1788, and Abigail Adams to Cotton Tufts, 20 February 1788, Adams Family Papers, MHi).

On 1 January 1788, Smith wrote Rufus King in New York City that "It may give you some satisfaction to know our friend Mr. Adams's opinion of the Constitution now under consideration, I send you a Copy of part of his last letter to me, which is to close the 3d. Vol: of his work–you may peruse it, shew it to fœderal men, (whom heaven preserve) or publish it as you think best" (King Papers, NHi). On 20 February King, who had just returned to New York City after serving as a delegate to the Massachusetts Convention, received Smith's letter and its enclosure. King sent a copy of the last two paragraphs of Adams's letter to Theophilus Parsons, who had also been a delegate to the Massachusetts Convention, noting that "Col. Smith observes in his letter that Mr. Adams wished no concealment of his Opinion on this subject; and I think its publicity may be useful. I am without a Frank; if the Doctor's Opinion is not worth the postage you value it much less than I do" (King Papers, NHi).

King, signing himself "A Customer," also sent Adams's letter to the *New York Journal* which published the entire letter on 23 February. The preface by "A Customer" and Adams's letter were reprinted in the *Pennsylvania Packet*, 4 March, and in the *Massachusetts Centinel*, 5 March. The *Massachusetts Gazette*, 4 March, omitted the preface but printed the entire letter. Excerpts from the letter, all of which included at least the last two paragraphs on the Constitution, were reprinted in fourteen other newspapers by 9 May: N.H. (1), Mass. (5), R.I. (1), Conn. (2), N.J. (1), Pa. (1), Md. (2), S.C. (1). The *New York Journal's* version of Adams's letter differs from the original in the *Defence* in paragraphing, italics, etc.

The day after the letter was reprinted in Boston, John Quincy Adams, who had reservations about the Constitution himself, noted in his diary that his father's letter "speaks very favourably of the System proposed by the federal Convention–I did not expect it, and am glad to find I was mistaken, since, it appears probable, the plan will be adopted" (5 March, Allen, *Adams Diary*, II, 371).

For other newspaper accounts of Adams's position on the Constitution, and the need for amendments, see "Accounts from England," 18 February–22 March (Appendix I). For a fuller discussion of Adams's *Defence*, see CC:16.

Mr. GREENLEAF, Upon a subject so interesting to the people of America, as the proposed federal constitution, the disquisitions of enlightened politicians are eagerly sought after, and the opinions of those, whose abilities and integrity have entitled them to the confidence and respect of their country, may justly be regarded as of the highest consequence.

The minister of the United States, at the court of London, has been constantly in the public employ, from the commencement of the American revolution. This gentleman was a delegate in Congress when the confederation was devised, and is said to have had no inconsiderable influence in its formation. His residence at London precluded him from any share in framing the constitution reported by the late federal convention; he cannot therefore be considered as a partizan for this system, or as its blind admirer.

Notwithstanding the uncandid attacks made by certain inferior critics upon a few expressions in the first volume of Mr. Adams' defence of the American constitutions, yet that performance has been read and approved by the sensible and candid part of the community. The second volume has been some time in America,[1] but hitherto has passed through but few hands. Mr. Adams has continued the work, and a third volume was ready for the press in the beginning of January. The following extract from the concluding letter of the third volume, contains Mr. Adams' opinion on the new constitution; its authenticity cannot be doubted, and the publication thereof will oblige   A CUSTOMER.

Extract[2] *of a letter from the honorable* J. ADAMS *to Col.* SMITH, *being the concluding letter of his* 3d *vol. on the American Constitutions, dated Grosvenor Square, December* 26, 1787.

"DEAR SIR, It should have been before observed, that the western empire fell in the 5th century, and the eastern in the 15th.

"Augustulus was compelled by Odoacer, king of the Hercili, in 475, to abdicate the western empire, and was the last Roman who possessed the imperial dignity at Rome. The dominion of Italy fell soon afterwards, into the hands of Theodoric the Goth.

"The eastern empire lasted many centuries after, until it was annihilated by Mahomet the Great, and Constantinople was taken in the year 1453. The interval between the fall of these two empires, making a period of about 1000 years, is called the middle age. During this term, republics, without number, arose in Italy; whirled upon their axles, or simple centres, foamed, raged; and burst, like so many water spouts upon the ocean. They were all alike ill-constituted; all alike miserable; and all ended in similar disgrace and despotism.

"It would be curious to pursue our subject through all of them whose records have survived the ravages of Goths, Saracens, and bigotted christians; through those other republics of Castile, Arragon, Catalonia, Gallicia, and all others in Spain; through those in Portugal; through the several provinces that now compose the kingdom of France; through those in Germany, Sweden, Denmark, Holland, England, Scotland, Ireland, &c. But if such a work should be sufficiently encouraged by the public (which is not probable, for mankind in general dare not as yet read or think upon constitutions) it is too extensive for my forces, and ought not to be done in so much haste. The preceding letters have been produced, upon the spur of a particular occasion, which made it necessary to write and publish with precipitation, or it might have been useless to have published at all. The whole has been done, in the midst of other occupations, in so much hurry, that scarce a moment could be spared to correct the style, adjust the method, pare off excrescences, or even obliterate repetitions, in all which respects it stands in need of an apology. You may pursue the investigation to any length you please. All nations, from the beginning, have been agitated by the same passions. The principles developed in these letters, will go a great way, in explaining every phenomenon that occurs in the history of government. The vegetable and animal kingdoms, and those heavenly bodies whose existence and movements we are, as yet, only permitted faintly to perceive, do not appear to be governed by laws more uniform or certain than those that regulate the moral and political world. Nations move by unalterable rules; and education, discipline, and laws, make the greatest difference in their accomplishments, happiness and perfection. It is the master artist alone who finishes his building, his picture, or his clock. The present actors on the stage, have been too little prepared by their early views, and too much occupied with turbulent scenes, to do more than they have done. Impartial justice will confess, that it is astonishing they have been able to do so much.

"It is for you, and your youthful companions, to make yourselves masters of what your predecessors have been able to comprehend and accomplish but imperfectly.

"A prospect into futurity, in America, is like contemplating the heavens through the telescope of Herschall.[3] Objects stupendous in their magnitudes and motions, strike us from all quarters, and fill us with amazement. When we recollect, that the wisdom or the folly, the virtue or the vice, the liberty or servitude, of those millions now beheld by us, only as Columbus saw these times in vision,[a] are certainly to be influenced, perhaps decided, by the manners, examples, principles, and the political institutions of the present generation. That mind must be hardened into stone, that is not melted into reverence and awe, with such affecting scenes before his eyes. Is there, can there be, a young American, indolent and incurious? Surrendered up to dissipation and frivolity? Vain of imitating the loosest manners of countries, which can never be made much better, or much worse? A profligate American youth must be profligate indeed, and richly merits the scorn of all mankind.

"The world has been too long abused with notions, that climate and soil decide the characters and political institutions of nations.

"The laws of Solon and the despotism of Mahomet, have at different times, prevailed at Athens, consuls, emperors and pontiffs, have ruled at Rome, can there be desired a stronger proof that policy and education, are able to triumph over every disadvantage of climate? Mankind have been still more injured by insinuations, that a certain celestial virtue, more than human, has been necessary to preserve liberty. Happiness, whether in despotism or democracy, whether in slavery or liberty, can never be found without virtue. The best republics will be virtuous, and have been so; but we may hazard a conjecture, that the virtues have been the effect of the well ordered constitutions, rather than the cause, and perhaps it would be impossible to prove that a republic cannot exist, even among highwaymen, by setting one rogue to watch another, and the knaves themselves may in time be made honest men by the struggle.

"It is now in our power to bring this work to a conclusion, with unexpected dignity. In the course of the last summer, two authorities have appeared, greater than any that have been before quoted, in which the principles we have attempted to defend have been acknowledged. The first is an ordinance of Congress of the 13th of July, 1787, for the government of the territory of the United States, north west of the river Ohio.[4] The second is the report of the convention at Philadelphia of the 17th of September, 1787. The former confederation of the United States was formed upon the model and example of all the confederacies ancient and modern, in which the federal council was only a diplomatic body. Even the Lycian which is thought to have been the best was no more. The magnitude of territory, the population[,] the wealth and commerce, and especially the rapid growth of the United States, have shewn such a government to be inadequate to their wants. And the new system, which seems admirably calculated to unite their interests and affections, and bring them to an uniformity of principles and sentiments, is equally well combined to unite their wills and forces, as a single nation; a result of accommodation cannot be supposed to reach the ideas of perfection of any one.

"But the conception of such an idea, and the deliberate union of so great and various a people, in such a plan, is, without all partiality or prejudice, if not the greatest exertion of human understanding, the greatest single effort of national deliberation that the world has ever seen. That it may be improved, is not to be doubted, and provision is made for that purpose, in the report itself. A people who could conceive, and can adopt it, we need not fear will be able to amend it, when by experience its inconveniences and imperfections shall be seen and felt."

(a) *Barlow's Poem.*[5]

1. Volume II was advertised for sale in the *New York Morning Post*, 23 January 1788; the Boston *Independent Chronicle*, 31 January; and the *Pennsylvania Herald*, 5 February.

2. This is not an extract of Adams's "letter," but the complete text of the "letter" as it appeared in the third volume of the *Defence.*

3. Sir William Herschel (1738–1822) was born in Germany but moved to England in 1757. He built his own telescope with which he discovered the planet Uranus in 1781 and two satellites of Uranus in 1787. He was appointed court astronomer in 1782.

4. For the Northwest Ordinance, see CDR, 168–74.

5. Joel Barlow's epic poem, "The Vision of Columbus," was published in Hartford in March 1787 (Evans 20220).

558. Publius: The Federalist 60
New York Independent Journal, 23 February

This essay, written by Alexander Hamilton, was reprinted in the *New York Packet*, 26 February. It is number 60 in the M'Lean edition and number 59 in the newspapers.

For a general discussion of the authorship, circulation, and impact of *The Federalist*, see CC:201, 639.

The FŒDERALIST. No. LIX.
To the People of the State of New-York.

We have seen that an incontroulable power over the elections for the federal government could not without hazard be committed to the state legislatures. Let us now see what would be the dangers on the other side; that is, from confiding the ultimate right of regulating its own elections to the union itself. It is not pretended, that this right would ever be used for the exclusion of any state from its share in the representation. The interest of all would in this respect at least be the security of all. But it is alledged that it might be employed in such a manner as to promote the election of some favourite class of men in exclusion of others; by confining the places of election to particular districts, and rendering it impracticable to the citizens at large to partake in the choice. Of all chimerical suppositions, this seems to be the most chimerical. On the one hand no rational calculation of probabilities would lead us to imagine, that the disposition, which a conduct so violent and extraordinary would imply, could ever find its way into the national councils; and on the other, it may be concluded with certainty, that if so improper a spirit should ever gain admittance into them, it would display itself in a form altogether different and far more decisive.

The improbability of the attempt may be satisfactorily inferred from this single reflection, that it could never be made without causing an immediate revolt of the great body of the people,–headed and directed by the state governments. It is not difficult to conceive that this characteristic right of freedom may, in certain turbulent and factious seasons, be violated in respect to a particular class of citizens by a victorious and overbearing[1] majority; but that so fundamental a privilege, in a country so situated and so enlightened, should be invaded to the prejudice of the great mass of the people, by the deliberate policy of the government; without occasioning a popular revolution, is altogether inconceivable and incredible.

In addition to this general reflection, there are considerations of a more precise nature, which forbid all apprehension on the subject. The dissimilarity in the ingredients, which will compose the national government; and still more in the manner in which they will be brought into action in its various branches must form a powerful obstacle to a concert of views, in any partial scheme of elections. There is sufficient diversity in the state of property, in the genius, manners, and habits of the people of the different parts of the union to occasion a material diversity of disposition in their representatives towards the different ranks and conditions in society. And though an intimate intercourse under the same government will promote a gradual assimilation, in some of these respects, yet there are causes as well physical as moral, which may in a greater or less degree permanently nourish different propensities and inclinations in this respect. But the circumstance, which will be likely to have the greatest influence in the matter, will be the dissimilar modes of constituting the several component parts of the government. The house of representatives being to be elected immediately by the people; the senate by the state legislatures; the president by electors chosen for that purpose by the people; there would be little probability of a common interest to cement these different branches in a predilection for any particular class of electors.

As to the senate it is impossible that any regulation of "time and manner," which is all that is proposed to be submitted to the national government in respect to that body, can affect the spirit which will direct the choice of its members. The collective sense of the state legislatures can never be influenced by extraneous circumstances of that sort: A consideration, which alone ought to satisfy us that the discrimination apprehended would never be attempted. For what inducement could the senate have to concur in a preference, in which itself would not be included? Or to what purpose would it be established in reference to one branch of the legislature; if it could not be extended to the other? The composition of the one would in this case counteract that of the other. And we can never suppose that it would embrace the appointments to the senate, unless we can at the same time suppose the voluntary co-operation of the state legislatures. If we make the latter supposition, it then becomes immaterial where the power in question is placed; whether in their hands or in those of the union.

But what is to be the object of this capricious partiality in the national councils? Is it to be exercised in a discrimination between the different departments of industry, or between the different kinds of property, or between the different degrees of property? Will it lean in favor of the landed interest, or the monied interest, or the mercantile interest, or the manufacturing interest? Or to speak in the fashionable language of the advarsaries of the Constitution; will it court the elevation of the "wealthy and the well born" to the exclusion and debasement of all the rest of the society?

If this partiality is to be exerted in favor of those who are concerned in any particular description of industry or property, I presume it will readily be admitted that the competition for it will lie between landed men and merchants. And I scruple not to affirm, that it is infinitely less likely, that either of them should gain an ascendant in the national councils, than that the one or the other of them should predominate in all the local councils. The inference will be, that a conduct tending to give an undue preference to either is much less to be dreaded from the former than from the latter.

The several states are in various degrees addicted to agriculture and commerce. In most, if not all of them, agriculture is predominant. In a few of them, however, commerce nearly divides its empire, and in most of them has a considerable share of influence. In proportion as either prevails, it will be conveyed into the national representation; and for the very reason that this will be an emanation from a greater variety of interests, and in much more various proportions, than are to be found in any single state, it will be much less apt to espouse either of them, with a decided partiality, than the representation of any single state.

In a country consisting chiefly of the cultivators of land where the rulers of an equal representation obtain the landed interest must upon the whole preponderate in the government. As long as this interest prevails in most of the state legislatures, so long it must maintain a correspondent superiority in the national senate, which will generally be a faithful copy of the majorities of those assemblies. It cannot therefore be presumed that a sacrifice of the landed to the mercantile class will ever be a favorite object of this branch of the federal legislature. In applying thus particularly to the senate a general observation suggested by the situation of the country, I am governed by the consideration, that the credulous votaries of state power, cannot upon their own principles suspect that the state legislatures would be warped from their duty by any external influence. But as in reality the same situation must have the same effect in the primitive composition at least of the federal house of representatives; an improper byass towards the mercantile class is as little to be expected from this quarter or from the other.

In order perhaps to give countenance to the objection at any rate, it may be asked, is there not danger of an opposite byass in the national government, which may dispose it to endeavour to secure a monopoly of the federal administration to the landed class? As there is little likelihood that the supposition of such a byass will have any terrors for those who would be immediately injured by it, a laboured answer to this question will be dispensed with. It will be sufficient to remark, first, that for the reasons elsewhere assigned,[2] it is less likely that any decided partiality should prevail in the councils of the union than in those of any of its members. Secondly that there would be no temptation to violate the constitution in favor of the landed class, because that class would in the natural course of things enjoy as great a preponderancy as itself could desire. And thirdly that men accustomed to investigate the sources of public prosperity, upon a large scale, must be too well convinced of the utility of commerce, to be inclined to inflict upon it so deep a wound as would result from the entire exclusion of those who would best understand its interest from a share in the management of them. The importance of commerce in the view of revenue alone must effectually guard it against the enmity of a body which would be continually importuned in its favour by the urgent calls of public necessity.

I the rather consult brevity in discussing the probability of a preference founded upon a discrimination between the different kinds of industry and property; because, as far as I understand the meaning of the objectors, they contemplate a discrimination of another kind. They appear to have in view, as the objects of the preference with which they endeavour to alarm us, those whom they designate by the description of the "wealthy and the well born." These, it seems, are to be exalted to an odious preeminence over the rest of their fellow citizens. At one time however their elevation is to be a necessary consequence of the smallness of the representative body; at another time it is to be effected by depriving the people at large of the opportunity of exercising their right of suffrage in the choice of that body.

But upon what principle is the discrimination of the places of election to be made in order to answer the purpose of the meditated preference? Are the wealthy and the well born, as they are called, confined to particular spots in the several states? Have they by some miraculous instinct or foresight set apart in each of them a common place of residence? Are they only to be met with in the towns or cities? Or are they, on the contrary, scattered over the face of the country as avarice or chance may have happened to cast their own lot, or that of their predecessors? If the latter is the case, (as every intelligent man knows it to be)[a] is it not evident that the policy of confining the places of elections to particular districts would be as subversive of its own aim as it would be exceptionable on every other account? The truth is that there is no method of securing to the rich the preference apprehended, but by prescribing qualifications of property either for those who may elect, or be elected. But this forms no part of the power to be conferred upon the national government. Its authority would be expressly restricted to the regulation of the *times*, the *places*, and the *manner* of elections. The qualifications of the persons who may choose or be chosen, as has been remarked upon another occasion,[3] are defined and fixed in the constitution; and are unalterable by the legislature.

Let it however be admitted, for argument sake, that the expedient suggested might be successful; and let it at the same time be equally taken for granted that all the scruples which a sense of duty or an apprehension of the danger of the experiment might inspire, were overcome in the breasts of the national rulers; still, I imagine, it will hardly be pretended, that they could ever hope to carry such an enterprise into execution, without the aid of a military force sufficient to subdue, the resistance of the great body of the people. The improbability of the existence of a force equal to that object, has been discussed and demonstrated in different parts of these papers;[4] but that the futility of the objection under consideration may appear in the strongest light, it shall be conceded for a moment that such a force might exist; and the national government shall be supposed to be in the actual possession of it. What will be the conclusion? With a disposition to invade the essential rights of the community, and with the means of gratifying that disposition, is it presumable that the persons who were actuated by it would amuse themselves in the rediculous task of fabricating election laws for securing a preferrence to a favourite class of men? Would they not be likely to prefer a conduct better adapted to their own immediate aggrandisement? Would they not rather boldly resolve to perpetuate themselves in office by one decisive act of usurpation, than to trust to precarious expedients, which in spite of all the precautions that might accompany them, might terminate in the dismission, disgrace and ruin of their authors? Would they not fear that citizens not less tenacious than conscious of their rights would flock from the remotest extremes of their respective states to the places of election, to overthrow their tyrants, and to substitute men who would be disposed to avenge the violated majesty of the people?

(a) *Particularly in the Southern States and in this State.*

1. "And overbearing" was omitted in the M'Lean edition.
2. *The Federalist* 35, New York *Independent Journal*, 5 January (CC:418).
3. *The Federalist* 59 (CC:555).
4. See especially *The Federalist* 24–29, published on 19, 21, 22, 25, 26 December, and 9 January (CC:355, 364, 366, 378, 381, 429).

559. John Williams on the Constitution
Albany Federal Herald, 25 February[1]

An Extract of a Letter from John Williams, Esq; at Poughkeepsie, to his Friends in Washington County, dated 29th *January,* 1788.

"The new constitution is not yet taken up, various are the opinions upon this subject; if I can have my opinion carried it will be this, let it come to the people without either recommending or disapprobation; let the people judge for themselves–if the majority is for it, let it be adopted– if they are against it, let it be rejected, as all powers are, or ought to be, in the people; they, and they only, have the right to say whether the form of government shall be altered. For my own part, I must confess, under the present situation of affairs, something must be done, but whether the present system is the best will be the question. The powers given to the president are very great. The elections may be so altered as to destroy the liberty of the people. The direct taxation, and to be collected by officers of Congress, are powers which cannot be granted agreeable to our present constitution, nor will it be very convenient for Congress officers, and our state collectors, to be collecting both at one time, and as Congress may lay a poll tax, how will that agree with us. I need not tell you the injustices of it. If the new constitution is adopted, Congress hath all the impost and excise; this latter may be laid heavy on taverns and spirits, so that the emoluments from taverns, which are now converted to the use of the poor, must go to Congress; and what is yet worse, all the duties arising from any duties or excise, are to be appropriated to the use of Congress.

"You will also observe that senators are for six years, and that small states have an equal number with large states, so that the advantage of having property in a maritime state, will be reduced to an equal value with the property where there is no navigation. If this is not taking our liberty, it is certainly diminishing our property, which is equal to it. What hath kept the taxes so low in this state–the reason is obvious, our impost duties. This is a privilege Providence hath endowed us with; our landed property will ever sell according to the conveniency of it; the lighter the tax, the higher the land; the nigher to market, the greater profits arising from our produce. Let our imposts and advantages be taken from us, shall we not be obliged to lay as heavy taxes as Connecticut, Boston, &c. What hath kept us from those burthens but the privileges, which we must lose if the present proposed constitution is adopted."

1. Reprints by 11 March (7): N.Y. (4), N.J. (1), Pa. (1), Md. (1). Williams (1752–1806)–a Washington County, N.Y., physician, country merchant, and large land-holder–was a judge of the county court and a state senator. On 1 February he voted in the state Senate against the calling of a state convention to ratify the Constitution. When it was learned that Williams intended to seek a seat in the state Convention, it was believed that "the federalists will be overpowered in that Quarter" (Leonard Gansevoort to Peter Gansevoort, 18 March, Gansevoort-Lansing Papers, NN). Williams

was elected to the state Convention from Washington County and voted against ratification of the Constitution on 26 July.

560. Hugh Williamson: Speech at Edenton, N.C.
New York Daily Advertiser, 25–27 February

On 8 November 1787 "a respectable number of Inhabitants" of Chowan County and the town of Edenton, in answer to a call of their representatives in the state legislature, met at the courthouse at Edenton and adopted several resolutions. These resolutions supported a strong Union, condemned the "anarchy, distress and dishonor" that followed the Revolution, praised the members of the Constitutional Convention (especially George Washington and Benjamin Franklin), and warned against any delays in ratifying the Constitution. The freemen asked their representatives to get the state legislature to call a state ratifying convention to meet at the earliest possible date. They thanked the state's delegates to the Constitutional Convention and expressed their particular obligation to Hugh Williamson "for the able and useful information he has this day given on the subject of the new Constitution proposed" (Newbern *State Gazette of North Carolina*, 29 November).

The "substance" of Williamson's speech was printed in the New York *Daily Advertiser* on 25, 26, and 27 February 1788. The printer had intended to publish it in two parts but was obliged to do so in three. The complete account was reprinted in the *Pennsylvania Packet*, 5 March; Charleston *Columbian Herald*, 17, 20 March; and the June issue of the Philadelphia *American Museum*. On 5 August the *Salem Mercury* printed two excerpts of the speech, each with a preface (see footnotes 9 and 13 below for the reprinting of these excerpts).

Hugh Williamson (1735–1819), a native of Pennsylvania, was educated at the College of Philadelphia, the University of Edinburgh, and the University of Utrecht. Before and during the Revolution, he was variously a licensed Presbyterian minister, a professor of mathematics, a physician, a scientist, and a merchant. He moved to Edenton in 1777 to engage in commerce and to practice medicine, and three years later he became head of the medical department of the North Carolina militia. He represented North Carolina in Congress, 1782–85, and Edenton and Chowan County in the state House of Commons in 1782 and 1785, respectively. In 1786 he was elected a delegate to the Annapolis Convention, but he arrived too late to attend its sessions. In 1787 Williamson's pamphlet, *Letters from Sylvius to the Freemen Inhabitants of the United States...* (Evans 20887), was published in New York. "Sylvius" attacked paper money and imported luxuries and advocated excises and import duties to encourage manufactures. The *Letters* were widely reprinted in newspapers. When Willie Jones and Governor Richard Caswell declined to attend the Constitutional Convention, Caswell appointed William Blount and Williamson to fill these vacancies. In the Constitutional Convention, Williamson spoke on many of the issues he later raised in his speech. He was elected again to Congress and attended from May to November 1788. Williamson represented Tyrrell County in the Fayetteville Convention in 1789 and voted for ratification of the Constitution. He served in the U.S. House of Representatives from 1790 to 1793, after which he retired from public life and lived in New York City.

[25 February] *The following Remarks on the New Plan of Government are handed us as the substance of Doctor* WILLIAMSON's *Address to the Freemen of Edenton and the County of Chowan, in North-Carolina, when assembled to instruct their Representatives.*

Though I am conscious that a subject of the greatest magnitude must suffer in the hands of such an advocate, I cannot refuse, at the request of my fellow-citizens, to make some observations on the new Plan of Government.

It seems to be generally admitted, that the system of Government which has been proposed by the late Convention, is well calculated to relieve us from many of the grievances under which we have been laboring. If I might express my particular sentiments on this subject, I should describe it as more free and more perfect than any form of government that ever has been adopted by any nation; but I would not say it has no faults. Imperfection is inseparable from every human device. Several objections were made to this system by two or three very respectable characters in the Convention, which have been the subject of much conversation;[1] and other objections, by citizens of this State, have lately reached our ears. It is proper that you should consider of these objections. They are of two kinds; they respect the things that are in the system, and the things that are not in it. We are told that there should have been a section for securing tha Trial by Jury in Civil cases, and the Liberty of the Press: that there should also have been a Declaration of Rights. In the new system it is provided, that *"The Trial of all crimes*, except in cases of Impeachment," *shall be by Jury*, but this provision could not possibly be extended to all *Civil* cases. For it is well known that the Trial by Jury is not general and uniform throughout the United States, either in cases of Admiralty or of Chancery; hence it became necessary to submit the question to the General Legislature, who might accommodate their laws on this occasion to the desires and habits of the nation. Surely there is no prohibition in a case that is untouched.

We have been told that the Liberty of the Press is not secured by the New Constitution. Be pleased to examine the plan, and you will find that the Liberty of the Press and the laws of Mahomet are equally affected by it. The New Government is to have the power of protecting literary property; the very power which you have by a special act delegated to the present Congress.[2] There was a time in England, when neither book, pamphlet, nor paper could be published without a licence from Government. That restraint was finally removed in the year 1694 and by such removal, their press became perfectly free, for it is not under the restraint of any licence.[3] Certainly the new Government can have no power to impose restraints. The citizens of the United States have no more occasion for a second Declaration of Rights, than they have for a section in favor of the press. Their rights, in the several States, have long since been explained and secured by particular declarations, which make a part of their several Constitutions. It is granted, and perfectly understood, that under the Government of the Assemblies of the States, and under the Government of the Congress, every right is reserved to the individual, which he has not expressly delegated to this, or that Legislature. The other objections that have been made to the new plan of Government, are: That it absorbs the powers of the several States: That the national Judiciary is too extensive: That a standing army is permitted: That Congress is allowed to regulate trade: That the several States are prevented from taxing exports, for their own benefit.

When Gentlemen are pleased to complain, that little power is left in the hands of the separate States; they should be advised to cast an eye upon the large code of laws, which have passed in this State since the peace. Let them consider how few of those laws have been framed, for the general benefit of the Nation. Nine out of ten of them, are domestic; calculated for the sole use of this State, or of particular citizens. There must still be use for such laws, though you should enable the Congress to collect a revenue for National purposes, and the collection of that revenue includes the chief of the new powers, which are now to be committed to the Congress.

Hitherto you have delegated certain powers to the Congress, and other powers to the Assemblies of the States. The portion that you have delegated to Congress is found to have been useless, because it is too small, and the powers that are committed to the assemblies of the several States, are also found to be absolutely ineffectual for national purposes, because they can never be so managed as to operate in concert. Of what use is that small portion of reserved power? It neither makes you respectable nor powerful. The consequence of such reservation is national contempt abroad, and a state of dangerous weakness at home. what avails the claim of power, which appears to be nothing better than the empty whistling of a name? The Congress will be chosen by yourselves, as your Members of Assembly are. They will be creatures of your hands, and subject to your advice. Protected and cherished by the small addition of power which you shall put into their hands, you may become a great and respectable nation.

[26 February] It is complained that the powers of the national Judiciary are too extensive. This objection appears to have the greatest weight in the eyes of gentlemen who have not carefully compared the powers which are to be delegated with those that had been formerly delegated to Congress. The powers that are now to be committed to the national Legislature, as they are detailed in the 8th section of the first article, have already been chiefly delegated to the Congress under one form or another, except those which are contained in the first paragraph of that section. And the objects that are now to be submitted to the Supreme Judiciary, or to the Inferior Courts, are those which naturally arise from the constitutional laws of Congress. If there is a single new case that can be exceptionable, it is that between a foreigner and a citizen, or that between the citizens of different States. These cases may come up by appeal. It is provided in this system that there shall be no fraudulent tender in the payments of debts. Foreigners, with whom we have treaties, will trust our citizens on the faith of this engagement. And the citizens of different States will do the same. If the Congress had a negative on the laws of the several States, they would certainly prevent all such laws as might endanger the honor or peace of the nation, by making a tender of base money; but they have no such power, and it is at least possible that some State may be found in this Union, disposed to break the Constitution, and abolish private debts by such tenders. In these cases the Courts of the offending States would probably decide according to its own laws. The foreigner would complain; and the nation might be involved in war for the support of such dishonest measures. Is it not better to have a Court of Appeals in which the Judges can only be determined by the laws of the nation? This Court is equally to be desired by the citizens of different States. But we are told that justice will be delayed, and the poor will be drawn away by the rich to a distant Court. The authors of this remark have not fully considered the question, else they must have recollected that the poor of this country have little to do with foreigners, or with the citizens of distant States. They do not consider that there may be an Inferior Court in every State; nor have they recollected that the appeals being *with such exceptions*, and *under such regulations* as Congress shall make, will never be permitted for trifling sums, or under trivial pretences, unless we can suppose that the national Legislature shall be composed of knaves and fools. The line that separates the powers of the national Legislature from those of the several States is clearly drawn. The several States reserve every power that can be exercised for the particular use and comfort of the State. They do not yield a single power which is not purely of a national concern; nor do they yield a single power which is not absolutely necessary to the safety and prosperity of the nation, nor one that could be employed to any effect in the hands of particular States. The powers of Judiciary naturally arise from those of the Legislature. Questions that are of a national concern, and those cases which are determinable by the general laws of the nation, are to be referred to the national Judiciary, but they have not any thing to do with a single case either civil or criminal, which respects the private and particular concerns of a State or its citizens.

The possibility of keeping regular troops in the public service has been urged as another objection against the new Constitution. It is very remarkable that the same objection has not been made against the original Confederation, in which the same grievance obtained without the same guards. It is now provided, that no appropriation of money for the use of the army shall be for a longer time than two years. Provision is also made for having a powerful militia, in which case there never can be occasion for many regular troops. It has been objected in some of the Southern States, that the Congress, by a majority of votes, is to have the power to regulate trade. It is universally admitted that Congress ought to have this power, else our commerce, which is nearly ruined, can never be restored; but some gentlemen think that the concurrence of two thirds of the votes in Congress should have been required.[4] By the sundry regulations of commerce, it will be in the power of Government not only to collect a vast revenue for the general benefit of the nation, but to secure the carrying

trade in the hands of citizens in preference to strangers. It has been alledged that there are few ships belonging to the Southern States, and that
the price of freight must rise in consequence of our excluding many foreign
vessels: but when we have not vessels of our own, it is certainly proper
that we should hire those of citizens in preference to strangers; for our
revenue is promoted and the nation is strengthened by the profits that
remain in the hands of citizens; we are injured by throwing it into the
hands of strangers; and though the price of freight should rise for two or
three years, this advantage is fully due to our brethren in the Eastern and
middle States, who, with great and exemplary candor, have given us equal
advantages in return. A small encrease in the price of freight would operate greatly in favor of the Southern States: it would promote the spirit of
ship building; it would promote a nursery for native seamen, and would
afford support to the poor who live near the sea coast; it would encrease
the value of their lands, and at the same time it would reduce their taxes.
It has finally been objected that the several States are not permitted to tax
their exports for the benefit of their particular Treasuries. This strange
objection has been occasionally repeated by citizens of this State. They
must have transplanted it from another State, for it could not have been
the growth of North-Carolina. Such have been the objections against the
new Constitution.

Whilst the honest patriot, who guards with a jealous eye the liberties of
his country, and apprehends danger under every form: the placeman in
every State, who fears lest his office should pass into other hands; the idle,
the factious, and the dishonest, who live by plunder or speculation on the
miseries of their country; while these, assisted by a numerous body of
secret enemies, who never have been reconciled to our Independence, are
seeking for objections to this Constitution; it is a remarkable circumstance,
and a very high encomium on the plan, that nothing more plausible has
been offered against it; for it is an easy matter to find faults.

Let us turn our eyes to a more fruitful subject; let us consider the present condition of the United States, and the particular benefits that North
Carolina must reap by the proposed form of Government. ⟨Without
money, no Government can be supported; and Congress can raise no
money under the present Constitution: They have not the power to make
commercial treaties, because they cannot preserve them when made.
Hence it is, that we are the prey of every nation: We are indulged in such
foreign commerce, as must be hurtful to us: We are prohibited from that
which might be profitable,[5] and we are accordingly told, that on the last
two years, the Thirteen States have hardly paid into the Treasury, as much
as should have been paid by a single State.[6] Intestine commotions in some
of the States: Paper Money in others, a want of inclination in some, and a
general suspicion throughout the Union, that the burthen is unequally
laid; added to the general loss of trade have produced a general bank-

ruptcy, and loss of honor. We have borrowed money of Spain–she demands the principal, but we cannot pay the interest. It is a circumstance
perfectly humiliating, that we should remain under obligations to that nation: We are Considerably indebted to France but she is too generous to
insist upon what she knows we cannot pay, either the principal or interest.
In the hour of our distress, we borrowed money in Holland; not from the
Government, but from private citizens.[7] Those who are called the Patriots
were our friends, and they are oppressed in their turn by hosts of enemies:
They will soon have need of money: At this hour we are not able to pay
the interests of their loan.[8] What is to be done? Will you borrow money
again from other citizens of that oppressed Republic, to pay the interest of
what you borrowed from their brethren? This would be a painful expedient, but our want of Government may render it necessary. You have two
or three Ministers abroad; they must soon return home, for they cannot
be supported. You have four or five hundred troops scattered along the
Ohio to protect the frontier inhabitants, and give some value to your lands;
those troops are ill paid, and in a fair way for being disbanded. There is
hardly a circumstance remaining; hardly one external mark by which you
can deserve to be called a nation. You are not in a condition to resist the
most contemptible enemy. What is there to prevent an Algerine Pirate
from landing on your coast, and carrying your citizens into slavery? You
have not a single sloop of war. Does one of the States attempt to raise a
little money by imposts or other commercial regulations.–A neighboring
State immediately alters her laws and defeats the revenue, by throwing the
trade into a different channel. Instead of supporting or assisting, we are
uniformly taking the advantage of one another. Such an assemblage of
people are not a nation. Like a dark cloud, without cohesion or firmness,
we are ready to be torn asunder and scattered abroad by every breeze of
external violence, or internal commotion.⟩[9]

[27 February] Is there a man in this State who believes it possible for us
to continue under such a Government?–Let us suppose but for a minute,
that such a measure should be attempted.–Let us suppose that the several
States shall be required and obliged to pay their several quotas according
to the original plan. You know that North-Carolina, on the last four years,
has not paid one dollar into the Treasury for eight dollars that she ought
to have paid.[10] We must encrease our taxes exceedingly, and those taxes
must be of the most grievous kind; they must be taxes on lands and heads;
taxes that cannot fail to grind the face of the poor; for it is clear that we
can raise little by imports and exports. Some foreign goods are imported
by water from the Northern States, such goods pay a duty for the benefit
of those States, which is seldom drawn back; this operates as a tax upon
our citizens. On this side, Virginia promotes her revenue to the amount
of 25,000 dollars every year, by a tax on our tobacco that she exports:
South-Carolina on the other side, may avail herself of similar opportuni-

ties. Two thirds of the foreign goods that are consumed in this State are imported by land from Virginia or South-Carolina; such goods pay a certain impost for the benefit of the importing States, but our Treasury is not profited by this commerce. By such means our citizens are taxed more than one hundred thousand dollars every year, but the State does not receive credit for a shilling of that money. Like a patient that is bleeding at both arms, North-Carolina must soon expire under such wasteful operations. Unless I am greatly mistaken, we have seen enough of the State of the Union, and of North-Carolina in particular, to be assured that another form of Government is become necessary. Is the form now proposed well calculated to give relief? To this, we must answer in the affirmative. All foreign goods that shall be imported into these States, are to pay a duty for the use of the nation. All the States will be on a footing, whether they have bad ports or good ones. No duties will be laid on exports; hence the planter will receive the true value of his produce, wherever it may be shipped. If excises are laid on wine, spirits, or other luxuries, they must be uniform throughout the States. By a careful management of imposts and excises, the national expences may be discharged without any other species of tax; but if a poll-tax, or land-tax shall ever become necessary, the weight must press equally on every part of the Union. For in all cases, such taxes must be according to the number of inhabitants. Is it not a pleasing consideration that North-Carolina, under all her natural disadvantages, must have the same facility of paying her share of the public debt as the most favored, or the most fortunate State? She gains no advantage by this plan, but she recovers from her misfortunes. She stands on the same footing with her sister States, and they are too generous to desire that she should stand on lower ground. When you consider those parts of the new System which are of the greatest import–those which respect the general question of liberty and safety, you will recollect that the States in Convention were unanimous; and you must remember that some of the members of that body have risqued their lives in defence of liberty; but the system does not require the help of such arguments; it will bear the most scrupulous examination.

When you refer the proposed system to the particular circumstances of North-Carolina, and consider how she is to be affected by this plan; you must find the utmost reason to rejoice in the prospect of better times–this is a sentiment that I have ventured with the greater confidence, because it is the general opinion of my late Honorable Colleagues, and I have the utmost reliance in their superior abilities.[11] But if our constituents shall discover faults where we could not see any, or if they shall suppose that a plan is formed for abridging their liberties when we imagined that we had been securing both liberty and property on a more stable foundation; if they perceive that they are to suffer a loss where we thought they must rise from a misfortune; they will at least do us the justice to charge those errors to the head, and not to the heart.

⟨The proposed system is now in your hands, and with it the fate of your country. We have a common interest, for we are embarked in the same vessel. At present she is in a sea of troubles, without sails, oars, or pilot; ready to be dashed into pieces by every flaw of wind. You may secure a port, unless you think it better to remain at sea. If there is any man among you that wishes for troubled times and fluctuating measures, that he may live by speculations, and thrive by the calamities of the State; this Government is not for him.[12]

If there is any man who envies the prosperity of a native citizen, who wishes that we should remain without native merchants or seamen, without shipping, without manufactures, without commerce; poor and contemptible, the tributaries of a foreign country; this Government is not for him.

And if there is any man who has never been reconciled to our Independence, who wishes to see us degraded and insulted abroad, oppressed by anarchy at home, and torn into pieces by factions; incapable of resistance and ready to become a prey to the first invader; this Government is not for him.

But it is a Government, unless I am greatly mistaken, that gives the fairest promise of being firm and honorable; safe from Foreign Invasion or Domestic Sedition. A Government by which our commerce must be protected and enlarged; the value of our produce and of our lands must be encreased; the labourer and the mechanic must be encouraged and supported. It is a form of Government that is perfectly fitted for protecting Liberty and Property, and for cherishing the good Citizen and the Honest Man.⟩[13]

1. Elbridge Gerry, George Mason, and Edmund Randolph refused to sign the Constitution. Gerry's objections were printed on 3 November, Mason's on 21 and 22 November, and Randolph's around 27 December (CC:227-A, 276, 385).

2. On 2 May 1783 Congress adopted a committee report, in Williamson's handwriting, urging the states to secure copyright protection for authors (JCC, XXIV, 326-27). In November 1785 Williamson, as a member of the North Carolina House of Commons, proposed a "Bill for securing Literary property." This bill, incorporating the language of the congressional committee report, became law on 29 December 1785 (NCSR, XVII, 280; XXIV, 747-48). The law did not delegate the power of copyright protection to Congress, but provided protection only to authors in other states that had passed similar laws.

3. The Printing Act of 1662 authorized the licensing of the press in England; it was renewed until 1679 and again in 1685 and 1692. In 1694 the House of Lords voted for renewal but the Commons opposed it, ending the licensing of the press (Frederick S. Siebert, *Freedom of the Press in England, 1476-1776* [Urbana, Ill., 1952], 237-63).

4. Williamson favored a two-thirds majority in the Constitutional Convention. He did not think it necesary, "but he knew the Southern people were apprehensive on this subject and would be pleased with the precaution" (Farrand, II, 450-51).

5. For a discussion of the restrictions placed on American commerce during the Confederation and the attempts to retaliate, see CC:Vol. 1, pp. 24-30.

6. See the 28 September 1787 report of the Board of Treasury on the requisitions of Congress (JCC, XXXIII, 569-85).

7. During the Revolution, Spain provided about $400,000 in subsidies, which were not considered loans and were never repaid, and $248,000 in loans. French subsidies amounted to nearly $2,000,000 and their loans to $6,350,000. Between 1782 and 1787 Dutch bankers floated loans of about $3,200,000 to the United States. Another loan of $400,000 was made in 1788. In August 1788 Williamson served on a congressional committee that reported unpaid interest on the foreign debt of $1,521,116 and principal payments due in 1787 and 1788 of $925,925 (JCC, XXXIV, 435).

8. During the early and mid-1780s, the Netherlands was split between the Patriots who supported a republic and the Orangists who advocated the return of the stadt-holder, William V. The Patriots had been sympathetic to the American Revolution and some of their leaders had been involved in the loans to America. In September 1787 Prussian forces invaded the Netherlands, routed the Patriots, and in October reinstated William V (Simon Schama, *Patriots and Liberators: Revolution in the Netherlands, 1780–1813* [New York, 1977], 64–135).

9. The text in angle brackets was reprinted in the *Salem Mercury*, 5 August, with this preface: "The following gloomy picture of '*the present condition of the United States*' is taken from a late 'address to the freemen of Edenton and County of Chowan, Northcarolina, by the Hon. HUGH WILLIAMSON, Esq. Delegate from said State to the late Continental Convention.'" This excerpt was reprinted four times with the one cited in note 13 below: N.H. (1), Conn. (2), N.Y. (1).

10. On 4 May 1790 the secretary of the treasury reported that North Carolina had paid about 10.5 percent of its specie quota of the congressional requisitions of 1784, 1785, and 1786 ($48,626 of $463,906), while it paid none of its indents quota of $674,739 (ASP, *Finance*, I, 56–57. See also a congressional committee report of September 1788 in JCC, XXXIV, 556–59. Williamson was a member of the committee.).

11. See North Carolina Delegates to Governor Richard Caswell, 18 September 1787 (CC:78).

12. Charles Johnson of Chowan County alluded to this portion of the speech while expressing his concern about adopting the Constitution unamended: "I only venture my doubts without any apprehension of your placing me in any of our friend Dr. W.'s classes, the burden of each verse of which, if I remember rightly is 'the government is not for him'" (to James Iredell, 14 January, CC:445).

13. The text in angle brackets was reprinted in the *Salem Mercury*, 5 August, with this preface: "In the conclusion of Mr. Williamson's address, we are relieved with a more pleasing representation than the foregoing [see note 9 above]-that of the probable ben-efits which the New Constitution is capable of affording." This excerpt was reprinted four times with the one cited in note 9: N.H. (1), Conn. (2), N.Y. (1). It was also reprinted alone in the Boston *Independent Chronicle*, 11 September, and the *Newport Herald*, 25 September.

561. Jeremiah Hill to George Thatcher
Biddeford, Maine, c. 26 February (excerpts)[1]

I can with a good deal of Pleasure anticipate the glory, of this young Empire, dedicated to the fair Godess of Liberty. a friend to his Country when he sees a fair prospect of its increase in Honor & happiness antici-pates the future Grandeur naturally resulting to its inhabitants from a well ordered Government. the same as we fond parents do the fair healthy promising boy rising to maturity–I am daily making Calculations for the United States to be adorned with her new *wedding Suit*. I will give you a short account of my Calculations. by the first of April next the present Congress will receive official Intelligence of nine States having adopted the

new Constitution. they will then make the proper Arrangements for sending official orders to the several States who have adopted it, to make the resiquite [i.e., requisite] Elections for organizing the new Congress. tho' they wont send out those orders untill every State in the Union has had the Constitution under debate and has either adopted or rejected it if they mean to do either, having made those necessary preresiquites Congress will adjourn leaving a Committee in the interregnum to manage such matters & things as may be necessary during that time, as the present Confederation authorises. then I shall expect to see my old friend again: I have made these Calculations to Mrss. Thatcher I assure you they were not disagreeable to her. ... To return the several States will receive these official orders by the first of August and by the first of October will have compleated the different Elections, then the present Congress will all return to induct the new Congress agreeable to the Constitution, then I hope we shall all see and enjoy those Halcyon days which has been so long prognosticated, when the *Lincolnians*[2] and *Shaysites* shall lie down together, beat their swords into plowshares and their spears into pruning hooks & learn *Insurgency* no more. then peace & good order shall invade this Asylum of Liberty where every one shall set in his own Orchard in the Summer, & by his own fire in the winter, and there shall be nothing to make us afraid, only the rod of Correction which shall slay the wicked and ungodly, who shall presume to trample on its laws or violate its Council–I made these Calculations previous to seeing your Letter to brother Lee[3] of the 10th. inst. which he has favored me with the perusal of–by that Letter I fear nine States won't have acted upon the new Constitution according to my Calculations. However, a month or so in the great Scale will be but in comparison of the great whole as a mote in the great Luminary of Heaven
. . . the post has not come this way week on Account of the heavy Snow. the man is waiting to carry this to Kennebunk therefore you must excuse my not filing up the third page–

1. RC, Chamberlain Collection, Thatcher Papers, MB. The letter was dated "Feby 1788," but it was postmarked "PORTSMOUTH/FEBRUARY 26." Portsmouth is about forty miles southwest of Biddeford.
2. General Benjamin Lincoln commanded the Massachusetts militia that crushed Shays's Rebellion.
3. Silas Lee.

562. Richard Henry Lee to James Gordon, Jr.
Chantilly, Va., 26 February[1]

Captain Merry delivered me the letter that you were pleased to write me, on the 11th instant, in which I find you propose the following questions, relative to the new constitution, proposed by the late general convention, and request my answer to them:

First. Whether the United States had not better receive than reject the said constitution?

Secondly. Whether it would not injure our credit in the European world, if we were to dissent therefrom; and whether our country would not thereby be endangered, as there are large demands in Europe against us?

Thirdly. Whether every objection to the plan may not, by instructions from the different states, be made as soon as the said Congress may be assembled?

Fourthly. Whether ruin would await us, unless we are consolidated in one general plan of government?

To the first question, namely, "Whether the United States," &c. I answer, that this question implies a *necessity* of either adopting or rejecting. But I know of no power on earth that has, or ever had, a right to propose such a question of extremity to the people, or any part of the people, of the United States. The happiness or misery of mankind depends so essentially upon government, that, when this is to be established by the people for themselves and their posterity, the right of the people cannot be questioned, of so acting with plans proposed, as to adopt them, reject them, or propose amendments to them.

To the second query, "Whether it would not injure," &c. I reply, that this second question is much founded on the first; and, so far as it is, may receive the same answer. It is divisible into two parts; the first, shall our credit be injured in Europe by *dissenting* from the proposed plan? It is presumable, that credit abroad depends much upon union and happiness at home, as it must always greatly do upon that industry and real strength which grows out of the possession of civil liberty. Those, therefore, who contend for the new plan, by propounding such a question, should prove, in the first place, that the adoption of this constitution will secure union and happiness at home, and those valuable consequences that flow from the possession of civil liberty; and this is the more necessary, as there are such numbers who think that the proffered plan, if admitted without amendments, will empower the administrators of the new government to destroy civil liberty. The second part of this question is, ["]whether our country will not be endangered by a *dissent*, as there are large demands against us in Europe." I presume that foreigners have no business with the nature of our government. Payment of their debts they are entitled to, but no possible reason can be assigned, why these debts may not as well be paid if the proposed constitution was to be so amended, as to secure the just rights and liberties of the people from violation, by a proper bill of rights; to retain the trial by jury in all cases, civil as well as criminal, as directed by the common law; to secure the rights of conscience, and freedom of the press. Will France, Holland, or Spain, be disturbed at our retaining these valuable privileges? or, will they quarrel with us for so amending this new plan, as to put it out of the power of the new rulers to carry every citizen of the state, by way of appeal, to be tried for every suit for debt, brought by all others than our own state citizens, in the supreme

federal court, where distance and expense may ruin multitudes? Have foreigners any thing to do with our amending the proposed constitution, so
as to put it out of the power of the rulers under it, to garble elections, by
ordering all the elections of any state to be held at any place they shall
choose–at Cape Henry,[2] for instance, if they so please at any time. See
section fourth, article first, where they have power over time, place, and
manner of holding elections for choosing representatives, without restraint
or limitation.

To the third query, "Whether every objection," &c. I answer, that the
constitution containing these objections, is made by the people of the
United States; "and the removal of them by the Congress, would only be
a common act of legislation, which may be revoked and repealed by every
subsequent meeting of the Congress.["] So that the power of oppressing
will be founded on the strong and lasting ground of a constitution made
by the people of the United States, and the remedies (if the new rulers
should ever please to declare any,) will rest on feeble and changeable acts
of a common legislature. Can it be safe or prudent to suffer this? As for
instructions, it is to be remarked, that the senators are chosen by the legislature of the states, and the representatives by all the freeholders–to instruct one, and not both branches of the new legislature, would be doing
nothing; and to render instructions of use, the general assembly, and the
freeholders of the community, must unite. The almost impossibility of
procuring such a union from the majority of the United States, is too
obvious, not to show the very little dependence that should be put on such
instructions. And, after all, the result could only be a legislative and mutable act against a fixed constitution. But how absurd would it be for the
people to agree to a constitutional evil to-day and to-morrow call for a
legislative redress of that evil!

The fourth and last question, "Whether ruin would await us," &c. I am
clearly of opinion, that our greater strength, safety, and happiness, depends on our union; but I am as clear that this union had infinitely better
be on principles that give security to the just rights and liberties of mankind, than on such principles as permit rulers to destroy them. Thus, sir,
I hope that I have fully, and to your satisfaction, answered your several
questions: so that you may think yourself warranted, if not bound to be a
friend to amendments that should be constitutional. To trust to future
events for remedy of evils that we have ourselves once created, is like
choosing to be sick, because a doctor may possibly cure us! A very capital
defect in this new project is, that the executive and legislative powers are
so blended and united, as to remove all chance for responsibility; and to
possess man with very great powers, without making him easily answerable for an abuse of these powers, is, in my opinion, neither safe nor wise.
I am glad to hear that Colonel Barbour[3] stands for the convention. It is
many years ago since I saw his conduct in the legislature, and observed it

to be both sensible and honest. I have been obliged to write in haste, so that you may be sure this letter is not intended for the press.

1. Printed: Richard H. Lee, *Memoir of the Life of Richard Henry Lee and His Correspondence...* (2 vols., Philadelphia, 1825), II, 84–86. Chantilly was the name of Lee's plantation in Westmoreland County, Va. Gordon (1759-1799) was an Orange County, Va., planter. In March he and James Madison were elected to represent Orange County in the Virginia Convention, where they voted to ratify the Constitution in June. In April Gordon was elected to the Virginia House of Delegates.

2. Cape Henry is in the southeastern corner of Virginia at the mouth of Chesapeake Bay.

3. Thomas Barbour (1735-1825), an Orange County planter and justice of the peace, was an ardent Antifederalist. See CC:574.

563. John Trumbull to Jonathan Trumbull, Jr.
London, 26 February (excerpt)[1]

. . . We entertain warm hopes of the adoption of the new constitution: it has the very general applause of Europe, tho' some of our Countrymen concieve some objections against it:–the want of a bill of rights–the want of a formal recognition of the liberty of the Press: & the perpetual eligibility of the President are the three points of imperfection most insisted on with us:–tho' from what I see of the American papers your objections seem to be not altogether the same.–the article of the President is thought to expose us in futurity to the intrigues of this quarter of the Globe, on the principle that it would be worth the expence of 2 or 300,000 Guineas even to continue a Man in that high office whose partialities should be known to favor a certain power:–an expence which would be ridiculous, if a Man must necessarily go out of office at a short period.–

Mr. Adams however, has just published a third volume of his defence of American Constitutions. in which He very fully, & with a Manliness highly honorable to him declares his opinions;–opinions which I am afraid will have no tendency at this moment, to place him higher in the popular estimation, but which appear to me founded in reason & the principles of human nature:–He gives the most pointed approbation to the division of Power into three equal portions, & the distinction of rank, even of hereditary rank.–He doubts the possibility of Elections to the highest Offices, being conducted for any number of years, without degenerating into scenes of corruption & tumult:–where domestic dissension will be fomented by foreign gold: & where the strength not of numbers but of Arms may decide the Choice.–

For my own part, I conceive that all Nations have & ever have had very nearly that form of Government which is best suited to their Manners & information & Merits:–I doubt not therefore but we shall continue to enjoy precisely as good a Constitution as we deserve, that supposing the present propos'd form to take place, we shall have the spirit to reform as many errors as we may have good sense to discover–& that after having made use of Elections as long as they are consonant with the state of our Morals:–we shall in the progress of our Existence pass thro' the various stages of encreasing power to that last stage when all other Empires have sunk.–where the governors are all, & the governed nothing. . . .

1. RC, John Trumbull Papers, CtY. Postmarked: "Boston 20 AP." John and Jonathan Trumbull were brothers.

564. Publius: The Federalist 61
New York Packet, 26 February

This essay, written by Alexander Hamilton, was reprinted in the New York *Independent Journal* on 27 February. It is number 61 in the M'Lean edition and number 60 in the newspapers.

For a general discussion of the authorship, circulation, and impact of *The Federalist*, see CC:201, 639.

The FŒDERALIST, No. 60.
To the People of the State of New-York.

The more candid opposers of the provision respecting elections contained in the plan of the Convention, when pressed in argument, will sometimes concede the propriety of that provision; with this qualification however that it ought to have been accompanied with a declaration that all elections should be had in the counties where the electors resided. This say they, was a necessary precaution against an abuse of the power. A declaration of this nature, would certainly have been harmless: So far as it would have had the effect of quieting apprehensions, it might not have been undesirable. But it would in fact have afforded little or no additional security against the danger apprehended; and the want of it will never be considered by an impartial and judicious examiner as a serious, still less, as an insuperable objection to the plan. The different views taken of the subject in the two preceding papers[1] must be sufficient to satisfy all dispassionate and discerning men, that if the public liberty should ever be the victim of the ambition of the national rulers, the power under examination at least will be guiltless of the sacrifice.

If those who are inclined to consult their jealousy only would exercise it in a careful inspection of the several State Constitutions, they would find little less room for disquietude and alarm from the latitude which most of them allow in respect to elections, than from the latitude which is proposed to be allowed to the National Government in the same respect. A review of their situation, in this particular, would tend greatly to remove any ill impressions which may remain in regard to this matter. But as that review would lead into lengthy and tedious details, I shall content myself with the single example of the State in which I write. The Constitution of New-York makes no other provision for *locality* of elections, than that the members of the Assembly shall be elected in the *counties*, those of the Senate in the great districts into which the State is or may be divided; these at present are four in number, and comprehend each from two to six counties. It may readily be perceived that it would not be more difficult to the Legislature of New-York to defeat the suffrages of the citizens of New-York by confining elections to particular places, than to the Legislature of the United States to defeat the suffrages of the citizens of the Union, by the like expedient. Suppose for instance, the city of Albany was to be appointed the sole place of election for the county and district of which it is a part, would not the inhabitants of that city speedily become the only electors of the members both of the Senate and Assembly, for that county and district? Can we imagine that the electors who reside in the remote subdivisions of the county of Albany, Saratoga, Cambridge, &c. or in any part of the county of Montgomery, would take the trouble to come to the city of Albany to give their votes for members of the Assembly or Senate, sooner than they would repair to the city of New-York to participate in the choice of the members of the Fœderal House of Representatives? The alarming indifference discoverable in the exercise of so invaluable a privilege under the existing laws, which afford every facility to it, furnishes a ready answer to this question. And, abstracted from any experience on the subject, we can be at no loss to determine that when the place of election is at an *inconvenient distance* from the elector, the effect upon his conduct will be the same whether that distance be twenty miles or twenty thousand miles. Hence it must appear that objections of the particular modification of the fœderal power of regulating elections will in substance apply with equal force to the modification of the like power in the Constitution of this State; and for this reason it will be impossible to acquit the one and to condemn the other. A similar comparison would lead to the same conclusion in respect to the Constitutions of most of the other States.

If it should be said that defects in the State Constitutions furnish no apology for those which are to be found in the plan proposed; I answer, that as the former have never been thought chargeable with inattention to the security of liberty, where the imputations thrown on the latter can be shown to be applicable to them also, the presumption is that they are rather the cavilling refinements of a predetermined opposition, than the well founded inferences of a candid research after truth. To those who are disposed to consider, as innocent omissions in the State Constitutions, what they regard as unpardonable blemishes in the plan of the Convention, nothing can be said; or at most they can only be asked to assign some substantial reason why the representatives of the people in a single State should be more impregnable to the lust of power or other sinister motives, than the representatives of the people of the United States? If they cannot do this, they ought at least to prove to us, that it is easier to subvert the liberties of three millions of people, with the advantage of local governments to head their opposition, than of two hundred thousand people, who are destitute of that advantage. And in relation to the point immediately under consideration, they ought to convince us that it is less probable a predominant faction in a single State, should, in order to maintain its superiority, incline to a preference of a particular class of electors, than that a similar spirit should take possession of the representatives of thirteen States spread over a vast region, and in several respects distinguishable from each other by a diversity of local circumstances, prejudices and interests.

Hitherto my observations have only aimed at a vindication of the provision in question, on the ground of theoretic propriety, on that of the danger of placing the power elsewhere, and on that of the safety of placing it in the manner proposed. But there remains to be mentioned a positive advantage which will result from this disposition, and which could not as well have been obtained from any other: I allude to the circumstance of uniformity in the time of elections for the Fœderal House of Representatives. It is more than possible, that this uniformity may be found by experience to be of great importance to the public welfare; both as a security against the perpetuation of the same spirit in the body; and as a cure for the diseases of faction. If each State may choose its own time of election, it is possible there may be at least as many different periods as there are months in the year. The times of election in the several States as they are now established for local purposes, vary between extremes as wide as March and November. The consequence of this diversity would be, that there could never happen a total dissolution or renovation of the body at one time. If an improper spirit of any kind should happen to prevail in it, that spirit would be apt to infuse itself into the new members as they come forward in succession. The mass would be likely to remain nearly the same; assimilating constantly to itself its gradual accretions. There is a contagion in example which few men have sufficient force of mind to resist. I am inclined to think that treble the duration in office, with the condition of a total dissolution of the body at the same time, might be less formidable to liberty, than one third of that duration, subject to gradual and successive alterations.

Uniformity in the time of elections seems not less requisite for executing the idea of a regular rotation in the Senate; and for conveniently assembling the Legislature at a stated period in each year.

It may be asked, why then could not a time have been fixed in the Constitution? As the most zealous adversaries of the plan of the Convention in this State, are in general not less zealous admirers of the Constitution of the State, the question may be retorted, and it may be asked, why was not a time for the like purpose fixed in the Constitution of this State? No better answer can be given, than that it was a matter which might safely be entrusted to legislative discretion, and that if a time had been appointed, it might upon experiment have been found less convenient than some other time. The same answer may be given to the question put on the other side. And it may be added, that the supposed danger of a gradual change being merely speculative, it would have been hardly adviseable upon that speculation to establish, as a fundamental point, what would deprive several States of the convenience of having the elections for their own governments, and for the National Government, at the same epochs.

1. See CC:555 and 558.

565. Centinel XVI
Philadelphia Independent Gazetteer, 26 February

On 26 February "Centinel" XVI made a new charge against the supporters of the Constitution–a charge that heightened political tension in Pennsylvania and sharpened the personal animosity between Federalists and Antifederalists. "Centinel" asserted that the ex post facto clause of the Constitution would prevent the United States from collecting money owed to it by former Confederation officers, such as Robert Morris, and by states which had not paid their quotas of the congressional requisitions.

Antifederalist writers quickly named other alleged defaulters–Thomas Mifflin, William Bingham, and Benjamin Franklin. Franklin, they charged, opposed the Constitution in the Constitutional Convention only until the ex post facto clause was adopted. The Convention contained nine of the "principal public defaulters," and the delinquent states of Connecticut, Delaware, and Georgia supported the Constitution only because of this provision. (See "James Bowdoin to James de Caledonia," "A Citizen of a Free and Independent State," "James de Caledonia to James Bowdoin," "A Countryman," and anonymous, *Independent Gazetteer*, 27 February, 3, 4, 6 March, CC:570; Mfm:Pa. 478, 481, 492, 494; and "Original Letters ... from Dr. R[ush] to Mr. H[ami]l[to]n, New York," Philadelphia *Freeman's Journal*, 5 March, Mfm:Pa. 487.)

Federalists defended the accused defaulters. The public was assured that all of the accounts of the alleged defaulters had been settled by Congress. Thomas Mifflin made available a certificate of the commissioners of accounts, showing that he owed only $42 in specie; if the expenses he had paid personally were included, "the balance would have appeared in his favor" (*Independent Gazetteer*, 6, 7 March, Mfm:Pa. 493, 495). "Z" defended William Bingham by citing resolutions in the Journals of Congress to prove that "so far from being in debt to the public, they were always so to him, and in times, when it was fashionable to be grateful, Congress nobly acknowledged their obligations..." (*ibid.*, 13 March, Mfm:Pa. 520). The charges against Robert Morris were called "a most wicked calumny, totally unsupported by even the shadow of truth," and certificates from treasury officers dated November 1784 were said to prove it. Morris had sacrificed his own interests to serve his country ("Z," *ibid.*, 8 March, Mfm:Pa. 500). Morris defended himself in a letter dated 21 March and published in the *Independent Gazetteer* on 8 April and the *Freeman's Journal* on 9 April (Mfm:Pa. 613). An anonymous writer regretted the charge made against "that philanthropic, patriotic sage, the venerable Franklin. ... It is also well known, that this venerable philosopher would have had his accounts adjusted long since, had his health and strength permitted him to make the journey to Congress" (*Pennsylvania Mercury*, 15 March, Mfm:Pa. 530).

Federalists also responded to the constitutional issue raised by "Centinel." "G.R." pointed out that Article IV, section 3 of the Constitution provides that "congress shall have power to dispose of, and make all needful rules and regulations respecting the territory OR OTHER PROPERTY BELONGING TO THE UNITED STATES, *and nothing in this constitution shall be so construed as to* PREJUDICE ANY CLAIMS OF THE UNITED STATES *or of any particular state*" (*Independent Gazetteer*, 18

March, Mfm:Pa. 537). Rufus King went even further. In a letter to Tench Coxe on 18 March, he called the Antifederalist interpretation an "egregious misconstruction." Even without Article IV, section 3, "as a Body politick the United States may recover their Debts..." (CC:623. Excerpts of King's letter were printed in the *Pennsylvania Gazette*, 26 March, and reprinted in Philadelphia, New York City, and Charleston.). "Antilon" made a similar argument. The debts are due to the people not the government of the United States. Even if the Constitution had not provided for the debts, they would have been collectible by the common law. If a law were required to collect the debt, it would not be ex post facto because the default had already been committed. "Antilon" complained that if the Constitution had not contained an ex post facto clause, "Centinel" would have criticized the omission (*Independent Gazetteer*, 28 March, Mfm:Pa. 577. See also "Reflection" V, *Carlisle Gazette*, 7 May, Mfm:Pa. 672.).

Sometime after 30 March, Benjamin Franklin prepared an essay for submission to the *Pennsylvania Gazette* in which he decried the personal attacks so common in newspaper articles. He noted that "it has long been the opinion of sober, judicious people, that nothing is more likely to endanger the liberty of the press, than the abuse of that liberty, by employing it in personal accusation, detraction, and calumny. The excesses some of our papers have been guilty of in this particular, have set this State in a bad light...." Franklin's piece, however, was never published (Mfm:Pa. 588).

In his next essay, "Centinel" renewed his charges that the defaulters and the delinquent states would be freed from their debts to the United States. He particularly rebutted the defenses made on behalf of Robert Morris and Thomas Mifflin. "For the honor of human nature," he chose not to pursue any further the conduct of Franklin, "whose name has given a false lustre to the new constitution, and been the occasion of sullying the laurels of a *Washington*..." (*Independent Gazetteer*, 24 March, CC:642).

"Centinel" XVI was reprinted in the *Freeman's Journal*, 27 February, and the *New York Journal*, 4 March. For a discussion of the authorship, circulation, and impact of "Centinel," see CC:133.

TO THE PEOPLE OF PENNSYLVANIA.

Fellow-Citizens, The new constitution instead of being the panecea or cure of every grievance so delusively represented by its advocates will be found upon examination like Pandora's box, replete with every evil. The most specious clauses of this system of ambition and iniquity contain latent mischief, and premedated villainy. By section 9th of the 1st article, "No *ex post facto* law shall be passed." This sounds very well upon a superficial consideration, and I dare say has been read by most people with approbation. Government undoubtedly ought to avoid retrospective laws as far as may be, as they are generally injurious and fraudulent: Yet there are occasions when such laws are not only just but highly requisite. An ex post facto law is a law made after the fact, so that the Congress under the new constitution are precluded from all controul over transactions prior to its establishment. This prohibition would skreen the numerous public defaulters, as no measure could be constitutionally taken to compel them to render an account and restore the public money; the unaccounted millions lying in their hands would become their private property. Hitherto these characters from their great weight and numbers have had the influence to prevent an investigation of their accounts, but if this constitution be established, they may set the public at defiance, as they would be completely exonerated of all demands of the United States against them.[1] This is not a strained construction of this section, but the proper evident meaning of the words,[2] which not even the ingenuity, or sophistry of the *Caledonian*,[3] can disguise from the meanest capacity. However if this matter admitted of any doubt, it would be removed by the following consideration, viz. that the new constitution is founded upon a dissolution of the present articles of confederation and is an original compact between those states, or rather those individuals who accede to it; consequently all contracts, debts and engagements in favor or against the United States, under the *old* government, are cancelled unless they are provided for in the *new* constitution. The framers of this constitution appear to have been aware of such consequence by stipulating in article 6th, that all debts contracted, and engagements entered into before the adoption of this constitution shall be valid *against* the United States under the new constitution,[4] but there is no provision that the debts, &c. due *to* the United States, shall be valid or recoverable. This is a striking omission, and must have been designed, as debts of the latter description would naturally occur and claim equal attention with the former. This article implied, cancels all debts due to the United States prior to the establishment of the new constitution. If equal provision had been made for the debts due *to* the United States, as *against* the United States, the ex post facto clause would not have so pernicious an operation.

The immaculate convention, that is said to have possessed the fullness of patriotism, wisdom and virtue, contained a number of the principal public defaulters; and these were the most influential members, and chiefly instrumental in the framing of the new constitution: There were several of this description in the deputation from the state of Pennsylvania, who have long standing and immense accounts to settle, and MILLIONS perhaps to refund. The late Financier alone, in the capacity of chairman of the commercial committee of Congress,[5] early in the late war, was entrusted with millions of public money, which to this day remain unaccounted for, nor has he settled his accounts as Financier. The others may also find it a convenient method to balance accounts with the public; they are sufficiently known and therefore need not be designated–This will account for the zealous attachment of such characters to the new constitution and their dread of investigation and discussion. It may be said that the new Congress would rather break through the constitution than suffer the public to be defrauded of so much treasure, when the burthens and distresses of the people are so very great; but this is not to be expected from the characters of which that Congress would in all probability be composed, if we may judge from the predominant influence and interest these defaulters now possess in many of the states. Besides, should Congress be disposed to violate the fundamental articles of the constitution for the sake of public justice, they would be prevented in so doing by their oaths,[a] but even if this should not prove an obstacle, if it can be supposed that any set of men would perjure themselves for the public good, and combat an host of enemies on such terms, still it would be of no avail, as there is a further barrier interposed between the public and these defaulters, namely, the supreme court of the union, whose province it would be to determine the constitutionality of any law that may be controverted; and supposing no bribery or corrupt influence practised on the bench of judges, it would be their sworn duty to refuse their sanction to laws made in the face and contrary to the letter and spirit of the constitution, as any law to compel the settlement of accounts and payment of monies depending and due under the old confederation would be. The 1st section of 3d article gives the supreme court cognizance of not only the laws, but of all cases arising under the constitution, which empowers this tribunal to decide upon the construction of the constitution itself in the last resort. This is so extraordinary, so unprecedented an authority, that the intention in vesting of it must have been to put it out of the power of Congress, even by breaking through the constitution, to compel these defaulters to restore the public treasure.

In the present circumstances these sections of the new constitution would be also productive of great injustice between the respective states; the delinquent states would be exonerated from all existing demands against them on account of the great arrearages of former requisitions, as they could not be constitutionally compelled to discharge them. And as the majority of the states are in this predicament, and have an equal voice in the senate, it would be their interest, and in their power by not only the constitution, but by a superiority of votes to prevent the levying of such arrearages; besides, the constitution, moreover, declares, that all taxes, &c. shall be uniform throughout the United States; which is an additional obstacle against noticing them.

The state of Pennsylvania in such case, would have no credit for her extraordinary exertions and punctuality heretofore; but would be taxed equally with those states which, for years past, have not contributed any thing to the common expences of the union; indeed, some of the states have paid nothing since the revolution.[6]

Philadelphia, 23d February, 1788.

(a) *Article* VI. *"The senators and representatives beforementioned and the members of the several state legislatures, and all executive and judicial officers, both of the United States and of the several states, shall be bound by oath to support this constitution." Were ever public defaulters so effectually skreened! Not only the administrators of the general government, but also of the state governments, are prevented by oath from doing justice to the public; and the legislature of Pennsylvania could not without perjury insist upon the delinquent states discharging their arrears.*

1. For a discussion of the effort to settle the wartime accounts of Confederation office-holders, see Merrill Jensen, *The New Nation: A History of the United States During the Confederation, 1781-1789* (New York, 1950), 379-81; and E. James Ferguson, *The Power of the Purse: A History of American Public Finance, 1776-1790* (Chapel Hill, N.C., 1961), 188-202.

2. The extent of ex post facto laws was not clear. On 14 September George Mason moved to delete the clause in the Constitutional Convention because "He thought it not sufficiently clear that the prohibition meant by this phrase was limited to cases of a criminal nature, and no Legislature ever did or can altogether avoid them in Civil cases." Elbridge Gerry "2ded. the motion but with a view to extend the prohibition to 'civil cases,' which he thought ought to be done" (CC:75). James Iredell in "Marcus" I wrote that the ex post facto clause assured that "the tenure of any property at any time held under the principles of the common law, cannot be altered by any act of the future general legislature" (CC:548).

3. James Wilson.

4. For a brief account of the circumstances under which this clause was adopted, see CC:371, note 3.

5. On 13 December 1775 Robert Morris was appointed to the Secret Committee–a body which exported goods in exchange for arms, ammunition, and other necessities to carry on the war. He became chairman of the committee on 14 March 1776 and served continuously on the committee until it was replaced by the Committee of Commerce on 5 July 1777. He was also chairman of this committee. In November 1777 he began a six-months leave from Congress, and there is no evidence that he returned to the Committee of Commerce at the end of his leave.

6. None of the states had paid its full quota of the requisitions. On the average, the states had paid 53 percent of the quotas payable in specie and 27 percent of the quotas payable in indents. Pennsylvania had paid 70 percent of its specie and 40 percent of its indents quota. Only Georgia had paid nothing. (See ASP, *Finance*, I, 56–57.) In 1793, when the Revolutionary War accounts were settled between the central government and the states, seven states were declared creditors and six were debtors; Pennsylvania was among the debtor states (see Ferguson, *Power of the Purse*, 332–33).

566 A–C. Governor John Hancock: Speech to the Massachusetts General Court, Boston, 27 February

On 24 November 1787 the Massachusetts General Court adjourned until 20 February 1788. In the meantime, the Massachusetts Convention convened on 9 January, ratified the Constitution with recommendatory amendments on 6 February, and adjourned the next day. On 4 February Governor John Hancock, the president of the Convention, issued a proclamation delaying the meeting of the General Court until 27 February so that Convention delegates, who were also legislators, would have time to return home.

On 27 February the General Court convened and at 5:00 p.m. Governor Hancock addressed a joint session of the two houses in the chambers of the House of Representatives. Among other things, Hancock praised the state Convention and the amendments to the Constitution that it had proposed (CC:566-A). Henry Jackson of Boston reported that Hancock's speech "is highly approved off, all is quiet & every body satisfied with respect to the adoption of the Federal constitution" (to Henry Knox, 2 March, Knox Papers, MHi). The Senate and the House of Representatives appointed members to a joint committee to draft a reply to the governor's address. The committee reported on 4 March and agreed with the governor's comments respecting the Constitution (CC:566-B). The same day the Senate accepted the report with minor amendments. (See notes 5 and 6 below.) Nathaniel Gorham, a member of the House from Charlestown who had signed the

Constitution in the Constitutional Convention and had voted for ratification in the state Convention, described the committee's report as "a very prudent-& decent answer-which passed the Senate without any dificulty" (to [Henry Knox?], 9 March, J.S.H. Fogg Autograph Collection, MeHi).

The House of Representatives read the committee report on 4 March and scheduled it for consideration on the 5th. On that day, "A warm debate" occurred in which Captain Phanuel Bishop of Rehoboth, who had voted against ratification in the state Convention, moved "to strike out all that related to the Constitution as reported by the Committe-& to insert a clause as prepared by himself or somebody for him in which the General Convention was charged with exceeding their powers & recommending measures which might involve the Country in blood:-by this amendment allso the Court were to say that they chose to suspend their opinion of the honor & integrity of the State Convention in consequence of their having ratified a Constitution so unfriendly to the rights of Men & States." Not all Antifederalists agreed with Bishop. William Widgery of New Gloucester, Maine, who had voted against ratification but who had agreed to support the Constitution, declared "that the Constitution had had a fair hearing and Discussion by a Body, authorised to recieve or reject it, and That the Opponents had been fairly beaten-and also that he thot the G. Court had nothing to do with it." The debate on Bishop's motion continued until 6 March, when the House voted "90 & od to 50 & od" that the consideration of Bishop's amendments should subside. The House then appointed a committee of five (including Bishop and Nathaniel Gorham) to report amendments to the reply to the governor's address which "when passed may not contain any opinion of the legislature upon the merits of the constitution" (Samuel Phillips Savage to George Thatcher, 7 March, CC:600; Gorham to [Knox?], 9 March, J.S.H. Fogg Autograph Collection, MeHi; and Journal of the House of Representatives, M-Ar. See also George R. Minot Journal, 27 February, Sedgwick [Minot] Papers, MHi.).

During the appointment of this committee it was said that the speaker of the House, Antifederalist James Warren of Milton, "cou'd readily hear the nomination of an *Anti* altho the Name of a *Fed* rung th[r]o the whole house without his being able to hear it-you will observe in the Fridays & Saturdays papers, some strikes upon him on that head" (Henry Jackson to Henry Knox, 10 March, Knox Papers, MHi). On Friday, 7 March, "A correspondent" observed in the *Massachusetts Gazette* "that the very palpable partiality of a certain honourable gentleman, in returning the nomination of a committee, (yesterday in the house) chosen to form an address to the governour, fully evinces his readiness to sacrifice truth and honour, in every instance, to the attainment of his favourite object." Six days later, "a correspondent" replied in the Antifederalist Boston *American Herald*: "should not the honorable House of Representatives resent the insult offered to their Speaker by a *paragraph* in the Massachusetts gazette of the 7th instant, and will not such *proceedings* soon produce a Removal of the Legislature from the town of Boston?"

On 11 March the House committee reported another reply which avoided any commentary on the Constitution: "We have observed the Communications which your Excellency has thought proper to make respecting the Federal System of Government and have postponed any Considerations on that important Subject" (Miscellaneous Legislative Papers, House Files, no. 2926, M-Ar). This reply was debated and then "it was Ordered that the consideration of the said answer subside." Representative Samuel Nasson of Sanford, Maine, who had voted against ratification in the state Convention, reported that "No answer is given to the Governors Address this Shew the Sence of the House but this was Disagreeable to me. I cannot Tell how it will Please the People. I cannot yet Say what Sutes them Sutes me I hope allways to Live in a Republicken Government" (to George Thatcher, 23 March, Thatcher Papers, MeHi). General Benjamin Lincoln of Hingham, who had voted for ratification in the state Convention, wrote that an answer was "omitted" in order "to avoid a greater evil" (to George Washington, 19 March, Washington Papers, DLC). On 6 April, after the legislative session ended, Nathaniel Gorham wrote that "The Legislature have ended the Session without doing any mischief–the utmost prudence & moderation was necessary & it was exerted" (to Rufus King, King Papers, NHi).

Governor John Hancock's speech was printed in Boston in the *Independent Chronicle* and the *American Herald* on 28 February with slightly different punctuation, spelling, capitalization, and italics, and with similar prefatory statements. By early June the complete speech was reprinted in the Philadelphia *American Museum* and in twenty-six newspapers: N.H. (1), Mass. (9), R.I. (2), Conn. (4), Pa. (3), Va. (2), S.C. (1). From 29 February to 9 April seven other newspapers reprinted excerpts from the speech that included at least three of the four paragraphs about the Constitution: N.H. (1), N.Y. (1), Pa. (2), Md. (1), Va. (1), N.C. (1).

On 24 March the Antifederalist *New York Journal* published an extract of a Massachusetts letter, dated 19 March, describing the actions of the legislature in trying to draft a reply to Hancock's speech and the text of Phanuel Bishop's amendment to that reply (CC:566–C). A correspondent in the Philadelphia *Independent Gazetteer* complained on 15 April that Ebenezer Hazard, the Confederation postmaster general, "still continues the practice of suppressing all useful information, and spreading delusion and falsehood"; he asserted that a New York newspaper had printed the Massachusetts House of Representative's critical answer to Hancock's speech. He also charged that Hazard was "determined" that only the governor's speech "should travel ... southward" (Appendix II).

The next day "A Bostonian," (Jonathan Williams, Jr.?), replying in the *Gazetteer*, questioned whether the Massachusetts House "ever did as a body reprobate the proceedings of the *general and state convention*." He requested that the *Gazetteer's* printer write his "correspondent printer in New-York ... for the very paper alluded to, and give us in your Gazetteer the full amount of this reprobation, cloathed with all the authority that it is capable of." If the printer was worried about the mails, he should order the newspaper by the stage. In an editorial note, the *Gazetteer's* printer said that he had already ordered the newspaper by stage because "no reliance or dependence can be placed on the present capricious and despotic *Post-Master-General*" (Appendix II).

The *Gazetteer* speculated on 17 April that "Time, that discoverer of all solid truths, will shew that the new constitution will never be received by the union as a government." Among the instances of Antifederalism listed by the *Gazetteer* was the answer to Hancock's speech in which the Massachusetts House of Representatives "reprobated" the Constitution "in the strongest terms, so it is probable it will be *reconsidered*" in Massachusetts (Mfm:Pa. 638).

On 28 April the *Gazetteer* reprinted the extract of the Massachusetts letter and Bishop's amendment, indicating that it had "at length procured" the *New York Journal* of 24 March and that it was taking "the earliest opportunity of laying before our readers, all that have reached us on the subject of the reply of the General Court of Massachusetts to Governor Hancock's late speech. The irregularity of our communications must be solely ascribed to the Post-Master General, who is still permitted to exercise the most execrable tyranny over the Printers, and to sport with the sacred liberties of the people" (Appendix II).

"A Bostonian" replied that the extract of the Massachusetts letter demonstrated "what some members of the Massachusetts Assembly *wished* the House to do, and what the House *did not do*, the matter (as the informant himself tells us) having subsided." In turn, "A Bostonian" produced an extract of a Boston letter, dated 9 March: "The next day the address was debated, and the amendment advocated by a very few only, many of these, finding it impossible to censure the Convention through the Legislature, voted for all conversation on the subject to subside; the address was recommitted with a vote of the House, that nothing for or against the constitution should be introduced; this I wish had not been done, as there was strength enough to have carried the address in its original form. I must do a leading part of the minority the justice to say, that their good conduct has continued in the trial of strength in the Legislature, they have given up their party, rather than sow sedition in the country, when it can no longer effect a decision" (*Independent Gazetteer*, 6 May, Mfm:Pa. 670. On 30 April a correspondent in the *Pennsylvania Gazette* had charged that the report the Massachusetts legislature disapproved the Constitution was an attempt "to deceive the public.").

Writing from New York City, Postmaster General Ebenezer Hazard was delighted that "A Bostonian" had disproved the "veracity" of the report published in the *New York Journal* on 24 March. Hazard himself challenged the authenticity of the Massachusetts letter of 19 March which he claimed could not have arrived by the 24th in New York by either post, stage, or vessel. Hazard concluded–"So much for Antifederal Veracity!" (See Hazard to Jeremy Belknap, 10 May, Appendix II.)

566–A. Governor John Hancock: Speech to the General Court
Boston Independent Chronicle, 28 February (excerpts)[1]

Yesterday, agreeably to Proclamation, the Hon. General Court of this Commonwealth, convened at the State-House, in this town–and a quorum of both Branches being assembled, a joint Committee was appointed to wait on his Excellency the Governour, to inform him, that they were ready to receive communications, &c.– Accordingly, at 5 o'clock, his Excellency, met both Branches, convened in the Representatives' Chamber, and delivered the following SPEECH:

Gentlemen of the Senate, and Gentlemen of the House of Representatives, The Letters which I have received in the recess, the Secretary will lay before you, they are not of such importance, as to claim any particular notice from me at this time.

The adjournment of the General Court, for the space of one week, became necessary, in order to give the members, who were also members of the late Convention, an opportunity of returning home before the meeting of the Legislature. I could have wished that the Proclamation of adjournment had been of an earlier date, but the Session of the Convention, by the importance of the business before that body, was protracted beyond what was expected. I flatter myself that this will be satisfactory, as well to those of you Gentlemen, who having not heard of the adjournment, have been some days waiting in town, as to those who may be apprehensive that the business of the present Session will demand a longer time, than can be conveniently afforded at this season of the year. . . .

In the beginning of your last Session, I laid before you the Constitution and Frame of Government for the United States of America, agreed upon by the late General Convention, and transmitted to me by Congress. As the System was to be submitted to the people, and to be decided upon by their Delegates in Convention, I forbore to make any remarks upon it.[2] The Convention which you appointed to deliberate upon that important subject, have concluded their Session, after having adopted & ratified the proposed plan, according to their resolution, a copy whereof, I have directed the Secretary to lay before you.

The obvious imbecility of the Confederation of the United States, has too long given pain to our friends, and pleasure to our enemies; but the forming a new System of Government, for so numerous a people, of very different views, and habits, spread upon such a vast extent of Territory, containing such a great variety of soils, and under such extremes of climate, was a task, which nothing less than the dreadful apprehension of losing our national existence, could have compelled the people to undertake.

We can be known to the world, only under the appellation of the *United States*; if we are robbed of the idea of our Union, we immediately become seperate nations, independent of each other, and no less liable to the depredations of foreign powers, than to wars and bloody contentions amongst ourselves. To pretend to exist as a nation without possessing those powers of coerce, which are necessarily incident to the national Character, would prove a fatal solecism in politicks. The objects of the proposed Constitution, are defence against external enemies, and the promotion of tranquility and happiness amongst the States. Whether it is well calculated for those important purposes, has been the subject of extensive and learned discussion in the Convention which you appointed. I believe there was never a body of men assembled, with greater purity of intention, or with higher zeal for the public interest. And although when the momentous Question was decided, there was a greater division than some expected, yet there appeared a candour, and a spirit of Conciliation, in the minority, which did them great honor, and afforded an happy presage of unanimity amongst the people at large.[3] Tho' so many of the members of the late Convention could not feel themselves convinced that they ought to vote for the ratification of this System, yet their opposition was conducted with a candid and manly firmness, and with such marks of integrity and real regard to the public interest, as did them the highest honor, and leaves no reason to suppose that the peace, and good order of the Government is not their object.

The amendments proposed by the Convention, are intended to obtain a constitutional security of the principles to which they refer themselves, and must meet the wishes of all the States. I feel myself assured, that they will very early become a part of the Constitution; and when they shall be added to the proposed plan, I shall consider it the most perfect System of government, as to the objects it embraces, that has been known amongst mankind.

Gentlemen, As that BEING, in whose hands is the government of all the Nations of the Earth, and who putteth down one, and raiseth up another according to His Sovereign Pleasure, has given to the People of these States, a rich and an extensive Country; has in a marvellous manner,

given them a name and a standing among the Nations of the World–has
blessed them with external Peace, and internal Tranquility;–I hope and
pray, that the gratitude of their Hearts may be expressed by a proper use
of those inestimable blessings,–by the greatest exertions of Patriotism,–by
forming and supporting Institutions for cultivating the human Understanding, and for the greatest Progress of the Arts and Sciences,–by establishing Laws for the support of Piety, Religion and Morality, as well as for
punishing Vice and Wickedness,–and by exibiting in the great Theatre of
the World, those social, public and private Virtues, which give more
Dignity to a People, possessing their own Sovereignty, than Crowns and
Diadems afford to Sovereign Princes. . . .

566–B. Draft of Answer to Governor's Speech
4 March (excerpt)[4]

. . . As the Constitution or frame of Government for these United States
which was laid before us by your Excellency in the beginning of the last
session was then to be submitted to the people for their unbiassed decision
there was the utmost propriety in your Excellencys conduct in not giving
your sentiments upon it at that period.[5] We feel with you, the strongest
conviction of the truth & justice of your remark "that the imbecility of the
Confederation has too long given pleasure to our enemies & pain to our
friends.–" Powerful and happy as this Country may become by its union;
its efforts will be proportionably feeble without a ~~federal~~ Government competent to the necessities of a people ~~extensively~~ diffused over an immense
territory and remarkable for the diversity of their habits manners & interests. This Idea Joined to the ~~dreadful~~ apprehension of our even loosing
our national existance must undoubtedly have originated ~~in~~ the late ~~Fed-
eral~~ continental Convention, the result of whose deliberations has since
been adopted in this State for our Federal Government–

As we are known only in our national Character we must be fully apprized that ~~where we to loose the Ideas of our~~ were the Ideas of an indissoluble union among the states to be abandoned we must become ~~separate
nations~~ distracted & unhappy exposed to foreign insults, and to the more
fatal evils of domestic & bloody contentions–We agree with your Excellency that the power of coercion is indispensibly requisite to the very ~~Idea~~
name of Government–And as the declared ~~object~~ end of the new constitution is defence against external enemies, & the maintenance & promotion
of liberty and happiness among the States–We fervently pray, that in the
progress of its operation it may fully ~~embrace attain~~ secure & perpetuate
these noble & essential purposes for which it was instituted–The Zeal
Knowledge & purity of intentions discovered by the members of the late
Convention of this State in discharge of the great & momentous trust which
has been assig[n]ed them leave no doubt of their integrity which we believe
with your Excellency has scarcely been exceeded–and we are fully agreed

that the candour & pleasing spirit of conciliation displayed by so large a minority ~~renders~~ confer on the Gentlemen who composed it the highest honor & affords an happy presage of our future Unanimity & Peace–

When we reflect on the nature of the amendments proposed by the convention and observe their design is to procure a Constitutional Security for those objects to which they refer, and also consider the liberal and extensive principles on which they are established we have reason to hope & *beleive*[6] that they will meet the approbation of the other States; and ~~we flatter ourselves that they will~~ early become a part of the proposed ~~federal~~ Constitution–And should this be the case we ⟨shou'd ~~consider~~ then view it ~~with respect to the objects it embraces & the principles on which it is constructed~~ as one of the most perfect Systems of *Federal* Government which we have known in the History of mankind–⟩[7]. . . .

566–C. New York Journal, 24 March[8]

Extract of a letter from Massachusetts, dated March 19, 1788.

"You have undoubtedly seen our governor's speech, and his encomiums therein on the proposed constitution; to which an answer, or rather *echo*, was prepared, and reported, to the legislature. The *whigs*, in the house of representatives were highly exasperated at the measure, and prepared an amendment. This terrified the federalists, *as they stile themselves* (that is, the gentry who opposed the British government because it was *arbitrary*, and who now are in favor of one *infinitely* more so) and produced a proposition from them, "that the matter should subside," as well the report as the amendment–thus you see that the representatives of the people of this state are not converts of *federalism*, a term which has the same meaning now which *toryism* had before the war."

The AMENDMENT *mentioned in the above letter.*

Your Excellency is pleased to inform us, that the convention which was appointed to deliberate upon the constitution and frame of government for the United States of America, agreed upon by the late general convention, have concluded their sessions after having adopted and ratified the proposed plan. We have long been sensible of the imbecility of the confederation of the United States, and of the consequences of that imbecility, and therefore appointed delegates to the late general convention, for the sole and express purpose of revising the articles of confederation, and reporting to Congress and the several legislatures such alterations and provisions therein, as shall, when agreed to in Congress, and confirmed by the states, render the federal constitution adequate to the exigencies of government and the preservation of the union! If they had observed, and acted agreeably to their commission, no difficulty perhaps would have arisen from the numbers of a people spread over a vast extent of territory, containing such a great variety of soils, and under such extremes of climate, and with such different views and habits while they were so well united in that one object, we are fully persuaded that our national existence might in that way have been preserved with unanimity, tranquility and peace. We do not wish to be known to the world under any other appellation than that of the United States.

In confederation and union with our sister states, we have happily baffled the intrigues and defeated the force of Great-Britain, have supported the rights of mankind, and secured the freedom and independence of America. While we wish to preserve the union entire, and are fully sensible of the ill consequences of an interruption of it, we are sorry to differ from your Excellency in the mode of effecting the first and avoiding the last.–Every good government should have for its objects defence against external enemies, and the promotion[9] of internal tranquility and happiness. While we suspend our opinion of the purity of intention, and of the great zeal for the interest[10] and welfare with which the late convention assembled, we are in justice to our constituents constrained to say that the result of their deliberations does not seem well calculated for those valuable purposes. We shall, under this head, only add, that the rights and liberties of a great country should stand on firmer ground than that of mere probability. If the amendments proposed with the ratification of the late convention, had been made a condition of ratification, they would have gone some way, though not fully, to a conciliation of our minds to the system, but your Excellency will permit us to say, that, as they now stand, they neither comport with the dignity or safety of the Commonwealth.

1. There are two manuscript versions of this address, both in the handwriting of the same clerk and both signed by Hancock, among the Miscellaneous Legislative Papers, House Files, nos. 2898 and 2899, in the Massachusetts Archives, Boston. One manuscript (no. 2898) is endorsed as read by the Senate and the House of Representatives on 28 February. The endorsements also indicate that two senators and three representatives were appointed a joint committee "to consider & report" on the address. The action of each house was signed respectively by Samuel Adams, president of the Senate, and James Warren, speaker of the House. The texts of both manuscripts differ from the text in the *Independent Chronicle* in punctuation, capitalization, spelling, paragraphing, and italics.

2. For Hancock's speech of 18 October, see CC:177.

3. The final vote to ratify the Constitution was 187 to 168. On the same day that Hancock delivered his address to the legislature, the *Massachusetts Centinel* printed an extract of a New York letter stating that the "minority have gained themselves immortal honour, by their honourable and candid behaviour." For widely circulated newspaper items commenting favorably on the Massachusetts minority, see *Pennsylvania Gazette*, 20 February, 12, 26 March, and *Pennsylvania Mercury*, 21 February (all in Appendix I), and the New York *Daily Advertiser*, 14, 18 February.

4. Dft, Miscellaneous Legislative Papers, House Files, no. 2690, M-Ar. The draft reply contains many emendations made by either the joint committee or the House, or both. An endorsement–signed by Samuel Adams, president of the Senate–indicates that the Senate read and accepted the reply with two amendments (see footnotes 6 and 7) and that two senators were appointed to be part of another joint committee to present the reply to the governor. The reply is docketed (probably by the clerk of the House):

"Answer to/the Govr's Speech/March 11th. 1788./consideration hereof/ordered to subside."

5. A marginal note indicates that this sentence was intended to be replaced by another sentence which reads: "We observe that your Excellency has been pleased to communicate respecting the doings of the late Convention in ratifying the proposed federal Governmt & sincerely wish that *if* that government should become the governt of the United States it may promote & establish the happiness of the People." There is no record that this change, which is on a separate piece of paper in the handwriting of the clerk of the Senate, was accepted by either house.

6. The Senate recommended the deletion of the words "*& believe.*"

7. The Senate recommended the deletion of the text within angle brackets and the insertion in its place of the following: "trust it will be calculated to promote the future welfare & happiness of the United States."

8. Reprinted: Boston *American Herald*, 31 March; Philadelphia *Independent Gazetteer*, 28 April; Philadelphia *Freeman's Journal*, 30 April; Baltimore *Maryland Gazette*, 13 May; Winchester *Virginia Centinel*, 14 May; Annapolis *Maryland Gazette*, 15 May. The *New York Journal's* version of Bishop's amendment differs only slightly from the version in the Journal of the House of Representatives (5 March) and the original draft manuscript in the Miscellaneous Legislative Papers, House Files, no. 2689, in the Massachusetts Archives. (See notes 9 and 10.)

9. "Preservation" in the House Journal and the original draft manuscript.

10. "Safety" in the House Journal and the original draft manuscript.

567. John Howard to George Thatcher
Smithtown, N.Y., 27 February (excerpt)[1]

. . . Soon after my recovery I heard that you had returned to Boston. This report has prevented my writing. But seeing an account in the public papers, that Congress were sitting, and that Massachusets was represented, I thought it likely that you were there, and therefore resolved to write; so that you might know that my negligence has not been owing to forgetfulness or want of respect for a worthy friend.

I have not written to Doctor Barker, being in some expectation of going to the eastward myself in the course of a few weeks. However this is uncertain, as it depends upon the determination of a few Merchants who talk of sending me thither to negotiate some business on their accounts. Be this as it may, I shall not go till I shall have done myself the honor of waiting on you at New York. In the mean time, I cannot suppress the satisfaction I feel on the conduct of the Massachusets-convention. I am charmed with the behavior of the minority, and am even constrained to love gentlemen of anticonstitutional principals. Their conduct was manly and generous, and will ever redound to the honor of that state. The candor of one side and the ingenuous concessions of the other, I am persuaded will have some weight upon the public mind, and facilitate the determination of other states in favour of the constitution. Should we be so happy as to have it adopted, how will the face of things be changed! Beside the common advantages of a well regulated trade, we shall see, as a consequence of it, the arts of Europe cross the Atlantic and settle here. Thousands of industrous inhabitants poor, which, by the by, are the wealth of a nation, are only waiting for our government to be well established–When this shall be done, and well known in Europe, they will transplant themselves into this happy soil, and enrich the United states at the expence of our enemies. We are now feeding and clothing multitudes of the inhabitants of Great britain & Irland at a most expensive rate, by an extravigant consumption of their manufactures. This I take to be one of the many evils, which result from the weakness of our old foederal government, and which appear to be well guarded against by the new. We must feed and clothe a certain proportion of the artisans of Europe; but it rests with us to chuse whether we will do it in Europe or America. The latter is doubtless most for our interest. Why then do we hesitate? Let us retrench a little (tho' a goodeal would do better) the use of foreign manufactures, and thousands of mechanics, which we now support in Europe, greatly to our prejudise, will be compelled hither to seek employment, to the infinite advantage of these states. Some may think, that a disuse of foreign goods would rather injure than benefit this country, by depriving many seamen and merchants of their means of living. Were all the foreign goods, that we consume, imported in American vessels, own'd and navigated by our own citizens, those objections would be part[l]y true: The reverse, however, is a meloncholy fact. Foreign luxries are exported to this country by foreigners, in their own ships, and sold here by their factors; while our own vessels are rotting in the docks, our seamen strolling the streets, and our merchants daily becoming bankrupts. By wise commercial regulations these evils might be removed, & our imports, at the same time, reduced to one tenth of what they now are. But some will say, "We can not manufacture yet–our country is too young–labour is too dear–we can import most articles cheaper than we can make them. Let us therefore attend to agriculture–export our raw materials to be worked in Europe, and import their manufactures." This is the policy of Europe, and has been so industrously inculcated upon the minds of our countrymen, that the greatest part of our fellow citizens believe it to be true; tho' nothing in fact can be more erroneous. But suppose an article of our own make cost 50 percent more than a similar article which is manufactured in Europe: would this be a sufficient excuse for neglecting our manufactures? By no means; for the difference is pay'd in our own labour. The raw materials of which cloths, for instance, are manufactured, are not on an average, more than one tenth part of their value: So that if we export 100 pounds of raw materials, and exchange them for cloths, we do, in fact, recieve but ten pounds for our hundred: And if we reckon freight & insurance, which will be about 20 percent, we shall give 120 pounds for 10. Thus it appears that in one millions worth of goods that we recieve from Europe 916,667 pounds of it are labour–the labour of those whose interest & wish it is to ruin us.–But I can confide in the wisdom of Congress, and doubt not, that when ever they shall have sufficient power, they will adopt such commercial regulations, as will, eventually, remove these evils, by inducing the artisans of Europe to transport themselves into this country, and to seek that livelihood here, which we refuse to supply them with on the other side [of] the Atlantic. Then, my dear friend, and never till then, shall we taste the sweets of independance. . . .

1. RC, Chamberlain Collection, Thatcher Papers, MB. Howard (1753–1816), a native of Bridgewater, Mass., was a Smithtown, N.Y., physician.

568. Charles Vaughan to Benjamin Franklin
Boston, 27 February[1]

I was prevented replying to your favour of the 12th. Instant, from the necessity of closing my English letters;–Indeed Mr. William's absence from Town, put it out of my power to give you any satisfactory answer;–He returned yesterday, & has promised to give me in a day or two a Statement of what is in his possession of Dr. Ingenhouse's:–He has drawn no part of the Intt. out of ye office.–I have made enquiries at the office, and find, from the Value of the facilities by which the Intt. is discharged,–it has been too trifling an object for remittance:–The Value of them is 3/8 in the £-. From conversation with persons possessed of large property in similar Securities, I find their confidence in them has encreased since the adoption of the Constitution in this State;–indeed the increased Value is a proof; they have risen 1/6,[2]–Some persons even expect that the Interest will be more valuable, it remains as yet the same depreciation.–I shall receive the Papers from Mr. Williams and shall wait your directions in what manner I am to conduct.–The Intt. can only be applyed to Taxes.–

It gives me much concern that New Hampshire did not adopt,–the circumstances of the Convention were such, that an adjournment was necessary to prevent a rejection.–By the last post I gave what appeared to me to be the true cause for adjournment–the reasons given in Convention I have inclosed to my brother.[3]–Russell's information may be depended on, and I took the paragraph from his Paper, The Centinel,[4]–There was a late moment when the minds of the People were prepared for any change that had the least prospect of amending this is past in New Hampshire–and the Constitution will be carried with some difficulty–as there are many Incendiaries thro' this country–and all most from situation interested in preventing good Govermt. The List of Yaes & Nays in the Massachusetts Convention[5] will at once shew that character & property are the Supporters of the New Government and the Debates are a sufficient Evidence that Men of Understanding or Information took no part in the opposition–Rhode Island met on Monday last and I understand they are resolved to censure the conduct of her *Sister* States for deserting the Confederation[6] they have so long indulged in bad measures that I fear your well timed Invitation to return to the Union will have no effect–I think it probable that all the *Sea Ports* will apply to be taken under the Protection of the Fœderal government if so it is to be hoped the opposition of the Interior parts will not obstruct the general good–Pray make my kind regards to your good family

1. RC, Franklin Papers, PPAmP. Vaughan (1759–1839) was a Boston merchant. On 12 February Franklin had asked Vaughan to settle Dr. Jan Ingenhousz's account with John Williams, a Boston merchant and grandnephew of Franklin (Franklin Papers, DLC). Ingenhousz (1730–1799), a renowned physician and chemist, was a close friend and frequent correspondent of Franklin. A native of Holland, Ingenhousz lived in London at this time.

2. Franklin had written Ingenhousz on 11 February that "we hope and believe" the certificates "will mend, when our new projected Constitution of Government is established" (Albert Henry Smyth, ed., *The Writings of Benjamin Franklin*... [10 vols., New York, 1905–1907], IX, 635).

3. John Vaughan (1756–1841) was a Philadelphia merchant.

4. See the *Massachusetts Centinel*, 27 February (CC:554–B).

5. The yeas and nays, taken on 6 February, were first printed in the *Massachusetts Gazette* on the 8th.

6. On 25 February the *Boston Gazette* printed an "Extract of a letter from Providence, dated Feb. 20," which stated that "Our Assembly convenes here next week:–it is asserted they intend PROTESTING against TREASONABLE ATTEMPTS made by their *Sister States* to *expunge* the *Old Constitution* by *adopting* the *New!!!*" The *Salem Mercury*, 26 February, printed a summary of this item which circulated widely (Appendix I).

569. Publius: The Federalist 62
New York Independent Journal, 27 February

The authorship of this essay was claimed by both James Madison and Alexander Hamilton, but it is generally attributed to Madison. This essay was reprinted in the *New York Packet* on 29 February. It is number 62 in the M'Lean edition and number 61 in the newspapers.

For a general discussion of the authorship, circulation, and impact of *The Federalist*, see CC:201, 639; and for the disputed authorship of this essay, see Cooke, xix–xxx, 644, and Rutland, *Madison*, X, 261–63.

The FŒDERALIST. No. LXI.
To the People of the State of New-York.

Having examined the constitution of the house of representatives,[1] and answered such of the objections against it as seemed to merit notice, I enter next on the examination of the senate. The heads into which this member of the government may be considered, are–I. the qualifications of senators–II. the appointment of them by the state legislatures–III. the equality of representation in the senate–IV. the number of senators, and the term for which they are to be elected–V. the powers vested in the senate.

I. The qualifications proposed for senators, as distinguished from those of representatives, consist in a more advanced age, and a longer period of citizenship. A senator must be thirty years of age at least; as a representative, must be twenty-five. And the former must have been a citizen nine years; as seven years are required for the latter. The propriety of these distinctions is explained by the nature of the senatorial trust; which requiring greater extent of information and stability of character, requires at the same time that the senator should have reached a period of life most likely to supply these advantages; and which participating immediately in transactions with foreign nations, ought to be exercised by none who are not thoroughly weaned from the prepossessions and habits incident to foreign birth and education. The term of nine years appears to be a prudent mediocrity between a total exclusion of adopted citizens, whose merit and talents may claim a share in the public confidence; and an indiscriminate and hasty admission of them, which might create a channel for foreign influence on the national councils.

II. It is equally unnecessary to dilate on the appointment of senators by the state legislatures. Among the various modes which might have been devised for constituting this branch of the government, that which has been proposed by the convention is probably the most congenial with the public opinion. It is recommended by the double advantage of favouring a select appointment, and of giving to the state governments such an agency in the formation of the federal government, as must secure the authority of the former; and may form a convenient link between the two systems.

III. The equality of representation in the senate is another point, which, being evidently the result of compromise between the opposite pretensions of the large and the small states, does not call for much discussion. If indeed it be right that among a people thoroughly incorporated into one nation, every district ought to have a *proportional* share in the government; and that among independent and sovereign states bound together by simple league, the parties however unequal in size, ought to have an *equal* share in the common councils, it does not appear to be without some reason, that in a compound republic partaking both of the national and federal character, the government ought to be founded on a mixture of the principles of proportional and equal representation. But it is superfluous to try by the standard of theory, a part of the constitution which is allowed on all hands to be the result not of theory, but "of a spirit of amity, and that mutual deference and concession which the peculiarity of our political situation rendered indispensable."[2] A common government with powers equal to its objects, is called for by the voice, and still more loudly by the political situation of America. A government founded on principles more consonant to the wishes of the larger states, is not likely to be obtained from the smaller states. The only option then for the former lies between the proposed government and a government still more objectionable. Under this alternative the advice of prudence must be, to embrace the lesser evil; and instead of indulging a fruitless anticipation of the possible mischiefs which may ensue, to contemplate rather the advantageous consequences which may qualify the sacrifice.

In this spirit it may be remarked, that the equal vote allowed to each state, is at once a constitutional recognition of the portion of sovereignty remaining in the individual states, and an instrument for preserving that residuary sovereignty. So far the equality ought to be no less acceptable to the large than to the small states; since they are not less solicitous to guard by every possible expedient against an improper consolidation of the states into one simple republic.

Another advantage accruing from this ingredient in the constitution of the senate, is the additional impediment it must prove against improper acts of legislation. No law or resolution can now be passed without the concurrence first of a majority of the people, and then of a majority of the states. It must be acknowledged that this complicated check on legislation may in some instances be injurious as well as beneficial; and that the peculiar defence which it involves in favour of the smaller states would be more rational, if any interests common to them, and distinct from those of the other states, would otherwise be exposed to peculiar danger. But as the larger states will always be able by their power over the supplies to defeat unreasonable exertions of this prerogative of the lesser states; and as the facility and excess of law-making seem to be the diseases to which our governments are most liable, it is not impossible that this part of the constitution may be more convenient in practice than it appears to many in contemplation.

IV. The number of senators and the duration of their appointment come next to be considered. In order to form an accurate judgment on both these points, it will be proper to enquire into the purposes which are to be answered by a senate; and in order to ascertain these it will be necessary to review the inconveniencies which a republic must suffer from the want of such an institution.

First. It is a misfortune incident to republican government, though in a less degree than to other governments, that those who administer it, may forget their obligations to their constituents, and prove unfaithful to their important trust. In this point of view, a senate, as a second branch of the legislative assembly, distinct from, and dividing the power with, a first, must be in all cases a salutary check on the government. It doubles the security to the people, by requiring the concurrence of two distinct bodies in schemes of usurpation or perfidy, where the ambition or corruption of one, would otherwise be sufficient. This is a precaution founded on such clear principles, and now so well understood in the United States, that it would be more than superfluous to enlarge on it. I will barely remark that as the improbability of sinister combinations will be in proportion to the dissimilarity in the genius of the two bodies; it must be politic to distinguish them from each other by every circumstance which will consist with a due harmony in all proper measures, and with the genuine principles of republican government.

Secondly. The necessity of a senate is not less indicated by the propensity of all single and numerous assemblies, to yield to the impulse of sudden and violent passions, and to be seduced by factious leaders, into intemperate and pernicious resolutions. Examples on this subject might be cited without number; and from proceedings within the United States, as well as from the history of other nations. But a position that will not be contradicted need not be proved. All that need be remarked is that a body which is to correct this infirmity ought itself be free from it, and consequently ought to be less numerous. It ought moreover to possess great firmness, and consequently ought to hold its authority by a tenure of considerable duration.

Thirdly. Another defect to be supplied by a senate lies in a want of due acquaintance with the objects and principles of legislation. It is not possible that an assembly of men called for the most part from pursuits of a private nature, continued in appointment for a short time, and led by no permanent motive to devote the intervals of public occupation to a study of the laws, the affairs and the comprehensive interests of their country, should, if left wholly to themselves, escape a variety of important errors in the exercise of their legislative trust. It may be affirmed, on the best grounds, that no small share of the present embarrassments of America is to be charged on the blunders of our governments; and that these have proceeded from the heads rather than the hearts of most of the authors of them. What indeed are all the repealing, explaining and amending laws, which fill and disgrace our voluminous codes, but so many monuments of deficient wisdom; so many impeachments exhibited by each succeeding, against each preceding session; so many admonitions to the people of the value of those aids which may be expected from a well constituted senate?

A good government implies two things; first, fidelity to the object of government, which is the happiness of the people; secondly, a knowledge of the means by which that object can be best attained. Some governments are deficient in both these qualities: Most governments are deficient in the first. I scruple not to assert that in the American governments, too little attention has been paid to the last. The federal constitution avoids this error; and what merits particular notice, it provides for the last in a mode which increases the security for the first.

Fourthly. The mutability in the public councils, arising from a rapid succession of new members, however qualified they may be, points out in the strongest manner, the necessity of some stable institution in the government. Every new election in the states, is found to change one half of the representatives. From this change of men must proceed a change of opinions; and from a change of opinions, a change of measures. But a continual change even of good measures is inconsistent with every rule of prudence, and every prospect of success. The remark is verified in private life, and becomes more just as well as more important, in national transactions.

To trace the mischievous effects of a mutable government would fill a volume. I will hint a few only, each of which will be perceived to be a source of innumerable others.

In the first place it forfeits the respect and confidence of other nations, and all the advantages connected with national character. An individual who is observed to be inconstant to his plans, or perhaps to carry on his affairs without any plan at all, is marked at once by all prudent people as a speedy victim to his own unsteadiness and folly. His more friendly neighbours may pity him; but all will decline to connect their fortunes with his; and not a few will seize the opportunity of making their fortunes out of his. One nation is to another what one individual is to another; with this melancholy distinction perhaps, that the former with fewer of the benevolent emotions than the latter, are under fewer restraints also from taking undue advantage of the indiscretions of each other. Every nation consequently whose affairs betray a want of wisdom and stability, may calculate on every loss which can be sustained from the more systematic policy of its wiser neighbours. But the best instruction on this subject is unhappliy conveyed to America by the example of her own situation. She finds that she is held in no respect by her friends; that she is the derision of her enemies; and that she is a prey to every nation which has an interest in speculating on her fluctuating councils and embarrassed affairs.

The internal effects of a mutable policy are still more calamitous. It poisons the blessings of liberty itself. It will be of little avail to the people that the laws are made by men of their own choice, if the laws be so voluminous that they cannot be read, or so incoherent that they cannot be understood; if they be repealed or revised before they are promulged, or undergo such incessant changes that no man who knows what the law is to day can guess what it will be to morrow. Law is defined to be a rule of action; but how can that be a rule, which is little known and less fixed?

Another effect of public instability is the unreasonable advantage it gives to the sagacious, the enterprising and the moneyed few, over the industrious and uninformed mass of the people. Every new regulation concerning commerce or revenue; or in any manner affecting the value of the different species of property, presents a new harvest to those who watch the change, and can trace its consequences; a harvest reared not by themselves but by the toils and cares of the great body of their fellow citizens. This is a state of things in which it may be said with some truth that laws are made for the *few* not for the *many*.

In another point of view great injury results from an unstable government. The want of confidence in the public councils damps every useful undertaking; the success and profit of which may depend on a continuance of existing arrangements. What prudent merchant will hazard his fortunes in any new branch of commerce, when he knows not but that his plans may be rendered unlawful before they can be executed? What farmer or manufacturer will lay himself out for the encouragement given to any particular cultivation or establishment, when he can have no assurance that his preparatory labors and advances will not render him a victim to an inconstant government? In a word no great improvement or laudable enterprise, can go forward, which requires the auspices of a steady system of national policy.

But the most deplorable effect of all is that diminution of attachment and revenue [reverence] which steals into the hearts of the people, towards a political system which betrays so many marks of infirmity, and disappoints so many of their flattering hopes. No government any more than an individual will long be respected, without being truly respectable, nor be truly respectable without possessing a certain portion of order and stability.

1. See *The Federalist* 52–59 (CC:514, 519, 524, 525, 533, 542, 546, 555).

2. Quoted from the President of the Constitutional Convention to the President of Congress, 17 September (CC:76; and CDR, 305–6).

570. James Bowdoin to James de Caledonia
Philadelphia Independent Gazetteer, 27 February

This satirical Antifederalist letter was addressed to James Wilson, a native of Scotland, who was sometimes called derisively James de Caledonia. Wilson's widely reprinted public speech of 6 October (CC:134) and his prominence in the Pennsylvania Convention made him one of the country's leading Federalist spokesmen.

James Bowdoin (1726–1790), a wealthy Boston merchant, had been governor of Massachusetts from 27 May 1785 to 1 June 1787. As governor, Bowdoin's main sources of strength were the state's powerful commercial interest, and as such, he was considered the leader of an aristocratic junto. He supported measures to strengthen the central government and to pay the federal debt; proposed heavy taxes to pay the state debt and congressional requisitions; and employed the state militia to crush Shays's Rebellion. In April 1787 Bowdoin was defeated in a bitterly contested gubernatorial election by John Hancock, whose adherents portrayed Bowdoin as a symbol of repressive and aristocratic government. Bowdoin represented Boston in the Massachusetts Convention, where he voted to ratify the Constitution on 6 February. Although he spoke infrequently, he was one of the principal Federalists in the Convention.

This fictitious letter and the statement by "QUID" were reprinted in the *New York Journal*, 6 March, and in the Boston *American Herald* and Boston *Independent Chronicle*, 20 March. The *Herald* prefaced both items with a statement by "A Federal Customer": "The following commendable production made its appearance in the '*New-York Weekly Register*,' of March *6, 1788*; and as it is a political Phœnomenon, you are requested to re-publish it in your boasted '*open, impartial, uninfluenced*' Herald of Thursday next, in order that the fallacy of its reasoning, &c. may be detected and exposed." The *Chronicle* prefaced the items with an editorial comment: "The following is inserted by desire.–The public must judge for themselves of the probability of its being *real* or *fictitious*."

The author of this Antifederalist satire did not end with this letter. On 4 March the *Independent Gazetteer* published a reply from "James de Caledonia" that discussed a number of points made in the earlier letter and elaborated upon the state of politics in Pennsylvania, in particular, and in several other states, including Massachusetts (Mfm:Pa. 481). Two more "James de Caledonia" responses considered the prospects of ratification in the states that had not ratified the Constitution and the question of the alleged public defaulters, especially Robert Morris (Philadelphia *Freeman's Journal*, 12 March; and *Independent Gazetteer*, 14 March,

Mfm:Pa. 512, 522. For a reply to the letter on the public defaulters, see the Philadelphia *Federal Gazette*, 15 March, Mfm:Pa. 527.).

Mr. Printer, I send you a copy of a real letter from one of the junto to
the *Eastward*, to his friend in this city, that you may lay it before the public, who may from it, form some faint idea of the *juggling* carrying on by
the *well born* few.

QUID.

February 23, 1788.

Boston, February 12, 1788.

To the Right Hon. James de Caledonia.

Dear Sir, I duly received yours of the 24th January, containing very
disagreeable accounts of our scheme being so ably opened up, and of the
people falling off from you, &c. it made us very unhappy here; however
do not despond; I am glad to find you have got your *"writing committee,"*[1]
appointed, and employed: I confess what you say is just, and that there is
somewhat disagreeable in writing, with the argument against you, and
with able compettitors. In your two first numbers of the *Freemen and Pennsylvanian*,[2] to be sure you exceed yourself: But I would not advise you to
continue the publication of them in the city, they will suit better for the
country; ha, ha, ha: You make bold assertions; you should take care not
to let it be known who the author of them is, the very name of a *lawyer*
would ruin a publication in our country.

Keep your committee hard at it; and fill *your weekly paper*[3] from top to
bottom: Your notion of answering your own pieces may do, if not found
out. Do try by all means to regain your lost ground, leave no stone un-
turned; much is gained by confusing the business, and you are really a
compleat *sophist*: You know your reward should it succeed; we have all
agreed you shall have £.8000 per annum, with the office of Attorney General (of the union.) As to the office of Chief Justice[4] which you wished for,
it would have been yours, but, necessity obliged us to close with J—y-[5] it
was his price.

I was glad to find you had stopped the publication of the debates of your
convention;[6] and that you had suited *your own* so well *to the tune*; you was
very right to hold back the second volume containing the speeches of the
minority, as perhaps the *real* ones might come out. But I was sorry you
could not *silence the press* entirely:[7] However as we have the P-t O—ce still
at our service,[8] you must prevent any of the newspapers which contain
publications against us, getting out of your state. We have been remarkably successful in this hitherto; every newspaper against us has been
stopped, even the reasons of dissent of your minority, and the information
of Mr. Martin, has been scarcely heard of here;[9] this was very fortunate,
as it would certainly have ruined us in this quarter. So great was the want
of information here, that we made the people believe all to the southward

of us, indeed that every state but our own were almost unanimous in favor
of our plan. You would have laughed to have seen our newspapers on the
day the final question was taken in our convention; there we published an
account of the almost unanimous adoption of the constitution by the convention of North-Carolina; that the state of New-York had called a convention at a very early day, without any opposition; and the *trifling*
opposition in your state had ceased; that Randolph, Mason, Lee, &c. had
joined our party;[10] and many other similar accounts.

In this situation, when such a variety of circumstances concurred in our
favor; although we had *juggled in* above 50 members of the convention, by
the assistance of country friends; and was so fortunate as to keep out any
Ciceros from the opposition in the convention: Although we bought off the
province of *Main* with the feather of a separate state;[11] although we had
such a number of able hands, among which were many as complete soph-
ists as yourself; although we gained the man of the people by holding out
to him the office of Vice President;[12] although we had the influence of the
town of Boston to assist us,[13] still we would have lost the question almost
two to one if we had not agreed to the amendments, which you find included in the ratification; and these not to be made by the first Congress
as you proposed, but according to the 5th article, that is, by another convention.[14] This was a fatal stroke, but we could not avoid it.

You have seen with much surprise, I dare say, the great parade we
made at the ratification;[15] it cost us a considerable sum, but I am in hopes
it will be of great service, these things have great effect on common minds.–
You see we have the town of Boston under our discipline; I wish I could
say so of the rest of the state, indeed it is far otherwise, four fifths of the
people are against us: But as you say, what need we care for the sentiments of the people, if we can only get the army a-foot.

I was happy to hear you was disarming your militia both for your own
safety,[16] and because you will want the arms for the troops; but at the
same time I thought it a bold push, and might cause alarm.

I have lately received a letter from Mr. J— A—, our A—d–r at London, he is pleased with my compliment on his volume, it was, I told him
of much service to us.[17] He has endeavoured through *Bobby's*[18] credit, to
contract for the *necessaries* we wrote for; but he found it would not do: He
then pledged the faith of the United States to fulfil the contracts he has
made. He has also entered into other treaties for the *other articles*, which I
shall be more particular about, by a safer opportunity.[19]

When these things were told to our friends here, many of them began to
stare; for they consider the matter as lost since this state, which, they say,
is the most important in the union, has called for amendments; the people
of your state, the states of Virginia, New-York, North-Carolina, and
Maryland so generally against it: to be sure, matters look blue; but I am
in hopes still that our exertions will be crowned with success. You know

that you or I have nothing to lose, and much to gain. Some of our milk
and water friends here think we had better stop, and submit again to another convention; because, say they, we will be envolved in a civil war, if
we persist; but I tell them we will not give it up while any hopes remain;
as now, we are found out, we shall never be trusted in another convention;
and so we shall lose every thing. But if we succeed in this plan, we shall
never again be troubled with the people, never dread the event of elections; we shall enjoy our places, honors, and preferments, and leave them
to our children after us. We shall be able to keep the people at a proper
distance, and establish our numerous friends and relations in lucrative and
substantial offices.

Present my compliments to *Bobby*, and also to *Billy* in the new big
house;[20] and tell them I congratulate them upon the prospect of all their
old *continental balances* being done away;[21] as I don't find that part of the
constitution is yet discovered.

You are an admirable man, the most useful in the convention; but you
was rather for taking too much at one time; the *double powers* of our little
sextentially elected senate; the controul over the press; the abolition of trial
by jury in civil cases, and the common law proceedings; internal taxation;
the pecuniary dependency of the judges, and their great powers; the standing army; the smallness of the lower house; the exclusion of rotation; and
the "powers to make all laws which we may think *necessary* and *proper*."
And that these *laws* and the *treaties* of the *little senate* should be the supreme
law of the land, over the constitutions and laws of the several states. These
would have been quite sufficient for us; with them alone we could chain
down all America; we might have given up the rest to the winds: the
controul over the elections; the command of the militia; the power of the
senate to alter money bills; the powers of president to pardon criminals, to
command in person the armies, navies, and militia, &c. and his long appointment, his right of being re-elected; omission of declarations in favor
of liberty of conscience, and twenty others, which have been of great hurt
to us, might have been left out. But between you and me, they will never
discover some of the most exceptionable parts.

I suppose you will soon hear of its adoption by *New-Hampshire*; but it
will be many months before any other can come into it. Pray, inform me
how Martin is going on; I hope he will be persuaded to discontinue his
publications; we have sent him an offer of the office of chief justice of the
federal court of his state, but I am afraid of him.[22]

We have gained much by deceiving one part of the continent, with plausible accounts from the other; pray, do not discontinue this; have you no
more town or county meetings to publish? What M—[23] says is very true;
almost all of our strength lies in the trading towns; and his remark is just
that they would consent to go to the devil, if they thought they could again
sell as many British goods, as they formerly did.

Keep up the spirits of your boys, and exert you[r]selves; I shall write you again shortly.

I am, dear sir, Your most obedient, And very humble servant,

J. B–wd–n.

1. For this alleged Federalist *"writing committee"* which was supposedly trying to inundate the state's newspapers to counteract Antifederalist propaganda, see *Pennsylvania Gazette*, 12 March, note 6 (Appendix I).

2. "A Freeman" I–III and "A Pennsylvanian" I–IV were written by Tench Coxe and printed in the *Pennsylvania Gazette* between 23 January and 27 February (CC:472, 488, 505; and Mfm:Pa. 408, 430, 439, 459).

3. Probably the *Pennsylvania Gazette*. On 24 November "Plain Truth" had accused Wilson of writing "numerous paragraphs . . . for a certain weekly paper–which contained the most glaring falsehoods, about Messrs. Mason, Gerry, Randolph, Clinton, Lee, &c, and all others who opposed the violent measures used by the advocates of this his favorite plan" (*Independent Gazetteer*, RCS:Pa., 292–93); while Federalist Benjamin Rush stated that the *Gazette* "is filled every week" with Federalist essays, anecdotes, and political intelligence (to Henry Muhlenberg, 15 February, Mfm:Pa. 432).

4. "Cincinnatus" VI, *New York Journal*, 6 December (CC:324) had also linked these two offices with Wilson.

5. Probably John Jay, who was appointed the first chief justice of the United States under the Constitution.

6. For Thomas Lloyd's publication on 7 February of the debates of the Pennsylvania Convention which consisted only of speeches by Federalists Wilson and Thomas McKean, see CC:511. Lloyd had promised to publish a second volume of Antifederalist speeches, which never appeared.

7. Probably a reference to the publication of the debates of the Pennsylvania Convention in the *Pennsylvania Herald*. Federalists objected to some of the *Herald's* reports and allegedly applied pressure on the publisher, who eventually fired the *Herald's* editor in early January before all of the lengthy debates were published. (See CC:Vol. 1, xxxix; CC:357; CC:470, note 7; and RCS:Pa., 40.)

8. For the alleged control of the post office by Federalists, see Appendix II.

9. See CC:353 (page 11) for the publication of the "Dissent of the Minority of the Pennsylvania Convention" in Boston in either mid-January or early February and for more on the Antifederalists' charge that Federalists prevented the "Dissent" from circulating in Boston during the meeting of the Massachusetts Convention from 9 January to 7 February. Luther Martin's *Genuine Information* I–II, V–X, and XII were reprinted in the Boston *American Herald* between 4 February and 8 May. For Martin's *Genuine Information*, see CC:389.

10. Massachusetts ratified the Constitution on 6 February. On 23 and 30 January and 6 February the *Massachusetts Centinel* contained items on Randolph, Pennsylvania, New York, and North Carolina (Mfm:Pa. 392; CC:Vol. 3, Appendix I; and Appendix I). On 5 February the *Massachusetts Gazette* contained an item on North Carolina (Appendix I); while on 31 January and 7 February the *Independent Chronicle* reprinted the items on New York and North Carolina that had appeared in the *Massachusetts Centinel*.

11. Five statehood conventions were held in Maine from October 1785 to September 1787, but by early 1788 separatist feeling in Maine had declined significantly. In the Massachusetts Convention the Maine delegates voted 25 to 21 to ratify the Constitution.

12. See "John Hancock and the Constitution," 3 January–4 February, CC:Vol. 3, Appendix I.

13. For an example of Boston's influence, see "Reports of the Boston Tradesmen Meeting," 8–9 January (CC:424).

14. See CC:508.

15. This parade took place on 8 February–the day after the state Convention adjourned. The "Grand Procession," totaling some 4,500 persons, was composed of representatives of the trades and professions of Boston and the adjacent towns (*Massachusetts Centinel*, 9 February).

16. On 4 December the Pennsylvania Supreme Executive Council ordered "That the Lieutenants of the city and several counties within the state, be directed to collect all the public arms within their respective counties, have them repaired" and report the expenses to the Council. For the newspaper debate over this order, see Mfm:Pa. 273.

17. For John Adams's *Defence of the Constitutions*, see CC:16, 557.

18. Robert Morris.

19. On 10 January Antifederalist "Philadelphiensis" VII had attacked John Adams for signing an agreement (1 June 1787) for a Dutch loan of one million florins ($400,000). The loan, thought to be "necessary, to prevent the total ruin of our Public Credit . . .," was ratified by Congress on 11 October (CC:438, note 3). In the same month, the Confederation Board of Treasury examined and approved Adams's accounts (JCC, XXXIII, 534, 609–10).

20. William Bingham was a prominent Philadelphia merchant. His recently completed "Mansion House" was one of the most luxurious and richly furnished houses in America.

21. See CC:565.

22. The twelfth and last installment of Luther Martin's *Genuine Information* was published on 8 February (CC:516). Martin was never a federal judge.

23. Possibly George Mason who objected to the Constitution's failure to provide for a two-thirds vote of each house of Congress on navigation acts.

571. Marcus II
Norfolk and Portsmouth Journal, 27 February[1]

Answers to Mr. Mason's *Objections* to the New Constitution, Recommended by the late Convention at Philadelphia.
IVth. Objection.

"The Judiciary of the United States is so constructed and extended, as to absorb and destroy the Judiciaries of the several States; thereby rendering law as tedious, intricate and expensive; and justice as unattainable by a great part of the community as in England; and enabling the rich to oppress and ruin the poor."
Answer.

Mr. Mason has here asserted, "That the Judiciary of the United States is so constructed and extended, as to absorb and destroy the Judiciaries of the several States." How is this the case? Are not the State Judiciaries left uncontrouled as to all the affairs of *that State only?* In this, as in all other cases, where there is a wise distribution, power is commensurate to its object. With the mere internal concerns of a State, Congress are to have nothing to do. In no case but where the Union is in some measure concerned, are the Fœderal Courts to have any jurisdiction. The State Judiciary will be a satellite waiting upon its proper planet: That of the Union like the sun, cherishing and preserving a whole planetary system.

In regard to a possible ill construction of this authority, we must depend upon our future Legislature in this case, as well as others, in respect to which it is impracticable to define every thing; that it will be provided for so as to occasion as little expence and distress to individuals as can be. In parting with the coercive authority over the States, as States, there must be a coercion allowed as to individuals. The former power no man of common sense can any longer seriously contend for: The latter is the only alternative. Suppose an objection should be made, that the future Legislature should not ascertain salaries, because they might divide among themselves and their officers all the revenue of the Union:[a] Will not every man see how irrational it is to expect that any government can exist, which is to be fettered in its most necessary operations, for fear of abuse?

Vth. Objection.

"The President of the United States, has no Constitutional Council (a thing unknown in any safe and regular government), he will therefore be unsupported by proper information and advice; and will generally be directed by minions and favorites–or he will become a tool to the Senate–or a Council of State will grow out of the principal officers of the great departments; the worst and most dangerous of all ingredients for such a Council in a free country; for they may be induced to join in any dangerous or oppressive measures; to shelter themselves, and prevent an enquiry into their own misconduct in office: Whereas, had a Constitutional Council been formed (as was proposed) of six Members, viz. two from the eastern, two from the middle, and two from the southern States; to be appointed by vote of the States in the House of Representatives, with the same duration and rotation of office as the Senate, the Executive would always have had safe and proper information and advice. The President of such a Council might have acted as Vice-President of the United States, *pro tempore*, upon any vacancy or disability of the Chief Magistrate; and long-continued Sessions of the Senate would, in a great measure have been prevented. From this fatal defect of a Constitutional Council, has arisen the improper power of the Senate, in the appointment of public officers, and the alarming dependence and connexion between that branch of the Legislature and the Supreme Executive. Hence also sprung that unnecessary and dangerous officer, the Vice-President; who, for want of other employment, is made President of the Senate; thereby dangerously blending the Executive and Legislative powers; besides always giving to some of the States an unnecessary and unjust pre-eminence over the others."

Answer.

Mr. Mason here reprobates the omission of a particular Council for the President, as a thing contrary to the example of all safe and regular governments. Perhaps there are very few governments now in being, deserving of that character, if under the idea of safety, he means to include safety for a proper share of personal freedom, without which their safety and regularity in other respects would be of little consequence to a people so justly jealous of liberty as I hope the people in America ever will be. Since however Mr. Mason refers us to such authority, I think I cannot do better than to select for the subject of our enquiry in this particular, a government which must be universally acknowledged to be the most safe and regular of any considerable government now in being (though I hope, America will soon be able to dispute that pre-eminence). Every body must know I speak of Great-Britain; and in this I think I give Mr. Mason all possible advantage; since, in my opinion, it is most probable he had Great-Britain principally in his eye when he made this remark. And in the very height of our quarrel with that country, so wedded were our ideas to the institution of a Council, that the practice was generally, if not universally followed, at the formation of our governments, though we instituted councils of a quite different nature; and so far as the little experience of the writer goes, have very little benefited by it. My enquiry into this subject shall not be confined to the actual present practice of Great-Britain. I shall take the liberty to state the constitutional ideas of Councils in England, as derived from their ancient laws subsisting long before the Union, not omitting however to shew what the present practice really is.–By the laws of England[b] the King is said to have four Councils. 1. The High Court of Parliament. 2. The Peers of the Realm. 3. His Judges. 4. His Privy Council.–By the first, I presume, is meant in regard to the making of laws; because the usual introductory expressions in most acts of Parliament, viz. "By the King's Most Excellent Majesty, by and with the advice and consent of the Lords Spiritual and Temporal, and Commons, &c." shew, that in a constitutional sense, they are deemed the King's laws, after a ratification in Parliament. The Peers of the Realm are, by their birth hereditary Counsellors of the Crown, and may be called upon for their advice either in time of Parliament, or when no Parliament is in being. They are called in some law books, *Magnum Concilium Regis*. (The King's Great Council). It is also considered the privilege of every particular Peer, to demand an audience of the King, and to lay before him any thing he may deem of public importance. The Judges, I presume, are called "A Council of the King," upon the same principle that the Parliament is, because the administration of justice is in his name, and the Judges are considered as his instruments in the distribution of it. We come now to the Privy Council, which I imagine, if Mr. Mason had any particular view towards England when he made this objection, was the one he intended as an example of a *Constitutional Council* in that kingdom. The Privy Council in that country is undoubtedly of very ancient institution; but it has one fixed property invariably annexed to it, that it is a mere creature of the Crown, dependent on its will both for number and duration, since the King may, whenever he thinks proper, discharge any particular Member, or the whole of it, and appoint another.[c] If this precedent is of moment to us, merely as a precedent, it should be followed in all its parts; and then what would there be in the regulation to prevent the President from being

governed by "minions and favorites?" It would only be the means of rivetting them on constitutional ground. So far as precedents in England
apply, the Peers being constitutionally the *Great Council of the King*, tho'
also a part of the Legislature, we have reason to hope, that there is by no
means, such gross impropriety as has been suggested, in giving the Senate, tho' a branch of the Legislature, a strong controul over the Executive.
The only difference in the two cases is, that the Crown may or may not
give this consequence to the Peers at its own pleasure; and accordingly we
find, that for a long time past, this Great Council has been very seldom
consulted: Under our Constitution, the President is allowed no option in
respect to certain points, wherein he cannot act without the Senate's concurrence. But we cannot infer from any example in England, that a concurrence between the Executive and a part of the Legislature is contrary
to the maxims of their government, since their government allows of such
a concurrence whenever the Executive pleases. The rule therefore from
the example of the freest government in Europe, that the Legislative and
Executive powers must be altogether distinct, is liable to exceptions. It
does not mean that the Executive shall not form a part of the Legislature
(for the King who has the whole Executive authority, is one entire branch
of the Legislature; and this, Montesquieu,[2] who recognizes the general
principle, declares is necessary): Neither can it mean (as the example above
evinces) that the Crown must consult neither house as to any exercise of
its Executive power: But its meaning must be, that one power shall not
include *both authorities:* The King, for instance, shall not have the sole Executive, and sole Legislative authority also. He may have the former, but
must participate the latter with the two Houses of Parliament. The rule
also would be infringed were the three branches of the Legislature to share
jointly the Executive power. But so long as the people's Representatives
are altogether distinct from the Executive authority, the liberties of the
people may be deemed secure. And in this point, surely there can be no
manner of comparison between the provisions by which the independence
of our House of Representatives is guarded, and the condition in which
the British House of Commons is left exposed to every species of corruption.–But Mr. Mason says, for want of a Council, the President may
become "a tool to the Senate." Why?–Because he cannot act without their
concurrence. Would not the same reason hold for his being "a tool to the
Council," if he could not act without their concurrence, supposing a
Council was to be imposed upon him without his own nomination (according to Mr. Mason's plan)? As great care is taken to make him independent
of the Senate; as I believe human precaution can provide. Whether the
President will be a tool to any persons, will depend upon the man; and the
same weakness of mind which would make him pliable to one body of
controul, would certainly attend him with another. But Mr. Mason objects, if he is not directed by minions and favorites, nor becomes a tool of

the Senate, "A Council of State will grow out of the principal officers of the great department[s], the worst and most dangerous of all ingredients for such a Council, in a free country; for they may be induced to join in any dangerous or oppressive measures to shelter themselves, and prevent an inquiry into their own misconduct in office." I beg leave again to carry him to my old authority, England, and ask him what efficient Council they have there, but one formed of their great officers? Notwithstanding their important *constitutional Council*, every body knows that the whole movements of their government, where a Council is consulted at all, are directed by their *Cabinet Council*, composed entirely of the principal officers of the great departments: That when a Privy Council is called, it is scarcely ever for any other purpose than to give a formal sanction to the previous determinations of the other; so much so that it is notorious that not one time in a thousand one Member of the Privy Council, except a known adherent of administration, is summoned to it. But though the President, under our Constitution, may have the aid of the "principal officers of the great departments," he is to have this aid, I think, in the most unexceptionable manner possible. He is not to be assisted by a Council, summoned to a jovial dinner perhaps, and giving their opinions according to the nod of the President–but the opinion is to be given with the utmost solemnity, *in writing*.[3] No after equivocation can explain it away. It must for ever afterwards speak for itself, and commit the character of the writer, in lasting colours either of fame or infamy, or neutral insignificance, to future ages, as well as the present. From those written reasons, weighed with care, surely the President can form as good a judgment as if they had been given by a dozen formal characters, carelessly met together on a slight appointment. And this further advantage would be derived from the proposed system (which would be wanting if he had constitutional advice to screen him) that the President must be *personally responsible* for every thing. For though an ingenious gentleman has proposed, that a Council should be formed, who should be responsible for *their opinions*; and the same sentiment of justice might be applied to these opinions of the great officers, I am persuaded it will in general be thought infinitely more *safe*, as well as more *just*, that the President who acts should be responsible for his *conduct*, following advice at his peril, than that there should be a danger of punishing any man for an erroneous opinion which might possibly be sincere. Besides the morality of this scheme, which may well be questioned, its inexpediency is glaring, since it would be so plausible an excuse, and the insincerity of it so difficult to detect; the hopes of impunity this avenue to escape, would afford, would nearly take away all dread of punishment. As to the temptations mentioned to the officers joining in dangerous or oppressive measures to shelter themselves, and prevent an enquiry into their own misconduct in office, this proceeds upon a supposition that the President and the great officers may form a very wicked combination to injure their country; a combination that in the first place it is utterly improbable, in a strong respectable government, should be formed for that purpose; and in the next, with such a government as this Constitution would give us, could have little chance of being successful, on account of the great superior strength, and natural and jealous vigilance of one at least, if not both the two weighty branches of Legislation. This evil however, of the possible depravity of *all public officers*, is one that can admit of no cure, since in every institution of government, the same danger in some degree or other must be risqued; it can only be guarded against by strong checks, and I believe it would be difficult for the objectors to our new Constitution, to provide stronger ones against any abuse of the Executive authority, than will exist in that. As to the Vice-President, it appears to me very proper he should be chosen much in the same manner as the President, in order that the States may be secure, upon any accidental loss by death or otherwise, of the President's service; of the services in the same important station of the man in whom they repose their second confidence. The complicated manner of election wisely prescribed, would necessarily occasion a considerable delay in the choice of another; and in the mean time the President of the Council, tho' very fit for the purpose of advising, might be very ill qualified, especially in a critical period, for an active executive department. I am concerned to see among Mr. Mason's other reasons, so trivial a one as the little advantage one State might accidentally gain by a Vice-President of their country having a seat, with merely a casting vote in the Senate. Such a reason is utterly unworthy that spirit of amity, and rejection of local views, which can alone save us from destruction. It was the glory of the late Convention, that by discarding such, they formed a general government upon principles that did as much honor to their hearts as to their understandings. God grant, that in all our deliberations, we may consider America as one body, and not divert our attention from so noble a prospect, to small considerations of partial jealousy and distrust. It is in vain to expect upon any system to secure an exact equilibrium of power for all the States. Some will occasionally have an advantage from the superior abilities of its Members; the field of emulation is however open to all. Suppose any one should now object to the superior influence of Virginia (and the writer of this is not a citizen of that State) on account of the high character of General Washington, confessedly the greatest man of the present age, and perhaps equal to any that has existed in any period of time: Would this be a reason for refusing a union with her, though the other States can scarcely hope for the consolation of ever producing his equal?

(To be continued.)

(a) *When I wrote the above, I had not seen Governor Randolph's letter:*[4] *Otherwise, I have so great a respect for that gentleman's character, I should have treated with more deference an idea in some*

measure countenanced by him. One of his objections relates to the
Congress fixing their own salaries. I am persuaded, upon a little
reflection, that gentleman must think this is one of those cases where a
trust must unavoidably be reposed. No salaries could certainly be fixed
now, so as to answer the various changes in the value of money, that
in the course of time must take place. And in what condition would
the Supreme Authority be, if their very subsistence depended on an
inferior power? An abuse in this case too, would be so gross, that it
is very unlikely to happen; but if it should, it would probably prove
much more fatal to the authors, than injurious to the people.

(b) *See Coke's Commentary upon Littleton,* 110. I. *Blackstone's*
Commentaries, 227 *and seq.*[5]

(c) I. *Blackstone's Commentaries,* 232.[6]

1. For the authorship and circulation of "Marcus," see CC:548.

2. *Spirit of Laws,* I, Book XI, chapter VI, 221–37, especially pp. 233–34.

3. Article II, section 2 of the Constitution reads: "he [the President] may require the Opinion, in writing, of the principal Officer in each of the executive Departments, upon any Subject relating to the Duties of their respective Offices. . . ."

4. In his letter to the speaker of the Virginia House of Delegates, Governor Edmund Randolph expressed the hope that Virginia would be joined by the other states "in incapacitating the Congress to determine their own salaries." The letter was published as a pamphlet in Richmond, Va., on or before 27 December and in Richmond newspapers as early as 2 January (CC:385).

5. Edward Coke, *The First Part of the Institutes of the Laws of England. Or, a Commentary upon Littleton* . . . (9th ed., London, 1684), Book II, chapter 10, section 164, p. 110; and Blackstone, *Commentaries,* Book I, chapter V, 227–32.

6. *Ibid.,* 232.

572. George Cabot to Theophilus Parsons
Beverly, Mass., 28 February[1]

I feel exceedingly disappointed in having you pass this way without stopping. I had so much relied on seeing you, that I could not believe you had left home, until yesterday I was informed that you had been very lately *seen* in Boston. I was about to inquire more particularly whether it was *you* or your *ghost;* but, recollecting that to determine this required more than common acuteness of sight and judgment, I waived a question which, by confounding my informant, might have placed him in a more humiliating point of view than a man is willing to be seen in. However, I am very glad to learn that you are still, *in any shape,* on this side the Styx; for I had begun very strongly to suspect that the old boatman had tumbled you into his scow, and paddled over the stream. As these apprehensions are of a nature that do not readily subside, I beg, before the old kidnapper takes advantage of you, that you would be doing whatever you have not already done toward rearing the *Conventional Edifice.* The impatience discovered by the few people I converse with, stimulated me to set about collecting such materials as were to be procured in this quarter. These I intended should pass your *sole* inspection, and only such of them as you should judge would be useful should be offered to the architects; but, having got into the depth of incertitude as to your *ubiety*, I forwarded all that I had collected in their rough state to Mr. Minot,[2] with a request that such of them as are not suitable for any part of the building may be used for firewood, which I am sure is much wanted [in] this cold weather. This last reflection is a very consolatory one to me, as I had felt much concern lest my lumber should not only fail of answering any good purpose, but might be prejudicial by encumbering the work-yard; whereas, if it arrives at the honor of warming the hands of my patriotic friends, and enables them more freely to execute the commands of their head, I shall be perfectly satisfied. With this sentiment operating in its full force on my mind, I proceed to make a little addition to what I had sent on before.

The objection to the fourth section of the first article is stated full as strongly in the paper I sent Mr. Minot as I remember to have heard or seen it made anywhere; and the argument that the people of one State have an interest in the elections of *every* State, may, if placed in the most striking light, be a satisfactory answer. But there is (in my mind) ground for an objection to that article, which, by going a little further back than the opponents have, may be taken and defended against anything I have ever thought of that could be brought against it. I mean that the objectors, instead of *conceding*, as they all do, by implication at least, that the powers of that article could not be fixed absolutely in the Constitution, and so reduce the question simply to what body it shall be lodged in,–if, instead of this, they should insist that it might and ought to have been fixed immovably in the Constitution, it will be difficult to answer them. For I cannot see why a rule might not have been made of a kind that should answer that description, and yet accommodate itself to the changes in population, &c. in all the different districts. The best answer to this which occurs to me is, "that, as the article now stands, the different States may each enjoy their own favorite mode," &c.; but this answer, if pursued, will very surely weaken the strongest argument we have ever used in favor of Congress having the right ultimately instead of the States. Pray think of the strongest objection possible to this article, and if you can answer it satisfactorily, it must be of infinite advantage.

I come now to the point for which I have thought it necessary to write to you at this time, and that is, to mention to you the two objections which, I am told, the people of the country find it the most difficult to get over. The first is that of the fourth section, mentioned above, and which I fear will never be entirely removed. The next is one which it seems to me may be pretty fully answered,–that of such a consolidation of the States as will dissolve their governments. Under the head of objections to the Senate, will it not be well to show how far the *injustice* of an equal representation in that body is balanced by the additional security it brings, that no

measures will ever pass tending in the smallest degree to consolidation?–
which must be always guarded against by small States: small States will
out-number great ones. This argument, well managed, in addition to the
dependence of the Federal Government for the elections of all its branches,
and the expressed and implied reference to the State governments in various parts of it, will show that the provisions for their existence are interwoven in the Constitution in such manner as not to be separated without
rending it in pieces. I wish you would introduce among the preliminary
observations of your address this idea,–that the General Government,
being an institution that is to affect States as well as people, will be obliged
to admit into one of its branches that equality which sovereigns independent of each other usually insist on. And there is *some fitness* in the principle
which requires that, as the laws affect States as well as people, the consent
of States as such, as well as individuals, should be first obtained, through
their representatives or ambassadors; and as sovereign States cannot be
expected to submit to an entire renunciation of claims which have been in
a degree sanctified by the long usage of nations, it is a strong motive why
the great States should concede something in this particular. *Verbum sap-
ienti.*

1. Printed: Theophilus Parsons, *Memoir of Theophilus Parsons* . . . (Boston, 1859),
463–65. Cabot (1752–1823), a Beverly merchant, was a special justice of the Court of
Common Pleas of Essex County, Mass., and a justice of the peace and of the quorum.
He represented Beverly in the state Convention. Parsons (1750–1813), a lawyer, represented Newburyport in the Massachusetts House of Representatives and was a justice
of the peace and of the quorum for Essex County. A Federalist leader in the Massachusetts Convention, Parsons was instrumental in persuading John Hancock to propose
recommendatory amendments to the Constitution (CC:508). Both Parsons and Cabot
voted to ratify the Constitution on 6 February.

2. George R. Minot (1758–1802), a Boston lawyer, was clerk of the Massachusetts
House of Representatives and secretary of the Massachusetts Convention. Later in the
year, Minot published a history of Shays's Rebellion (Evans 21259).

573. Benjamin Rush to Jeremy Belknap
Philadelphia, 28 February[1]

In answer to your question respecting the conduct & opinions of the
quakers in Pennsylvania,[2] I am very happy in being able to inform you
that they are all (with an exception of three or four persons only) highly
fœderal.–There was a respectable representation of that Society in our
Convention, all of whom voted in favor of the New Constitution.[3] They
consider very wisely that the Abolition of slavery in our country must be
gradual in order to be effectual, and that the Section of the Constitution
which will put it in the power of Congress twenty years hence to ~~prohibit~~
restrain it altogether, was a great point obtained from the Southern States.
The appeals therefore that have been made to the humane & laudable
prejudices of our quakers by our Antifœderal writers, upon the Subject of

Negro Slavery, have been treated by that prudent Society with Silence and Contempt.-[4]

Some of the same reasons have operated upon me, that have influenced you to admire & prefer the new government. If it held forth no other advantages that a future exemption from paper money & tender laws, it would be eno' to recommend it to honest men. To look up to a government that encourages Virtue–establishes justice ensures order, secures property–and protects from every Species of Violence, affords a pleasure that can only be exceeded by looking up in all circumstances to a *general providence*. Such a pleasure I hope is before us & our posterity under the influence of the new Government.-

The arguments, or to express myself more properly–the Objections of your minority, were in many respects the same as those which were urged by the Speakers in behalf of the minority of Pennsylvania. They both suppose that the men who are to be entrusted with the supreme power of our Country will become at once the receptacles of all the depravity of human nature.–They forget that they are to be part of ourselves, and if we may judge of their future conduct by what we have too Often Observed in the State governments, the Members of the fœderal legislature, will much Oftener injure their constituents by voting agreeably to their inclinations, than *against* them.

But in cherishing jealousies of our rulers, we are too apt to overlook the weaknesses & vices of the people. Is not history as full of examples of both in them, as it is of the crimes of kings? What is the present moral character of the inhabitants of the united States? I need not describe it. It proves too plainly that the *people*, are as much disposed to Vice, as their rulers, and that nothing but a vigorous & efficient government can prevent their degenerating into Savages, or devouring each other like beasts of prey.-

I pant for the time when the establishment of the new government, and the Safety to individuals which shall arise from it, shall excuse men who like myself wish only to be passengers, from performing the duty of Sailors on board the political Ship in which our all is embarked.–I have yeilded to a deep Sense of the extreme danger of my Country, in quitting the [cabin?] for a Station at the pump. As soon as the storm is over, and our bark safely moored, the first wish of my heart will be to devote the whole of my time to the peaceable pursuits of Science, and to the pleasures of social and domestic life.-

1. RC, Belknap Papers, MHi.
2. On 12 February Belknap had asked Rush how Pennsylvania Quakers interpreted the slave trade clause of the Constitution. Belknap became concerned when Antifederalist James Neal, a Quaker preacher from Kittery, Maine, criticized the Constitution in the Massachusetts Convention for prohibiting Congress from interfering with the importation of slaves for twenty years. Neal was answered by Theophilus Parsons "who construed that article [slave-trade clause] into a dawn of hope for the final abolition of the horrid Traffick" (CC:Vol. 2, Appendix III, 529–30).

3. "Undeniable Facts" stated that eight of the sixty-nine members of the Pennsylvania Convention were Quakers and that they all voted to ratify the Constitution (Philadelphia *Independent Gazetteer*, 15 January, Mfm:Pa. 333).

4. For Pennsylvania Quakers and the Constitution, see CC:Vol. 2, Appendix III, *passim*; and RCS:Pa., 133, 135, 137–38, 207, 721–22, 724n–25n.

574. Joseph Spencer to James Madison
Orange County, Va., 28 February[1]

The Federal Constitution, has it Enimyes in Orange as well as in other parts, Col. Thos. Barber offers as a Candedit for our March Election, he is as grate an Enimy to it as he posably can be, & if not as grate as any it has, as grate as his abiliteys will alow him to be, which if our County men admired his Politickes no more than I do, the Constitution would have but Little to fear from that Quarter, but his unwared Labours riding his Carquits & the Instruments he makes use of to Obtain his Election, misrepresents things in such Horred carrecters that the weker clas of the people are much predegessed agains it. by which meens he has many which as yet, appears grately in favour of him, amoungs his Friends appears, in a General way the Baptus's,[2] the Prechers of that Society are much alarm'd fearing relegious liberty is not Sufficiently secur'd thay pretend to other objections but that I think is the principle objection, could that be removed by sum one Caperable of the Task. I think thay would become friends to it, that body of people has become very formible in pint of Elections, as I can think of no Gentln. of my Acquaintance so Suitible to the Task as your Self. I have taken the liberty to Request it of you, several of your Conections in Orange Joines me in oppinion, thinking it would answer a Valuable purpus for I am Cartain that pople relye much on your integerity & Candure,[3] Mr. Leeland & Mr. Bledsoe and Sanders[4] are the most publick men of that Society in Orange, therefore as Mr. Leeland Lyes in your Way home from Fredricksburg to Orange would advise you'l call on him[5] & spend a few Howers in his Company, in Clos'd youl receive his objections, which was Sent by me to, Barber, a Coppy I tooke, this copy was first Design'd for Capt Walker,[6] but as I hoped youl be in this state in a few days thought proper to Send it to you, by which means youl be made Acquainted with their objections [& have] time to Consider them should you think it an Object worth yr Attention, my fears are that Except you & yr friends do Exerte yr Selves Very much youl not obtain yr Election in Orange Such are the predegeses of the people for in short there is nothing so Vile, but what the Constitution is Charged with, hope to See you in Orange in a few days

[Enclosure][7]

According, to your request, I have send you my objections to the *Fœderal Constitution*, which are as follows,

1st. There is no Bill Rights, whenever Number of men enter into a State of Socity, a Number of individual Rights must be given up to Socity, but there should always be a memorial of those not surrendred, otherwise every natural & domestic Right becomes alianable, which raises Tyranny at once, & this is as necessary in one Form of Goverment as in another–

2nd. There is a Contradiction in the Constitution, we are first inform'd that all Legislative Powers therein granted shall be Vested in a Congress, composed of *two houses*, & yet afterwards all the power that lies between a Majority two thirds, which is one Sixth part, is taken from these *two Houses*, and given to one man, who is not only chosen two removes from the people, but also the head of the executive Department–

3rd. The House of Representatives is the only free, direct Representation of the body of the people, & yet in Treaties which are to be some of the Supreme Laws of the Land, this House has no Voice–

4th. The time place & Manner of chusing the Members of the Lower house is intirely at the Mercy of Congress, if they Appoint Pepin or Japan, or their ten Miles Square for the place, no man can help it.–how can Congress guarantee to each state a republican form of Goverment, when every principle of Republicanism is Sapped–

5th. The Senators are chosen for Six years, & when they are once Chosen, they are impeachable to nun but themselves, No Counterpoize is left in the hands of the People, or even in Legislative Bodys to check them, Vote as they will, there they sit, paying themselves at Pleasure–

6th I utterly oppose any Division in Legislative Body, the more Houses, the more parties,–the more they are Divided; the more the Wisdom is Scattered, sometimes one house may prevent the Error of another & the same stands true of twenty Houses But the Question is, whether they do more good then harm the Business is cartainly thereby retarded & the Expence inhansed

7th. We are not informed whether Votes in all cases in the lower house are to be by Members or by States,–I Question wheather a man could find out the Riddle by plowing with Sampsons Heifer,[8] if each Member is not to have a Vote why are they to be chosen according to the Numbers of Inhabitants, & why should Virginia be at ten-times the Expence of Deleware for the same power, if the Votes are always to be by States, why is it not Expressed as in the choise of a President, in cartain Cases, If each member is to have a Vote, Why is it Expressed concarning Senators, & not Concarning Representatives, this Blank appears to me, to be designed, to encourage the Small States with hops of Equality, & the Large States with Hopes of Superiority–

8ly. We have no assurance that the liberty of the press will be allowed under this Constitution–

9ly. We have been always taught that it was dangerous Mixing the Legislative & Executive powers together in the same body of People but in this Constitution, we are taught better, or worse–

10ly. What is dearest of all–*Religious Liberty*, is not Sufficiently Secured, No religious test is required as a Qualification to fill any office under the United States, but if a Majority of Congress with the presedent favour one Systom more then another, they may oblige all others to pay to the Support of their System as Much as they please, & if Oppression dose not ensue, it will be owing to the Mildness of Administration & not to any Constitutional defense, & if the Manners of People are so far Corrupted, that they cannot live by republican principles, it is Very Dangerous leaving religious Liberty at their Marcy–

1. RC, Madison Papers, DLC. Spencer wrote the date "Feby. 26th 1788" under his signature, and Madison endorsed the letter "Joseph Spencer/Feby. 26. 1788." Nevertheless, the letter is placed under 28 February, the date appearing at the top of the letter. Spencer addressed the letter "To the care of Mr. F Murey [Maury]/in Fredricksburg," expecting Madison to pass through Fredericksburg on his way home to Orange County from Congress in New York City. Spencer was possibly the Joseph Spencer (d. 1829) who served as a captain in the Continental Army, 1776–77, and as an Orange County delegate to the Virginia House of Delegates, 1780–81.

2. On 30 January Madison's father informed him that "The Baptists are now generally opposed to it [the Constitution], as it is said; Col. Barbour has been down on Pamunky amongst them, & on his return, I hear, publicly declared himself a candidate" for the Virginia Convention (Rutland, *Madison*, X, 446). In March the Virginia Baptist General Committee met and asked the question: "Whether the new Federal Constitution . . . made sufficient provision for the secure enjoyment of religious liberty. . . ." The General Committee "agreed unanimously" that "it did not" (L.H. Butterfield, "Elder John Leland, Jeffersonian Itinerant," American Antiquarian Society *Proceedings*, 62 [1952], 183–84).

3. For other efforts in January and February to get Madison to attend the state Convention election in Orange County and to run as a candidate for the Convention, see CC:499; and Rutland, *Madison*, X, 446, 454–55, 515–16, 518. For Madison's notice that he would attend the election and be a candidate, see his letter of 20 February to George Washington, *ibid.*, 526–27.

4. Aaron Bledsoe (c. 1730–1809) and Nathaniel Saunders (d. 1808). Bledsoe preached at "North Fork of Pamunkey," located about eight miles southeast of Orange. For Leland, see note 5 below.

5. John Leland (1754–1841), a native of Massachusetts, had been in Virginia since 1776 and was the leading Baptist in the state. Throughout the 1770s and 1780s, he was a strong and active supporter of religious liberty and the separation of church and state. Madison supposedly met Leland somewhere between Fredericksburg and Orange before the convention election of 24 March and convinced him to support candidates who favored the Constitution. Leland's support probably won over other Baptists. Madison assured the Baptists that amendments to the Constitution would protect their civil and religious liberties (Butterfield, "Elder John Leland," 188–91).

6. James Walker, a state senator in 1777 and 1778, was defeated for election to the state Convention from Culpeper County.

7. The enclosure is in Spencer's handwriting. At the end of these objections, Spencer wrote: "Revd. John Leeland's Objections to the Federal Constitution Sent to Col. Thos. Barber by his Request, a Coppy taken by Jos. Spencer, entended for the Consideration of Capt Jas. Walker Culpeper."

8. Judges 14:18.

575. Ezra Stiles to John Adams
Yale College, New Haven, 28 February[1]

Last Sumer I wrote you acknowleding the Receipt of the Abbe Mably's Pamphlet,[2] and your Letter accompanying it. On the 19th. Inst. I received the two Volumes of your Letters in a most neat & elegant Edition, thro' the Hands of Mr Andrew Craige of New York.[3] I am greatly honored by these repeated Testimonials of your Excellencys Friendship. These last Volumes shew a more thorough Investigation upon the Policies of antient & modern States, than has I believe ever been made before. It is with Pleasure that I observe your leading Ideas have given the Complexion to the Constitution of the State of the Massachusetts formerly and now lately to the new improved Polity of the fœderal Constitution, already adopted by six States of the Union; and which I hope will be finally adopted by all the States. For altho' a ꝑfect System of Policy may not yet be investigated, and if investigated could ꝑhaps not be introduced to general Reception without some unhappy Alterations; yet we have to rejoyce that Liberty & public Right are so well established, and an efficacious Government & competent unfrustrable Revenue, for the public Purposes of the Union, are so well secured & provided for as we find in the new fœderal Constitution. I do not hear that Hampshire Convention, now sittg, hath come to a Decision. But we have good Informn that they will adopt it. N York & Pensylva[4] have delayed. But we believe will finally accede. Be pleased to accept my Thanks for your kind & most acceptable Present.

1. RC, Adams Family Papers, MHi.
2. The Abbé de Mably had published four letters addressed to John Adams in a volume entitled *Observations sur le Gouvernement et les Loix des États-Unis d'Amérique* (Amsterdam, 1784). In 1784 this volume was published in English in London and in Philadelphia the next year (Evans 19065).
3. Craigie (1754–1819), a wealthy New York apothecary and speculator in public securities, sent Stiles volumes 1 and 2 of Adams's *Defence of the Constitutions* (CC:16). On 1 August 1788 Stiles wrote Adams that he had received a duplicate of volume 1, and he asked for a copy of the third volume (Adams Family Papers, MHi).
4. Stiles probably mistakenly wrote Pennsylvania instead of Virginia.

576. Brutus XIV
New York Journal, 28 February[1]

The second paragraph of sect. 2d. art. 3, is in these words: "In all cases affecting ambassadors, other public ministers and consuls, and those in which a state shall be a party, the supreme court shall have original jurisdiction. In all the other cases before mentioned, the supreme court shall have appellate jurisdiction, both as to law and fact, with such exceptions, and under such regulations as the Congress shall make."

Although it is proper that the courts of the general government should have cognizance of all matters affecting ambassadors, foreign ministers, and consuls; yet I question much the propriety of giving the supreme court original jurisdiction in all cases of this kind.

Ambassadors, and other public ministers, claim, and are entitled by the law of nations, to certain privileges, and exemptions, both for their persons and their servants.

The meanest servant of an ambassador is exempted by the law of nations from being sued for debt. Should a suit be brought against such an one by a citizen, through inadvertency or want of information, he will be subject to an action in the supreme court. All the officers concerned in issuing or executing the process will be liable to like actions. Thus may a citizen of a state be compelled, at great expence and inconveniency, to defend himself against a suit, brought against him in the supreme court, for inadvertently commencing an action against the most menial servant of an ambassador for a just debt.

The appellate jurisdiction granted to the supreme court, in this paragraph, has justly been considered as one of the most objectionable parts of the constitution: under this power, appeals may be had from the inferior courts to the supreme, in every case to which the judicial power extends, except in the few instances in which the supreme court will have original jurisdiction.

By this article, appeals will lie to the supreme court, in all criminal as well as civil causes. This I know, has been disputed by some; but I presume the point will appear clear to any one, who will attend to the connection of this paragraph with the one that precedes it. In the former, all the cases, to which the power of the judicial shall extend, whether civil or criminal, are enumerated. There is no criminal matter, to which the judicial power of the United States will extend; but such as are included under some one of the cases specified in this section. For this section is extended to define all the cases, of every description, to which the power of the judicial shall reach. But in all these cases it is declared, the supreme court shall have appellate jurisdiction, except in those which affect ambassadors, other public ministers and consuls, and those in which a state shall be a party. If then this section extends the power of the judicial, to criminal cases, it allows appeals in such cases. If the power of the judicial is not extended to criminal matters by this section, I ask, by what part of this system does it appear, that they have any cognizance of them?

I believe it is a new and unusual thing to allow appeals in criminal matters. It is contrary to the sense of our laws, and dangerous to the lives and liberties of the citizen. As our law now stands, a person charged with a crime has a right to a fair and impartial trial by a jury of his country, and their verdict is final. If he is acquitted no other court can call upon him to answer for the same crime. But by this system, a man may have had ever so fair a trial, have been acquitted by ever so respectable a jury of his country; and still the officer of the government who prosecutes, may appeal to the supreme court. The whole matter may have a second hearing. By this means, persons who may have disobliged those who execute the general government, may be subjected to intolerable oppression. They may be kept in long and ruinous confinement, and exposed to heavy and insupportable charges, to procure the attendence of witnesses, and provide the means of their defence, at a great distance from their places of residence.

I can scarcely believe there can be a considerate citizen of the United States, that will approve of this appellate jurisdiction, as extending to criminal cases, if they will give themselves time for reflection.

Whether the appellate jurisdiction as it respects civil matters, will not prove injurious to the rights of the citizens, and destructive of those privileges which have ever been held sacred by Americans, and whether it will not render the administration of justice intolerably burthensome, intricate, and dilatory, will best appear, when we have considered the nature and operation of this power.

It has been the fate of this clause, as it has of most of those, against which unanswerable objections have been offered, to be explained different ways, by the advocates and opponents to the constitution. I confess I do not know what the advocates of the system, would make it mean, for I have not been fortunate enough to see in any publication this clause taken up and considered. It is certain however, they do not admit the explanation which those who oppose the constitution give it, or otherwise they would not so frequently charge them with want of candor, for alledging that it takes away the trial by jury, appeals from an inferior to a superior court, as practised in the civil law courts, are well understood. In these courts, the judges determine both on the law and the fact; and appeals are allowed from the inferior to the superior courts, on the whole merits: the superior tribunal will re-examine all the facts as well as the law, and frequently new facts will be introduced, so as many times to render the cause in the court of appeals very different from what it was in the court below.

If the appellate jurisdiction of the supreme court, be understood in the above sense, the term is perfectly intelligible. The meaning then is, that in all the civil causes enumerated, the supreme court shall have authority to re-examine the whole merits of the case, both with respect to the facts and the law which may arise under it, without the intervention of a jury; that this is the sense of this part of the system appears to me clear, from the express words of it, "in all the other cases before mentioned, the supreme court shall have appellate jurisdiction, both as to law and fact, &c." Who are the supreme court? Does it not consist of the judges? and they are to have the same jurisdiction of the fact as they are to have of the law. They will therefore have the same authority to determine the fact as they will have to determine the law, and no room is left for a jury on appeals to the supreme court.

If we understand the appellate jurisdiction in any other way, we shall be left utterly at a loss to give it a meaning; the common law is a stranger to any such jurisdiction: no appeals can lie from any of our common law courts, upon the merits of the case; the only way in which they can go up from an inferior to a superior tribunal is by habeas corpus before a hearing, or by certiorari, or writ of error, after they are determined in the subordinate courts; but in no case, when they are carried up, are the facts re-examined, but they are always taken as established in the inferior court.

(To be continued.)

1. Reprinted: Boston *American Herald*, 13 March. The conclusion of "Brutus" XIV was printed in the *New York Journal*, 6 March (CC:598).

577. The Arraignment of Centinel
Pennsylvania Mercury, 28 February

On 26 February Daniel Humphreys, the publisher of the triweekly *Pennsylvania Mercury*, noted that "The Arraignment of — Centinel, Esq. at the Bar of the most illustrious United States, will appear in our next." On the day the *Mercury* printed "The Arraignment of Centinel," Benjamin Rush wrote Stephen Chambers of Lancaster: "Enclosed you have Hall's paper [*Pennsylvania Gazette*] of yesterday–and Humphries's of this day.–I wish you would get the tryal of the Centinel & the character of the *old woman* translated & published in your paper [*Lancaster Zeitung*].–When you have done with Humphries's paper please to send it forward to have the above pieces, published in the York town, or Carlisle papers [*Pennsylvania Chronicle* and *Carlisle Gazette*]" (Mfm:Pa. 462). "The character of the *old woman*" refers to a series of eight satirical Federalist letters signed "Margery" (i.e., Antifederalist George Bryan) that were published in the *Pennsylvania Mercury* between 21 February and 20 March (Mfm:Pa. 444, 445, 449, 450, 472, 473, 501, 549). It is possible that Benjamin Rush was the author of both this series and "The Arraignment of Centinel." An Antifederalist had charged that Rush, in order "to *save his bacon*," had become "the *humble* copyist" of the publisher of the *Pennsylvania Mercury* (Philadelphia *Independent Gazetteer*, 19 February, Mfm:Pa. 436). Despite Rush's request to Chambers, "The Arraignment of Centinel" was reprinted only in the New York *Daily Advertiser* on 4 March.

The ARRAIGNMENT *of* — CENTINEL, Esq.
February 27, 1788.

— CENTINEL, Esq. was brought to the bar of the most illustrious the United States; and the clerk having read the return, Mr. A—y G—l informed the court, there was an indictment against the prisoner, and prayed he might be charged with it.

Clerk. — Centinel, hold up your hand, which he (reluctantly) did.
Pennsylvania, ss.

The jurors for the most illustrious United States of America, upon their oaths do present, that — Centinel, late of the Northern Liberties, in the county of Philadelphia, Esq.[1] and within the jurisdiction of the aforesaid most illustrious United States, as a false traitor, not having the fear of God in his heart, neither in his eyes, nor weighing the duties of citizenship and allegiance, but moved and seduced by the instigation of Satan, Belzebub,

Lucifer, Belial, and the whole herd of Devils, withdrawing the due obedience, which a true and faithful subject ought, should, and of right is bound to bear, towards the aforesaid most illustrious United States; contriving, and with all his strength, soul, body, and goose quill (even to an unprecedented degree of flaming zeal and enthusiasm) to disturb the peace and common tranquillity of the aforesaid most illustrious United States, by dogmatical, proditorious publications, (lies and other hellish devices) to stir up and move opposition, faction, riot, sedition, insurrection, civil wars, rebellion and murder, against the aforesaid most illustrious United States, the Honorable the Congress, His Excellency General Washington,[2] and divers others members of the honorable the continental and state conventions, and against their new proposed glorious frame of government, for promoting the peace, liberty and safety of the aforesaid most illustrious United States; for which purposes the aforesaid Centinel, as a false traitor, maliciously, traiterously, and diabolically, did conspire, compass, imagine and intend, and with the artifices and plausibility of a thorough-paced Jesuit, to frustrate their designs, &c. by holding a secret correspondence and cabal on the 18th day of September, in the year of our Lord 1787, and in the 12th year of the independence of the aforesaid most illustrious United States; and divers times, as well before as after, did meet and consult with other false traitors, as Philadelphiensis,[3] the Red Nos'd Vicar,[4] the Old Militia Man, the Old Whig,[5] Timmy the Rover,[6] and other false and scurrilous traitors, to the jurors at present unknown, at their sedition and libel-shop, at College-Green,[7] in the state of Pennsylvania aforesaid.

And then and there did distil, in large quantities, false, factious, opprobrious, disgraceful, shameful, vile, defamatory, scandalous, libellous, traiterous, malicious, infamous and stinkabuss pieces, to the number of sixteen, entituled the "Centinel," and which said infamous libels, &c. the said — Centinel as aforesaid, as a false traitor, &c. with the most unparalleled and audacious effrontery, did cause to be printed and published, from time to time, and from day to day, in the paper by him called the "impartial and immaculate paper,"[8] which said libels, &c. were filled with lies, false quotations, trifling tales, fears, suggestions, prognostications, broken-hearted sighs, enthusiastic rhapsodies, tautological repetitions, and the whole palladium of nonsense and absurdities, liberally and spontaneously embellished, with the words, miscreants, infernal wretches, conclave, aristocratics, well-born, accursed villains, conspirators, and other Billingsgate expressions, abounding with scandalum magnatum, by wholesale, ad infinitum; and which libellous papers, together with handbills, in both German and English, the aforesaid Centinel, as a false traitor, &c. did clandestinely convey by private hands, into some of the back counties, particularly Cumberland, Franklin and Fayette,[9] to raise and stir up riot, opposition, civil wars, and rebellion, and which actually took effect in the town of Carlisle.[10]

And also this same Centinel, as a false traitor, &c. did hold a treasonable correspondence with certain other well known traitors of the minority, by the names of W—, F— and S—,[11] a detestable triumviri, disturbers of the peace of society, insignificant babblers, noisy, ignorant, impertinent politicasters, assiduous seekers of their own interest, office hunters, makers of paper money and test laws, seceders,[12] protestors, promoters of riot, faction, sedition, discord, civil wars and rebellion; and at the same time impudently, ungraciously, burlesquically and ironically, together (with a very small number of other low, trifling slubberdegullions of an inferior class) calling themselves Patriots!

And moreover, the aforesaid Centinel, as a false traitor, &c. in order to fulfil those his most horrid and diabolical treasons, and traiterous compassings, imaginations and purposes aforesaid, and to leave nothing undone, which envy, hatred, malice, ambition and a diabolical heart could suggest, did collogue with certain wheel-barrow men, convicts and criminals, now in the new gaol of the city and county of Philadelphia, making use of all his interest and influence with divers others, sneakups, time-serving, pickthanks, sycophants, and traitors, &c. of his gang, to get him the aforesaid Centinel, chosen president of their society; and actually succeeded therein, as fully appears by the treasonable and traitorous resolves of the aforesaid society printed and published in the Pennsylvania Gazette,[13] of which he the said Centinel, &c. is now president, and L— M—[14] vice-president, against the duty of his allegiance, against the peace of the aforesaid most illustrious United States, against the dignity and independence thereof, and against the form of the statutes in this case made and provided.

How say you, — Centinel, are you guilty of this high treason and other matters, whereof you stand indicted, or not guilty?

Centinel–Not guilty.

Clerk–Culprit, how will you be tried?

Centinel–By God and the minority.

Clerk–God send you a good deliverance.

The prisoner then was remanded back to gaol, and the court adjourned *sine die.*

1. George Bryan was thought to be "Centinel" (CC:133).

2. For "Centinel's" criticism of George Washington, see CC:133, pp. 327n, 330.

3. For "Philadhiensis" (i.e., Benjamin Workman, tutor at the University of Pennsylvania) and his writings against the Constitution, see CC:237.

4. A reference to the Reverend Dr. John Ewing, provost of the University of Pennsylvania, whose use of snuff evidently gave him a red nose. See also "Margery, Letter VI, To Doctor Snuffle of Cogue-Hall, College-Green," *Pennsylvania Mercury*, 1 March (Mfm:Pa. 473).

5. On 22 November Antifederalist William Shippen, Jr., a Philadelphia physician, stated that the essays by "An Old Whig" were said to be written by George Bryan, James Hutchinson, and John Smilie. Bryan and Hutchinson were from Philadelphia,

while Smilie was from Fayette County. For the writings of "An Old Whig" against the Constitution, see CC:157.

6. Possibly Timothy Matlack (1730-1829), an old Revolutionary and a leader of Philadelphia's Constitutionalist Party. For an exchange of letters between "Margery" and "Timmy the Rover," see *Pennsylvania Mercury*, 23 February, 1 March (Mfm:Pa. 449, 450, 472). In one of these letters (CC:450), "Timmy the Rover" reveals that he is the author of the "Philadelphiensis" essays.

7. At this time, the University of Pennsylvania was controlled by members of the Constitutionalist Party.

8. The Philadelphia *Independent Gazetteer*.

9. In the Pennsylvania Convention, the delegates of these counties voted seven to one against ratifying the Constitution.

10. For the Carlisle riot which took place on 26 December, see the Philadelphia *Independent Gazetteer*, 4 March (Appendix I).

11. Robert Whitehill, William Findley, and John Smilie were Antifederalist leaders in the Pennsylvania Convention (RCS:Pa., *passim*).

12. Whitehill and Findley were two of the nineteen assemblymen who, on 28 September, had hoped to forestall the calling of a state convention by seceding from the Assembly, thereby preventing that body from attaining a quorum (RCS:Pa., 95, 117, and CC:125).

13. A reference to Federalist Francis Hopkinson's "Meeting of the *Wheel-barrow Society* in the Prison-yard, Philadelphia, February the 8th, 1788" which was published in the *Pennsylvania Gazette* on 20 February (Mfm:Pa. 440).

14. Antifederalist Luther Martin of Maryland, the author of the *Genuine Information* (CC:389).

578. Samuel McDowell et al. to the Court of Fayette County, Ky., 28 February[1]

Each of the eight signers of this petition was a member of Kentucky's "court party"–a group so-called because it included the judges of the district court, the attorney general, and the most prominent lawyers. They were bound by ties of marriage, religion, and education; and they were also connected with General James Wilkinson and his scheme to bring Kentucky under Spanish control. The "court party" supported separate statehood for Kentucky and opposed the new federal Constitution. These men believed that the Constitution granted too much power to the central government. In particular, the "court party" insisted that the state courts try all land disputes between residents and nonresidents, and it wanted the state legislature to have the right to tax imports in order to encourage local manufacturing. It also thought that the Eastern States would not support America's right to the free navigation of the Mississippi River–a right particularly important to Westerners. In fact, the "court party" believed that little could be expected from the East because its views were so diametrically opposed to those of the West. (See Patricia Watlington, *The Partisan Spirit: Kentucky Politics, 1779-1792* [Chapel Hill, N.C., 1972], 83-89, 139-51.) With one possible exception, each of the eight signers served in at least one of the nine Kentucky statehood conventions held between 1784 and 1790, and with the exception of Benjamin Logan and Caleb Wallace, each signer was a member of The Political Club of Danville–a group of thirty men who debated the merits of the Constitution between February and May 1788. The club was sharply critical of the Constitution and recommended many changes, including the addition of a bill of rights. (See Thomas Speed, "The Political Club, Danville, Kentucky, 1786-1790," *Filson Club Publications*, No. 9 [Louisville, Ky., 1894], 38, 143-50.)

Samuel McDowell (1735–1817) of Mercer County and his son-in-law Caleb Wallace (1742–1814) of Fayette County were justices of the district court of Kentucky; George Muter (d. 1811) of Mercer County was chief justice; and Christopher Greenup (1750–1818) of Mercer County, a lawyer, was clerk. Harry Innes (1752–1816) of Mercer County was attorney general of the District of Kentucky. Benjamin Sebastian (c. 1745–1834) of Jefferson County was an Anglican minister and a lawyer; while Benjamin Logan (1743–1802), a brigadier general of militia, represented Lincoln County in the Virginia House of Delegates, 1781–82, 1785–87. Thomas Allin (1757–1833), the clerk of the Mercer County court, voted against ratification of the Constitution in the Virginia Convention in June 1788.

The petition printed below was apparently one of several addressed to all of the Kentucky county courts. A copy of this petition addressed to the Mercer County court, found in a clipping from a nineteenth- or twentieth-century newspaper, is in the Harry Innes Papers at the Library of Congress. The Mercer County petition was signed by nine members of the "court party," including the men below (except Thomas Allin) and William McDowell and William M'Clung. (For an earlier circular letter of four members of the "court party" which related only to the question of the free navigation of the Mississippi River, see note 2 below.)

In all general questions which affect a community at large it is Usual for them in some Manner to Signify their dislike, or approbation to it, and wherever it hath proved inconvenient for the whole Society to convene together, it hath heretofore been Judged expedient for them to elect representatives to declare their sentiments upon the Occasion. There Never was and we may Venture to declare there Never will be a greater call to the inhabitants of the Western Country than at the present Moment to consider coolly and dispassionately the effects which will insue to them and their posterity by the Adoption or rejection of the proposed Fœdral Constitution.

There are many Objections thrown Out against it which are of a general Nature and affect the interests of the States at large, but there are Others of a local Nature which in Our Opinion Strike immediately at the happiness & greatness of the Western Country. These local Objections arise by the Vesting in Congress the power To regulate commerce with foreign Nations.

To lay duties & imposts which shall be uniform thro'out the United states.

The Power Over the Militia.

The prohibition of a Tax or a duty on Articles exported from any State. And the power of the Fœdral Court

By the power to regulate commerce, we loose the Navigation of the Mississippi;[2] population will cease, and Our lands become of little Value. By Uniform duties and imposts, and the prohibition of a tax or duty on Articles exported from any State, we Never shall be able to encourage Manufactaries and our wealth be carried to the Eastern & Southern States. The power Over the Militia, may leave us in a defenceless State and subject us to the ravages of the Merciless Savages; And Upon Our Separation being established, a Number of our Citizens will be draged by the power of the Fœdral Court Six or eight hundred Miles to contest their Legal Claims.

These are Objects Worthy the attention of the western Settlers, and require a Minute investigation. We have therefore Ventured thro' your Body to recommend it to the Good people of your Country to elect three representatives at your ensuing March Court, to meet Other representatives from the several Counties of this district at Danville on the first Monday in April,[3] to consider the proposed Fœdral Constitution, &c if Necessary to instruct our delegates to the State Convention, & address that Body Upon the Occasion.

That the people may have an Opportunity of Making a Judicious Choice of representatives upon this Occasion, we recommend that the Election be kept Open each day during the sitting of the Court, & that this letter be read each day preceeding the Opning of the poles.

We asure the Court of Fayette, that the only Motive which hath induced us to address you at this time, is from a desire of promoting our general interest and We hope that we shall Stand acquitted from any idea of arrogance & presumption in recommending this Measure which we Most ardently wish to See adopted.

We are Gent. your mo. ob Servts

Saml. McDowell	Ben Sebastian
Caleb Wallace	Benjamin Logan
George Muter	Christo. Greenup
Harry Innes	Tho. Allin

1. DS, Draper Manuscripts, George Rogers Clark, WHi. The petition was attested by Levi Todd, clerk of the county court: "The Court recommend that the Sheriff* read this Letter as is therein requested & notify the People that an Election as is therein directed will be held from Day to day until Saturday Evening & proceed to hold the Same immediately after the Election for Delegats is over & hold the Poll in some convenient place not to interrupt the Court Business." The asterisk was inserted after "Sheriff " in the mid-nineteenth century by Lyman Copeland Draper, secretary of the State Historical Society of Wisconsin, who indicated that the sheriff was Colonel Robert Patterson, among whose papers he found this document.

2. On 29 March 1787 Muter, Innes, Sebastian, and John Brown, after meeting with other members of the "court party," had sent a circular letter "to the different Courts in the Western Country," expressing alarm at Congress' proposed cession of America's right to the navigation of the Mississippi River for twenty-five or thirty years in exchange for commercial concessions from Spain. They recommended that the counties in the Kentucky District send delegates to a convention in Danville on 7 May to prepare a petition to Congress protesting such a cession. In turn, this convention would appoint delegates to a convention of "the several districts on the Western Waters" since "all the inhabitants residing on the Western Waters are equally affected by this partial conduct of Congress." This letter was printed in the *Maryland Journal* on 3 July and widely reprinted. There is no evidence that either convention took place. For the impact of the question of the navigation of the Mississippi on the politics of the United States, see CC:46.

3. There is no record that this convention ever met.

579. Thomas B. Wait to George Thatcher
Portland, 29 February[1]

In your last Letter to Brother Silas[2] you inquired concerning our Separation from Massachusetts–I do not know how your Biddeford correspondent will answer the interrogation–Nor do I care–I am determin'd to say something about it–

The vastness of the object that has, since your departure, ~~and still does~~ attracted the public mind, hath left not a crack or crevise for the territory of *Sagadahock*[3]–But when the general agitation occasioned by any Phenomenon shall subside, then will an opportunity offer to contemplate its effects–

The adoption of the proposed national Constitution, which I now begin to look upon as certain, will alter the opinion of our Boston Brethren–instead of opposing, they will assuredly advocate our separation–so will every man on this side Philadelphia.–The acquisition of two Senators in the northern interest, will be considered as an object of magnitude–The independence of Vermont will, also, on the same principles, be contended for–and obtained–What say you?–

I have actually written my vote for the Governour of Main;–but it is for a man who I am very certain *you* would not vote for.–

I think you have written to, and received Letters from Genl. Thompson–Do for God's sake write him once more–he conducts as if the Devil had possessed him. His opposition to the new Constitution continues.–When he left Boston, his last words were–*I will throw the state into Confusion*–It is true, these were *great swelling words*; but he may do a great deal of mischief.–Can not you contrive a Letter that will do him good?–For I do not believe Thompson to be a man of a bad heart–Should you tell him that the Consti– with the proposed *amendments*, which will certainly take place, will operate less injuriously than many suppose–that other amendments if found necessary will certainly take place–that you admire the submissive conduct of the minority &c. &c.–(richly interlarding the whole with Republicanism)–something of this kind might be serviceable–Yours–Dictator

1. RC, Thatcher Papers, MB.
2. Silas Lee of Biddeford, Maine, had read law with Thatcher and was married to his niece Temperance Hedge. Thatcher had written to Lee on 16 February (not found), and on 29 February and 20 March Lee responded (Chamberlain Collection, Thatcher Papers, MB, and CC:631). For more on Maine's separation from Massachusetts, see CC:570, note 11.
3. Sagadahock was the early name for a great part of Maine that had been granted to the Duke of York by his brother Charles II in 1664.

Editors' Note
George Washington to Caleb Gibbs
Mount Vernon, 29 February

Excerpts from this letter were printed in the *Massachusetts Centinel* on 22 March. (See CC:638.)

580. The Landholder No. X
Maryland Journal, 29 February[1]

"Landholder" IV, V, and VIII criticized Elbridge Gerry for his actions in the Constitutional Convention and his objections to the Constitution (*Connecticut Courant* and Hartford *American Mercury*, 26 November, 3 and 24 December 1787, CC:295, 316, 371). Gerry responded on 5 January in the *Massachusetts Centinel* (CC:419), and Luther Martin, a Maryland delegate to the Constitutional Convention, defended Gerry in the *Maryland Journal* on 18 January (CC:460). On 29 February "Landholder" X replied to Martin.

Unlike the first nine "Landholder" essays, "Landholder" X was not printed in Connecticut, casting serious doubt whether or not it was written by the Connecticut "Landholder." When the Connecticut "Landholder" series was revived on 3 March, the first essay printed was numbered X (CC:588). Martin himself questioned the identity of the Maryland "Landholder," declaring that "Whether the Landholder of the Connecticut Courant, and of the Maryland Journal, is the same person, or different, is not very material;–I however incline to the former opinion, as I hope, for the honour of human nature, it would be difficult to find more than one individual, who could be capable of so total a disregard to the principles of truth and honour" (CC:604).

Because of his knowledge of the Constitutional Convention, in general, and Luther Martin's actions in the Convention, in particular, it seems likely that the Maryland "Landholder" was one of Martin's fellow Convention delegates from Maryland who supported the Constitution–Daniel of St. Thomas Jenifer, Daniel Carroll, or James McHenry. Jenifer is a good possibility. When the Maryland Convention delegates reported to the Maryland House of Delegates in late November 1787, Jenifer publicly challenged Martin's assertion that Robert Yates and John Lansing, Jr., two of New York's Convention delegates, "had left the Convention in disgust, and with the fixed intention not to return" (*Pennsylvania Packet*, 14 February). Martin defended his statement in a letter to the speaker of the Maryland House of Delegates, pointing out that the recently published letter by Yates and Lansing to the governor of New York supported his contention (Baltimore *Maryland Gazette*, 29 January). There is good evidence that Martin and Jenifer were at odds in the Constitutional Convention. On 6 August, the day that the Committee of Detail presented the first draft of the Constitution, the Maryland delegation met to confer on the report and to prepare themselves "to act in unison." In describing the meeting, James McHenry reported that Martin declared that ". . . he was against the system, that a compromise only had enabled its abettors to bring it into its present stage–that had Mr. Jenifer voted with him, things would have taken a different turn. Mr. Jenifer said he voted with him till he saw it was in vain to oppose its progress. I begged the gentlemen to observe some order to enable us to do the business we had convened upon" (Farrand, II, 190).

The Maryland "Landholder," No. X was answered by Luther Martin in three essays published in the *Maryland Journal* on 7, 18, and 21 March (CC:604, 626, 636). Gerry reentered the battle as "A Friend and Customer" in the Boston *American Herald* on 18 April (CC:691). On 10 April a Federalist essayist, identifying himself as Martin, published a satirical item in the Philadelphia *Federal Gazette* on the debate between the "Landholder" and Martin. The essay was prefaced: "I observe, that you have republished the Landholder, No. X. against me. Your publishing my fifth Number to the Citizens of Maryland, will be a proof of your impartiality, and will much oblige your humble servant." Only two days earlier, the real Luther Martin had challenged the publisher of the *Pennsylvania Mercury*, who had reprinted the "Landholder," No. X, to print his defenses of Gerry and himself that had been published in the *Maryland Journal* on 7, 18, and 21 March. In the satirical essay, the fictitious Luther Martin described himself as the Constitu-

tional Convention's "*only honest man*" who "opposed every measure of that body;
because I knew them, *every man*, to be aspiring tyrants."

The Maryland "Landholder," No. X was reprinted in the Philadelphia *Federal
Gazette*, 15, 18 March; *Pennsylvania Mercury*, 18 March; *Massachusetts Centinel*, 5 April;
and Providence *United States Chronicle*, 8 May.

To the Honourable LUTHER MARTIN, Esq;

SIR, I have just met with your performance, in favour of the Honourable Mr. Gerry, published in the Maryland Journal of the 18th January,
1788.

As the Public may be ignorant of the sacrifice you have made of your
resentments on this occasion, you will excuse me for communicating what
your extreme modesty must have induced you to conceal. You, no doubt,
remember that you and Mr. Gerry never voted alike in Convention, except in the instances I shall hereafter enumerate. He uniformly opposed
your principles, and so far did you carry your abhorrence of his politics,
as to inform certain members to be on their guard against his wiles, for
that, he and Mr. Mason held private meetings, where plans were concerted "to aggrandise, at the expence of the small States, Old Massachusetts and the Ancient Dominion." After having thus opposed him and
accused him, to appear his Champion and *intimate acquaintance*, has placed
you beyond the reach of ordinary panegyric.

Having done this justice to your magnanimity, I cannot resist drawing
the veil of the Convention a little further aside; not, I assure you, with any
intention to give pain to your Constituents, but merely to induce them to
pity you for the many piercing mortifications you met with in the discharge of your duty.

The day you took your seat must be long remembered by those who
were present; nor will it be possible for you to forget the astonishment
your behaviour almost instantaneously produced. You had scarcely time
to read the propositions which had been agreed to after the fullest investigation, when, without requesting information, or to be let into the reasons
of the adoption of what you might not approve, you opened against them,
in a speech which held during two days,[2] and which might have continued
two months, but for those marks of fatigue and disgust you saw strongly
expressed on whichever side of the house you turned your mortified eyes.–
There needed no other display to fix your character and the rank of your
abilities, which the Convention would have confirmed by the most distinguishing silence, had not a certain similarity in genius provoked a sarcastic
reply from the pleasant Mr. Gerry;[3] in which he admired the strength of
your lungs and your profound knowledge in the first principles of government; mixing and illustrating his little remarks with a profusion of those
hems, that never fail to lengthen out and enliven his oratory. This reply
(from your *intimate acquaintance*) the match being so equal and the contrast
so comic, had the happy effect to put the house in good humour, and leave
you a prey to the most humiliating reflections. But these did not teach you

to bound your future speeches by the lines of moderation; for the very next day you exhibited, without a blush, another specimen of eternal volubility. It was not however to the duration of your speeches, you owed the perfection of your reputation. You, *alone*, advocated the political heresy, that the people *ought not to be trusted with the election of representatives*.[4] You held the jargon, that notwithstanding each State had an equal number of votes in the Senate, yet the States were *unequally* represented in the Senate.[5] You espoused the tyrannic principle, that where a State refused to comply with a requisition of Congress for money, that an army should be marched into its bowels, to fall indiscriminately upon the property of the innocent and the guilty, instead of having it collected, as the Constitution proposed, by the mild and equal operation of laws.[6] One hour you sported the opinion, that Congress, afraid of the militia resisting their measures, would neither arm nor organize them: and the next, as if men required no time to breathe between such contradictions, that they would harrass them by long and unnecessary marches, till they wore down their spirit and rendered them fit subjects for despotism.[7] You too contended that the *powers* and *authorities* of the new Constitution must destroy the liberties of the people; but that the same powers and authorities might be safely trusted with the old Congress.[8] You cannot have forgotten, that by such ignorance in politics and contradictory opinions, you exhausted the politeness of the Convention, which at length prepared to slumber when you rose to speak: nor can you have forgotten, you were only twice appointed a member of a Committee,[9] or that these appointments were made, merely to avoid your endless garrulity, and if possible, lead you to reason, by the easy road of familiar conversation.

But lest you should say that I am a record only of the bad, I shall faithfully recognize whatever occurred to your advantage. You originated that clause in the Constitution which enacts, that "*This Constitution and the laws of the United States which shall be made in pursuance thereof, and all treaties made, or which shall be made, under the authority of the United States, shall be the supreme law of the land, and the judges in every State shall be bound thereby, any thing in the Constitution or the law of any State to the contrary notwithstanding.*"[10] You voted that an *appeal* should lay to the supreme judiciary of the United States, for the correction of all errors both in *law and fact*.[11] You also agreed to the clause that declares *nine States to be sufficient to put the government in motion*.(a)[12] These are among the greater positive virtues you exhibited in the Convention; but it would be doing you injustice were I to omit those of a negative nature.

Since the publication of the Constitution, every topic of vulgar declamation has been employed to persuade the people, that it will destroy the *trial by jury*, and is defective for being without a *bill of rights*. You, Sir, had more candour in the Convention than we can allow to those declaimers out of it; there you never signified by any motion or expression whatever, that it stood in need of a bill of rights, or in anywise endangered the trial by jury. In these respects the Constitution met your entire approbation: for had you believed it defective in these essentials, you ought to have mentioned it in Convention, or had you thought it wanted further guards, it was your *indispensable duty to have proposed them*. I hope to hear that the same candour that influenced you on this occasion, has induced you to obviate any improper impressions such publications may have excited in your constituents, when you had the honour to appear before the General Assembly.[13]

From such high instances of your approbation (for every member, like you, had made objections to parts of the Constitution) the Convention were led to conclude that you would have honoured it with your signature, had you not been called to Maryland upon some indispensable business; nor ought it to be withheld from you, that your colleagues informed many Gentlemen of the House, that you told them you intended to return before its completion.

Durst I proceed beyond these *facts*, to which the whole Convention can witness, I would ask you why you changed your opinion of the Constitution after leaving Philadelphia. I have it from good authority, that you complained to an intimate acquaintance, that nothing grieved you so much as the apprehension of being detained in Maryland longer than you could wish; for that you had rather lose one hundred guineas, than not have your name appear to the Constitution. But as this circumstance seems to have been overlooked when you composed your defence of Mr. Gerry, you may have your recollection of it revived by applying to Mr. Young, of Spruce-Street, Philadelphia, to whom you made your complaint.

But leaving this curious piece of human vanity to such further investigation as you may think it deserves, let us come to those matters more particularly between us.

You have said, that you "never heard Mr. Gerry, or any other member, introduce a proposition for the redemption of continental money, according to its nominal or any other value; nor did you ever hear that such a proposition had been offered to the Convention, or had been thought of."[14]

That the Public may clearly comprehend what degree of credit ought to be given to this kind of evidence, they should know the time you were *absent* from the Convention, as well as the time you *attended*. If it should appear that you were only *a few days absent*, when unimportant business was the object, they will conclude in your favour, provided they entertain a good opinion of your veracity; on the other hand, should it appear that you were absent *nearly half the session*, however your veracity may be esteemed, they must reject your evidence. As you have not stated this necessary information, I shall do it for you.–

The Session of Convention commenced the 14th of May, and ended the 17th of September, which makes 126 days–You took your seat the 10th of

June, and left it the 4th of September, of which period you were absent at Baltimore 10 days, and as many at New-York, so that you attended only 66 days out of 126.[15]

Now, Sir, is it to be presumed that you could have been minutely informed of all that happened in Convention, and *committees of Convention*, during the 60 days of your absence; or does it follow by any rule of reasoning or logic, that because a thing did not happen in the 66 days you were present, that it did not happen in the 60 days which you did not attend?– Is it anywise likely that you could have heard what passed, especially during the last 13 days, within which period the Landholder has fixed the apostacy of Mr. Gerry; or if it is likely that your particular *intimacy* with Mr. Gerry, would stimulate to inquiries respecting his conduct, why is it that we do not see Mr. M'Henry's verification of your assertion, who was of the *committee* for considering a provision for the debts of the Union?[16]

Your reply to my second charge against this gentleman may be soon dismissed. Compare his letter to the Legislature of his State[17] with your defence, and you will find that you have put into his mouth objections different from any thing it contains, so that if your representation be *true*, his must be *false*. But there is another circumstance which militates against your new friend. Though he was *face to face* with his colleagues at the State Convention of Massachusetts,[18] he has not ventured to call upon them to clear him either of this charge, or that respecting the continental money. But as the Public seemed to require that something should be said on the occasion, an anonymous writer, denies that he made such a motion, and endeavours to abate the force of my second allegation, merely by supposing, that "his colleagues were men of too much honour to assert that his reasons in Convention were *totally different*[19] from those which he has published." But alas! his colleagues would not acquit him in this way, and he was of too proud a spirit to ask them to do it in person.[(b)] Hence the charge remains on its original grounds, while you, for want of proper concert, have joined his accusers, and reduced him to the humiliating necessity of endeavouring to stifle your justification.

These points being dismissed, it remains only to reconcile the contradictory parts you have acted on the great political stage.

You entered the Convention without a sufficient knowledge in the science of government, where you committed a succession of memorable blunders; as the work advanced, some rays of light penetrated your understanding, and enabled you (as has been shewn) to assist in raising some of its pillars, when the desire of having your name enrolled with the other labourers, drew from you that remarkable complaint so expressive of vanity and conviction. But self-interest soon gained the ascendant. You quickly comprehended the delicacy of your situation, and this restored your first impressions in all their original force. You thought the *Deputy Attorney-General of the United States for the State of Maryland*, destined for a different character, and that inspired you with the hope, that you might derive from a desperate opposition what you saw no prospect of gaining by a contrary conduct. But I will venture to predict, that though you were to double your efforts, you would fail in your object. I leave you now to your own reflections, under a promise, however, to give my name to the Public, should you be able to procure any indifferent testimony to contradict a single fact I have stated.

February–, 1788.

(a) Mr. Gerry agreed with Mr. Martin on these questions.

(b) To prevent any misconstruction, the following is the publication entire. From the MASSACHUSETTS CENTINEL.[20]

"That Mr. Gerry, by giving his dissent to the proposed Constitution, could have no motives for preserving an office–for he holds none under the United States, or any of them; that he has not, as has been asserted, exchanged Continental for State Securities, and if he had, it would have been for his interest to have supported the new system, because thereby the States are restrained from impairing the obligation of contracts, and by a transfer of such securities, they may be recovered in the new federal court; that he never heard, in the Convention, a motion made, much less did make any, 'for the redemption of the old continental money;' but that he proposed the public debt should be made neither better nor worse by the new system; but stand precisely on the same ground it now does by the Articles of Confederation; that had there been such a motion, he was not interested in it, as he did not then, neither does he now, own the value of ten pounds in continental money; that he never was called on for his reasons for not signing, but stated them fully in the progress of the business–his objections are chiefly contained in his letter to the Legislature; that he believes his colleagues men of too much honour to assert what is not truth; that his reasons in the Convention 'were totally different from those which he published,' that his only motive for dissenting from the new Constitution, was, a firm persuasion that it would endanger the liberties of America; that if the people are of a different opinion, they have a right to adopt it; but he was not authorized to an act, which appeared to him was a surrender of their liberties; that as a representative of a free State, he thought he was bound in honour, to vote according to his idea of her true interest, and that he should do the same in similar circumstances."

"Cambridge, January 3, 1788."

I will not say this writer makes a distinction between a thing done in *Convention*, and a thing done in *Committee*. Be this as it may, he confesses more than Mr. Martin; for it seems that Mr. Gerry proposed that the public debt should stand "on the same ground it now stands on by the articles of confederation." He might have subjoined that Mr. Gerry prefaced this motion by observing, that it was the same in substance as his first, in as much as it included his first. But notwithstanding this motion was readily agreed to without his explanation being contradicted, yet he never afterwards favoured the Convention with a look of peace, or a word of reconcilement.

1. On 26 February the printer of the *Maryland Journal* noted: "The LANDHOLDER, No. X, addressed to the Honourable LUTHER MARTIN, Esq; is just come to Hand, and will be inserted in our next."

2. Martin first attended the Convention on Saturday, 9 June, but he did not speak. On Monday, the 11th, he made a motion (Farrand, I, 203). "Landholder" is possibly referring to a lengthy speech that Martin made on 27–28 June. According to James Madison, Martin ended the first part of his speech on the 27th by stating that "He was too much exhausted . . . to finish his remarks, and reminded the House that he should tomorrow, resume them." Robert Yates said that Martin's ". . . arguments were too diffuse and in many instances desultory, it was not possible to trace him through the whole, or to methodize his ideas into a systematic or argumentative arrangement." Martin continued his speech the next day, and Madison noted at the end of Martin's remarks that "This was the substance of the residue of his discourse which was delivered with much diffuseness & considerable vehemence" (Farrand, I, 436–59).

3. No other record of Gerry's comments has been found, and Gerry himself denied the "Landholder's" assertions (Boston *American Herald*, 18 April, CC:691).

4. On 20 June Martin stated that "He considered Congs as representing the people, being chosen by the Legislatures who were chosen by the people. At any rate Congress represented the Legislatures. . . ." On 6 August Martin declared in a private meeting of the Maryland delegates (described by James McHenry) that "he was against two branches–that he was against the people electing the representatives of the national government . . ." (Farrand, I, 340; II, 191. See also *ibid.*, 437, 444, 457.).

5. There is no record of Luther Martin having made such a statement. He favored an unicameral legislature with equality of suffrage for the states. When it became evident that the Convention favored a bicameral legislature, Martin strongly supported equality of suffrage in the Senate (Farrand, I, 437–38, 438–40, 444–45, 453–55, 499, 510; II, 4).

6. On 21 August Martin declared that "The power of taxation is most likely to be criticised by the public. Direct taxation should not be used but in cases of absolute necessity; and then the States will be best Judges of the mode. He therefore moved 'And whenever the Legislature of the U:S: shall find it necessary that revenue should be raised by direct taxation, having apportioned the same, according to the above rule on the several States,–requisitions shall be made of the respective States to pay into the Continental Treasury their respective quotas within a time in the said requisitions specified; and in case of any of the States failing to comply with such requisitions, then and then only to devise and pass acts directing the mode, and authorizing the collections of the same' " (Farrand, II, 359. See also Luther Martin, *Genuine Information* VI, Baltimore *Maryland Gazette*, 15 January, CC:451, pp. 377–78.).

7. In his only recorded speech on the militia, Martin stated that he "was confident that the States would never give up the power over the Militia; and that, if they were [to do so,] the militia would be less attended to by the Genl. than by the State Governments" (23 August, Farrand, II, 387).

8. On 20 June Martin said that "I consider the present system as a system of slavery. . . . I confess that when the confederation was made, congress ought to have been invested with more extensive powers; but when the states saw that congress indirectly aimed at sovereignty, they were jealous, and therefore refused any farther concessions" (Farrand, I, 347).

9. On 2 July and 22 August Martin was appointed to two grand committees that fashioned important compromises. The first committee was concerned with the question of representation in the two houses of Congress and the second with the slave trade and navigation acts. In all, the Convention appointed eleven committees, and Martin was in attendance when eight of them were appointed (Farrand, I, 509, 524; II, 366, 396; IV, 140–41).

10. Martin made his motion on the supremacy clause on 17 July after the Convention defeated a motion (which he opposed) giving Congress the power to veto state laws (Farrand, II, 28–29). For the text of this motion, see CC:636, note 1.

11. This clause was adopted "nem: con:" on 27 August (Farrand, II, 431).

12. On 31 August a motion by Martin and Daniel Carroll that the Constitution be ratified by thirteen states was defeated. The Convention also rejected a motion that the Constitution be ratified by ten states, but adopted a motion requiring nine states to ratify. Maryland voted "aye" in each case. When the final vote was taken on the article as amended (Article VII of the Constitution), every state except Maryland voted for it. Jenifer was the only member of the Maryland delegation who voted "aye" (Farrand, II, 477).

13. On 29–30 November the Maryland delegates to the Convention reported to the state House of Delegates. For Martin's address to the House and for his *Genuine Information*, which is an expansion of his address, see CC:304, 389.

14. For a full discussion of this matter, see "Landholder" VIII, *Connecticut Courant*, 24 December (CC:371, note 3).

15. The Convention was scheduled to convene on 14 May but it did not attain a quorum until the 25th. It adjourned *sine die* on 17 September. It did not meet on Sundays, the 4th of July, and between 27 July and 4 August, when the Committee of Detail met to write the first draft of the Constitution. From 25 May to 17 September, then, the Convention met a total of eighty-nine days. Martin arrived in the Convention on Saturday, 9 June; was absent from 7 to 11 August; and left on 4 September, a total of sixty days in attendance.

16. James McHenry was appointed to the committee on state debts on 18 August (Farrand, II, 322, 328).

17. For Gerry's 18 October letter to the Massachusetts legislature, first published in the *Massachusetts Centinel* on 3 November, see CC:227-A.

18. On 14 January the Massachusetts Convention resolved that Elbridge Gerry be invited to attend the Convention in order to answer questions about the drafting of the Constitution. Gerry attended only a few days.

19. The italics are "Landholder's."

20. This item, written by Elbridge Gerry, was printed in the *Massachusetts Centinel* on 5 January (CC:419).

581. A Columbian Patriot: Observations on the Constitution
Boston, February

The author of the pamphlet signed "A Columbian Patriot" was Mercy Warren of Milton, Mass. In mid-May 1788, Warren wrote an English friend that "If you wish to know more of the present ideas of your friend and the consequences apprehended from the hasty adoption of the new form of government, I will whisper you–You may find them at large in the subjoined manuscripts I now enclose with a printed pamphlet entitled the Columbian Patriot by the same hand" (to Catherine Macaulay Graham, c. 16 May, Mercy Warren Papers, MHi. Graham replied that the pamphlet was "written with spirit and energy," 29 October, *ibid.*). Contemporaries, however, suspected others of being "A Columbian Patriot." In early March Rufus King, a Massachusetts Convention delegate who had just returned to his family in New York City, asserted that Elbridge Gerry was "A Columbian Patriot" and that he "sinks daily in public esteem, and his bantling goes unnoticed" (to John Alsop, 2 March, Ford, *Pamphlets*, 2). Almost two months later Samuel A. Otis, a Massachusetts delegate to Congress in New York City, wrote Mercy's husband James Warren, that he had "heard in the Circles here, you, or Sister W have written the Columbian patriot, I suspect you, but wish to have it ascertained . . ." ([24?] April, Mercy Warren Papers, MHi. Historians and bibliographers accepted Gerry as "A Columbian Patriot" until 1930 when Charles Warren, a descendant of James and Mercy Warren, discovered family papers which indicated that Mercy Warren was "A Columbian Patriot." See Charles Warren, "Elbridge Gerry, James Warren, Mercy Warren and the Ratification of the Federal Constitution in Massachusetts," *Massachusetts Historical Society Proceedings*, LXIV [1930–32], 142–64.).

Mercy Warren (1728–1814), historian, playwright, and poet, was the sister of James Otis, a leading opponent of British imperial policy before the Revolution. Her husband James Warren was a prominent Antifederalist and speaker of the Massachusetts House of Representatives. Mercy Warren was a critic of British policy and published three satirical plays between 1772 and 1775 in the *Massachusetts Spy* and the *Boston Gazette*. In these plays, she attacked Governor Thomas Hutchinson and his family, leading supporters of the royal prerogative in America, and the mandamus councillors who held office under the Massachusetts Government Act (1774) at the pleasure of the Crown. By 1787 she was deeply engaged in writing a history of the American Revolution which was eventually published in three volumes in 1805 (see note 10).

In late February, "A Columbian Patriot" was printed in Boston as a nineteen-page pamphlet entitled *Observations on the New Constitution, and on the Federal and State Conventions.* The title page included the epigraph–"*Sic transit gloria Americana.*" The printer was probably Edward E. Powars, but none of the extant copies of the pamphlet has a title page and no advertisements have been found. (Powars of the Boston *American Herald* had recently printed two other Antifederalist pamphlets, *Letters from the Federal Farmer* and *The Dissent of the Minority of the Pennsylvania Convention*, CC:242, 353. On 19 March the *Massachusetts Centinel* noted with some sarcasm that the pamphlet had "ascended from a certain press."). Mercy Warren stated that the pamphlet "circulated in the Massachusetts immediately on their ratification" of the Constitution which took place on 6 February (to Catherine Macaulay Graham, c. 16 May, Mercy Warren Papers, MHi). The entire pamphlet was reprinted in two Philadelphia Antifederalist newspapers–the *Freeman's Journal*, 12, 19, and 26 March, and the *Independent Gazetteer*, 13, 20, and 27 March. The *Journal* prefaced its reprinting with a statement by "A.B.": "The inclosed Pamphlet was written in Massachusetts since the ratification of the proposed Constitution by that State. The author's mode of reasoning is good, in my opinion. Give it to us 'wholesale or retail' as best suits you, and oblige yours, &c."

In late March or early April Thomas Greenleaf of the *New York Journal* reprinted "A Columbian Patriot" as a twenty-two page pamphlet with this colophon: "Boston printed, New York re-printed, M, DCC, LXXX, VIII." The Boston and New York versions of the pamphlet are identical except for slight differences in punctuation, paragraphing, capitalization, italics, and spelling. Using the same plates, Greenleaf reprinted the pamphlet, "*by request*," in the *New York Journal* on 2, 4, and 5 April.

On 6 April–about three weeks before the election of delegates to the New York Convention–the New York City Antifederal Committee forwarded 1,700 copies of Greenleaf's edition of "A Columbian Patriot" to Antifederal county committees throughout the state, requesting that the pamphlets be distributed. The New York City committee also wanted the county committees to pay for the cost of printing (New York City Antifederal Committee Circular Letter, 6 April, and an undated document signed "C.T.," Lamb Papers, NHi). The Albany Antifederal Committee replied that it had received the pamphlets and promised to distribute them, but it refused to pay the costs of printing. It had other "considerable" expenses. The committee described the pamphlet as "a well composed piece but in a Stile too sublime & florid for us common people in this Part of the Country" (12 April, *ibid.*).

On 11 June the printers of the North Carolina *Wilmington Centinel* noted that they had just received copies of "A Columbian Patriot" from New York and that they would sell the pamphlet for two shillings each. The advertisement was run in the issues of 18, 25 June, and 2 July. On 12 March 1789 Thomas Greenleaf advertised the pamphlet for sale, with a number of other Antifederalist pamphlets, in his *New York Journal*.

Federalist attacks on the pamphlet were few but sharp. Rufus King called it "a pitiful performance" (to John Alsop, 2 March, Ford, *Pamphlets*, 2). On 19 March the *Massachusetts Centinel* noted that "Every real friend to his country, must feel his indignation greatly excited at a recent attempt of the antifederal JUNTO to poison the publick mind, by the circulation of a malicious pamphlet, which, like the locusts from the bottomless pit, hath ascended from a certain press, and are scattered over the country–This effort of a detestable faction, to traduce the late Federal and State Conventions, is however a mere piece of bombast and declamation, like the *cant, whinings,* and *ravings* of the CENTINEL and PHILADELPHIENSIS of Pennsylvania–we trust our good friends will be on their guard against the attempts of these *desperadoes*; but, should they unfortunately effect their purposes in any degree, the prime agents may assure themselves of being the earliest victims to the resentment of an enraged people."

Mankind may amuse themselves with theoretick systems of liberty, and trace its social and moral effects on sciences, virtue, industry, and every improvement of which the human mind is capable; but we can only discern its true value by the practical and wretched effects of slavery; and thus dreadfully will they be realized, when the inhabitants of the Eastern States are dragging out a miserable existence, *only* on the gleanings of their fields; and the Southern, blessed with a softer and more fertile climate, are languishing in hopeless poverty; and when asked, what is become of the flower of their crop, and the rich produce of their farms–they may answer in the hapless stile of the Man of *La Mancha*,–"The steward of my Lord has seized and sent it to *Madrid*."[1]–Or, in the more literal language of truth, The *exigencies* of government require that the collectors of the revenue should transmit it to the *Federal City*.

Animated with the firmest zeal for the interest of this country, the peace and union of the American States, and the freedom and happiness of a people who have made the most costly sacrifices in the cause of liberty,–who have braved the power of Britain, weathered the convulsions of war, and waded thro' the blood of friends and foes to establish their independence and to support the freedom of the human mind; I cannot silently witness this degradation without calling on them, before they are compelled to blush at their own servitude, and to turn back their languid eyes on their lost liberties–to consider, that the character of nations generally changes at the moment of revolution.–And when patriotism is discountenanced and publick virtue becomes the ridicule of the sycophant–when every man of liberality, firmness, and penetration, who cannot lick the hand stretched out to oppress, is deemed an enemy to the State–then is the gulph of despotism set open, and the grades to slavery, though rapid, are scarce perceptible–then genius drags heavily its iron chain–science is neglected, and real merit flies to the shades for security from reproach–the mind becomes enervated, and the national character sinks to a kind of apathy with only energy sufficient to curse the breast that gave it milk, and as an elegant writer observes, "To bewail every new birth as an encrease of misery, under a government where the mind is necessarily debased, and talents are seduced to become the panegyrists of usurpation and tyranny." He adds, "that even sedition is not the most indubitable enemy to the publick welfare; but that its most dreadful foe is despotism, which always changes the character of nations for the worse, and is productive of nothing but vice, that the tyrant no longer excites to the pursuits of glory or virtue; it is not talents, it is baseness and servility that he cherishes, and the weight of arbitrary power destroys the spring of emulation."[a][2] If such is the influence of government on the character and manners, and undoubtedly the observation is just, must we not subscribe to the opinion of the celebrated *Abbé Mablé?* "That there are disagreeable seasons in the unhappy situation of human affairs, when policy requires both the intention and the power of doing mischief to be punished; and that when the senate proscribed the memory of *Cæsar* they ought to have put *Anthony* to death, and extinguished the hopes of *Octavius.*"[3] Self defence is a primary law of nature, which no subsequent law of society can abolish; this primœval principle, the immediate gift of the Creator, obliges every one to remonstrate against the strides of ambition, and a wanton lust of domination, and to resist the first approaches of tyranny, which at this day threaten to sweep away the rights for which the brave sons of America have fought with an heroism scarcely paralleled even in ancient republicks. It may be repeated, they have purchased it with their blood, and have gloried in their independence with a dignity of spirit, which has made them the admiration of philosophy, the pride of America, and the wonder of Europe. It has been observed, with great propriety, that "the virtues and vices of a people when a revolution happens in their government, are the measure of the liberty or slavery they ought to expect–An heroic love for the publick good, a profound reverence for the laws, a contempt of riches, and a noble haughtiness of soul, are the only foundations of a free

government."(b)4 Do not their dignified principles still exist among us? Or
are they extinguished in the breasts of Americans, whose fields have been
so recently crimsoned to repel the potent arm of a foreign Monarch, who
had planted his engines of slavery in every city, with design to erase the
vestiges of freedom in this his last asylum. It is yet to be hoped, for the
honour of human nature, that no combinations either foreign or domestick
have thus darkned this Western hemisphere.—On these shores freedom has
planted her standard, diped in the purple tide that flowed from the veins
of her martyred heroes; and here every uncorrupted American yet hopes
to see it supported by the vigour, the justice, the wisdom and unanimity
of the people, in spite of the deep-laid plots, the secret intrigues, or the
bold effrontery of those interested and avaricious adventurers for place,
who intoxicated with the ideas of distinction and preferment, have pros-
trated every worthy principle beneath the shrine of ambition. Yet these are
the men who tell us republicanism is dwindled into theory—that we are
incapable of enjoying our liberties—and that we must have a master.—Let
us retrospect the days of our adversity, and recollect who were then our
friends; do we find them among the sticklers for aristocratick authority?
No, they were generally the same men who now wish to save us from the
distractions of anarchy on the one hand, and the jaws of tyranny on the
other; where then were the class who now come forth importunately urging that our political salvation depends on the adoption of a system at
which freedom spurns?—Were not some of them hidden in the corners of
obscurity, and others wrapping themselves in the bosom of our enemies
for safety? Some of them were in the arms of infancy; and others speculating for fortune, by sporting with public money; while a few, a very few of
them were magnanimously defending their country, and raising a character, which I pray heaven may never be sullied by aiding measures derogatory to their former exertions. But the revolutions in principle which time
produces among mankind, frequently exhibits the most mortifying instances of human weakness; and this alone can account for the extraordinary appearance of a few names, once distinguished in the honourable
walks of patriotism, but now found on the list of the Massachusetts assent
to the ratification of a Constitution,5 which, by the undefined meaning of
some parts, and the ambiguities of expression in others, is dangerously
adapted to the purposes of an immediate *aristocratic tyranny*; that from the
difficulty, if not impracticability of its operation, must soon terminate in
the most *uncontrouled despotism*.

All writers on government agree, and the feelings of the human mind
witness the truth of these political axioms, that man is born free and possessed of certain unalienable rights—that government is instituted for the
protection, safety, and happiness of the people, and not for the profit,
honour, or private interest of any man, family, or class of men—That the
origin of all power is in the people, and that they have an incontestible

right to check the creatures of their own creation, vested with certain powers to guard the life, liberty and property of the community: And if certain selected bodies of men, deputed on these principles, determine contrary to the wishes and expectations of their constituents, the people have an undoubted right to reject their decisions, to call for a revision of their conduct, to depute others in their room, or if they think proper, to demand further time for deliberation on matters of the greatest moment: it therefore is an unwarrantable stretch of authority or influence, if any methods are taken to preclude this reasonable, and peaceful mode of enquiry and decision. And it is with inexpressible anxiety, that many of the best friends to the Union of the States–to the peaceable and equal participation of the rights of nature, and to the glory and dignity of this country, behold the insiduous arts, and the strenuous efforts of the partisans of arbitrary power, by their vague definitions of the best established truths, endeavoring to envelope the mind in darkness the concomitant of slavery, and to lock the strong chains of domestic despotism on a country, which by the most glorious and successful struggles is but newly emancipated from the sceptre of foreign dominion.–But there are certain seasons in the course of human affairs, when Genius, Virtue, and Patriotism, seems to nod over the vices of the times, and perhaps never more remarkably, than at the present period; or we should not see such a passive disposition prevail in some, who we must candidly suppose, have liberal and enlarged sentiments; while a supple multitude are paying a blind and idolatrous homage to the opinions of those who by the most precipitate steps are treading down their dear bought privileges; and who are endeavouring by all the arts of insinuation, and influence, to betray the people of the United States, into an acceptance of a most complicated system of government; marked on the one side with the *dark, secret* and *profound intrigues*, of the statesman, long practised in the purlieus of despotism; and on the other, with the ideal projects of *young ambition*, with its wings just expanded to soar to a summit, which imagination has painted in such gawdy colours as to intoxicate the *inexperienced votary*, and send *him* rambling from State to State, to collect materials to construct the ladder of preferment.

[1.] But as a variety of objections to the *heterogeneous phantom*, have been repeatedly laid before the public, by men of the best abilities and intentions; I will not expatiate long on a Republican *form* of government, founded on the principles of monarchy–a democratick branch with the *features* of aristocracy–and the extravagance of nobility pervading the minds of many of the candidates for office, with the poverty of peasantry hanging heavily on them, and insurmountable, from their taste for expence, unless a generous provision should be made in the arrangement of the civil list, which may enable them with the champions of their cause to "*sail down the new pactolean channel.*"[6] Some gentlemen with laboured zeal, have spent much time in urging the necessity of government, from the embarrass-

ments of trade–the want of respectability abroad and confidence in the
public engagements at home:–These are obvious truths which no one denies; and there are few who do not unite in the general wish for the
restoration of public faith, the revival of commerce, arts, agriculture, and
industry, under a lenient, peaceable and energetick government: But the
most sagacious advocates for the party have not by fair discusion, and
rational argumentation, evinced the necessity of adopting this many-
headed monster; of such motley mixture, that its enemies cannot trace a
feature of Democratick or Republican extract; nor have its friends the
courage to denominate it a Monarchy, an Aristocracy, or an Oligarchy,
and the favoured bantling must have passed through the short period of its
existence without a name, had not Mr. *Wilson*, in the fertility of his genius, suggested the happy epithet of a *Federal Republic*.[7]–But I leave the
field of general censure on the secrecy of its birth, the rapidity of its growth,
and the fatal consequences of suffering it to live to the age of maturity, and
will particularize some of the most weighty objections to its passing through
this continent in a gigantic size.–It will be allowed by every one that the
fundamental principle of a free government, is the equal representation of
a free people–And I will *first* observe with a justly celebrated writer, "That
the principal aim of society is to protect individuals in the absolute rights
which were vested in them by the immediate laws of nature, but which
could not be preserved in peace, without the mutual intercourse which is
gained by the institution of friendly and social communities."[8] And when
society has thus deputed a certain number of their equals to take care of
their personal rights, and the interest of the whole community, it must be
considered that responsibility is the great security of integrity and honour;
and that annual election is the basis of responsibility.–Man is not immediately corrupted, but power without limitation, or amenability, may endanger the brightest virtue–whereas a frequent return to the bar of their
Constituents is the strongest check against the corruptions to which men
are liable, either from the intrigues of others of more subtle genius, or the
propensities of their own hearts,–and the gentlemen who have so warmly
advocated in the late Convention of the Massachusetts, the change from
annual to biennial elections;[9] may have been in the same predicament,
and perhaps with the same views that Mr. *Hutchinson* once acknowledged
himself, when in a letter to *Lord Hillsborough*, he observed, "that the grand
difficulty of making a change in government against the general bent of
the people had caused him to turn his thoughts to a variety of plans, in
order to find one that might be executed in spite of opposition," and the
first he proposed was that, "instead of annual, the elections should be only
once in three years:"[10] but the Minister had not the hardiness to attempt
such an innovation, even in the revision of colonial charters: nor has any
one ever defended Beinnial, Triennial, or Septennial, Elections, either in
the British House of Commons, or in the debates of Provincial assemblies,

on general and free principles: but it is unnecessary to dwell long on this article, as the best political writers have supported the principles of annual elections with a precision, that cannot be confuted, though they may be darkned, by the sophistical arguments that have been thrown out with design, to undermine all the barriers of freedom.

2. There is no security in the profered system, either for the rights of conscience, or the liberty of the Press: Despotism usually while it is gaining ground, will suffer men to think, say, or write what they please; but when once established, if it is thought necessary to subserve the purposes of arbitrary power, the most unjust restrictions may take place in the first instance, and an *imprimator* on the Press in the next, may silence the complaints, and forbid the most decent remonstrances of an injured and oppressed people.

3. There are no well defined limits of the Judiciary Powers, they seem to be left as a boundless ocean, that has broken over the chart of the Supreme Lawgiver *"thus far shalt thou go and no further,"*[11] and as they cannot be comprehended by the clearest capacity, or the most sagacious mind, it would be an Herculean labour to attempt to describe the dangers with which they are replete.

4. The Executive and the Legislative are so dangerously blended as to give just cause of alarm, and every thing relative thereto, is couched in such ambiguous terms–in such vague and indifinite expression, as is a sufficient ground without any other objection, for the reprobation of a system, that the authors dare not hazard to a clear investigation.

5. The abolition of trial by jury in civil causes.–This mode of trial the learned Judge Blackstone observes, "has been coeval with the first rudiments of civil government, that property, liberty and life, depend on maintaining in its legal force the constitutional trial by jury." He bids his readers pause, and with Sir Matthew Hale observes, how admirably this mode is adapted to the investigation of truth beyond any other the world can produce.[12] Even the party who have been disposed to swallow, without examination, the proposals of the *secret conclave*, have started on a discovery that this essential right was curtailed; and shall a privilege, the origin of which may be traced to our Saxon ancestors–that has been a part of the law of nations, even in the fewdatory systems of France, Germany and Italy–and from the earliest records has been held so sacred, both in ancient and modern Britain, that it could never be shaken by the introduction of Norman customs, or any other conquests or change of government–shall this inestimable privilege be relinquished in America–either thro' the fear of inquisition for unaccounted thousands of public monies in the hands of some who have been officious in the fabrication of the *consolidated system*, or from the apprehension that some future delinquent possessed of more power than integrity, may be called to a trial by his peers in the hour of investigation?

6. Though it has been said by Mr. *Wilson*[13] and many others, that a Standing-Army is necessary for the dignity and safety of America, yet freedom revolts at the idea, when the Divan, or the Despot, may draw out his dragoons to suppress the murmurs of a few, who may yet cherish those sublime principles which call forth the exertions, and lead to the best improvement of the human mind. It is hoped this country may yet be governed by milder methods than are usually displayed beneath the bannerets of military law.–Standing armies have been the nursery of vice and the bane of liberty from the Roman legions, to the establishment of the artful Ximenes, and from the ruin of the Cortes of Spain, to the planting the British cohorts in the capitals of America:–By the edicts of authority vested in the sovereign power by the proposed constitution, the militia of the country, the bulwark of defence, and the security of national liberty is no longer under the controul of civil authority; but at the rescript of the Monarch, or the aristocracy, they may either be employed to extort the enormous sums that will be necessary to support the civil list–to maintain the regalia of power–and the splendour of the most useless part of the community, or they may be sent into foreign countries for the fulfilment of treaties, stipulated by the President and two thirds of the Senate.

7. Notwithstanding the delusory promise to guarantee a Republican form of government to every State in the Union–If the most discerning eye could discover any meaning at all in the engagement, there are no resources left for the support of internal government, or the liquidation of the debts of the State. Every source of revenue is in the monopoly of Congress, and if the several legislatures in their enfebled state, should against their own feelings be necessitated to attempt a dry tax for the payment of their debts, and the support of internal police, even this may be required for the purposes of the general government.

8. As the new Congress are empowered to determine their own salaries, the requisitions for this purpose may not be very moderate, and the drain for public moneys will probably rise past all calculation: and it is to be feared when America has consolidated its despotism, the world will witness the truth of the assertion–"that the pomp of an eastern monarch may impose on the vulgar who may estimate the force of a nation by the magnificence of its palaces; but the wise man, judges differently, it is by that very magnificence he estimates its weakness. He sees nothing more in the midst of this imposing pomp, where the tyrant sets enthroned, than a sumptuous and mournful decoration of the dead; the apparatus of a fastuous funeral, in the centre of which is a cold and lifeless lump of unanimated earth, a phantom of power ready to disappear before the enemy, by whom it is despised!"

9. There is no provision for a rotation, nor any thing to prevent the perpetuity of office in the same hands for life; which by a little well timed bribery, will probably be done, to the exclusion of men of the best abilities

from their share in the offices of government.–By this neglect we lose the advantages of that check to the overbearing insolence of office, which by rendering him ineligible at certain periods, keeps the mind of man in equilibrio, and teaches him the feelings of the governed, and better qualifies him to govern in his turn.

10. The inhabitants of the United States, are liable to be draged from the vicinity of their own county, or state, to answer to the litigious or unjust suit of an adversary, on the most distant borders of the Continent: in short the appelate jurisdiction of the Supreme Federal Court, includes an unwarrantable stretch of power over the liberty, life, and property of the subject, through the wide Continent of America.

11. One Representative to thirty thousand inhabitants is a very inadequate representation; and every man who is not lost to all sense of freedom to his country, must reprobate the idea of Congress altering by law, or on any pretence whatever, interfering with any regulations for the time, places, and manner of choosing our own Representatives.

12. If the sovereignty of America is designed to be elective, the circumscribing the votes to only ten electors in this State, and the same proportion in all the others, is nearly tantamount to the exclusion of the voice of the people in the choice of their first magistrate. It is vesting the choice solely in an aristocratic junto, who may easily combine in each State to place at the head of the Union the most convenient instrument for despotic sway.

13. A Senate chosen for six years will, in most instances, be an appointment for life, as the influence of such a body over the minds of the people will be coequal to the extensive powers with which they are vested, and they will not only forget, but be forgotten by their constituents–a branch of the Supreme Legislature thus set beyond all responsibility is totally repugnant to every principle of a free government.

14. There is no provision by a bill of rights to guard against the dangerous encroachments of power in too many instances to be named: but I cannot pass over in silence the insecurity in which we are left with regard to warrants unsupported by evidence–the daring experiment of granting *writs of assistance* in a former arbitrary administration is not yet forgotten in the Massachusetts;[14] nor can we be so ungrateful to the memory of the patriots who counteracted their operation, as so soon after their manly exertions to save us from such a detestable instrument of arbitrary power, to subject ourselves to the insolence of any petty revenue officer to enter our houses, search, insult, and seize at pleasure. We are told by a gentleman of too much virtue and real probity to suspect he has a design to deceive–"that the whole constitution is a declaration of rights"–but mankind must think for themselves, and to many very judicious and discerning characters, the whole constitution with very few exceptions appears a perversion of the rights of particular states, and of private citizens.–But the

gentleman goes on to tell us, "that the primary object is the general government, and that the rights of individuals are only incidentally mentioned, and that there was a clear impropriety in being very particular about them."[15] But, asking pardon for dissenting from such respectable authority, who has been led into several mistakes, more from his prediliction in favour of certain modes of government, than from a want of understanding or veracity. The rights of individuals ought to be the primary object of all government, and cannot be too securely guarded by the most explicit declarations in their favor. This has been the opinion of the Hampdens, the Pyms, and many other illustrious names, that have stood forth in defence of English liberties; and even the Italian master in politicks, the subtle and renouned Machiavel acknowledges, that no republic ever yet stood on a stable foundation without satisfying the common people.[16]

15. The difficulty, if not impracticability, of exercising the equal and equitable powers of government by a single legislature over an extent of territory that reaches from the Missisippi to the Western lakes, and from them to the Atlantic ocean, is an insuperable objection to the adoption of the new system.–Mr. *Hutchinson*, the great champion for arbitrary power, in the multitude of his machinations to subvert the liberties of this country, was obliged to acknowledge in one of his letters, that, "from the extent of country from north to south, the scheme of one government was impracticable."[17] But if the authors of the present visionary project, can by the arts of deception, precipitation and address, obtain a majority of suffrages in the conventions of the states to try the hazardous experiment, they may then make the same inglorious boast with this insidious politician, who may perhaps be their model, that "the union of the colonies was pretty well broken, and that he hoped never to see it renewed."[18]

16. It is an indisputed fact, that not one legislature in the United States had the most distant idea when they first appointed members for a convention, entirely commercial, or when they afterwards authorised them to consider on some amendments of the Federal union, that they would without any warrant from their constituents, presume on so bold and daring a stride, as ultimately to destroy the state governments, and offer a *consolidated system*, irreversible but on conditions that the smallest degree of penetration must discover to be impracticable.

17. The first appearance of the article which declares the ratification of nine states sufficient for the establishment of the new system, wears the face of dissention, is a subversion of the union of the Confederated States, and tends to the introduction of anarchy and civil convulsions, and may be a means of involving the whole country in blood.

18. The mode in which this constitution is recommended to the people to judge without either the advice of Congress, or the legislatures of the several states, is very reprehensible–it is an attempt to force it upon them

before it could be thoroughly understood, and may leave us in that situation, that in the first moments of slavery the minds of the people agitated by the remembrance of their lost liberties, will be like the sea in a tempest, that sweeps down every mound of security.

But it is needless to enumerate other instances, in which the proposed constitution appears contradictory to the first principles which ought to govern mankind; and it is equally so to enquire into the motives that induced to so bold a step as the annihilation of the independence and sovereignty of the thirteen distinct states.–They are but too obvious through the whole progress of the business, from the first shutting up the doors of the federal convention and resolving that no member should correspond with gentlemen in the different states on the subject under discussion; till the trivial proposition of *recommending* a few amendments was artfully ushered into the convention of the Massachusetts. The questions that were then before that honorable assembly were profound and important, they were of such magnitude and extent, that the consequences may run parallel with the existence of the country; and to see them waved and hastily terminated by a measure too absurd to require a serious refutation, raises the honest indignation of every true lover of his country. Nor are they less grieved that the ill policy and arbitrary disposition of some of the sons of America has thus precipitated to the contemplation and discussion of questions that no one could rationally suppose would have been agitated among us, till time had blotted out the principles on which the late revolution was grounded; or till the last traits of the many political tracts, which defended the seperation from Britain, and the rights of men were consigned to everlasting oblivion. After the severe conflicts this country has suffered, it is presumed that they are disposed to make every reasonable sacrifice before the altar of peace.–But when we contemplate the nature of men and consider them originally on an equal footing, subject to the same feelings, stimulated by the same passions, and recollecting the struggles they have recently made, for the security of their civil rights; it cannot be expected that the inhabitants of the Massachusetts, can be easily lulled into a fatal security, by the declamatory effusions of gentlemen, who, contrary to the experience of all ages would perswade them there is no danger to be apprehended, from vesting discretionary powers in the hands of man, which he may, or may not abuse. The very suggestion, that we ought to trust to the precarious hope of amendments and redress, after we have voluntarily fixed the shackles on our own necks should have awakened to a double degree of caution.–This people have not forgotten the artful insinuations of a former Governor, when pleading the unlimited authority of parliament before the legislature of the Massachusetts; nor that his arguments were very similar to some lately urged by gentlemen who boast of opposing his measure, "*with halters about their necks.*"[19]

We were then told by him, in all the soft language of insinuation, that no form of government of human construction can be perfect–that we had nothing to fear-that we had no reason to complain-that we had only to acquiesce in their illegal claims, and to submit to the requisitions of parliament, and doubtless the lenient hand of government would redress all grievances, and remove the oppressions of the people:[20]-Yet we soon saw armies of mercenaries encamped on our plains-our commerce ruined-our harbours blockaded-and our cities burnt. It may be replied, that this was in consequence of an obstinate defence of our privileges; this may be true; and when the *"ultima ratio"* is called to aid, the weakest must fall. But let the best informed historian produce an instance when bodies of men were intrusted with power, and the proper checks relinquished, if they were ever found destitute of ingenuity sufficient to furnish pretences to abuse it. And the people at large are already sensible, that the liberties which America has claimed, which reason has justified, and which have been so gloriously defended by the sword of the brave; are not about to fall before the tyranny of foreign conquest: it is native usurpation that is shaking the foundations of peace, and spreading the sable curtain of despotism over the United States. The banners of freedom were erected in the wilds of America by our ancestors, while the wolf prowled for his prey on the one hand, and more savage man on the other; they have been since rescued from the invading hand of foreign power, by the valor and blood of their posterity; and there was reason to hope they would continue for ages to illumine a quarter of the globe, by nature kindly seperated from the proud monarchies of Europe, and the infernal darkness of Asiatic slavery.-And it is to be feared we shall soon see this country rushing into the extremes of confusion and violence, in consequence of the proceedings of a set of gentlemen, who disregarding the purposes of their appointment, have assumed powers unauthorised by any commission, have unnecessarily rejected the confederation of the United States, and annihilated the sovereignty and independence of the individual governments.-The causes which have inspired a few men assembled for very different purposes with such a degree of temerity as to break with a single stroke the union of America, and disseminate the seeds of discord through the land may be easily investigated, when we survey the pa[r]tizans of monarchy in the state conventions, urging the adoption of a mode of government that militates with the former professions and exertions of this country, and with all ideas of republicanism, and the equal rights of men.

Passion, prejudice, and error, are characteristics of human nature; and as it cannot be accounted for on any principles of philosophy, religion, or good policy; to these shades in the human character must be attributed the mad zeal of some, to precipitate to a blind adoption of the measures of the late federal convention, without giving opportunity for better information to those who are misled by influence or ignorance into erroneous opinions.-Litterary talents may be prostituted, and the powers of genius debased to subserve the purposes of ambition, or avarice; but the feelings of the heart will dictate the language of truth, and the simplicity of her accents will proclaim the infamy of those, who betray the rights of the people, under the specious, and popular pretence of *justice, consolidation,* and *dignity.*

It is presumed the great body of the people unite in sentiment with the writer of these observations, who most devoutly prays that public credit may rear her declining head, and remunerative justice pervade the land; nor is there a doubt if a free government is continued, that time and industry will enable both the public and private debtor to liquidate their arrearages in the most equitable manner. They wish to see the Confederated States bound together by the most indissoluble union, but without renouncing their seperate sovereignties and independence, and becoming tributaries to a consolidated fabrick of aristocratick tyranny.–They wish to see government established, and peaceably holding the reins with honour, energy, and dignity; but they wish for no *federal city* whose "*cloud cap't towers*"[21] may screen the state culprit from the hand of justice; while its exclusive jurisdiction may protect the riot of armies encamped within its limits.–They deprecate discord and civil convulsions, but they are not yet generally prepared with the ungrateful Israelites to ask a King, nor are their spirits sufficiently broken to yield the best of their olive grounds to his servants, and to see their sons appointed to run before his chariots[22]–It has been observed by a zealous advocate for the new system, that most governments are the result of fraud or violence, and this with design to recommend its acceptance[23]–but has not almost every step towards its fabrication been fraudulent in the extreme? Did not the prohibition strictly enjoined by the general Convention, that no member should make any communication to his Constituents, or to gentlemen of consideration and abilities in the other States, bear evident marks of fraudulent designs?– This circumstance is regretted in strong terms by Mr. Martin, a member from Maryland, who acknowledges "He had no idea that all the wisdom, integrity, and virtue of the States was contained in that Convention, and that he wished to have corresponded with gentlemen of eminent political characters abroad, and to give their sentiments due weight"–he adds, "so extremely solicitous were they, that their proceedings should not transpire, that the members were prohibited from taking copies of their resolutions, or extracts from the Journals, without express permission, by vote."[24]– And the hurry with which it has been urged to the acceptance of the people, without giving time, by adjournments, for better information, and more unanimity has a deceptive appearance; and if finally driven to resistance, as the only alternative between that and servitude, till in the confusion of discord, the reins should be seized by the violence of some enterprizing genius, that may sweep down the last barrier of liberty, it must be added to the score of criminality with which the fraudulent usurpation at Philadelphia, may be chargeable.–Heaven avert such a tremendous scene! and let us still hope a more happy termination of the present ferment:–may the people be calm, and wait a legal redress; may the mad transport of some of our infatuated capitals subside; and every influential character through the States, make the most prudent exertions for a new general Convention, who may vest adequate powers in Congress, for all national purposes, without annihilating the individual governments, and drawing blood from every pore by taxes, impositions and illegal restrictions.–This step might again re-establish the Union, restore tranquility to the ruffled mind of the inhabitants, and save America from distresses, dreadful even in contemplation.–"The great art of governing is to lay aside all prejudices and attachments to particular opinions, classes or individual characters; to consult the spirit of the people; to give way to it; and in so doing, to give it a turn capable of inspiring those sentiments, which may induce them to relish a change, which an alteration of circumstances may hereafter make necessary."–The education of the advocates for monarchy should have taught them, and their memory should have suggested that "monarchy is a species of government fit only for a people too much corrupted by luxury, avarice, and a passion for pleasure, to have any love for their country, and whose vices the fear of punishment alone is able to restrain; but by no means calculated for a nation that is poor, and at the same time tenacious of their liberty–animated with a disgust to tyranny– and inspired with the generous feelings of patriotism and liberty, and at the same time, like the ancient Spartans have been hardened by temperance and manly exertions, and equally despising the fatigues of the field, and the fear of enemies,"–and while they change their ground they should recollect, that Aristocracy is still a more formidable foe to public virtue, and the prosperity of a nation–that under such a government her patriots become mercenaries–her soldiers, cowards, and the people slaves.–Though several State Conventions have assented to, and ratified, yet the voice of the people appears at present strong against the adoption of the Constitution.–By the chicanery, intrigue, and false colouring of those who plume themselves, more on their education and abilities, than their political, patriotic, or private virtues–by the imbecility of some, and the duplicity of others, a majority of the Convention of Massachusetts have been flattered with the ideas of amendments, when it will be too late to complain–While several very worthy characters, too timid for their situation, magnified the hopeless alternative, between the dissolution of the bands of all government, and receiving the proffered system *in toto*, after long endeavouring to reconcile it to their consciences, swallowed the indigestible penacea, and in a kind of sudden desperation lent their signature to the dereliction of the honorable station they held in the Union, and have broken over the solemn compact, by which they were bound to support their own excellent constitution till the period of revision.–Yet Virginia, equally large and respectable, and who have done honour to themselves, by their vigorous exertions from the first dawn of independence, have not yet acted upon the question; they have wisely taken time to consider before they introduce innovations of a most dangerous nature:–her inhabitants are brave, her burgesses are free, and they have a Governor who dares to think for himself, and to speak his opinion (without first pouring libations on the altar of popularity) though it should militate with some of the most accomplished and illustrious characters.[25]

Maryland, who has no local interest to lead her to adopt, will doubtless reject the system–I hope the same characters still live, and that the same spirit which dictated to them a wise and cautious care, against sudden revolutions in government, and made them the last State that acceded to the independence of America, will lead them to support what they so deliberately claimed.–Georgia apprehensive of a war with the Savages, has acceded in order to insure protection.–Pennsylvania has struggled through much in the same manner, as the Massachusetts, against the manly feelings, and the masterly reasonings of a very respectable part of the Convention:[26] They have adopted the system, and seen some of its authors burnt in effigy–their towns thrown into riot[27] and confusion, and the minds of the people agitated by apprehension and discord.

New-Jersey and Delaware have united in the measure, from the locality of their situation, and the selfish motives which too generally govern mankind; the Federal City, and the seat of government, will naturally attract the intercourse of strangers–the youth of enterprize, and the wealth of the nation to the central States.

Connecticut has pushed it through with the precipitation of her neighbour, with few dissentient voices;–but more from irritation and resentment to a sister State, perhaps partiality to herself in her commercial regulations, than from a comprehensive view of the system, as a regard to the welfare of all.[28]–But New-York has motives, that will undoubtedly lead her to a rejection, without being afraid to appeal to the understanding of mankind, to justify the grounds of their refusal to adopt a Constitution, that even the framers dare not risque to the hazard of revision, amendment, or reconsideration, least the whole superstructure should be demolished by more skilful and discreet architects.–I know not what part the Carolinas will take; but I hope their determinations will comport with the dignity and freedom of this country–their decisions will have great weight in the scale.–But equally important are the small States of New-Hampshire and Rhode-Island:–New-York, the Carolinas, Virginia, Maryland, and these two lesser States may yet support the liberties of the Continent; if they refuse a ratification, or postpone their proceedings till the spirits of the community have time to cool, there is little doubt but the wise measure of another federal convention will be adopted, when the members would have the advantage of viewing, at large, through the medium of truth, the objections that have been made from various quarters; such a measure

might be attended with the most salutary effects, and prevent the dread
consequences of civil feuds.–But even if some of those large states should
hastily accede, yet we have frequently seen in the story of revolution, relief
spring from a quarter least expected.

Though the virtues of a Cato could not save Rome, nor the abilities of a
Padilla defend the citizens of Castile from falling under the yoke of Charles;
yet a *Tell* once suddenly rose from a little obscure city, and boldly rescued
the liberties of his country.–Every age has its Bruti and its Decii, as well
as its Cæsars and Sejani:–The happiness of mankind depends much on the
modes of government, and the virtues of the governors; and America may
yet produce characters who have genius and capacity sufficient to form the
manners and correct the morals of the people, and virtue enough to lead
their country to freedom. Since her dismemberment from the British empire, America has, in many instances, resembled the conduct of a restless,
vigorous, luxurious youth, prematurely emancipated from the authority of
a parent, but without the experience necessary to direct him to act with
dignity or discretion. Thus we have seen her break the shackles of foreign
dominion, and all the blessings of peace restored on the most honourable
terms: She acquired the liberty of framing her own laws, choosing her own
magistrates, and adopting manners and modes of government the most
favourable to the freedom and happiness of society. But how little have we
availed ourselves of these superior advantages: The glorious fabric of liberty successfully reared with so much labour and assiduity totters to the
foundation, and may be blown away as the bubble of fancy by the rude
breath of military combinations, and politicians of yesterday.

It is true this country lately armed in opposition to regal despotism–
impoverished by the expences of a long war, and unable immediately to
fulfil their public or private engagements, have appeared in some instances, with a boldness of spirit that seemed to set at defiance all authority, government, or order, on the one hand; while on the other, there has
been, not only a secret wish, but an open avowal of the necessity of drawing the reins of government much too taught, not only for republicanism,
but for a wise and limited monarchy.–But the character of this people is
not averse to a degree of subordination: the truth of this appears from the
easy restoration of tranquility, after a dangerous insurrection in one of the
states; this also evinces the little necessity of a complete revolution of government throughout the union. But it is a republican principle that the
majority should rule; and if a spirit of moderation could be cultivated on
both sides, till the voice of the people at large could be fairly heard it
should be held sacred.–And if, on such a scrutiny, the proposed constitution should appear repugnant to their character and wishes; if they, in the
language of a late elegant pen, should acknowledge that "no confusion in
my mind, is more terrible to them than the stern disciplined regularity and
vaunted police of arbitrary governments, where every heart is depraved

by fear, where mankind dare not assume their natural characters, where the free spirit must crouch to the slave in office, where genius must repress her effusions, or like the Egyptian worshippers, offer them in sacrifice to the calves in power, and where the human mind, always in shackles, shrinks from every generous effort." Who would then have the effrontery to say, it ought not to be thrown out with indignation, however some respectable names have appeared to support it.–But if after all, on a dispassionate and fair discussion, the people generally give their voice for a voluntary dereliction of their privileges, let every individual who chooses the active scenes of life, strive to support the peace and unanimity of his country, though every other blessing may expire–And while the statesman is plodding for power, and the courtier practising the arts of dissimulation without check–while the rapacious are growing rich by oppression, and fortune throwing her gifts into the lap of fools, let the sublimer characters, the philosophic lovers of freedom who have wept over her exit, retire to the calm shades of contemplation, there they may look down with pity on the inconsistency of human nature, the revolutions of states, the rise of kingdoms, and the fall of empires.

(a) Helvitius.

(b) Abbe Mable.

1. An apparent reference to Miguel de Cervantes Saavedra's (1547–1616) *Don Quixote* which was published in two parts in 1605 and 1615 and translated almost immediately into English.

2. A reference to Claude Adrien Helvétius (1715–1771), who published *De l'Esprit* in 1758 and its supplement, *De l'Homme, de Ses Facultés Intellectuelles et de Son Éducation* in 1773. The former work rivalled Montesquieu's *L'Esprit des Lois* which had been published in 1748. *De l'Homme* was translated into English in 1777.

3. *Observations sur les Romains* in *Œuvres Complètes de L'Abbé de Mably* (19 vols., Toulouse and Nismes, 1793), VI, 100. *Observations* was first published in Geneva in 1751.

4. *Ibid.*, 121.

5. Probably a reference to such patriots as Samuel Adams, James Bowdoin, and John Hancock, especially Adams who had opposed the Constitution. The list of yeas and nays was first printed in the *Massachusetts Gazette* on 8 February.

6. A reference to the river Pactolus, in Lydia, noted for its golden sands.

7. See James Wilson's speech of 24 November to the Pennsylvania Convention. On 28 November a summary of the speech appeared in the *Pennsylvania Herald* and a lengthy account, taken from shorthand notes, was printed as a pamphlet (RCS:Pa., 335–36, 340–50; and CC:289). Each of these versions was reprinted in five Massachusetts newspapers. Only in Pennsylvania did Wilson's speech have a wider circulation. "Helvidius Priscus" (James Warren?) described the speech as "insidious" (Boston *Independent Chronicle*, 27 December).

8. Blackstone, *Commentaries*, Book I, chapter I, 124. Blackstone used the phrase "immutable laws of nature" not "immediate laws of nature."

9. On 14 and 15 January the Massachusetts Convention debated the question of annual *versus* biennial elections (*Massachusetts Centinel*, 16, 19 January).

10. This letter, dated October 1770, was printed in the *Boston Gazette* on 14 August 1775, under the heading "*Further Account of Tom.* Hutchinson's *Assiduity in rooting up our ONCE happy Constitution, and of his Endeavours to disunite the AMERICAN COLONIES.*" The *Gazette* indicated that the text of the letter was taken from Hutchinson's letterbook

which was found by the popular party after he left for England on 1 June 1774. Governor Hutchinson was the most hated man in revolutionary Massachusetts. In her history of the American Revolution, Mercy Warren described him as "dark, intriguing, insinuating, haughty and ambitious, while the extreme of avarice marked each feature of his character" (*History of the Rise, Progress and Termination of the American Revolution. Interspersed with Biographical, Political and Moral Observations* [3 vols., Boston, 1805], I, 79). The Earl of Hillsborough (Wills Hill) was secretary of state for America and president of the Board of Trade from 1768 to 1772.

11. Job 38:11. See also General Samuel Thompson's remarks in note 15 below.

12. Blackstone, *Commentaries*, Book III, chapter XXIII, 349, 350, 355. The quoted passage is from two separate sections of Blackstone's sketch of the history of trial by jury. Sir Matthew Hale (1609–1676) was lord chief justice of the Court of King's Bench from 1671 to 1676 and the author of a history of the common law that was published after his death.

13. See James Wilson's public speech of 6 October (CC:134).

14. In February 1761, following the death of George II, the surveyor general of customs in Massachusetts requested that the superior court issue new writs of assistance that would permit customs officers to search for smuggled goods. (The court had been issuing such writs since 1755.) Boston merchants protested and hired James Otis as one of their lawyers to question the legality of the writs. Otis argued that the writs were void because they violated the fundamental principles of law. In December 1761 the Superior Court of Massachusetts, of which Thomas Hutchinson was chief justice, ordered that the writs be issued. In 1766 a Boston mob helped a merchant resist the sheriff who had a writ of assistance.

15. On 23 January the Massachusetts Convention debated the extent of Congress' powers outlined in Article I, section 8. Antifederalist General Samuel Thompson of Topsham, Maine, stated "Gentlemen say this sect. is as clear as the sun, and that all power is retained which is not given. But where is the bill of rights which shall check the power of this Congress, which shall say, *thus far shall ye come and no farther.*–The safety of the people depends on a bill of rights." In a lengthy speech, former Governor James Bowdoin replied: "With regard to rights, the whole Constitution is a declaration of rights, which primarily and principally respect the general government intended to be formed by it. The rights of particular States and private citizens not being the object or subject of the Constitution, they are incidentally mentioned. In regard to the former, it would require a volume to describe them, as they extend to every subject of legislation, not included in the powers vested in Congress: And in regard to the latter, as all government is founded on the relinquishment of personal rights in a certain degree, there was a clear impropriety in being very particular about them" (*Massachusetts Centinel*, 6 February).

16. See "A Discourse on Remodeling the Government of Florence," in Allan Gilbert, trans., *Machiavelli: The Chief Works and Others* (3 vols., Durham, N.C., 1965), I, 110. This "Discourse" was written about 1520.

17. In February 1770 Hutchinson wrote John Pownall, undersecretary of state for America, that the colonies were becoming increasingly independent. Unlike some royal officials, Hutchinson opposed a single government for all of the colonies, preferring the erection of three separate governments or confederacies (*Boston Gazette*, 19 June 1775. As in the case of Hutchinson's October 1770 letter [note 10 above], this letter was probably printed from Hutchinson's letterbook.).

18. On 22 June 1772, during the so-called period of quiet following the collapse of the non-importation movement, Hutchinson wrote Thomas Pownall, a former governor of Massachusetts, that "The union of the colonies is pretty well broke; I hope I shall never see it renewed. Indeed our sons of liberty are hated and despised by their former brethren in New York and Pennsylvania, and it must be something very ex-

traordinary ever to reconcile them" (quoted in Warren's, *History of the American Revolution*, I, 422).

19. In a lengthy speech in the Massachusetts Convention on 18 January, Judge Francis Dana of Cambridge defended the power of Congress to lay direct taxes and the Convention delegates who supported this clause. These men, he said, were not enemies to the rights of their country. "After dilating on this matter a short time, the learned judge begged gentlemen to look around them, and see who were the men that composed the assembly–Are they not, he asked, men who have been formost in the cause of their country, both in the cabinet and the field, and who with halters about their necks boldly and intrepidly advocated the rights of America, and of humanity, at home and in foreign countries? and are THEY not to be trusted?" (*Massachusetts Centinel*, 26 January).

20. In July 1772 a committee of the General Court reported that, according to the charter of the colony, the governor should be paid by a grant of the General Court from taxes imposed by that body. The committee charged that "the governor's having and receiving his support, independent of the grants and acts of the general assembly, is a dangerous innovation" and a violation of the charter. The General Court accepted the report and sent it to Governor Thomas Hutchinson for a reply. Hutchinson defended the prerogative of the Crown to pay him his salary. He declared:

"I am sensible, that, when all other exceptions to this representation of your constitution are taken away, you will ask, what security have we then against the oppression of a governor? The answer is obvious. The law and the constitution are your security; if he departs from them, there is a power superior to him, to which he is accountable for his mal-administration. This is all the redress that can consist with the nature of a subordinate government.

"No state of government is perfect: if we have all that perfection which the state we are in will admit of, we have no reason to complain. Indeed we have no reason to fear redress from any opposition. So tender has been our most gracious sovereign of the rights of his subjects, that although I should humbly hope for royal forgiveness, in case of inattention to some point of no great importance, which might affect the prerogative, yet I may not expect the forgiveness of any wilful invasion of your liberties" (Thomas Hutchinson, *The History of the Colony of Massachusets Bay* . . . [3 vols., 1764, 1767, and 1828; reprint ed., New York, 1972], III, 545-51).

21. William Shakespeare, *The Tempest*, act 4, scene 1.

22. I Samuel 8:6-14.

23. In his speech to the Pennsylvania Convention on 24 November, James Wilson said governments had been "the result of force, fraud, or accident" (RCS:Pa., 342).

24. Luther Martin, *Genuine Information* I, Baltimore *Maryland Gazette*, 28 December (CC:389, p. 151).

25. See Governor Edmund Randolph's letter to the Speaker of the Virginia House of Delegates, 10 October, which was printed as a pamphlet in Richmond around 27 December (CC:385). It was reprinted in three Massachusetts newspapers.

26. See the "Dissent of the Minority of the Pennsylvania Convention," *Pennsylvania Packet*, 18 December (CC:353), which was published as a pamphlet in Boston in mid-January.

27. For an account of a riot in Carlisle, Pa., on 26 December, during which James Wilson and Thomas McKean were burned in effigy, see CC:407. This account was reprinted seven times in Massachusetts.

28. For Connecticut's commercial dependence on and animosity toward New York, see RCS:Conn., *passim*.

582. Publius: The Federalist 63
New York Independent Journal, 1 March

James Madison and Alexander Hamilton both claimed authorship of this essay, but it is generally attributed to Madison. This essay was reprinted in the *New York Packet* on 4 March. It is number 63 in the M'Lean edition and number 62 in the newspapers.

For a general discussion of the authorship, circulation, and impact of *The Federalist*, see CC:201, 639; and for the disputed authorship of this essay, see Cooke, xix–xxx, 644–45, and Rutland, *Madison*, X, 261–63.

The FŒDERALIST. No. LXII.
To the People of the State of New-York.

A *fifth* desideratum illustrating the utility of a senate, is the want of a due sense of national character. Without a select and stable member of the government, the esteem of foreign powers will not only be forfeited by an unenlightened and variable policy, proceeding from the causes already mentioned;[1] but the national councils will not possess that sensibility to the opinion of the world, which is perhaps not less necessary in order to merit, than it is to obtain, its respect and confidence.

An attention to the judgment of other nations is important to every government for two reasons: The one is, that independently of the merits of any particular plan or measure, it is desireable on various accounts, that it should appear to other nations as the offspring of a wise and honorable policy: The second is, that in doubtful cases, particularly where the national councils may be warped by some strong passion, or momentary interest, the presumed or known opinion of the impartial world, may be the best guide that can be followed. What has not America lost by her want of character with foreign nations? And how many errors and follies would she not have avoided, if the justice and propriety of her measures had in every instance been previously tried by the light in which they would probably appear to the unbiassed part of mankind.

Yet however requisite a sense of national character may be, it is evident that it can never be sufficiently possessed by a numerous and changeable body. It can only be found in a number so small, that a sensible degree of the praise and blame of public measures may be the portion of each individual; or in an assembly so durably invested with public trust, that the pride and consequence of its members may be sensibly incorporated with the reputation and prosperity of the community. The half-yearly representatives of Rhode-Island, would probably have been little affected in their deliberations on the iniquitous measures of that state, by arguments drawn from the light in which such measures would be viewed by foreign nations, or even by the sister states; whilst it can scarcely be doubted, that if the concurrence of a select and stable body had been necessary, a regard to national character alone, would have prevented the calamities under which that misguided people is now labouring.

I add as a *sixth* defect, the want in some important cases of a due responsibility in the government to the people, arising from that frequency of elections, which in other cases produces this responsibility. This remark will perhaps appear not only new but paradoxical. It must nevertheless be acknowledged, when explained, to be as undeniable as it is important.

Responsibility in order to be reasonable must be limited to objects within the power of the responsible party; and in order to be effectual, must relate to operations of that power, of which a ready and proper judgment can be formed by the constituents. The objects of government may be divided into two general classes; the one depending on measures which have singly an immediate and sensible operation; the other depending on a succession of well chosen and well connected measures, which have a gradual and perhaps unobserved operation. The importance of the latter description to the collective and permanent welfare of every country needs no explanation. And yet it is evident, that an assembly elected for so short a term as to be unable to provide more than one or two links in a chain of measures, on which the general welfare may essentially depend, ought not to be answerable for the final result, any more than a steward or tenant, engaged for one year, could be justly made to answer for places or improvements, which could not be accomplished in less than half a dozen years. Nor is it possible for the people to estimate the *share* of influence which their annual assemblies may respectively have on events resulting from the mixed transactions of several years. It is sufficiently difficult to preserve a personal responsibility in the members of a *numerous* body, for such acts of the body as have an immediate, detached and palpable operation on its constituents.

The proper remedy for this defect must be an additional body in the legislative department, which, having sufficient permanency to provide for such objects as require a continued attention, and a train of measures, may be justly and effectually answerable for the attainment of those objects.

Thus far I have considered the circumstances which point out the necessity of a well constructed senate, only as they relate to the representatives of the people. To a people as little blinded by prejudice, or corrupted by flattery, as those whom I address, I shall not scruple to add, that such an institution may be sometimes necessary, as a defence to the people against their own temporary errors and delusions. As the cool and deliberate sense of the community ought in all governments, and actually will in all free governments, ultimately prevail over the views of its rulers; so there are particular moments in public affairs, when the people stimulated by some irregular passion, or some illicit advantage, or misled by the artful misrepresentations of interested men, may call for measures which they themselves will afterwards be the most ready to lament and condemn. In these critical moments, how salutary will be the interference of some temperate and respectable body of citizens, in order to check the misguided career, and to suspend the blow meditated by the people against themselves, until reason, justice and truth, can regain their authority over the public mind? What bitter anguish would not the people of Athens have often escaped, if their government had contained so provident a safeguard against the tyranny of their own passions? Popular liberty might then have escaped the indelible reproach of decreeing to the same citizens, the hemlock on one day, and statues on the next.

It may be suggested that a people spread over an extensive region, cannot like the crouded inhabitants of a small district, be subject to the infection of violent passions; or to the danger of combining in pursuit of unjust measures. I am far from denying that this is a distinction of peculiar importance. I have on the contrary endeavoured in a former paper, to shew that it is one of the principal recommendations of a confederated republic.[2] At the same time this advantage ought not to be considered as superseding the use of auxiliary precautions. It may even be remarked that the same extended situation which will exempt the people of America from some of the dangers incident to lesser republics, will expose them to the inconveniency of remaining for a longer time, under the influence of those misrepresentations which the combined industry of interested men may succeed in distributing among them.

It adds no small weight to all these considerations, to recollect, that history informs us of no long lived republic which had not a senate. Sparta, Rome and Carthage are in fact the only states to whom that character can be applied. In each of the two first there was a senate for life. The constitution of the senate in the last, is less known. Circumstantial evidence makes it probable that it was not different in this particular from the two others. It is at least certain that it had some quality or other which rendered it an anchor against popular fluctuations; and that a smaller council drawn out of the senate was appointed not only for life; but filled up vacancies itself. These examples, though as unfit for the imitation, as they are repugnant to the genius of America, are notwithstanding, when compared with the fugitive and turbulent existence of other antient republics, very instructive proofs of the necessity of some institution that will blend stability with liberty. I am not unaware of the circumstances which distinguish the American from other popular governments, as well antient as modern; and which render extreme circumspection necessary in reasoning from the one case to the other. But after allowing due weight to this consideration, it may still be maintained that there are many points of similitude which render these examples not unworthy of our attention. Many of the defects as we have seen, which can only be supplied by a senatorial institution, are common to a numerous assembly frequently elected by the people, and to the people themselves. There are others peculiar to the former, which require the controul of such an institution. The people can never wilfully betray their own interests: But they may possibly be betrayed by the representatives of the people; and the danger will be evidently greater where the whole legislative trust is lodged in the hands of one body of men, than where the concurrence of separate and dissimilar bodies is required in every public act.

The difference most relied on between the American and other republics, consists in the principle of representation, which is the pivot on which the former move, and which is supposed to have been unknown to the latter, or at least to the antient part of them. The use which has been made of this difference, in reasonings contained in former papers, will have shewn that I am disposed neither to deny its existence nor to undervalue its importance.[3] I feel the less restraint therefore in observing that the position concerning the ignorance of the antient government on the subject of representation is by no means precisely true in the latitude commonly given to it. Without entering into a disquisition which here would be misplaced. I will refer to a few known facts in support of what I advance.

In the most pure democracies of Greece, many of the executive functions were performed not by the people themselves, but by officers elected by the people, and *representing* the people in their *executive* capacity.

Prior to the reform of Solon, Athens was governed by nine Archons, annually *elected by the people at large*. The degree of power delegated to them seems to be left in great obscurity. Subsequent to that period, we find an assembly first of four and afterwards of six hundred members, annually *elected by the people*; and *partially* representing them in their *legislative* capacity; since they were not only associated with the people in the function of making laws; but had the exclusive right of originating legislative propositions to the people. The senate of Carthage also, whatever might be its power or the duration of its appointment, appears to have been *elective* by the suffrages of the people. Similar instances might be traced in most if not all the popular governments of antiquity.

Lastly in Sparta, we meet with the Ephori, and in Rome with the Tribunes; two bodies, small indeed in number, but annually *elected by the whole body of the people*, and considered as the *representatives* of the people, almost in their *plenipotentiary* capacity. The Cosme of Crete were also annually *elected by the people;* and have been considered by some authors as an institution analogous to those of Sparta and Rome; with this difference only that in the election of that representative body, the right of suffrage was communicated to a part only of the people.

From these facts, to which many others might be added, it is clear that the principle of representation was neither unknown to the antients, nor wholly overlooked in their political constitutions. The true distinction between these and the American Governments lies *in the total exclusion of the people in their collective capacity* from any share in the *latter*, and not in the *total exclusion of representatives of the people*, from the administration of the *former*. The distinction however thus qualified must be admitted to leave a most advantageous superiority in favor of the United States. But to ensure to this advantage its full effect, we must be careful not to separate it from the other advantage, of an extensive territory. For it cannot be believed that any form of representative government, could have succeeded within the narrow limits occupied by the democracies of Greece.

In answer to all these arguments, suggested by reason, illustrated by other examples, and enforced by our own experience, the jealous adversary of the constitution will probably content himself with repeating, that a senate appointed not immediately by the people, and for the term of six years, must gradually acquire a dangerous preeminence in the government, and finally transform it into a tyrannical aristocracy.

To this general answer the general reply ought to be sufficient; that liberty may be endangered by the abuses of liberty, as well as by the abuses of power; that there are numerous instances of the former as well as of the latter; and that the former rather than the latter is apparently most to be apprehended by the United States. But a more particular reply may be given.

Before such a revolution can be effected, the senate, it is to be observed, must in the first place corrupt itself; must next corrupt the state legislatures, must then corrupt the house of representatives, and must finally corrupt the people at large. It is evident that the senate must be first corrupted, before it can attempt an establishment of tyranny. Without corrupting the state legislatures, it cannot prosecute the attempt, because the periodical change of members would otherwise regenerate the whole body. Without exerting the means of corruption with equal succession the house of representatives, the opposition of that co-equal branch of the government would inevitably defeat the attempt; and without corrupting the people themselves, a succession of new representatives would speedily restore all things to their pristine order. Is there any man who can seriously persuade himself, that the proposed senate can, by any possible means within the compass of human address, arrive at the object of a lawless ambition, through all these obstructions?

If reason condemns the suspicion, the same sentence is pronounced by experience. The constitution of Maryland furnishes the most apposite example. The senate of that state is elected, as the federal senate will be, indirectly by the people; and for a term less by one year only, than the federal senate. It is distinguished also by the remarkable prerogative of filling up its own vacancies within the term of its appointment: and at the same time, is not under the controul of any such rotation, as is provided for the federal senate.[4] There are some other lesser distinctions, which would expose the former to colorable objections[5] that do not lie against the latter. If the federal senate therefore really contained the danger which has been so loudly proclaimed, some symptoms at least of a like danger ought by this time to have been betrayed by the senate of Maryland; but no such symptoms have appeared. On the contrary the jealousies at first entertained by men of the same description with those who view with terror the correspondent part of the federal constitution, have been gradually extinguished by the progress of the experiment; and the Maryland constitution is daily deriving from the salutary operations of this part of it, a reputation in which it will probably not be rivalled by that of any state in the union.

But if any thing could silence the jealousies on this subject, it ought to be the British example. The senate there, instead of being elected for a term of six years, and of being unconfined to particular families or fortunes, is an hereditary assembly of opulent nobles. The house of representatives, instead of being elected for two years and by the whole body of the people, is elected for seven years; and in very great proportion, by a very small proportion of the people. Here unquestionably ought to be seen in full display, the aristocratic usurpations and tyranny, which are at some future period to be exemplified in the United States. Unfortunately however for the antifederal argument in the British history informs us, that this hereditary assembly has not even been able to defend itself against the continual encroachments of the house of representatives; and that it no sooner lost the support of the monarch, than it was actually crushed by the weight of the popular branch.

As far as antiquity can instruct us on this subject, its examples support the reasoning which we have employed. In Sparta the Ephori, the annual representatives of the people, were found an overmatch for the senate for life, continually gained on its authority, and finally drew all power into their own hands. The tribunes of Rome, who were the representatives of the people, prevailed, it is well known, in almost every contest with the senate for life, and in the end gained the most complete triumph over it. This fact is the more remarkable, as unanimity was required in every act of the tribunes, even after their number was augmented to ten. It proves the irresistable force possessed by that branch of a free government, which has the people on its side. To these examples might be added that of Carthage, whose senate, according to the testimony of Polybius, instead of drawing all power into its vortex, had at the commencement of the second punic war, lost almost the whole of its original portion.[6]

Besides the conclusive evidence resulting from this assemblage of facts, that the federal senate will never be able to transform itself, by gradual usurpations, into an independent and aristocratic body; we are warranted in believing that if such a revolution should ever happen from causes which the foresight of man cannot guard against, the house of representatives with the people on their side will at all times be able to bring back the constitution to its primitive form and principles. Against the force of the immediate representatives of the people, nothing will be able to maintain

even the constitutional authority of the senate, but such a display of enlightened policy, and attachment to the public good, as will divide with
that branch of the legislature, the affections and support of the entire body
of the people themselves.

1. See *The Federalist* 62 (CC:569).
2. See *The Federalist* 10, New York *Daily Advertiser*, 22 November (CC:285).
3. See *The Federalist* 14, *New York Packet*, 30 November (CC:310).
4. Thorpe, III, 1693–94.
5. "Subjections" was substituted in the M'Lean edition.
6. F. Hultsch and Evelyn S. Shuckburgh, trans., *The Histories of Polybius* (2 vols.,
Bloomington, Ind., 1962), I, Book VI, chapter 51, pp. 501–2.

583. George Washington to James Madison
Mount Vernon, 2 March[1]

The decision of Massachusetts, notwithstanding its concomitants,[2] is a
severe stroke to the opponents of the proposed Constitution in this State;
and with the favorable determinations of the States which have gone before, and such as are likely to follow after, will have a powerful operation
on the Minds of men who are not actuated more by disappointment,[3]
passion and resentment, than they are by moderation, prudence & candor.–Of the first description however, it is to be lamented that there are so
many–and among them, *some* who would hazard *every* thing rather than
their opposition should fail, or the sagacity of their prognostications should
be impeached by an issue contrary to their predictions.

The determination you have come to, will give pleasure to your friends.–
From those in your own County you will learn with more certainty than
from me, the expediency of your attending the Election in it.[4]–With *some*,
to have differed in sentiment, is to have passed the Rubicon of their friendship, altho' you should go no further–with others (for the honor of humanity) I hope there is more liberallity; but the consciousness of having
discharged that duty which we owe to our Country, is superior to all other
considerations, and will place smaller matters in a secondary point of
view.–

His Most Ch—n M—y[5] speaks, & acts in a style not very pleasing to
republican ears, or to Republican forms;–nor do I think this language is
altogether so to the temper of his own Subjects at *this* day.–Liberty, when
it begins to take root, is a plant of rapid growth.–The checks he endeavors
to give it, however warrantable by ancient usage, will, more than probably, kindle a flame which may not easily be extinguished; tho' for a while
it may be smothered by the Armies at his command, & the Nobility in his
interest.–When the people are oppressed with Taxes, & have cause to suspect that there has been a misapplication of their money, the language of
despotizm is but illy brooked.–This, & the mortification which the pride of
the Nation has sustained in the affairs of Holland (if one may judge from

appearances) may be productive of events which prudence will not mention

To-morrow, the Elections for delegates to the Convention of this State commences–and as they will tread close on the heels of each other this month becomes interesting and important.–

1. RC, Lee-Kohns Collection, NN.
2. On 15 February Madison sent Washington a copy of the Massachusetts form of ratification that included the state's proposed amendments to the Constitution (Rutland, *Madison*, X, 510–11). For the Massachusetts amendments, see CC:508.
3. The letterbook version has "Peak" instead of "disappointment."
4. On 20 February Madison informed Washington that he had decided to seek election to the Virginia Convention from Orange County, and that he would leave Congress in New York City, if he were informed that his presence at the election was "indispensable" (Rutland, *Madison*, X, 526–27).
5. His Most Christian Majesty, Louis XVI of France.

584. Pierce Butler to Elbridge Gerry
Mary-Ville, S.C., 3 March (excerpts)[1]

Your two much esteemed favours of ye 27th. of Novbr. and 18th. of December reached my hand within twenty hours of each other, about three weeks ago. . . . Your sentiments my worthy friend, respecting the effect that politicks shoud have on Our feelings in private life intirely coincide with mine–An honorable Man is respectable in every vicissitude of life– more do I respect and esteem such a Man, thō differing from me in political opinions, than the Interested Tyrants who may draw with me–Believe my dear Sir, I felt it a misfortune that I shoud be compell'd by such judgement as it pleased God to endow me with, to draw in politicks so differently from a Man whose judgement I so highly revere–whose independence and wise integrity I bore witness to during the whole session[2]–I ardently wished my friend Gerry to think as I did, that the Constitution, with all its imperfections is the only thing at this critical moment that can rescue the States from Civil discord and foreign contempt–Reflecting maturely on Circumstances, on the too little disposition of most of the States to submit to any Government, I preferd giving my consent to a trial of the Constitution in question with all its deficiencies, to what appeared to me the innevitable alternative–that there are parts of it I do not like, *You well Know*, but still I prefer a trial of it, having within itself a power of amendment, to seeing the Gordian Knot cut–the Knot of Union in my judgement will be no more if this Constitution is Rejected–I coud ardently wish to Draw in publick, as I ever shall in private, life in Unison with a person I have so great an affection for as Mr Gerry, but I shall not less admire his independent Spirit–His disinterested Conduct–His many Virtues because he may not think with me on publick measures–, Sans Complement, Your objections to the adoption of the Constitution are in my opinion at the head of opposition Sentiments–I find by a late Boston paper the Conven-

tion of Massachusets have adopted it.[3] You had a different opinion–I am
satisfied from the liberality of Your sentiments and feelings, that when
You find opposition can have no good effect, You will give the Constitution Your support, to carry it into effect–Our Legislature have agreed to
call a Convention to meet in May. I am of opinion there is scarce a doubt
of this States adopting the Constitution: there was but a feeble opposition
to calling the Convention–We adjourned *last Saturday* after a long unpro-
ductive session–

In Your last letter You say *some dignified* falsehoods have been published
in Charleston respecting You[4]–It was the first information I had of it, and
it hurt me exceedingly–I did all in my power to find out the Paper, but
never met with any person here that even saw it–We have several different
Papers publishd in Charleston, which makes it impossible for me to trace
it, but if You will inform me of the Name of the Printer, and the date of
the Paper, I will spare no pains in finding out the Auther, and telling him
my mind *freely*–pray inclose me the publication–I seldom go to Charleston
thõ I live so near to it, and I scarce ever look at their Newspapers they are
in general so barren; but I am anxious to trace out the traducer of my
friend. . . .

1. RC (photostat), Gerry Papers, DLC. Mary-Ville was the name of Butler's plantation on the Ashley River in Prince William Parish, S.C.

2. Butler represented South Carolina in the Constitutional Convention, while Gerry
was a Massachusetts delegate.

3. On the same day that Butler wrote this letter, the Charleston *Columbian Herald*
reprinted the Massachusetts Convention's form of ratification which had been printed
by every Boston newspaper.

4. Possibly a reference to an item printed in the Charleston *City Gazette*, 10 November: "The new Constitution is so very popular in the states of Massachusetts and Maryland, a gentleman informs us that Mr. Geary has been burnt in effigy in Massachusetts,
and when Col. Mason arrived in Alexandria, on his way home, the Corporation waited
on him, with an intimation, that, although they entertained the highest sense of his
amiable character, yet such party spirit prevailed amongst the people that they could
not protect him, and advised his speedy departure from that place." The remarks concerning Gerry were apparently based upon "Curtius" III, printed in the New York
Daily Advertiser on 3 November. "Curtius" stated that "Boston warmly espouses the
opinion of her worthy Governor [John Hancock]; but it is to be hoped she has not burnt
in effigy a seceding member of the Convention. . . ."

585. Phineas Bond to the Marquis of Carmarthen
Philadelphia, 3 March (excerpt)[1]

. . . The Convention of Massachusetts Bay, having ratified the federal
Constitution, six States have now adopted it–every other State, my Lord,
Rhode Island alone excepted, has nominated a Convention; and there
seems every Prospect, at present, of a Recognition of 12 States of the 13.–
It will be a fortunate Thing for this Country, and for those, whose Inter-
ests are connected with it, to enjoy a System of Goverment whose Energy

may correct the present relaxed Situation of the Laws, and restore public Faith & private Credit.—

In some Parts of America, my Lord, particularly in the Southern States, the Rights of British Subjects are most severely oppressed; and no means of immediate Redress presents itself.[2]. . .

1. RC, Foreign Office, Class 4, America, Volume 6, ff. 85–86, Public Record Office, London, England. Printed: J. Franklin Jameson, ed., "Letters of Phineas Bond, British Consul at Philadelphia, to the Foreign Office of Great Britain, 1787, 1788, 1789," American Historical Association *Annual Report . . . 1896* (2 vols., Washington, D.C., 1897), I, 559–61. Docketed: "R[eceived] 29th. [March]."

2. The remainder of Bond's letter, not printed here, is concerned with an act of the Virginia legislature (12 December 1787), which, upon the recommendation of Congress, repealed state laws impeding the collection of British debts. The act, however, would not take effect until Great Britain surrendered its Western posts and compensated Virginians for the slaves confiscated during the war. Also discussed by Bond was a decision of the Superior Court of North Carolina in the case of *Bayard* v. *Singleton* (1787), declaring a state law unconstitutional and deciding that aliens could not hold land in North Carolina.

586. Thomas Hartley to Tench Coxe
York, Pa., 3 March[1]

I received your Favour of last Month, and am highly obliged to you for your Information.

It must give Pleasure to the Friends of real Liberty on this Side the Atlantic to find that their Conduct meets with the Approbation of the good, and wise on the other Side of the Ocean.

The late general Convention had so many Difficulties to encounter that it must be surprizing to most Men of Observation that so good a System has been offered—had the Difficulties of a capital Nature not been so numerous it is possible that the Convention might have descended into Particulars the Want of which in the Opinion of some Minds furnishes Exceptions against the Constitution: but as I have said upon a former Occasion, the cardinal Principles are generally laid down right, and any Improvements which the Wisdom of this Country may think proper to devise may at a future Day be introduced in a constitutional Manner.

Those Improvements should not be the Whim of an Hour, but founded on real Observation and Experience. Holding out the Idea of too much Flexibility, might give a Cast of Unsteadiness to our Goverment.

New York seems to put herself last on the List—the Risque of the Loaves and Fishes has I imagine more Weight with the Opponents to the Constitution in that State than any pretended Objections against the Plan, however she must at length become one of the Pillars of the Grand Fabric.

The Demagogues of Part of Maryland are exerting themselves; I trust they will fail in their Opposition and that the Constitution will be adopted in that State.

Virginia I presume will assume the Air of Wisdom and Importance; and the Leaders of the Antifœdralists will endeavour to carry their Point by Embarrassments such as adding other Amendments to those of Massachusetts &c. The good Sense of those Gentlemen who will watch them will I hope prevent any bad Consequences.

North Carolina is a weak State on account of the Extent of her Territory, and the Thinness of her Inhabitants. it is certainly her Interest to become a Part of a Government which can protect her. The Objection that the more Northern States may be her Carriers or rather the Cultivators of her Fields, when she wants Strength to do either herself, is neither founded in sound Reason or Policy

In South Carolina from all Appearances we have a Right to expect a Majority in our Favour. The Men of the Mountains or Frontiers unacquainted with the Principles of good Government, but verging towards extreme Liberty the Sister of Anarchy may be averse–yet I would fondly hope their Number will be small.

Upon a view of the several States their Interests and their Circumstances we may reasonably expect that the new Fœderal Constitution will be adopted.

This brings us naturally forward to the Administration of it in our own State.

You speak of Mr. George Clymer[2] as one of the Senate it is only to know him–to agree to the Choice, amongst a virtuous People.

So far as my Knowledge goes and I have been acquainted with his Character several Years, he is a Man of Virtue, Understanding and Firmness fit to take a Part in this or any other Government that is founded on Liberty or Justice–among the Circle of my Acquaintance he stands high.

General Irvine has been spoke of as Country Senator–he is a Man of Prudence, Understanding and Steadiness, and well affected to the Constitution notwithstanding some Insinuations against him upon the latter Head.[3]

When Parties run very high in a popular Assembly a Person is necessarily obliged to act under one Party or another–but when a Gentleman is in a distinct Body as Mr. Irvine lately in Congress and not obliged to give his Sentiments officially, his Silence to the general World should not be an Objection: He stands well with the People beyond the Mountains–he lived with them and protected them–he opposed them in the Council of Censors and so he will (if I am not mistaken in the Man) again in any improper Measures, which they may attempt in any public Body of which he may be a Member.

Perhaps at the present Sessions of Assembly it would be improper (and indeed the Attempt might prove unsuccessful) to make a provisional Law (in Case nine States should adopt the present Constitution) to chuse Members of the House of Representatives for the Fœderal Congress, &c.[4]

If Members were to be chosen out of the State at large you might possibly elect the best Men, but when we find considerable Disaffection in the back Counties; Districts well settled might be more acceptable.

The Pieces you speak of will be occasionally published here[5]–we are all serene and quiet in this County:[6] Cumberland is a little agitated[7]–I shall be highly pleased to hear from you as frequently as possible

1. RC, Tench Coxe Papers, Series II, Correspondence and General Papers, PHi. Hartley (1748–1800), a York, Pa., lawyer, was a lieutenant-colonel in the Continental Army who resigned his commission in early 1779 to represent York County in the Pennsylvania Assembly. As a member of the Council of Censors in 1783–84, he supported radical revision of the state constitution. In December 1787 he voted to ratify the federal Constitution in the state Convention. He was a U.S. Representative from 1789 until his resignation in 1800 due to ill health.

2. Clymer (1739–1813), a Philadelphia merchant, was a member of Congress, 1776–77, 1780–82, and signed the Declaration of Independence in 1776. He was a member of the Pennsylvania Assembly, 1776–79 and 1785–89, and in September 1787 he was a leader in the fight to have the Assembly call a state convention to consider the Constitution. As a delegate to the Constitutional Convention, he signed the Constitution. Clymer was a U.S. Representative from 1789 to 1791.

3. General William Irvine of Carlisle had represented Cumberland County in the Council of Censors, where, as a member of the Republican Party, he sought radical revision of the state constitution. He had been a member of Congress since January 1787. His letters do not indicate his personal opinion of the Constitution, but the letters to him indicate that he was perceived as a Federalist. By September 1788, however, he was distrusted by Federalists because he was a member of a committee of Congress that charged Robert Morris, the leader of the Republican Party, with the mismanagement of wartime finances. Irvine was narrowly defeated by Morris for the U.S. Senate. He then was defeated as a candidate for the U.S. House of Representatives on the Harrisburg or Antifederalist ticket.

4. The Pennsylvania Assembly passed election laws on 4 October and 13 November 1788.

5. On 6 February Coxe sent Hartley copies of his "Freeman" essays for reprinting in the York newspaper (CC:472).

6. For two contradictory descriptions of the attitude of the "country people" in York County, see Philadelphia *Independent Gazetteer*, 3 March (Appendix I).

7. Cumberland County was agitated by the aftermath of the Carlisle riots and the petition campaign to overthrow Pennsylvania's ratification of the Constitution (*Independent Gazetteer*, 4 March, and *Pennsylvania Gazette*, 26 March, note 2, both in Appendix I).

587. James Madison to Edmund Randolph
New York, 3 March[1]

The Convention of N. Hampshire have disappointed the general expectation. They have not rejected the Constitution, but they have adjourned without adopting it. It was found that on a final question there would be a majority of 3 or 4 in the negative but in this number were included some who with instructions from their Towns against the Constitution, had been proselyted by the discussions. These concurring with the fœderalists in the adjournment carried it by 57 agst. 47. if I am rightly informed as to the numbers. The second meeting is not to be till the last week in June. I have

enquired from the gentlemen from that quarter what particularly reco-
m̃ended so late a day, supposing it might refer to the times fixed by N.Y.
& Virga. They tell me it was governed by the intermediate annual elections and Courts.[2] If the opposition in that State be such as they are described it is not probable that they. pursue any sort of plan, more than that
of Massts. This event whatever causes may have produced it, or whatever
consequences it may have in N.H. is no small check to the progress of the
business. The opposition here which is unquestionably hostile to every
thing beyond the fœderal principle, will take new spirits. The event in
Massts. had almost extinguished their hopes. That in Pena. will probably
be equally encouraged.

Col. Heth arrived a day or two ago with the proceedings of the Com̃-
issrs.[3] They will be laid before Congress today. I have been detained from
setting out for Virga. by this circumstance having fixed on yesterday for
the purpose. I shall probably get away tomorrow, and possibly this afternoon.[4]

1. RC, Madison Papers, DLC. On the same day, Madison wrote similar letters to
George Washington and Edmund Pendleton (Rutland, *Madison*, X, 554, 555).

2. Most of the text to this point was printed in the *Virginia Independent Chronicle* on 19
March. The printer of the *Chronicle* began the item: "By accounts from New-York, of
the 3d instant, received by last Saturday's [15 March's] mail. . . ." On the 3rd Madison was attending Congress and Governor Randolph was in Richmond.

3. William Heth (1735–1808), a member of the Virginia Council of State, was one of
the state commissioners appointed to liquidate the claim of Virginia against the United
States on account of Virginia's earlier cession of the Northwest Territory. (See Rutland, *Madison*, X, 352–54.)

4. Madison reached his Orange County home on 23 March, having stopped off at
Mount Vernon to visit George Washington on 18 and 19 March (*ibid.*, 542n, 556n).
On 24 March he was elected to represent Orange County in the state Convention.

588. The Landholder X
Connecticut Courant, 3 March

The adjournment of the New Hampshire Convention on 22 February, without
taking a vote on the ratification of the Constitution (CC:554), stimulated a revival
of the "Landholder" series which had last appeared on 31 December (CC:397).
"Landholder" X and XI, published on 3 and 10 March, urged New Hampshire to
ratify the Constitution when the state Convention reconvened in June (CC:588,
611).

"Landholder" X was also printed in the Hartford *American Mercury* on 3 March.
The *Courant* and *Mercury* versions differ in paragraphing, capitalization, spelling,
and punctuation. (See also note 2 below.) By 5 May "Landholder" X was reprinted thirteen times: N.H. (4), Mass. (5), Conn. (2), N.Y. (1), S.C. (1). On 11
March the *Salem Mercury* also reprinted excerpts.

For the authorship, circulation, and impact of "Landholder," see CC:230.

To the CITIZENS of NEW-HAMPSHIRE.

The opposition[1] in your State to the new[2] Constitution[3] is an event
surprising to your New-England Brethren, yet we are not disposed to criminate a people which made such gallant efforts in the establishment of
the American empire. It is the prerogative of freemen to determine their

own form of government, and if this Constitution is not addressed to your interest; if it is not calculated to preserve your freedom, and make you glorious, we wish you not to accept it. We have fought by your side, we have long been connected in interest, and with many of you by consanguinity, and wish that you may share with us in all the benefits of a great and free empire. Brethren who differ in their opinions how a common interest may be best governed, ought to deliberate with coolness and not wantonly accuse each other, either of folly or design. Massachusetts and Connecticut have decidedly judged the new government well calculated not only for the whole, but for the northern states.–Either you or these states have judged wrong. Your interests are similar to theirs, and cannot be separated from them without counteracting nature. If there be any one state more interested than the others in the adoption of this system, it is New-Hampshire. Your local situation which can never be altered is a solemn argument in its favour. Though separated from the government of Britain, at no less price than the blood of your bravest sons, you border on her dominions–She is our enemy, and wishes nothing more than your submission to her laws, and to the will of her proud servants. Her force may easily be pointed through your whole territory, and a few regiments would effectually banish resistance. New-Hampshire, though growing in population, and among the first states in personal bravery cannot yet stand alone. Should a disunion of the states tempt Britain to make another effort for recovering her former greatness, you will be the first to fall under her sway. In such case you will have nothing to expect from the other states.– Dispirited with a fruitless attempt to unite in some plan of general government and protection, they will say, let the dissenting states abide the consequences of their own false opinions. Though such a reply might not be wise, it would be exactly conformable to what we have ever found in human nature; and nature will have its course, let policy be what it may. You are the northern barrier of the United States, and by your situation, must first meet any hostile animosity from that quarter, designed against any part of them. It is certainly for the interest of a barrier country, to have a general government on such efficient principles, as can point the force of the whole for its relief when attacked[4]–The old Constitution could not do this; that now under consideration, if accepted, we trust will produce a circulation of riches and the powers of protection, to the most extreme parts of the body.–On these principles it has generally been said, that New-Hampshire and Georgia would be among the first in adopting– Georgia has done it, not perhaps because they are more wise than New-Hampshire, but being pressed with a dangerous war in the very moment of decision, they felt its necessity; and feeling is an argument none can resist. Trust not to any complaisance of those British provinces on your northern borders, or those artful men who govern them, who were selected on purpose to beguile your politics, and divide and weaken the union– When the hour for a permanent connection between the states is past, the teeth of the Lion will be again made bare, and you must either be devoured or become his Jackall to hunt for prey in the other states.

We believe those among you who are opposed to the system as honest and brave as any part of the community, and cannot suspect them of any design against American independence; but such persons ought to consider what will be the probable consequence of their dissent; and whether this is not the only hour in which this country can be saved from a condition, which is on all hands allowed to be dangerous and unhappy. There are certain critical periods in which nations as well individuals, who have fallen into perplexity, by a wise exertion may save themselves and be glorious.–Such is the present æra in American policy; but if we do not see the hour of our salvation, there is no reason to expect that Heaven will repeat it.–The unexpected harmony of the Federal Convention–their mutual condescension in the reconcilement of jarring interests and opposing claims between the several states–the formation of a system so efficient in appearance, and at the same time, so well guarded against an oppression of the subject–the concurring sentiments of a vast majority through the United States, of those persons who have been most experienced in policy and most eminent in wisdom and virtue, are events which must be attributed to the special influence of Heaven.

To be jealous for our liberties is lawful, but jealousy in excess is a delirium of the imagination by no means favourable to liberty. If you would be free and happy a power must be created to protect your persons and properties; otherwise you are slaves to all mankind. Your British neighbours have long known these truths, and will not fail by their emissaries to seminate such jealousies as favour their own designs–To prophesy evil is an ungrateful business; but forgive me when I predict, that the adoption of this Constitution, is the only probable means of saving the greatest part of your state from becoming an appendage of Canada or Nova-Scotia.–In some future paper I shall assign other reasons why New-Hampshire more than any other state is interested in this event.[5]

1. This word was italicized in the *New Hampshire Mercury*, 12 March, *New Hampshire Spy*, 14 March, and Exeter, N.H., *Freeman's Oracle*, 14 March.
2. The *American Mercury* inserted the word "Federal" at this point.
3. The words "new Constitution" were italicized by the three New Hampshire newspapers listed in note 1.
4. This last phrase, beginning "as can . . .," was italicized by the three New Hampshire newspapers listed in note 1.
5. For "Landholder" XI, see CC:611.

589. Tobias Lear to William Prescott, Jr.
Mount Vernon, 4 March (excerpt)[1]

. . . I congratulate you upon the adoption of the proposed Government in your State.–The majority in favor of it, tho' small, was very respectable, and the decent behaviour of the minority will have more influence than the decision itself.–What *will* be its fate in this State is impossible to

foretell at this distant period from our convention, but from every information I can gain (and my situation is such as enables me to gain the best)
I have not a doubt of its being accepted–its opponents here are men of
great influence & abilities, but their arguments have not that decided
weight with the people which they would have upon any other subject–this
is an important one upon which they chuse to think for themselves, and
the favourable decisions of other States have more influence than the persuasive Rhetoric of a Mason, a Lee, a Henry or a Randolph.–I was not in
the convention, but I suppose no person, who was not a member of that
body, has had a better opportunity of knowing what were the sentiments
& doings of almost every man there than myself.–The Constitution and its
circumstances have been almost the sole topics of conversation here for
some months past, and as we are visited by few Characters but the first &
best informed[2] I have had more LIGHT thrown upon the subject than Mr
Gerry[3] could have diffused had he possessed ten-times the abilities, knowledge & information than he does.–The report that General Washington
was *drawn in* to sign it is as false as it is artful;[4]–he looks up to it as the
rock of our political salvation–he knows it is not perfect, but he knows, at
the same time that it approaches much nearer to perfection than any person, who knew the variety of views, interēts & prejudices which were to
conciliate, could have expected.–Thus much for great & political matters. . . .

1. RC, William Prescott Papers, MHi. The address page of this letter, postmarked
"ALEX, MARCH 24," included this note in George Washington's handwriting: "Free/
Go: Washington." In the omitted part of this letter, Lear wrote that Washington had
given him permission to use his franking privileges. Lear and Prescott (1762–1844) had
been graduated from Harvard College in 1783. Lear was Washington's private secretary, a position Prescott had been offered but which he had rejected. Instead, Prescott
studied law in Beverly, Mass., with Nathan Dane, and in 1787 began practicing law in
Beverly.

2. Since late October 1787, Washington had been visited by such members of the
Constitutional Convention as George Mason and Gouverneur and Robert Morris and
by such congressmen as Richard Henry Lee, Henry Lee, and Edward Carrington.
James Madison, who served in both bodies, visited Washington about two weeks after
Lear wrote this letter.

3. In his letter of 27 January (not found), Prescott probably informed Lear that the
Massachusetts Convention had invited Gerry to answer questions about the drafting of
the Constitution.

4. For Antifederalist charges that Washington was duped into signing the Constitution and that he signed only because he was president of the Constitutional Convention,
see "Centinel" I, Philadelphia *Independent Gazetteer*, 5 October (CC:133), and *Pennsylvania Herald*, 19, 22 December, note 3 (CC:Vol. 3, Appendix I).

590. Collin McGregor to Neil Jamieson
New York, 4 March (excerpt)[1]

. . . Within these few days Final Settlements have rose & fallen.–After
the Adoption of the New Constitution by Boston State they rose to near
4/.; but New-Hampshire havg Adjourned their Convention till June, has

had the effect to reduce these securities abt. 6d..–we trust that this last
mentd. State will adopt it at their next meetg and in the meantime other
States will come into the Measure which will again give a Spring to securities.–There are great doubts abt. Virga.; and also of this State.–when I
was at Alb[an]y the other day[2] I found a formidable Party in favor of the
New Governt. But in the Country I was told they are much agt. it; This
~~doctrine~~ last is the friendly Party of our chief Magistrate[3] & his influence
is great.–"*Whig & Tory*" is entirely done away, and we have substituted in
their Stead "Fœderalists & *Antifœderalists*,"–These Parties carry on their
disputes in many instances with much ~~resentment~~ warmth ill-humour &
sometimes too personal.–I beg pardon for this digression from business.–it
is the securities which is the cause of it, as they are more or less blended
wt. the Politics of the day. . . .

   1. FC, Collin McGregor Letterbook, 1787-1788, NN. Duplicates of this letter and
another dated 18 February were sent to Jamieson by McGregor on 2 April. (See
CC:538, note 1.)
   2. In a part of the letter not printed, McGregor indicated that he had left New York
City for Albany on 21 February.
   3. Governor George Clinton.

591. Archibald Maclaine to James Iredell
Wilmington, N.C., 4 March[1]

   . . . You have no doubt seen that in New York there was very nearly
one half of the Assembly against calling a convention;[2] yet I am informed
by a letter from that place, it is the general opinion that the new constitution will be adopted. This opinion is probably founded on the belief that it
will be ratified by nine States, in which case, it will be certainly embraced
by the remaining four. That this is the idea of those in the opposition, I
have no doubt, for a number of their emissaries were at Boston, during
the deliberation of the convention, endeavoring to scatter their poison
among the members.[3] It is, however, extraordinary, that though there
were in the convention a majority, and that considerable, against the proposed government, it should have been ratified by a majority of nineteen.
This is attributed to the Good Genius of America. A rejection in Massachusetts would probably have proved fatal. As the convention of New
Hampshire have been sitting now near three weeks, and are said to be
unanimous, we may conclude that seven States have come into the measure; South Carolina is certain. Among the other four we shall probably
have a ninth. My principal reliance is on Maryland.

   I expect in a few weeks the Federalist in a volume. He is certainly a
judicious and ingenious writer, though not well calculated for the common
people.

   Your old friend Huske, and Col. Read,[4] have joined all the low scoundrels in the county, and by every underhand means, are prejudicing the
common people against the new constitution. The former is a candidate

for the county; but although in the beginning he was ridiculously loud, and even clamorous, he has been taught prudence by his associates. As a proof that he is not actuated by principle, he condemned the whole, after having a slight view of one half only over the shoulders of another person. In truth his objections are a disgrace to his understanding as well as his principles, &c., &c.

1. Printed: McRee, *Iredell*, II, 219-20. The excerpt published by McRee is printed here in its entirety. Maclaine (d. 1791), a lawyer-planter, was a native of Scotland who emigrated to North Carolina from Ireland before 1750. Maclaine represented Brunswick County in the state Senate, 1777, 1780-81, 1782-3, and Wilmington in the House of Commons, 1783-87. As Wilmington's representative, he supported the Constitution in the Hillsborough Convention in July and August 1788.

2. The resolution calling the state convention was passed by the Senate 11 to 8 and by the Assembly 27 to 25 (*Massachusetts Centinel*, 13 February, Appendix I).

3. No record has been found of such Antifederalist "emissaries," but just before the Massachusetts Convention convened on 9 January, a New York Antifederalist pamphlet, *Letters from the Federal Farmer*, actively distributed by New York Antifederalists, had reached Massachusetts and was about to be reprinted (see CC:242, 390).

4. In January Maclaine had described John Huske (d. 1792), a justice of the peace for New Hanover County, as "the loudest man in Wilmington against the new Constitution. Whether ambition, or avarice, or a compound of both, actuates him, I leave you to judge" (to Iredell, 15 January, McRee, *Iredell*, II, 217). Huske represented New Hanover County and opposed the Constitution in both the Hillsborough Convention of 1788 and the Fayetteville Convention of 1789. Colonel James Read of Wilmington (d. 1803), a Revolutionary War officer, was a justice of the peace for New Hanover County and collector of Port Brunswick.

592 A–B. Publius: The Federalist 64
New York Independent Journal, 5 March

This essay was written by John Jay, who, because of illness, had not contributed to the series since *The Federalist* 5 was published on 10 November (CC:252). The manuscript draft of the essay is among the Jay Papers at the New-York Historical Society. Because the draft differs significantly from the newspaper version, it is also published below (CC:592-B). The draft was found among John Jay's family papers and given to the Historical Society in 1863. It was printed by Henry B. Dawson in *The Historical Magazine*, 2nd series, I (1867), 257-61. (See also note 4 below.)

The Federalist 64 was reprinted on 7 March in the *New York Packet* which had announced, on 4 March, that the essay was "unavoidably omitted, for want of room." The essay is number 64 in the M'Lean edition and number 63 in the newspapers.

For a general discussion of the authorship, circulation, and impact of *The Federalist*, see CC:201, 639.

592-A. Newspaper Version

The FŒDERALIST. No. LXIII.
To the People of the State of New-York.

It is a just and not a new observation that enemies to particular persons and opponents to particular measures, seldom confine their censures to such things only in either, as are worthy of blame, unless on this principle it is difficult to explain the motives of their conduct, who condemn the proposed constitution in the aggregate, and treat with severity some of the most unexceptionable articles in it–

The 2d. section gives power to the president *"by and with the advice and consent of the senate to make treaties* PROVIDED TWO THIRDS OF THE SENATORS PRESENT CONCUR.*"*

The power of making treaties is an important one, especially as it relates to war, peace and commerce; and it should not be delegated but in such a mode, and with such precautions, as will afford the highest security, that it will be exercised by men the best qualified for the purpose, and in the manner most conducive to the public good. The convention appears to have been attentive to both these points–they have directed the president to be chosen by select bodies of electors to be deputed by the people for that express purpose; and they have committed the appointment of senators to the state legislatures. This mode has in such cases, vastly the advantage of elections by the people in their collective capacity, where the activity of party zeal taking advantage of the supiness, the ignorance, and the hopes and fears of the unwary and interested, often places men in office by the votes of a small proportion of the electors.

As the select assemblies for choosing the president, as well as the state legislatures who appoint the senators will in general be composed of the most enlightened and respectable citizens, there is reason to presume that their attention and their votes will be directed to those men only who have become the most distinguished by their abilities and virtue, and in whom the people perceive just grounds for confidence. The constitution manifests very particular attention to this object. By excluding men under thirty five from the first office, and those under thirty from the second, it confines the electors[1] to men of whom the people have had time to form a judgment, and with respect to whom they will not be liable to be deceived by those brilliant appearances of genius and patriotism, which like transient meteors sometimes mislead as well as dazzle. If the observation be well founded, that wise kings will always be served by able ministers, it is fair to argue that as an assembly of select electors possess in a greater degree than kings, the means of extensive and accurate information relative to men and characters, so will their appointments bear at least equal marks of discretion and discernment. The inference which naturally results from these considerations is this, that the president and senators so chosen will always be of the number of those who best understand our national interests, whether considered in relation to the several states or to foreign nations, who are best able to promote those interests,[2] and whose reputation for integrity inspires and merits confidence. With such men the power of making treaties may be safely lodged.

Although the absolute necessity of system in the conduct of any business, is universally known and acknowledged, yet the high importance of

it in national affairs has not yet become sufficiently impressed on the public mind. They who wish to commit the power under consideration to a
popular assembly, composed of members constantly coming and going in
quick succession, seem not to recollect that such a body must necessarily
be unadequate to the attainment of those great objects, which require to
be steadily contemplated in all their relations and circumstances, and which
can only be approached and atchieved by measures, which not only talents, but also exact information and often much time are necessary to
concert and to execute. It was wise therefore in the convention to provide
not only that the power of making treaties should be committed to able
and honest men, but also that they should continue in place a sufficient
time to become perfectly acquainted with our national concerns, and to
form and introduce a system for the management of them. The duration
prescribed is such as will give them an opportunity of greatly extending
their political informations and of rendering their accumulating experience
more and more beneficial to their country. Nor has the convention discovered less prudence in providing for the frequent elections of senators in
such a way, as to obviate the inconvenience of periodically transferring
those great affairs entirely to new men, for by leaving a considerable residue of the old ones in place, uniformity and order, as well as a constant
succession of official information, will be preserved.

There are few who will not admit that the affairs of trade and navigation
should be regulated by a system cautiously formed and steadily pursued;
and that both our treaties and our laws should correspond with, and be
made to promote it. It is of much consequence that this correspondence
and conformity be carefully maintained, and they who assent to the truth
of this position, will see and confess that it is well provided for by making
the concurrence of the senate necessary both to treaties and to laws.

It seldom happens in the negotiation of treaties of whatever nature, but
that perfect *secrecy* and immediate *dispatch* are sometimes requisite.[3] There
are cases where the most useful intelligence may be obtained, if the persons possessing it can be relieved from apprehensions of discovery. Those
apprehensions will operate on those persons whether they are actuated by
mercenary or friendly motives, and there doubtless are many of both descriptions, who would rely on the secrecy of the president, but who would
not confide in that of the senate, and still less in that of a large popular
assembly. The convention have done well therefore in so disposing of the
power of making treaties, that although the president must in forming
them act by the advice and consent of the senate, yet he will be able to
manage the business of intelligence in such manner as prudence may suggest.

They who have turned their attention to the affairs of men, must have
perceived that there are tides in them. Tides, very irregular in their duration, strength and direction, and seldom found to run twice exactly in the

same manner or measure. To discern and to profit by these tides in national affairs, is the business of those who preside over them; and they who have had much experience on this head inform us, that there frequently are occasions when days, nay even when hours are precious. The loss of a battle, the death of a prince, the removal of a minister, or other circumstances intervening to change the present posture and aspect of affairs, may turn the most favorable tide into a course opposite to our wishes. As in the field, so in the cabinet, there are moments to be seized as they pass, and they who preside in either, should be left in capacity to improve them. So often and so essentially have we heretofore suffered from the want of secrecy and dispatch, that the constitution would have been inexcusably defective if no attention had been paid to those objects. Those matters which in negociations usually require the most secrecy and the most dispatch, are those preparatory and auxiliary measures which are no otherwise important in a national view, than as they tend to facilitate the attainment of the objects of the negotiation. For these the president will find no difficulty to provide, and should any circumstance occur which requires the advice and consent of the senate, he may at any time convene them. Thus we see that the constitution provides that our negotiations for treaties shall have every advantage which can be derived from talents, information, integrity, and deliberate investigations on the one hand, and from secrecy and dispatch on the other.

But to this plan as to most others that have ever appeared, objections are contrived and urged.

Some are displeased with it, not on account of any errors or defects in it, but because as the treaties when made are to have the force of laws, they should be made only by men invested with legislative authority. These gentlemen seem not to consider that the judgments of our courts, and the commissions constitutionally given by our governor, are as valid and as binding on all persons whom they concern, as the laws passed by our legislature are. All constitutional acts of power, whether in the executive or in the judicial departments, have as much legal validity and obligation as if they proceeded from the legislature, and therefore whatever name be given to the power of making treaties, or however obligatory they may be when made, certain it is that the people may with much propriety commit the power to a distinct body from the legislature, the executive or the judicial. It surely does not follow that because they have given the power of making laws to the legislature, that therefore they should likewise give them power to do every other act of sovereignty by which the citizens are to be bound and affected.

Others, though content that treaties should be made in the mode proposed, are averse to their being the *supreme* laws of the land. They insist and profess to believe, that treaties, like acts of assembly, should be repealable at pleasure. This idea seems to be new and peculiar to this country, but new errors as well as new truths often appear. These gentlemen would do well to reflect that a treaty is only another name for a bargain; and that it would be impossible to find a nation who would make any bargain with us, which should be binding on them *absolutely*, but on us only so long and so far as we may think proper to be bound by it. They who make laws may without doubt amend or repeal them, and it will not be disputed that they who make treaties may alter or cancel them; but still let us not forget that treaties are made not by only one of the contracting parties but by both, and consequently that as the consent of both was essential to their formation at first, so must it ever afterwards be to alter or cancel them. The proposed constitution therefore has not in the least extended the obligation of treaties. They are just as binding, and just as far beyond the lawful reach of legislative acts now, as they will be at any future period, or under any form of government.

However useful jealousy may be in republics, yet when, like Bile in the natural, it abounds too much in the body politic; the eyes of both become very liable to be deceived by the delusive appearances which that malady casts on surrounding objects. From this cause probably proceed the fears and apprehensions of some, that the president and senate may make treaties without an equal eye to the interests of all the states. Others suspect that the two-thirds will oppress the remaining third, and ask whether those gentlemen are made sufficiently responsible for their conduct–whether if they act corruptly they can be punished; and if they make disadvantageous treaties, how are we to get rid of those treaties?

As all the states are equally represented in the senate, and by men the most able and the most willing to promote the interest of their constituents, they will all have an equal degree of influence in that body, especially while they continue to be careful in appointing proper persons, and to insist on their punctual attendance. In proportion as the United States assume a national form, and a national character, so will the good of the whole be more and more an object of attention; and the government must be a weak one indeed, if it should forget that the good of the whole can only be promoted by advancing the good of each of the parts or members which compose the whole. It will not be in the power of the president and senate to make any treaties, by which they and their families and estates will not be equally bound and affected with the rest of the community; and having no private interest distinct from that of the nation, they will be under no temptations to neglect the latter.

As to corruption, the case is not supposable, he must either have been very unfortunate in his intercourse with the world, or possess a heart very susceptible of such impressions, who can think it probable that the president and two-thirds of the senate will ever be capable of such unworthy conduct. The idea is too gross and too invidious to be entertained. But in such a case, if it should ever happen, the treaty so obtained from us would, like all other fraudulent contracts, be null and void by the laws of nations.

With respect to their responsibility, it is difficult to conceive how it could be encreased. Every consideration that can influence the human mind, such as honor, oaths, reputation, conscience, the love of country, and family affections and attatchments, afford security for their fidelity. In short, as the constitution has taken the utmost care that they shall be men of talents and integrity, we have reason to be persuaded that the treaties they make will be as advantageous as all circumstances considered could be made; and so far as the fear of punishment and disgrace can operate, that motive to good behaviour is amply afforded by the article on the subject of impeachments.

592–B. Draft Version

It is unhappily the law both with Respect to Measures and to Persons that their opponents seldom confine their Censures to such things only as are worthy of Blame–unless on this Principle it is difficult to account for the Conduct of those who condemn the proposed Constitution in the aggregate, and treat with Severity some of the most unexceptionable articles in it–

The 2 Sec. gives Power to the President "by and with ye Advice and consent of the Senate to make Treaties provided two thirds of the Senators present concur–["]

The power of making Treaties is unquestionably a very important one, especially as it relates to war Peace & commerce, and should not be ~~vested in any Man or Body of Men~~ delegated, without such precautions ~~in the mode of constituting them~~ as that the nation ~~shall~~ may have the highest Security wh. the nature of the Case will admit of, that it will be exercised by men the best qualified for the purpose, and in the manner most conducive to the public good–The framers of the constitution appear to have been ~~particularly~~ attentive to both these Points–They have directed the President to be chosen by select bodies of Electors to be convened for that express purpose, and have referred the appointment of Senators to the State Legislatures.

This mode has in such Cases vastly the advantage of Elections by the People in their collective Capacity, where the activity of Party Zeal taking advantage of the Supiness the Ignorance the Hopes and the Fears of the unwary & interested frequently places Men in office by the votes of a small Proportion of the Electors, ~~and men too with whom the great body of Electors have not always Reason to be satisfied–~~

as the ~~assemblys~~ State Electors for President as well as the State Legislatures, will in general be composed of the most enlightened and respectable Citizens, there is ~~the highest~~ Reason to presume that their appointments to these ~~great~~ national offices will be ~~discreet~~ judicious, or in other words that the federal President & Senators ~~so chosen~~ will be ~~those~~ men who had become eminently distinguished by their vertue and Talents–nay so exceedingly cautious and attentive were [the] Convention in providing for this object, that by excluding men und[er] 35 from the first office, and under 30 from the second, they have confined the Electors to men of whom the People have had Experience, and with Respect to whom they will be in no Danger of being deceived by those brilliant appearances of Genius and Patriotism which like transient Meteors sometimes mislead as well as dazzle–

From the manner in which they are to be appointed it is reasonable to infer that the power of making Treaties will be exercised by ~~the most~~ able and honest men ~~to be found in the Country~~ U.S. for if the observation be just that wise Kings will always be served by ~~wise~~ able ministers, it is natural to presume that *as* an assembly of select Electors possess in a higher Degree than Kings, the means of extensive & accurate Information relative to men & ~~their~~ characters, so in the same Degree will their appointments be in general more discreet, ~~and less liable to~~ and judicious

The Presidt. & Senrs so chosen will doubtless be of the number of those in each State who best understand its Interests, whether considered in Relation to the other States or to foreign Nations; and we must suppose that the members from each State however well disposed to promote the general good of the whole, will yet be still more Strongly disposed to promote that of their immediate constituents–

altho the absolute necessity of System in the conduct of any Business is universally known & acknowledged, yet the high Importance of it in national affairs has not yet become sufficiently impressed on the public mind– They who wish to commit the power under Consideration to a popular assembly composed of members constantly coming and going in quick Succession, seem not to ~~be apprized~~ recollect that such a Body must necessarily be inadequate to the attainmt. of those great objects which require to be steadily contemplated in their various Relations and Circumstances, and which can only be approached and atchieved by measures which not only Talents but accurate Information & often much Time are necessary to concert and to execute

It was wise therefore in the Convention to provide not only that this power shd. be exercised by the ablest men, but also that they should continue in Place a sufficient Time to become well acquainted with our national Concerns, and to form and introduce a System for the management of them–by this Provision they will be in Capacity to make daily additions to their Stock of political Information and be enabled by experience to render it more & more beneficial to the Country–nor did the Convention manifest less prudence in so prescribing for the frequent Election of Senators in such a way as to obviate the Inconvenience of periodically committing those great affairs to new Men unacquainted with their exact Situation & circumstances, ~~but on ye contrary~~ for by leaving a considerable Residue of the old ones in place uniformity and order as well a constant Succession of Information from the first to the latter members, will be preserved–

It will not be denied that the affairs of Trade and navigation should be regulated by a System wisely formed and steadily pursued–It is also well known ~~that these affairs will be regulated~~ that whatever may be the System our Treaties with foreign nations as well as our Laws on the Subject shd. be conformable to it–It is highly important therefore that this ~~uniformity~~ conformity shd be preserved and the Convention ~~appears to have been apprized, for~~ by making the Concurrence of the Senate necessary to both, ~~there is little Danger of the~~ have taken effectual Care ~~is taken~~ that our Treaties & our Laws shall always harmonize and unite in promoting the attainment of the same ~~interesting~~ national objects–

Let it also be remembered that in forming Treaties of Peace & of Commerce & particulary the former, it often happens that perfect Secrecy and ~~great~~ immediate Dispatch are requisite There are Cases when the most useful Intelligence ~~of great Importance~~ may be obtained provided the Parties possessing & conveying it have no Reason to apprehend a Discovery–whether those Parties be influenced by mercenary or by friendly motives will make but little Difference, for in either Case a Discovery might be equally fatal to them–It is not rash to presume that there are many of both Descriptions who would rely on the Secrecy of the President, but who would not confide in that of the Senate, and still less in that of a large popular Assembly–The Convention have done well therefore in so disposing of this power of making Treaties, as that altho the president ~~is restrained by~~ must in forming them act by the Advice and Consent of the Senate, yet ~~that all he will be under [– – –] obligations to~~ he will be able to manage all affairs of secret Intelligence in the Way which Prudence and Circumstances may suggest–The Propriety of these Remarks might be illustrated by Facts well known to many but which it would not be adviseable to render more public.

They who have turned their attention to the Affairs of men well know that there are Tides in them–Tides exceedingly irregular in their Duration Strength & Direction, and seldom found to run twice exactly in the same Manner and Measure–To discern and profit by these Tides in national affairs, is the Business of those Politicians who preside over ~~nations~~ them–in doing this Days and even Hours are often precious, and Dispatch indispensable–The intervening Death of a Prince, the removal of a Minister in short the least change in the present posture of affairs may give a favorable Tide an opposite Course

as in the Field so in the Cabinet there are moments to be seized as they pass; neither our Governors or our Generals should be restrained from improving them–~~these observations~~ we have in more Instances than one suffered exceedingly from the Delays inseparable from our present Govt. and we have much Reason to rejoice that the proposed Constitution has so well provided agt. them–for many preparatory and collateral Measures relative to Negociations may be taken by the President and when such as require the Concurrence of the Senate occur, he may at any time convene them–thus does the constitution give to the formation of Treaties all the advantages of Secy and Dispatch on the one Hand and of deliberate Council on the other–

But to this Plan as to all others that have ever appeared in the World, ~~without excepting even those which descended from heaven,~~ objections have been contrived and urged

Some object because the Treaties so made are to have the Force of Laws, and therefore that the makers of them will so far have legislative power This objection is a mere play on the word legislative–Is not the Commission of the King of Great Britain to a Judge or a general as valid in Law and as obligatory on all whom it may concern, as if the Judge or the General had been commissioned by Act of Parliament–If the People from whom only civil Power can be derived think it expedient by their Constitution to give to a King the power of issuing such Commissions, they must be as much bound by such royal acts, as they are by those acts which they authorize their Legislature to pass–

~~The People of america knowing that they would have occasion to make Treaties or Bargains with other Nations appoint certain men in their name to make those Bargains for them–again the People of america knowing that Laws regulating their general affairs would be necessary, think proper to appoint certain other men to make such Laws then–surely in the one Case as in the other the acts of these men must have equall~~

Whatever name therefore be given to the obligation of Treaties or whether the making them be called the Exercise of legislative or of any other kind of authority certain it is that the people have a Right to dispose of the power to make them as they think expedient–& when made conformably to the power delegated must be valid and inviolable

others seem uneasy that Treaties are to be the sup. Laws of the Land It is not easy even to suspect Gentlemen of being serious when they profess to believe and insist that Treaties like acts of assembly should be repealable at our will & pleasure–a Treaty is only another name for a Bargain or a Contract, and have no Reason to expect or hope that any Nation or any private man of Common Sense can be found, who would consent to make any bargain with us which so far from being mutually binding, should by us be carved, and construed, extended, contracted or annulled just as our Legislature or Legislatures might think most convenient and advantageous

They who make Laws may without doubt repeal them and it is equally true that they who make Treaties may alter or annul them–but we are not to forget that Treaties are made not by one of the contracting Parties but by both, and consequently that as the Consent of both was essential to making them at first, so must it ever afterwards be to alter or cancel them– The proposed Constitution therefore has not in the least extended the obligation of Treaties–they are just as binding and just as far beyond the

lawful Reach of legislative acts ~~before the Convention convened~~ now as
they will be at any future period or under future Govt–

Altho how useful Jealousy may be a ~~republican~~ republics ~~Requisite~~
Qualification (for a virtue it never was nor will be) yet when like Bile in
the natural too much in the Body politic the Eyes of become very liable to
be deceived by the delusive appearances which that malady gives to surrounding Objects–

will the President and Senate make Treaties with an equal Eye to the
Interests of all the States–will not the two thirds often be tempted to oppress the remaining third–~~will not the Influence of the eastern & middle~~
~~States generally preponderate in that Body~~ are these Gent. made sufficiently responsible for their Conduct? if they act corruptly can they be
punished? and if they make disadvantageous Treaties can we get rid of
such Treaties–

Such Questions really betray an undue Degree of Jealousy every objection to the fœderal Constitution wh they imply may at least with equal
force be applied to that of this State

will the Govr & Legislature of New York make Laws with an equal Eye
to the Interests of all the Counties–will not the majority often oppress the
minority–are these Gentlemen made sufficiently responsible for their Conduct–if they act corruptly can they be punished–and if the commissioners
make disadvantageous Treaties or Bargains with the Indians or others can
we get rid of them–

as all the States are represented equally in the senate which is to vote
per Capita, they will all have an equal Degree of Influence there, especially if they are careful to appoint ~~their best men~~ proper persons to that
Body, and insist on their punctual attendance–In Proportion as the United
States assume a national Form and a national Character, so will the good
of the whole become more and more an object of attention; and the Govt.
must be a weake one indeed if it should forget that the good of the whole
cannot be promoted without attending to the good of each of the parts or
members which compose the whole–It will not be in the power of the President and Senate to form any Treaty by which they & their Estates and
Families will not be equally bound and affected with Rest of the Community, and having no private interest distinct from that of the Nation they
will be under no temptations to neglect the latter–

as to corruption the Case is not supposable–a man must either have
been very unfortunate in his Intercourse with the world, or possess a Heart
very susceptible of such Impressions; who can think it probable that the
President and two-thirds of the Senate will ever be capable of such unworthy Conduct–The Idea is too gross and too black to be entertained – – –
But even in such a Case if it shd. ever happen the Treaty so obtained from
us would like all other fraudulent Contracts be null and void by the Laws
of Nations–

with Respect to the Responsibility of the President and Senate, it is difficult to concieve how it could be increased–Every Consideration that can influence the human mind, such as Honor, Oaths, Reputation, the Love of Country, and domestic affections & attachments afford Security for their Fidelity–

as the Constitution has provided that they shall be men of Talents and Integrity we have good Reason to be persuaded that the Treaties they make will be as advantageous as all Circumstances considered could be expected–~~Besides such Individuals among them as may now~~ and so far as the Fear of Punishment and Disgrace can operate, that motive to good Behaviour is amply supplied and afforded by the article on the Subject of Empeachments

~~In short no Plan If Talent and Integrity, if political Information respecting the State of things at Home and abroad, if Secrecy & Dispatch and the benefit of joint Counsels be desirable~~

In short as this Plan appears at least in Theory to have greatly the advantage of any that has yet appeared, it certainly merits a fair Trial.[4] in Relation to foreign nations–

Altho the People at large may sometimes by Negligence or other Causes be led into indiscreet appointments yet Experience tells us that the State Legislatures very seldom lose Sight of their obvious Interests, or commit their management to men in whom they have little or no Confidence–It is natural therefore to presume that in chusing their Senators they will turn their Eyes to those Citizens who have become destinguished by their Knowledge Abilities & steady good Conduct–and surely Men so destinguished are the men of all others who will carry into the Senate the most political Information both with Respect to their own State & with Respect also to the United States, and to foreign nations–

Let it also be remembered that neither the President nor the members of ye Senate are to pass thro those offices so rapidly as to have little Time or opportunity while in them to encrease their Stock of Information and Experience or become extensively acquainted with the Business they are to transact–The Duration of their offices tho short, will still enable them to digest and introduce some System [and] order into our affairs, before they retire; and as only a Part of the Senate will retire at a Time, a sufficient number of the old ones will remain to carry it on and give necessary Information to the new ones that come in–altho the absolute necessity of order and System in the Conduct of any Business is universally known & acknowledged yet the People of america have not been hitherto sufficiently sensible of its Importance–a popular assembly made up of members constantly coming & going in quick Succession, must necessar[il]y be inadequate to the attainment of any great objects which require to be contemplated in all their Relations and circumstances, and approached by Measures which accurate Information as well as Talents are necessary to concert and to execute–when indeed Danger and Destruction are at our Doors, & men are more anxious for Safety than for Honors, the best men in the Community will be called forth, & will unite their Endeavours & abilities in and this must be the Case not only from the want of Time to mature & to execute, but also from the Difficulty of prevailing on the best Men to place themselves in Situations where they can do little good, and where they are sure to experience the Pain of regretting that under such Circumstances much cannot be done

1. "Elections" in the M'Lean edition.
2. The draft reads: "The Presidt. & Senrs so chosen will doubtless be of the number of those in each State who best understand its Interests, whether considered in Relation to the other States or to foreign Nations; and we must suppose that the members from each State however well disposed to promote the general good of the whole, will yet be still more Strongly disposed to promote that of their immediate constituents."
3. In the draft this sentence reads: "Let it also be remembered that in forming Treaties of Peace & of Commerce & particularly the former, it often happens that perfect Secrecy and immediate Dispatch are requisite[.]"
4. Dawson's printing of the draft stopped at this point. The following material begins a new page and may be an earlier version of the draft.

593. Philadelphia Freeman's Journal, 5 March[1]

One of the principal arguments which the advocates for a *change* in government hold out, is, that if after a trial of the new constitution it will not answer, we can mend it; but such fairy tales cannot deceive people of any understanding, they must only be invented to amuse the weak and foolish among themselves. The fable of the ax-man treacherously supplicating the trees in the forest for a handle to his ax, with which he afterwards destroyed them all, is a sufficient explanation of such a fallacious argument.[2] The freemen of America will remember, that it is very easy to change a *free* government into an arbitrary, despotic, or *military* one: but it is very difficult, almost impossible to reverse the matter–very difficult to regain *freedom* once lost. The struggles now existing between the *people* of France and their government is a striking proof of this; for, that government has lately laid (in addition to the other enormous existing taxes) a very heavy *land tax* of 30 per cent. The people complain of it loudly, but what does this avail? their complaints are treated with contempt, as that government has a large *standing army* at their command, and we find those who dare to complain are banished, or sent to the *Bastile!*–So much for the government of the *well-born few*, and standing armies.

1. Reprints by 7 April (7): Mass. (1), R.I. (2), N.Y. (3), Pa. (1).
2. See CC:506, note 3.

594. Pennsylvania Gazette, 5 March[1]

The American character, says a correspondent, has been traduced as turbulent and disorderly by some foreign nations. The treatment which the great question of the fœderal constitution has received from *all the people* of America fully contradicts that opinion. Though there are individuals in every part of the union, who wish alterations and though there is a majority of that sentiment in a few districts, and although great pains have been taken (probably from a sense of duty in some) to exhibit the constitution in an unfavorable light, yet we have heard of no popular body that has risen against it. While this proves the great majority, who are desirous to obtain or disposed to accept the proposed constitution, it shews the orderly and good dispositions that prevail among that part of the people, who have not yet seen reason to think favorably of the new fœderal government. The Americans seem to be duly impressed with the propriety and duty of making the voice of the majority the law of the land. Could a minority of 49 govern a majority of 51, there would be no possibility of saying at what number it would end. The ambitious and designing, by lessening the minority by degrees, might bring us under the government even of ONE. How dangerous, then, must it appear to every jealous and sincere friend of liberty, to dispense, upon any occasion, with the great rule of republics, that the voice of the majority of the people is *the unalterable law*.

1. Reprints by 15 April (7): N.H. (1), Mass. (1), N.Y. (2), N.J. (1), Pa. (1), Va. (1).

595. "A.B.C."
Pennsylvania Gazette, 5 March[1]

Messieurs PRINTERS, The words FEDERAL and ANTIFEDERAL, like many others, have departed already from their original signification. Instead of being applied only to the friends and enemies of the new government, I find they are applied as epithets to many other things, a short account of which I shall endeavour to furnish you with for your useful paper.

The following is a list of such persons, qualities and articles, as are designated with the epithet of FEDERAL.

General Washington, Dr. Franklin, and all the first and most useful characters in the American revolution.

The mechanics in every part of the United States.

The war-worn officers and soldiers of the late American army.

Widows, orphans, and aged citizens, who have deposited their fortunes in the funds of the United States.

The friends of public credit and national faith are all federal.

Patriotism, integrity and industry, are all *federal* qualities.

Gold and silver are *federal* mediums of commerce.

American nails and paper, cloth buttons, leather breeches, and leather pockets for cloth cloaths, American beer, Hare's porter, New-Jersey and Connecticut cheese, and cyder, Massachusetts womens' shoes, and all other things manufactured in the United States, are *federal*.

In my next address to you, I shall send you a list of *antifederal* persons, qualities and articles.[2]

1. Reprinted: *Massachusetts Centinel*, 19 March; *Massachusetts Gazette*, 21 March; *New Hampshire Spy*, 25 March.
2. No subsequent address has been located.

596. Marcus III
Norfolk and Portsmouth Journal, 5 March[1]

Answers to Mr. Mason's *Objections* to the New Constitution, Recommended by the late Convention at Philadelphia.

VIth. Objection.

"The President of the United States, has the unrestrained power of granting pardons for treason, which may be sometimes exercised to screen from punishment those whom he had secretly instigated to commit the crime, and thereby prevent a discovery of his own guilt."

Answer.

Nobody can contend upon any rational principles, that a power of pardoning should not exist somewhere in every government, because it will often happen in every country, that men are obnoxious to a legal conviction, who yet are entitled, from some favorable circumstances in their case, to a merciful interposition in their favor. The advocates of monarchy have accordingly boasted of this, as one of the advantages of that form of government, in preference to a Republican; nevertheless this authority is vested in the Stadtholder in Holland, and I believe is vested in every Executive power in America. It seems to have been wisely the aim of the late Convention in forming a general government for America, to combine the acknowledged advantages of the British Constitution with proper Republican checks, to guard as much as possible against abuses; and it would have been very strange if they had omitted this which has the sanction of such great antiquity in that country, and if I am not mistaken, an universal adoption in America.[a] Those gentlemen who object to other parts of the Constitution, as introducing innovations, contrary to long experience, with a very ill grace attempt to reject an experience so unexceptionable as this, to introduce an innovation (perhaps the first ever suggested) of their own. When a power is acknowledged to be necessary, it is a very dangerous thing to prescribe limits to it; for men must have a greater confidence in their own wisdom than I think any men are entitled to, who imagine they can form such exact ideas of all possible contingencies as to be sure that the restriction they propose will not do more harm than good. The probability of the President of the United States committing an act of treason against his country is very slight; he is so well guarded by the other powers of government, and the natural strength of the people at large must be so weighty, that in my opinion it is the most chimerical apprehension that can be entertained. Such a thing is however possible, and accordingly he is not exempt from a trial, if he should be guilty, or supposed guilty, of that or any other offence. I entirely lay out of the consideration, the improbability of a man honored in such a manner by his country, risquing, like General Arnold, the damnation of his fame to all future ages, though it is a circumstance of some weight in considering, whether, for the sake of such a remote and improbable danger as this, it would be prudent to abridge this power of pardoning in a manner altogether unexampled, and which might produce mischiefs, the extent of which, it is not perhaps easy at present to foresee. In estimating the value of any power it is possible to bestow, we have to chuse between inconveniences of some sort or other, since no institution of man can be entirely free from all. Let us now therefore consider some of the actual inconveniencies which would attend an abridgement of the power of the President in this respect. One of the great advantages attending a single Executive power is, the degree of secrecy and dispatch with which, on critical occasions, such a power can act. In war this advantage will often counterballance the want of many others. Now suppose, in the very midst of a war of extreme consequence to our safety or prosperity, the President could prevail upon a gentleman of abilities to go into the enemy's country, to serve in the useful, but dishonorable character of a spy: Such are certainly maintained by all vigilant governments, and in proportion to the ignominy of the character, and the danger sustained in the enemy's country, ought to be his protection and security in his own. This man renders very useful services; perhaps, by timely information prevents the destruction of his country. Nobody knows of these secret services but the President himself; his adherence however to the enemy is notorious: He is afterwards intercepted in endeavouring to return to his own country, and having been perhaps a man of distinction before, he is proportionably obnoxious to his country at large for his supposed treason. Would it not be monstrous, that the President should not have it in his power to pardon this man? or that it should depend upon mere solicitation and favor, and perhaps, though the President should state the fact as it really was, some zealous partizan, with his jealousy constantly fixed upon the President, might insinuate that in fact the President and he were secret traitors together, and thus obtain a rejection of the President's application. It is a consideration also of some moment, that there is scarcely any accusation more apt to excite popular prejudice than the charge of treason. There is perhaps no country in the world where justice is in general more impartially administered than in England; yet let any man read some of the trials for treason in that country even since the Revolution, he will see sometimes a fury influencing the Judges, as well as the Jury, that is extremely disgraceful. There may happen a case in our country, where a man in reality innocent, but with strong plausible circumstances against him, would be so obnoxious to popular resentment, that he might be convicted upon very slight and insufficient proof. In such a case it would certainly be very proper for a cool, temperate man of high authority, and who might be supposed uninfluenced by private motives, to interfere, and prevent the popular current proving an innocent man's ruin. I know men who write with a view to flatter the people, and not to give them honest information, may misrepresent this account, as an invidious imputation on the usual impartiality of Juries. God knows, no man more highly reverences that blessed institution than I do: I consider them the natural safeguard of the personal liberties of a free people, and I believe they would much seldomer err in the administration of justice, than any other tribunal whatever. But no man of experience and candor will deny the probability of such a case as I have supposed, sometimes, tho' rarely happening; and whenever it did happen, surely so safe a remedy as a prerogative of mercy in the chief magistrate of a great country, ought to be at hand. There is little danger of an abuse of such a power, when we know how apt most men are in a Republican government, to court popularity at too great an expence, rather than to do a just and beneficent action, in opposition to strong prevailing prejudices, among the people. But, says Mr. Mason, "The President may sometimes exercise this power to screen from punishment those whom he had secretly instigated to commit the crime, and thereby prevent a discovery of his own guilt." This is possible, but the probability of it is surely too slight to endanger the consequences of abridging a power which seems so generally to have been deemed necessary in every well regulated government. It may also be questioned, whether, supposing such a participation of guilt, the President would not expose himself to greater danger by pardoning, than by suffering the law to have its course. Was it not supposed, by a great number of intelligent men, that Admiral Byng's execution was urged on to satisfy a discontented populace, when the Administration, by the weakness of the force he was entrusted with, were, perhaps the real cause of the miscarriage before Minorca?[2] Had he been acquitted, or pardoned he could perhaps have exposed the real fault: As a prisoner under so heavy a charge, his recrimination would have been discredited as merely the effort of a man in despair to save himself from an ignominious punishment. If a President should pardon an accomplice, that accomplice then would be an unexceptionable witness. Before, he would be a witness with a rope about his own neck, struggling to get clear of it at all events. Would any men of understanding, or at least ought they to credit an accusation from a person under such circumstances?[b]

VIIth. Objection.

"By declaring all treaties supreme laws of the land, the Executive and the Senate have in many cases an exclusive power of legislation, which might have been avoided by proper distinctions with respect to treaties, and requiring the assent of the House of Representatives, where it could be done with safety."

Answer.

Did not Congress very lately unanimously resolve in adopting the very sensible letter of Mr. Jay, that a treaty when once made pursuant to the sovereign authority, *ex vi termini* became immediately the law of the land?[3] It seems to result unavoidably from the nature of the thing, that when the constitutional right to make treaties is exercised, the treaty so made should be binding upon those who delegated authority for that purpose. If it was not, what foreign power would trust us? And if this right was restricted by any such fine checks as Mr. Mason has in his imagination, but has not thought proper to disclose, a critical occasion might arise, when for want of a little rational confidence in our own government, we might be obliged to submit to a master in an enemy. Mr. Mason wishes the House of Representatives to have some share in this business; but he is immediately sensible of the impropriety of it, and adds, "Where it could be done with safety." And how is it to be known whether it can be done with safety or not, but during the pendency of a negociation? Must not the President and Senate judge, whether it can be done with safety or not? If they are of opinion it is unsafe, and the House of Representatives of course not consulted, what becomes of this boasted check, since if it amounts to no more than that the President and Senate may consult the House of Representatives if they please, they may do this as well without such a provision as with it? Nothing would be more easy than to assign plausible reasons after the negociation was over, to shew that a communication was unsafe, and therefore surely a precaution that could be so easily eluded, if it was not impolitic to the greatest degree, must be thought trifling indeed. It is also to be observed, that this authority so obnoxious in the new Constitution (which is unfortunate in having little power to please some persons, either as containing new things or old) is vested indefinitely and without restriction in our present Congress,[4] who are a body constituted in the same manner as the Senate is to be; but there is this material difference in the two cases, that we shall have an additional check under the new system of a President of high personal character, chosen by the immediate body of the people.

(To be continued.)

(a) *I have since found, that in the Constitutions of some of the States, there are much stronger restrictions on the Executive authority, in this particular, than I was aware of. In others the restriction only extends to prosecutions carried on by the General Assembly, or the most numerous branch of Legislature; or a contrary provision by law: Virginia is in the latter class.*[5] *But when we consider how necessary it is in many cases to make use of accomplices to convict their associates, and what little regard ought in general to be paid to a guilty man swearing to save his own life, we shall probably think that the jealousies which (by prohibiting pardons before conviction) ever disabled the Executive authority from procuring unexceptionable testimony of this sort, may more fairly be ascribed to the natural irritation of the public mind at the time when the Constitutions were formed, than to an enlarged and full consideration of the whole subject. Indeed, it could scarcely be avoided, that when arms were first taken up in the cause of liberty, to save us from the immediate crush of arbitrary power, we should lean too much rather to the extreme, of weakening than of strengthening the Executive power in our own government. In England, the only restriction upon this power in the King, in case of Crown prosecutions (one or two slight cases excepted) is, that his pardon is not pleadable in bar of an impeachment; but he may pardon after conviction, even on an impeachment; which is an authority not given to our President, who in cases of impeachment has no power either of pardoning or reprieving.*

(b) The evidence of a man confessing himself guilty of the same crime, is undoubtedly admissible; but it is generally, and ought to be always viewed with great suspicion, and other circumstances should be required to corroborate it.

1. For the authorship and circulation of "Marcus," see CC:548.

2. British public opinion was outraged when Admiral John Byng (1704–1757) failed to reinforce the British garrison at Fort St. Philip during the French invasion of Minorca in 1756. Byng was court-martialed; although acquitted of cowardice, he was convicted of not having done his utmost and was executed.

3. On 13 October 1786 Secretary for Foreign Affairs John Jay sent Congress a long report concerning infractions of the Treaty of Peace. Among other things, the report proposed a resolution stating that treaties could not be interpreted or limited by the states because once "constitutionally made, ratified and published, they become, in virtue of the Confederation, part of the law of the land, and are not only independent of the will and power of such Legislatures, but also binding and obligatory on them." This resolution was unanimously adopted by Congress on 21 March 1787 and was sent to the states on 13 April (JCC, XXXI, 869-70; XXXII, 124-25; and LMCC, VIII, 575).

4. Article IX of the Articles of Confederation gave Congress "the sole and exclusive right and power of . . . entering into treaties and alliances, provided that no treaty" restrain the states from imposing the same imposts and duties on foreigners as their own people were charged or prohibiting the importation or exportation of any commodity (CDR, 89).

5. Every state constitution except South Carolina's provided for pardons. Four prohibited pardons in impeachments and five prior to conviction. In Rhode Island and Connecticut, pardons were granted by the legislature, and in the other states, the power generally resided in the governor, sometimes shared with the council. In Maryland, the power to pardon was given to the governor "except in such cases where the law shall otherwise direct"; in Delaware, Virginia, and North Carolina, the governor could not issue pardons if the prosecution was done by the legislature or the lower house, or if the pardoning power was otherwise directed by law. In New York, Pennsylvania, and Georgia, the legislatures had the ultimate power to grant pardons in cases of treason, the governor being limited to issuing a reprieve and reporting to the legislature (Thorpe, I, 534, 563; II, 788; III, 1696, 1901; IV, 2464; V, 2596, 2633, 2791, 3087; VI, 3215; VII, 3817).

597. Jeremiah Hill to George Thatcher
Biddeford, Maine, 6 March (excerpt)[1]

. . . you say that you are convinced of your former Error respecting two or three branches in legislation, when any one voluntarily acknowledges an Error it is a sure index of an open mind and in politicks of a diligent inquirer, for nothing will make a man a great Politician but a thorough examination into humane Nature, the rise and progress of different States and like wise and prudent navigators set up perches on every Rock & quick sand where others have struck, split & totally sunk–while Man is Man *self* will be a darling favorite, and when new States are forming every one who have Ideas of selfishness, (and if a man has nothing of that it is a sure mark he don't deserve any thing) will be planing for *one at least* and if he can plan in an honest way so as to take Care of one, he must sustain the Character of a good Citizen, and ought to be encouraged according to his Abilities, for if he dont take Care for himself and those of his own household how can the State expect he will take Care for them–the Conversation respecting the new Constitution is chiefly subsided. I believe the people in general are satisfied in favor of its adoption, Esqr. Staple[2] you know is a mighty Christian he says it is for the best for the Powers that be are ordained of God and he that resisteth the ordinance must receive a dreadful Sentence, therefore he submits not only for wrath but also for Conscience sake, you seem to predict the destruction of the state debts or rather what we call state securities I have been fully convinced of that doctrine ever since I first went to the general Court–you say the impost & Excise at present does not exceed a Million Dollars a year, how do you mean? thrō the united States? does all the States have excise Laws & if they have do they operate in that uniformity they would if there were a Chain of Continental revenue officers under the general System from Florida to Nova-Scotia when all smugling from State to State will be prevented which it is now almost impossible to do. I never was very famous in Castle-building, therefore never have planned for those great matters taking place under the new Constitution, however I dare predict it will be better than it is at present under the old rack which we are now sinking on. a general System of Revenue Laws put in opperation thrō the united States will be twenty per Cent more in the Treasury than it now is, with the same duties on every Article only think how easy it is to smuggle from Rhode Island to the adjacent States as also from New hampshire &c. &c. which upon a general System will be prevented. . . .

1. RC, Chamberlain Collection, Thatcher Papers, MB. Postmarked: "PORTSMOUTH/ MARCH 11."
2. Either Benjamin or David Staples of Washington Plantation which was about fifteen miles northwest of Biddeford–Jeremiah Hill's home. As a justice of the peace for Biddeford, Hill's area of jurisdiction included Washington Plantation.

598. Brutus XIV
New York Journal, 6 March[1]

(Continued.)

It may still be insisted that this clause does not take away the trial by jury on appeals, but that this may be provided for by the legislature, under that paragraph which authorises them to form regulations and restrictions for the court in the exercise of this power.

The natural meaning of this paragraph seems to be no more than this, that Congress may declare, that certain cases shall not be subject to the appellate jurisdiction, and they may point out the mode in which the court shall proceed in bringing up the causes before them, the manner of their taking evidence to establish the facts, and the method of the courts proceeding. But I presume they cannot take from the court the right of deciding on the fact, any more than they can deprive them of the right of determining on the law, when a cause is once before them; for they have the same jurisdiction as to fact, as they have as to the law. But supposing the Congress may under this clause establish the trial by jury on appeals. It does not seem to me that it will render this article much less exceptionable. An appeal from one court and jury, to another court and jury, is a thing altogether unknown in the laws of our state, and in most of the states in the union. A practice of this kind prevails in the eastern states; actions are there commenced in the inferior courts, and an appeal lies from them on the whole merits to the superior courts: the consequence is well known, very few actions are determined in the lower courts; it is rare that a case of any importance is not carried by appeal to the supreme court, and the jurisdiction of the inferior courts is merely nominal; this has proved so burthensome to the people in Massachusetts, that it was one of the principal causes which excited the insurrection in that state, in the year past;[2] very few sensible and moderate men in that state but what will admit, that the inferior courts are almost entirely useless, and answer very little purpose, save only to accumulate costs against the poor debtors who are already unable to pay their just debts.

But the operation of the appellate power in the supreme judicial of the United States, would work infinitely more mischief than any such power can do in a single state.

The trouble and expence to the parties would be endless and intolerable. No man can say where the supreme court are to hold their sessions, the presumption is, however, that it must be at the seat of the general government: in this case parties must travel many hundred miles, with their witnesses and lawyers, to prosecute or defend a suit; no man of midling fortune, can sustain the expence of such a law suit, and therefore the poorer and midling class of citizens will be under the necessity of submitting to the demands of the rich and the lordly, in cases that will come under the cognizance of this court. If it be said, that to prevent this oppression, the supreme court will set in different parts of the union, it may be replied, that this would only make the oppression somewhat more tolerable, but by no means so much as to give a chance of justice to the poor and midling class. It is utterly impossible that the supreme court can move into so many different parts of the Union, as to make it convenient or even tolerable to attend before them with witnesses to try causes from every part of the United states; if to avoid the expence and inconvenience of calling witnesses from a great distance, to give evidence before the supreme court, the expedient of taking the deposition of witnesses in writing should be adopted, it would not help the matter. It is of great importance in the distribution of justice that witnesses should be examined face to face, that the parties should have the fairest opportunity of cross examining them in order to bring out the whole truth; there is something in the manner in which a witness delivers his testimony which cannot be committed to paper, and which yet very frequently gives a complexion to his evidence, very different from what it would bear if committed to writing, besides the expence of taking written testimony would be enormous; those who are acquainted with the costs that arise in the courts, where all the evidence is taken in writing, well know that they exceed beyond all comparison those of the common law courts, where witnesses are examined viva voce.

The costs accruing in courts generally advance with the grade of the court; thus the charges attending a suit in our common pleas, is much less than those in the supreme court, and these are much lower than those in the court of chancery; indeed the costs in the last mentioned court, are in many cases so exorbitant and the proceedings so dilatory that the suitor had almost as well give up his demand as to prosecute his suit. We have just reason to suppose, that the costs in the supreme general court will exceed either of our courts; the officers of the general court will be more dignified than those of the states, the lawyers of the most ability will practice in them, and the trouble and expence of attending them will be greater. From all these considerations, it appears, that the expence attending suits in the supreme court will be so great, as to put it out of the power of the poor and midling class of citizens to contest a suit in it.

From these remarks it appears, that the administration of justice under the powers of the judicial will be dilatory; that it will be attended with such an heavy expence as to amount to little short of a denial of justice to the poor and middling class of people who in every government stand most in need of the protection of the law; and that the trial by jury, which has so justly been the boast of our fore fathers as well as ourselves is taken away under them.

These extraordinary powers in this court are the more objectionable, because there does not appear the least necessity for them, in order to secure a due and impartial distribution of justice.

The want of ability or integrity, or a disposition to render justice to every suitor, has not been objected against the courts of the respective states: so far as I have been informed, the courts of justice in all the states, have ever been found ready, to administer justice with promptitude and impartiality according to the laws of the land; It is true in some of the states, paper money has been made, and the debtor authorised to discharge his debts with it, at a depreciated value, in others, tender laws have been passed, obliging the creditor to receive on execution other property than money in discharge of his demand, and in several of the states laws have been made unfavorable to the creditor and tending to render property insecure.

But these evils have not happened from any defect in the judicial departments of the states; the courts indeed are bound to take notice of these laws, and so will the courts of the general government be under obligation to observe the laws made by the general legislature; not repugnant to the constitution; but so far have the judicial been from giving undue latitude of construction to laws of this kind, that they have invariably strongly inclined to the other side. All the acts of our legislature, which have been charged with being of this complexion, have uniformly received the strictest construction by the judges, and have been extended to no cases but to such as came within the strict letter of the law. In this way, have our courts, I will not say evaded the law, but so limited it in its operation as to work the least possible injustice: the same thing has taken place in Rhode-Island, which has justly rendered herself infamous, by her tenaciously adhering to her paper money system. The judges there gave a decision, in opposition to the words of the Statute, on this principle, that a construction according to the words of it, would contradict the fundamental maxims of their laws and constitution.[3]

No pretext therefore, can be formed, from the conduct of the judicial courts which will justify giving such powers to the supreme general court, for their decisions have been such as to give just ground of confidence in them, that they will firmly adhere to the principles of rectitude, and there is no necessity of lodging these powers in the courts, in order to guard against the evils justly complained of, on the subject of security of property under this constitution. For it has provided, "that no state shall emit bills of credit, or make any thing but gold and silver coin a tender in payment of debts." It has also declared, that "no state shall pass any law impairing the obligation of contracts."–These prohibitions give the most perfect security against those attacks upon property which I am sorry to say some of the states have but too wantonly made, by passing laws sanctioning fraud in the debtor against his creditor. For "this constitution will be the supreme law of the land, and the judges in every state will be bound thereby; any thing in the constitution and laws of any state to the contrary notwithstanding."

The courts of the respective states might therefore have been securely trusted, with deciding all cases between man and man, whether citizens of the same state or of different states, or between foreigners and citizens, and indeed for ought I see every case that can arise under the constitution or laws of the United States, ought in the first instance to be tried in the court of the state, except those which might arise between states, such as respect ambassadors, or other public ministers, and perhaps such as call in question the claim of lands under grants from different states. The state courts would be under sufficient controul, if writs of error were allowed from the state courts to the supreme court of the union, according to the practice of the courts in England and of this state, on all cases in which the laws of the union are concerned, and perhaps to all cases in which a foreigner is a party.

This method would preserve the good old way of administering justice, would bring justice to every man's door, and preserve the inestimable right of trial by jury. It would be following, as near as our circumstances will admit, the practice of the courts in England, which is almost the only thing I would wish to copy in their government.

But as this system now stands, there is to be as many inferior courts as Congress may see fit to appoint, who are to be authorised to originate and in the first instance to try all the cases falling under the description of this article; there is no security that a trial by jury shall be had in these courts, but the trial here will soon become, as it is in Massachusetts' inferior courts, mere matter of form; for an appeal may be had to the supreme court on the whole merits. This court is to have power to determine in law and in equity, on the law and the fact, and this court is exalted above all other power in the government, subject to no controul, and so fixed as not to be removeable, but upon impeachment, which I shall hereafter shew, is much the same thing as not to be removeable at all.

To obviate the objections made to the judicial power it has been said, that the Congress, in forming the regulations and exceptions which they are authorised to make respecting the appellate jurisdiction, will make provision against all the evils which are apprehended from this article. On this I would remark, that this way of answering the objection made to the power, implies an admission that the power is in itself improper without restraint, and if so, why not restrict it in the first instance.

The just way of investigating any power given to a government, is to examine its operation supposing it to be put in exercise. If upon enquiry, it appears that the power, if exercised, would be prejudicial, it ought not to be given. For to answer objections made to a power given to a government, by saying it will never be exercised, is really admitting that the power ought not to be exercised, and therefore ought not to be granted.

1. For the first part of "Brutus" XIV, see CC:576. The second part was not reprinted.

2. The county courts of common pleas in Massachusetts had only civil jurisdiction, many of their cases being concerned with debts. The fees paid by the litigants were high. The costs were escalated because most parties appealed the decisions of these

courts to the supreme judicial court. For example, between 1784 and 1786 the supreme judicial court heard 3,800 cases for recognizance of debts already upheld by county courts. Some people even went so far as to call for the abolition of the county courts because all their cases could be appealed to the supreme judicial court (Van Beck Hall, *Politics Without Parties: Massachusetts, 1780–1791* [Pittsburgh, 1972], 48, 192–98).

3. In September 1786 the Rhode Island Superior Court, in the case of *Trevett* v. *Weeden*, declared unconstitutional a law that provided penalties for anyone convicted of depreciating the state's paper money. The justices who supported the decision were not reappointed by the Assembly in May 1787.

599. John Page to Thomas Jefferson
Rosewell, Va., 7 March (excerpt)[1]

. . . I have long wished for a leisure Hour to write to you, but really could not command one till now; when by means of an uncommon spell of severe Weather, & a deep Snow, I am caught at Home alone, having left my Family at York, to attend on the Election of Delegates to serve in Convention in June next–I came over, offered my Services to the Free-holders in a long Address which took me an Hour & an half to deliver it, in which I explained the Principles of the Plan of the fœderal Constitution & shewed the Defects of the Confederation declaring myself a Friend to the former; & that I wished it might be adopted without losing Time in fruitless Attempts to make Amendments which might be made with more probablility of Success in the Manner pointed out by the Constitution itself–I candidly confessed that I had been at first an Enemy to the Constitution proposed,[2] & had endeavoured to fix on some Plan of Amendments; but finding that Govr. Randolph, Col. Mason, & Col. Lee differed in their Ideas of Amendments, & not one of them agreed with me in Objections, I began to suspect that our Objections were founded on wrong Principles; or that we should have agreed; & therefore I set to work; & examined over again the Plan of the Constitution; & soon found, that the Principles we had applied were such as might apply to the Government of a single State, but not to the complicated Government, of 13, perhaps 30 States which were to be *united*, so as to be *one* in Interest Strength & Glory; & yet to be severally sovereign & independent, as to their municipal Laws, & local Circumstances (except in a few Instances which might clash with the general Good); that such a general Government was necessary as could command the Means of mutual Support, more effectually than mere Confederacies Leagues & Alliances, that is, a Government which for fœderal Purposes should have all the Activity Secresy & Energy which the best regulated Governments in the World have; & yet that this, should be brought about, without establishg a Monarchy or an Aristocracy; & without violating the [just?] Principles of democratical Governments. I say I confessed, that, when I considered, that this was to be the Nature of the Government which was necessary to be adopted in the United States I found that the Objections which might be made [---] a single State thus governed, would not apply to this great delicate & complicated Machinery of Government, & that the Plan proposed by the Convention was perhaps the best which could be devised–I have run myself out of Breath in a long winded Sentence, & lost a deal of Time in telling you what I might as well have said in three Words,–vizt, that after all my Trouble the Freeholders left me far behind, Warner Lewis & Thos. Smith[3] on the Lists of Candidates. I had however this Consolation, that I was not rejected on Account of my Attachment to the Constitution–for those two Gentlemen openly avowed the same Sentiments which I had declared in my Address to the People. Many of my Friends were very much mortified at the Disappointment we met with, & thought they comforted me by telling me of the extreme badness of the Weather which they said prevented many Freeholders from attending on the Election, but I comforted myself with the Reflection that I had adhered to my Resolution of treating the Freeholders like free Men; having never insulted them upon such Occasions by Solicitations & Caresses; & that they would now see clearly the Impropriety of engaging their Votes; & I comfort myself now, with the Reflection, that I shall have a little more Leisure to attend to my Affairs & to my Friends. . . .

1. RC, Jefferson Papers, DLC. Printed: Boyd, XII, 650–54. Page (1744–1808), the owner of a Gloucester County, Va., plantation named Rosewell, was a member of the House of Burgesses, 1771–73, and the House of Delegates, 1781–83, 1785, 1786, 1788, 1797, and 1800; a member of the Council of State and lieutenant governor, 1776–80; a member of the U.S. House of Representatives, 1789–97; and governor, 1802–5. He had attended William and Mary College with Jefferson, and they were lifelong friends.

2. On 9 December James Madison wrote Jefferson that "Genl. Nelson, Mr. Jno. Page, Col. Bland, &c. are also opponents, but on what principle and to what extent, I am equally at a loss to say" (CC:334). But on 14 January Archibald Stuart informed Madison that "Mr. Page of Rosewell has become a Convert" (Rutland, *Madison*, X, 374).

3. Lewis, a former state senator, and Smith, a member of the House of Delegates, voted to ratify the Constitution in the state Convention in June.

600. Samuel Phillips Savage to George Thatcher
Weston, Mass., 7 March[1]

The little I have in the World, is in consolidated, or what is called consolidated, Notes of this Goverment, Loan Office Certificates and Soldiers final settlements, of all which, I never bought one, and a person with a thousand pounds, nominal value, in his pocket, may be carried to a Goal for a Debt he owes the Goverment, the united States, or even a private person of one quarter of the Sum, altho they were given for money lent or Service done–Is it in the least probable the debt will ever be paid? or is there reason to hope the sum will be funded and an Interest annually be paid thereon? If the latter, it is perhaps as much as the Creditors of Governts can at present expect, and, if punctuality observed in payment, it may be as much as they ever wish for: for altho every body is clamoring, yet all are convinced, it is not, at present in the power of Government to pay the principal, while few, very few believe that the Intt. might not be discharg'd as it arises. I have somewhere met with that wise saying, "this ought ye to have done and not leave the others undone" it is undoubtedly right that the Interest of those large sums, so generously lent us by France &c &c should be punctually paid, but to what cause can it be assigned that the poor Soldier, who stood between us and bullets wingd with Death, should be turnd off with his Intt. once in 3 or 4 years, & then paid in paper, which he sells for 3/ or 4/ in the pound.–

Every thinking man laments the want of Energy in your Body, and the mighty Clamor & Opposition to the new Goverment arises *chiefly* from the Enimies of all good Governmts, who wish it ever may remain so, let the pretentions be what they may, this is the sole, bottom and only reason for the Opposition with them–some there be, who really act conscientiously, and if any fault there be in them, it lays not in their hearts.–the political Creed of the former is that as the Earth was given to the Children of Men, & that every Man ought to go Share and Share alike, let the Industry, Services or Merit of some be what it may: this Creed I believe is not confined only to the Northern States, it seems at present to be too much the temper of the idle, the lazy and the Debtors throughout all the States, and I fear unless ~~some~~ there be more energy in Govt than there is at present, it will ere long be the sine qua non of every one whose election is made sure among us.–blessed times these! when a Shaise or some other daring, desperate and enterprising Genius, may, with less trouble, take the reins of Governt than a Cromwell.

I said above there were two Sorts of Men, who opposed the adoption of the new Governmt–does not the Conduct of N Hampshire prove there are others–think you not, that selfish motives influenced some, from the hope of Commerce being forced to their ports by the wholsome Duties that will (if the Constitution be adopted) undoubtedly be laid by Congress on those States who do adopt it. It is this narrow contracted Spirit, that has led us on thus far to distruction, and which if pursued, will seal our political Misery.–

This leaves us all well. Mrs. Savage begs her remembrance–I cordially wish you all happiness and am affectionately Yours–

[P.S.] Since I finished the foregoing I am informed that the fa[mous] or [in]famous Dr. Tayler,[2] with many others of the same kidney, who were members of the late Convention, & are members also of the Genl Court, have in the Week past been trying to raise a Storm in the Court, about the new proposed Constitution, in which your Neighbour Wedgery[3] of new Glocesters, did himself singular honour; by declaring that the Constitution had had a fair ~~hearing and~~ Discussion by a Body, authorised to recieve or reject it, and that the Opponents had been fairly beaten–and also that he thot the G. Court had nothing to do with it–After 3 or 4 Days scolding, a Question was put and carried by the federalists 60 to 30–here ~~ended~~ rests the Matter until some evil Spirit shall again canjur it up.–[4]

1. RC, Thatcher Papers, MB. Savage (1718-1797), a farmer and former Boston merchant, was Thatcher's father-in-law. He was a Boston selectman, 1760-61, and, for most of the Revolution, was president of the Massachusetts Board of War. Savage was a judge of the Middlesex County Inferior Court, 1775-82, and of the Court of Common Pleas, 1782-97.

2. John Taylor (1734-1794) of Douglas, Worcester County, was a physician. He was one of the most frequent spokesmen against the Constitution in the Massachusetts Convention, where he voted against ratification on 6 February. After the vote on ratification, Taylor told the Convention that "he had uniformly opposed the constitution, that he found himself fairly beat, and expressed his determination to go home, and endeavour to infuse a spirit of harmony and love, among the people" (*Massachusetts Gazette*, 8 February).

3. William Widgery of New Gloucester, Cumberland County, Maine, was also a frequent spokesman against the Constitution who voted against ratification. After the vote, he had preceded Dr. Taylor in making conciliatory remarks. Widgery said "that he should return to his constituents, and inform them, that he had opposed the adoption of this constitution, but that he had been overruled, and that he had been carried by a majority of wise and understanding men: that he should endeavour to sow the seeds of union and peace among the people he represented–and that he hoped, and believed, that no person would wish for, or suggest the measure of a PROTEST; for, said he, we must consider that this body is as full a representation of the people, as can be conceived. . . . he concluded by saying he should support, as much as in him lay, the constitution, and believed, as this state had adopted it, not only 9, but the whole 13 would come into the measure" (*ibid.*).

4. See CC:566.

601. Publius: The Federalist 65
New York Packet, 7 March

This and all of the remaining "Publius" essays were written by Alexander Hamilton. Madison had returned to his Virginia home on 3 or 4 March (CC:587); while Jay's contributions ended with number 64 (CC:592). Essay number 65 was reprinted in the New York *Independent Journal* on 8 March. It is number 65 in the M'Lean edition and number 64 in the newspapers.

For a general discussion of the authorship, circulation, and impact of *The Federalist*, see CC:201, 639.

The FŒDERALIST, No. 64.
To the People of the State of New-York.

The remaining powers, which the plan of the Convention allots to the Senate, in a distinct capacity, are comprised in their participation with the Executive in the appointment to offices, and in their judicial character as a court for the trial of impeachments. As in the business of appointments the Executive will be the principal agent, the provisions relating to it will most properly be discussed in the examination of that department.[1] We will therefore conclude this head with a view of the judicial character of the Senate.

A well constituted court for the trial of impeachments, is an object not more to be desired than difficult to be obtained in a government wholly elective. The subjects of its jurisdiction are those offences which proceed from the misconduct of public men, or in other words from the abuse or

violation of some public trust. They are of a nature which may with peculiar propriety be denominated POLITICAL, as they relate chiefly to injuries
done immediately to the society itself. The prosecution of them, for this
reason, will seldom fail to agitate the passions of the whole community,
and to divide it into parties, more or less friendly, or inimical, to the
accused. In many cases, it will connect itself with the pre-existing factions,
and will inlist all their animosities, partialities, influence and interest on
one side, or on the other; and in such cases there will always be the greatest danger, that the decision will be regulated more by the comparitive
strength of parties than by the real demonstrations of innocence or guilt.

The delicacy and magnitude of a trust, which so deeply concerns the
political reputation and existence of every man engaged in the administration of public affairs, speak for themselves. The difficulty of placing it
rightly in a government resting entirely on the basis of periodical elections
will as readily be perceived, when it is considered that the most conspicuous characters in it will, from that circumstance, be too often the leaders,
or the tools of the most cunning or the most numerous faction; and on this
account can hardly be expected to possess the requisite neutrality towards
those, whose conduct may be the subject of scrutiny.

The Convention, it appears, thought the Senate the most fit depositary
of this important trust. Those who can best discern the intrinsic difficulty
of the thing will be least hasty in condemning that opinion; and will be
most inclined to allow due weight to the arguments which may be supposed to have produced it.

What it may be asked is the true spirit of the institution itself? Is it not
designed as a method of NATIONAL INQUEST into the conduct of public men?
If this be the design of it, who can so properly be the inquisitors for the
nation, as the representatives of the nation themselves? It is not disputed
that the power of originating the inquiry, or in other words of preferring
the impeachment ought to be lodged in the hands of one branch of the
legislative body; will not the reasons which indicate the propriety of this
arrangement, strongly plead for an admission of the other branch of that
body to a share in the inquiry? The model, from which the idea of this
institution has been borrowed, pointed out that course to the Convention:
In Great Britain, it is the province of the house of commons to prefer the
impeachment; and of the house of lords to decide upon it. Several of the
State constitutions have followed the example. As well the latter as the
former seem to have regarded the practice of impeachments, as a bridle in
the hands of the legislative body upon the executive servants of the government. Is not this the true light in which it ought to be regarded?

Where else, than in the Senate could have been found a tribunal sufficiently dignified, or sufficiently independent? What other body would be
likely to feel *confidence enough in its own situation*, to preserve unawed and
uninfluenced the necessary impartiality between an *individual* accused, and
the *representatives of the people, his accusers*?

Could the Supreme Court have been relied upon as answering this description? It is much to be doubted whether the members of that tribunal would, at all times, be endowed with so eminent a portion of fortitude, as would be called for in the execution of so difficult a task; & it is still more to be doubted, whether they would possess the degree of credit and authority, which might, on certain occasions, be indispensable, towards reconciling the people to a decision, that should happen to clash with an accusation brought by their immediate representatives. A deficiency in the first would be fatal to the accused; in the last, dangerous to the public tranquility. The hazard in both these respects could only be avoided, if at all, by rendering that tribunal more numerous than would consist with a reasonable attention to œconomy. The necessity of a numerous court for the trial of impeachments is equally dictated by the nature of the proceeding. This can never be tied down by such strict rules, either in the delineation of the offence by the prosecutors, or in the construction of it by the Judges, as in common cases serve to limit the discretion of courts in favor of personal security. There will be no jury to stand between the Judges, who are to pronounce the sentence of the law and the party who is to receive or suffer it. The awful discretion, which a court of impeachments must necessarily have, to doom to honor or to infamy the most confidential and the most distinguished characters of the community, forbids the commitment of the trust to a small number of persons.

These considerations seem alone sufficient to authorise a conclusion, that the Supreme Court would have been an improper substitute for the Senate, as a court of impeachments. There remains a further consideration which will not a little strengthen this conclusion. It is this–The punishment, which may be the consequence of conviction upon impeachment, is not to terminate the chastisement of the offender. After having been sentenced to a perpetual ostracism from the esteem and confidence, the honors and emoluments of his country; he will still be liable to prosecution and punishment in the ordinary course of law. Would it be proper that the persons, who had disposed of his fame and his most valuable rights as a citizen in one trial, should in another trial, for the same offence, be also the disposers of his life and his fortune? Would there not be the greatest reason to apprehend, that error in the first sentence would be the parent of error in the second sentence? That the strong bias of one decision would be apt to overrule the influence of any new lights, which might be brought to vary the complexion of another decision? Those, who know any thing of human nature, will not hesitate to answer these questions in the affirmative; and will be at no loss to perceive, that by making the same persons Judges in both cases, those who might happen to be the objects of prosecution would in a great measure be deprived of the double security, intended them by a double trial. The loss of life and estate would often be virtually included in a sentence, which, in its terms, imported nothing more than dismission from a present, and disqualification for a future office. It may be said, that the intervention of a jury, in the second instance, would obviate the danger. But juries are frequently influenced by the opinions of Judges. They are sometimes induced to find special verdicts which refer the main question to the decision of the court. Who would be willing to stake his life and his estate upon the verdict of a jury, acting under the auspices of Judges, who had predetermined his guilt?

Would it have been an improvement of the plan, to have united the Supreme Court with the Senate, in the formation of the court of impeachments? This Union would certainly have been attended with several advantages; but would they not have been overballanced by the signal disadvantage, already stated, arising from the agency of the same Judges in the double prosecution to which the offender would be liable? To a certain extent, the benefits of that Union will be obtained from making the Chief Justice of the Supreme Court the President of the court of impeachments, as is proposed to be done in the plan of the Convention; while the inconveniences of an intire incorporation of the former into the latter will be substantially avoided. This was perhaps the prudent mean. I forbear to remark upon the additional pretext for clamour, against the Judiciary, which so considerable an augmentation of its authority would have afforded.

Would it have been desirable to have composed the court for the trial of impeachments of persons wholly distinct from the other departments of the government? There are weighty arguments, as well against, as in favor of such a plan. To some minds, it will not appear a trivial objection, that it could tend[2] to increase the complexity of the political machine; and to add a new spring to the government, the utility of which would at best be questionable. But an objection, which will not be thought by any unworthy of attention, is this–A court formed upon such a plan would either be attended with a heavy expence, or might in practice be subject to a variety of casualties and inconveniencies. It must either consist of permanent officers stationary at the seat of government, and of course entitled to fixed and regular stipends, or of certain officers of the State governments, to be called upon whenever an impeachment was actually depending. It will not be easy to imagine any third mode materially different, which could rationally be proposed. As the court, for reasons already given, ought to be numerous; the first scheme will be reprobated by every man, who can compare the extent of the public wants, with the means of supplying them; the second will be espoused with caution by those, who will seriously consider the difficulty of collecting men dispersed over the whole union; the injury to the innocent, from the procrastinated determination of the charges which might be brought against them; the advantage to the guilty, from the opportunities which delay would afford to intrigue and corruption; and in some cases the detriment to the State, from the prolonged inaction of men, whose firm and faithful execution of their duty might have exposed them to the persecution of an intemperate or designing majority in the House of Representatives. Though this latter supposition may seem harsh, and might not be likely often to be verified; yet it ought not to be forgotten, that the dœmon of faction will at certain seasons extend his sceptre over all numerous bodies of men.

But though one or the other of the substitutes which have been examined, or some other that might be devised, should be thought preferable to the plan, in this respect, reported by the Convention, it will not follow, that the Constitution ought for this reason to be rejected. If mankind were to resolve to agree in no institution of government, until every part of it had been adjusted to the most exact standard of perfection, society would soon become a general scene of anarchy, and the world a desart. Where is the standard of perfection to be found? Who will undertake to unite the discordant opinions of a whole community, in the same judgment of it; and to prevail upon one conceited projector to renounce his *infallible* criterion, for the *fallible* criterion of his more *conceited neighbor?* To answer the purpose of the adversaries of the Constitution, they ought to prove, not merely, that particular provisions in it are not the best, which might have been imagined; but that the plan upon the whole is bad and pernicious.

1. See *The Federalist* 67–77, 11 March–2 April (CC:612, 615, 617, 619, 625, 628, 635, 644, 646, 656, 657).

2. "Would" in the M'Lean edition.

602. Arthur Lee's Report of Virginia Antifederalism
7 March

On 7 March the Philadelphia *Independent Gazetteer*, in a widely reprinted article, noted that Arthur Lee, a member of the Confederation's Board of Treasury passing through the city enroute to New York from his Virginia home, had declared that four-fifths of all Virginians were against the Constitution (printed below). A satirical Antifederalist letter–dated Philadelphia, 10 March, and supposedly written by James de Caledonia (James Wilson) to James Bowdoin–stated that "a long time ago" Philadelphia Federalists published items indicating "that most in Virginia were in favor of it [the Constitution], and that *Mason, Lee*, &c. had given up all opposition, when you know it is just the reverse; and unluckily *Lee* passed through this city some days since, and contradicted all we had said" (Philadelphia *Freeman's Journal*, 12 March, Mfm:Pa. 512).

On 11 March the *New York Morning Post*, which had reprinted the *Gazetteer's* original report on the 10th, printed a denial: "The Printer is requested to undeceive the public relative to the intelligence from Virginia, said to have been brought to Philadelphia by the Honourable A. Lee; that gentleman not having given, nor authorised any such intelligence to be given." Also on the 11th the report and a denial appeared in the *New York Packet* and the *New York Journal*. The *Packet's* denial reads: "We are requested to assure the public, that the above intelligence from Virginia, said to have been brought to Philadelphia, by the Hon. Arthur Lee, is *destitute of truth*; that gentleman not having given, nor authorized such information to be given." The denial, in one form or another, was reprinted, by 21 March, in seven of the eleven newspapers which had published the report: N.Y. (4), Pa. (2),

Md. (1). The denial was also printed in two newspapers that had not published the *Gazetteer's* report–the New York *Daily Advertiser*, 11 March, and the Winchester *Virginia Gazette*, 9 April.

Thomas Greenleaf printed a slightly different version of the *Independent Gazetteer's* report in his *New York Journal*. He failed, however, to mention that the report originated in Philadelphia, and since he ran it under a New York dateline, it seemed as if it had originated in New York. Nor did Greenleaf mention Arthur Lee, but only "a gentleman of distinction." Greenleaf's denial–by referring "to the Intelligence from Virginia, said to have been brought to Philadelphia by the Honorable A. Lee" and printed in the *New York Morning Post* on 10 March–made it less than obvious that his denial was repudiating the report that he had printed immediately above it.

Writing for the *New York Morning Post* on 13 March, "W" accused Greenleaf of intentional deception for partisan purposes. He warned Greenleaf that "when his party fails, he must fail with them;–and it will be well for him to remember, that LOW CUNNING has been the beginning of many a man's career to the *Gallows*." The next day Greenleaf defended himself by explaining that he had intended to omit the *Independent Gazetteer's* report entirely and publish only the denial, but that the report was printed "*inadvertently*." He labeled "W's" charge as "too contemptible to be despised."

Arthur Lee was attacked in the *Pennsylvania Mercury* on 15 March by "Inspector," who identified Lee as "an old crazy crony" of Pennsylvania Antifederalist leader George Bryan and as a constant enemy both of George Washington and the state of Pennsylvania. On 17 March the denial got back to Philadelphia. It was printed in the *Independent Gazetteer* under a "New-York, March 11" dateline, with this tag line: ". . . that gentleman [Arthur Lee] not having given nor authorised any such intelligence to be published–although it happens to be *true*." "Dick a Dick," writing in the *New York Journal* on 29 March, also questioned the truthfulness of the denial and criticized Lee for not openly disavowing the report. Lee was told that his original "manuscript was handed to the press by one of your most *intimate* friends; and until you come forward yourself, and declare it to be false, every candid inquirer will view it as an established fact, and that you have on this occasion played the part of a *Janus*."

Philadelphia Independent Gazetteer, 7 March[1]

We hear, that on Monday last passed thro' this city, on his way from Virginia to New-York, the honorable *Arthur Lee*; this gentleman informs, that four-fifths of the people of Virginia are opposed to the new constitution:[2] and that so far from there being any chance of its adoption by that state, that there is great fear they will not allow the necessary additional powers to congress, because they have been so much alarmed by the present conspiracy against their liberties. The same gentleman says, so great a game of deception is carrying on there; that it is generally believed all opposition is at an end in Pennsylvania and elsewhere.

1. Reprints by 2 April (10): N.Y. (4), N.J. (1), Pa. (1), Md. (2), Va. (2).

2. On 26 March the Winchester *Virginia Gazette* reported that "Various are the opinions of our domestic politicians, as to what reception the Federal Constitution will meet with in this State, at the ensuing Convention; some assert that four fifths of the people are against it; in the lower counties, it is generally believed, a great majority is decidedly opposed to it. Time only can determine the important event." This report was

reprinted in the Philadelphia *Independent Gazetteer*, 8 April, and the Baltimore *Maryland Gazette*, 15 April.

603. Philadelphia Independent Gazetteer, 7 March[1]

A real state of the proposed constitution in the
United States.

Adopted by the delinquent counties of *Jersey, Delaware, Connecticut, Georgia*: that is, by a few leading men in those counties; for the *people* in them, have never been allowed any information on this important business, their news-papers having been all mufled by these leading characters. Still the opposition to it among the people in those states is considerable.

In the state of *Pennsylvania* it was adopted by an illegal mob convention, under the direction of the city junto: the majority in this convention were only elected by about 1-12th[2] of the suffrages of the freemen of the state: And so entirely against the real sense of the state that it will be all undone.

In the state of *Massachusetts*, above three-fourths of the people are warmly opposed to it, even the friends of it themselves would not dare to adopt it without considerable amendment. Much fraud at the election of that convention.

Maryland, three-fourths of that state are against it since the *press* has been opened; convention to meet the latter end of April, supposed they will adjourn till they see what their sister southern states will do.

Virginia, 4-5ths of the people[3] and most of the leading characters are decided against it; their convention not to meet till June. That state will not allow Congress farther than commercial and such general powers, and the impost. They will not allow standing armies, &c. nor part with that grand bulwark of freedom, annual elections and rotation.

North-Carolina is generally opposed to it, convention meets late in July, she will act the same part that Virginia will.

South-Carolina convention meets 12th May, but supposed she will adjourn till July. The country interest, which is two to one in that state, is opposed to it.

New-Hampshire convention adjourned to the third Wednesday in June (to meet in Concord) three-fourths of that state have instructed their respective deputies to vote against it.

New-York convention meets 17th June; except in the city there is few advocates for it: it is expected the city members will be alone in the convention in favor of it.

Rhode-Island, it is almost certain will have nothing to do with it, except it is reduced down to a federal government.

The friends of the proposed constitution will now have to tread back every step they have taken, the people have now discovered their schemes, and will come forward to defend their liberties which was in such danger of being overturned.

The system of deception practised by its advocates, is pretty generally found out by the people; their arts of making each place on the continent believe that every other part but their own was in favor of it, will serve them no longer. Their *runners* and story carriers will no longer be attended to.

1. Reprinted: *New York Morning Post*, 11 March; *New York Journal*, 21 March; *Providence Gazette*, 5 April; Boston *American Herald*, 7 April.
2. See RCS:Pa., 264–65, 553, 587–88.
3. See CC:602.

604. Luther Martin: Reply to Maryland Landholder No. X
Maryland Journal, 7 March

On 26 November and 3 and 24 December the Connecticut "Landholder" IV, V, and VIII attacked Elbridge Gerry for his opposition to the Constitution (*Connecticut Courant*, CC:295, 316, 371). Luther Martin defended Gerry in the *Maryland Journal* on 18 January (CC:460), and on 29 February he was answered by the Maryland "Landholder," No. X (CC:580). The essay printed below is Martin's rejoinder. Martin continued his defense of Gerry and himself in the first two of four numbered addresses to the citizens of Maryland that were published in the *Maryland Journal* on 18 and 21 March (CC:626, 636). Finally, Gerry defended himself as "A Friend and Customer" in the Boston *American Herald* on 18 April (CC:691).

Luther Martin's defense of 7 March, which was announced for publication on 4 March, was reprinted in the Philadelphia *Independent Gazetteer* on 7 April and in the New Jersey *Brunswick Gazette* on 29 July and 5 August. The *Gazette's* reprint was prefaced: "As a publication under the signature of a Landholder addressed to the Hon. Luther Martin, Esq. of the state of Maryland, was circulated in this state; and as I have not seen republished in the papers of this state the Address to Mr. Goddard, and to the Citizens of Maryland, by that gentleman, in answer to the Landholder, I shall esteem it a favor if you will republish them in your paper, by doing which you will oblige many of your readers; and I the more particularly wish them to be republished in your paper, because it circulates through that part of the state where Mr. Martin was born, and where he has many respectable friends and connections." (Martin, the son of a farmer, was born in New Brunswick, N.J., and was graduated from Princeton College.)

On 8 April the *Pennsylvania Mercury* published a letter dated 30 March from Luther Martin requesting that the *Mercury* reprint his defenses from the *Maryland Journal* of 7, 18, and 21 March because the *Mercury* had already reprinted the Maryland "Landholder," No. X. Martin continued: "As I have no doubt your press is conducted upon principles of freedom and impartiality, and that you have no desire to print falsehood and obloquy against me, rather than truth in my favour, I flatter myself you will consider, as an act of justice, that which I request as a favour." Martin did not include copies of his defenses because he assumed that the *Mercury* regularly received the *Maryland Journal*. As a footnote to Martin's letter, the printer of the *Mercury* said that he had not received the *Maryland Journal* of 7 March. (Immediately below this footnote, the *Mercury* reprinted Martin's letter of 18 March.)

A Federalist satirist, apparently influenced by Martin's letter to the *Pennsylvania Mercury*, wrote a fictitious essay that was published in the Philadelphia *Federal Gazette* on 10 April. The address was signed "L-R M-N" and entitled "NUMBER V. *To the Citizens of Maryland*." The Federalist prefaced his essay with this letter to the printer of the *Federal Gazette*: "I observe, that you have republished the Landholder, No. X. against me. Your publishing my fifth Number to the Citizens of Maryland, will be a proof of your impartiality, and will much oblige your humble servant."

Mr. GODDARD, SIR, In consequence of the justice I did Mr. Gerry, on a former occasion, I find myself complimented with an Address in your last Paper.–Whether the Landholder of the Connecticut Courant, and of the Maryland Journal, is the same person, or different, is not very material;– I however incline to the former opinion, as I hope, for the honour of human nature, it would be difficult to find more than one individual, who could be capable of so total a disregard to the principles of truth and honour.

After having made the most unjust and illiberal attack on Mr. Gerry, and stigmatized him as an enemy to his country, and the basest of mankind, for no other reason than a firm and conscientious discharge of an important trust reposed in that gentleman, had I not come in for a share of his censure, I confess I should have been both disappointed and mortified–It would have had at least the appearance, that the Landholder had discovered something in my principles, which he considered congenial with his own–However great may be my political sins, to be cursed with his approbation and applause, would be a punishment much beyond their demerit. But, Sir, at *present*, I mean to confine myself to the original subject of controversy, the injustice of the charges made against Mr. Gerry.

That my veracity will not be questioned when giving my negative to *anonymous* slander, I have the fullest confidence–I have equal confidence that it will be as little questioned by any who know me, even should the Landholder vouchsafe to give the Public his name[1]–a *respectable* name I am sure it *cannot* be–His absolute want of truth and candour in assertions meant to injure the reputation of individuals, whose names are given to the Public, and to hold them up to the indignation of their fellow-citizens, will ever justify this assertion, even should the name belong to one decorated with wealth, or dignified by station.

But the Landholder wishes it to be supposed, that though my veracity should not be doubted, yet my evidence ought to be rejected, and observes, that to comprehend what *credit* ought to be given to it, (by which, I suppose, he means its *sufficiency* if credited) it ought to be known how long I was absent from Convention, as well as the time I attended.

I believe, Sir, whoever will read my former publication, will in a moment perceive, that I there "stated" all the "information" on this subject, that was "necessary" or material, and that I left no defect for the Landholder to supply–I *there* mentioned, that "I took my seat early in June, that I left Philadelphia on the fourth of September, and during that period, was not absent from the Convention *while sitting*, except only five days in the beginning of August, immediately after the Committee of Detail had reported."

I did not state the precise day of June when I took my seat–it was the ninth, not the tenth–a very inconsiderable mistake of the Landholder–But between that day and the fourth of September, he says, that I was absent ten days at Baltimore, and as many at New-York; and thereby insinuates, that an *absence* of *twenty* days *from the Convention* intervened during that period, in *which time* Mr. Gerry might have *made*, and *failed in*, his motion concerning continental money.

A short state of facts is all that is necessary to shew the disingenuity of the Landholder, and that it is very possible to convey a falsehood, or something very much like it, almost in the words of truth–On the twenty-fifth [sixth] of July the Convention *adjourned*, to meet again on the sixth of August–I embraced that opportunity to come to Baltimore, and left Philadelphia on the twenty seventh; I returned on the fourth of August, and on the sixth attended the Convention, with such members as were in town, at which time the Committee of Detail made their report, and many of the members being yet absent, we adjourned to the next day–Mr. Gerry left Philadelphia to go to New-York, the day before I left there to come to Baltimore; he had not returned on Tuesday the seventh of August,[2] when I set out for New-York, from whence I returned and took my seat in Convention on Monday the thirteenth.

It is true that from the twenty-fifth of July to the thirteenth of August, eighteen (not twenty) days had elapsed; but on *one* of those days *I attended*, and on *twelve* of them the *Convention did not meet*; I was therefore perfectly correct in my *original* statement, that from early in June till the fourth of September, I was absent but five days from the Convention while sitting, and in that statement omitted no "necessary information"–It is also true, that of *those eighteen* days Mr. Gerry was absent *twelve* or *thirteen*, and that one of those days when he was not absent was Sunday, on which day the Convention did not meet.

Thus, Sir, by relating facts as they really occurred, we find the only time between early in June and the fourth of September, when such a motion could have been made by Mr. Gerry, without my being present, is narrowed down to four, or at most five days, as I originally stated it, although the Landholder wishes it should be supposed there were twenty days during that period, when it might have taken place without my knowledge, to wit, ten while I was at Baltimore, and as many more while at New-York.

The Landholder also states, that the Convention commenced the fourteenth day of May, and that I did not take my seat till the tenth day of June, by which, if he means any thing, I presume he means to insinuate, that within that portion of time, Mr. Gerry's motion might have been made and rejected. He is here, Sir, equally unfortunate and disingenuous–Though the Convention was to have met by appointment on the fourteenth of May, yet no material business was entered upon till on or about

the *thirtieth* of that month: It was on *that day* that the Convention, having
had certain propositions laid before them by the Honourable Governor of
Virginia, *resolved* to go into a consideration of those propositions[3]–In this
fact I am confident I am not mistaken, as I state the *day* not merely from
my own recollection, from minutes, which I believe to be very correct, in
my possession, of the information given by the Honourable Mr. M'Henry,
to the assembly.[4] The truth is, Sir, that very little progress had been made
by the Convention before I arrived, and that they had not been more than
ten days, or about that time, seriously engaged in business.–The first thing
I did after I took my seat was carefully to examine the journals for information of what had already been done or proposed–I was also furnished
with notes of the debates which had taken place, and can with truth say,
that I made myself "minutely informed" of what had happened before
that period–In the same manner, after my return from New-York, I consulted the *journals*, (for we *were* permitted to *read* them, although we were
not always permitted *to take copies*)–If the motion attributed to Mr. Gerry,
had been made and rejected either before I first took my seat, or while at
New-York, it would have *there* appeared; and that no such motion was
made and rejected during either of those periods, I appeal to the highest
possible authority–I appeal to those very journals, which ought to have
been published, and which we are informed are placed in the possession of
our late Honourable President[5]–But why, Sir, should I appeal to those
journals, or to any other authority? Let the Landholder turn to his *eighth*
number, addressed to the Honourable Mr. Gerry–let him blush, unless
incapable of that sensation, while he reads the following passage! "*Almost
the whole time* during the sitting of the Convention, and until the *constitution*
had received its *present* form, no man was more plausible and conciliating
on every subject than Mr. Gerry," &c. "Thus stood Mr. Gerry till towards the *close of the business*, he introduced a motion respecting the redemption of paper-money"[6]–The *whole time* of the sitting of the Convention
was not *almost* past–The *Constitution* had not received its *present* form–nor
was the *business* drawing towards a *close* until long after I took my seat in
Convention. It is therefore proved by the Landholder himself, that Mr.
Gerry did not make this motion at any time *before* the ninth day of June–
Nay more, in the paper now before me *he* acknowledges, that in his eighth
number he meant (and surely no one ought to know his meaning better
than himself) "to *fix* Mr. Gerry's apostacy to a *period within the last thirteen
days.*"[7] Why then all this misrepresentation of my absence at Baltimore
and New-York? Why the attempt to induce a belief that the Convention
had been engaged in business from the fourteenth of May, and the insinuation that it might have happened in those periods? And why the charge
that in not stating *those facts* I had withheld from the public information
necessary to its forming a right judgment of the credit which ought to be
given to my evidence?

But, Sir, I am really at a loss which most to admire, the depravity of this writer's heart, or the weakness of his head!–Is it possible he should not perceive that the moment he *fixes* the time of Mr. Gerry's motion to the last thirteen days of the Convention, he proves incontestibly the falshood and malice of his charges against that gentleman? for he has expressly stated that this motion and the rejection it received was the cause, and the sole cause, of his apostacy; that "before, there was nothing in the system, as it *now* stands, to which he had any objection, but that *afterwards* he was inspired with the utmost rage and intemperate opposition to the whole system he had formerly praised;"[8]–whereas I have shewn to the clearest demonstration, that a considerable time before the last thirteen days, Mr. Gerry had given the most decided opposition to the system; I have shewn this by recital of facts, which if credited, incontestibly prove it–facts which I again repeat, will never by contradicted by any member of the Convention–I ground this assertion upon the fullest conviction, that it is impossible to find a single person in that number so wicked, as publicly and deliberately to prostitute his name in support of falsehood, and at the same time so weak as to do this when he must be sure of detection.

But the Landholder is willing to have it supposed, that Mr. Gerry might have made the motion in a "*Committee*," and that *there* it might have happened without my knowledge; to such wretched subterfuges is he driven. This evasion, however, will be equally unavailing.

The business of the committees were not of a secret nature, nor were they conducted in a secret manner; I mean as to the members of the Convention. I am satisfied that there was no committee while I was there, of whose proceedings I was not at least "so minutely informed,"[9] that an attempt of so extraordinary a nature as that attributed to Mr. Gerry, and attended with such an immediate and remarkable revolution in his conduct, could not have taken place without my having heard something concerning it.–The non-adoption of a measure by a committee did not preclude its being proposed to the Convention, and being there adopted. Can it be presumed that a question in which Mr. Gerry is represented to have been so deeply interested, and by the fate of which his conduct was entirely influenced, would, for want of success in a *committee*, have been totally relinquished by him, without a single effort to carry it in *Convention?*–If any other proof is wanting, I appeal again to the Landholder himself:–In his *eighth* number he states that the motion was rejected "by the Convention"–Let it be remembered also, as I have before observed, in the paper now before me, he declares it was his intention in *that* number to fix Mr. Gerry's apostacy to a period within the last thirteen days; and in the *same* number he observes, that Mr. Gerry's resentment could only embarrass and delay the *completion* of the business for a *few days*; all which equally militates against every idea of the motion being made before I left Philadelphia, whether in Committee, or in Convention.

The Landholder hath also asserted, that I have "put into Mr. Gerry's mouth, objections different from any thing his letter to the legislature of his state contains, so that if my representation is *true*, his must be *false*."[10] In this charge he is just as well founded as in those I have already noticed.-Mr. Gerry has more than once published to the world, under the sanction of his name, that he opposed the system from a firm persuasion that it would endanger the liberties of America, and destroy the freedom of the states and their citizens.[11] Every word which I have stated as coming from his mouth, so far from being inconsistent with those declarations, are perfectly correspondent thereto, and direct proofs of their truth.

When the Landholder informed us that Mr. Gerry was "face to face with his colleagues in the Convention of Massachusetts,"[12] why did he not, unless he wished to mislead the public, also inform us for what purpose he was there? That it was only to *answer* questions that might be proposed to him, not himself to *ask* questions–that he could not consistently interfere in any manner in the debates–and that he was even prohibited an opportunity of explaining such parts of his conduct as were censured in his presence.[13]

By the anonymous publication alluded to by the Landholder,[14] and inserted in the note, Mr. Gerry's colleagues are not called upon to *acquit* him; it only declares "that he believes them to be men of too much honour to assert that his reasons in Convention were totally different from those he published;"-and in this, I presume, he was not disappointed–the Landholder otherwise would have published it with triumph;-but if Mr. Gerry, as it is insinuated, was only prevented by pride from, in person, requesting them to acquit him, it amounts to a proof of his consciousness that, as men of honour, they could not have refused it, had he made the request.

No person, who views the absurdities and inconsistencies of the Landholder, can, I think, have a very respectable opinion of his understanding; but I, who am not much prejudiced in his favour, could scarcely have conceived him so superlatively weak as to expect to deceive the public and obtain credit to himself, by asking "if the charges against Mr. Gerry are not true, why do not his colleagues contradict them?"[15] and "why is it that we do not see Mr. M'Henry's verification of your assertions?"[16]-If *these* gentlemen were to do Mr. Gerry that justice, he might as well inquire "why is it we do not also see the verification" of A, B, C and D, and so on to the last letter of the conventional alphabet.

When the Landholder, in his eighth number, addressed himself to Mr. Gerry, he introduced his charges by saying, "you doubtless will recollect the following state of facts;-if you do not, *every member* of the Convention will *attest them.*"[17]

One member of the Convention has had firmness sufficient to contradict them with his name, although he was well apprised that he thereby exposed himself as a mark for the arrows of his political adversaries, and as to some of them, he was not unacquainted with what kind of men he had to deal: But of all the members who composed that body, not one has yet stepped forward to make good the Landholder's *prediction*; nor has one been found to *"attest"* his statement of *facts*.

Many reasons may be assigned why the members of the Convention should not think themselves under a *moral* obligation of involving themselves in controversy, by giving their names in vindication of Mr. Gerry; and I do not believe any of those who signed the proposed Constitution would consider themselves bound to do this by any *political* obligation:- But, Sir, I can hardly suppose that Mr. Gerry is so perfectly esteemed and respected by *every* person who had a seat in that body, that not a single individual could possibly be procured to give his sanction to the Landholder's charges, if it could be done with justice; and as to *myself*, I much question whether it would be easy to convince any person, who was present at our information to the assembly, that *every one* of my honourable colleagues (to each of whose merit I cordially subscribe, though compelled to differ from them in political sentiments) would be prevented by motives of personal delicacy to myself, from contradicting the facts I have stated relative to Mr. Gerry, if it could be done consistent with truth.

If the Landholder was a member of the Convention, to facilitate the adoption of a favourite system, or to gratify his resentment against its opposers, he has originally invented, and is now labouring to support, charges the most unjust and ungenerous, contrary to his own knowledge of facts.-If he was not a member, he is acting the same part, without any knowledge of the subject, and in this has the merit of either following his own invention, or of dealing out the information he receives from some person of whom he is the wretched tool and dupe, at the same time expressing himself with a decision, and making such professions of being perfectly in every secret, as naturally tends, unless contradicted, to deceive and delude the unsuspecting multitude.

In *one* of these predicaments the Landholder *must* stand-he is welcome to take his choice-in either case he only wants to be known to be despised.

Now, Sir, let the Landholder come forward and give his name to the public-It is the only thing necessary to finish his character-and to convince the world that he is as dead to shame, as he is lost to truth and destitute of honour.

If I, Sir, can be instrumental in procuring him to disclose himself; even in this I shall consider myself as rendering a service to my country.-I flatter myself, for the dignity of human kind, there are few such characters; but there is no situation in life, in which they may not prove the bane and curse of society;-they, therefore, ought to be known, that they may be guarded against.

Baltimore, March 3, 1788.

1. The Maryland "Landholder," No. X concluded his essay: "I leave you now to your own reflections, under a promise, however, to give my name to the Public, should you be able to procure any indifferent testimony to contradict a single fact I have stated."

2. Gerry first attended the Convention on 29 May. After the Convention adjourned on 26 July to allow the Committee of Detail to draft a constitution, Gerry visited his wife and child who were staying at his father-in-law's home in New York City. Gerry returned to Philadelphia on the evening of 9 August and attended the Convention until it adjourned on 17 September.

3. The Virginia Resolutions were presented to the Convention by Governor Edmund Randolph on 29 May (CDR, 243–45), and the next day the Convention began consideration of them.

4. On 29 November James McHenry read the Virginia Resolutions to the Maryland House of Delegates (CC:304–A). In the first installment of his *Genuine Information*, Martin declared that McHenry had "very faithfully detailed the substance" of Randolph's speech and that, although he was not present, Martin "saw notes which had been taken" of the speech (Baltimore *Maryland Gazette*, 28 December, CC:389).

5. On 17 September the Convention voted ten states to one to deposit "the Journals and other papers of the Convention in the hands of the President" (George Washington). The Maryland delegation–James McHenry, Daniel of St. Thomas Jenifer, and Daniel Carroll–voted against the motion. The Convention then resolved unanimously that the President of the Convention "retain the Journal and other papers, subject to the order of Congress, if ever formed under the Constitution." Washington kept the Journal and papers until 1796 when he turned them over to the Department of State. The Journal was not printed until 1819 (Farrand, I, xi–xii; II, 648).

6. The italics in the quoted material are Martin's.

7. The italics in the quoted material are Martin's. In the Maryland "Landholder," No. X this passage reads: "Is it anywise likely that you could have heard what passed, especially during the last 13 days, within which period the Landholder has fixed the apostacy of Mr. Gerry. . . ."

8. See "Landholder" VIII (CC:371). The italics in the quoted material are Martin's.

9. See Maryland "Landholder," No. X.

10. *Ibid.*

11. See Gerry's letter of 18 October to the Massachusetts legislature published on 3 November (CC:227–A); and his unsigned letter of 3 January to the printer of the *Massachusetts Centinel* published on 5 January (CC:419 and 580).

12. See Maryland "Landholder," No. X.

13. For Gerry's explanation of the limits placed by the Massachusetts Convention upon his activities while appearing before that body, see "State of Facts," Boston *American Herald*, 28 January.

14. Gerry wrote this anonymous defense which was printed in the *Massachusetts Centinel* on 5 January (CC:419). The Maryland "Landholder," No. X included it as a note at the end of the essay.

15. Paraphrased from the Maryland "Landholder," No. X who says: "But alas! his colleagues would not acquit him in this way. . . ."

16. See Maryland "Landholder," No. X.

17. The italics in the quoted material are Martin's.

605. Simeon Baldwin to James Kent
New Haven, 8 March (excerpt)[1]

A thousand unforeseen accidents have prevented my writing to you before, but principally the want of conveyance–nothing will induce me my friend to sacrifice to it, the pleasure & advantage of your Correspondence–your last Letter I have not by me or I would give it a particular answer.–I think it contained some Law Questions which ought before this to have been answered, but the short notice I had of this conveyance will not allow me to search for authorities–You was so kind as to give me your opinion upon one point of Law, which I have since tried & had established (after a warm dispute,) agreeable to your Sentiments–Action on Note–*plea*. Infancy when the Note was given–*Reply*. that it was given in N Y. for Necessaries suitable &c. & that by the Laws of the state of N Y. Notes given by minors for necessaries are good valid, & binding in Law–to this reply there was a demurrer, & the Court ruled the reply sufficient–It would indeed make very wild work with contracts should we establish the principle that the Lex Loci must not govern them–The property of Individuals who reside in States, connected with such intercourse as there is between the US. of America, would be very precarious upon a contrary System–A greater uniformity in Laws will probably follow the adoption of the proposed Constitution–I have not heard your sentiments upon that subject, & I know that the State of New York is much divided upon it–But I'll venter to write to you as a friend to it–for I cannot think that a man of your candour & discernment–unbiased by Interest–can stand forth, & wield the weapons of Anarchy–against the Salvation of our Country–who are they in general who oppose the Constitution?–none but the uninformed or the interested– I have frequently been diverted to hear the very trifling & yet very different objections which are made to it by different peasants of this State–for you know that in this State the farmers are all politicians–many will condemn the same Articles which others with zeal recommend. none of them agree in their objections–even this Circumstance must convince an unbiassed mind that the wisdom of that venerable Body who framed the Constitution has led them thro' that central point of Gravity whh. must support the interest of all–

The conduct of New Hamshire has surprized us all this way–we did not expect it–but had ever calculated upon that State as sure–our fears were centered upon New York–we are sensible that more self-interest must be sacrificed to the general Good in that State–from their darling impost[2]– than in any other. Yet as there is a pretty equal consumption thro' the States of Articles subject to impost–Justice will certainly require that the avails should go to the advantage of those from whom the Impost is colle[c]ted–let the Ports at which they are landed & from whence they are scattered be one or many–I wish for your Sentiments upon the Constitution & the prospect of its adoption in the State–Many of your influential Characters we are told are against it–I must believe that the supreme being, whose hand is so visible in the settlement of this Country–in its rapid population–the extent of territory over which the People have spread–in the general diffusion of knowledge among them, which is not equalled by the people of any territory on earth–& in the surprizing union of the whole in the Cause of Liberty–has designed something great, noble, glorious from such a Country–such a people–such a revolution. And I will add from such a change in the Consti[tu]tion as the United Wisdom of the

U.S. has proposed, from the most perfect models of Govt. both in Theory & practice which have appeared on earth & been sanctioned by the approbation of the wise politicians who have gone before us–

This State is at present very quiet in its politics–the federal party have evidently obtained the superiority, & both sides seem qu[i]etly disposed to lay down their Arms–but it has not ever been a circumstance in the politics of this State that those who are concerned in them remain long in a State of Apathy. The leading Characters among our antifederalist are in general willful & Dogmatical–no Speakers are found among them–all their influence is by a low clandestine intrigue Our Leaders in the federal Party are the Leaders in the House of Assembly–Men who despise secrecy in their Sentiments & attempt more by solid Reason & an overbearing Eloquence, than by intreague–Their foible is–they do not try to reconcile–but frequintly irritate by sarcastic reflections–

The situation of this State as it respects their property, is far from being flourishing–we seem to have arrived to the turning point, between a Commerce in wh. the balance has long been against us, & the introduction of manufactures among ourselves whh. will supercede the Necessity of such a Commerce–The fact is we have too many inhabitants for the extent of territory–considering our mode of Cultivation & the employments of the people–All have not farms nor can they obtain them–of course untill Manufactures are introduced, the people must be idle, or crowd into those professions which do not immediately depend on the soil–The people thus employed, consume the produce of the farmer–till nothing is left for a remittance for those Articles which our stage of Society has to a Degree rendered necessary–Some attempts were made in this Town the last year for the introduction of a linnen manufactory, that is coarse linnen–for Sails &c. which succeded so as to yield a profit to the subscribers far beyond their expectation–the same is continued & another subscription for a Wollen manufac[tory] is filling up fast–The introduction of a few such manufactures by men of fortune & enterprize will doubtless opperate to the advantage of the State–we can never expect to be in so flourishing Circumstances as the State of New York–their situation gives them a superiority which industry cannot equal–& I must think that the Policy of that State as it respects their finance is managed with admirable ~~economy~~ foresight– & the circumstances of the Citizens are very different from ours–I rejoice my friend that you are placed among them–that you are sharing in its riches & can toil with the prospect of reaping a reward for your Labour–I have frequently lamented that I did not attend enough to my own advantage when I could have tarried & probably have pursued my professional employment there[3]–A bubble brought me back & local attachments bind me here. . . .

1. FC, Simeon E. Baldwin Collection, CtY. James Kent and Simeon Baldwin (1761–1851) were graduated from Yale College in 1781. Baldwin, a New Haven, Conn., lawyer and a son-in-law of Roger Sherman, was clerk of the U.S. district and circuit

courts for Connecticut, 1790–1803, 1805–6; U.S. Representative, 1803–5; and associate justice of the Connecticut Superior Court and Supreme Court of Errors, 1806–17. He was also New Haven city clerk, 1789–1800; councilman, 1798–99; alderman, 1800–16, 1823, 1825; and mayor, 1826.

2. In 1787, for example, New York collected almost half its revenue from its state impost (CC:457, note 5).

3. Baldwin served as senior preceptor at the academy in Albany, N.Y., in 1782 and 1783.

606 A–B. Arthur Campbell on the Constitution
Washington County, Va., 8, 9 March

606–A. To Francis Bailey, 8 March (excerpt)[1]

. . . The bearer Colo. Orth,[2] will forward you a revised Copy of the Federal Constitution;–It is the work of a Society of Western Gentlemen,[3] who took this method to investigate and understand the piece & to some of them it has lately been hinted, that the most of the pieces wrote for and against the Constitution, were rather declamatory, and bewildered common readers in the perusal; but by our mode it may be shewn at one view, what is deamed right or what is wrong–In order to embrace so safe and direct a conveyance, too little time was afforded, to digest the amendments, and to make out a correct copy. May we request it of you, if you judge it worthy of a place in the Freemans Journal, first to give it a careful perusal, and have all inaccuracies removed. We would wish to see it in the first Page of your Paper, embellished with proper Capitals and a neat type. I suppose it will take part of two Weeks Papers, to compleat the insertion. we have thoughts of soliciting your patronage to have it inserted in the American Museum. We might venture to asure the Editor that it is nearer the sentiments of the great body of the Yeomanry of America, especially in the Southern States, than the original.–We have thought ourselves sufficiently disposed to "amity, concession and mutual deference"[4] to be willing to surrender so much of our liberties to preserve the union, which is a great object with us: nor are we yet convinced, but that the States might be more safe, united, and prosperous, under something like what we now offer, than the other, which on a near view, seems to have too many of the features of despotism.–We for ourselves, for the sake of peace, and unity could submit for a course of years, by way of experiment say four, to absolute rule, provided we had security that a door would then be really open, whereby amendments might be offered.

Should any of the friends to the original Plan offer sensible strictures on our amendments, we have so well considered the subject that we are not without arguments to support them.–By means of Capt. Robert Craig late of Lancaster County[5] we expect in future to get the Freemans Journal, regularly.

The inclosed copy of a letter will inform you of some late commotions in [State of] Franklin, which you will please to insert.–I also send an extract of a letter received the other day from Kentuckey. I have a desire to attend the Synod next May,[6] if I do, I will then be happy, in personally acknowleging how much I esteem and love a character impressed with a true stamp of freedom.

P.S. I need not remind you, of the propriety of keeping my name secret in all communications sent you.

606–B. To Adam Orth, 9 March[7]

I came here on purpose to see you and converse on the subject of the proposed Federal Constitution, a matter that now so highly interests all America.

I keep up an extensive correspondence in the Southern States and have a few intelligent friend[s] convenient to me; from all which information, we have ventured to forward to be printed a revised Copy of the Constitution, as nearer the sentiments of the People of America, than the original & yet energetic enough for all the purposes of good government.

I have proposed to Mr. Bailey to print it in his News-Paper; but since on consideration I think it would be more extensively useful if first published in a Pamphlet, and speedily dispersed, especially in Pensylvania, N. York and Virginia.–Could not two or three of the Printers undertake to publish at their own risque I am sure several hundred copys would sell in Virginia, besides the clause in the Constitution in favour of the Press,[8] may be of more value to them than ten thousand copys.–But should that mode of publication be found impracticable I would submit it to you, and the other worthy Patriots of the Minority, whether you had not risque the publication in a Pamphlet at your own expence taking care to sell them low and I am sure 500 Copies forwarded to a trusty correspondent in Petersburg Virginia would sell fast. And would it not be right to have it published in the German tongue also.–After you return to Pensylvania could you not, have a consultation with Messr. Findley Whitehill and Smilie,–or a Mr. M'Clean[9] near Carlisle on the subject, and communicate your sentiments to Mr. Bailey who no doubt will act with secrecy, and propriety agreeable to your desire. I am not acquainted with Dr. Ewing[10] but conclude it would be of great service, should he revise the Piece, and give his assistance.

I dare say you are as fully as I am impressed with the importance of the subject; if the original piece has the seeds of despotism in it, we may be forging chains for our posterity; on the other hand the preservation of the union, ought to be a first object of all our cares: These two considerations combined produced the work now sent by you; which has a *Declaration* of *Rights*[11] that I believe will please most, and has amendments to the original, that will make it a more mild & we hope a more just plan of government.

1. RC, George Bryan Papers, PHi. Campbell (1743–1811), a planter, was a justice of the peace and county lieutenant for Washington County, Va. He represented Fincastle County in the Virginia House of Delegates in 1776, and Washington County in 1778, 1782–83, 1786–88. In 1784–85 he was the leader of a movement to separate southwestern Virginia and place it in the State of Franklin. He also supported separate statehood for Kentucky. (For an article he wrote under the pseudonym "Many" attacking the Constitution, see *Virginia Independent Chronicle*, 18 June 1788. Washington County voted against ratification of the Constitution in the Virginia Convention in June.) Bailey (c. 1735–1815) was the printer of the rabidly Antifederalist Philadelphia *Freeman's Journal* (CC:Vol. 1, xxxiv–xxxv).

2. Adam Orth (1733–1794) operated an iron forge in Lebanon township, Lancaster County, Pa. He voted against ratification of the Constitution in the Pennsylvania Convention in December 1787 and signed the "Dissent of the Minority of the Pennsylvania Convention" (CC:353).

3. Neither a manuscript nor a printed copy of this revised Constitution has been located. A similar document, however, does exist. In December 1786 thirty men met in Danville, Ky., and organized "The Political Club." (Campbell was not a member.) The club debated the Constitution from February through May 1788, amending and revising it. The results of the club's deliberations are embodied in a twenty-page manuscript entitled: "The Constitution/of the United States of America/as amended and approved by/The Political Club," found among the club's records in the Filson Club, Louisville, Ky. These records also include an annotated printed copy of the Constitution and drafts of the amendments to the Constitution, as well as the club's minutes and debates. For a history of the club, see Thomas Speed, *The Political Club, Danville, Kentucky, 1786–1790* . . . (Louisville, Ky., 1894).

4. A paraphrasing of a passage from the letter of the President of the Constitutional Convention to the President of Congress, 17 September (CC:76).

5. Craig, a militia captain during the Revolution, was a Lancaster County commissioner in 1778 and a member of the General Assembly in 1784. He was related to the Whitehills by marriage (see note 9 below).

6. A reference to the New York and Philadelphia synod of the Presbyterian Church which adjourned on 29 May (*Pennsylvania Packet*, 5 June).

7. RC, George Bryan Papers, PHi.

8. The amended Constitution of the Danville Political Club does not include such a clause. One of the club's resolutions, however, states "That the Federal Constitution ought to be preceded by a Declaration of Rights."

9. William Findley, Robert Whitehill, and John Smilie were the principal Antifederalist speakers in the Pennsylvania Convention. They voted against the Constitution in the Convention and signed the "Dissent of the Minority of the Pennsylvania Convention" (CC:353). Antifederalist James McLene of Franklin County had been a member of the Supreme Executive Council until he was elected to the House of Assembly in October 1787.

10. John Ewing (1732–1802), a Presbyterian minister and Philadelphia Antifederalist leader, was provost of the University of Pennsylvania.

11. The Danville Political Club records do not include a declaration of rights.

607. Publius: The Federalist 66
New York Independent Journal, 8 March

This essay, written by Alexander Hamilton, was reprinted in the *New York Packet* on 11 March. It is number 66 in the M'Lean edition and number 65 in the newspapers.

For a general discussion of the authorship, circulation, and impact of *The Federalist*, see CC:201, 639.

The FŒDERALIST. No. LXV.
To the People of the State of New-York.

A review of the principal objections that have appeared against the proposed court for the trial of impeachments, will not improbably eradicate the remains of any unfavourable impressions, which may still exist, in regard to this matter.

The *first* of these objections is, that the provision in question confounds legislative and judiciary authorities in the same body; in violation of that important and well established maxim, which requires a separation between the different departments of power. The true meaning of this maxim has been discussed and ascertained in another place, and has been shewn to be entirely compatible with a partial intermixture of those departments for special purposes, preserving them in the main distinct and unconnected.[1] This partial intermixture is even in some cases not only proper, but necessary to the mutual defence of the several members of the government, against each other. An absolute or qualified negative in the executive, upon the acts of the legislative body, is admitted by the ablest adepts in political science, to be an indispensable barrier against the encroachments of the latter upon the former. And it may perhaps with not less reason be contended that the powers relating to impeachments are as before intimated,[2] an essential check in the hands of that body upon the encroachments of the executive. The division of them between the two branches of the legislature; assigning to one the right of accusing, to the other the right of judging; avoids the inconvenience of making the same persons both accusers and judges; and guards against the danger of persecution from the prevalency of a factious spirit in either of those branches. As the concurrence of two-thirds of the senate will be requisite to a condemnation, the security to innocence, from this additional circumstance, will be as complete as itself can desire.

It is curious to observe with what vehemence this part of the plan is assailed, on the principle here taken notice of, by men who profess to admire without exception the constitution of this state; while that constitution makes the senate, together with the chancellor and judges of the supreme court, not only a court of impeachments, but the highest judicatory in the state in all causes, civil and criminal. The proportion, in point of numbers, of the chancellor and judges to the senators, is so inconsiderable, that the judiciary authority of New-York in the last resort may, with truth, be said to reside in its senate.[3] If the plan of the convention be in this respect chargeable with a departure from the celebrated maxim which has been so often mentioned, and seems to be so little understood, how much more culpable must be the constitution of New-York?[(a)]

A *second* objection to the senate, as a court of impeachments, is, that it contributes to an undue accumulation of power in that body, tending to give to the government a countenance too aristocratic. The senate, it is

observed, is to have concurrent authority with the executive in the formation of treaties, and in the appointment to offices: If, say the objectors, to
these prerogatives is added that of deciding in all cases of impeachment, it
will give a decided predominancy to senatorial influence. To an objection
so little precise in itself, it is not easy to find a very precise answer. Where
is the measure or criterion to which we can appeal, for determining what
will give the senate too much, too little, or barely the proper degree of
influence? Will it not be more safe, as well as more simple, to dismiss such
vague and uncertain calculations, to examine each power by itself, and to
decide on general principles where it may be deposited with most advantage and least inconvenience?

If we take this course it will lead to a more intelligible, if not to a more
certain result. The disposition of the power of making treaties, which has
obtained in the plan of the convention, will then, if I mistake not, appear
to be fully justified by the considerations stated in a former number,[4] and
by others which will occur under the next head of our enquiries.[5] The
expediency of the junction of the senate with the executive[6] will, I trust,
be placed in a light not less satisfactory, in the disquisitions under the
same head. And I flatter myself the observations in my last paper[7] must
have gone no inconsiderable way towards proving that it was not easy, if
practicable, to find a more fit receptacle for the power of determining impeachments, than that which has been chosen. If this be truly the case, the
hypothetical dread[8] of the too great weight of the senate ought to be dis-
carded from our reasonings.

But this hypothesis, such as it is has already been refuted in the remarks
applied to the duration in office prescribed for the senators.[9] It was by
them shewn, as well on the credit of historical examples, as from the reason of the thing, that the most *popular* branch of every government, partaking of the republican genius, by being generally the favorite of the people,
will be as generally a full match, if not an overmatch, for every other
member of the government.

But independent of this most active and operative principle, to secure
the equilibrium of the national house of representatives, the plan of the
convention has provided in its favor, several important counterpoises to
the additional authorities, to be conferred upon the senate. The exclusive
privilege of originating money bills will belong to the house of representatives. The same house will possess the sole right of instituting impeachments: Is not this a complete counterballance to that of determining them?—
The same house will be the umpire in all elections of the president, which
do not unite the suffrages of a majority of the whole number of electors; a
case which it cannot be doubted will sometimes, if not frequently, happen.
The constant possibility of the thing must be a fruitful source of influence
to that body. The more it is contemplated, the more important will appear
this ultimate, though contingent power of deciding the competitions of the

most illustrious citizens of the union, for the first office in it. It would not perhaps be rash to predict, that as a mean of influence it will be found to outweigh all the peculiar attributes of the senate.

A third objection to the senate as a court of impeachments is drawn from the agency they are to have in the appointments to office. It is imagined that they would be too indulgent judges of the conduct of men, in whose official creation they had participated. The principle of this objection would condemn a practice, which is to be seen in all the state governments, if not in all the governments, with which we are acquainted: I mean that of rendering those, who hold offices during pleasure, dependent on the pleasure of those, who appoint them. With equal plausibility might it be alledged in this case that the favoritism of the latter would always be an asylum for the misbehavior of the former. But that practice, in contradiction to this principle, proceeds upon the presumption, that the responsibility of those who appoint, for the fitness and competency of the persons, on whom they bestow their choice, and the interest they will[10] have in the respectable and prosperous administration of affairs, will inspire a sufficient disposition, to dismiss from a share in it, all such, who, by their conduct, shall[11] have proved themselves unworthy of the confidence reposed in them. Though facts may not always correspond with this presumption, yet if it be in the main just, it must destroy the supposition, that the senate, who will merely sanction the choice of the executive, should feel a byass towards the objects of that choice, strong enough to blind them to the evidences of guilt so extraordinary as to have induced the representatives of the nation to become its accusers.

If any further argument were necessary to evince the improbability of such a byass, it might be found in the nature of the agency of the senate, in the business of appointments. It will be the office of the president to *nominate*, and with the advice and consent of the senate to *appoint*. There will of course be no exertion of *choice* on the part of the senate. They may defeat one choice of the executive, and oblige him to make another; but they cannot themselves *choose*–they can only ratify or reject the choice, of the president. They might even entertain a preference to some other person, at the very moment they were assenting to the one proposed; because there might be no positive ground of opposition to him; and they could not be sure, if they withheld their assent, that the subsequent nomination would fall upon their own favorite, or upon any other person in their estimation more meritorious than the one rejected. Thus it could hardly happen that the majority of the senate would feel any other complacency towards the object of an appointment, than such, as the appearances of merit, might inspire, and the proofs of the want of it, destroy.

A fourth objection to the senate, in the capacity of a court of impeachments, is derived from their union with the executive in the power of making treaties. This, it has been said, would constitute the senators their own judges, in every case of a corrupt or perfidious execution of that trust. After having combined with the executive in betraying the interests of the nation in a ruinous treaty, what prospect, it is asked, would there be of their being made to suffer the punishment, they would deserve, when they were themselves to decide upon the accusation brought against them for the treachery of which they had been guilty?

This objection has been calculated[12] with more earnestness and with greater show of reason, than any other which has appeared against this part of the plan; and yet I am deceived if it does not rest upon an erroneous foundation.

The security essentially intended by the constitution against corruption and treachery in the formation of treaties, is to be sought for in the numbers and characters of those who are to make them. The JOINT AGENCY of the chief magistrate of the union, and of two-thirds of the members of a body selected by the collective wisdom of the legislatures of the several states, is designed to be the pledge for the fidelity of the national councils in this particular. The convention might with propriety have meditated the punishment of the executive, for a deviation from the instructions of the senate, or a want of integrity in the conduct of the negociations committed to him: They might also have had in view the punishment of a few leading individuals in the senate, who should have prostituted their influence in that body, as the mercenary instruments of foreign corruption: But they could not with more or with equal propriety have contemplated the impeachment and punishment of two-thirds of the senate, consenting to an improper treaty, than of a majority of that or of the other branch of the national legislature, consenting to a pernicious or unconstitutional law: a principle which I believe has never been admitted into any government. How in fact could a majority of the house of representatives impeach themselves? Not better, it is evident, than two-thirds of the senate might try themselves. And yet what reason is there, that a majority of the house of representatives, sacrificing the interests of the society, by an unjust and tyrannical act of legislation, should escape with impunity more than two-thirds of the senate, sacrificing the same interests in an injurious treaty with a foreign power? The truth is, that in all such cases it is essential to the freedom and to the necessary independence of the deliberations of the body, that the members of it should be exempt from punishment for acts done in a collective capacity; and the security to the society must depend on the care which is taken to confide the trust to proper hands, to make it their interest to execute it with fidelity, and to make it as difficult as possible for them to combine in any interest opposite to that of the public good.

So far as might concern the misbehaviour of the executive in perverting the instructions, or contravening the views of the senate, we need not be apprehensive of the want of a disposition in that body to punish the abuse of their confidence, or to vindicate their own authority. We may thus far count upon their pride, if not upon their virtue. And so far even as might concern the corruption of leading members, by whose arts and influence the majority may have been inveigled into measures odious to the community; if the proofs of that corruption should be satisfactory, the usual propensity of human nature will warrant us in concluding, that there would be commonly no defect of inclination in the body, to divert the public resentment from themselves, by a ready sacrifice of the authors of their mismanagement and disgrace.

> (a) *In that of New-Jersey also the final judiciary authority is in a branch of the legislature. In New-Hampshire, Massachusetts, Pennsylvania, and South-Carolina, one branch of the legislative is the court for the trial of impeachments.*[13]

1. See *The Federalist* 47–51, 30 January–6 February (CC:486, 492, 495, 500, 503).
2. See *The Federalist* 65 (CC:601).
3. See Thorpe, V, 2635. In March 1788 there were three supreme court judges and twenty-four senators.
4. See *The Federalist* 64 (CC:592).
5. See *The Federalist* 69 and 75 (CC:617, 646).
6. "In the power of appointing to offices" inserted at this point in the M'Lean edition.
7. See *The Federalist* 65 (CC:601).
8. "Danger" substituted in the M'Lean edition.
9. See *The Federalist* 63 (CC:582).
10. "Will" deleted in the M'Lean edition.
11. "May" substituted in the M'Lean edition.
12. "Circulated" substituted in the M'Lean edition.
13. In New Jersey, the governor and council were a "Court of Appeals, in the last resort, in all clauses of law." In New Hampshire, Massachusetts, and South Carolina, the senate was the court of impeachment, while in Pennsylvania, the unicameral state assembly was the court of impeachment (Thorpe, III, 1897; IV, 2461; V, 2596, 3085; VI, 3253–54).

608 A–B. The Fabrick of Freedom
Philadelphia Federal Gazette, 8, 13 March

"The Fabrick of Freedom" (CC:608–A) was written by Jonathan Williams, Jr. (1750–1815), a native of Boston and a grandnephew of Benjamin Franklin. The son of a Boston merchant, Williams went to England in 1770 to complete his business training. Six years later he left for France to join Franklin, one of the American commissioners. Almost immediately he was appointed by the commissioners to be their commercial agent in the port of Nantes. In 1778 Arthur Lee, one of the commissioners, accused him of embezzlement and had John Adams, another commissioner, dismiss him. The next year, Williams was exonerated, but Franklin would not risk appointing him to another public office. Williams went into business for himself in Nantes but by 1783 he was bankrupt. In September 1785 he returned to America with Franklin, and between 1785 and 1788 he engaged in various business ventures and traveled to several states trying to collect debts due him. While on visits to Boston in 1786, Williams published a three-part essay entitled "A View of the Federal Government of America. Its Defects, and a proposed Remedy," under the pseudonym "A Bostonian" (Boston *Independent*

Chronicle, 3, 10 August, and 28 December 1786). "A Bostonian" emphasized the importance of giving Congress legislative, judicial, and executive powers–the "three grand immutable principles in good government." In particular, Congress had to have power over commerce. According to Williams, "A Bostonian" was reprinted in several states and excerpts from it were "quoted twenty times" (to Mariamne Williams, 27 October 1787, Jonathan Williams Mss, InU-Li). In the latter part of 1787 and in 1788, Williams spent most of his time in Philadelphia, where he contributed essays to the newspapers. For two essays, signed "A Bostonian," which were probably written by Williams, see *Independent Gazetteer*, 16 April and 6 May (Appendix II and CC:566 headnote). By 1790 he had become a prosperous Philadelphia merchant. After 1796 he held such positions as associate judge of the Court of Common Pleas for the City and County of Philadelphia; the first superintendent of the U.S. Military Academy at West Point, N.Y.; and chief engineer of the U.S. Army.

"The Fabrick of Freedom" was printed on 8 March in the first issue of the triweekly Philadelphia *Federal Gazette*. Three days later the *Gazette* announced that "The music of the lines which appeared in our last, entitled 'The Fabrick of Freedom,' shall, to oblige a number of our correspondents, be given in our next." On 13 March the *Gazette* printed "*the Vocal Music*" to the first stanza of the poem (CC:608-B).

"The Fabrick of Freedom" was reprinted in the *Virginia Independent Chronicle*, 19 March; Charleston *Columbian Herald*, 28 April; *Georgia State Gazette*, 17 May; and the New Jersey *Brunswick Gazette*, 21 October, which identified Williams as the author.

608-A. The Fabrick of Freedom, 8 March

Air. *The Topsail shivers in the Wind.*

I.

Fair *Freedom!* lend thy gracious aid,
    To sing our fabrick's fame,
By patriots rais'd, celestial maid!
    It boasts thy sacred name:
On thy broad basis may it be!
The pride and safeguard of the *free*.

II.

Here *Justice* holds her even scales,
    And grasps her rightful sword;
As *Truth* directs she never fails,
    To punish or reward:
Her equal law is *Virtue's* guide,
And *Virtue's sons* therein confide.

III.

Here blue ey'd *Peace* with gentle sway,
    Extends her blessings far;
Though by her dictates rul'd, we may
    Be still prepar'd for war:
The force which from our union grows,
Shall aid our friends and crush our foes.

IV.

Thus is our constitution rear'd,
  On *Freedom Strength* and *Peace*;
By *Virtue* lov'd, by *Faction* fear'd,
  For faction's self must cease.
Contented now we'll happy live,
While *Industry* and *Trade* shall thrive.

V.

Come! *Ceres*, come! in golden pride,
  Adorn each waving field;
Come! with *Pomona* by thy side,
  And fruitful harvests yield:
The heavenly pair their favors show'r,
And agriculture owns their power.

VI.

See *Commerce* with extended hand,
  Flies the restraint of kings;
And foreign riches to this land,
  From ev'ry climate brings:
Bless'd by her smiles, we soon shall find,
That where she's free, she's always kind.

VII.

May *Science* and her handmaid *Art*,
  To this new world belong!
And infant muses joy impart
  In strains of sportive song!-
Apollo see! with glory drest,
Appears refulgent in the west.

VIII.

America is thus become.
  A seat to *freedom* dear,
Where virtuous strangers find a home,
  And no oppression fear.
These rising States shall be renown'd,
By *Plenty*, *Art*, and *Science* crown'd.

608–B. Vocal Music: The Fabrick of Freedom, 13 March

The following is the Vocal Music for the Lines entitled, The Fabric of Freedom, *in our first number.*

Fair Freedom lend thy gracious aid

to sing our fa—bric's fame

By patriots rais'd ce—les—tial maid

It boasts thy sa—cred name

On thy broad ba—sis may it be

The pride and safeguard of the free

On thy broad basis may it be

The pride and safeguard of the free.

609. Philadelphiensis XI
Philadelphia Independent Gazetteer, 8 March[1]

My Fellow Citizens, Every day opens a new scene of the baseness of the conspirators, their intentions of screening themselves from rendering an account of the public money so fraudulently detained, will rank them among the meanest traitors, that ever dishonoured the human character.[2] How must their consciences condemn them, when avarice and lust of dominion are suffered for a moment to subside, and reason and reflection take their place? Let these men but cooly consider the misery that must inevitably befal millions of their countrymen, in consequence of their treachery in framing this system of fraud and oppression; and remorse and deep anguish of soul must await them! Humanity brings a tear of sympathetic pity from the eye of their fellow men, whose ruin they had secretly projected. As our holy religion expressly enjoins it as a duty, not to return evil for evil, but to overcome evil with good;[3] consequently our resentment against these ungrateful men should be moderated by christian charity: Yet as freemen and citizens, determined to hand down to posterity sacred liberty unimpaired, we are solemnly bound, at the hazard of our fortunes and lives, to oppose this base attempt of theirs to enslave our country.

If on the broad basis of equity and justice, crimes and punishments have their proper proportion: What punishment then, on the scale of moderation, could counterpoise, or atone, for a crime so aggravated as that charged to the majority of the members of the late federal convention? I assert roundly, that another assembly of men never met in this, or any other country, possessing so fully the confidence of so many freemen: and to their shame be it said, they abused this confidence; their own private interest, private emolument, and hopes of dominion, overcame every consideration of duty, honor, and gratitude.

The citizens of Pennsylvania have nobly shown their love for liberty, and attachment to the true interests of the union, by their generous exertions in favor of public credit. They have rigidly fulfilled their engagements in regard to the general debt; the requisitions of Congress have been strictly attended to, and fully answered.[4] Add to this, that we have sunk a considerable part of the domestic debt, and in fact assumed a larger portion of it than in justice belonged to us.[5] These spirited exertions, while they contributed to the general welfare of the union, and raised the reputation of the state, did not fail however to distress our farmers and every other class and description of citizens, very sensibly indeed.

But what is the result of their unshaken loyalty to the cause of liberty, and the honor of their country? What recompence will the honest and industrious Pennsylvanians receive for their patriotism, if the new government be established? Such a return as perhaps history does not afford a single instance similar to. So base a violation of public justice and plighted faith, is certainly a novelty in politics, and begins a new epoch in history.

Pennsylvania, instead of receiving credit for the immense sums she has paid into the general treasury, will be placed on a footing with the most delinquent state in the union; and which is highly probable she and all the other states will be taxed hereafter in an exact ratio of the sums they have hitherto raised. Consequently our former acts of generosity, in support of public faith, is to terminate in a two-fold loss to our citizens. In the first place we have nearly ruined ourselves already, through our punctuality in paying our quota of the public debt; and secondly, to complete the scene, our future quotas of continental revenue will be apportioned to the exertions we have heretofore made: That is in plain terms, Pennsylvania will be much worse under this cruel system of tyranny in consequence of her fidelity and honor, than she would have been had she never attempted to pay a shilling of public debt; or if she be not worse, the uniformity of internal taxation through the union, which is expressly stipulated by the constitution, necessarily places her citizens on a parallel with those of that state which has not paid a shilling of public debt since the peace.

The people of the delinquent states might inconsiderately be induced to triumph in the new system of government; for they may conclude, now our public debts are paid as far forward as those of any other state, but attentive consideration will soon convince them of their mistake. Although the new constitution advances them as high in the public scale as if they had strictly and honorably made good the requisitions of the old Congress; yet the unbounded powers of the new Congress in respect to internal taxation, must eventually fleece them of their all; and from their inability heretofore to pay their just quotas as levied by Congress, we may rationally conclude, that, even the states of Pennsylvania and New-York,[6] which are in advance at present, will still be above them, supposing the extra payments of these two states not to be carried to the credit of their account, which they certainly will not, on the principles of this constitution.

The truth of this matter is simply this; the taxes will hereafter be uniform in all the states, and as oppressive as tyranny can make them. In every state the face of the poor must be ground to dust; and where any appearance of prosperity or wealth is observed, an additional tax will be devised; for so complicated and uncontrouled a government, will find ways and means to apply all the revenue that America can raise; indeed the whole produce of the lands cultivated by three millions and an half of people, could not satiate the desires of such a government. If the *lesser*, or rather *weaker* states would moderate their precipitancy, in urging forward the constitution, by reason and the certainty of misery that stares them in the face, I imagine they would find their advantage in the measure. Lenity in the old Congress has in some degree screened them; and besides their fellow citizens in the other states befriend them; but the high hand of power, so completely vested in the new Congress, will exact the uttermost farthing, both from the states and individuals: No excuse will satisfy the demands of a cruel *excise-man*; we must instantly pay the federal tax, or have our property seized, and ourselves dragged to prison by a federal soldier.

That this government, should it be ratified by nine states, will not possess the confidence of the majority of the people, is a truth incontrovertible. I admit, that through fraud and surprise, many have inconsiderately joined themselves to its deceptive standard; but their number is diminishing rapidly; and I sincerely believe, that in a few months the *office-hunters*, the *well born*, and their sycophants, will be left alone: The farmer, the mechanic, and even the merchant, would be ruined if it took effect; their interest is to oppose it, and to endeavor to have another convention called immediately.

Who is so dimsighted as to suppose that a constitution so essentially differing from the principles of the revolution, and from freedom, and opposed by so respectable a body of freemen, could be established in America; or if it were possible by force or surprise to put it in motion, could it exist any space of time? Nay, the idea is futile, and common sense spurns at it. While it would exist, it must be by the power of a standing army alone; but its warmest advocates know, that all their credit, and influence could not support a standing army, equal to the business, six months.

It is admitted, that in Great Britain they are scarce ever without violent factions and parties, and yet no injury is apprehended to the country on that account, but generally much good: But let us attend to this matter seriously, and we must see clearly that factions and parties in America in respect to the present important object, would eventually ruin this country. The parties, factions, and cabals, so frequent in Britain, are not from a dislike to the fundamentals of their constitution, but on account of maladministration: All parties glory in the constitution, and disagree only, when it is infringed, or violated.

To infer then, from the example of Britain, that the opposition to the new government would not terminate in our ruin, if it were adopted by a majority in nine states, would be a dangerous mistake; for there is no analogy between the premises, the conclusions are therefore different. The opposition in America is against the fundamentals of the constitution itself; but this is not so in England. No constitution that is not popular can possibly be established in America; or if for a short time it were established, we would have nothing but anarchy and civil war, while it was in existence.

Let us not be deceived by delusive tales, that it shall be amended after the meeting of the first Congress; since it is admitted almost universally that it wants amendments; now is the time to have them done, while we are at peace abroad, and among ourselves. A fragment of liberty cannot remain, if we once set it in motion in its imperfect state. How can we suppose, that the president general, being once in full possession of his unlimited powers, would deliver them back again to the people; the supposition is preposterous; he must be more than *man* if he would; a more dangerous king is not in the world than he will be; liberty will be lost in America the day on which he is proclaimed, and must be recovered by the *sword*, if ever we are to enjoy it again.

1. This essay was not reprinted. Three days after it appeared, Francis Hopkinson of Philadelphia, writing as "A.B.," identified "Philadelphiensis" as "no less a personage than BENJAMIN WORKMAN, one of the *well-born tutors in the University of Pennsylvania*," thereby touching off a heated newspaper debate among Workman, Hopkinson, and their supporters (CC:237, headnote).

Commenting on the first eleven numbers of "Philadelphiensis," "A Retailer of Scraps," noted that he had "patiently submitted to the drudgery of reading" these essays, "and, for my soul, I cannot discover a single argument, in the whole of them, which has any thing to do with the merits or demerits, of the new plan of federal government." "Philadelphiensis," continued "A Retailer of Scraps," had "excelled" in "genuine" and "sublime Billingsgate" (Philadelphia *Federal Gazette*, 1 April, Mfm:Pa. 590).

2. See "Centinel" XVI (CC:565).

3. See Romans 12:21 and 1 Peter 3:9.

4. In May 1790 a report of the Department of the Treasury revealed that Pennsylvania had paid 70 percent of its specie quota and 40 percent of its indent quota for a total of 53 percent of its assessed portion of the congressional requisitions–second best only to New York (ASP, *Finance*, I, 56–57. See also note 5 below.).

5. By the end of 1787, Pennsylvania had assumed federal securities worth about $6,000,000 in specie (CC:85, note 2).

6. By 1790 New York had paid 89 percent of its specie quota and 58 percent of its indent quota for a total of 70 percent of its assessed portion of the congressional requisitions–the best state record (ASP, *Finance*, I, 56–57).

610. Henry Knox to George Washington
New York, 10 March[1]

Your favor of the 11th ultimo was duly received.[2]

The publication signed *Publius* is attributed to the joint efforts of Mr Jay, Mr Maddison and Colo Hamilton It is highly probable that the general conjecture in this case is well founded

I have not written to you since the untoward event of New Hampshire The conduct of the convention was so contrary to expectations of every person who conceived themselves informed of the dispositions of that State, that I knew not what to write[3]

I have received a letter from President Sullivan in which he says that the adjournment will be attended with the hapiest consequences, and that the convention in their next session will adopt the constitution by a majority of three to one[4]

The business in this state is critically circumstanced, and the parties nearly balanced–The issue will depend greatly on the industry of the different sides–I am apprehensive that the antifederalists will be the most indefatigable. The federalists say they shall have a small majority certainly–but it is to be apprehended that their confidence will prove highly injurious to the cause–Nothing has been received from Rhode Island that can give any immediate hopes that state will endevor to establish a different character

I beg the favor that you would present Mrs Knox and myself to Mrs Washington–and my Compliments to Colo Humphrieys–[5]

1. RC, Washington Papers, DLC.

2. Knox probably refers to Washington's letter of 5 February which has this postscript: "Pray, if it is not a secret, who is the author, or authors of Publius" (Fitzpatrick, XXIX, 400-1).

3. The New Hampshire Convention adjourned on 22 February without voting on whether or not to ratify the Constitution. On 14 February, the day after the Convention began its sessions, Knox had written Washington that "About 20 days hence I hope to have the pleasure of informing you of the adoption of the constitution in that State" (Washington Papers, DLC).

4. Sullivan's letter to Knox has not been found. On 28 February, however, Sullivan had written Nicholas Gilman, a New Hampshire delegate to Congress, who, like Knox, was in New York City. Sullivan predicted that the New Hampshire Convention would ratify the Constitution "by three Quarters of the members present" when it reconvened in June (Gratz Collection, PHi).

5. In November 1787 Colonel David Humphreys of Derby, Conn., went to Mount Vernon where he remained until 1789, serving for a time as Washington's secretary.

611. The Landholder XI
Connecticut Courant, 10 March[1]

To the CITIZENS of NEW-HAMPSHIRE.

Those who wish to enjoy the blessings of society must be willing to suffer some restraint of personal liberty, and devote some part of their property to the public that the remainder may be secured and protected. The cheapest form of government is not always best; for parsimony though it spends little, generally gains nothing. Neither is that the best government which imposes the least restraint on its subjects; for the benefit of having others restrained, may be greater than the disadvantage of being restrained ourselves. That is the best form of government which returns the greatest number of advantages in proportion to the disadvantages with which it is attended. Measured by this rule, the state of New-Hampshire cannot expect a Constitution preferable to that now proposed for the union: In point of defence it gives you the force of the whole empire, so arranged as to act speedily and in concert, which is an article of greatest importance to the frontier states. With the present generation of men, national interest is the measure by which war or peace are determined; and when we see the British nation, by a late treaty paying an enormous annual subsidy to the little principality of Hesse Cassel for the purpose of retaining her in military alliance, it should teach us the necessity of those parts in the Constitution, which enable the efficient force of the whole to be opposed to an invasion of any part.

A national revenue and the manner of collecting it is another very interesting matter, and here the citizens of New-Hampshire have better terms offered them, than their local situation can ever enable them to demand or enforce. Impost and duties on trade which must be collected in the great importing towns, are the means by which an American revenue will be principally, and perhaps, wholly raised. But a point of your state comes near the sea, and that point so situated that it never can collect commerce, and become an emporium for the whole state–Nineteen parts in twenty of New-Hampshire are greatly inland, so that local situation necessitates you to be an agricultural people; and this is not a hard necessity if you now form such a political connection with the other states, as will entitle you to a just share in that revenue they raise on commerce. New-York, the trading towns on Connecticut River, and Boston, are the sources from which a great part of your foreign supplies will be obtained, and where your produce will be exposed for market.–In all these places an impost is collected, of which, as consumers, you pay a share without deriving any public benefit. You cannot expect any alteration in the private systems of these states, unless effected by the proposed government, neither to remedy the evil can you command trade from the natural channels; but must sit down contented under the burden, if the present hour of deliverance be not accepted. This argument alone, if there were no other, ought to decide you in favour of adoption.

It has been said that you object to the number of inhabitants being a ratio to determine your proportion of the national expence–that your lands are poor but the climate favourable to population, which will draw a share of expence beyond your ability to pay. I do not think this objection well founded. Long experience hath taught that the number of industrious inhabitants in any climate is not only the strength, but the wealth of a state, and very justly measures their ability for defraying public expences, without encroaching on the necessary support of life.–If a great proportion of your lands are barren, you ought likewise to remember another rule of nature; that the population and fertility in any tract of country will be proportioned to each other. Accidental causes for a short time may interrupt the rule, but they cannot be of dangerous continuance. Force may controul in a despotic government, and commerce may interrupt it in an advantageous situation for trade; but from the first of these causes you have no reason to fear, and the last should it happen will increase wealth with numbers.

The fishery is a source of wealth and an object of immense consequence to all the eastern coasts. The jealousy of European nations, ought to teach us its value. So far as you become a navigating people, the fishery should be an object of your first attention. It cannot flourish until patronized and protected by the general government. All the interests of navigation and commerce must be protected by the union or come to ruin, and in our present system where is the power to do it. When Americans are debarred the fishery, as will soon be the case unless a remedy is provided, all the eastern shores will become miserably poor.

Your forests embosom an immense quantity of timber for ship-building and the lumber trade,–but of how little value at present you cannot be ignorant, and the value cannot increase until American navigation and commerce are placed on a respectable footing, which no single state can do for itself–The embarrassments of trade lower the price of your produce, which with the distance of transportation almost absorbs the value; and when by a long journey we have arrived at the place of market, even the finest of your grain will not command cash, at that season of the year most convenient for you to transport. Hence arises that scarcity of *specie* of which you complain. Your interest is intimately connected with that of the most commercial states, and you cannot separate it. When trade is embarrassed the merchant is the first to complain, but the farmer in event bears more than his share of the loss.

Let the citizens of New-Hampshire candidly consider these facts, and they must be convinced that no other state is so much interested in adopting that system of government now under consideration.

1. This essay, a continuation of "Landholder's" address to the citizens of New Hampshire (3 March, CC:588), was also printed in the Hartford *American Mercury* on 10 March. The *Courant* and *Mercury* versions differ in paragraphing, spelling, capitalization, and punctuation. "Landholder" XI was reprinted seven times by 4 April: N.H. (3), Mass. (3), Conn. (1).

For the authorship, circulation, and impact of "Landholder," see CC:230.

612. Publius: The Federalist 67
New York Packet, 11 March

This essay, written by Alexander Hamilton, was reprinted in the New York *Independent Journal* on 12 March. It was number 67 in the M'Lean edition and number 66 in the newspapers. A reviewer, probably editor Noah Webster, in the June issue of the New York *American Magazine*, wrote that "In this and the ten succeeding numbers, Publius enters into an examination of the Constitution and powers of the President, or Supreme Executive. He begins by detecting some gross misrepresentations of this part of the systems, on the side of the opposition. He shews the singular advantages of the mode of appointment. He institutes a comparison between the powers of the Executive in Great Britain and in this State, and shows that they can in no respect be dangerous to liberty. He proves the utility of a *single* Executive, and the inconvenience of an Executive Council. His remarks on the continuance of the President in office, and his re-eligibility, are deemed just and well worthy of particular attention in States where the principle of rotation is established. His reasonings on the powers of the President are clear and forceable; calculated to satisfy every candid enquirer, that the Executive is clothed with no more power than is necessary to a just administration of the laws; nor more than is necessary to secure the rights of the citizens and States."

For a general discussion of the authorship, circulation, and impact of *The Federalist*, see CC:201, 639.

The FŒDERALIST. No. 66.

To the People of the State of New-York.

The Constitution of the executive department of the proposed government claims next our attention.

There is hardly any part of the system, which could have been attended with great[1] difficulty in the arrangement of it than this; and there is perhaps none, which has been inveighed against with less candor, or criticised with less judgment.

Here the writers against the Constitution seem to have taken pains to signalize their talent of misrepresentation, calculating upon the aversion of the people to monarchy, they have endeavoured to inlist all their jealousies and apprehensions in opposition to the intended President of the United States; not merely as the embryo but as the full grown progeny of that detested parent. To establish the pretended affinity they have not scrupled to draw resources even from the regions of fiction. The authorities of a magistrate, in few instances greater, and in some instances less, than those of a Governor of New-York, have been magnified into more than royal prerogatives. He has been decorated with attributes superior in dignity and splendor to those of a King of Great-Britain. He has been shown to us with the diadem sparkling on his brow, and the imperial purple flowing in his train. He has been seated on a throne surrounded with minions and mistresses; giving audience to the envoys of foreign potentates, in all the supercilious pomp of majesty. The images of Asiatic despotism and voluptuousness have scarcely been wanting to crown the exaggerated scene. We have been almost taught to tremble at the terrific visages of murdering janizaries; and to blush at the unveiled mysteries of a future seraglio.

Attempts so extravagant as these to disfigure, or it might rather be said, to metamorphose the object, render it necessary to take an accurate view of its real nature and form; in order as well to ascertain its true aspect and genuine appearance, as to unmask the disingenuity and expose the fallacy of the counterfeit resemblances which have been so insidiously as well as industriously propagated.

In the execution of this task there is no man, who would not find it an arduous effort, either to behold with moderation or to treat with seriousness the devices, not less weak than wicked, which have been contrived to pervert the public opinion in relation to the subject. They so far exceed the usual, though unjustifiable, licenses of party-artifice, that even in a disposition the most candid and tolerant they must force the sentiments which favor an indulgent construction of the conduct of political adversaries to give place to a voluntary and unreserved indignation. It is impossible not to bestow the imputation of deliberate imposture and deception upon the gross pretence of a similitude between a King of Great-Britain and a magistrate of the character marked out for that of the President of the United States. It is still more impossible to withhold that imputation from the rash and barefaced expedients which have been employed to give success to the attempted imposition.

In one instance, which I cite as a sample of the general spirit, the temerity has proceeded so far as to ascribe to the President of the United States a power, which by the instrument reported is *expressly* allotted to the executives of the individual States.-I mean the power of filling casual vacancies in the Senate.

This bold experiment upon the discernment of his countrymen, has been hazarded by a writer who (whatever may be his real merit) has had no inconsiderable share in the applauses of his party;[a]-and who upon this false and unfounded suggestion, has built a series of observations equally false and unfounded. Let him now be confronted with the evidence of the fact; and let him, if he be able, justify or extenuate the shameful outrage he has offered to the dictates of truth and to the rules of fair dealing.

The second clause of the second section of the second article empowers the President of the United States "to nominate, and by and with the advice and consent of the Senate to appoint ambassadors, other public ministers and consuls, judges of the Supreme Court, and all other *officers* of the United States, whose appointments are *not* in the Constitution *otherwise provided for*, and *which shall be established by law*." Immediately after this clause follows another in these words-"The President shall have power to fill up all *vacancies* that may happen *during the recess of the Senate*, by granting commissions which shall *expire at the end of their next session*." It is from this last provision that the pretended power of the President to fill vacancies in the Senate has been deduced. A slight attention to the connection of the clauses and to the obvious meaning of the terms will satisfy us that the deduction is not even colorable.

The first of these two clauses it is clear only provides a mode for appointing such officers, "whose appointments are *not otherwise provided for* in the Constitution, and which *shall be established by law*;" of course it cannot extend to the appointment of senators; whose appointments are *otherwise provided for* in the Constitution,[b] and who are *established by the Constitution*, and will not require a future establishment by law. This position will hardly be contested.

The last of these two clauses, it is equally clear, cannot be understood to comprehend the power of filling vacancies in the Senate, for the following reasons-*First*. The relation in which that clause stands to the other, which declares the general mode of appointing officers of the United States, denotes it to be nothing more than a supplement to the other; for the purpose of establishing an auxiliary method of appointment in cases, to which the general method was inadequate. The ordinary power of appointment is confided to the President and Senate *jointly*, and can therefore only be exercised during the session of the Senate; but as it would have been improper to oblige this body to be continually in session for the appointment of officers; and as vacancies might happen *in their recess*, which it might be necessary for the public service to fill without delay, the succeeding clause is evidently intended to authorise the President *singly* to make temporary appointments "during the recess of the Senate, by granting commissions which should expire at the end of their next session."-*Secondly*. If this clause is to be considered as supplementary to the one which precedes, the *vacancies* of which it speaks must be construed to relate to the "officers" described in the preceding one; and this we have seen excludes from its description the members of the Senate.-*Thirdly*. The time within which the power is to operate "during the recess of the Senate" and the duration of the appointments "to the end of the next session" of that body, conspire to elucidate the sense of the provision; which if it had been intended to comprehend Senators would naturally have referred the temporary power of filling vacancies to the recess of the State Legislatures, who are to make the permanent appointments, and not to the recess of the national Senate, who are to have no concern in those appointments; and would have extended the duration in office of the temporary Senators to the next session of the Legislature of the State, in whose representation the vacancies had happened, instead of making it to expire at the end of the ensuing session of the national Senate. The circumstances of the body authorised to make the permanent appointments, would of course have governed the modification of a power which related to the temporary appointments; and as the national Senate is the body whose situation is alone contemplated in the clause upon which the suggestion under examination has been founded, the vacancies to which it alludes can only be deemed to respect those officers, in whose appointment that body has a concurrent agency with the President.-But, *lastly*, the first and second clauses of the third section of the first article, not only obviate the possibility of doubt, but destroy the pretext of misconception. The former provides that "the Senate of the United States shall be composed of two Senators from each State, chosen *by the Legislature thereof* for six years," and the latter directs that "if vacancies in that body should happen by resignation or otherwise *during the recess of the Legislature of* ANY STATE, the Executive THEREOF may make temporary appointments until the *next meeting of the Legislature*, which shall then fill such vacancies." Here is an express power given, in clear and unambiguous terms, to the State executives to fill the casual vacancies in the Senate by temporary appointments; which not only invalidates the supposition, that the clause before considered could have been intended to confer that power upon the President of the United States; but proves that this supposition, destitute as it is even of the merit of plausibility, must have originated in an intention to deceive the people, too palpable to be obscured by sophistry, and too atrocious to be palliated by hypocrisy.

I have taken the pains to select this instance of misrepresentation, and to place it in a clear and strong light, as an unequivocal proof of the unwarrantable arts which are practised to prevent a fair and impartial judgment of the real merits of the constitution submitted to the consideration of the people. Nor have I scrupled in so flagrant a case to allow myself in a severity of animadversion little congenial with the general spirit of these papers. I hesitate not to submit it to the decision of any candid and honest adversary of the proposed government, whether language can furnish epithets of too much asperity for so shameless and so prostitute an attempt to impose on the citizens of America.

(a) *See Cato No.* 5.[2]
(b) *Article* I. §3. *Clause* I.

1. "Greater" substituted in the M'Lean edition.
2. "Cato" V stated that the Constitutional Convention had "given to the executive the unprecedented power of making temporary senators, in case of vacancies, by resignation or otherwise" (*New York Journal*, 22 November, CC:286).

613. William Findley to William Irvine
Philadelphia, 12 March (excerpt)[1]

. . . With respect to the publication Subscribed Aristides[2] which you were pleased to in[s]cribe to me, I have by being too tedious already precluded the oppertunity of making particuliar remarks, and shall only observe in general–that the Auther ~~makes~~ gaves greater evidences of his good will to Support, and his enthusiastical abilitys to declaim, in favour of the new System, than of his digested knowledge of the operation of political principles upon Government or candour in stating the objections which he pretends to refute or his good Sense in aranging the principles which he professes to explain. I conclude that the Auther hath never passed the threshold of politics or else considers his readers to have little understanding, permitt me Sir to conclude with some of my own Sentiments.–I do not object to the construction of the new System but to the powers as they extend to internal objects, and eventually leaves us no means of relief or protection in the State governments, I believe the System is impracticable, because that from our extended situation and our thinness of Settling, our proportioned Scarcity of men for Armys, and Small resourses of Supporting them, from the independence of our habits and Situation and Consequent Jealousys now much ex[c]ited, our Goverment must be a Government of confidence, it must be a Goverment Supported by affection arising from an apprehension of mutual interest, and Seccurity, and not of fear and apprehension, I wish the powers at present practi[c]able only had been given and the door left open for encreasing those powers with greater ease when Circumstances would have required it–had the Federal Convention given Such powers only as we had ground to expect, or as congress ever expressed a wish to enjoy; and altered the Construction of the General Government as they have done, and rendered nine states agreeing Sufficient for future alterations; Congress would have had all the powers they could venture at the beginning to exercise at any rate, and the future encrease of authority would have been Sufficiently facicilitated; under the existing confederation I believe Nine or more states have agreed to almost every new power that hath been asked[3]- [I not?] only lament the plan but the methods that have been all along taken in Pennsylvania at least, to have it adopted–these methods of Violence and deception were not only calculated to ex[c]ite Jealousys, but resentments–I am Sorry that the Federalists addressed our implicite faith So much with great Names, instead of addressing our reason with Solid Arguments–it hath at last as might have have been expected, brought our most esteemed chara[c]ters to be treated as common things–You will find by our papers, one of which I enclose you as a Sample, that the triffling and Scourilous fictious Letters of Margery,[4] have produced the more masterly Satirecal though perhaps not Less Scurilous letters of — De. Calidonia[5] &c–but having greatly transgressed the bounds of a Letter. I shall request you not to neglect writing to me for fear of Such Lengthy replys–I expect we will adjourn in about two weeks, and should be very glad to hear from Genl. Irwin before that time–Messrs. McClene, Smily Smith[6] &c, are well.

1. RC, Irvine Papers, PHi. Postmarked 14 March. Findley (1741-1821), a native of northern Ireland who had emigrated to Pennsylvania in 1763, was in Philadelphia representing Westmoreland County in the state Assembly. Findley held many state offices: Council of Censors, 1783-84; Assembly, 1784-88; Supreme Executive Council, 1789-90; constitutional convention, 1789-90; House of Representatives, 1790-91; and Senate, 1799-1803. He was one of the leading opponents of the Constitution in the state Convention in November-December 1787. He also served in the U.S. House of Representatives from 1791 to 1799 and from 1803 to 1817.

2. A Federalist pamphlet, written by "Aristides" (Alexander Contee Hanson) and entitled *Remarks on the Proposed Plan of a Federal Government* . . ., went on sale in Annapolis on 31 January. Hanson sent "a large pacquet of Pamphlets" to his uncle, Benjamin Contee of Maryland, who, like Irvine, was in New York as a delegate to Congress (CC:490).

3. The Impost of 1781 was adopted by every state except Rhode Island, although Virginia and New York rescinded their ratifications in December 1782 and March 1783, respectively. The Impost of 1783 and the grant of commercial power of 1784 were adopted by every state, although, in both cases, the ratifications of some states were unacceptable to Congress. Consequently, neither measure ever became law. Moreover, by August 1786 only five states had granted Congress the supplementary funds that were tied to the Impost of 1783. The Impost could not go into effect until every state granted Congress these funds. The amendment to the Articles changing the method of apportioning expenses among the states was adopted by every state except New Hampshire and Rhode Island. (For these grants of additional power, see CDR, 140-41, 146-50, 153-54; and CC:Vol. 1, pp. 11-25.)

4. Seven satirical articles, in the form of "Letters of Margery," were printed in the Federalist *Pennsylvania Mercury* from 21 February to 8 March (Mfm:Pa. 444-45, 449-50, 472-73, 501). "Margery" was a nickname for Antifederalist leader George Bryan who Federalists believed was the author of the "Centinel" essays.

5. Four satirical articles, in the form of letters between James Bowdoin and James de Caledonia (i.e., James Wilson), were published in Philadelphia in the Antifederalist *Independent Gazetteer* and *Freeman's Journal* between 27 February and 14 March (CC:570; and Mfm:Pa. 457, 481, 512, 522).

6. Antifederalist leaders James McLene, John Smilie, and Abraham Smith were in Philadelphia as members of the Supreme Executive Council.

614. Philadelphia Freeman's Journal, 12 March[1]

Even the *partial* success of the new Constitution (says a correspondent) is now at an end: its advocates themselves now give the matter over, tho' they set the best face on their affairs. The four trifling States of Delaware, Connecticut, Georgia and Jersey, have adopted it, but this was only obtained by precipitancy, the suppression of discussion, and the stoppage of newspapers in the Post-Office; the leaders in these states too were led into it, in some measure, by their states being delinquent, and by the new system they would be discharged from repaying to Pennsylvania, &c. vast sums she lent the Union.[2]

Pennsylvania is said to have adopted it; but it is far otherwise, it was done only by one twelfth of the people, and illegally too.[3]

Massachusetts has been procured by a very small majority, and that too with considerable amendments.

New-Hampshire convention has adjourned till summer; 100 miles farther back in the country; above three fourths of that convention are instructed to vote against it.

The other State Conventions will be all opposed to it; they do not meet this long time. Would it not be adviseable to recommend a general thanksgiving throughout the State, to that Providence which has thus defeated such a deep laid scheme against the peace and happiness of America.

It has been the constant practice of the advocates of the new Constitution, ever since its publication, to abuse the characters of all who differed in opinion with them, and in the same moment to extol to the heavens the characters of its advocates; thus we find in the beginning of their paragraphs the illustrious, pious, magnanimous names of its friends, and in the conclusion the nefarious, villainarious, and scoundelarious names of Gerry, Martin, Lee, Clinton, Mason, &c. who have been constantly abused with torrents of scurrility: But when a part of the new system is discovered, which makes it necessary to call on the public defaulters and delinquent States for the *millions* detained by them from the public treasury, as they will by this system be skreened from public justice; Oh they then cry out, Shame upon you, low born gentry, to call such grand big men public defaulters, their characters are sacred; it is blasphemy to touch their names: if they owe the public millions, the people must sit down and bear it patiently, without so much as a murmur.

1. The last paragraph was reprinted in the *New York Journal*, 22 March, and the Boston *American Herald*, 31 March.
2. By 1790 Delaware paid 53 percent of its specie requisitions and 42 percent of its indents requisitions; Connecticut, 36 and 14 percent, respectively; New Jersey, 42 percent in specie; and Georgia nothing at all (ASP, *Finance*, I, 56–57).

3. The minority of the Pennsylvania Convention declared that more than 70,000 freemen could vote in Pennsylvania, but that the forty-six Convention delegates who voted for ratification were elected by only 6,800 freemen (CC:353, p. 17. See also RCS:Pa., 264–65, and CC:394.). On the questionable legality of the calling of the state convention, see CC:125.

615. Publius: The Federalist 68
New York Independent Journal, 12 March

This essay, written by Alexander Hamilton, was reprinted in the *New York Packet* on 14 March. It was number 68 in the M'Lean edition and number 67 in the newspapers.

For a general discussion of the authorship, circulation, and impact of *The Federalist*, see CC:201, 639.

The FEDERALIST. No. LXVII.

To the People of the State of New-York.

The mode of appointment of the chief magistrate of the United States is almost the only part of the system, of any consequence, which has escaped without severe censure, or which has received the slightest mark of approbation from its opponents. The most plausible of these, who has appeared in print, has even deigned to admit, that the election of the president is pretty well guarded.[a] I venture somewhat further; and hesitate not to affirm, that if the manner of it be not perfect, it is at least excellent. It unites in an eminent degree all the advantages; the union of which was to be desired.

It was desireable, that the sense of the people should operate in the choice of the person to whom so important a trust was to be confided. This end will be answered by committing the right of making it, not to any pre-established body, but to men, chosen by the people for the special purpose, and at the particular conjuncture.

It was equally desirable, that the immediate election should be made by men most capable of analizing the qualities adapted to the station, and acting under circumstances favourable to deliberation and to a judicious combination of all the reasons and inducements, which were proper to govern their choice. A small number of persons, selected by their fellow citizens from the general mass, will be most likely to possess the information and discernment requisite to such complicated investigations.

It was also peculiarly desirable, to afford as little opportunity as possible to tumult and disorder. This evil was not least to be dreaded in the election of a magistrate, who was to have so important an agency in the administration of the government, as the president of the United States. But the precautions which have been so happily concerted in the system under consideration, promise an effectual security against this mischief. The choice of *several* to form an intermediate body of electors, will be much less apt to convulse the community, with any extraordinary or violent movements, than the choice of *one* who was himself to be the final object of the public wishes. And as the electors, chosen in each state, are to assemble and vote in the state, in which they are chosen, this detatched and divided situation will expose them much less to heats and ferments, which might be communicated from them to the people, than if they were all to be convened at one time, in one place.

Nothing was more to be desired, than that every practicable obstacle should be opposed to cabal, intrigue and corruption. These most deadly adversaries of republican government might naturally have been expected to make their aproaches from more than one quarter, but chiefly from the desire in foreign powers to gain an improper ascendant in our councils. How could they better gratify this, than by raising a creature of their own to the chief magistracy of the union? But the convention have guarded against all danger of this sort with the most provident and judicious attention. They have not made the appointment of the president to depend on any pre-existing bodies of men who might be tampered with before hand to prostitute their votes; but they have referred it in the first instance to an immediate act of the people of America, to be exerted in the choice of persons for the temporary and sole purpose of making the appointment. And they have excluded from elegibility to this trust, all those who from situation might be suspected of too great devotion to the president in office. No senator, representative, or other person holding a place of trust or profit under the United States, can be of the number of the electors. Thus, without corrupting the body of the people, the immediate agents in the election will at least enter upon the task, free from any sinister byass. Their transient existence, and their detached situation, already taken notice of, afford a satisfactory prospect of their continuing so, to the conclusion of it. The business of corruption, when it is to embrace so considerable a number of men, requires time, as well as means. Nor would it be found easy suddenly to embark them, dispersed as they would be over thirteen states, in any combinations, founded upon motives, which though they could not properly be denominated corrupt, might yet be of a nature to mislead them from their duty.

Another and no less important desideratum was, that the executive should be independent for his continuance in office on all, but the people themselves. He might otherwise be tempted to sacrifice his duty to his complaisance for those whose favor was necessary to the duration of his official consequence. This advantage will also be secured, by making his re-election to depend on a special body of representatives, deputed by the society for the single purpose of making the important choice.

All these advantages will be happily combined in the plan devised by the convention; which is, that the people of each state shall choose a number of persons as electors, equal to the number of senators and representatives of such state in the national government, who shall assemble within the state and vote for some fit person as president. Their votes, thus given, are to be transmitted to the seat of the national government; and the person who may happen to have a majority of the whole number of votes will be the president. But as a majority of the votes might not always happen to centre on one man and as it might be unsafe to permit less than a majority to be conclusive, it is provided, that in such a contingency, the house of representatives shall select out of the candidates, who shall have the five highest numbers of votes, the man who in their opinion may be best qualified for the office.

This process of election affords a moral certainty, that the office of president, will never[1] fall to the lot of any man, who is not in an eminent degree endowed with the requisite qualifications. Talents for low intrigue and the little arts of popularity may alone suffice to elevate a man to the first honors in a single state; but it will require other talents and a different kind of merit to establish him in the esteem and confidence of the whole union, or of so considerable a portion of it as would be necessary to make him a successful candidate for the distinguished office of president of the United States. It will not be too strong to say, that there will be a constant probability of seeing the station filled by characters pre-eminent for ability and virtue. And this will be thought no inconsiderable recommendation of the constitution, by those, who are able to estimate the share, which the executive in every government must necessarily have in its good or ill administration. Though we cannot acquiesce in the political heresy of the poet who says–

> "For forms of government let facts[2] contest–
> That which is best administered is best."[3]

–yet we may safely pronounce, that the true test of a good government is its aptitude and tendency to produce a good administration.

The vice-president is to be chosen in the same manner with the president; with this difference, that the senate is to do, in respect to the former, what is to be done by the house of representatives, in respect to the latter.

The appointment of an extraordinary person, as vice president, has been objected to as superfluous, if not mischievous. It has been alledged, that it would have been preferable to have authorised the senate to elect out of their own body an officer, answering that description. But two considerations seem to justify the ideas of the convention in this respect. One is, that to secure at all times the possibility of a definitive resolution of the body, it is necessary that the president should have only a casting vote. And to take the senator of any state from his seat as senator, to place him in that of president of the senate, would be to exchange, in regard to the state from which he came, a constant for a contingent vote. The other consideration is, that as the vice-president may occasionally become a substitute for the president, in the supreme executive magistracy, all the reasons, which recommend the mode of election prescribed for the one, apply with great, if not with equal, force to the manner of appointing the other. It is remarkable, that in this as in most other instances, the objection, which is made, would be against the constitution of this state. We have a Lieutenant Governor chosen by the people at large, who presides in the senate, and is the constitutional substitute for the Governor in casualties similar to those, which would authorise the vice-president to exercise the authorities and discharge the duties of the president.

> (a) *Vide Federal Farmer.*[4]

1. "Seldom" substituted in the M'Lean edition.
2. The M'Lean edition substituted the correct word "fools."
3. Alexander Pope, *An Essay on Man* . . . (London, 1758), Epistle III, 30. The third epistle was first published in 1733. Pope's line "That which is best administered is best" was also quoted in Letter I of the *Letters from the Federal Farmer*, 8 November (CC:242), another part of which "Publius" refers to in this essay (see note 4 below).
4. See Letter III in *Letters from the Federal Farmer*, 8 November (CC:242, p. 33).

616. Marcus IV
Norfolk and Portsmouth Journal, 12 March[1]

Answers to Mr. Mason's *Objections* to the New Constitution, Recommended by the late Convention at Philadelphia.
VIIIth. Objection.

"Under their own construction of the general clause at the end of the enumerated powers, the Congress may grant monopolies in trade and commerce, constitute new crimes, inflict unusual and severe punishments, and extend their power as far as they shall think proper; so that the State Legislatures have no security for the powers now presumed to remain to them, or the people for their rights. There is no declaration of any kind for preserving the Liberty of the Press–the Trial by Jury in civil cases–nor against the danger of standing armies in time of peace."

Answer.

The general clause at the end of the enumerated powers is as follows:–

"To make all laws which shall be necessary and proper for carrying into execution the *foregoing powers, and all other powers vested by this Constitution in the United States, or in any department or office*[2] *thereof.*"

Those powers would be useless, except acts of Legislation could be exercised upon them. It was not possible for the Convention, nor is it for any human body, to foresee and provide for all contingent cases that may arise. Such cases must therefore be left to be provided for by the general Legislature, as they shall happen to come into existence. If Congress, under pretence of exercising the power delegated to them, should, in fact, by the exercise of any other power, usurp upon the rights of the different Legislatures, or of any private citizens, the people will be exactly in the same situation as if there had been an express provision against such power in particular, and yet they had presumed to exercise it. It would be an act of tyranny, against which no parchment stipulations can guard; and the Convention surely can be only answerable for the propriety of the powers given, not for the future virtues of all with whom those powers may be entrusted. It does not therefore appear to me, that there is any weight in this objection more than in others–but, that I may give it every fair advantage, I will take notice of every particular injurious act of power which Mr. Mason points out as exerciseable by the authority of Congress, under this general clause.

The first mentioned is, "That the Congress may grant monopolies in trade and commerce." Upon examining the Constitution, I find it expressly provided, "That no preference shall be given to the ports of one State over those of another;" and that "Citizens of each State shall be entitled to all privileges and immunities of citizens in the several States." These provisions appear to me to be calculated for the very purpose Mr. Mason wishes to secure. Can they be consistent with any monopoly in trade and commerce?[(a)] I apprehend therefore, under this expression must be intended more than is expressed; and if I may conjecture from another publication of a gentleman of the same State and in the same party of opposition,[3] I should suppose it arose from a jealousy of the Eastern States, very well known to be often expressed by some gentlemen of Virginia. They fear, that a majority of the States may establish regulations of commerce which will give great advantage to the carrying trade of America, and be a means of encouraging New England vessels rather than old England.–Be it so.–No regulations can give such advantage to New England vessels, which will not be enjoyed by all other American vessels, and many States can build as well as New England, tho' not at present perhaps in equal proportion.[(b)] And what could conduce more to the preservation of the union, than allowing to every kind of industry in America a peculiar preference! Each State exerting itself in its own way, but the exertions of all contributing to the common security, and increasing the rising greatness of our country! Is it not the aim of every wise country to be as much the carriers of their own produce as can be? And would not this be the means in our own of producing a new source of activity among the people, giving to our own fellow citizens what otherwise must be given to strangers, and laying the foundation of an independent trade among ourselves, and of gradually raising a navy in America, which, however distant the prospect, ought certainly not to be out of our sight. There is no great probability however that our country is likely soon to enjoy so glorious an advantage. We must have treaties of commerce, because without them we cannot trade to other countries. We already have such with some nations–we have none with Great-Britain; which can be imputed to no other cause but our not having a strong respectable government to bring that nation to terms. And surely no man who feels for the honor of his country, but must view our present degrading commerce with that country with the highest indignation, and the most ardent wish to extricate ourselves from so disgraceful a situation. This only can be done by a powerful government, which can dictate conditions of advantage to ourselves, as an equivalent for advantages to them; and this could undoubtedly be easily done by such a government, without diminishing the value of any articles of our own produce; or if there was any diminution it would be too slight to be felt by any patriot in competition with the honor and interest of his country.

As to the constituting new crimes, and inflicting unusual and severe punishment, certainly the cases enumerated wherein the Congress are empowered either to define offences, or prescribe punishments, are such as are proper for the exercise of such authority in the general Legislature of the union. They only relate to "counterfeiting the securities and current coin of the United States; to piracies and felonies committed on the high seas, and offences against the law of nations, and to treason against the United States." These are offences immediately affecting the security, the honor or the interest of the United States at large, and of course must come within the sphere of the Legislative authority which is entrusted with their protection. Beyond these authorities Congress can exercise no other power of this kind, except in the enacting of penalties to enforce their acts of Legislation in the cases where express authority is delegated to them, and if they could not enforce such acts by the enacting of penalties, those powers would be altogether useless, since a legislative regulation without some sanction would be an absurd thing indeed. The Congress having, for these reasons, a just right to authority in the above particulars, the question is, whether it is practicable and proper to prescribe the limits to its exercise, for fear that they should inflict punishments unusual and severe? It may be observed in the first place, that a declaration against "cruel and unusual punishments," formed part of an article in the Bill of Rights at the Revolution in England, in 1688. The prerogative of the Crown having been grossly abused in some preceding reigns, it was thought proper to notice every grievance they had endured, and those declarations went to an abuse of power in the crown only, but were never intended to limit the authority of Parliament. Many of these articles of the Bill of Rights in England, without a due attention to the difference of the cases, were eagerly adopted when our Constitutions were formed, the minds of men then being so warmed with their exertions in the cause of liberty, as to lean too much perhaps towards a jealousy of power to repose a proper confidence in their own government. From these articles in the State Constitutions, many things were attempted to be transplanted into our new Constitution, which would either have been nugatory or improper: This is one of them. The expressions "unusual and severe," or "cruel and unusual," surely would have been too vague to have been of any consequence, since they admit of no clear and precise signification. If to guard against punishments being too severe, the Convention had enumerated a vast variety of cruel punishments, and prohibited the use of any of them, let the number have been ever so great, an inexhaustible fund must have been unmentioned, and if our government had been disposed to be cruel, their invention would only have been put to a little more trouble. If to avoid this difficulty, they had determined, not negatively, what punishments should not be exercised, but positively what punishments should, this must have led them into a labyrinth of detail which in the original constitution of a government would have appeared perfectly ridiculous, and not left a room for such changes according to circumstances, as must be in the power of every Legislature that is rationally formed. Thus, when we enter into particulars, we must be convinced that the proposition of such a restriction would have led to nothing useful, or to something dangerous, and therefore that its omission is not chargeable as a fault in the new Constitution. Let us also remember, that as those who are to make those laws must, themselves be subject to them, their own interest and feelings will dictate to them not to make them unnecessarily severe; and that in the case of treason, which usually in every country exposes men most to the avarice and rapacity of government, care is taken that the innocent family of the offender shall not suffer for the treason of their relation. This is the crime with respect to which a jealousy is of the most importance, and accordingly it is defined with great plainness and accuracy, and the temptations to abusive prosecutions guarded against as much as possible. I now proceed to the three great cases:–The Liberty of the Press–The Trial by Jury in civil cases, and a Standing Army in time of peace.

The Liberty of the Press is always a grand topic for declamation; but the future Congress will have no other authority over this than to secure to authors for a limited time the exclusive privilege of publishing their works. This authority has long been exercised in England, where the press is as free as among ourselves, or in any country in the world, and surely such an encouragement to genius is no restraint on the liberty of the press, since men are allowed to publish what they please of their own; and so far as this may be deemed a restraint upon others it is certainly a reasonable one, and can be attended with no danger of copies not being sufficiently multiplied, because the interest of the proprietor will always induce him to publish a quantity fully equal to the demand–besides, that such encouragement may give birth to many excellent writings which would otherwise have never appeared.[c] If the Congress should exercise any other power over the press than this, they will do it without any warrant from this Constitution, and must answer for it as for any other act of tyranny.

In respect to the trial by jury in civil cases, it must be observed, it is a mistake to suppose, that such a trial takes place in all civil cases now. Even in the common law Courts, such a trial is only had where facts are disputed between the parties, and there are even some facts triable by other methods. In the Chancery and Admiralty Courts, in many of the States, I am told, they have no Juries at all. The States in these particulars differ very much in their practice from each other: A general declaration therefore to preserve the trial by Jury in all civil cases, would only have produced confusion, so that the Courts afterwards in a thousand instances would not have known how to have proceeded. If they had added "as heretofore accustomed," that would not have answered the purpose, because there has been no uniform custom about it. If therefore the Convention had interfered, it must have been by entering into a detail highly unsuitable to a fundamental constitution of government: If they had pleased some States, they must have displeased others, by innovating upon modes of administering justice perhaps endeared to them by habit, and agreeable to their settled conviction of propriety. As this was the case it appears to me it was infinitely better, rather than endanger every thing by attempting too much, to leave this complicated business of detail, to the regulation of the future Legislature, where it can be adjusted coolly and at ease, and upon full and exact information.–There is no danger of the trial by Jury being rejected, when so justly a favorite of the whole people. The Representatives of the people surely can have no interest in making themselves odious for the mere pleasure of being hated; and when a Member of the House of Representatives is only sure of being so for two years, but must continue a citizen all his life, his interest as a citizen, if he is a man of common sense, to say nothing of his being a man of common honesty, must ever be uppermost in his mind. We know the great influence of the monarchy in the British government, and upon what a different tenure the Commons there have their seats in Parliament, from that prescribed to our Representatives. We know also, they have a large standing army. It is in the power of the Parliament if they dare to exercise it, to abolish the trial by jury altogether–but woe be to the man who should dare to attempt it–it would undoubtedly produce an insurrection that would hurl every tyrant to the ground who attempted to destroy that great and just favorite of the English nation. We certainly shall be always sure of this guard at least, upon any such act of folly or insanity in our Representatives: They soon would be taught the consequence of sporting with the feelings of a free people. But when it is evident that such an attempt cannot be rationally apprehended, we have no reason to anticipate unpleasing emotions of that nature. There is indeed little probability, that any degree of tyranny which can be figured to the most discoloured imagination, as likely to arise out of our government, could find an interest in attacking the trial by Jury in civil cases; and in criminal ones, where no such difficulties intervened as in the other, and where there might be supposed temptations to violate the personal security of a citizen, it is sacredly preserved.

The subject of a standing army has been exhausted in so masterly a manner in two or three numbers of the Fœderalist[4] (a work which I hope will soon be in every body's hands)[5] that, but for the sake of regularity in answering Mr. Mason's objections, I should not venture upon the same topic; and shall only presume to do so, with a reference for fuller satisfaction to that able performance. It is certainly one of the most delicate and proper cases for the consideration of a free people, and so far as a jealousy of this kind leads to any degree of caution not incompatible with the public safety, it is undoubtedly to be commended. Our jealousy of this danger has descended to us from our British ancestors: In that country they have a monarch, whose power being limited, and at the same time his prerogatives very considerable, a constant jealousy of him is both natural and proper. The two last of the Stuarts having kept up a considerable body of standing forces in time of peace, for the clear and almost avowed purpose of subduing the liberties of the people, it was made an article of the Bill of Rights at the Revolution, "That the raising or keeping a standing army within the kingdom in time of peace, unless it be with the consent of Parliament, is against law;" but no attempt was made, or I dare say, ever thought of, to restrain the Parliament from the exercise of that right. An army has been since kept on foot annually by authority of Parliament, and I believe ever since the Revolution they have had some standing troops; disputes have frequently happened about the number, but I don't recollect any objection by the most zealous patriot, to the keeping up of any at all. At the same time, notwithstanding the above practice of an annual vote (arising from a very judicious caution) it is still in the power of Parliament to authorise the keeping up of any number of troops for any indefinite time, and to provide for their subsistence for any number of years: Considerations of prudence, not constitutional limits to their authority, alone restrain such an exercise of it. Our Legislature however will be strongly guarded, though that of Great Britain is without any check at all. No appropriations of money for military service can continue longer than two years. Considering the extensive services the general government may have to provide for upon this vast continent, no forces with any serious prospect of success, could be attempted to be raised for a shorter time. Its being done for so short a period, if there were any appearances of ill designs in the government, would afford time enough for the real friends of their country to sound an alarm; and when we know how easy it is to excite jealousy of any government, how difficult for the people to distinguish from their real friends, those factious men, who in every country are ready to disturb its peace for personal gratifications of their own, and those desperate ones to whom every change is welcome, we shall have much more reason to fear that the government may be overawed by groundless discontents, than that it should be able, if contrary to every probability such a government could be supposed willing, to effect any designs for the destruction of their own liberties, as well as those of their constituents: For surely we ought ever to remember, that there will not be a man in the government but who has been either mediately or immediately recently chosen by the people, and that for too limited a time to make any arbitrary designs, consistent with common sense, when every two years a new body of Representatives, with all the energy of popular feelings, will come to carry the strong force of a severe national controul, into every department of government; to say nothing of the one-third to compose the Senate, coming at the same time warm with popular sentiments from their respective Assemblies. Men may, to be sure, suggest dangers from any thing; but it may truly be said, that those who can seriously suggest the danger of a premeditated attack on the liberties of the people from such a government as this, could with ease assign reasons equally plausible for distrusting the integrity of any government formed in any manner whatever; and really it does seem to me, that all their reasons may be fairly carried to this position,–that in as much as any confidence in any men would be unwise, as we can give no power but what may be grossly abused, we had better give none at all, but continue as we are, or resolve into total anarchy at once, of which indeed, our present condition falls very little short. What sort of a government must that be, which, upon the most certain intelligence that hostilities were meditated against it, could take no method for its defence, till after a formal declaration, of war, or the enemy's standard was actually fixed upon the shore. The first has for some time been out of fashion; but if it had not, the restraint these gentlemen recommend, would certainly have brought it into disuse with every Power who meant to make war upon America. They would not be such fools as to give us the only warning we had informed them we would accept of, before we would take any steps to counteract their designs. The absurdity of our being prohibited from preparing to resist an invasion till after it had actually taken place,[d] is so glaring that no man can consider it for a moment without being struck with astonishment, to see how rashly, and with how little consideration gentlemen, whose characters are certainly respectable, have suffered themselves to be led away by so delusive an idea. The example of other countries, so far from warranting any such limitation of power, is directly against it. That of England is particularly noticed. In our present articles of Confederation there is no such restriction. It has been observed by the Fœderalist, that Pennsylvania and North-Carolina appear to be the only States in the union, which have attempted any restraint of the Legislative authority in this particular, and that their restraint appears rather in the light of a caution than a prohibition; but, that notwithstanding that, Pennsylvania had been obliged to raise forces in the very face of that article of her Bill of Rights.[6] That great writer, from the remoteness of his situation, did not know that North-Carolina had equally violated her Bill of Rights in a similar manner. The Legislature of that State, in November 1786, passed an act for raising 201 men for the protection of a County called Davidson County, against hostilities from the Indians; they were to continue for *two years* from the time of their first rendezvous, unless sooner disbanded by the Assembly; and were to be "subject to the same rules with respect to their government as were established in the time of the late war by the Congress of the United States, for the government of the Continental army:"[7] These are the very words of the act. Thus, for the example of the only two countries in the world, that I believe ever attempted such a restriction, it appears to be a thing incompatible with the safety of government. Whether their restriction is to be considered as a caution or a prohibition, in less than five years after peace the caution has been disregarded, or the prohibition disobeyed.[e] Can the most credulous or suspicious man, require stronger proof of the weakness and impolicy of such restraints?

(To be concluded in our next.)

(a) *One of the powers given to Congress is, "To promote the progress of science and useful arts, by securing for limited times to authors and inventors, the exclusive right to their respective writings and discoveries." I am convinced Mr. Mason did not mean to refer to this clause. He is a gentleman of too much taste and knowledge himself to wish to have our government established upon such principles of barbarism as to be able to afford no encouragement to genius.*

(b) *Some might apprehend, that in this case as New England would at first have the greatest share of the carrying trade, that the vessels of that country might demand an unreasonable freight; but no attempt could be more injurious to them, as it would immediately set the Southern States to building, which they could easily do, and thus a temporary loss would be compensated with a lasting advantage to us. The very reverse would be the case with them; besides, that from that country alone there would probably be competition enough for freight to keep it upon reasonable terms.*

(c) *If this provision had not been made in the new Constitution, no author could have enjoyed such an advantage in all the United States, unless a similar law constantly subsisted in each of the States separately.*

(d) *Those gentlemen who gravely tell us the militia will be sufficient for this purpose, do not recollect that they themselves do not desire we should rely solely on a militia in case of actual war, and therefore in the case I have supposed, they cannot be deemed sufficient even by themselves, for when the enemy landed it would undoubtedly be a time of war, but the misfortune would be, that they would be prepared—we not. Certainly all possible encouragement should be given to the training of our militia, but no man can really believe that they will be sufficient without the aid of any regular troops, in a time of foreign hostility. A powerful militia may make fewer regulars necessary, but will not make it safe to dispense with them altogether.*

(e) *I presume we are not to be deemed in a state of war whenever any Indian hostilities are committed on our frontiers. If that is the case, I don't suppose we have had six years of peace since the first settlement of the country, or shall have for fifty years to come. A distinction between peace and war would be idle indeed, if it can be frittered away by such pretences as those.*

1. For the authorship and circulation of "Marcus," see CC:548.
2. The word in the Constitution is "officer." The italics are "Marcus'."
3. See Richard Henry Lee to Governor Edmund Randolph, 16 October, Petersburg *Virginia Gazette*, 6 December (CC:325).
4. See *The Federalist* 24–28, which were published in New York between 19 and 26 December (CC:355, 364, 366, 378, 381).
5. On 30 January the *Norfolk and Portsmouth Journal* printed an advertisement, dated 16 January, announcing that the printer was taking subscriptions for a pamphlet of *The Federalist*. (The *Journal* issues of 16 and 23 January are not extant.) For the publication of *The Federalist* in book form, see CC:406, and for Iredell's subscription to *The Federalist*, see CC:548.
6. See *The Federalist* 25 (CC:364).
7. See NCSR, XXIV, 783–86.

617. Publius: The Federalist 69
New York Packet, 14 March

This essay, written by Alexander Hamilton, was reprinted in the New York *Independent Journal* on 15 March. It was number 69 in the M'Lean edition and number 68 in the newspapers.

For a general discussion of the authorship, circulation, and impact of *The Federalist*, see CC:201, 639.

The FŒDERALIST, No. 68.
To the People of the State of New-York.

I proceed now to trace the real characters of the proposed executive as they are marked out in the plan of the Convention. This will serve to place in a strong light the unfairness of the representations which have been made in regard to it.

The first thing which strikes our attention is that the executive authority, with few exceptions, is to be vested in a single magistrate. This will scarcely however be considered as a point upon which any comparison can be grounded; for if in this particular there be a resemblance to the King of Great-Britain, there is not less a resemblance to the Grand Signior, to the Khan of Tartary, to the man of the seven mountains, or to the Governor of New-York.

That magistrate is to be elected for *four* years; and is to be re-eligible as often as the People of the United States shall think him worthy of their confidence. In these circumstances, there is a total dissimilitude between *him* and a King of Great-Britain; who is an *hereditary* monarch, possessing the crown as a patrimony descendible to his heirs forever; but there is a close analogy between *him* and a Governor of New-York, who is elected for *three* years, and is re-eligible without limitation or intermission. If we consider how much less time would be requisite for establishing a dangerous influence in a single State, than for establishing a like influence throughout the United States, we must conclude that a duration of *four* years for the Chief Magistrate of the Union, is a degree of permanency far less to be dreaded in that office, than a duration of *three* years for a correspondent office in a single State.

The President of the United States would be liable to be impeached, tried, and upon conviction of treason, bribery, or other high crimes or misdemeanors, removed from office; and would afterwards be liable to prosecution and punishment in the ordinary course of law. The person of the King of Great-Britain is sacred and inviolable: There is no constitutional tribunal to which he is amenable; no punishment to which he can be subjected without involving the crisis of a national revolution. In this delicate and important circumstance of personal responsibility, the President of confederated America would stand upon no better ground than a Governor of New-York, and upon worse ground than the Governors of Maryland and Delaware.[1]

The President of the United States is to have power to return a bill, which shall have passed the two branches of the Legislature, for re-consideration; but the bill so returned is to become a law, if upon that re-consideration it be approved by two thirds of both houses.[2] The King of Great Britain, on his part, has an absolute negative upon the acts of the two houses of Parliament. The disuse of that power for a considerable time past, does not affect the reality of its existence; and is to be ascribed wholly to the crown's having found the means of substituting influence to authority, or the art of gaining a majority in one or the other of the two houses, to the necessity of exerting a prerogative which could seldom be exerted without hazarding some degree of national agitation. The qualified negative of the President differs widely from this absolute negative of the British sovereign; and tallies exactly with the revisionary authority of the Council of revision of this State, of which the Governor is a constituent part. In this respect, the power of the President would exceed that of the Governor of New-York; because the former would possess singly what the latter shares with the Chancellor and Judges:[3] But it would be precisely the same with that of the Governor of Massachusetts, whose constitution, as to this article, seems to have been the original from which the Convention have copied.[4]

The President is to be the "Commander in Chief of the army and navy of the United States, and of the militia of the several States, when called into the actual service of the United States. He is to have power to grant reprieves and pardons for offences against the United States, *except in cases of impeachment*; to recommend to the consideration of Congress such measures as he shall judge necessary and expedient; to convene on extraordinary occasions both houses of the Legislature, or either of them, and in case of disagreement between them *with respect to the time of adjournment*, to adjourn them to such time as he shall think proper; to take care that the laws be faithfully executed; and to commission all officers of the United States." In most of these particulars the power of the President will resemble equally that of the King of Great-Britain and the Governor of New-York. The most material points of difference are these–First; the President will have only the occasional command of such part of the militia of the nation, as by legislative provision may be called into the actual service of the Union–The King of Great-Britain and the Governor of New-York have at all times the entire command of all the militia within their several jurisdictions. In this article therefore the power of the President would be inferior to that of either the Monarch or the Governor.–Secondly; the President is to be Commander in Chief of the army and navy of the United States. In this respect his authority would be nominally the same with that of the King of Great-Britain, but in substance much inferior to it. It would amount to nothing more than the supreme command and direction of the military and naval forces, as first General and Admiral of the confederacy; while that of the British King extends to the *declaring* of war and to the *raising* and *regulating* of fleets and armies; all which by the Constitution under consideration would appertain to the Legislature.[a] The Governor of New-York on the other hand, is by the Constitution of the State vested only with the command of its militia and navy.[5] But the Constitutions of several of the States, expressly declare their Governors to be the Commanders in Chief as well of the army as navy;[6] and it may well be a question whether those of New-Hampshire and Massachusetts,[7] in particular, do not in this instance confer larger powers upon their respective Governors, than could be claimed by a President of the United States.–Thirdly; the power of the President in respect to pardons would extend to all cases, *except those of impeachment*. The Governor of New-York may pardon in all cases, even in those of impeachment, except for treason and murder.[8] Is not the power of the Governor in this article, on a calculation of political consequences, greater than that of the President? All conspiracies and plots against the government, which have not been matured into actual treason, may be screened from punishment of every kind, by the interposition of the prerogative of pardoning. If a Governor of New-York therefore should be at the head of any such conspiracy, until the design had been ripened into actual hostility, he could ensure his accomplices and adherents an entire impunity. A President of the Union on the other hand, though he may even pardon treason, when prosecuted in the ordinary course of law, could shelter no offender in any degree from the effects of impeachment & conviction. Would not the prospect of a total indemnity for all the preliminary steps be a greater temptation to undertake and persevere in an enterprise against the public liberty than the mere prospect of an exemption from death and confiscation, if the final execution of the design, upon an actual appeal to arms, should miscarry? Would this last expectation have any influence at all, when the probability was computed that the person who was to afford that exemption might himself be involved in the consequences of the measure; and might be incapacitated by his agency in it, from affording the desired impunity. The better to judge of this matter, it will be necessary to recollect that by the proposed Constitution the offence of treason is limitted "to levying war upon the United States, and adhering to their enemies, giving them aid and comfort," and that by the laws of New-York it is confined within similar bounds.[9]– Fourthly; the President can only adjourn the national Legislature in the single case of disagreement about the time of adjournment. The British monarch may prorogue or even dissolve the Parliament. The Governor of New-York may also prorogue the Legislature of this State for a limited time; a power which in certain situations may be employed to very important purposes.[10]

The President is to have power with the advice and consent of the Senate to make treaties; provided two thirds of the Senators present concur. The King of Great-Britain is the sole and absolute representative of the nation in all foreign transactions. He can of his own accord make treaties of peace, commerce, alliance, and of every other description. It has been insinuated, that his authority in this respect is not conclusive, and that his conventions with foreign powers are subject to revision, and stand in need of the ratification of Parliament. But I believe this doctrine was never heard of 'till it was broached upon the present occasion. Every jurist[b] of that kingdom, and every other man acquainted with its constitution knows, as an established fact, that the prerogative of making treaties exists in the crown in its utmost plenitude; and that the compacts entered into by the royal authority have the most complete legal validity and perfection, independent of any other sanction. The Parliament, it is true, is sometimes seen employing itself in altering the existing laws to conform them to the speculations in a new treaty; and this may have possibly given birth to the imagination that its co-operation was necessary to the obligatory efficacy of the treaty. But this parliamentary interposition proceeds from a different cause; from the necessity of adjusting a most artificial and intricate system of revenue and commercial laws to the changes made in them by the operation of the treaty; and of adapting new provisions and precautions to the new state of things, to keep the machine from running into disorder. In this respect therefore, there is no comparison between the intended power of the President, and the actual power of the British sovereign. The one can perform alone, what the other can only do with the concurrence of a branch of the Legislature. It must be admitted that in this instance the power of the fœderal executive would exceed that of any State executive. But this arises naturally from the exclusive possession by the Union of that part of the sovereign power, which relates to treaties. If the confederacy were to be dissolved, it would become a question, whether the executives of the several States were not solely invested with that delicate and important prerogative.

The President is also to be authorised to receive Ambassadors and other public Ministers. This, though it has been a rich theme of declamation, is more a matter of dignity than of authority. It is a circumstance, which will be without consequence in the administration of the government, and it was far more convenient that it should be arranged in this manner, than that there should be a necessity of convening the Legislature, or one of its branches, upon every arrival of a foreign minister; though it were merely to take the place of a departed predecessor.

The President is to nominate and *with the advice and consent of the Senate* to appoint Ambassadors and other public Ministers, Judges of the Supreme Court, and in general all officers of the United States established by law and whose appointments are not otherwise provided for by the Constitution. The King of Great-Britain is emphatically and truly stiled the fountain of honor. He not only appoints to all offices, but can create offices. He can confer titles of nobility at pleasure; and has the disposal of an immense number of church preferments. There is evidently a great inferiority, in the power of the President in this particular, to that of the British King; nor is it equal to that of the Governor of New-York, if we are to interpret the meaning of the constitution of the State by the practice which has obtained under it. The power of appointment is with us lodged in a Council composed of the Governor and four members of the Senate chosen by the Assembly. The Governor *claims* and has frequently *exercised* the right of nomination, and is *entitled* to a casting vote in the appointment. If he really has the right of nominating, his authority is in this respect equal to that of the President, and exceeds it in the article of the casting vote.[11] In the national government, if the Senate should be divided, no appointment could be made: In the government of New-York, if the Council should be divided the Governor can turn the scale and confirm his own nomination.(c) If we compare the publicity which must necessarily attend the mode of appointment by the President and an entire branch of the national Legislature, with the privacy in the mode of appointment by the Governor of New-York, closeted in a secret apartment with at most four, and frequently with only two persons, and if we at the same time consider how much more easy it must be to influence the small number of which a Council of Appointment consist than the considerable number of which the national Senate would consist, we cannot hesitate to pronounce, that the power of the Chief Magistrate of this State in the disposition of offices must in practice be greatly superior to that of the Chief Magistrate of the Union.

Hence it appears, that except as to the concurrent authority of the President in the article of treaties, it would be difficult to determine whether that Magistrate would in the aggregate, possess more or less power than the Governor of New-York. And it appears yet more unequivocally that there is no pretence for the parallel which has been attempted between him and the King of Great-Britain. But to render the contrast, in this respect, still more striking, it may be of use to throw the principal circumstances of dissimilitude into a closer groupe.

The President of the United States would be an officer elected by the people for *four* years. The King of Great-Britain is a perpetual and *hereditary* prince. The one would be amenable to personal punishment and disgrace: The person of the other is sacred and inviolable. The one would have a *qualified* negative upon the acts of the legislative body: The other has an *absolute* negative. The one would have a right to command the military and naval forces of the nation: The other in addition to this right, possesses that of *declaring* war, and of *raising* and *regulating* fleets and armies by his own authority. The one would have a concurrent power with a branch of the Legislature in the formation of treaties: The other is the *sole possessor* of the power of making treaties. The one would have a like concurrent authority in appointing to offices: The other is the sole author of all appointments. The one can infer no privileges whatever: The other can make denizens of aliens, noblemen of commoners, can erect corporations with all the rights incident to corporate bodies. The one can prescribe no rules concerning the commerce or currency of the nation: The other is in several respects the arbiter of commerce, and in this capacity can establish markets and fairs, can regulate weights and measures, can lay embargoes for a limited time, can coin money, can authorise or prohibit the circulation of foreign coin. The one has no particle of spiritual jurisdiction: The other is the supreme head and Governor of the national church!–What answer shall we give to those who would persuade us that things so unlike resemble each other?–The same that ought to be given to those who tell us, that a government, the whole power of which would be in the hands of the elective and periodical servants of the people, is an aristocracy, a monarchy, and a despotism.

(a) *A writer in a Pennsylvania paper, under the signature of* Tamony *has asserted that the King of Great-Britain owes his prerogatives as Commander in Chief to an annual mutiny bill.* [12] *– The truth is on the contrary that his prerogative in this respect is immemorial, and was only disputed "contrary to all reason and precedent," as* Blackstone, *vol.* I, *p.* 262, *expresses it, by the long parliament of* Charles the first, *but by the statute the* 13, *of* Charles second, *ch.* 6, *it was declared to be in the King alone, for that the sole supreme government and command of the militia within his Majesty's realms and dominions, and of all forces by sea and land, and of all forts and places of strength,* ever was and is *the undoubted right of his Majesty and his royal predecessors Kings and Queens of England,*

and that both or either House of Parliament cannot nor ought to pretend to the same.[13]

(b) *Vide Blackstone's Commentaries, page* 257.[14]

(c) *Candor however demands an acknowledgment, that I do not think the claim of the Governor to a right of nomination well founded. Yet it is always justifiable to reason from the practice of a government till its propriety has been constitutionally questioned. And independent of this claim, when we take into view the other consideration[s] and pursue them through all their consequences, we shall be inclined to draw much the same conclusion.*

1. The New York constitution provided that state officials could be impeached for "crimes and misdemeanors." The judgment of impeachment could not extend any farther "than to removal from office, and disqualification to hold or enjoy any place of honor, trust, or profit under this State. But the party so convicted shall be, nevertheless, liable and subject to indictment, trial, judgment, and punishment, according to the laws of the land" (Thorpe, V, 2635). The constitutions of Virginia (it was substituted for Maryland in the M'Lean edition) and Delaware have identical provisions: "If found guilty, he or they shall be either forever disabled to hold any office under government, or removed from office *pro tempore*, or subjected to such pains and penalties as the laws shall direct" (Thorpe, I, 566; VII, 3818).

2. The phrase in the M'Lean edition reads: "but the bill so returned is not to become a law, unless upon that re-consideration it be approved by two thirds of both houses."

3. For the Council of Revision, see CC:486, note 5.

4. The veto provisions of the U.S. and Massachusetts constitutions are almost identical, except for the fact that the governor of Massachusetts had to return a vetoed bill within five days (Thorpe, III, 1893–94).

5. The New York constitution provided that the governor "shall, by virtue of his office, be general and commander-in-chief of all the militia, and admiral of the navy of this State" (Thorpe, V, 2632).

6. The constitutions of Delaware, Georgia, Massachusetts, New Hampshire, and South Carolina all provided that the governor was to be commander in chief of the army and navy. The Maryland constitution gave the governor the command of the land and sea forces but he could not command them in person without the advice of the Council (Thorpe, I, 611; II, 782; III, 1696, 1901; IV, 2463–64; VI, 3249ff. See also note 7 below.).

7. The Massachusetts and New Hampshire constitutions granted several military powers to their state executives that were not given to the President of the United States by the U.S. Constitution. For example, the state executives of these two states could train, instruct, and exercise the state militias; could assemble and lead the inhabitants of the states in repelling and expelling invaders; and could declare martial law over the army, navy, and militia during times of war and invasion (Thorpe, III, 1901; IV, 2463–64).

8. The New York constitution gave the governor the power "to grant reprieves and pardons to persons convicted of crimes, other than treason or murder, in which he may suspend the execution of the sentence, until it shall be reported to the legislature at their subsequent meeting; and they shall either pardon or direct the execution of the criminal, or grant a further reprieve" (Thorpe, V, 2633).

9. An act passed on 16 February 1787 stated "That if any person do levy war against the people of this State, within this State, or be adherent to the enemies of the People of this State or of the United-States of America, within this State, giving to them aid and comfort in this State, or elsewhere, and be thereof by good proof attainted of open deed, such offences and none other, shall be adjudged treason against the People of the State

of New-York." No one could be indicted, tried, or attainted of treason, except "by and upon the oath and testimony of two lawful witnesses, either both of them to the same overt act, or one of them to one, and the other of them to another overt act of the same treason" (*Laws of the State of New-York, Passed by the Legislature of Said State, at Their Tenth Session* [New York, 1787], 53–55 [Evans 20578]). Hamilton was a member of the legislature that passed this act.

10. The New York constitution gave the governor the power to prorogue the legislature "from time to time, provided such prorogations shall not exceed sixty days in the space of any one year" (Thorpe, V, 2632–33).

11. For the Council of Appointment, see Thorpe, V, 2633–34. George Clinton, the governor of New York since the constitution was adopted in 1777, had assumed the sole right to nominate appointees, and for years this right went virtually unchallenged. In early 1794, while Clinton was still governor, the right to nominate was seized, against Clinton's strenuous objections, by the majority party (i.e., Federalists) in the House of Assembly.

12. "Tamony" was first printed in the *Virginia Independent Chronicle* on 9 January (CC:430) and reprinted in the Philadelphia *Independent Gazetteer* on 1 February and in the *New York Journal* on 8 February. "Tamony" noted that "The office of president is treated with levity and intimated to be a machine calculated for state pageantry–Suffer me to view the commander of the fleets and armies of America, with a reverential awe, inspired by the contemplation of his great prerogatives, though not dignified with the magic name of King, he will possess more supreme power, than Great Britain allows her hereditary monarchs, who derive ability to support an army from annual supplies, and owe the command of one to an annual mutiny law. The American President may be granted supplies for two years, and his command of a standing army is unrestrained by law or limitation."

13. *Commentaries*, I, chapter VII, 262–63.

14. *Ibid.*, 257.

618. Nathan Dane to Samuel Holten
New York, 15 March (excerpt)[1]

It was my intentions to have done myself the honor to have called on you before I left Massachusetts–but several circumstances prevented–I arrived here the 20th. of the last month–there has been a Congress most of the time for two months past, and part of the time nine States assembled– but we do but very little business–indeed we have but very little to do–It does not appear to be the intentions of Congress to engage in any important business–an adjournment has been mentioned for a few months–the reasons offered against it are such as were offered against an adjournment last year, with which you are well acquainted–many of the members are of opinion that the particular situation of our public Affairs, at this time, requires that Congress should be in Sessions and the forms of the Government kept up–this idea naturally leads us to contemplate public affairs on a large Scale, and to observe the present State of the New Constitution– when Massachusetts adopted it in the manner She did–both parties seemed rather to consider the question as settled–that it must be adopted also by the other States, and amended afterwards–But the unexpected Conduct of New Hamshire and late intilligence from Virginia and North Carolina, appear to make the adoption of the Constitution much more doubtful–and all parties here consider the great question far from being dicided–the opponents in this State, in Virginia and North Carolina I find say they have a very considerable majority–the Supporters of the Constitution are doubtful–I confess it is my opinion, notwithstanding, that all these States will adopt it–recommending amendments–perhaps, some in addition to those recommended by Massa–I need not mention to you how important it is to keep the minds of men Cool and temperate at this time, particularly by keeping up the forms of Government and the appearances of Tranquility

Matters seem to be in a State of quiet in Europe at present,–but I do not think they will remain so long–we hear nothing from that quarter that respects us particularly–except that our friends the Dutch are very pressing for their Interest money, and I expect Congress will make a short Statement to the States on this Subject[2]–the States must apply some small sums, at least, to the use of the Union or the federal Government must be dissolved–I am at a loss to know how the board of Treasury have done so well as they have, to pay the civil list, the Dutch Interest and troops in a considerable part–I believe the Union has been Supported almost wholly for a year or two past on the payments of New York, the gleanings of New Emission money, and a little tobacco from North Carolina–[3]

We have as usual much said about an Indian war–I doubt whether there will be any thing more than party disputes among the plundering individuals–

Kentucky and Virginia have formaly applied to Congress to acknowledge the Independance of the former and to admit it into the union–nothing of importance has yet been done in Congress relative to the subject and, probably, there will not be at present.[4] . . .

1. RC, Edward Lawrence Doheny Library, St. John's Seminary, Camarillo, California. Dane (1752-1835), a Beverly, Mass., lawyer, was a state representative, 1782-86; a state senator, 1793-99; and a delegate to Congress, 1785-88. In September 1787 he opposed the Constitution in the congressional debates on transmitting the Constitution to the states, but by July 1788 he had acquiesced in the Constitution and urged ratification by all states (CC:95; and CC:392, note 12). Dane was an unsuccessful candidate for the U.S. Senate and the U.S. House of Representatives in 1788. Holten (1738-1816), a Danvers, Mass., physician, was a member of the colonial House of Representatives, 1768-76; a state councillor, 1780-82, 1784, 1786, 1789-92, 1795-96; a delegate to Congress, 1778-80, 1783-85, 1787; and a member of the U.S. House of Representatives, 1793-95. An opponent of the Constitution, he was a delegate to the state ratifying Convention but illness forced him to leave early. Holten was an unsuccessful candidate for the U.S. Senate and the U.S. House of Representatives in 1788. For over thirty years, he was justice of the Court of Common Pleas for Essex County, a justice of the Court of General Sessions, and a justice of the peace and quorum; and for nineteen years (1796-1815), he was a judge of the probate court.

2. For the Dutch debt, see CC:560, notes 7 and 8.

3. For the amounts paid into the treasury on the various congressional requisitions, see the September 1787 report of the Board of Treasury on the requisition of 1787 (JCC, XXXIII, 569-85). In return for tobacco receipts from North Carolina, the Board credited the state with $28,487 in specie payments on 1 November 1787.

4. See CC:480, note 2.

619. Publius: The Federalist 70
New York Independent Journal, 15 March

This essay, written by Alexander Hamilton, was reprinted in the *New York Packet* on 18 March. It is number 70 in the M'Lean edition and number 69 in the newspapers.

For a general discussion of the authorship, circulation, and impact of *The Federalist*, see CC:201, 639.

The FEDERALIST. No. LXIX.
To the People of the State of New-York.

There is an idea, which is not without its advocates, that a vigorous executive is inconsistent with the genius of republican government. The enlightened well wishers to this species of government must at least hope that the supposition is destitute of foundation; since they can never admit its truth, without at the same time admitting the condemnation of their own principles. Energy in the executive is a leading character in the definition of good government. It is essential to the protection of the community against foreign attacks: It is not less essential to the steady administration of the laws, to the protection of property against those irregular and high handed combinations, which sometimes interrupt the ordinary course of justice to the security of liberty against the enterprises and assaults of ambition, of faction and of anarchy. Every man the least conversant in Roman [hi]story knows how often that republic was obliged to take refuge in the absolute power of a single man, under the formidable title of dictator, as well against the intrigues of ambitious individuals, who aspired to the tyranny, and the seditions of whole classes of the community, whose conduct threatened the existence of all government, as against the invasions of external enemies, who menaced the conquest and destruction of Rome.

There can be no need however to multiply arguments or examples on this head. A feeble executive implies a feeble execution of the government. A feeble executive is but another phrase for a bad execution: And a government ill executed, whatever it may be in theory, must be in practice a bad government.

Taking it for granted, therefore, that all men of sense will agree in the necessity of an energetic executive; it will only remain to inquire, what are the ingredients which constitute this energy–how far can they be combined with those other ingredients which constitute safety in the republican sense? And how far does this combination characterise the plan, which has been reported by the convention?

The ingredients, which constitute energy in the executive, are first unity, secondly duration, thirdly an adequate provision for its support, fourthly competent powers.

The circumstances which constitute safety in the republican sense are, 1st. a due dependence on the people, secondly a due responsibility.

Those politicians and statesmen, who have been the most celebrated for the soundness of their principles, and for the justness of their views, have declared in favor of a single executive and a numerous legislative. They have with great propriety considered energy as the most necessary qualification of the former, and have regarded this as most applicable to power in a single hand; while they have with equal propriety considered the latter as best adapted to deliberation and wisdom, and best calculated to conciliate the confidence of the people and to secure their privileges and interests.

That unity is conducive to energy will not be disputed. Decision, activity, secrecy, dispatch will generally characterise the proceeding of one man, in a much more eminent degree, than the proceedings of any greater number; and in proportion as the number is increased, these qualities will be diminished.

This unity may be destroyed in two ways; either by vesting the power in two or more magistrates of equal dignity and authority; or by vesting it ostensibly in one man, subject in whole or in part to the controul and co-operation of others, in the capacity of counsellors to him. Of the first the two consuls of Rome may serve as an example; of the last we shall find examples in the constitutions of several of the states. New-York and New-Jersey, if I recollect right, are the only states, which have entrusted the executive authority wholly to single men.[a] Both these methods of destroying the unity of the executive have their partisans; but the votaries of an executive council are the most numerous. They are both liable, if not to equal, to similar objections; and may in most lights be examined in conjunction.

The experience of other nations will afford little instruction on this head. As far however as it teaches any thing, it teaches us not to be inamoured of plurality in the executive. We have seen that the Achæns on an experiment of two Prætors, were induced to abolish one.[1] The Roman history records many instances of mischiefs to the republic from the dissentions between the consuls, and between the military tribunes, who were at times substituted to the consuls. But it gives us no specimens of any peculiar advantages derived to the state, from the circumstance of the plurality of those magistrates. That the dissentions between them were not more frequent, or more fatal, is matter of astonishment; until we advert to the singular position in which the republic was almost continually placed and to the prudent policy pointed out by the circumstances of the state, and pursued by the consuls, of making a division of the government between them. The Patricians engaged in a perpetual struggle with the Plebians for the preservation of their antient authorities and dignities; the consuls, who were generally chosen out of the former body, were commonly united by the personal interest they had in the defence of the privileges of their order. In addition to this motive of union, after the arms of the republic had considerably expanded the bounds of its empire, it became an established custom with the consuls to divide the administration between themselves by lot; one of them remaining at Rome to govern the city and its environs; the other taking the command in the more distant provinces. This expedient must no doubt have had great influence in preventing those collisions and rivalships, which might otherwise have embroiled the peace of the republic.

But quitting the dim light of historical research, and attaching ourselves purely to the dictates of reason and good sense, we shall discover much greater cause to reject than to approve the idea of plurality in the executive, under any modification whatever.

Wherever two or more persons are engaged in any common enterprize or pursuit, there is always danger of difference of opinion. If it be a public trust or office in which they are cloathed with equal dignity and authority, there is peculiar danger of personal emulation and even animosity. From either and especially from all these causes, the most bitter dissentions are apt to spring. Whenever these happen, they lessen the respectability, weaken the authority, and distract the plans and operations of those whom they divide. If they should unfortunately assail the supreme executive magistracy of a country, consisting of a plurality of persons, they might impede or frustrate the most important measures of the government, in the most[2] critical emergencies of the state. And what is still worse, they might split the community into the most violent and irreconcilable factions, adhering differently to the different individuals who composed the magistracy.

Men often oppose a thing merely because they have had no agency in planning it, or because it may have been planned by those whom they dislike. But if they have been consulted and have happened to disapprove, opposition then becomes in their estimation an indispensable duty of self love. They seem to think themselves bound in honor, and by all the motives of personal infallibility to defeat the success of what has been resolved upon, contrary to their sentiments. Men of upright, benevolent tempers have too many opportunities of remarking with horror, to what desperate lengths this disposition is sometimes carried, and how often the great interests of society are sacrificed to the vanity, to the conceit and to the obstinacy of individuals, who have credit enough to make their passions and their caprices interesting to mankind. Perhaps the question now before the public may in its consequences afford melancholy proofs of the effects of this despicable frailty, or rather detestable vice in the human character.

Upon the principles of a free government, inconveniencies from the source just mentioned must necessarily be submitted to in the formation of the legislature; but it is unnecessary and therefore unwise to introduce them into the constitution of the executive. It is here too that they may be most pernicious–In the legislature, promptitude of decision is oftener an evil than a benefit. The differences of opinion, and the jarrings of parties in that department of the government, though they may sometimes obstruct salutary plans, yet often promote deliberation and circumspection; and serve to check excesses in the majority. When a resolution too is once taken, the opposition must be at an end. That resolution is a law, and resistance to it punishable. But no favourable circumstances palliate or atone for the disadvantages of dissention in the executive department. Here they are pure and unmixed. There is no point at which they cease to operate. They serve to embarrass and weaken the execution of the plan or measure, to which they relate, from the first step to the final conclusion of it. They constantly counteract those qualities in the executive, which are the most necessary ingredients in its composition, vigour and expedition, and this without any counterballancing good. In the conduct of war, in which the energy of the executive is the bulwark of the national security, every thing would be to be apprehended from its plurality.

It must be confessed that these observations apply with principal weight to the full[3] case supposed, that is to a plurality of magistrates of equal dignity and authority; a scheme the advocates for which are not likely to form a numerous sect: But they apply, though not with equal, yet with considerable weight, to the project of a council, whose concurrence is made constitutionally necessary to the operations of the ostensible executive. An artful cabal in that council would be able to distract and to enervate the whole system of administration. If no such cabal should exist, the mere diversity of views and opinions would alone be sufficient to tincture the exercise of the executive authority with a spirit of habitual feebleness and delatoriness.

But one of the weightiest objections to a plurality in the executive, and which lies as much against the last as the first plan, is that it tends to conceal faults, and destroy responsibility. Responsibility is of two kinds, to censure and to punishment. The first is the most important of the two; especially in an elective office. Man, in public trust, will much oftener act in such a manner as to render him unworthy of being any longer trusted, than in such a manner as to make him obnoxious to legal punishment. But the multiplication of the executive adds to the difficulty of detection in either case. It often becomes impossible, amidst mutual accusations, to determine on whom the blame or the punishment of a pernicious measure, or series of pernicious measures ought really to fall. It is shifted from one to another with so much dexterity, and under such plausible appearances, that the public opinion is left in suspense about the real author. The circumstances which may have led to any national miscarriage or misfortune are sometimes so complicated, that where there are a number of actors who may have had different degrees and kinds of agency, though we may clearly see upon the whole that there has been mismanagement, yet it may be impracticable to pronounce to whose account the evil which may have been incurred is truly chargeable.

"I was overruled by my council.–The council were so divided in their opinions, that it was impossible to obtain any better resolution on the point." These and similar pretexts are constantly at hand, whether true or false. And who is there that will either take the trouble or incur the odium of a strict scrutiny into the secret springs of the transaction? Should there be found a citizen zealous enough to undertake the unpromising task, if there happen to be a collusion between the parties concerned, how easy is it to cloath the circumstances with so much ambiguity, as to render it uncertain what was the precise conduct of any of those parties?

In the single instance in which the governor of this state is coupled with a council, that is in the appointment to offices, we have seen the mischiefs of it in the view now under consideration.[4] Scandalous appointments to important offices have been made. Some cases indeed have been so flagrant, that ALL PARTIES have agreed in the impropriety of the thing. When enquiry has been made, the blame has been laid by the governor on the members of the council; who on their part have charged it upon his nomination: While the people remain altogether at a loss to determine by whose influence their interests have been commited to hands so unqualified, and so manifestly improper. In tenderness to individuals, I forbear to descend to particulars.

It is evident from these considerations, that the plurality of the executive tends to deprive the people of the two greatest securities they can have for the faithful exercise of any delegated power; first, the restraints of public opinion, which lose their efficacy as well on account of the division of the censure attendant on bad measures among a number, as on account of the uncertainty on whom it ought to fall; and secondly, the opportunity of discovering with facility and clearness the misconduct of the persons they trust, in order either to their removal from office, or to their actual punishment, in cases which admit of it.

In England the king is a perpetual magistrate; and it is a maxim, which has obtained for the sake of the public peace, that he is unaccountable for his administration, and his person sacred. Nothing therefore can be wiser in that kingdom than to annex to the king a constitutional council, who may be responsible to the nation for the advice they give. Without this there would be no responsibility whatever in the executive department; an idea inadmissible in a free government. But even there the king is not bound by the resolutions of his council, though they are answerable for the advice they give. He is the absolute master of his own conduct, in the exercise of his office; and may observe or disregard the council given to him at his sole discretion.

But in a republic, where every magistrate ought to be personally responsible for his behaviour in office, the reason which in the British constitution dictates the propriety of a council not only ceases to apply, but turns against the institution. In the monarchy of Great-Britain, it furnishes a substitute for the prohibited responsiblity of the chief magistrate; which serves in some degree as a hostage to the national justice for his good behaviour. In the American republic it would serve to destroy, or would greatly diminish the intended and necessary responsibility of the chief magistrate himself.

The idea of a council to the executive, which has so generally obtained in the state constitutions, has been derived from that maxim of republican jealousy, which considers power as safer in the hands of a number of men than of a single man. If the maxim should be admitted to be applicable to the case, I should contend that the advantage on that side would not counterballance the numerous disadvantages on the opposite side. But I do not think the rule at all applicable to the executive power. I clearly concur in opinion in this particular with a writer whom the celebrated Junius[5] pronounces to be "deep, solid and ingenious," that, "the executive power is more easily confined when it is one:"[b] That it is far more safe there should be a single object for the jealousy and watchfulness of the people; and in a word that all multiplication of the executive is rather dangerous than friendly to liberty.

A little consideration will satisfy us, that the species of security sought for in the multiplication of the executive is unattainable. Numbers must be so great as to render combination difficult; or they are rather a source of danger than of security. The united credit and influence of several individuals must be more formidable to liberty than the credit and influence of either of them separately. When power therefore is placed in the hands of so small a number of men, as to admit of their interests and views being easily combined in a common enterprise, by an artful leader, it becomes more liable to abuse and more dangerous when abused, than if it be lodged in the hands of one man; who from the very circumstance of his being alone will be more narrowly watched and more readily suspected, and who cannot unite so great a mass of influence as when he is associated with others. The Decemvres of Rome, whose name denotes their number,[c] were more to be dreaded in their usurpation than any ONE of them would have been. No person would think of proposing an executive much more numerous than that body, from six to a dozen have been suggested for the number of the council. The extreme of these numbers is not too great for an easy combination; and from such a combination America would have more to fear, than from the ambition of any single individual. A council to a magistrate, who is himself responsible for what he does, are generally nothing better than a clog upon his good intentions; are often the instruments and accomplices of his bad, and are almost always a cloak to his faults.

I forbear to dwell upon the subject of expence; though it be evident that if the council should be numerous enough to answer the principal end, aimed at by the institution, the salaries of the members, who must be drawn from their home to reside at the seat of government, would form an item in the catalogue of public expenditures, too serious to be incurred for an object of equivocal utility.

I will only add, that prior to the appearance of the constitution, I rarely met with an intelligent man from any of the states, who did not admit as the result of experience, that the UNITY of the Executive of this state was one of the best of the distinguishing features of our constitution.

> (a) *New-York has no council except for the single purpose of appointing to offices; New-Jersey has a council, whom the governor may consult. But I think from the terms of the constitution their resolutions do not bind him.*[6]
>
> (b) *De Loslme.*[7]
>
> (c) *Ten.*

1. See *The Federalist* 18, *New York Packet*, 7 December (CC:330).

2. "Most" deleted in the M'Lean edition.

3. "First" substituted in the M'Lean edition.

4. See *The Federalist* 69 (CC:617). For the New York Council of Appointment, see CC:617, note 11.

5. See C.W. Everett, ed., *The Letters of Junius* (London, 1927), "Preface by Junius," page 17. This preface was apparently written in 1771 and was published in Henry Sampson Woodfall's edition of *The Letters* which appeared in 1772 (*ibid.*, vii, 311).

6. In New Jersey, three or more members of the Legislative Council were to be a privy council which the governor could consult (Thorpe, V, 2596).

7. "De Lome" substituted in the M'Lean edition. See Jean Louis De Lolme, *The Constitution of England . . .* (London, 1816), Book II, chapter II, 215. *The Constitution of England* was first printed in 1771.

620. Comte de Moustier to Comte de Montmorin
New York, 16 March (excerpt)[1]

The general expectation has been singularly disappointed by the resolution made by the Convention of the State of Newhampshire to adjourn to the third tuesday of June, which will be the 17th. The majority of votes against the new Constitution there was 70. to 40. It seems certain that most of the members of the Convention, who have voted against the Constitution were bound by the instructions of their constituents, which forced them to vote contrary to the belief, with which the federalists inspired them afterwards, in the necessity and usefulness of the new plan. It is only in this way that one can explain the adherence of a great number to the proposition of the minority to adjourn to reconsider the proposed Constitution after having allowed the people the time to give new instructions to their representatives. This motion passed with a plurality of 53. to 51.

The State of Rhodeisland, which for a long time has separated itself from the others by the singularity of its conduct and where the common people entirely dominate, made a rather peculiar resolution. Instead of taking the advice of the people through the channel of its representatives in a general Convention, the Legislature has submitted the examination of the new federal Constitution to the conventicles formed in each district.[2] The majority of the districts must decide on its adoption. The Demagogues, who govern the people by flattering them, undoubtedly hope in this way to cause the rejection of the Constitution, whose design is to curb their excesses. However they could be deluded in their expectation, if the Quakers who are quite numerous in that State align themselves with the Federalists for fear of the abuse of paper money, the terrible weapon, with which the demagogues attack and destroy the propertied class in general.[3]

The fear of little security for their property disturbs all who possess any; the eagerness to acquire property or to be absolved of their debts arouses a great number of opponents to the new Constitution. Those of this opinion find in paper money a means to free themselves or to become rich by forcing the acceptance of this imaginary money, which they create and abolish at will, when they are able to dominate the State Legislatures. Thus one can count among the Federalists the majority of landowners and among the Antifederalists the Bankrupts, the men of bad faith, the needy and the men who could not exercise any power whatsoever in their States, except if it did not exist in the general Government. The generality of the people divide themselves among their Leaders. Until now there seemed to be more moderation among the Federalists than among their adversaries. But every day it becomes more difficult to judge what the outcome of this power struggle will be. Just as a Government can be built that is solid, united, durable, it is equally possible for one to see it dissipate into the shadow of a body which until now seemed invested with the power of the Confederation. The dissolution of Congress is an event as likely to happen as its regeneration. Interested observers consequently cannot stop themselves from speculating according to these two hypotheses.

It would be principally in a political report that the difference between the consolidation or the division of the American Confederation would be touched. . . .

1. RC (Tr), Correspondance Politique, États-Unis, Vol. 33, ff. 152–53, Archives du Ministère des Affaires Étrangères, Paris, France. This letter, dispatch number 8, was endorsed as received on 25 May.

2. On 1 March the Rhode Island legislature called for a referendum on the Constitution to be held in the towns on 24 March. Many Federalists, especially in Providence and Newport, boycotted the referendum, and the Constitution was rejected 2,711 to 239.

3. In February 1788 the Rhode Island legislature received a petition from the Society of Friends denouncing the depreciation of paper money and calling for the repeal of the legal tender aspects of paper money. The petition also requested the repeal of an act calling for the redemption of all promissory notes and other forms of short-term business credits within a period of two years. (Federalists supported both positions.) The legislature turned the Quaker petition over to the freemen who were to vote on it in their town meetings. The towns approved the repeal of the act concerning business credits, but they upheld the legal tender aspects of the paper-money system. In April the legislature repealed the act concerning business credits. Despite the agreement of

Quakers and Federalists on the paper-money system, there were many Quakers who opposed the Constitution because it permitted the importation of African slaves until 1808. In time, the failure of the Quaker petition on the tender question caused considerable controversy. Some Federalists charged that Quakers and Antifederalists had exchanged Quaker silence on paper money for Antifederalist support on slave-trade legislation.

621. John Brown to James Breckinridge
New York, 17 March (excerpt)[1]

. . . I have at length presented the Kentucky address to Congress & from the apparent disposition of Congress at present relative to that Business I fear I shall meet with no small difficulty in obtaining the Independence of that District The objections are the want of power by the Articles of Confederation to admit a new State into the Union–That the admission of Kentucky is contrary to the Eastern Interest as it woud throw another Vote into the Western or rather Southern Scale–that therefore it would affect the adoption of the New Plan of Govt. in Eastern States–The reasonableness of the request of the District is admitted by all–but the Policy of the Measure is disputed–I shall spare no Pains or Arguments in my power to effect this Measure which I have much at heart–as I am fully convinced that the future tranquility & Glory of that Country very much depend upon the event–Knowing you to be much interested in the issue of this Business I shall from time to time give you a particular account of its progress It now stands refered to a committee of the *Whole*–I am sorry that I have it not in my power to give you a favorable Account relative to the Success of the New Constitution The Convention of N. Hampshire adjd. without adopting it 'till June next a majority of the Members having been instructed to reject it; there is little doubt but that it will finally be adopted in that State, yet I fear the present failure will be productive of bad consequences as it will give fresh spirits & Confidence to the Malcontents who were begining to dispair & relax in their opposition–Altho Pensilva. has adopted it yet there is a very powerful party opposed who are growing very tumultuous having been exasperated by the intemperate Zeal of the friends to the Plan–I really dread the Consequences of its rejection–It has already damn'd the present Govt. in the estimation of the World, it cannot it will not drag on much longer, & should the New be rejected God only knows what will be the event–From the present Situation & disposition of the States there is little foundation to hope that any new plan can be brought forward less exceptionable than that now proposed–I hope Virginia will not be so blind to her own Interest & that of the Union as not to adopt it–The Necessity of the Case, with me precludes even the Idea of Hesitation. . . .

1. RC, Breckinridge Family Papers, ViU.

622. The Landholder XII
Connecticut Courant, 17 March

"Landholder" XII was addressed to the Antifederalist majority of the state of Rhode Island whose voters were scheduled to have a referendum on the Constitution on 24 March and another on the state's paper-money system (CC:620, notes 2 and 3). The essay was also printed in the Hartford *American Mercury* on 17 March. The *Courant* and *Mercury* versions differ in paragraphing, capitalization, spelling, and punctuation. By 11 April the complete essay was reprinted in ten newspapers: N.H. (2), Mass. (3), R.I. (3), Conn. (1), N.Y. (1). It was also reprinted in the October 1788 issue of the Philadelphia *American Museum*. The reprint in the Providence *United States Chronicle*, 27 March, included a preface signed by "A": "A Number of your Readers request you to publish, in your impartial Chronicle, the following ADDRESS.–That it may have a proper Effect upon the Minds of our present Rulers, as well as upon the great Body of the Freeholders, is the earnest Wish of every real Friend to the State." The reprint in the *Providence Gazette*, 29 March, noted that "Landholder" had been "Inserted by Request." Excerpts from "Landholder" XII were reprinted in the *Salem Mercury* on 25 March (see text in angle brackets). By 9 April these excerpts were printed in seven other newspapers: Mass. (1), N.Y. (1), N.J. (1), Pa. (4).

For the authorship, circulation, and impact of "Landholder," see CC:230.

To the Rhode-Island Friends of PAPER-MONEY, TENDER-ACTS and ANTIFEDERALISM.

The singular system of policy adopted by your state, no longer excites either the surprize or indignation of mankind. There are certain extremes of iniquity, which are beheld with patience, from a fixed conviction that the transgressor is inveterate, and that his example from its great injustice hath no longer a seducing influence. Milton's lapse of the angels and their expulsion from Heaven, produces deeper regret in a benevolent mind, than all the evil tricks they have played, or torments they have suffered since the bottomless pit became their proper home. Something similar to this is excited[1] in beholding the progress of human depravity. Our minds cannot bear to be always pained, the Creator hath therefore wisely provided that our tender sentiments should subside, in those desperate cases where there is no longer a probability, that any effort to which we may be excited, will have a power to reclaim.–But though our benevolence is no longer distressed with the injustice of your measures, as philosophers above the feelings of passion, we can speculate on them to our advantage. ⟨The sentiment thrown out by some of our adventurous divines, that the permission of sin is the highest display of supreme wisdom, and the greatest blessing to the universe, is most successfully illustrated by the effects of your general policy.

In point of magnitude, your little state bears much this same proportion to the united American empire, as the little world doth to the immense intelligent universe, and if the apostacy of man hath conveyed such solemn warning and instruction to the whole, as your councils have to every part of the union, no one will doubt the usefulness of Adams fall.⟩ At the commencement of peace, America was placed in a singular situation. Fear of a common danger could no longer bind us together–patriotism had done its best and was wearied with exertions rewarded only by ingratitude–our federal system was inadequate for national government and justice, and from inexperience the great body of the people were ignorant what consequences should flow from the want of them. Experiments in public credit, though ruinous to thousands, and a disregard to the promises of government had been pardoned in the moment of extreme necessity, and many honest men did not realize that a repetition of them in an hour less critical would shake the existence of society. Men full of evil and of desperate fortune were ready to propose every method of public fraud that can be effected by a violation of public faith and depreciating promises. This poison of the community, was their only preservative from deserved poverty, and from prisons appointed to be the reward of indolence and knavery. An easement of the poor and necessitous was plead as a reason for measures which have reduced them to more extreme necessity. Most of the states have had their prejudices against an efficient and just government, and have made their experiments in a false policy; but it was done with a timorous mind, and seeing the evil they have receded. A sense of subordination and moral right was their check. Most of the people were convinced–and but few remained who wished to establish iniquity by law. ⟨To silence such opposition as might be made to the new constitution, it was fit that public injustice should be exhibited in its greatest degree and most extreme effects. For this end Heaven permitted your apostacy from all the principles of good and just government. By your system we see unrighteousness in the essence, in its effects, and in its native miseries.[2] The rogues of every other state blush at the exhibition, and say you have betrayed them by carrying the matter too far. The very naming of your measures is a complete refutation of antifederalism, paper money and tender acts, for no man chooses such company in argument.⟩

The distress to which many of your best citizens are reduced–the groans of ruined creditors, of widows and orphans demonstrates that unhappiness follows vice, by the unalterable laws of nature and society. I did not mention the stings of conscience, but the authors of public distress ought to remember that there is a world where conscience will not sleep.

Is it not at length time to consider. ⟨The great end for which your infatuation was permitted is now become compleat. The whole union has seen and fears, and while history gives true information, no other people will ever repeat the studied process of fraud.–You may again shew the distorted features of injustice, but never in more lively colours, or by more able hands than had been done already.–As virtue and good government have derived all possible advantage from your experiment, and every other state thanks you for putting their own rogues and fools out of countenance, begin to have mercy on yourselves.⟩ You may not expect to exist in this course any longer than is necessary for public good; and there is no need that such a kind of warning as you set before us should be eternal. Secure as you may feel in prosecuting what all the rest of mankind condemn, the hour of your political revolution is at hand. The cause is within yourselves, and needs but the permission of your neighbours to take its full effect. Every moral and social law calls for a review, and a volume of penal statutes cannot prevent it.[3] They are in the first instance nullified by injustice, and five years hence not a man in your territories will presume their vindication.[4] Passion and obstinacy, which were called in to aid injustice, have had their reign, and can support you no longer. By a change of policy give us evidence that you are returned to manhood and honour. The inventors of such councils can never be forgiven in this world, but the people at large who acted by their guidance may break from the connection and restore themselves to virtue.

There are among you characters eminent through the union for their wisdom and integrity.[5] Penetrated with grief and astonishment they stand in silence, waiting the return of your reason. They are the only men who can remove the impassable gulph that is between you, and the rest of mankind. In your situation there must be some sacrifice.–It is required by the necessity of the case, and for the dignity of government. You have guilty victims enough for whom even benevolence will not plead; let them make the atonement and save your state. The large body of a people are rarely guilty of any crime greater than indiscretion, in following those who have no qualification to lead but an unblushing assurance in fraud. Acknowledge the indiscretion and leave those whom you have followed into the quicksands of death to the infamy prepared for them, and from which they cannot be reserved.[6] Your situation admits no compounding of opposite systems, or halving with justice, but to make the cure there must be an entire change of measures.[7] The Creator of nature and its laws, made justice as necessary for nations as for individuals and this necessity hath been sealed by the fate of all obstinate offenders. ⟨If you will not hear your own groans, nor feel the pangs of your own torture it must continue until removed by a political anihilation.⟩ Such as do not pity themselves cannot be long pitied.

Determined that our feelings shall be no longer wounded by any thing to which dispair may lead you, with philosophic coolness we wait to continue our speculations on the event.

1. "Experienced" in the *American Mercury*.

2. "Essence," "effects," and "native miseries" were italicized in the *Salem Mercury*, 25 March, and in most of the newspapers that reprinted this excerpt from it.

3. Penalty acts were passed by the Rhode Island legislature in June and August 1786. The first act provided that anyone convicted of depreciating the state's new paper money would be fined £100 for the first offense and a similar fine and disenfranchisement for

the second offense. The second act reduced the fines but provided that cases could be tried before a court without juries and without the right to appeal.

4. This sentence was italicized in the Providence *United States Chronicle*, 27 March.

5. See note 4.

6. "Saved" in the *American Mercury*.

7. See note 4.

623. Rufus King to Tench Coxe
New York, 18 March (excerpt)[1]

. . . We have nothing new in politicks in this Quarter; the Decision of the Question concerning the Constitution is very doubtful in this State–The conduct of New Hampshire, although by no means explanatory of what will be the Fate of the Question in that State, seems to have checked the spirit of Federalism–⟨I have no Doubt however but that the Constitution will be adopted by New Hampshire–⟩the Assembly of Rhode Island have referred the constitution to the people of that State to be decided on in Town Meetings on the last monday of this month; I think they will negative it by a majority of two to one; probably by a still larger majority–

⟨I dont see so much virulence, and illiberal party zeal, from any part of the Union, nor indeed from all the other States together, as from Pennsylvania–The great Question before the people can, and ought to, be determined, without so much personal abuse as is exhibited in your Gazettes. The constitution ought to be examined by its own merits & Demerits, and not by those of the members of the federal Convention, or of any other Assembly–a charge has been made by some of your writers against the Constitution that if the system is adopted, it will operate a discharge to all persons who are indebted to the United States, & several Gentlemen are held up as Debtors to the Union[2]–this is a mischievous and I think a very uncandid construction–nothing but the spirit of party could have originated it, against express clauses in the constitution to the contrary–I have been however Surprized that instead of attempts to exculpate the Persons charged as Defaulters, some person has not thought proper to expose this egregious misconstruction, and degrade its authors by stating the Truth–independent of the clauses in the 3. Sect. of the 4th. Art: as a Body politick the United States may recover their Debts; and it is in this sense only, they are entitled under the present Confederation, for there is no particular clause in that Instrument on this point⟩

1. RC, Coxe Papers, Series II, Correspondence and General Papers, PHi. The text within angle brackets was marked with "x's" presumably by Coxe and was printed in the *Pennsylvania Gazette*, 26 March, as an "Extract of a letter from a gentleman in New-York, to his friend in this city, dated March 18, 1788." The extract was reprinted in the *New York Morning Post*, 29 March; *Pennsylvania Packet*, 1 April; and *State Gazette of South Carolina*, 1 May.

2. See CC:565.

624. Poughkeepsie Country Journal, 18 March[1]

Copy of a letter from one of the people called *Friends* in New York, to an acquaintance of the same profession in Dutchess County.

New-York, the third day of the third month, 1788.

Friend * * *, I thank thee for thy communications of the 21st last month, and join with thee in praising that alone fountain from whence domestic happiness as well as eternal felicity floweth: To that great source I commend thee and thine.

The concern thou manifestest respecting the situation of this the land of our nativity is equally shared by me: with thee, I have beheld with anxiety the clouds of public commotion gathering, and with thee dread the fearful explosion. To bear up manfully against calamities, whether of a public or private nature, consistent with those principles of christian meekness, which they of our profession have adopted, is a course, assisted by divine grace, I mean to pursue. To unsheath the blade of human vengeance, and moisten the earth with my brother's blood, because his sentinents or practices are different from my own, is, I think abhorrent to that religion which speaketh peace, as well as to the conviction of my own mind which has adopted that religion.–I may not kill. But altho' restrained from sporting with an existence which when gone I cannot restore, I may, consistent with the word of truth prevent by unsanguinary exertions the evils feared. Thus in the present case, however ill it would become friends to enlist under the banners of heated party, and thereby add fuel to that fire which already blazeth too high; yet I think as a body, they might exhibit their united weight in the legal line of suffrage, and perhaps be a means of giving tranquility to their country.

⟨How differently people in dissimilar situations view the same object! here, a very decided majority think (and with them thy friend) that a union of the American States, as exemplified in the new constitution, is friendly to *property*; consistent with *freedom*; and favorable to *morality* and *religion*. Whereas in thy county I am told many think exactly the reverse.⟩

I believe it will not be contradicted that in proportion to the respectability of a nation, so its commerce flourishes and its prosperity is advanced: experience and reason both corroborate this idea.

If at only a frown of a potent State, its puny neighbour is thrown into convulsions, what must be its situation if a stroke succeeds the frown? Nothing less than public distraction and wreck of private fortune. Since the American revolution the people of this country have undoubtedly multiplied, houses have been reared, and arable acres wrested from the wilderness; but has the situation of the people at large been remarkably easy? I think not.–A shackled commerce, a decreasing medium, and a degenerating punctuality, is felt and acknowledged by all. And it must from the nature of things continue so, till a permanent union of the States gives energy in every department, and system and order to the whole.

Why a nation consisting of only three millions of souls, (and the whole American empire contains scarcely that number) should be more in danger of losing its liberty, than thirteen disunited seperate communities each on an average containing but little more than two hundred thousand inhabitants is mysterious.

I believe the history of mankind is pretty full in evidence, that, like the Magicians serpents, small communities have generally fallen a prey to some devouring neighbour. If an individual State's unremitted exertion of cabal, of stratagem, and of force, to support its pigmy omnipotence be called its *liberty*, from such liberty may thee and I my friend be set free. The wars of powerful empires occur but seldom, are unwieldly in their operation, and are generally felt but on the extremity of boundary; whereas the conflicts of more contracted districts affect every member and agitate the very base of the political structure. In this point of view the new constitution certainly looketh with a friendly aspect on the *freedom* of this country.

I think it also favorable to the morals of the people. For if jealousies, factions, cabals and war have a tendency to corrupt the manners that political situation which prevents jealousies, factions, cabals and war is desirable on a moral account: and if on a moral, certainly on a *religious.*–We my brother have seen the ship-wreck of both in the time of recent hostility.

If this State in convention finally rejects the constitution, how perilous our situation! Massachusetts, Connecticut, New-Jersey, and Pennsylvania, our immediate neighbours and all differing from us in political Ideas! without the spirit of prophecy, one may anticipating, behold Massachusetts uniting its western property to its eastern dominion,[2] and forming a huge parrellelogram from the pine clad banks of the Kennebeck to lake Erie.–Connecticut in one campaign making the shore of the Hudson its western boundary–and New-Jersey adding the whole territory between the Hudson and Delaware to its former domain.

I know it may be said, that treaties with foreign powers may be contracted, and compacts made with the few antifederal States (if any such) to secure to this State its soil and its rights: However contradictory to cool reason this hypothesis may be, I will for a moment suppose it practicable; and what a scene of carnage and devastation rises to view!–Again will our cities be wrapt in flames–The country desolated, the peaceful husbandman drenching with his blood, that field which would have been his support; and the wife of his bosom, and the children of his love, forlorn and unbefriended flying from one destruction only to meet another.

In order to avoid these monstrous evils and to procure those solid benefits which I think a firmer union of the States bids fair to introduce, I would seriously recommend to *Friends* in every part of the State to make it a matter of real concern to give their suffrages in such a manner as to make their importance as a body felt, and felt for the general good. In this city the friends, as far as my intelligence has reached, will to a man vote for such to represent them in convention as are the avowed friends to UNION and PEACE. May the sons of peace in thy country do the same.

After all my brother, whatever the highest may determine concerning this land, may thee and I and all who are in fellowship with us, be ever found sincere followers of him who has made it the peculiar tenet of his religion to LOVE ONE ANOTHER.

Thy sincere well wisher.

* * * *.

1. Reprinted: Hartford *American Mercury*, 31 March; Albany *Federal Herald*, 7 April; *Massachusetts Gazette*, 8 April; *Pennsylvania Gazette*, 30 April; Charleston *City Gazette*, 23 June. The text within angle brackets was reprinted in the *Pennsylvania Mercury* on 25 March, and by 16 April eight more newspapers reprinted this excerpt: N.H. (1), Mass. (1), N.Y. (1), Pa. (2), Md. (2), Va. (1).

2. A reference to Massachusetts' landholdings in western New York. When Massachusetts ceded its western lands to Congress in 1784, it specifically retained its colonial charter rights to western New York. Commissioners from the two states met in Hartford in 1786 and settled the dispute. New York retained jurisdiction over all land within its borders, but Massachusetts was given title to more than six million acres in western New York.

625. Publius: The Federalist 71
New York Packet, 18 March

This essay, written by Alexander Hamilton, was reprinted in the New York *Independent Journal* on 19 March. It was number 71 in the M'Lean edition and number 70 in the newspapers.

For a general discussion of the authorship, circulation, and impact of *The Federalist*, see CC:201, 639.

The FŒDERALIST, No. 70.
To the People of the State of New-York.

Duration in office has been mentioned as the second requisite to the energy of the executive authority. This has relation to two objects: To the personal firmness of the Executive Magistrate in the employment of his constitutional powers; and to the stability of the system of administration which may have been adopted under his auspices.–With regard to the first, it must be evident, that the longer the duration in office, the greater will be the probability of obtaining so important an advantage. It is a general principle of human nature, that a man will be interested in whatever he possesses, in proportion to the firmness or precariousness of the tenure, by which he holds it; will be less attached to what he holds by a momentary or uncertain title, than to what he enjoys by a durable or certain title; and of course will be willing to risk more for the sake of the one, than for the sake of the other. This remark is not less applicable to a political privilege, or honor, or trust, than to any article of ordinary property. The inference from it is, that a man acting in the capacity of Chief Magistrate, under a consciousness, that in a very short time he *must* lay down his office, will be apt to feel himself too little interested in it, to hazard any material censure or perplexity, from the independent exertion of his powers, or from encountering the ill-humors, however transient, which may happen to prevail either in a considerable part of the society itself, or even in a predominant faction in the legislative body. If the case should only be, that he *might* lay it down, unless continued by a new choice; and if he should be desirous of being continued, his wishes conspiring with his fears would tend still more powerfully to corrupt his integrity, or debase his fortitude. In either case feebleness and irresolution must be the characteristics of the station.

There are some, who would be inclined to regard the servile pliancy of the executive to a prevailing current, either in the community, or in the Legislature, as its best recommendation. But such men entertain very crude notions, as well of the purposes for which government was instituted, as of the true means by which the public happiness may be promoted. The republican principle demands, that the deliberate sense of the community should govern the conduct of those to whom they entrust the management of their affairs; but it does not require an unqualified complaisance to every sudden breese of passion, or to every transient impulse which the people may receive from the arts of men, who flatter their prejudices to betray their interests. It is a just observation, that the people commonly *intend* the PUBLIC GOOD. This often applies to their very errors. But their good sense would despise the adulator, who should pretend that they always *reason right* about the *means* of promoting it. They know from experience, that they sometimes err; and the wonder is, that they so seldom err as they do; beset as they continually are by the wiles of parasites and sycophants, by the snares of the ambitious, the avaricious, the desperate; by the artifices of men, who possess their confidence more than they deserve it, and of those who seek to possess, rather than to deserve it. When occasions present themselves in which the interests of the people are at variance with their inclinations, it is the duty of the persons whom they have appointed to be the guardians of those interests, to withstand the temporary delusion, in order to give them time and opportunity for more cool and sedate reflection. Instances might be cited, in which a conduct of this kind has saved the people from very fatal consequences of their own mistakes, and has procured lasting monuments of their gratitude to the men, who had courage and magnanimity enough to serve them at the peril of their displeasure.

But however inclined we might be to insist upon an unbounded complaisance in the executive to the inclinations of the people, we can with no propriety contend for a like complaisance to the humors of the Legislature. The latter may sometimes stand in opposition to the former; and at other times the people may be entirely neutral. In either supposition, it is certainly desirable that the executive should be in a situation to dare to act his own opinion with vigor and decision.

The same rule, which teaches the propriety of a partition between the various branches of power, teaches us likewise that this partition ought to be so contrived as to render the one independent of the other. To what purpose separate the executive, or the judiciary, from the legislative, if both the executive and the judiciary are so constituted as to be at the absolute devotion of the legislative? Such a separation must be merely nominal and incapable of producing the ends for which it was established. It is one thing to be subordinate to the laws, and another to be dependent on the legislative body. The first comports with, the last violates, the fundamental principles of good government; and whatever may be the forms of the Constitution, unites all power in the same hands. The tendency of the legislative authority to absorb every other, has been fully displayed and illustrated by examples, in some preceding numbers.[1] In governments purely republican, this tendency is almost irresistable. The representatives of the people, in a popular assembly, seem sometimes to fancy that they are the people themselves; and betray strong symptoms of impatience and disgust at the least sign of opposition from any other quarter; as if the exercise of its rights by either the executive or judiciary, were a breach of their privilege and an outrage to their dignity. They often appear disposed to exert an imperious controul over the other departments; and as they commonly have the people on their side, they always act with such momentum as to make it very difficult for the other members of the government to maintain the balance of the Constitution.

It may perhaps be asked how the shortness of the duration in office can affect the independence of the executive on the legislative, unless the one were possessed of the power of appointing or displacing the other? One answer to this enquiry may be drawn from the principle already remarked, that is from the slender interest a man is apt to take in a short lived advantage, and the little inducement it affords him to expose himself on account of it to any considerable inconvenience or hazard. Another answer, perhaps more obvious, though not more conclusive, will result from the consideration of the influence of the legislative body over the people, which might be employed to prevent the re-election of a man, who by an upright resistance to any sinister project of that body, should have made himself obnoxious to its resentment.

It may be asked also whether a duration of four years would answer the end proposed, and if it would not, whether a less period which would at least be recommended by greater security against ambitious designs, would not for that reason be preferable to a longer period, which was at the same time too short for the purpose of inspiring the desired firmness and independence of the magistrate?

It cannot be affirmed, that a duration of four years or any other limited duration would completely answer the end proposed; but it would contribute towards it in a degree which would have a material influence upon the spirit and character of the government. Between the commencement and termination of such a period there would always be a considerable interval, in which the prospect of annihilation would be sufficiently remote not to have an improper effect upon the conduct of a man endued with a tolerable portion of fortitude; and in which he might reasonably promise himself, that there would be time enough, before it arrived, to make the community sensible of the propriety of the measures he might incline to pursue. Though it be probable, that as he approached the moment when the public were by a new election to signify their sense of his conduct, his confidence and with it, his firmness would decline; yet both the one and the other would derive support from the opportunities, which his previous continuance in the station had afforded him of establishing himself in the esteem and good will of his constituents. He might then hazard with safety, in proportion to the proofs he had given of his wisdom and integrity, and to the title he had acquired to the respect and attachment of his fellow citizens. As on the one hand, a duration of four years will contribute to the firmness of the executive in a sufficient degree to render it a very valuable ingredient in the composition; so on the other, it is not long enough to justify any alarm for the public liberty. If a British House of Commons, from the most feeble beginnings, *from the mere power of assenting or disagreeing to the imposition of a new tax*, have by rapid strides, reduced the prerogatives of the crown and the privileges of the nobility within the limits they conceived to be compatible with the principles of a free government; while they raised themselves to the rank and consequence of a coequal branch of the Legislature; if they have been able in one instance to abolish both the royalty and the aristocracy, and to overturn all the ancient establishments as well in the church as State; if they have been able on a recent occasion to make the monarch tremble at the prospect of an innovation[(a)] attempted by them; what would be to be feared from an elective magistrate of four years duration, with the confined authorities of a President of the United States? What but that he might be unequal to the task which the Constitution assigns him?–I shall only add that if his duration be such as to leave a doubt of his firmness, that doubt is inconsistent with a jealousy of his encroachments.

> (a) *This was the case with respect to Mr. Fox's India bill which was carried in the House of Commons, and rejected in the House of Lords, to the entire satisfaction, as it is said, of the people.*[2]

1. See *The Federalist* 48–49 (CC:492, 495).

2. In November 1783 Charles James Fox, secretary of state for foreign affairs, introduced a bill in the House of Commons calling for the reorganization of the government of India. The control of India was transferred from the East India Company to commissioners first appointed by Parliament and later by the Crown. All of the original commissioners were named in the bill. The bill passed by a vote of 208 to 102. Viewing the bill as an opportunity to destroy a coalition government he disliked, George III let it be known to the members of the House of Lords "that he should consider all who voted

for it as his enemies." Consequently, the bill was defeated in the Lords. The Fox-North coalition fell, and William Pitt the Younger formed a new government. The House of Commons voted 153 to 80 that it was a breach of privilege to report the King's personal opinion on a bill (J. Steven Watson, *The Reign of George III, 1760–1815* [Oxford, Eng., 1960], 261–67).

626. Luther Martin: Address No. I
Maryland Journal, 18 March

Four addresses by Luther Martin to the citizens of Maryland were published in the *Maryland Journal* on 18, 21, and 28 March, and 4 April. The first two (CC:626, 636) answered the Maryland "Landholder," No. X (CC:580) who had criticized Martin and Elbridge Gerry for their activities in the Constitutional Convention. (For Martin's earlier defense against the Maryland "Landholder's" charges, see CC:604.) In his third and fourth addresses, Martin called for a second constitutional convention that would amend the Constitution so that the rights and liberties of the people would be protected and some powers would be restored to the states (CC:650, 662). For a Federalist satire on Martin's four addresses, see "Luther Martin," Address No. V, Philadelphia *Federal Gazette*, 10 April.

Luther Martin's first address (CC:626), announced for publication on 14 March, was reprinted in the Philadelphia *Independent Gazetteer* and *Pennsylvania Mercury*, 8 April; Boston *American Herald*, 5 May; *Salem Mercury*, 10 June; and New Jersey *Brunswick Gazette*, 12 August. The reprinting in the *Pennsylvania Mercury* was requested by Luther Martin himself; while those in the *Salem Mercury* and *Brunswick Gazette* were requested by readers and customers.

To the CITIZENS of MARYLAND.

To you, my fellow-citizens, I hold myself in a particular manner accountable for every part of my conduct in the exercise of a trust reposed in me by you, and should consider myself highly culpable if I was to withhold from you any information in my possession, the knowledge of which may be material to enable you to form a right judgment on questions wherein the happiness of yourselves and your posterity are involved–Nor shall I ever consider it an act of condescension when impeached in my *public* conduct, or character, to vindicate myself at your bar, and to submit myself to your decision. In conformity to these sentiments, which have regulated my conduct since my return from the Convention, and which will be the rule of my actions in the sequel, I shall, at this time, beg your indulgence, while I make some observations on a Publication which the Landholder has done me the honour to address to me, in the Maryland Journal, of the 29th of February last.

In my controversy with that writer, on the subject of Mr. Gerry, I have already enabled you to decide, without difficulty, on the credit which ought to be given to his most positive assertions, and should scarce think it worth my time to notice his charges against myself, was it not for the opportunity it affords me of stating certain facts and transactions, of which you ought to be informed, some of which were *undesignedly* omitted by me when I had the honour of being called before the House of Delegates.[1]

No "extreme modesty" on my part was requisite to induce me to conceal the "sacrifice of resentments" against Mr. Gerry–since no such sacri-. fice had ever been made–nor had any such resentments ever existed–The *principal* opposition in sentiment between Mr. Gerry and myself, was on the subject of representation; but even on that subject, he was much more conceding than his colleagues, two of whom obstinately persisted in voting against the equality of representation in the Senate, when the question was taken in Convention upon the adoption of the conciliatory propositions, on the fate of which depended, I believe, the *continuance* of the Convention.[2]

In many important questions we perfectly harmonized in opinion, and where we differed, it never was attended with warmth or animosity, nor did it in any respect interfere with a friendly intercourse, and interchange of attention and civilities.–We both opposed the extraordinary powers over the militia, given to the general government[3]–we were both against the re-eligibility of the president[4]–we both concurred in the attempt to prevent members of each branch of the legislature from being appointable to offices,[5] and in many other instances, although the Landholder, with his usual regard to truth, and his usual *imposing* effrontery, tells me, that I "doubtless must remember Mr. Gerry and myself never voted alike, except in the instances" he has mentioned. As little foundation is there in his assertion, that I "cautioned certain members to be on their guard against his wiles, for that he and Mr. Mason held private meetings, where the plans were concerted to aggrandize, at the expence of the small States, old Massachusetts and the ancient dominion." I need only state facts to refute the assertion. Some time in the month of August, a number of members who considered the system, as then under consideration, and likely to be adopted, extremely exceptionable, and of a tendency to destroy the rights and liberties of the United States, thought it advisable to meet together in the evenings, in order to have a communication of sentiments, and to concert a plan of *conventional* opposition to, and amendment of that system, so as, if possible, to render it less dangerous. Mr. Gerry was the first who proposed this measure to me, and that before any meeting had taken place, and wished we might assemble at my lodgings; but not having a room convenient, we fixed upon another place–There Mr. Gerry and Mr. Mason *did* hold meetings; but with them also met the Delegates from New-Jersey and Connecticut, a part of the delegation from Delaware, an honourable member from South-Carolina, one other from Georgia, and myself–These were the only "private meetings" that ever I knew or heard to be held by Mr. Gerry and Mr. Mason–meetings at which I myself attended until I left the Convention–and of which the sole object was not to aggrandize the *great* at the expence of the *small*, but to protect and preserve, if possible, the existence and essential rights of *all* the States, and the liberty and freedom of their citizens.[6] Thus, my fellow-citizens, I am obliged, unless I could accept the compliment at an expence of truth equal to the Landholder's, to give up all claim to being "placed beyond the reach of ordinary panegyrick," and to that "magnanimity" which he was so solicitous to bestow upon me, that he has wandered the regions of falsehood to seek the occasion.

When we find such disregard of truth even in the introduction, while only on the threshold, we may form some judgment what respect is to be paid to the information he shall give us of what passed in the Convention, when he "draws aside the veil"–a veil which was interposed between our proceedings and the Public, in my opinion, for the most dangerous of purposes, and which was *never* designed by the advocates of the system to be drawn aside, or if ever, not till it should be *too late* for any beneficial purpose[7]–which as far as it is done or pretended to be done, on the present occasion, is only for the purpose of deception and misrepresentation.

It was on Saturday[8] that I first took my seat–I obtained that day a copy of the propositions that had been laid before the Convention, and which were then the subject of discussion in a committee of the whole.[9] The secretary was so polite as, at my request, to wait upon me at the State-House the next day (being Sunday) and there gave me an opportunity of examining the journals, and making myself acquainted with the little that had been done before my arrival–I was not a little surprised at the system brought forward, and was solicitous to learn the reasons which had been assigned in its support; for this purpose the journals could be of no service, I therefore conversed on the subject with different members of the Convention, and was favoured with minutes of the debates, which had taken place before my arrival–I applied to history for what lights it could afford me–and I procured every thing the most valuable I could find in Philadelphia, on the subject of governments in general, and on the American revolution and governments in particular–I devoted my whole time and attention to the business in which we were engaged, and made use of all the opportunities I had, and abilities I possessed, conscientiously to decide what part I ought to adopt in the discharge of that sacred duty I owed to my country, in the exercise of the trust you had reposed in me–I attended the Convention many days without taking any share in the debates, listening in silence to the eloquence of others, and offering no other proof that I possessed the powers of speech, than giving my yea or nay when a question was taken, and notwithstanding my propensity to "endless garrulity," should have been extremely happy if I could have continued that line of conduct, without making a sacrifice of your rights and political happiness.

The committee of the whole house had made but small progress, at the time I arrived, in the discussion of the propositions which had been referred to them; they completed that discussion, and made their report–The propositions of the minority were then brought forward and rejected[10]–The Convention had resumed the report of the committee, and had employed some days in its consideration–*Thirty* days,[11] I believe, or more, had elapsed from my taking my seat before, in the language of the Landholder, I "opened in a speech which held during two days".[12]–Such, my fellow-citizens, is the true state of the conduct I pursued when I took my seat in Convention, and which the Landholder, to whom falshood appears more familiar than truth, with his usual effrontery, has misrepresented by a positive declaration, that without obtaining, or endeavouring to obtain, any information on the subject, I hastily and insolently obtruded my sentiments on the Convention, and, to the astonishment of every member present, on the very day I took my seat, began a speech, which continued two days, in opposition to those measures, which, on mature deliberation, had been adopted by the Convention.

But I "alone advocated the political heresy, that the people ought not to be trusted with the election of representatives." On this subject, as I would wish to be on every other, my fellow-citizens, I have been perfectly explicit in the information I gave to the House of Delegates, and which has since been published.[13]–In a *state* government, I consider all power flowing *immediately* from the people in their individual capacity, and that the people, in their individual capacity, have, and ever ought to have, the right of choosing delegates in a state legislature; the business of which is to make laws, regulating their concerns, as individuals, and operating upon them as such; but, in a *federal* government, formed over free states, the power flows from the people, and the right of choosing delegates belongs to them *only mediately* through their respective state governments, which are the members composing the federal government, and from whom all its power *immediately* proceeds; to which state governments, the choice of the *federal* delegates *immediately* belongs.–I should blush, indeed, for my ignorance of the first elements of government, was I to entertain different sentiments on this subject; and if this is "political heresy," I have no ambition to be ranked with those who are orthodox.–Let me here, my fellow-citizens, by way of caution, add an observation, which will prove to be founded in truth–those who are the most liberal in complimenting you with powers which do not belong to you, act commonly from improper and interested motives, and most generally have in view thereby to prepare the way for depriving you of those rights to which you are justly entitled.–Every thing that weakens and impairs the bands of *legitimate* authority, smooths the road of ambition; nor can there be a surer method of supporting and preserving the just rights of the *people*, than by *supporting* and *protecting* the *just rights* of *Government*.

As to the "jargon" attributed to me of maintaining "that notwithstanding each state had an equal number of votes in the Senate, yet the states were unequally represented in the Senate," the Landholder has all the merit of its absurdity; nor can I conceive what sentiment it is that I ever have expressed, to which he, with his usual perversion and misrepresentation, could give such a colouring.

That I ever suggested the idea of letting loose an army indiscriminately on the innocent and guilty, in a state refusing to comply with the requisitions of Congress, or that such an idea ever had place in my mind, is a falsehood so groundless, so base and malignant, that it could only have originated or been devised by a heart which would dishonour the midnight assassin. My sentiments on this subject are well known; it was *only* in the case where a state refused to comply with the requisitions of Congress, that *I* was willing to grant the general government those powers which the *proposed constitution* gives it in *every* case.[(a)14]–Had I been a greater friend to a standing army, and not quite so averse to exposing your liberties to a soldiery, I do not believe the Landholder would have chose me for the object on whom to expend his artillery of falsehood.

That a system may enable government wantonly to exercise power over the militia, to call out an unreasonable number from any particular state without its permission, and to march them upon, and continue them in, remote and improper services–that the same system should enable the government totally to discard, render useless, and even disarm the militia, when it would remove them out of the way of opposing its ambitious views, is by no means inconsistent, and is really the case in the proposed constitution:–In both these respects it is, in my opinion, highly faulty, and ought to be amended. In the proposed system, the general government has a power not only *without* the *consent*, but *contrary* to the *will* of the *state government*, to call out the *whole* of its militia, without regard to *religious scruples*, or any other consideration, and to continue them in service as long as it pleases, thereby subjecting the *freemen* of a whole state to *martial* law, and reducing them to the situation of *slaves*.–It has also, by another clause, the powers, by *which only* the militia can be organized and armed, and by the neglect of which they may be rendered utterly useless and insignificant, when it suits the ambitious purposes of government:–Nor is the suggestion unreasonable, even if it had been made, that the government might improperly oppress and harrass the militia, the better to reconcile them to the idea of regular troops, who might relieve them from the burthen, and to render them less opposed to the measures it might be disposed to adopt for the purpose of reducing them to that state of insignificancy and uselessness.

When the Landholder declared that "I contended the powers and authorities of the new constitution must destroy the liberties of the people," he, for once, stumbled on the truth; but even this he could not avoid coupling with an assertion utterly false. I never suggested that "the same powers could be safely entrusted to the old Congress;"–on the contrary, I opposed many of the powers as being of that nature that, in my opinion, they could not be entrusted to any government whatever, consistent with the freedom of the states and their citizens; and earnestly recommended, what I wish, my fellow-citizens, deeply to impress on your minds, that in altering or amending our federal government, no *greater powers* ought to be given than *experience has shewn to be necessary*, since it will be *easy to delegate further power* when *time* shall dictate the *expediency* or *necessity*; but powers *once bestowed* upon a government, should they be found ever so *dangerous* or *destructive* to freedom, *cannot be resumed or wrested from government*, but by *another revolution*.

Baltimore, March 14, 1788.

> (a) *According to this idea, I endeavoured to obtain as an amendment to the system, the following clause: "And whenever the legislature of the United States shall find it necessary that revenue shall be raised by direct taxation, having apportioned the same by the above rule,* requisitions *shall be made of the respective states to pay into the continental treasury their respective quotas, within a* time *in the said requisition to be specified; and in case of any of the states* failing *to comply with such requisition,* then, *and* then only, *to have power to devise and pass acts directing the mode, and authorizing the same in the state failing therein."-This was rejected, and that power, which I wished to have given the government only in this* particular instance, *is given to it, without any restraint or limitation, in* every case.

1. For Martin's address to the Maryland House of Delegates on 29 November, see CC:304-B; and for his *Genuine Information*, a published expansion of this address, see CC:389.

2. On 16 July the Convention adopted, by a vote of five states to four, a compromise which provided for representation according to population in the House of Representatives and equal state suffrage in the Senate. The Massachusetts delegation was divided: Elbridge Gerry and Caleb Strong voted for the compromise; Rufus King and Nathaniel Gorham against it (Farrand, II, 15).

3. For Martin's and Gerry's opposition to giving the central government "extraordinary powers over the militia," see Farrand, II, 332, 385-88.

4. For Martin's and Gerry's leadership of the opposition to the reeligibility of the president, see Farrand, II, 52, 58, 101, 102. At one point, however, they suggested long terms for the president-Martin, eleven years, and Gerry, fifteen years.

5. For Gerry's support of the provision making congressmen ineligible for appointment to federal offices, see Farrand, I, 388, 393; II, 285-86, 491. There is no record that Martin spoke on the issue.

6. For a discussion of these meetings, see Forrest McDonald, *E Pluribus Unum: The Formation of the American Republic, 1776-1790* (2nd ed., Indianapolis, Ind., 1979), 295-302; and George Athan Billias, *Elbridge Gerry: Founding Father and Republican Statesman* (New York, 1976), 193, 387n-88n.

7. The rule of secrecy was especially galling to Martin. On 25 July, just before the Convention adjourned to permit the Committee of Detail to draft a constitution, Martin moved that the delegates might "take copies of the resolutions which have been agreed to." The motion was defeated six states to five, with Maryland voting in the majority (Farrand, II, 107, 108, 115; and Luther Martin, *Genuine Information* I, Baltimore *Maryland Gazette*, 28 December, CC:389). When the Convention adjourned on 17 September, James McHenry wrote in his notes: "Injunction of secrecy taken off" (Farrand, II, 650).

8. 9 June 1787.

9. A reference to the Virginia Resolutions which were presented to the Convention on 29 May (CDR, 243–45).

10. A reference to the New Jersey Amendments to the Articles of Confederation which were presented to the Convention on 15 June and rejected on the 19th (CDR, 250–53).

11. After the Convention rejected the New Jersey Amendments, it accepted the Amended Virginia Resolutions and debated them until 26 July, when it adjourned to allow the Committee of Detail to draft a constitution (CDR, 247–50, 255–60).

12. Martin delivered his two-day speech on 27–28 June (CC:580, note 2).

13. See *Genuine Information* IV, Baltimore *Maryland Gazette*, 8 January (CC:425).

14. See *Genuine Information* VI, *ibid.*, 15 January (CC:451, note 3).

627. Massachusetts Centinel, 19 March[1]

Extract of a letter from a gentleman in Richmond, Virginia, to his friend in this town, dated Feb. 24, 1788.

"Our Governour has expressed quite different sentiments respecting the new Constitution since its adoption by your State.[2] Although the majority was made, yet the speeches of some of the minority after its adoption has gained more proselytes to federalism here, than if the majority had been much larger, and the Convention had dissolved with any animosity.[3] Our politicians are much pleased with the candour and liberality with which the important matter was discussed; and the little appearance of party discovered by your minority, has caused many worthy characters here to view the matter in quite a different light, and I believe from quite a large majority against the Constitution, we can now boast of at least equal numbers, and the superiour excellence of the new plan cannot help forcing conviction on the minds of many more good men—Most of those now opposed to it, are persons whose estates are much involved, by owing large British debts, which they think must be paid when we have a federal head: But as Governour *Randolph* now speaks in favour of it, and as he has much influence, I am confident that it will not only be adopted, but by a very respectable majority. North-Carolina follows of course."

1. Reprints, in whole or in part, by 1 May (25): N.H. (1), Mass. (4), R.I. (2), Conn. (3), N.Y. (3), N.J. (2), Pa. (5), Md. (1), Va. (2), S.C. (2).

2. See Governor Edmund Randolph's letter of 10 October to the speaker of the Virginia House of Delegates which was published around 27 December (CC:385).

3. These conciliatory speeches, first printed in the *Massachusetts Gazette* on 8 February, were reprinted throughout the United States. (For two of these speeches, see CC:600, notes 2–3.)

628. Publius: The Federalist 72
New York Independent Journal, 19 March

This essay, written by Alexander Hamilton, was reprinted in the *New York Packet* on 21 March. It is number 72 in the M'Lean edition and number 71 in the newspapers.

For a general discussion of the authorship, circulation, and impact of *The Federalist*, see CC:201, 639.

The FEDERALIST. No. LXXI.

To the People of the State of New-York.

The ADMINISTRATION of government, in its largest sense, comprehends all the operations of the body politic, whether legislative, executive or judiciary, but in its most usual and perhaps in its most precise signification, it is limited to executive details, and falls peculiarly within the province of the executive department. The actual conduct of foreign negotiations, the preparatory plans of finance, the application and disbursement of the public monies, in conformity to the general appropriations of the legislature, the arrangement of the army and navy, the direction of the operations of war; these and other matters of a like nature constitute what seems to be most properly understood by the administration of government. The persons therefore, to whose immediate management these different matters are committed, ought to be considered as the assistants or deputies of the chief magistrate; and, on this account, they ought to derive their offices from his appointment, at least from his nomination, and ought to be subject to his superintendence. This view of the subject will at once suggest to us the intimate connection between the duration of the executive magistrate in office, and the stability of the system of administration. To reverse and undo what has been done by a predecessor is very often considered by a successor, as the best proof he can give of his own capacity and desert; and, in addition to this propensity, where the alteration has been the result of public choice, the person substituted is warranted in supposing, that the dismission of his predecessor has proceeded from a dislike to his measures, and that the less he resembles him the more he will recommend himself to the favor of his constituents. These considerations, and the influence of personal confidences and attachments, would be likely to induce every new president to promote a change of men to fill the subordinate stations; and these causes together could not fail to occasion a disgraceful and ruinous mutability in the administration of the government.

With a positive duration of considerable extent, I connect the circumstance of re-eligibility. The first is necessary to give to the officer himself the inclination and the resolution to act his part well, and to the community time and leisure to observe the tendency of his measures, and thence to form an experimental estimate of their merits. The last is necessary to enable the people, when they see reason to approve of his conduct, to continue him in the station, in order to prolong the utility of his talents and virtues, and to secure to the government, the advantage of permanency in a wise system of administration.

Nothing appears more plausible at first sight, nor more ill founded upon close inspection, than a scheme, which in relation to the present point has had some respectable advocates–I mean that of continuing the chief magistrate in office for a certain time, and then excluding him from it, either for a limited period, or for ever after. This exclusion whether temporary or perpetual would have nearly the same effects; and these effects would be for the most part rather pernicious than salutary.

One ill effect of the exclusion would be a diminution of the inducements to good behaviour. There are few men who would not feel much less zeal in the discharge of a duty, when they were conscious that the advantages of the station, with which it was connected, must be relinquished at a determinate period, then when they were permitted to entertain a hope of *obtaining* by *meriting* a continuance of them. This position will not be disputed, so long as it is admitted that the desire of reward is one of the strongest incentives of human conduct, or that the best security for the fidelity of mankind is to make their interest coincide with their duty. Even the love of fame, the ruling passion of the noblest minds, which would prompt a man to plan and undertake extensive and arduous enterprises for the public benefit, requiring considerable time to mature and perfect them, if he could flatter himself with the prospect of being allowed to finish what he had begun, would on the contrary deter him from the undertaking, when he foresaw that he must quit the scene, before he could accomplish the work, and must commit that, together with his own reputation, to hands which might be unequal or unfriendly to the task. The most to be expected from the generality of men, in such a situation, is the negative merit of not doing harm instead of the positive merit of doing good.

Another ill effect of the exclusion would be the temptation to sacred[1] views, to peculation, and in some instances, to usurpation. An avaricious man, who might happen to fill the offices, looking forward to a time when he must at all events yield up the emoluments[2] he enjoyed, would feel a propensity, not easy to be resisted by such a man, to make the best use of the opportunity he enjoyed, while it lasted; and might not scruple to have recourse to the most corrupt expedients to make the harvest as abundant as it was transient; though the same man probably, with a different prospect before him, might content himself with the regular perquisites of his situation, and might even be unwilling to risk the consequences of an abuse of his opportunities. His avarice might be a guard upon his avarice. Add to this, that the same man might be vain or ambitious as well as avaricious. And if he could expect to prolong his honors, by his good conduct, he might hesitate to sacrifice his appetite for them to his appetite for gain. But with the prospect before him of approaching and inevitable annihilation, his avarice would be likely to get the victory over his caution, his vanity or his ambition.

An ambitious man too, when he found himself seated on the summit of his country's honors, when he looked forward to the time at which he must descend from the exalted eminence forever; and reflected that no exertion of merit on his part could save him from the unwelcome reverse: Such a man, in such a situation, would be much more violently tempted to embrace a favorable conjuncture for attempting the prolongation of his power,

at every personal hazard, than if he had the probability of answering the
same end by doing his duty.

Would it promote the peace of the community, or the stability of the
government, to have half a dozen men who had had credit enough to be
raised to the seat of the supreme magistracy, wandering among the people
like discontented ghosts, and sighing for a place which they were descried[3]
never more to possess?

A third ill effect of the exclusion would be the depriving the community
of the advantage of the experience gained by the chief magistrate in the
exercise of his office. That experience is the parent of wisdom is an adage,
the truth of which is recognized by the wisest as well as the simplest of
mankind. What more desireable or more essential than this quality in the
governors of nations? Where more desirable or more essential than in the
first magistrate of a nation? Can it be wise to put this desirable and essential quality under the ban of the constitution; and to declare that the moment it is acquired, its possessor shall be compelled to abandon the station
in which it was acquired, and to which it is adapted? This nevertheless is
the precise import of all those regulations, which exclude men from serving their country, by the choice of their fellow citizens, after they have, by
a course of service filled themselves for doing it with a greater degree of
utility.

A fourth ill effect of the exclusion would be the banishing men from
stations, in which in certain emergencies of the state their presence might
be of the greatest moment to the public interest or safety. There is no
nation which has not at one period or another experienced an absolute
necessity of the services of particular men, in particular situations, perhaps
it would not be too strong to say, to the preservation of its political existence. How unwise therefore must be every such self-denying ordinance,
as serves to prohibit a nation from making use of its own citizens, in the
manner best suited to its exigences and circumstances! Without supposing
the personal essentiality of the man, it is evident that a change of the chief
magistrate, at the breaking out of a war, or at any similar crisis, for another even of equal merit, would at all times be detrimental to the community; inasmuch as it would substitute inexperience to experience, and
would tend to unhinge and set afloat the already settled train of the administration.

A fifth ill effect of the exclusion would be, that it would operate as a
constitutional interdiction of stability in the administration. By *necessitating*
a change of men, in the first office in the nation, it would necessitate a
mutability of measures. It is not generally to be expected, that men will
vary; and measures remain uniform. The contrary is the usual course of
things. And we need not be apprehensive there will [be] too much stability, while there is even the option of changing; nor need we desire to
prohibit the people from continuing their confidence, where they think it

may be safely placed, and where by constancy on their part, they may obviate the fatal inconveniences of fluctuating councils and a variable policy.

These are some of the disadvantages, which would flow from the principle of exclusion. They apply most forcibly to the scheme of a perpetual exclusion; but when we consider that even a partial exclusion would always render the re-admission of the person a remote and precarious object, the observations which have been made will apply nearly as fully to one case as to the other.

What are the advantages premised to counterballance these advantages?[4] They are represented to be 1st. Greater independence in the magistrate: 2dly. Greater security to the people. Unless the exclusion be perpetual there will be no pretence to infer the first advantage. But even in that case, may he have no object beyond his present station to which he may sacrifice his independence? May he have no connections, no friends, for whom he may sacrifice it? May he not be less willing, by a firm conduct, to make personal enemies, when he acts under the impression, that a time is fast approaching, on the arrival of which he not only MAY, but MUST be exposed to their resentments, upon an equal, perhaps upon an inferior footing? It is not an easy point to determine whether his independence would be most promoted or impaired by such an arrangement.

As to the second supposed advantage, there is still greater reason to entertain doubts concerning it. If the exclusion were to be perpetual, a man of irregular ambition, of whom alone there could be reason in any case to entertain apprehensions, would with infinite reluctance yield to the necessity of taking his leave forever of a post, in which his passion for power and pre-eminence had acquired the force of habit. And if he had been fortunate or adroit enough to conciliate the good will of the people he might induce them to consider as a very odious and unjustifiable restraint upon themselves, a provision which was calculated to debar them of the right of giving a fresh proof of their attachment to a favorite. There may be conceived circumstances, in which this disgust of the people, seconding the thwarted ambition of such a favourite, might occasion greater danger to liberty, than could ever reasonably be dreaded from the possibility of a perpetuation in office, by the voluntary suffrages of the community, exercising a constitutional privilege.

There is an excess of refinement in the idea of disabling the people to continue in office men, who had entitled themselves, in their opinion, to approbation and confidence; the advantages of which are at best speculative and equivocal; and are overbalanced by disadvantages far more certain and decisive.

1. "Sordid" substituted in the M'Lean edition.
2. "Advantages" substituted in the M'Lean edition.
3. "Destined" substituted in the M'Lean edition.
4. "Disadvantages" substituted in the M'Lean edition.

629. Virginia Independent Chronicle, 19 March[1]

From CORRESPONDENTS.

Out of all the members as yet returned to the Convention there are only three or four against the new constitution–and it is the general opinion that there will scarcely be found ten men in the whole state, who, when they meet here in June, will be hardy enough to set their opinions in competition with those of all the great and good patriots in America, and thus suffer themselves to be branded with the *odious* and *disgraceful* appellation of *antifœderalists*.[2]

Those are to be accounted such who talk of amendments *before* the adoption of the constitution. The true friends to union, that is, to liberty, happiness and national glory, are those who wish to go hand in hand with Massachusetts–adopt the constitution as they have done–*and then* propose such amendments as may be thought necessary–By uniting with her we shall, as the two largest states in the union, be sure to accomplish every just, honorable and impartial amendment–But if we pull one way and Massachusetts another–both of us may lose what each may have in view.[3]

Six states have adopted the new constitution, and those, in which are included, after our own, the two largest states in the union, already make a majority of the free people of America.[4]

It is somewhat remarkable that all who are real friends to the union, and who act honestly and openly, take great pains to remove the groundless prejudices which prevail among the people by distributing copies of the new constitution–whilst, on the other hand, those who are in their hearts against a union–that is, those who talk of amendments *before* ratification–endeavor to keep the people in the *dark* by *telling* them what the constitution is, without *shewing* them what it is–or *giving* it to them to read and *judge for themselves*. All their little artifices and low cunning, all their misconstructions and misrepresentations may serve to confirm the obstinate and to deceive the ignorant–but the honest and well meaning with only common understandings see through their designs and despise them for their wickedness–It will be fortunate for them if the resentment of the people should terminate in contempt alone–When they have been misled–it will be but a small consolation to them to be told by those who have deceived them–that they *thought so and so*.–[5]

1. Fifteen newspapers reprinted all four of these paragraphs by 5 May: Mass. (3), Conn. (3), N.Y. (3), N.J. (1), Pa. (4), S.C. (1). (For the reprinting of an excerpt from the fourth paragraph, see note 5.) The individual paragraphs were each reprinted between sixteen and twenty-six times. (See notes 2–5 below.)

2. By 5 May this paragraph was reprinted twenty-six times: N.H. (4), Mass. (6), R.I. (3), Conn. (4), N.Y. (3), N.J. (1), Pa. (4), S.C. (1).

3. By 5 May this paragraph was reprinted twenty-four times: N.H. (4), Mass. (5), R.I. (3), Conn. (3), N.Y. (3), N.J. (1), Pa. (4), S.C. (1).

4. By 5 May this paragraph was reprinted twenty-five times: N.H. (3), Mass. (6), R.I. (3), Conn. (4), N.Y. (3), N.J.(1), Pa. (4), S.C. (1).

5. By 5 May this paragraph was reprinted sixteen times: N.H. (1), Mass. (3), Conn. (3), N.Y. (3), N.J.(1), Pa. (4), S.C. (1). The reprints in the Philadelphia *Federal Gazette*, 27 March, and in five subsequent newspapers excluded the last sentence of this paragraph.

630. Marcus V
Norfolk and Portsmouth Journal, 19 March[1]

Answers to Mr. Mason's *Objections* to the New Constitution, Recommended by the late Convention at Philadelphia.
(Concluded from our last.)

IXth. Objection.

"The State Legislatures are restrained from laying export duties on their own exports."

Answer.

Duties upon exports, though they may answer in some particulars a convenience to the country which imposes them, are certainly not things to be contended for, as if the very being of a State was interested in preserving them. Where there is a kind of monopoly this may sometimes be ventured upon, but even there perhaps more is lost by imposing such duties than is compensated for by any advantage. Where there is not a species of monopoly no policy can be more absurd. The American States are so circumstanced, that some of the States necessarily export part of the produce of neighbouring ones. Every duty laid upon such exported produce, operates in fact as a tax by the exporting State upon the non-exporting State. In a system expressly formed to produce concord among all, it would have been very unwise to have left such a source of discord open; and upon the same principle, and to remove as much as possible every ground of discontent, Congress itself are prohibited from laying duties on exports, because by that means those States which have a great deal of produce to export, would be taxed much more heavily than those which have little or none for exportation.

Xth. Objection.

"The general Legislature is restrained from prohibiting the further importation of slaves for twenty odd years, though such importations render the United States weaker, more vulnerable, and less capable of defence."

Answer.

If all the States had been willing to adopt this regulation, I should, as an individual, most heartily have approved of it, because, even if the importation of slaves in fact rendered us stronger, less vulnerable, and more capable of defence, I should rejoice in the prohibition of it, as putting a stop to a trade which has already continued too long for the honor and humanity of those concerned in it. But as it was well known that South-Carolina and Georgia thought a further continuance of such importations useful to them, and would not perhaps otherwise have agreed to the new

Constitution, those States which had been importing till they were satisfied, could not with decency have insisted upon their relinquishing advantages [which they] themselves had already enjoyed.[2] Our situation makes it necessary to bear the evil as it is. It will be left to the future Legislatures to allow such importations or not. If any, in violation of their clear conviction of the injustice of this trade, persist in pursuing it, this is a matter between God and their own consciences. The interests of humanity will however have gained something by a prohibition of this inhuman trade, though at the distance of twenty odd years.

XIth. Objection.

"Both the general Legislature, and the State Legislatures are expressly prohibited making *ex post facto* laws, though there never was, nor can be a Legislature but must and will make such laws when necessity and the public safety require them; which will hereafter be a breach of all the Constitutions in the union, and afford precedents for other innovations."

Answer.

My ideas of liberty are so different from those of Mr. Mason, that in my opinion this very prohibition is one of the most valuable parts of the new Constitution. *Ex post facto* laws may some times be convenient, but that they are ever absolutely necessary I shall take the liberty to doubt, till that necessity can be made apparent. Sure I am, they have been the instrument of some of the grossest acts of tyranny that were ever exercised, and have this never failing consequence, to put the minority in the power of a passionate and unprincipled majority, as to the most sacred things; and the plea of necessity is never wanting where it can be of any avail. This very clause, I think, is worth ten thousand Declarations of Rights, if this the most essential right of all was omitted in them. A man may feel some pride in his security, when he knows that what he does innocently and safely to-day, according to the laws of his country, cannot be tortured into guilt and danger to-morrow. But if it should happen, that a great and over-ruling necessity, acknowledged and felt by all, should make a deviation from this prohibition excusable, shall we not be more safe in leaving the excuse for an extraordinary exercise of power to rest upon the apparent equity of it alone, than to leave the door open to a tyranny it would be intolerable to bear? In the one case every one must be sensible of its justice, and therefore excuse it: In the other, whether its exercise was just or unjust, its being lawful would be sufficient to command obedience. Nor would a case like that, resting entirely on its own bottom, from a conviction of invincible necessity, warrant an avowed abuse of another authority where no such necessity existed or could be pretended.

I have now gone through Mr. Mason's objections; one thing still remains to be taken notice of; his prediction, which he is pleased to express in these words: "This government will commence in a modern[3] aristocracy; it is at present impossible to foresee, whether it will, in its operation, produce a monarchy or a corrupt oppressive aristocracy; it will most probably vibrate some years between the two, and then terminate in the one or the other." From the uncertainty of this prediction, we may hope Mr. Mason was not divinely inspired when he made it, and of course that it may as fairly be questioned as any of his particular objections. If my answers to his objections are in general solid, a very different government will arise from the new Constitution if the several States should adopt it, as I hope they will. It will not probably be too much to flatter ourselves with, that it may present a spectacle of combined strength in government; and genuine liberty in the people the world has never yet beheld. In the mean time our situation is critical to the greatest degree. Those gentlemen who think we may at our ease go on from one Convention to another, to try if all objections cannot be conquered by perseverance, have much more sanguine expectations that I can presume to form. There are critical periods in the fate of nations, as well as in the life of man, which are not to be neglected with impunity. I am much mistaken if this is not such a one with us. When we were at the very brink of despair, the late excellent Convention, with an unanimity that none could have hoped for, generously discarding all little considerations, formed a system of government which I am convinced can stand the nicest examination, if reason and not prejudice is employed in viewing it. With a happiness of thought, which in our present awful situation ought to silence much more powerful objections than any I have heard, they have provided in the very frame of government a safe, easy and unexceptionable method of correcting any errors it may be thought to contain. These errors may be corrected at leisure; in the mean time the acknowledged advantages likely to flow from this Constitution may be enjoyed. We may venture to hold up our head among the other powers of the world. We may talk to them with the confidence of an independent people, having strength to resent insults, and avail ourselves of all our natural advantages. We may be assured of once more beholding justice, order and dignity taking place of the present anarchical confusion prevailing almost every where, and drawing upon us universal disgrace. We may hope, by proper exertions of industry, to recover thoroughly from the shock of the late war, and truly to become an independent, great and prosperous people. But if we continue as we now are, wrangling about every trifle, listening to the opinion of a small minority in preference to a large and most respectable majority of the first men in our country, and among them some of the first in the world; if our minds in short, are bent rather on indulging a captious discontent, than bestowing a generous and well-placed confidence in those who we have every reason to believe are entirely worthy of it, we shall too probably present a spectacle for malicious exultation to our enemies, and melancholy dejection to our friends; and the honor, glory and prosperity which were just within our reach, will, perhaps be snatched from us for ever.

January, 1788.

1. For the authorship and circulation of "Marcus," see CC:548.

2. For the debate in the Constitutional Convention on the slave-trade clause, see Farrand, II, 364–65, 369–74, 400, 414–17. During the debate, Hugh Williamson of North Carolina said "He thought the S. States could not be members of the Union if the clause should be rejected, and that it was wrong to force any thing down, not absolutely necessary, and which any State must disagree to" (*ibid.*, 373).

3. In Mason's objections the word is "moderate." The pamphlet version of "Marcus" printed it correctly.

631. Silas Lee to George Thatcher
Biddeford, Maine, 20 March (excerpt)[1]

. . . We have no News of any kind–Seperation,[2] & Constitution seemed to have entirely subsided–the former for the want of Scribblers–the latter from it's having been decided–Thus at present we seem to be at peace–Many who have been much opposed to the Constitution are become warm advocates for it–a circumstance that will ever afford pleasure to every Friend to good Government–In my last letter you say, if our situation, which is admitted to be very deplorable & not to be worsted, is the greatest reason to Justify its adoption, it must be thought to be very bad indeed–perhaps not–There may be many good reasons besides, I think, & yet that the greatest–yes, for the greatest–indeed, I think, that argument alone is unanswerable & sufficient, when we consider that the *worst* of Governments is *better* than none–and that our situation was such, that we must have had this, or none–The old articles of confederation were found totally inadaquate to the purposes, & therefore very little or no better than nothing at all–and principally for the want of energy or power in the federal Head–the proposed Govt. remedies that evil, but as one extreme generally follows another, so it is said, that this Constitution errs on the other side–but as anarchy & confusion, nay perhaps a total dissolution of the States, would probably be the consequence of a continuance in our present situation, (than which state of confusion, nothing ought to be more avoided) & as that Constitution would probably afford immediate relief, & if prudently amended, would undoubtedly be productive of great & lasting happiness, wisdom & Self preservation would indubitally, I think, Justify it's adoption had it been ten times as bad as it is–Nay the worst in the world except our own–than which I think, it would be impossible to find a worse such a one–how then do you conclude, that, if our situation is the greatest reason to Justify it's adoption, that it must be thought to be very bad?

P.S. I intended to have transcribed this before I sent it but have not time–

1. RC, Thatcher Papers, MB.

2. A reference to the movement to establish Maine as a separate state (see CC:570, note 11).

632. Brutus XV
New York Journal, 20 March[1]

(Continued.)

I said in my last number,[2] that the supreme court under this constitution would be exalted above all other power in the government, and subject to no controul. The business of this paper will be to illustrate this, and to shew the danger that will result from it. I question whether the world ever saw, in any period of it, a court of justice invested with such immense powers, and yet placed in a situation so little responsible. Certain it is, that in England, and in the several states, where we have been taught to believe, the courts of law are put upon the most prudent establishment, they are on a very different footing.

The judges in England, it is true, hold their offices during their good behaviour, but then their determinations are subject to correction by the house of lords; and their power is by no means so extensive as that of the proposed supreme court of the union.-I believe they in no instance assume the authority to set aside an act of parliament under the idea that it is inconsistent with their constitution. They consider themselves bound to decide according to the existing laws of the land, and never undertake to controul them by adjudging that they are inconsistent with the constitution-much less are they vested with the power of giv[ing] an *equitable* construction to the constitution.

The judges in England are under the controul of the legislature, for they are bound to determine according to the laws passed by them. But the judges under this constitution will controul the legislature, for the supreme court are authorised in the last resort, to determine what is the extent of the powers of the Congress; they are to give the constitution an explanation, and there is no power above them to sit aside their judgment. The framers of this constitution appear to have followed that of the British, in rendering the judges independent, by granting them their offices during good behaviour, without following the constitution of England, in instituting a tribunal in which their errors may be corrected; and without adverting to this, that the judicial under this system have a power which is above the legislative, and which indeed transcends any power before given to a judicial by any free government under heaven.

I do not object to the judges holding their commissions during good behaviour. I suppose it a proper provision provided they were made properly responsible. But I say, this system has followed the English government in this, while it has departed from almost every other principle of their jurisprudence, under the idea, of rendering the judges independent; which, in the British constitution, means no more than that they hold their places during good behaviour, and have fixed salaries, they have made the judges *independent*, in the fullest sense of the word. There is no power above them, to controul any of their decisions. There is no authority that can remove them, and they cannot be controuled by the laws of the legislature. In short, they are independent of the people, of the legislature, and of every power under heaven. Men placed in this situation will generally soon feel themselves independent of heaven itself. Before I proceed to illustrate the truth of these assertions, I beg liberty to make one remark–Though in my opinion the judges ought to hold their offices during good behaviour, yet I think it is clear, that the reasons in favour of this establishment of the judges in England, do by no means apply to this country.

The great reason assigned, why the judges in Britain ought to be commissioned during good behaviour, is this, that they may be placed in a situation, not to be influenced by the crown, to give such decisions, as would tend to increase its powers and prerogatives. While the judges held their places at the will and pleasure of the king, on whom they depended not only for their offices, but also for their salaries, they were subject to every undue influence. If the crown wished to carry a favorite point, to accomplish which the aid of the courts of law was necessary, the pleasure of the king would be signified to the judges. And it required the spirit of a martyr, for the judges to determine contrary to the king's will.–They were absolutely dependent upon him both for their offices and livings. The king, holding his office during life, and transmitting it to his posterity as an inheritance, has much stronger inducements to increase the prerogatives of his office than those who hold their offices for stated periods, or even for life. Hence the English nation gained a great point, in favour of liberty. When they obtained the appointment of the judges, during good behaviour, they got from the crown a concession, which deprived it of one of the most powerful engines with which it might enlarge the boundaries of the royal prerogative and encroach on the liberties of the people. But these reasons do not apply to this country, we have no hereditary monarch; those who appoint the judges do not hold their offices for life, nor do they descend to their children. The same arguments, therefore, which will conclude in favor of the tenor of the judge's offices for good behaviour, lose a considerable part of their weight when applied to the state and condition of America. But much less can it be shewn, that the nature of our government requires that the courts should be placed beyond all account more independent, so much so as to be above controul.

I have said that the judges under this system will be *independent* in the strict sense of the word: To prove this I will shew–That there is no power above them that can controul their decisions, or correct their errors. There is no authority that can remove them from office for any errors or want of capacity, or lower their salaries, and in many cases their power is superior to that of the legislature.

1st. There is no power above them that can correct their errors or controul their decisions–The adjudications of this court are final and irreversible, for there is no court above them to which appeals can lie, either in error or on the merits.–In this respect it differs from the courts in England, for there the house of lords is the highest court, to whom appeals, in error, are carried from the highest of the courts of law.

2d. They cannot be removed from office or suffer a dimunition of their salaries, for any error in judgement or want of capacity.

It is expressly declared by the constitution,–"That they shall at stated times receive a compensation for their services which shall not be diminished during their continuance in office."

The only clause in the constitution which provides for the removal of the judges from offices, is that which declares, that "the president, vice-president, and all civil officers of the United States, shall be removed from office, on impeachment for, and conviction of treason, bribery, or other high crimes and misdemeanors." By this paragraph, civil officers, in which the judges are included, are removable only for crimes. Treason and bribery are named, and the rest are included under the general terms of high crimes and misdemeanors.–Errors in judgement, or want of capacity to discharge the duties of the office, can never be supposed to be included in these words, *high crimes and misdemeanors*. A man may mistake a case in giving judgment, or manifest that he is incompetent to the discharge of the duties of a judge, and yet give no evidence of corruption or want of integrity. To support the charge, it will be necessary to give in evidence some facts that will shew, that the judges commited the error from wicked and corrupt motives.

3d. The power of this court is in many cases superior to that of the legislature. I have shewed, in a former paper,[3] that this court will be authorised to decide upon the meaning of the constitution, and that, not only according to the natural and ob[vious] meaning of the words, but also according to the spirit and intention of it. In the exercise of this power they will not be subordinate to, but above the legislature. For all the departments of this government will receive their powers, so far as they are expressed in the constitution, from the people immediately, who are the source of power. The legislature can only exercise such powers as are given them by the constitution, they cannot assume any of the rights annexed to the judicial, for this plain reason, that the same authority which vested the legislature with their powers, vested the judicial with theirs–both are derived from the same source, both therefore are equally valid, and the judicial hold their powers independently of the legislature, as the legislature do of the judicial.–The supreme court then have a right, independent of the legislature, to give a construction to the constitution and every part of it, and there is no power provided in this system to correct their construction or do it away. If, therefore, the legislature pass any laws, inconsistent with the sense the judges put upon the constitution, they will declare it void; and therefore in this respect their power is superior to that of the legislature. In England the judges are not only subject to have their decisions set aside by the house of lords, for error, but in cases where they give an explanation to the laws or constitution of the country, contrary to the sense of the parliament, though the parliament will not set aside the judgement of the court, yet, they have authority, by a new law, to explain a former one, and by this means to prevent a reception of such decisions. But no such power is in the legislature. The judges are supreme–and no law, explanatory of the constitution, will be binding on them.

From the preceding remarks, which have been made on the judicial powers proposed in this system, the policy of it may be fully developed.

I have, in the course of my observation on this constitution, affirmed and endeavored to shew, that it was calculated to abolish entirely the state governments, and to melt down the states into one entire government, for every purpose as well internal and local, as external and national. In this opinion the opposers of the system have generally agreed–and this has been uniformly denied by its advocates in public. Some individuals, indeed, among them, will confess, that it has this tendency, and scruple not to say, it is what they wish; and I will venture to predict, without the spirit of prophecy, that if it is adopted without amendments, or some such precautions as will ensure amendments immediately after its adoption, that the same gentlemen who have employed their talents and abilities with such success to influence the public mind to adopt this plan, will employ the same to persuade the people, that it will be for their good to abolish the state governments as useless and burdensome.

Perhaps nothing could have been better conceived to facilitate the abolition of the state governments than the constitution of the judicial. They will be able to extend the limits of the general government gradually, and by insensible degrees, and to accomodate themselves to the temper of the people. Their decisions on the meaning of the constitution will commonly take place in cases which arise between individuals, with which the public will not be generally acquainted; one adjudication will form a precedent to the next, and this to a following one. These cases will immediately affect individuals only; so that a series of determinations will probably take place before even the people will be informed of them. In the mean time all the art and address of those who wish for the change will be employed to make converts to their opinion. The people will be told, that their state officers, and state legislatures are a burden and expence without affording any solid advantage, for that all the laws passed by them, might be equally well made by the general legislature. If to those who will be interested in the change, be added, those who will be under their influence, and such who will submit to almost any change of government, which they can be persuaded to believe will ease them of taxes, it is easy to see, the party who will favor the abolition of the state governments would be far from being inconsiderable.–In this situation, the general legislature, might pass one law after another, extending the general and abridging the state jurisdictions, and to sanction their proceedings would have a course of decisions of the judicial to whom the constitution has committed the power of explaining the constitution.–If the states remonstrated, the constitutional mode of deciding upon the validity of the law, is with the supreme court, and neither people, nor state legislatures, nor the general legislature can remove them or reverse their decrees.

Had the construction of the constitution been left with the legislature, they would have explained it at their peril; if they exceed their powers, or sought to find, in the spirit of the constitution, more than was expressed in the letter, the people from whom they derived their power could remove them, and do themselves right; and indeed I can see no other remedy that the people can have against their rulers for encroachments of this nature. A constitution is a compact of a people with their rulers; if the rulers break the compact, the people have a right and ought to remove them and do themselves justice; but in order to enable them to do this with the greater facility, those whom the people chuse at stated periods, should have the power in the last resort to determine the sense of the compact; if they determine contrary to the understanding of the people, an appeal will lie to the people at the period when the rulers are to be elected, and they will have it in their power to remedy the evil; but when this power is lodged in the hands of men independent of the people, and of their representatives, and who are not, constitutionally, accountable for their opinions, no way is left to controul them but *with a high hand and an outstretched arm.*

1. Reprinted: Boston *American Herald,* 14 April; Providence *United States Chronicle,* 24 April. "A.B." asked the editor of the *United States Chronicle* to reprint "Brutus" in his "impartial Paper" because it was "worthy the Perusal of every Freeman." For the authorship, circulation, and impact of "Brutus," see CC:178.
2. See "Brutus" XIV (CC:576, 598).
3. See "Brutus" XI, *New York Journal,* 31 January (CC:489).

633. Publicola: An Address to the Freemen of North Carolina
State Gazette of North Carolina, 20 March

"Publicola" was written by Archibald Maclaine, a Wilmington, N.C., lawyer-planter. It first appeared in the Newbern *State Gazette of North Carolina* in two installments on 20 and 27 March. The former issue is not extant; the latter contains the concluding portion of the essay which was prefaced: "Continued from our last." Hodge and Wills, printers of the *State Gazette,* also announced in their 27 March issue that they had published a pamphlet edition (Evans 45276) of "Marcus" (CC:548) and "Publicola." Maclaine wrote James Iredell, the author of the "Marcus" essay, that "I perceive that Hodge has published in a pamphlet your answers to Mr Mason's objections, to which he has appended the piece I sent him" (2 April, Iredell Papers, NcD). Maclaine was also identified as the author of "Publicola" by Iredell in a copy of the pamphlet now at the New-York Historical Society.

The text of "Publicola" printed below is taken from the pamphlet edition. For the second part of "Publicola," see CC:648.

To the Freemen of the state of North-Carolina.

The constitution proposed by the late general Convention, being in some states opposed with great warmth, and uncommon perseverance; and among ourselves being a common topic of discussion, tho' apparently little understood; it becomes the duty of every citizen who conceives he can throw any light upon the subject, to communicate his sentiments to you.

We have among us some characters who have uniformly opposed giving Congress any additional powers–what idea such persons have of a government, which by its constitution is empowered to make treaties, contract debts and to demand monies from the several states, without being able to raise a single shilling, or inforce obedience to any one of its acts, they would do well to inform us. They had better acknowledge with candour, what they avow in principle, that we have no occasion for a federal government. Congress, in its present state of imbecility, is a considerable expence to the states. If it cannot be rendered more useful, we had much better keep the money among ourselves, than part with it to so little purpose. Our present *form* of federal government (for it is no more) is the only one in the known world altogether without energy.

There are others who acknowledge that a reform is necessary, but at the same time start numerous objections to the remedy proposed. These objections are indeed so various and contradictory, that they destroy themselves–Scarcely any two of those who oppose the new constitution agree together; nor is there among the whole any thing proposed to substitute in the place of that which they reject. It is evident from this, that whatever may be their professions, they do not wish for any reform–Their strength lies in cavilling; convinced that if they can successfully oppose the proposed government, nothing better can be substituted in its place.

I very sincerely believe that there are many averse from the new constitution upon principle. They conceive that some parts of it may prove dangerous to liberty–It is to such I would wish to offer my remarks; for as to those who are opposed, without reasoning upon, or even reading, what they condemn, I consider them as incorrigible; and however respectable they may appear from station or capacity, I cannot view their conduct without discovering some degree of contempt for their selfish meanness.

Every man of common understanding, and common honesty, will readily acknowledge that something more than a bare federal union is necessary to make us a great and respectable nation–Mixed governments are universally acknowledged to be the best, as partaking of the different forms which are necessary for securing the rights of the people, and at the same time for promoting that dispatch and energy which is necessary for defence against enemies. The new government is partly federal, and partly national. The confederation still subsists, where it is not altered by the new form. To prove this, if it should be doubted, take part of the preamble to the latter: "We the people of the *United States* in order to form a *more perfect union.*" The constitution of the respective states, and the rights of the people, are to remain as under the confederation, excepting such parts as interfere with the express powers given to Congress by the new constitution. All the clamour therefore, which has been raised about the trial by jury, and the liberty of the press, might have been spared, as altogether unfounded. To those who wish to trust themselves under separate state-governments, which may, as they have hitherto done, disregard the recommendations and requisitions of the union, I would recommend an attentive perusal of history, and as they do not seem to place any dependance on the reasoning of their fellow citizens, learn to be wise from the experience of past ages. They will find that in all countries, a strict union among the people, has been the only means of preserving liberty. Spain, composed of a number of kingdoms, principalities and provinces, which in the beginning of the reign of the Emperor Charles the Fifth, the first sovereign of that united country, enjoyed more liberty than any other country in Europe; but for want of union among the people, lost the whole; and their Kings from being the most limited, became in a few years to be some of the most absolute monarchs in Europe. At this day, there is not the shadow of liberty among them–every species of tyranny, which could be devised, has reduced the people to the most abject slavery. When people enter into society, they must, in order to obtain protection, give up some part of their natural liberty, in order to secure the rest–the more we retain in our hands, consistent with that protection, which is necessary for society, will be so much the better, and this is called civil liberty–In small states, the people generally retain more than in those which are extensive; but at the same time, they are more subject to violence and oppression, from their powerful neighbours. There is no possible way of uniting the force of a number of small states, but under one head. If each one is left to its own deliberations, it may determine, for want of knowing what is most salutary for the whole, contrary to the general interest; and thus defeat the purposes of the union–In all events, the very time taken in deliberating may prove fatal.–Instead of searching for objections against the new constitution, something should be proposed that will better answer the purpose, and at the same time secure the liberties of the people.–There are no powers granted by the new constitution, but what are necessary in all governments, and if we cannot entrust them in the hands of our own citizens; persons of our own choice, and whom we may remove at stated, and short periods, we must be contented to live without any effective government–We must be contented to remain at the mercy of the first foreign invader who may think us worth subduing; or, what will unquestionably be much worse, to fall into civil wars, and at last become the prey of the most daring desperado among ourselves. There is scarcely an objection made to the new constitution, but what will operate with equal force against any form of government that can be devised.

It is very remarkable that the principal opponents among us, are either those whose private interest may be affected by the proposed constitution;

or those who conceive that their importance may be lessened by the intended change. Had the interested and ambitious acted honestly, and taken as much pains to explain and elucidate, as they have done to prevent; those among you, who have little or no means of information but from your wealthy, or dignified neighbours, would not at this day have raised your voices against a work that does honour, even to the most celebrated of those names who assisted in forming it. The new constitution is not pretended to be a work of perfection–such is not to be expected from imperfect beings; but it is perfect, compared to what we had reason to expect, from the jarring interests, and dissonant opinions of those who composed it–It is not a work intended for this, or that state, but for the whole body of the union. But were it completely adapted to our present situation, so as to be unexceptionable to all, time would render it defective–Improvements in commerce and manufactures, in arts and sciences; an increase in population, and an alteration in manners, would render amendments to the new constitution necessary–nothing in this world can be permanent; but it has been truly and elegantly observed by one of the framers of the new constitution, that the seeds of reformation are sown in the work itself–there is express provision made for amendments, when its defects and imperfections shall be discovered in its operation.[1]

There is reason to believe that those who are predetermined against the new constitution, have insidiously endeavoured to poison your minds so far, as to prevail on many of you to make it a previous condition with your representatives, to vote against it;–those who will take the trouble to reflect upon the consequences of such a measure, must be convinced of the absurdity, as well as the fatal tendency of it. It is putting a negative upon the proposed constitution before debate; and should your delegates be convinced hereafter, that it is worthy of adoption, they will be embarrassed with your instructions. The greatest part of you have not the means of information, and being unaccustomed to think of government, few of you are competent judges of it. Why do the people chuse representatives but to decide for them? Why do the representatives want instructions, but to give them a plausible pretext for voting against the conviction of their own minds? It must be a bad cause that will not admit of a free investigation. Instructions to reject the new constitution, defeats the very purpose for which the Convention is to meet. We are, by the resolves of the Congress and Assembly, to elect persons "for the purpose of *deliberating* and *determining* on the said constitution;"[2] not for the purpose either of adoption or rejection, without deliberation and debate. Were that to be the case, the members of the Convention would have no more to do than to examine all the different instructions; to *count noses*, and by that summary method, to adopt, or reject. This method, if not the most rational, that might be adopted, will at least be equal to the *throw of a die*, or any other species of gaming; though by some persons it may not be thought altogether so eligible as that, which is authorised; of collecting the united wisdom of the state in order, to *deliberate* and *determine.*

The arguments which mislead you are as weak as they are dishonest. You are told that by adopting the new constitution, the dignity of the state will be lost; that you will be drained of your money by *foreign* taxes (for so the taxes of Congress are as *modestly as wisely* called) and be obliged to attend *foreign* Courts, at a great distance, and an enormous expence; whereas, say the objectors, we are able to support our own state; the taxes imposed by our legislature, will be consumed among ourselves; and we can have justice as well administered at home, as at six or seven hundred miles distance, and at a much cheaper rate. To those who do not look further, but consider this state, not only as the guardian of our liberties, but as bulwark of defence, these are flattering arguments; and when they are applied to a man heated with zeal, he will be apt to set all the powers of Europe at defiance. If however he should happen to recollect that a handful of men during the late war, took possession of one of the principal ports of the state, and kept possession of it ten months, even when a body of militia, three times their number, advanced against them; and that, that very handful of men, marched a hundred miles through the country un-molested, and plundered a principal seaport before their return, it is pos-sible he may begin to doubt his own prowess, and even question whether the state can be depended upon for a guard against the depredations of a single privateer.[3] It is not material what resources we have–experience may teach us, that under our present government, we cannot make a proper use of them. The United States are, and for some years have been, without any national character–Foreigners say, and they say truly, that we have no government–Even in this state, our policy is so wretched, that we have lost all credit, the very soul of commerce. No foreigner, no not an individual of any of our sister states, will trust us with a shilling. Our paper money, and our judicial decisions, banish all confidence; and the former has banished all gold and silver–Let paper money be no longer a tender, and justice be done to those who have transactions with us, and I will venture to assert that we shall soon have among us, a pound value in gold and silver, for every shilling in paper which we now possess. Wher-ever depreciated money is a lawful tender, that which is good vanishes, as if by inchantment.[4]

I am astonished to hear that appeals are held up as a bugbear by men of understanding, if indeed they are in earnest. It is well known to every one who has looked into the new constitution, with any degree of attention, that the federal courts can have nothing to do with suits between citizens of the same state, unless where they claim lands under grants of different states. This [is] a power reserved by the confederation, and it is necessary for the purpose of giving each party a fair and impartial trial, before Judges who may be supposed indifferent to both states–The citizen of this state will have the benefit of this regulation, when he claims land in another state, either under a grant of that state, or his own. Appeals will be regulated by your own representatives in Congress, and will undoubtedly be confined to suits where the value contended for, will bear the expence and trouble. This is a sufficient security for us, as a great majority of the states must necessarily be at a considerable distance from the seat of government; and in framing laws the members will be attentive to the interest of their respective constituents. But I find some people are so strangely infatuated, as to think that Congress can, and therefore will, usurp powers not given them by the states, and do any thing, however oppressive and tyrannical. I know no good grounds for such a supposition, but this, that the legislative and judicial powers of the state have too often stepped over the bounds prescribed for them by the constitution; and yet, strange to tell, few of those, whose arguments I am now considering, think such measures censurable–The conclusion to be drawn here is obvious–The objectors hope to enjoy the same latitude of doing evil with impunity, and they are fearful of being restricted, if an efficient government takes place. But in truth many of the arguments used against the new constitution are utterly unaccountable; such for instance, that taxes are to be levied at the point of the bayonet–I would be glad to know the reason for this extraordinary assertion–Who has informed those worthy objectors all over the United States (for they catch at the arguments of each other) that the people would refuse to pay taxes for the support of the union? For to make soldiers necessary in the collection, resistance in the people is pre-supposed. That the people in this state should raise any objections to federal courts, and to appeals, is to me past all comprehension. After complaining for some years past, of the delays in our own courts, and of frequent decisions which have given great offence to the people in general, it would naturally occur that some reform should be thought necessary, and that any scheme that would effect such a salutary purpose, would readily be adopted.[5] All criminal matters must be tried, and finally determined, in the state where the offence may be committed, even if it should be treason against the United States; and though the federal courts must be confined to some particular cases specified in the new constitution, yet the rules of their conduct will have a powerful influence upon the courts of the state. If business is transacted in the former upon settled and uniform principles, and without unnecessary delays, the latter will be ashamed to neglect their duty. I am informed that our Judges see clearly that this will be one of the consequences of adopting the new constitution, and one of them, fearful of being restricted to do what is right, expressed his apprehensions, that the *great federal courts* would *overshadow* the courts of the state: So unwilling are men possessed of absolute power to relinquish any part of it.[6] For this, and several reasons, altogether as good, our Judges are decidedly opposed to the new constitution. But I suppose no good citizen will think it any degradation to the state, that our courts should undergo a reform from the example of the courts of the union (of which we are a part) or even from the example of the courts of any other country. The apprehensions of paying taxes for the support of the union, should not influence our conduct in deciding whether we shall receive the new constitution–We should have paid them long since, towards discharging the interest of our debts, and had our government been judiciously conducted, we might have done it with ease.[7] Taxes are necessary for the support of every government, and though we shall always have a state establishment to support, the taxes for the union will be applied for our protection and defence from foreign enemies–Besides they will be rated by our own immediate representatives, and they and their families will be equally liable with ourselves. But it is not probable, in our present situation, that the federal government will want any direct taxes from the states, for a considerable time to come–I am persuaded that nothing but a rupture with some foreign power will make taxation necessary; and if we are enabled to make good our past engagements, there will be little or no danger of a war on our parts–But if it should be unavoidable, it is certainly better for us to pay a moderate tax, in order to be prepared to repel an enemy, than to suffer the country to be invaded and plundered. We have had sufficient experience of that already, and no good man wishes for a repetition of it.–But the sale of the western territory, and the duties arising from imposts, will, in all probability, be more than equal to our wants while we continue in peace–These last will increase yearly beyond all exception, and our exports in proportion; so that every succeeding year we shall be the better able to pay. Much of the sums collected at the different ports will center among ourselves. The different federal departments must be supported, and commerce will make us ample returns for whatever monies may be drawn from us. Exclusive of the advantages of a general trade, we must supply many, and might in time supply almost all of the materials necessary for equiping a navy.

1. See James Wilson's 6 October speech, CC:134.

2. The resolution of Congress, 28 September, recommended that the Constitution "be submitted to a convention of Delegates chosen in each state by the people thereof" (CC:95). The Assembly resolutions of 6 December called for the election of delegates "for the purpose of deliberating and determining on the said Constitution."

3. Between January and November 1781, a British force occupied Wilmington and raided beyond Newbern. The North Carolina militia unsuccessfully challenged this force.

4. During the war North Carolina issued large amounts of paper money which eventually became almost worthless. After the war, the state emitted a total of £200,000 in legal tender paper money in 1783 and 1785. These issues served as a medium of exchange within the state, but depreciated as much as fifty percent by 1789.

5. In January 1787 Maclaine was chairman of a joint legislative committee that prepared charges against the judges of the Superior Court, and he was one of those who protested when the Assembly not only rejected the charges but thanked the judges "for their long and faithful services" (NCSR, XVIII, 421-25, 428-29, 461, 476, 477-83).

These proceedings are described in Peter Charles Hoffer and N.E.H. Hull, *Impeachment in America, 1635–1805* (New Haven, 1984), 87–91. See also CC:648, note 4.

6. All three Superior Court judges–Samuel Ashe, Samuel Spencer, and John Williams–opposed ratification of the Constitution. In July and August 1788 Spencer was a leader of the Antifederalists at the Hillsborough Convention and argued that the federal courts would overwhelm the state courts.

7. See CC:560, note 10.

634. Gazette of the State of Georgia, 20 March[1]

Extract of a letter from the Hon. William Pierce, *Esq. to* St. George Tucker, *Esq. dated New York, Sept.* 28, 1787.

"You ask me for such information as I can, with propriety, give you, respecting the proceedings of the Convention. In my letter from Philadelphia, in July last, I informed you that every thing was covered with the veil of secresy.[2] It is now taken off, and the great work is presented to the public for their consideration. I enclose you a copy of it, with the letter which accompanies the Constitution.[3]

"You will probably be surprised at not finding my name affixed to it; and will, no doubt, be desirous of having a reason for it. Know then, Sir, that I was absent in New York on a piece of business so necessary that it became unavoidable. I approve of its principles, and would have signed it with all my heart, had I been present. To say, however, that I consider it as perfect, would be to make an acknowledgment immediately opposed to my judgment. Perhaps it is the only one that will suit our present situation. The wisdom of the Convention was equal to something greater; but a variety of local circumstances, the inequality of states, and the dissonant interests of the different parts of the Union, made it impossible to give it any other shape or form.

"The great object of this new government is to consolidate the Union, and to give us the appearance and power of a nation. The inconvenience of the different states meeting on the footing of compleat equality, and as so many sovereign powers confederated, has been severely felt by the Union at large; and it is to remedy this evil that something like a national institution has become necessary. The condition of America demands a change; we must sooner or later be convulsed if we do not have some other government than the one under which we at present live. The old Federal Constitution is like a ship bearing under the weight of a tempest; it is trembling, and just on the point of sinking. If we have not another bark to take us up we shall all go down together. There are periods in the existence of a political society that require prompt and decisive measures; I mean that point of time between a people's running into anarchy and an anxious state of the public mind to be rescued from its approaching mischiefs by the intervention of some good and efficient government. That is precisely the situation in which we seem to be placed. A question then arises, Shall we have this government, or shall we run into confusion? It is with the people to decide the alternative.

"I am well aware that objections will be made to this new government when examined in the different states; some will oppose it from pride, some from self-interest, some from ignorance, but the greater number will be of that class who will oppose it from a dread of its swallowing up the individuality of the states. Local circumstances will weigh against the general interest, and no respect will be paid to all the parts aggregated which compose the Confederacy. Good as well as bad men will probably unite their interest to oppose it, and some small convulsions may possibly happen in some of the states before it is adopted, but I am certain it is the ark that is to save us. I therefore hope and trust it will be accepted. It is a difficult point to concentrate thirteen different interests so as to give general and compleat satisfaction: But as individuals in society (to use an old hackneyed and well known principle) give up a part of their natural rights to secure the rest, so the different states should render a portion of their interests to secure the good of the whole. Was this question proposed to each of the states separately, 'What kind of government is best calculated for the people of the United States?' there would be as many different opinions as there are different Interests. It would be like the decisions of the seven wise men of Greece, who were called on, at the Court of Periander, to give their sentiments on the nature of a perfect commonwealth,– they all judged differently, but they all judged right, in the view each man had of it.

"Many objections have been already started to the Constitution because it was not founded on a Bill of Rights; but I ask how such a thing could have been effected; I believe it would have been difficult in the extreme to have brought the different states to agree in what probably would have been proposed as the very first principle, and that is, 'that all men are born equally free and independent.' Would a Virginian have accepted it in this form? Would he not have modified some of the expressions in such a manner as to have injured *the strong sense of them*, if not to have buried them altogether in *ambiguity and uncertainty?*

"In my judgment, when there are restraints on power to prevent its invading the positive rights of a people, there is no necessity for any such thing as a Bill of Rights. I conceive civil liberty is sufficiently guarded when personal security, personal liberty, and private property, are made the peculiar care of government. Now the defined powers of each department of the government, and the restraints that naturally follow, will be sufficient to prevent the invasion of either of those rights. Where then can be the necessity for a Bill of Rights? It is with diffidence I start this question; I confess I cannot help doubting the negative quality which it conveys, as some of the greatest men I ever knew have objected to the government for no other reason but because it was not *bottomed with a Bill*

of Rights; men whose experience and wisdom are sufficient to give authority and support to almost any opinion they may choose to advance.

"I set this down as a truth founded in nature, that a nation habituated
to freedom will never remain quiet under an invasion of its liberties. The
English history presents us with a proof of this. At the Conquest that nation lost their freedom, but they never were easy or quiet until the true
balance between liberty and prerogative was established in the reign of
Charles the second. The absolute rights of Englishmen are founded in
nature and reason, and are coeval with the English Constitution itself.
They were always understood and insisted on by them as well without as
with a Bill of Rights. This same spirit was breathed into the Americans,
and they still retain it, nor will they, I flatter myself, ever resign it to any
power, however plausible it may seem. The Bill of Rights was not introduced into England until the Revolution of 1688, (upwards of 600 years
after the Conquest) when the Lords and Commons presented it to the
Prince and Princess of Orange. And afterwards the same rights were asserted in the Act of Settlement[4] at the commencement of the present century, when the Crown was limited to the House of Hanover. It was deemed
necessary to introduce such an instrument to satisfy the public mind in
England, not as a bottom to the Constitution, but as a prop to it; and
hereafter, if the same necessity should exist in America, it may be done by
an act of the Legislature here, so that the Constitution not being founded
on a Bill of Rights I conceive will not deprive it at any future time of being
propt by one, should it become necessary.

"A defect is found by some people in this new Constitution, because it
has not provided, except in criminal cases, for Trial by Jury.[5] I ask if the
trial by jury in civil cases is really and substantially of any security to the
liberties of a people. In my idea the opinion of its utility is founded more
in prejudice than in reason. I cannot but think that an able Judge is better
qualified to decide between man and man than any twelve men possibly
can be. The trial by jury appears to me to have been introduced originally
to soften some of the rigors of the feudal system, as in all the countries
where that strange policy prevailed, they had, according to Blackstone, 'a
tribunal composed of twelve good men, true *boni homines*, usually the vassals or tenants of the Lord, being the equals or peers of the parties liti-
gant.'[6] This style of trial was evidently meant to give the tenants a check
upon the enormous power and influence of their respective Lords; and,
considered in that point of view, it may be said to be a wise scheme of
juridical polity; but applied to us in America, where every man stands
upon a footing of independence, and where there is not, and I trust never
will be, such an odious inequality between Lord and tenant as marked the
times of a Regner or an Egbert, is useless, and I think altogether unnecessary; and, if I was not in the habit of respecting some of the *prejudices* of
very sensible men, I should declare it ridiculous. An Englishman to be

sure will talk of it in raptures; it is a virtue in him to do so, because it is insisted on in Magna Charta (that favorite instrument of English liberty) as the great bulwark of the nation's happiness. But we in America never were in a situation to feel the same benefits from it that the English nation have. We never had any thing like the Norman trial by battel, nor great Lords presiding at the heads of numerous tribes of tenants whose influence and power we wished to set bounds to.

"As to trial by jury in criminal cases, it is right, it is just, perhaps it is indispensable,–the life of a citizen ought not to depend on the fiat of a single person. Prejudice, resentment, and partiality, are among the weaknesses of human nature, and are apt to pervert the judgment of the greatest and best of men. The solemnity of the trial by jury is suited to the nature of criminal cases, because, before a man is brought to answer the indictment, the fact or truth of every accusation is inquired into by the Grand Jury, composed of his fellow citizens, and the same truth or fact afterwards (should the Grand Jury find the accusation well founded) is to be confirmed by the unanimous suffrage of twelve good men, 'superior to all suspicion.' I do not think there can be a greater guard to the liberties of a people than such a mode of trial on the affairs of life and death. But here let it rest.

"The most solid objection I think that can be made to any part of the new government is the power which is given to the Executive Department; it appears rather too highly mounted to preserve exactly the equilibrium. The authority which the President holds is as great as that possessed by the King of England. Fleets and armies must support him in it. I confess however that I am at a loss to know whether any government can have sufficient energy to effect its own ends without the aid of a military power. Some of the greatest men differ in opinion about this point. I will not pretend to decide it.

"It requires very little wisdom or foresight to see into the consequences of the government when put compleatly in motion. You will observe that one branch of the Legislature is to come from the People, the other from the several State Legislatures; one is to sympathize with the people at large, the other with the sovereignty of the states, but the suffrages of the two are unequal; the House of Commons will have sixty-five votes, whilst the Senate has only twenty-six. Some of the states will have eight and ten Members in the Lower House, some only two or three, but all will have an equal number in the Senate. The Judicial Power is to extend 'to controversies between two or more states, between a state and citizens of another state, between citizens of different states, between citizens of the same state claiming lands under grants of different states, and between a state and the citizens thereof, and foreign states, citizens, or subjects.' And the President is to be Commander in Chief of the Fleets and Armies of the United States and the Militia of the states when called into the service of the

Union. All this taken collectively forms such a power independent of the states as must eventually draw from them all their remaining sovereignty. Whether such a thing is desirable or not let every man appeal to his own judgment to determine. It is clearly my opinion that we had better be consolidated than to remain any longer a confederated republic.

"I would say something about the Article of Commerce, but it involves in it so much inquiry and calculation that I will reserve it for another letter. I know the most popular opposition in Virginia will be founded on this head, but I think it can be proven beyond a doubt that a uniform regulation of its principles will secure lasting and equal advantages to every part of the empire. If this right had at first been lodged in the hands of Congress, we should not at this day be in the condition we are."

1. Pierce (c. 1740–1789) was a Continental Army officer from 1776 to 1783, serving for a time as General Nathanael Greene's aide-de-camp. St. George Tucker, a judge of the General Court of Virginia, had also served with the Virginia militia which assisted Greene in his southern campaign. In 1786 Pierce, a Savannah merchant, represented Chatham County in the Georgia Assembly. In 1787 he attended Congress from 17 January to 24 May, 6 July to 1 August, and 27 August to 1 October. From 31 May to 1 July, Pierce sat almost continuously in the Constitutional Convention, where he favored strengthening the central government at the expense of the states. His sketches of the Convention's delegates and notes of debates are printed in Max Farrand's *Records of the Federal Convention*. In 1789 Pierce was elected vice president of the Georgia Society of the Cincinnati.

The first four paragraphs of Pierce's letter to Tucker were reprinted in the *Massachusetts Centinel* on 21 May.

2. On 27 June 1787 Pierce wrote Tucker that "I wish it was in my power to give you some information respecting the proceedings of the Convention, but we are enjoined to secrecy,–I dare not say any thing.–

"You may suppose that where there are a variety of interests, there will be a variety of projects.–Nothing can conquer the force of local habits; some are for one thing, and some for another, but I believe we shall ultimately agree on one sort of Government.–

"Burlamiqui relates a circumstance which he has borrowed from Herodotus, that is a good deal in the style of our various sentiments.–On the death of Cambyses of Persia there was an attempt made to reestablish the Government, and to effect the punishment of the Magus, who had usurped the Throne as a descendant from Cyrus.–A question was proposed in the Council of the seven chiefs, of this sort,–what is the best kind of Government for the present state of Persia?–One was of opinion that Persia ought to be a Republic;–another was of opinion that it ought to be a strong Aristocracy,–and a third (who I think was Darius) was convinced that no other Government would suit it but a Monarchy.–" [Jean Jacques Burlamaqui, *The Principles of Natural and Politic Law* (2nd ed., 2 vols., London, 1763), II, 82–86.]

"I pray you not from this story to conclude that we are to have a Monarchy,–I relate it merely to give you some idea of the various opinions which we have sometimes started," (Tucker-Coleman Papers, Swem Library, William and Mary College).

3. Probably the official four-page broadside printing of the Constitution made by John M'Lean of the New York *Independent Journal* and the circular letter of Charles Thomson, the secretary of Congress (CDR, 340, 342, note 25).

4. Passed in 1701.

5. For an extended critique of Pierce's defense of the Constitution's failure to provide for a jury trial in civil cases, see "A Planter," *Gazette of the State of Georgia*, 3 April (RCS:Ga., 298–300).

6. *Commentaries*, III, chapter XXIII, 349.

635. Publius: The Federalist 73
New York Packet, 21 March

This essay, written by Alexander Hamilton, was reprinted in the New York *Independent Journal* on 22 March. It is number 73 in the M'Lean edition and number 72 in the newspapers.

For a general discussion of the authorship, circulation, and impact of *The Federalist*, see CC:201, 639.

The FŒDERALIST, No. 72.

To the People of the State of New-York.

The third ingredient towards constituting the vigor of the executive authority is an adequate provision for its support. It is evident that without proper attention to this article, the separation of the executive from the legislative department would be merely nominal and nugatory. The Legislature, with a discretionary power over the salary and emoluments of the Chief Magistrate, could render him as obsequious to their will, as they might think proper to make him. They might in most cases either reduce him by famine, or tempt him by largesses, to surrender at discretion his judgment to their inclinations. These expressions taken in all the latitude of the terms would no doubt convey more than is intended.–There are men who could neither be distressed nor won into a sacrifice of their duty; but this stern virtue is the growth of few soils: And in the main it will be found, that a power over a man's support is a power over his will. If it were necessary to confirm so plain a truth by facts, examples would not be wanting, even in this country, of the intimidation or seduction of the executive by the terrors, or allurements, of the pecuniary arrangements of the legislative body.

It is not easy therefore to commend too highly the judicious attention which has been paid to this subject in the proposed Constitution. It is there provided that "The President of the United States shall, at stated times, receive for his services a compensation, *which shall neither be increased nor diminished, during the period for which he shall have been elected*, and he shall *not receive within that period any other emolument* from the United States or any of them." It is impossible to imagine any provision which would have been more eligible than this–The Legislature on the appointment of a President is once for all to declare what shall be the compensation for his services during the time for which he shall have been elected. This done, they will have no power to alter it either by increase or diminution, till a new period of service by a new election commences–They can neither weaken his fortitude by operating upon his necessities; nor corrupt his integrity, by appealing to his avarice. Neither the Union nor any of its members will be at liberty to give, nor will he be at liberty to receive any other emolument, than that which may have been determined by the first act. He can of course have no pecuniary inducement to renounce or desert the independence intended for him by the Constitution.

The last of the requisites to energy which have been enumerated are competent powers. Let us proceed to consider those which are proposed to be vested in the President of the United States.

The first thing that offers itself to our observation, is the qualified negative of the President upon the acts or resolutions of the two Houses of the Legislature; or in other words his power of returning all bills with objections; to have the effect of preventing their becoming laws, unless they should afterwards be ratified by two thirds of each of the component members of the legislative body.

The propensity of the legislative department to intrude upon the rights and to absorb the powers of the other departments, has been already suggested and repeated; the insufficiency of a mere parchment delineation of the boundaries of each, has also been remarked upon; and the necessity of furnishing each with constitutional arms for its own defence, has been inferred and proved.[1] From these clear and indubitable principles results the propriety of a negative, either absolute or qualified, in the executive, upon the acts of the legislative branches. Without the one or the other the former would be absolutely unable to defend himself against the depredations of the latter. He might gradually be stripped of his authorities by successive resolutions, or annihilated by a single vote. And in the one mode or the other, the legislative and executive powers might speedily come to be blended in the same hands. If even no propensity had ever discovered itself in the legislative body, to invade the rights of the executive, the rules of just reasoning and theoretic propriety would of themselves teach us, that the one ought not to be left at the mercy of the other, but ought to possess a constitutional and effectual power of self defence.

But the power in question has a further use. It not only serves as a shield to the executive, but it furnishes an additional security against the enaction of improper laws. It establishes a salutary check upon the legislative body calculated to guard the community against the effects of faction, precipitancy, or of any impulse unfriendly to the public good, which may happen to influence a majority of that body.

The propriety of a negative, has upon some occasions been combated by an observation, that it was not to be presumed a single man would possess more virtue or wisdom, than a number of men; and that unless this presumption should be entertained, it would be improper to give the executive magistrate any species of controul over the legislative body.

But this observation when examined will appear rather specious than solid. The propriety of the thing does not turn upon the supposition of superior wisdom or virtue in the executive: But upon the supposition that the legislative will not be infallible: That the love of power may sometimes betray it into a disposition to encroach upon the rights of the other members of the government; that a spirit of faction may sometimes pervert its deliberations; that impressions of the moment may sometimes hurry it into measures which itself on maturer reflection would condemn. The primary inducement to conferring the power in question upon the executive, is to enable him to defend himself; the secondary one is to encrease the chances in favor of the community, against the passing of bad laws, through haste, inadvertence, or design. The oftner a measure is brought under examination, the greater the diversity in the situations of those who are to examine it, the less must be the danger of those errors which flow from want of due deliberation, or of those misteps which proceed from the contagion of some common passion or interest. It is far less probable, that culpable views of any kind should infect all the parts of the government, at the same moment and in relation to the same object, than that they should by turns govern and mislead every one of them.

It may perhaps be said, that the power of preventing bad laws includes that of preventing good ones; and may be used to the one purpose as well as to the other. But this objection will have little weight with those who can properly estimate the mischiefs of that inconstancy and mutability in the laws, which forms the greatest blemish in the character and genius of our governments. They will consider every institution calculated to restrain the excess of law-making, and to keep things in the same state, in which they may happen to be at any given period, as much more likely to do good than harm; because it is favorable to greater stability in the system of legislation. The injury which may possibly be done by defeating a few good laws will be amply compensated by the advantage of preventing a number of bad ones.

Nor is this all. The superior weight and influence of the legislative body in a free government, and the hazard to the executive in a trial of strength with that body, afford a satisfactory security, that the negative would generally be employed with great caution, and that there would oftener be room for a charge of timidity than of rashness, in the exercise of it. A King of Great-Britain, with all his train of sovereign attributes, and with all the influence he draws from a thousand sources, would at this day hesitate to put a negative upon the joint resolutions of the two houses of Parliament. He would not fail to exert the utmost resources of that influence to strangle a measure disagreeable to him, in its progress to the throne, to avoid being reduced to the dilemma of permitting it to take effect, or of risking the displeasure of the nation, by an opposition to the sense of the legislative body. Nor is it probable that he would ultimately venture to exert his prerogatives, but in a case of manifest propriety, or extreme necessity. All well informed men in that kingdom will accede to the justness of this remark. A very considerable period has elapsed since the negative of the crown has been exercised.

If a magistrate, so powerful and so well fortified as a British monarch, would have scruples about the exercise of the power under consideration, how much greater caution may be reasonably expected in a President of the United States, cloathed for the short period of four years with the executive authority of a government wholly and purely republican?

It is evident that there would be greater danger of his not using his power when necessary, than of his using it too often, or too much. An argument indeed against its expediency has been drawn from this very source.[2] It has been represented on this account as a power odious in appearance; useless in practice. But it will not follow, that because it might be rarely exercised, it would never be exercised. In the case for which it is chiefly designed, that of an immediate attack upon the constitutional rights of the executive, or in a case in which the public good was evidently and palpably sacrificed, a man of tolerable firmness would avail himself of his constitutional means of defence, and would listen to the admonitions of duty and responsibility.[3] In the former supposition, his fortitude would be stimulated by his immediate interest in the power of his office; in the latter by the probability of the sanction of his constituents; who though they would naturally incline to the legislative body in a doubtful case, would hardly suffer their partiality to delude them in a very plain case. I speak now with an eye to a magistrate possessing only a common share of firmness. There are men, who under any circumstances will have the courage to do their duty at every hazard.

But the Convention have pursued a mean in this business; which will both facilitate the exercise of the power vested in this respect in the executive magistrate, and make its efficacy to depend on the sense of a considerable part of the legislative body. Instead of an absolute negative, it is proposed to give the executive the qualified negative already described. This is a power, which would be much more readily exercised than the other. A man who might be afraid to defeat a law by his single VETO, might not scruple to return it for re-consideration; subject to being finally rejected only in the event of more than one third of each house concurring in the sufficiency of his objections. He would be encouraged by the reflection, that if his opposition should prevail, it would embark in it a very respectable proportion of the legislative body, whose influence would be united with his in supporting the propriety of his conduct, in the public opinion. A direct and categorical negative has something in the appearance of it more harsh, and more apt to irritate, than the mere suggestion of argumentative objections to be approved or disapproved, by those to whom they are addressed–In proportion as it would be less apt to offend, it would be more apt to be exercised; and for this very reason it may in practice be found more effectual. It is to be hoped that it will not often happen, that improper views will govern so large a proportion as two-thirds of both branches of the Legislature at the same time; and this too in spite[4] of the counterpoising weight of the executive. It is at any rate far less probable, that this should be the case, than that such views should

taint the resolutions and conduct of a bare majority. A power of this nature, in the executive, will often have a silent and unpercieved though
forcible operation. When men engaged in unjustifiable pursuits are aware,
that obstructions may come from a quarter which they cannot controul,
they will often be restrained, by the bare apprehension of opposition, from
doing what they would with eagerness rush into, if no such external impediments were to be feared.

This qualified negative, as has been elsewhere remarked, is in this State
vested in a council, consisting of the Governor, with the Chancellor and
Judges of the Supreme Court, or any two of them.[5] It has been freely
employed upon a variety of occasions, and frequently with success. And
its utility has become so apparent, that persons who in compiling the Constitution were violent opposers of it, have from experience become its declared admirers.[a]

I have in another place remarked, that the Convention in the formation
of this part of their plan, had departed from the model of the Constitution
of this State, in favor of that of Massachusetts[6]–two strong reasons may be
imagined for this preference. One is that the Judges, who are to be the
interpreters of the law, might receive an improper bias from having given
a previous opinion in their revisionary capacities. The other is that by
being often associated with the executive they might be induced to embark
too far in the political views of that magistrate, and thus a dangerous
combination might by degrees be cemented between the executive and
judiciary departments. It is impossible to keep the Judges too distinct from
every other avocation than that of expounding the laws. It is peculiarly
dangerous to place them in a situation to be either corrupted or influenced
by the executive.

(a) *Mr. Abraham Yates, a warm opponent of the plan of the Convention, is of this number.*[7]

1. See *The Federalist* 47–51 and 71 (CC:486, 492, 495, 500, 503, 625).
2. See "Centinel" II, Philadelphia *Freeman's Journal*, 24 October (CC:190).
3. In a review of *The Federalist* in the June issue of the New York *American Magazine*,
the reviewer (probably editor Noah Webster) found some stylistic inaccuracies in this
sentence. Webster noted that "The past tense is here used for the future or conditional
should be or *might be*; and many such examples occur in the course of the work. The haste
in which these essays were written is an apology for all such inaccuracies. But the
author has a better apology.

"This kind of inaccuracy is very common with the best writers, and has never before
been noticed. The silence of critics on the point, is astonishing; but it is also real, and
will excuse the faults of those writers whose principal business is with *ideas* rather than
with *words*.

"On the whole, it must be allowed that these essays compose one of the most complete dissertations on government that ever has appeared in America, perhaps in Europe. . . ."
4. "Defiance" substituted in the M'Lean edition.
5. See *The Federalist* 47, New York *Independent Journal*, 30 January (CC:486, note 5),
and *The Federalist* 69 (CC:617).

6. See *The Federalist* 69 (CC:617).

7. Abraham Yates, Jr. (1724–1796), a native and resident of Albany, was a strong supporter of American independence and a delegate to all of the New York provincial congresses, 1775–77. He was chairman of the committee that drafted the state constitution in 1777. He was a state senator, 1777–90; a delegate to Congress, 1787–88; and mayor of Albany, 1790–96. Throughout the 1780s, Yates wrote pamphlets and newspaper articles opposing the increase of Congress' powers at the expense of the states. As an Antifederalist leader, he also wrote newspaper articles attacking the Constitution under such pseudonyms as "Rough Hewer," "Rough Hewer, Jr.," "Sidney," and "Sydney." One Antifederalist even thought Yates wrote the "Brutus" essays (CC:298).

636. Luther Martin: Address No. II
Maryland Journal, 21 March

This essay is a continuation of Luther Martin's reply to the Maryland "Landholder," No. X, *Maryland Journal*, 29 February (CC:580. For Martin's earlier replies, see CC:604, 626.). It was reprinted in three Philadelphia newspapers: *Freeman's Journal*, 2, 9 April (excerpts); *Independent Gazetteer*, 10 April; and *Pennsylvania Mercury*, 10, 12 April.

To the CITIZENS of MARYLAND.

In the recognition which the Landholder professes to make "of what occurred to my advantage," he equally deals in the arts of misrepresentation, as while he was "only the record of the bad," and I am equally obliged, from a regard to truth, to disclaim his pretended approbation as his avowed censure.

He declares, that I originated the clause which enacts, that "this Constitution, and the laws of the United States, which shall be made in pursuance thereof, and all treaties made, or which shall be made, under the authority of the United States, shall be the supreme law of the land, and the judges in every state shall be bound thereby, any thing in the Constitution or the laws of any state to the contrary notwithstanding." To place this matter in a proper point of view, it will be necessary to state, that as the propositions were reported by the committee of the whole house, a power was given to the general government to *negative* the laws passed by the state legislatures–a power which I considered as totally inadmissible;– in substitution of this, I proposed the following clause, which you will find very materially different from the clause adopted by the Constitution, "that the legislative acts of the United States, made by virtue and in pursuance of the articles of the union, and all treaties made and *ratified* under the authority of the United States, shall be the supreme law of the respective states, so far as those acts or treaties shall relate to the said states, or their citizens; and that the judiciaries of the several states shall be bound thereby in their decisions, any thing in the respective laws of the individual states to the contrary notwithstanding."[1]

When this clause was introduced, it was not established that *inferior* continental courts should be appointed for trial of all questions arising on treaties and on the laws of the general government,[2] and it was my wish and hope that every question of that kind would have been determined, in the first instance, in the courts of the respective states; had this been the case, the propriety and the necessity that treaties duly made and ratified, and the laws of the general government should be *binding* on the state judiciaries, which were to decide upon them, must be evident to every capacity, while, at the same time, if such treaties or laws were inconsistent with our constitution and bill of rights, the judiciaries of this state would be bound to *reject* the *first* and *abide* by the *last*; since in the form *I* introduced the clause, notwithstanding treaties and the laws of the general government were intended to be superior to the laws of our state government, where they should be opposed to each other, yet that they were not proposed, nor meant to be superior to our *constitution* and bill of rights. It was afterwards altered and amended (if it can be called an amendment) to the form in which it stands in the system now published,[3] and, as inferior continental, and not state, courts are originally to decide on those questions, it is *now worse* than *useless*; for being so altered as to render the treaties and laws made under the general government superior to our constitution, if the system is adopted, it will amount to a total and unconditional surrender to that government, by the citizens of this state, of every right and privilege secured to them by our constitution, and an express compact and stipulation with the general government, that it may, at its discretion, make laws in direct violation of those rights: But on this subject I shall enlarge in a future number.[4]

That I "voted an appeal should lay to the supreme judiciary of the United States, for the *correction* of all *errors* both in law and fact," in *rendering judgment*, is most true; and it is equally true that if it had been so ordained by the Constitution, the supreme judiciary would only have had an appellate jurisdiction, of the *same nature* with that possessed by our high court of appeals, and could not in any respect intermeddle with any fact decided by a jury; but as the clause now stands, an appeal being given in general terms from the inferior courts, both as to law and fact, it not only doth, but was *avowedly intended* to give a power very different from what our court of appeals, or any court of appeals in the United States or in England enjoys–a power of the most dangerous and alarming nature, that of setting at nought the verdict of a jury, and having the same facts which they had determined, without any regard or respect to their determination, examined and ultimately decided by the judges themselves; and that by judges immediately appointed by the government.

But the Landholder also says, that "I agreed to the clause that declares nine states to be sufficient to put the government in motion."–

I cannot take to myself the merit even of this, without too great a sacrifice of truth.–

It was proposed that if *seven* states agreed, that should be sufficient;–by a rule of convention in filling up blanks, if different numbers were mentioned, the question was always to be taken on the highest: It was my opinion, that to agree upon a ratification of the constitution by any less number than the whole thirteen states, is so directly *repugnant* to our present articles of confederation, and the mode therein prescribed for their alteration, and such a *violation* of the compact which the states, in the most solemn manner, have entered into with each other, that those who could advocate a contrary proposition, ought never to be confided in and entrusted in public life–I availed myself of this rule, and had the question taken on thirteen, which was rejected–Twelve, eleven, ten and nine were proposed in succession; the last was adopted by a majority of the members–I voted successively for each of these numbers, to prevent a less number being agreed on–Had nine not been adopted, I should on the *same* principle have voted for eight: But so far was I from giving my approbation that the assent of a less number of states than thirteen should be sufficient to put the government in motion, that I most explicitly expressed my sentiments to the contrary, and always intended, had I been present when the ultimate vote was taken on the constitution, to have given it my decided negative, accompanied with a solem[n] protest against it, assigning this reason among others for my dissent. Thus, my fellow-citizens, that candour with which I have conducted myself through the whole of this business, obliges me, however reluctantly, and however "mortifying it may be to my vanity" to disavow all "those greater positive virtues" which the Landholder has so obligingly attributed to me in Convention, and which he was so desirous of conferring upon me as to consider the guilt of misrepresentation and falsehood but a trifling sacrifice for that purpose, and to increase my mortification, you will find I am equally compelled to yield up every pretence, even to those of a negative nature, which a regard to justice has, as he says, obliged him not to omit.–These consist, as he tells us, in giving my entire approbation to the system, as to those parts which are said to endanger a trial by jury, and as to its want of a bill of rights, and in having too much candour there to signify that I thought it deficient in either of these respects:–But how, I pray can the Landholder be *certain* that I deserve this encomium? Is it not possible, as I so frequently exhausted the politeness of the Convention, that some of those marks of fatigue and disgust, with which he intimates I was mortified as oft as I attempted to speak, might, at that time, have taken place, and have been of such a nature as to attract his attention;–or, perhaps, as the Convention was prepared to slumber whenever I rose, the Landholder, among others, might have sunk into sleep, and at that very moment might have been feasting his imagination with the completion of his ambitious views, and dreams of future greatness:–But supposing I never did declare in Convention, that I thought the system defective in those essential points, will it amount to a positive proof that I approved the system in those respects, or that I culpably neglected an indispensable duty? Is it not possible, whatever might have been my insolence and assurance when I first took my seat, and however fond I might be at that time of obtruding my sentiments, that the many rebuffs with which I met–the repeated mortifications I experienced–the marks of fatigue and disgust with which my eyes were sure to be assailed wherever I turned them–one gaping here–another yawning there–a third slumbering in this place–and a fourth snoring in that–might so effectually have put to flight all my original arrogance, that, as we are apt to run into extremes, having at length become convinced of my comparative nothingness, in so august an assembly, and one in which the science of government was so perfectly understood, I might sink into such a state of modesty and diffidence, as not to be able to muster up resolution enough to break the seal of silence and open my lips, even after the rays of light had begun to penetrate my understanding, and in some measure to chase away those clouds of error and ignorance, in which it was enveloped on my first arrival.–Perhaps, had I been treated with a more forbearing indulgence while committing those memorable blunders, for want of a sufficient knowledge in the science of Government, I might, after the rays of light had illuminated my mind, have rendered my country much more important services, and not only assisted in raising some of the pillars, but have furnished the edifice with a new roof of my own construction, rather better calculated for the convenience and security of those who might wish to take shelter beneath it, than that which it at present enjoys.–Or even admitting I was not mortified, as I certainly ought to have been, from the Landholder's account of the matter, into a total loss of speech, was it in me, who considered the system, for a *variety* of reasons, absolutely inconsistent with your political welfare and happiness, a culpable neglect of duty in not endeavouring, and that against every chance of success, to remove one or two defects, when I had before ineffectually endeavoured to clear it of the others, which, therefore, I knew must remain.

But to be serious; as to what relates to the appellate jurisdiction in the extent given by the system proposed, I am positive there were objections made to it, and as far as my memory will serve me, I think I was in the number of those who actually objected; but I am sure that the objections met with my approbation.[5]

With respect to a bill of rights–Had the government been formed upon principles truly federal, as I wished it, legislating over and acting upon the states only in their collective or political capacity, and not on individuals, there would have been no need of a bill of rights, as far as related to the rights of individuals, but only as to the rights of states:–But the proposed constitution being intended and empowered to act not only on states, but also immediately on individuals, it renders a recognition and a stipulation in favour of the rights both of states and of men, not only proper, but in my opinion, *absolutely* necessary.–I endeavoured to obtain a restraint on the powers of the general government, as to standing armies, but it was rejected.[6] It was my wish that the general government should not have the power of suspending the privilege of the writ of *Habeas Corpus*, as it appears to me altogether unnecessary, and that the power given to it, may and will be used as a dangerous engine of oppression; but I could not succeed.[7]

An honourable member from South-Carolina, most anxiously sought to have a clause inserted, securing the Liberty of the Press, and *repeatedly* brought this subject before the Convention, but could not obtain it.[8]–I am almost positive he made the same attempt to have a stipulation in favour of Liberty of Conscience, but in vain.[9]–The more the system advanced, the more was I impressed with the necessity of not merely attempting to secure a few rights, but of digesting and forming a complete bill of rights, including those of states and of individuals, which should be assented to, and prefixed to the constitution, to serve as a barrier between the general government and the respective states and their citizens; because the more the system advanced, the more clearly it appeared to me that the framers of it did not consider that either states or men had any rights at all, or that they meant to secure the enjoyment of any to either the one or the other; accordingly, I devoted a part of my time to the actually preparing and draughting such a bill of rights, and had it in readiness before I left the Convention, to have laid it before a committee.–I conversed with several members on the subject; they agreed with me on the propriety of the measure, but, at the same time, expressed their sentiments that it would be impossible to procure its adoption if attempted.–A very few days before I left the Convention, I shewed to an honourable member sitting by me, a proposition, which I then had in my hand, couched in the following words, "Resolved, that a committee be appointed to prepare and report a bill of rights, to be prefixed to the proposed constitution," and I then would instantly have moved for the appointment of a committee for that purpose, if he would have agreed to second the motion, to do which he hesitated, not as I understood from any objection to the measure, but from a conviction in his own mind, that the motion would be in vain.[10]

Thus, my fellow-citizens, you see that so far from having no objections to the system on this account, while I was at Convention, I not only then thought a bill of rights necessary, but I took some pains to have the subject brought forward, which would have been done, had it not been for the difficulties I have stated:–At the same time I declare, that when I drew up the motion, and was about to have proposed it to the Convention, I had not the most distant hope it would meet with success.–The rejection of the clauses attempted in favour of particular rights, and to check and restrain the dangerous and exorbitant powers of the general government from being abused, had sufficiently taught me what to expect:–And from the best judgment I could form while in Convention, I then was, and yet remain, decidedly of the opinion, that ambition and interest had so far blinded the understanding of some of the principal framers of the constitution, that while they were labouring to erect a fabrick by which they themselves might be exalted and benefited, they were rendered insensible to the sacrifice of the freedom and happiness of the states and their citizens, which must, inevitably, be the consequence.–I most sacredly believe their object is the total abolition and destruction of all state governments, and the erection, on their ruins, of one great and extensive empire, calculated to aggrandize and elevate its rulers and chief officers, far above the common herd of mankind–to enrich them with wealth, and to encircle them with honours and glory–and which, according to my judgment, on the maturest reflection, must, inevitably, be attended with the most humiliating and abject slavery of their fellow-citizens, by the sweat of whose brows, and by the toil of whose bodies, it can only be effected:–And so anxious were its zealous promoters to hasten to a birth this misshapen, heterogeneous monster of ambition and interest, that, for some time before the Convention rose, upon the least attempt to alter its form, or modify its powers, the most fretful impatience was shewn, such as would not have done much honour to a state assembly, had they been sitting as long a time, and their treasury empty; while it was repeatedly urged on the contrary, but urged in vain, that in so momentous an undertaking, in forming a system for such an extensive continent, on which the political happiness of so many millions, even to the latest ages, may depend, no time could be too long– no thought and reflection too great–and that if by continuing six months, or even as many years, we could free the system from all its errors and defects, it would be the best use to which we could possibly devote our time.

Thus, my fellow-citizens, am I under the necessity of resigning again into the hands of the Landholder, all those virtues both of a positive and negative kind, which, from an excess of goodness, he bestowed upon me, and give him my full permission to dispose of them hereafter in favour of some other person, who may be more deserving, and to whom they will be more acceptable; at the same time, I must frankly acknowledge, however it may operate as a proof of my dullness and stupidity, that the "ignorance in the science of government" under which I laboured at first, was not removed by more than two months close application, under those august and enlightened masters of the science, with which the Convention abounded, nor was I able to discover during that time, either by my own researches, or by any light borrowed from those luminaries, any thing in the history of mankind, or in the sentiments of those who have favoured the world with their ideas on government, to warrant or countenance the motley mixture of a system proposed; a system which is an innovation in government of the most extraordinary kind;–a system neither wholly *federal*, nor wholly *national*–but a strange hotch-potch of both–just so much federal in appearance as to give its advocates, in some measure, an opportunity of passing it as such upon the unsuspecting multitude, before they had time and opportunity to examine it, and yet so predominantly national, as to put it in the power of its movers, whenever the machine shall be set agoing, to strike out every part that has the appearance of being federal, and to render it wholly and entirely a national government:–And if the framing and approving the constitution now offered to our acceptance, is a proof of knowledge in the science of government, I not only admit, but I glory in my ignorance; and if my rising to speak had such a *somnific* influence on the Convention as the Landholder represents, I have no doubt the time will come, should this system be adopted, when my countrymen will ardently wish I had never left the Convention, but remained there to the last, daily administering to my associates, the salutary opiate. Happy, thrice happy, would it have been for my country, if the whole of that time had been devoted to sleep, or been a blank in our lives, rather than employed in forging its chains!

As I fully intended to have returned to the Convention before the completion of its business, my colleagues very probably might, and were certainly well warranted to, give that information the Landholder mentions; but whether the Convention was led to conclude that I "would have honoured the constitution with my signature, had not indispensable business called me away," may be easily determined after stating a few facts.–The Landholder admits I was *at first* against the system.–When the compromise took place on the subject of representation, I in the most explicit manner declared in Convention, that though I had concurred in the report, so far as to consent to proceed upon it, that we might see what kind of a system might be formed, yet I disclaimed every idea of being bound to give it my assent, but reserved to myself the full liberty of finally giving it my negative, if it appeared to me inconsistent with the happiness of my country.– In a desultory conversation, which long after took place in Convention, one morning before our honourable president[11] took the chair, he was observing how unhappy it would be should there be such a diversity of sentiment as to cause any of the members to oppose the system when they returned to their states;–on that occasion I replied, that I was confident no state in the union would more readily accede to a proper system of government than Maryland, but that the system under consideration was of such a nature, that I never could recommend it for acceptance;–that I thought the state never ought to adopt it, and expressed my firm belief that it never would.

An honourable member from Pennsylvania, objected against that part of the sixth article which requires an oath to be taken by the persons there mentioned, in support of the constitution, observing (as he justly might from the conduct the convention was then pursuing) how little such oaths were regarded:[12] I immediately joined in the objection, but declared my reason to be, that I thought it such a constitution as no friend of his country ought to bind himself to support.–And not more than two days before

I left Philadelphia, another honourable member from the same state, urged most strenuously that the convention ought to hasten their deliberations to a conclusion, assigning as a reason, *that the assembly of Pennsylvania was just then about to meet, and that it would be of the greatest importance to bring the system before that session of the legislature, in order that a convention of the state might be immediately called to ratify it, before the enemies of the system should have an opportunity of making the people acquainted with their objections, at the same time declaring that if the matter should be delayed, and the people have time to hear the variety of objections which would be made to it by its opposers, he thought it doubtful whether that state, or any state in the union, would adopt it.*[a] As soon as the honourable member took his seat, I rose and observed, that I was precisely of the same opinion, that the people of America never would, nor did I think they ought to, adopt the system, if they had time to consider and understand it, whereas a proneness for novelty and change–a conviction that some alteration was necessary, and a confidence in the members who composed the Convention might possibly procure its adoption, if brought hastily before them–but that these sentiments induced me to wish that a very different line of conduct should be pursued from that recommended by the honourable member–I wished the people to have every opportunity of information, as I thought it much preferable that a bad system should be rejected at first, than hastily adopted, and afterwards be unavailingly repented of. If these were instances of my "high approbation," I gave them in abundance, as all the Convention can testify, and continued so to do till I left them.–[13]

That I expressed great regret at being obliged to leave Philadelphia, and a fixed determination to return, if possible, before the Convention rose, is certain–That I might declare that I had rather lose an hundred guineas than not to be there at the close of the business is very probable–and it is possible that some who heard me say this, not knowing my reasons, which could not be expressed without a breach of that secrecy to which we were enjoined, might erroneously have concluded that my motive was the gratification of vanity, in having my name enrolled with those of a Franklin and a Washington. As to the *first,* I cordially join in the tribute of praise so justly paid to the enlightened philosopher and statesman, while the polite friendly and affectionate treatment myself and my family received from that venerable sage, and the worthy family in which he is embosomed, will ever endear him to my heart–The name of Washington is far above my praise!–Would to Heaven that, on this occasion, one more wreath had been added to the number of those which are twined around his amiable brow!–that those with which it is already surrounded, may flourish with immortal verdure, nor wither or fade till time shall be no more, is my fervent prayer! and may that glory which encircles his head, ever shine with undiminished rays!

To find myself under the necessity of opposing such illustrious characters, whom I venerated and loved, filled me with regret, but viewing the system in the light I then did, and yet do view it, to have hesitated would have been criminal; complaisance would have been guilt.

If it was the idea of my State, that whatever a Washington or Franklin approved, was to be blindly adopted, she ought to have spared herself the expence of sending any members to the Convention, or to have instructed them implicitly to follow where they led the way.

It was not to have my "name enrolled with the other labourers," that I wished to return to Philadelphia–that sacrifice which I must have made of my principles by putting my name to the constitution, could not have been effaced by any derivative lustre it could possibly receive from the bright constellation with which it would have been surrounded.–My object was, in truth, the very reverse, as I had uniformly opposed the system in its progress, I wished to have been present at the conclusion, to have then given it my solemn negative, which I certainly should have done, even had I stood single and alone, being perfectly willing to leave it to the cool and impartial investigation both of the present and of future ages to decide who best understood the science of government–who best knew the rights of men and of states–who best consulted the true interest of America, and who most faithfully discharged the trust reposed in them, those who agreed to, or those who opposed, the new Constitution–and so fully have I made up my own mind on this subject, that as long as the history of mankind shall record the appointment of the late Convention, and the system which has been proposed by them, it is my highest ambition that my name may be also recorded as one who considered the system injurious to my country, and as such opposed it.

Having shewn that I did not "alter my opinion after I left Philadelphia," and that I acted no "contradictory parts on the great political stage," and, therefore, that there are none such to *reconcile*, the reason assigned by the Landholder for *that purpose*, doth not deserve my notice, except only to observe, that he shrewdly intimates there is already a junto established, who are to share in, and deal out the offices of this new government at their will and pleasure, and that they have already fixed upon the character who is to be "Deputy Attorney-General of the United States for the State of Maryland." If this is true, it is worth while to inquire of whom this junto consists, as it might lead to a discovery of the persons, for the gratification of whose ambition and interest this system is prepared, and is, if possible, to be enforced; and from the disposition of offices already allotted in the various and numerous departments, we possibly might discover whence proceeds the conviction and zeal of some of its advocates.

Baltimore, March 19, 1788.

> (a) *How exactly agreeable to the sentiments of that honourable member has been the conduct of the friends of the constitution in Pennsylvania and some other states, I need not mention.*[14]

1. Martin's motion was made on 17 July and adopted *nemine contradicente*. The italics are not in the original motion (Farrand, II, 28-29).

2. On 18 July the Convention voted to give Congress the power to create "inferior tribunals." Martin spoke against the proposal. The Convention then revised the language concerning the jurisdiction of the federal judiciary, providing "that the jurisdiction shall extend to all cases arising under the Natl. laws: And to such other questions as may involve the Natl. peace & harmony" (*ibid.*, 45-46).

3. For the evolution of the supremacy clause from 17 July (note 1) to the final adoption of the Constitution, see CDR, 257, 265, 277, 296.

4. Luther Martin: Address No. III, 28 March (CC:650).

5. There is no evidence indicating Martin's position on the appellate jurisdiction of the federal judiciary, although one amendment was adopted nine states to one, with Maryland the only dissenting state (Farrand, II, 437-38).

6. On 18 August Martin and Elbridge Gerry's motion attempting to limit the size of a peacetime army "was disagreed to nem. con." (*ibid.*, 330).

7. On 28 August the clause allowing the suspension of the writ of habeas corpus was adopted seven states to three, with Maryland voting in the majority (*ibid.*, 438).

8. On 20 August Charles Pinckney presented several propositions, some of which amount to a bill of rights, to the Convention. One proposition stated that "The liberty of the Press shall be inviolably preserved." Pinckney's "propositions were referred to the Committee of detail without debate or consideration." On 14 September Pinckney and Elbridge Gerry moved "that the liberty of the Press should be inviolably observed," and the Convention rejected the motion (*ibid.*, 340-42, 617-18, 620).

9. Pinckney did not include this right among the propositions he offered on 20 August.

10. Martin left the Convention on 4 September. Eight days later Gerry moved that a committee be appointed to prepare a bill of rights, and the Convention rejected the motion ten states to none (CC:75).

11. George Washington.

12. On 23 July James Wilson "said he was never fond of oaths, considering them as a left handed security only. A good Govt. did not need them. and a bad one could not or ought not to be supported" (Farrand, II, 87).

13. On 31 August the Convention took up Article XXII of the report of the Committee of Detail. On a motion of Gouverneur Morris and Charles Pinckney, the Convention voted eight states to three to eliminate the requirement that the Constitution be submitted to Congress "for their approbation" before being submitted for ratification to state conventions called by state legislatures. (Maryland voted in the minority.) Morris and Pinckney then moved a substitute for Article XXII that called upon the state legislatures to summon "Conventions within their respective States as speedily as circumstances will permit." Morris's "object was to impress in stronger terms the necessity of calling Conventions in order to prevent enemies to the plan, from giving it the go by. When it first appears, with the sanction of this Convention, the people will be favorable to it. By degrees the State officers, & those interested in the State Govts will intrigue & turn the popular current against it."

Martin agreed with Morris "that after a while the people would be agst. it. but for a different reason from that alledged. He believed they would not ratify it unless hurried into it by surprize." The Convention rejected this motion seven states to four, with Maryland in the majority (*ibid.*, 478-79).

14. For the events in Pennsylvania on 28-29 September, see CC:125.

637. Nicholas Gilman to John Sullivan
New York, 22 March (excerpts)[1]

I am honored with your Excellencys favor of the 28th ultimo and beg leave to express my thanks for the particulars of the action at Exeter[2]– That the defence of the System was great as the ground was advantageous

I have no doubt; but have still to regret (with much apprehension) that the victory was not more compleat.–your Excellencys expectations of success in the next engagement affords some consolation–yet I am sorry the field assigned for the scene of action is so much in favor of the adverse party.[3]

Those that have not been in the way of seeing and hearing can hardly imagine what pernicious effects our Convention business has produced in a number of the States–New Hampshire had been counted on by friends & foes as being perfectly federal–so that from the ratification of the new System in Massachusetts–the opposers began to make excuses and change sides in all Quarters but immediately on your adjournment they augmented their forces took possession of their old ground and seem determined to maintain it at all hazards–

The Governor of this State[4] acts no longer under Covert but is open and indefatigable in the opposition In Pennsylvania, I am informed, affairs have a most unfavourable aspect–The Antis. are forming associations–holding County Conventions &c. much in the stile of the Massachusetts rebellion[5]–by all late accounts from Virginia the opposition is there increasing and there is reason to apprehend that North Carolina is too highly tinctured with the same spirit–Patrick Henry is intirely antifederal and Grayson is warmly opposed to the present plan–The adoption of it is certainly doubtful in New York–Virginia–North Carolina & Rhode Island–this being the case I hope no pains will be wanting to secure a Majority in the next meeting of our Convention–I do assure, Sir, Our present situation appears truly alarming and I am more and more confirmed in an opinion I have long entertained that the tranquility of our Country is suspended solely on the great question of the day. . . .

I think Mr. Wingate informed your Excellency of the application of Kentucky to be set off as a seperate State and taken into the union, which Virginia will accede to on condition of her being exonerated from a proportion of her federal obligations &c. The affair has been once debated in Congress in Committee of the whole and postponed, since which it has not been taken up. It is an application that cannot, in the present State of affairs be complied with–but there is such a spirit of avulsion among the people of that Country they are so impatient and importunate as to make it a Subject that requires, at this critical juncture, the most prudent management. . . .

I take the liberty to enclose for your Excellencys perusal, the remarks of Aristides (Alia Judge Harrison our old friend who was Secretary to General Washington) on the new plan of government[6]–and as I cannot procure another, shall be obliged if you will please to lend it to the Treasurer–[7]

Having drawn my letter to some length I will not trespass further than to add the perfect Respect with which I have the honor to be

1. RC, State Papers Relating to the Revolution, II (1785–89), 131–35, New Hampshire State Archives, Concord.

2. In this letter, New Hampshire Convention president John Sullivan described and analyzed the Convention's adjournment without taking a vote on whether or not to ratify the Constitution (Gratz Collection, PHi).

3. The second session of the New Hampshire Convention was scheduled to convene on 18 June in Concord, a principal town in the Merrimack Valley. Concord's delegate voted against ratification at the second session.

4. George Clinton.

5. For the petition campaign in Pennsylvania to overthrow the state's ratification of the Constitution, see RCS:Pa., 709–25. Gilman was comparing the activity in Pennsylvania to Shays's Rebellion.

6. See "Aristides" (Alexander Contee Hanson of Maryland), *Remarks on the Proposed Plan of a Federal Government . . .*, 31 January (CC:490).

7. State treasurer John Taylor Gilman (1753–1828), Nicholas Gilman's brother, represented Exeter in the state Convention, where he voted to ratify the Constitution in June.

638 A–B. George Washington on the Ratification of the Constitution by Massachusetts

On 20 December 1787 James Madison, concerned about the prospects of ratification in Massachusetts, wrote George Washington that "I have good reason to believe that if you are in correspondence with any gentlemen in that quarter, and a proper occasion offered for an explicit communication of your good wishes for the plan, so as barely to warrant an explicit assertion of the fact, that it would be attended with valuable effects. I barely drop the idea. The circumstances on which the propriety of it depends, are best known to, as they will be best judged of, by yourself" (CC:359). Washington replied on 10 January that he had "no regular corrispondt. in Massachusetts; otherwise, as the occasional subject of a letter I should have had no objection to the communication of my sentiments on the proposed Government as they are unequivocal & decided" (Rutland, *Madison*, X, 358).

Two days later Washington was upset when he learned that his letter of 14 December to Charles Carter of Stafford County, Va., in support of the Constitution, had been published in the Fredericksburg *Virginia Herald* on 27 December. Washington informed Carter that, although he was not averse to the publication of his sentiments on the Constitution, he was pained "to see the hasty, and indigested production of a private letter, handed to the public, to be animadverted upon by the adversaries of the new Government." Carter replied on 17 January that he had disseminated copies of Washington's remarks with the understanding "that they should not go to the press." On 22 January Washington accepted Carter's explanation, absolved him of any wrongdoing, and apologized for having given Carter "so much trouble." (For Washington's exchange of letters with Carter, and for the public reaction to the publication of Washington's letter, especially with respect to its authenticity, see CC:386.)

On 31 January Washington wrote his wartime friend General Benjamin Lincoln, who was representing Hingham in the Massachusetts Convention in Boston, about the publication of his letter to Carter. Washington declared that, although he had no objection to seeing his opinion on the Constitution in print, the letter had been intended only for Carter's eyes. Consequently, he "did not attend to the manner of expressing my ideas, or dress them in the language I should have done, if I had had the smallest suspicion of their ever coming to the public eye–through that channel" (The Original Letters of George Washington to Benjamin Lincoln, Houghton Library, MH). A week later Washington reiterated these sentiments in a letter to Madison. Washington also recalled Madison's letter of 20 December

1787: "At the time you suggested for my consideration, the expediency of a com-munication of my sentiments on the proposed Constitution, to any corrispondent I might have in Massachusetts, it did not occur to me that Genl Lincoln & myself frequently interchanged letters" (5 February, CC:499. Washington and Lincoln had not corresponded since early 1787, but had renewed their correspondence when Lincoln wrote Washington on 9, 13 January concerning the Massachusetts Con-vention [Washington Papers, DLC].).

The Massachusetts Convention met on 9 January and ratified the Constitution on 6 February by a vote of 187 to 168. On 9 February Lincoln sent Washington a copy of the *Massachusetts Centinel* of that day which contained the conciliatory speeches of a number of Antifederalists. Lincoln informed Washington that from the paper "you will learn what was the temper of many of those who had been in the oposition. I think they discovered a candour which does them honor and prom-ises quiet in the State." Some Antifederalists, however, still opposed the Constitu-tion. Considering Shays's Rebellion and the large majority against the Constitution at the beginning of the Convention, Lincoln believed "that we have got through this business pretty well." "Every exertion," he continued, "will be made to in-form the people & to quiet their minds. It is very fortunate for us that the Clergy are pretty generally with us they have in this State a very great influence over the people and they will contribute much to the general peace and happiness" (Wash-ington Papers, DLC). On the same day Major Caleb Gibbs of Boston also sent Washington a newspaper illustrating the conciliatory attitude of the Convention's minority (*ibid.*). Gibbs (1748–1818) had commanded Washington's bodyguard during the Revolution and both he and Lincoln fought at Yorktown in 1781. (Gibbs was not mentioned by Washington in his 5 February letter to Madison because the two men had apparently not corresponded since 1785.)

Washington's letterbook contains two similar letters to Lincoln and Gibbs, both dated 28 February (Washington Papers, DLC). The next day Washington copied the letter to Lincoln and probably the one to Gibbs and sent them out. On this day he also wrote a similar letter to Rufus King, who had been a member of the Mas-sachusetts Convention but who was now in New York City. (The recipient's copy of the letter to Lincoln, endorsed by Lincoln, is in The Original Letters of George Washington to Benjamin Lincoln in the Houghton Library at Harvard University; while that to King is in the King Papers at the New-York Historical Society.) In his letters to Lincoln, Gibbs, and King, Washington expressed his pleasure with Massachusetts' ratification of the Constitution and with the conciliatory stance of the Convention's minority. Washington also stated that the prospects for ratifica-tion in Virginia were good. Lincoln was still in Boston, as perhaps Gibbs was also, on 19 March, when Washington's letter arrived (Lincoln to Washington, 19 March, Washington Papers, DLC). On the same day the *Massachusetts Centinel* stated: "A letter from General Washington, to a gentleman in this town, acquaints, that from the best information he was able to collect from gentlemen from various parts of the State, there was every prospect of the Constitution being ratified by Virginia." This item was reprinted six times by 31 March: N.H. (2), Mass. (3), Conn. (1).

Excerpts of Washington's letter to Major Gibbs, dated 29 February, were printed in the *Massachusetts Centinel* on 22 March with a prefatory statement, which among other things, attested to the authenticity of the letter (CC:638-A. For the letter-book copy of the letter to Gibbs, dated 28 February, see CC:638-B.). The *Centi-nel's* interest in affirming that the letter had indeed been written by Washington was probably a consequence of the debate that had taken place in the Boston newspapers over the authenticity of Washington's earlier letter to Charles Carter (CC:386). The *Centinel's* excerpted version of Washington's letter to Gibbs was reprinted forty-nine times by 10 May: Vt. (2), N.H. (3), Mass. (7), R.I. (3), Conn. (9), N.Y. (6), N.J. (2), Pa. (10), Md. (1), Va. (3), S.C. (1), Ga. (2). Only six of these newspapers reprinted the *Centinel's* preface: N.H. (2), N.Y. (3), Pa. (1). The *New York Journal*, 31 March, followed its reprinting with this statement: "Whoever reads the above are requested to recollect the *false* annunciation of the ratification of the constitution by North-Carolina, two days previous to the *grand question*, TO BE, or NOT TO BE, in the Massachusetts convention." (See "False Reports of North Carolina's Ratification of the Constitution," 5 February–5 March, Appendix I.)

The reaction to the publication of Washington's 29 February letter to Caleb Gibbs was minimal. "A Federalist" noted that the letter induced "a belief that Virginia would undoubtedly ratify the Constitution" (Poughkeepsie *Country Journal*, 22 April). A Virginia writer declared that the "great Washington has honoured" the minority of the Massachusetts Convention "with his approbation . . . and is alone a sufficient reward for the disinterested love of their country" (*Norfolk and Portsmouth Journal*, 23 April). The Comte de Moustier, France's minister plenipotentiary to the United States, was surprised to see the letter in print: "In the uncertainty existing at this time over the success of the new plan of Constitution, the General will be pained to see that his opinion has been published, which after all that has been said on the election of a President, he will not appear to be impartial" (30 March, Extraits du Journal de M. de Moustier, Extraits des Papiers de La Légation de France aux États-Unis, Vol. I, Part II [3rd Cahier], 10–11, Franklin Collection, CtY). No record has been found of Washington commenting on the publication of his letter to Gibbs.

638–A. Massachusetts Centinel, 22 March

We feel a peculiar pleasure in laying before the publick, the following authentick extract of a letter from that great–and good as he is great–man, the American Fabius.–To receive the tribute of applause from him, must make the breasts of the gentlemen in the minority of our Convention, feelingly alive to the most agreeable sensations: And as citizens of Massachusetts, we feel a superiour degree of consequence, in knowing his opinion of the importance of the proceedings of this Commonwealth, in the affairs of the Continent.

Extract of a letter from his Excellency Gen. WASHINGTON, *to a gentleman in this town, dated Mount Vernon, Feb.* 29, 1788.

"The candid and conciliatory behaviour of your minority, places them in a more favourable point of view than the debates of the Convention gave room to expect, and sufficiently shews the good efforts which were produced by a full and fair discussion of the subject.

"The adoption of the Constitution in Massachusetts, will, I presume, be greatly influential in obtaining a favourable determination upon it in these States where the question is yet to be agitated.

"No person can, at this moment, pretend to say what *will* be its fate here–But from what I can collect, I have no doubt of its being accepted."

638–B. George Washington to Caleb Gibbs
Mount Vernon, 28 February[1]

I have received your letter of the 9th. inst. accompanied by the papers which you was so polite as to send me.[2]–I must beg you to accept my thanks for your attention in forwarding to me the pleasing decision of your convention upon the proposed Government.–The candid and conciliating behav[i]our of the minority places them in a more favourable point of view than the debates of the Convention gave room to expect, and sufficiently shews the good effects of the full and fair discussion which the subject met with.–

The adoption of the Constitution in Massachusetts will, I presume, be greatly influential in obtaining a favourable determination upon it in those States where the question is yet to be agitated.–

No person can, at this moment pretend to say what *will* be its fate here, and I am perhaps less qualified to give an opinion upon it, from my own observation, than almost any one, as I very seldom ride off my farms, and am indebted to Gentlemen who call upon me for any information which I have of the disposition of the people towards it, but from what I can collect, I have no doubt of its being accepted here.–

1. FC, Washington Papers, DLC.
2. In addition to sending Washington the newspaper illustrating the conciliatory attitude of the Convention's minority, Gibbs sent Washington newspapers of "allmost all the debates of the Convention" (Washington Papers, DLC).

639 A–C. Publication and Sale of the Book Edition of The Federalist, 22 March

On 2 December 1787 James Madison, who had recently started to contribute essays to *The Federalist*, sent two numbers to Governor Edmund Randolph of Virginia and apologized for not being able to forward all of the numbers that had been printed. He was not, however, too concerned because he understood that "the printer means to make a pamphlet of them" (CC:314). Two weeks later Connecticut Federalist Jeremiah Wadsworth asked Rufus King to send him two dozen copies of *The Federalist* if it was published as a pamphlet. Wadsworth hoped that a pamphlet edition of *The Federalist* would counteract the Antifederalist material that was being sent from New York into Connecticut (16 December. See also Wadsworth to Henry Knox, RCS:Conn., 496–97, 501.). King replied that *The Federalist* "will be published in a pamphlet or rather in a small volume; for the work will be voluminous" (23 December, CC:368).

New York City printers John and Archibald M'Lean were commissioned by Alexander Hamilton and a committee of gentlemen to produce 500 copies of a pamphlet containing 20 to 25 essays, at a total cost of £30. However, by 2 January 1788, when the M'Leans first announced their publication plans in John M'Lean's New York *Independent Journal*, thirty-one essays had already been published in the newspapers. The M'Lean advertisement solicited advance subscribers promising them a price of five shillings for a 200-page pamphlet or six shillings for one of 250 pages or more. In general, the work would be "printed on a fine Paper and good Type" in a duodecimo volume, although "a few Copies" would be printed on "superfine Royal Writing Paper," at ten shillings a volume. Printers and booksellers throughout America were authorized to accept subscriptions. From January to March, the M'Lean advertisement was run several times in the *Independent Journal* and the *New York Packet* and one or more times in the New York *Daily Advertiser*, the Poughkeepsie *Country Journal*, the *Virginia Independent Chronicle*, and John M'Lean's *Norfolk and Portsmouth Journal* (CC:406).

As news of the proposed publication of the volume spread, people from various parts of America requested copies. Federalist essayist Tench Coxe of Philadelphia sent money to James Madison in New York asking to have the printer put him down for a copy. Coxe thought that "the letters of Publius" were the "most valuable disquisitions of Government in its peculiar relations and connexions with this Country" (16 January, Rutland, *Madison*, X, 375). Philadelphia merchant William Bingham requested that John Jay, another contributor to *The Federalist*, send him a pamphlet, declaring that "various detached Numbers . . . have much pleased me, as the Author has treated the Subject in a Strong masterly Manner" (29 January, Jay Collection, NNC). In Virginia, George Washington–who had received newspapers containing at least twenty-two numbers–asked Madison to forward him "three or four Copies; one of which to be neatly bound" (5 February, CC:499). George Nicholas, a Virginia Federalist and a delegate to the state Convention, asked Madison to obtain 30 or 40 copies for distribution to the Convention delegates (5 April, Rutland, *Madison*, XI, 10). In North Carolina, James Iredell, Archibald Maclaine, and Richard Dobbs Spaight ordered copies of the pamphlet (John M'Lean to Iredell, 15 February, Iredell Papers, NcD; Maclaine to Iredell, 4 March, CC:591; and Spaight to Levi Hollingsworth, 25 April, Hollingsworth Papers, PHi). Maclaine described *The Federalist* as "a judicious and ingenious writer, though not well calculated for the common people." Stephen Van Rensselaer, the patroon of vast estates in northern New York, subscribed for twenty copies and possibly as many as fifty copies were subscribed in Albany and twenty in Montgomery County (Archibald M'Lean to Van Rensselaer, 10 April, Miscellaneous Collection, CSmH; and Leonard Gansevoort to Van Rensselaer, 11 April, Miscellaneous Manuscripts, NHi). George Cabot, a Beverly, Mass., merchant, put his name to "a Paper of Proposals" in Boston (Cabot to Nathan Dane, 9 May, Dane Papers, Beverly Historical Society).

On 19 March the New York *Independent Journal* announced that "Those Gentlemen, who were intrusted with Subscription Lists for the *FEDERALIST*, are requested to send them to the Printing-Office, No. 41, Hanover-Square, as *the* first Volume of that Valuable Work will be published on Saturday next."

On 22 March, the *Independent Journal* informed its readers that the first volume of *The Federalist* had just been published and was selling for three shillings to subscribers, who were asked to send for their copies. The *Journal* also stated that a second volume was in press (CC:639–A). This advertisement, which was also printed in the *Daily Advertiser* on the 22nd, ran in the *Journal* until 28 May when the second volume appeared containing forty-nine essays in 390 pages (Evans 21127). On 2 April the *Norfolk and Portsmouth Journal* reprinted the first three paragraphs of the *Independent Journal's* advertisement and appended the following statement: "Subscribers to the above valuable work in Norfolk and Portsmouth, will be waited on with the *First Volume* immediately; those who from their remote distance in the Country cannot be attended, are requested to send without loss of time, as the rapid demand for this book will render it impossible to preserve them long in the Store." Subscribers were charged three shillings per volume, non-subscribers three shillings and nine pence. This advertisement was run again on 9 and 16 April and was reprinted, in part, in the *Virginia Independent Chronicle* on 23 and 30 April.

Volume I–entitled *The Federalist: A Collection of Essays, Written in Favour of the New Constitution, as Agreed Upon by the Federal Convention, September 17, 1787* (CC:639–B)– contains a preface (CC:639–C); a table of contents giving descriptive titles for each essay; and the texts of the first thirty-six essays. The preliminary material runs to six pages, the essays to 227 pages. The unsigned preface, dated "NEW-YORK, March 17, 1788," was written by Alexander Hamilton who also corrected a number of the essays (James Madison to James K. Paulding, 23 July 1818, Gaillard Hunt, ed., *The Writings of James Madison* [9 vols., New York, 1900–1910], VIII,

411n). Newspaper essay 35 became number 29 in the pamphlet and newspaper essay 31 became numbers 32 and 33. The signature "A Citizen of New-York," as proposed in the *Independent Journal* advertisement of 2 January, was not used. According to James Madison, "a reason for the change was that one of the writers was not a Citizen of that State; another that the publication had diffused itself among most of the other States" (to Paulding, 23 July 1818, Hunt, *Madison*, VIII, 410–11n).

Copies of Volume I were distributed to subscribers and others throughout America, most particularly in Virginia and New York whose conventions were scheduled to meet on 2 and 17 June, respectively. The authors actively disseminated the volume. On 24 March John Jay, perhaps at the request of James Madison who had left New York City for his Virginia home in early March, forwarded the *The Federalist* to George Washington (Washington Papers, DLC). In mid-May Alexander Hamilton, at Madison's direction, sent "40 of the common copies & twelve of the finer ones" to Governor Edmund Randolph, a delegate to the Virginia Convention, for distribution among the members of that body. These were probably the volumes requested by George Nicholas, another Convention delegate (Hamilton to Madison, 19 May, Rutland, *Madison*, XI, 54; and Madison to Nicholas, 8 April, CC:667). Convention delegate John Marshall had received a copy of *The Federalist* in mid-April, apparently through his own subscription (Herbert A. Johnson, ed., *The Papers of John Marshall* [Williamsburg, Va., 1974–], I, 409).

In April, two and a half weeks before the election of New York Convention delegates, at least sixty copies of *The Federalist* volume were forwarded to Albany and Montgomery counties on subscription. Another twenty copies were sent upon request to Stephen Van Rensselaer. If he desired more volumes, Van Rensselaer was asked to contact Alexander Hamilton, Leonard Gansevoort, or the printers (Archibald M'Lean to Van Rensselaer, 10 April, Miscellaneous Collection, CSmH; and Gansevoort to Van Rensselaer, 11 April, Miscellaneous Manuscripts, NHi). James Kent and Egbert Benson distributed the volume, "to the best of our judgments," in a Dutchess County meeting called to nominate candidates for the state Convention (William Kent, *Memoirs and Letters of James Kent . . .* [Boston, 1898], 302).

Copies of *The Federalist* were sent to other states and abroad. John Jay, as requested, sent a copy to William Bingham in Philadelphia (24 March, Henry P. Johnston, ed., *The Correspondence and Public Papers of John Jay . . .* [4 vols., New York and London, 1890–1893], III, 325). John Vaughan of Philadelphia borrowed a volume and, as soon as he finished reading it, he planned to send it to John Dickinson in Delaware (9 April, Dickinson Papers, PPL). Charles Thomson, secretary of Congress, forwarded *The Federalist* to James McHenry, a delegate to the Maryland Convention which was scheduled to meet on 21 April (19 April, LMCC, VIII, 722). And Virginia delegate to Congress Edward Carrington sent a volume to Thomas Jefferson in Paris (14 May, Boyd, XIII, 157).

John and Archibald M'Lean were not satisfied with their compensation as printers of *The Federalist*. On 14 October 1788, four and a half months after the appearance of Volume II, Archibald M'Lean sent a bill to the New York committee that had commissioned the publication. M'Lean stated that when he and his brother first agreed to print the pamphlet edition, they anticipated one volume of no more than twenty-five essays, for which they planned to charge six shillings. However, "The Work encreased from 25 Numbers to 85, so that instead of giving the Subscribers one vollume containing 200 Pages for six shillings, I was obliged to give them two vollumes containing upwards of 600 pages

"The Money expended for Printing Paper, Journeymens Wages and Binding was upwards of two hundred and seventy Pounds; of which sum I have charged

Coll: Hamilton with 144 Pounds, which is not three shillings per Vol: I have several hundred Copies remaining on hand, and even allowing they were all sold, at the low Price I am obliged to sell them at, I would not clear five Pounds on the whole impression" (to Robert Troup, Hamilton-McLane Papers, DLC). On 22 May and 14 August 1789, Archibald M'Lean advertised in his *New York Daily Gazette* (a successor to the *Independent Journal*) "that a few Copies" of *The Federalist* remained for sale. In 1799 the remaining copies of the M'Lean edition were republished by John Tiebout of New York City with new title pages.

Soon after its appearance, Volume I of *The Federalist* was reviewed in the March and April issues of the New York *American Magazine*. The reviewer, probably editor Noah Webster, summarized the essays and asserted that "it would be difficult to find a treatise, which, in so small a compass, contains so much valuable information, or in which the true principles of republican government are unfolded with such precision." Volume II of *The Federalist* was reviewed in the May and June issues of the *Magazine*.

For a general discussion of the authorship, circulation, and impact of *The Federalist*, see CC:201.

639–A. New York Independent Journal, 22 March

THIS DAY IS PUBLISHED,
Price to Subscribers, *only* THREE SHILLINGS,
The FEDERALIST,
VOLUME FIRST.

A desire to throw full light upon so interesting a subject has led, in a great measure unavoidably, to a more copious discussion than was at first intended; and the undertaking not being yet completed, it is judged adviseable to divide the collection into two Volumes.

The several matters which are contained in these Papers, are immediately interwoven with the very existence of this new Empire, and ought to be well understood by every Citizen of America. The Editor entertains no doubt that they will be thought by the judicious reader, the cheapest as well as most valuable publication ever offered to the American Public.

The second Volume is in the Press, and will be published with all possible expedition.

☞Subscribers will be pleased to send for their Copies, to the Printing-Office, No. 41, Hanover-Square, four Doors from the Old-Slip.

∴ Those Gentlemen who were intrusted with Subscription Lists, will please to return them to the Printers; and those in the Country are desired to forward theirs immediately.

New-York, March 22, 1788.

639–B. Title Page

THE

FEDERALIST:

A COLLECTION

O F

E   S   S   A   Y   S,

WRITTEN IN FAVOUR OF THE

NEW CONSTITUTION,

AS AGREED UPON BY THE FEDERAL CONVENTION,
SEPTEMBER 17, 1787.

IN TWO VOLUMES.

VOL. I.

NEW-YORK:

PRINTED AND SOLD BY J. AND A. M'LEAN,
No. 41, HANOVER-SQUARE.
M,DCC,LXXXVIII.

639-C. Preface

It is supposed that a collection of the papers which have made their appearance, in the Gazettes of this City, under the Title of the FEDER-ALIST, may not be without effect in assisting the public judgment on the momentous question of the Constitution for the United States, now under the consideration of the people of America. A desire to throw full light upon so interesting a subject has led, in a great measure unavoidably, to a more copious discussion than was at first intended. And the undertaking not being yet completed, it is judged adviseable to divide the collection into two Volumes, of which the ensuing Numbers constitute the first. The second Volume will follow as speedily as the Editor can get it ready for publication.

The particular circumstances under which these papers have been written, have rendered it impracticable to avoid violations of method and repetitions of ideas which cannot but displease a critical reader. The latter defect has even been intentionally indulged, in order the better to impress particular arguments which were most material to the general scope of the reasoning. Respect for public opinion, not anxiety for the literary character of the performance, dictates this remark. The great wish is, that it may promote the cause of truth, and lead to a right judgment of the true interests of the community.

NEW-YORK, March 17, 1788.

640. Cyrus Griffin to James Madison
New York, 24 March[1]

before the date of this letter I hope you are gotten safe to orange, and found all things in a situation the most agreeable.[2]

we are still going forward in the same tract of seven states, of course not a great deal can be done, and indeed not a great deal to do.

a prospect of the new Constitution seems to deaden the activity of the human mind as to all other matters; and yet I greatly fear that constitution may never take place; a melancholy Judgment most certainly–and would to heaven that nothing under the sun shall be more erroneous!

The adjournment of N. Hampshire, the small majority of Massachusets, a certainty of rejection in Rhode Island, the formidable opposition in the state of n. york, the convulsions and Committee meetings in pennsylvania,[3] and above all the antipathy of virginia to the system, operating together, I am apprehensive will prevent the noble fabrick from being erected. The constitution is beautiful in Theory–I wish the experiment to be made–in my opinion it would be found a government of sufficient energy *only*.

neither of the packets have yet arrived, and what has detained the french no one at this place can determine.

not a word from our Ministers abroad.

Congress have taken final leave of the Chavalier by a very polite and friendly letter.[4]

The Marchioness is recovering rapidly, and the Count in good health;[5] I mention them because they entertain a very exalted [opinion] of you and talk much upon that subject.

Daniel Shays and Eli parsons have petitioned the Legislature of Massachusets for pardon–and *will succeed*.[6]

The frequent attacks upon the post-office has produced the enclosed performance.[7]

The customary papers are sent to you within this cover.

1. RC, Madison Papers, DLC.

2. Madison, a Virginia delegate to Congress, left New York City on 3 or 4 March and reached his home in Orange County on the 23rd (Rutland, *Madison*, X, 542n).

3. For the Carlisle riots, see the Philadelphia *Independent Gazetteer*, 4 March (Appendix I), and for the petition campaign to overthrow Pennsylvania's ratification of the Constitution, see the *Pennsylvania Gazette*, 26 March, note 2 (Appendix I).

4. On 18 March Congress instructed the Secretary of Foreign Affairs to congratulate the Chevalier de la Luzerne, former minister plenipotentiary to the United States who had been promoted to the position of minister of marine by the King of France (JCC, XXXIV, 93).

5. Griffin refers to Madame de Bréhan, mistress to the Comte de Moustier, France's new minister plenipotentiary to the United States.

6. On 10 March the petition of Daniel Shays and Eli Parsons was read in the Massachusetts House of Representatives. Three days later it was printed in the Boston *Independent Chronicle* and on 21 March it was reprinted in the *New York Morning Post*. In June a pardon was granted to all those who had taken part in Shays's Rebellion.

7. Probably Postmaster General Ebenezer Hazard's defense of himself that was printed in the *New York Journal* on 21 March (Appendix II).

641. The Landholder XIII
Connecticut Courant, 24 March

"Landholder" XIII, the last essay in the series, was also printed in the Hartford *American Mercury* on 24 March. The *Courant* and *Mercury* versions differ in paragraphing, capitalization, spelling, and punctuation. By 18 April "Landholder" XIII was reprinted nine times: N.H. (3), Mass. (2), R.I. (1), Conn. (3). The Providence *United States Chronicle*, 10 April, prefaced its reprinting with this statement: "The following *Remarks* apply, in a particular Manner, to the State of Rhode-Island–we have therefore copied them, not doubting but that they will be acceptable to our Readers."

For the authorship, circulation, and impact of the "Landholder," see CC:230.

The attempt to amend our federal Constitution, which for some time past hath engrossed the public regard, is doubtless become an old and unwelcome topic to many readers whose opinions are fixed, or who are not concerned for the event. There are other subjects which claim a share of attention, both from the public and from private citizens. It is good government which secures the fruits of industry and virtue; but the best system of government cannot produce general happiness unless the people are virtuous, industrious and œconomical.

The love of wealth is a passion common to men, and when justly regulated it is condusive to human happiness. Industry may be encouraged by good laws–wealth may be protected by civil regulations; but we are not to depend on these to create it for us, while we are indolent and luxurious. Industry is most favourable to the moral virtue of the world, it is therefore wisely ordered by the Author of Nature, that the blessings of this world should be acquired by our own application in some business useful to society; so that we have no reason to expect any climate or soil will be found, or any age take place, in which plenty and wealth will be spontaneously produced. The industry and labour of a people furnish a general rule to measure their wealth, and if we use the means we may promise ourselves the reward. The present state of America will limit the greatest part of its inhabitants to agriculture; for as the art of tilling the earth is easily acquired, the price of land low, and the produce immediately necessary for life, greater encouragement to this is offered here than in any country on earth.–But still suffer me to enquire whether we are not happily circumstanced and actually able to manage some principal Manufactories with success, and encrease our wealth by encreasing the labour of the people, and saving the surplus of our earnings, for a better purpose than to purchase the labour of European nations. It is a remark often made, and generally believed, that in a country so new as this, where the price of lands is low and the price of labour high, manufactories cannot be conducted with profit. This may be true of some manufactures, but of others it is grossly false. It is now in the power of New-England to make itself more formidable to Great-Britain, by rivaling some of her principal manufactures, than ever it was by separating from her government. Woolen cloaths the principal English manufacture, may more easily be rivaled than any other. Purchasing all the materials and labour at the common price of the country, cloths of three quarters width, may be fabricated for six shillings per yard, of fineness and beauty equal to English cloths of six quarters width, which sell at twenty shillings. The cost of our own manufacture is little more than half of the imported, and for service it is allowed to be much preferable. It is found that our wool is of equal quality with the English, and that what we once supposed the defect of our wool, is only a deficiency in cleansing, sorting and dressing it.

It gives me pleasure to hear that a number of gentlemen in Hartford and the neighbouring towns are forming a fund for the establishment of a great Woolen Manufactory[1]–The plan will doubtless succeed, and be more profitable to the stockholders than money deposited in trade. As the manufacture of cloths is introduced, the raising of wool and flax the raw materials, will become an object of the farmers attention.

Sheep are the most profitable part of our stock, and the breed is much sooner multiplied than horses or cattle. Why do not our opulent farmers avail themselves of the profit? An experiment would soon convince them there is no better method of advancing property, and their country would thank them for the trial. Sheep are found to thrive and the wool to be of a good quality in every part of New-England, but as this animal delights in grazing, and is made healthy by coming often to the earth, our sea coasts with the adjacent country, where snow is of short continuance, are particularly favourable to their propagation. Our hilly coasts were designed by nature for this, and every part of the country that abounds in hills ought to make an experiment by which they will be enriched.

In Connecticut, the eastern and south-eastern counties, with the highlands on Connecticut river towards the sea, ought to produce more wool than would cloath the inhabitants of the state. At present the quantity falls short of what is needed for our own consumption; if a surplusage could be produced, it would find a ready market and the best pay.

The culture of flax, another principal material for manufacturing, affords great profit to the farmer. The seed of this crop when it succeeds well will pay the husbandman for his labour, and return a better ground rent than many other crops which are cultivated. The seed is one of our best articles for remittance and exportation abroad. Dressing and preparing the flax for use is done in the most leisure part of the year, when labour is cheap, and we had better work for six pence a day and become wealthy, than to be idle and poor.

It is not probable the market can be overstocked, or if it should chance for a single season to be the case, no article is more meliorated by time, or will better pay for keeping, by an increase of quality. A large flax crop is one most certain sign of a thrifty husbandman. The present method of agriculture in a course of different crops is well calculated to give the husbandman a sufficiency of flax ground, as it is well known that this vegetable will not thrive when sown successively in the same place.

The Nail Manufacture might be another source of wealth to the northern states. Why should we twice transport our own iron, and pay other nations for labour which our boys might perform as well. The art of nail making is easily acquired. Three thousand men and boys in Connecticut, might spend our long and idle winters in this business, without detriment to their agricultural service. Remittances have actually been made from some parts of the state in this article, the example is laudable and ought to be imitated. The sources of wealth are open to us, and there needs but industry to become as rich as we are free.

1. "Landholder" refers to the Hartford Woolen Manufactory which was established as a joint stock company in 1788 with a capital of £1,200 and which remained in existence until 1797.

642. Centinel XVII
Philadelphia Independent Gazetteer, 24 March

This essay continues "Centinel's" assault upon alleged public defaulters that he had launched in his sixteenth number on 26 February (CC:565). "Philanthropos," a pseudonym previously used by Tench Coxe (CC:454), attacked "Centinel" XVII for criticizing George Washington, Benjamin Franklin, the members of the Constitutional Convention in general, Robert Morris, William Bingham, and Francis Hopkinson. Referring to Supreme Court Judge George Bryan, the assumed author of "Centinel," "Philanthropos" asserted "I expect to pay my part of the public taxes, while he expects to live by them." "Philanthropos" asked his readers "to look into the proposed constitution carefully, and disdain to be led by any old interested Parasite, or any young inexperienced stranger [Benjamin Workman, note 7], who may come among us, and fall a bellowing and braying like a wild asses colt" (*Pennsylvania Mercury*, 29 March, Mfm:Pa. 583).

"Centinel" XVII was reprinted in the Philadelphia *Freeman's Journal*, on 26 March. For a discussion of the authorship, circulation, and impact of "Centinel," see CC:133.

To the People of Pennsylvania.

Fellow-Citizens, In my last number I exposed the villainous intention of the framers of the new constitution, to defraud the public out of the millions lying in the hands of individuals by the construction of this system, which would, if established, cancel all debts now due to the United States. I also shewed that thereby the delinquent states would be exonerated of all arrearages due by them on former requisitions of Congress; and to prove that the cancelling of the public dues was premeditated in regard to individuals, I stated that the general convention contained a number of the principal public defaulters, and that these were the most influential members, and chiefly instrumental in framing the new constitution: In answer to which, the conspirators have, by bold assertions, spurious vouchers, and insufficient certificates, endeavoured to exculpate one member, and to alleviate the weight of the charge of delinquency against another.[1] In the face of a resolution of Congress of the 20th June, 1785, declaring their intention of appointing 3 commissioners, to settle and adjust the receipts and expenditures of the late financier; the conspirators have asserted, that his accounts were finally settled in November, 1784, for which they pretend to have vouchers, and by a pompous display of certain resolutions of Congress, respecting a particular charge of fraud against him, as commercial agent to the United States, they vainly hope to divert the public attention from his great delinquency, in never accounting for the millions of public money, entrusted to him in that line. When we consider the immense sums of money taken up by Mr. M—s, as commercial agent, to import military supplies, and even to trade in behalf of the United States, at a time when the risque was so great, that individuals would not venture their property; that all these transactions were conducted under the private firm of W—g and M—,[2] which afforded unrestrained scope to peculation and embezzlement of the public property, by enabling Mr. M—s to throw the loss of all captures by the enemy, at that hazardous period, on the public, and converting most of the safe arrivals (which were consequently very valuable) into his private property; and when we add to these considerations, the principles of the MAN, his bankrupt situation at the commencement of the late war, and the immense wealth he has dazzled the world with since, can it be thought unreasonable to conclude, that the principal source of his affluence was the commercial agency of the United States, during the war, not that I would derogate from his successful ingenuity in his numerous speculations in the paper monies, Havannah monopoly and job, or in the sphere of financiering.

The certificate published in behalf of general M–ffl–n, the quarter master gen–l,[3] will not satisfy a discerning public, or acquit him of the charge of delinquency, as this certificate was procured to serve an electioneering purpose, upon a superficial and hasty inspection of his general account, unchecked by the accounts of his deputies, whose receipts and expenditures had not been examined, and consequently, by errors, collusion between him and them, or otherwise g—l M–ffl–n may retain a large balance in his hands; in such case a *quietus* may have been thought expedient to continue his affluence.

For the honor of human nature, I wish to draw a veil over the situation and conduct of another weighty character,[4] whose name has given a false lustre to the new constitution, and been the occasion of sullying the laurels of a *Washington*, by inducing him to acquiesce in a system of despotism and villainy, at which enlightened patriotism shudders.

The discovery of the intended fraud, which for magnitude and audacity, is unparalelled, must open the eyes of the deluded to the true character and principles of the men who had assumed the garb of patriotism, with an insidious design of enslaving and robbing their fellow-citizens–of establishing those odious distinctions between the well born and the great body of the people, of degrading the latter to the level of slaves, and elevating the former to the rank of nobility.

The citizens of this state, which is in advance in its payments to the federal treasury, whilst some of the others have not paid a farthing since the war,[5] ought in a peculiar manner to resent the intended imposition, and make its authors experience their just resentment; it is incumbent upon them in a particular manner, to exert themselves to frustrate the measures of the conspirators, and set an example to those parts of the union, who have not enjoyed the blessing of a free press on this occasion, but are still enveloped in the darkness of delusion, and enthralled by the fascination of names.

Could it have been supposed seven years ago, that, before the wounds received in the late conflict for liberty were scarcely healed, a post master-general and his deputies would have had the daring presumption to convert an establishment intended to promote and secure the public welfare into an engine of despotism, by suppressing all those newspapers that contain the essays of patriotism and real intelligence, and propagating instead thereof falsehoods and delusion?[6] Such a supposition at that time, would have been treated as chimerical; but how must our indignation rise when we find this flagitious practice is persevered in, after being publicly detected! Must not the bribe from the conspirators be very great to compensate the post master-general and his deputies, for the loss of character and infamy consequent upon such conduct, and for the danger they incur of being impeached and turned out of office?

The scurrilous attack of the *little Fiddler* upon Mr. Workman of the university, on a suspicion, perhaps, unfounded of his being the author of a series of essays under the signature of *Philadelphiensis*,[7] is characteristical of the man; he has ever been the base parasite and tool of the wealthy and great, at the expence of truth, honor, friendship, treachery to benefactors, nay to the nearest relatives; all have been sacrificed by him at the shrine of the great: he ought however, to have avoided a contrast with so worthy and highly respected a character as Mr. Workman, who had an equal right with himself to offer his sentiments on the new constitution; and if he viewed it as a system of despotism, and had talents to unfold its nature and tendency, he deserves the thanks of every patriotic American, if he has exerted them under the character of Philadelphiensis.–His not being above four years in the country can be no objection; the celebrated Thomas Paine wrote his Common Sense before he had been two years in America,[8] which was not the less useful or acceptable upon that account. The public have nothing to do with the author of a piece; it is the merits of the writing that are alone to be considered.–Mr. Workman, prior to his coming to America, was a professor in an eminent academy in Dublin.–Little Francis should have been cautious in giving provocation, for insignificance alone could have preserved him the smallest remnant of character; I hope he will take the hint, or such a scene will be laid open as will disgrace even his patrons; the suit of cloaths, and the quarter cask of wine, will not be forgot.

Philadelphia, March 19th, 1788.

1. For the defense of Robert Morris and William Bingham, see "Z," *Independent Gazetteer*, 8, 13 March (Mfm:Pa. 500, 520). For Morris' defense of himself, see *ibid.*, 8 April (Mfm:Pa. 613).

2. The firm of Thomas Willing and Robert Morris of Philadelphia.

3. For the defense of Thomas Mifflin, see *Independent Gazetteer*, 6, 7 March (Mfm:Pa. 493, 495).

4. Benjamin Franklin.

5. See CC:565, note 6.

6. For the attacks upon Postmaster General Ebenezer Hazard and the post office, see Appendix II.

7. For Francis Hopkinson's attacks on Benjamin Workman, see "A.B.," *Independent Gazetteer*, 11 March, and "Philadelphiensis" I (CC:237).

8. Paine arrived in Philadelphia in November 1774 and *Common Sense* was printed in January 1776.

643. Salem Mercury, 25 March[1]

An obliging correspondent has favoured us with the following extract of a letter from a Member of Congress to his friend in this county–dated March 1, 1788.

"We were, last evening, informed that the Convention of Newhampshire has adjourned to June, without coming to any decision respecting the Constitution. This was so unexpected, that we could scarcely realize it. ⟨I fear it will have a bad effect. The publick mind has been fluctuating, with regard to the system proposed–at least in considerable districts of the community: The first impressions were favourable to the adoption of the plan: The next, occasioned by various pieces written against it, and the intemperate conduct of its zealous friends in Pennsylvania,[2] &c. were much less favourable. The adoption of it in Massachusetts again turned the current of opinion much in its favour: The principal men in opposition in the State of Newyork, Maryland, &c. appeared to be agreed to acquiese in the adoption of it, in the form in which it has been adopted in Massachusetts; but I am quite unable to say, what effect this unexpected conduct in Newhampshire may have.⟩[3] Tho' my opinion, on fully examining all that has been said and written, respecting this plan, is not altered as to the amendable parts of it; yet I have been long satisfied we must, and ought to, put it into operation, and afterwards engraft the amendments into it, which time and experience shall direct. ⟨It is dangerous to remain long in our present situation, and the more so, in my opinion, on account of the storm evidently gathering in Europe. The present calm there, is, I am fully persuaded, momentary, and that a war will take place among the European nations with which we are principally connected, at no very distant period. And I think we may clearly observe in their plans already, evident intentions to entangle us in their disputes. It will be impossible for us to remain neuter, and pursue our true interest, unless we shall have a national Government for effectually regulating our affairs, and controuling the conduct of our own citizens."⟩[4]

1. Reprints in whole by 20 May (11): N.H. (1), Mass. (1), R.I. (1), Conn. (2), N.Y. (1), Pa. (3), Va. (1), S.C. (1). (See also notes 3 and 4.)

2. Probably a reference to the forcible return, on 29 September, of two Antifederalists to the Pennsylvania Assembly so that there would be a quorum to adopt resolutions calling a state convention (CC:125).

3. The text in angle brackets was omitted in the Providence *United States Chronicle*, 3 April.

4. The text in angle brackets was reprinted in the Newburyport *Essex Journal*, 2 April; the Exeter, N.H., *Freeman's Oracle*, 4 April; and the *New Hampshire Spy*, 8 April. The excerpt was prefaced: "A letter from a member of Congress, dated March 1, 1788, after speaking of the Federal Constitution, says."

644. Publius: The Federalist 74
New York Packet, 25 March

This essay, written by Alexander Hamilton, was reprinted in the New York *Independent Journal* on 26 March. It is number 74 in the M'Lean edition and number 73 in the newspapers.

For a general discussion of the authorship, circulation, and impact of *The Federalist*, see CC:201, 639.

The FŒDERALIST, No. 73.
To the People of the State of New-York.

The President of the United States is to be "Commander in Chief of the army and navy of the United States, and of the militia of the several States *when called into the actual service* of the United States." The propriety of this provision is so evident in itself; and it is at the same time so consonant to the precedents of the State constitutions in general, that little need be said to explain or enforce it.[1] Even those of them, which have in other respects coupled the Chief Magistrate with a Council, have for the most part concentred the military authority in him alone. Of all the cares or concerns of government, the direction of war most peculiarly demands those qualities which distinguish the exercise of power by a single hand. The direction of war implies the direction of the common strength; and the power of directing and employing the common strength, forms an usual and essential part in the definition of the executive authority.

"The President may require the opinion in writing of the principal officer in each of the executive departments upon any subject relating to the duties of their respective offices." This I consider as a mere redundancy in the plan; as the right for which it provides would result of itself from the office.

He is also to be authorised "to grant reprieves and pardons for offences against the United States *except in cases of impeachment.*" Humanity and good policy conspire to dictate, that the benign prerogative of pardoning should be as little as possible fettered or embarrassed. The criminal code of every country partakes so much of necessary severity, that without an easy access to exceptions in favor of unfortunate guilt, justice would wear a countenance too sanguinary and cruel. As the sense of responsibility is always strongest in proportion as it is undivided, it may be inferred that a single man would be most ready to attend to the force of those motives, which might plead for a mitigation of the rigor of the law, and least apt to yield to considerations, which were calculated to shelter a fit object of its vengeance. The reflection, that the fate of a fellow creature depended on his *sole fiat*, would naturally inspire scrupulousness and caution: The dread of being accused of weakness or connivance would beget equal circumspection, though of a different kind. On the other hand, as men generally derive confidence from their numbers, they might often encourage each other in an act of obduracy, and might be less sensible to the apprehension of suspicion or censure for an injudicious or affected clemency. On these accounts, one man appears to be a more eligible dispenser of the mercy of the government than a body of men.

The expediency of vesting the power of pardoning in the President has, if I mistake not, been only contested in relation to the crime of treason.

This, it has been urged, ought to have depended upon the assent of one or both of the branches of the legislative body. I shall not deny that there are strong reasons to be assigned for requiring in this particular the concurrence of that body or of a part of it. As treason is a crime levelled at the immediate being of the society, when the laws have once ascertained the guilt of the offender, there seems a fitness in refering the expediency of an act of mercy towards him to the judgment of the Legislature. And this ought the rather to be the case, as the supposition of the connivance of the Chief Magistrate ought not to be entirely excluded. But there are also strong objections to such a plan. It is not to be doubted that a single man of prudence and good sense, is better fitted, in delicate conjunctures, to balance the motives, which may plead for and against the remission of the punishment, than any numerous body whatever. It deserves particular attention, that treason will often be connected with seditions, which embrace a large proportion of the community; as lately happened in Massachusetts.[2] In every such case, we might expect to see the representation of the people tainted with the same spirit, which had given birth to the offence. And when parties were pretty equally matched, the secret sympathy of the friends and favorers of the condemned person, availing itself of the good nature and weakness of others, might frequently bestow impunity where the terror of an example was necessary.[3] On the other hand, when the sedition had proceeded from causes which had inflamed the resentments of the major party, they might often be found obstinate and inexorable, when policy demanded a conduct of forbearance and clemency. But the principal argument for reposing the power of pardoning in this case in the Chief Magistrate is this–In seasons of insurrection or rebellion, there are often critical moments, when a well timed offer of pardon to the insurgents or rebels may restore the tranquility of the commonwealth; and which, if suffered to pass unimproved, it may never be possible afterwards to recall. The dilatory process of convening the Legislature, or one of its branches, for the purpose of obtaining its sanction to the measure, would frequently be the occasion of letting slip the golden opportunity. The loss of a week, a day, an hour, may sometimes be fatal. If it should be observed that a discretionary power with a view to such contingencies might be occasionally confered upon the President; it may be answered in the first place, that it is questionable whether, in a limited constitution, that power could be delegated by law; and in the second place, that it would generally be impolitic before-hand to take any step which might hold out the prospect of impunity. A proceeding of this kind, out of the usual course, would be likely to be construed into an argument of timidity or of weakness, and would have a tendency to embolden guilt.

1. See *The Federalist* 69 (CC:617, notes 5–7).
2. Shays's Rebellion.
3. Commenting on this sentence, the reviewer (probably Noah Webster) of *The Federalist* in the June issue of the New York *American Magazine* noted that "The past tense is

here used for the future or conditional *should be* or *might be*. . . ." (For more on this review, see CC:635, note 3.)

645. John Adams to Governor George Clinton
London, 26 March (excerpt)[1]

. . . It is expected in Europe that the new Constitution for the United States will be soon adopted by all. it is a general opinion that the old one, stood in great need of a Reform, and that the projected Change, will be much for our Prosperity. a fœderal Republick of independent sovereign states was never known to exist, over a large Territory. innumerable Difficulties have been found in those which have been tried in Small Countries. The Question really Seems to be, whether the Union shall be broken; or whether all shall come under one sovereignty.–The Union is an object of such Magnitude: that every Thing but constitutional Liberty should be sacrificed to it.–What is Switzerland? What is Holland. What was Lisia [Lycia], Achaia or Tuscany, in Extent & Numbers, Wealth & Power to what our states are or will be in a very few years?–But I must restrain myself

1. RC, Emmet Collection, NN. Adams was writing Governor Clinton of New York to introduce his daughter and son-in-law, Abigail and William Stephens Smith. "Mrs Smith as a Young Stranger will Stand in need of the Candour and benevolence of the Citizens of New York, and as your Excellencies Example and that of your Family has great Influence, let me recommend her to your Protection and Patronage and to the Friendship of your Family." The Smiths arrived in New York City from England in May 1788 and settled in Jamaica, N.Y.

646. Publius: The Federalist 75
New York Independent Journal, 26 March

This essay, written by Alexander Hamilton, was reprinted in the *New York Packet* on 28 March. It is number 75 in the M'Lean edition and number 74 in the newspapers.

For a general discussion of the authorship, circulation, and impact of *The Federalist*, see CC:201, 639.

The FEDERALIST. No. LXXIV.
To the People of the State of New-York.

The president is to have power "by and with the advice and consent of the senate, to make treaties, provided two-thirds of the senators present concur." Though this provision has been assailed on different grounds, with no small degree of vehemence, I scruple not to declare my firm persuasion, that it is one of the best digested and most unexceptionable parts of the plan. One ground of objection is, the trite topic of the intermixture of powers; some contending that the president ought alone to possess the power of making treaties; and others, that it ought to have been exclusively deposited in the senate. Another source of objection is derived from the small number of persons by whom a treaty may be made: Of those who espouse this objection, a part are of opinion that the house of representatives ought to have been associated in the business, while another part seem to think that nothing more was necessary than to have substituted two-thirds of *all* the members of the senate to two-thirds of the members *present*. As I flatter myself the observations made in a preceding number, upon this part of the plan, must have sufficed to place it to a discerning eye in a very favourable light,[1] I shall here content myself with offering only some supplementary remarks, principally with a view to the objections which have been just stated.

With regard to the intermixture of powers, I shall rely upon the explanations already given, in other places, of the true sense of the rule,[2] upon which that objection is founded; and shall take it for granted, as an inference from them, that the union of the executive with the senate, in the article of treaties, is no infringement of that rule. I venture to add that the particular nature of the power of making treaties indicates a peculiar propriety in that union. Though several writers on the subject of government place that power in the class of executive authorities, yet this is evidently an arbitrary disposition: For if we attend carefully to its operation, it will be found to partake more of the legislative than of the executive character, though it does not seem strictly to fall within the definition of either of them. The essence of the legislative authority is to enact laws, or in other words to prescribe rules for the regulation of the society. While the execution of the laws and the employment of the common strength, either for this purpose or for the common defence, seem to comprise all the functions of the executive magistrate. The power of making treaties is plainly neither the one nor the other. It relates neither to the execution of the subsisting laws, nor to the enaction of new ones, and still less to an exertion of the common strength. Its objects are CONTRACTS with foreign nations, which have the force of law, but derive it from the obligations of good faith. They are not rules prescribed by the sovereign to the subject, but agreements between sovereign and sovereign. The power in question seems therefore to form a distinct department, and to belong properly neither to the legislative nor to the executive. The qualities elsewhere detailed, as indispensable in the management of foreign negotiations,[3] point out the executive as the most fit agent in those transactions; while the vast importance of the trust, and the operation of treaties as laws, plead strongly for the participation of the whole or a part of the legislative body in the effect[4] of making them.

However proper or safe it may be in governments where the executive magistrate is an hereditary monarch, to commit to him the entire power of making treaties, it would be utterly unsafe and improper to entrust that power to an elective magistrate of four years duration. It has been remarked upon another occasion, and the remark is unquestionably just, that an hereditary monarch, though often the oppressor of his people, has personally too much at stake in the government to be in any material danger of being corrupted by foreign powers.[5] But a man raised from the station of a private citizen to the rank of chief magistrate, possessed of but a moderate or slender fortune, and looking forward to a period not very remote, when he may probably be obliged to return to the station from which he was taken, might sometimes be under temptations to sacrifice his duty to his interest, which it would require superlative virtue to withstand. An avaricious man might be tempted to betray the interests of the state to the acquisition of wealth. An ambitious man might make his own aggrandisement, by the aid of a foreign power, the price of his treachery to his constituents. The history of human conduct does not warrant that exalted opinion of human virtue which would make it wise in a nation to commit interests of so delicate and momentous a kind as those which concern its intercourse with the rest of the world to the sole disposal of a magistrate, created and circumstanced, as would be a president of the United States.

To have entrusted the power of making treaties to the senate alone, would have been to relinquish the benefits of the constitutional agency of the president, in the conduct of foreign negotiations. It is true, that the senate would in that case have the option of employing him in this capacity; but they would also have the option of letting it alone; and pique or cabal might induce the latter rather than the former. Besides this, the ministerial servant of the senate could not be expected to enjoy the confidence and respect of foreign powers in the same degree with the constitutional representative of the nation; and of course would not be able to act with an equal degree of weight or efficacy. While the union would from this cause lose a considerable advantage in the management of its external concerns, the people would lose the additional security, which would result from the co-operation of the executive. Though it would be imprudent to confide in him solely so important a trust; yet it cannot be doubted, that his participation in it would materially add to the safety of the society. It must indeed be clear to a demonstration, that the joint possession of the power in question by the president and senate would afford a greater prospect of security, than the separate possession of it by either of them. And whoever has maturely weighed the circumstances, which must concur in the appointment of a president will be satisfied, that the office will always bid fair to be filled by men of such characters as to render their concurrence in the formation of treaties peculiarly desirable, as well on the score of wisdom as on that of integrity.

The remarks made in a former number, which has been alluded to in an other part of this paper, will apply with conclusive force against the admission of the house of representatives to a share in the formation of treaties.[6] The fluctuating and taking its future increase into the account, the multitudinous composition of that body, forbid us to expect in it those qualities which are essential to the proper execution of such a trust. Accurate and comprehensive knowledge of foreign politics; a steady and systematic adherence to the same views; a nice and uniform sensibility to national character, decision, *secrecy* and dispatch; are incompatible with the genius of a body so valuable and so numerous. The very complication of the business by introducing a necessity of the concurrence of so many different bodies, would of itself afford a solid objection. The greater frequency of the calls upon the house of representatives, and the greater length of time which it would often be necessary to keep them together when convened, to obtain their sanction in the progressive stages of a treaty, would be source of so great inconvenience and expence, as alone ought to condemn the project.

The only objection which remains to be canvassed is that which would substitute the proportion of two thirds of all the members composing the senatorial body to that of two [thirds of the][7] members *present*. It has been shewn under the second head of our inquiries that all provisions which require more than the majority of any body to its resolutions have a direct tendency to embarrass the operations of the government and an indirect one to subject the sense of the majority to that of the minority. This consideration seems sufficient to determine our opinion, that the convention have gone as far in the endeavour to secure the advantage of numbers in the formation of treaties as could have[8] reconciled either with the activity of the public councils or with a reasonable regard to the major sense of the community. If two thirds of the whole number of members had been required, it would in many cases from the non attendance of a part amount in practice to a necessity of unanimity. And the history of every political establishment in which this principle has prevailed is a history of impotence, perplexity and disorder. Proofs of this position might be adduced from the examples of the Roman tribuneship, the Polish diet and the states general of the Netherlands; did not an example at home render foreign precedents unnecessary.

To require a fixed proportion of the whole body would not in all probability contribute to the advantages of a numerous agency, better than merely to require a proportion of the attending members. The former by making a determinate number at all times requisite to a resolution diminishes the motives to punctual attendance. The latter by making the capacity of the body to depend on a *proportion* which may be varied by the absence or presence of a single member, has the contrary effect. And as, by promoting punctuality, it tends to keep the body complete, there is great likelihood that its resolutions would generally be dictated by as great a number in this case as in the other; while there would be much fewer occasions of delay. It ought not to be forgotten that under the existing confederation two members *may* and usually *do* represent a state; whence it happens that Congress, who now are solely invested with *all the powers* of the union, rarely consists of a greater number of persons than would compose the intended senate. If we add to this, that as the members vote by states, and that where there is only a single member present from a state, his vote is lost, it will justify a supposition that the active voices in the senate, where the members are to vote individually, would rarely fall short in number of the active voices in the existing Congress. When in addition to these considerations we take into view the co-operation of the president, we shall not hesitate to infer that the people of America would have greater security against an improper use of the power of making treaties, under the new constitution, than they now enjoy under the confederation. And when we proceed still one step further, and look forward to the probable augmentation of the senate, by the erection of new states, we shall not only perceive ample ground of confidence in the sufficiency of the members, to whose agency that power will be entrusted; but we shall probably be led to conclude that a body more numerous than the senate would be likely to become, would be very little fit for the proper discharge of the trust.

1. See *The Federalist* 64, by John Jay (CC:592).
2. See *The Federalist* 47–51, 71, and 73 (CC:486, 492, 495, 500, 503, 625, 644).
3. See *The Federalist* 64 (CC:592).
4. "Office" substituted in the M'Lean edition.
5. See *The Federalist* 22, *New York Packet*, 14 December (CC:347).
6. See *The Federalist* 64 (CC:592).
7. The reprint in the *New York Packet*, 28 March, and the M'Lean edition both corrected the error in the *Independent Journal* by adding the words "thirds of the" that are enclosed in brackets here.
8. "Been" inserted at this point in the M'Lean edition.

647. Purported Letters from George Bryan to John Ralston
Pennsylvania Gazette, 26 March

On 26 March the Federalist *Pennsylvania Gazette* printed two letters, dated 7 and 12 March, allegedly written by George Bryan to John Ralston. Bryan, one of the judges of the Pennsylvania Supreme Court, was thought to be the author of the "Centinel" essays (CC:133). Ralston (1735–1795), a Northampton County farmer, was a delegate to the state constitutional convention in 1776, a major in the state militia during the Revolution, and a state assemblyman from 1776 to 1780 and from 1784 to 1785. The "Bryan letters" were given to the *Pennsylvania Gazette* for publication by "X," who, in a prefatory statement, attacked Bryan as "the indefatigable Monster, The *CENTINEL*" and Ralston as "one of the sourest, narrowest, and most illiterate creatures in the state." According to "Q" in the Philadelphia *Freeman's Journal* of 9 April, "the world is indebted" for the publication of the letters "to the zeal of a TRUE FEDERALIST, whose *amor patriæ* beat so high that it beat down the battlements of civil society, arresting confidential letters, violating their seals and publishing them to the world.

"—*I would not be the Villain*
For the whole space that's in the tyrant's grasp
And the rich EAST to boot."

George Bryan neither denied nor affirmed that he had written the letters, although some Antifederalists insisted that he had not.

The letters argued that the prospects for ratification of the Constitution in several states were not good and that the opposition in Pennsylvania was growing rapidly. They described the Carlisle riot of 26 December 1787, the legal proceedings following it, and the attitude toward the Constitution in Carlisle and its surrounding area. (For the Carlisle riot and its aftermath, see Philadelphia *Independent Gazetteer*, 4 March, Appendix I.) The letters attacked the Federalists' use of force and intimidation; their use of the post office to suppress newspapers and Antifederalist literature; and their use of newspapers to disseminate false reports. The commercial community of Philadelphia was also criticized for supporting the Constitution out of economic self-interest. A postscript claimed that Marylander Andrew Ellicott had said that the Constitution would not be ratified by Maryland.

The Antifederalist response to the publication of these letters was swift. An unidentified Montgomery County Antifederalist termed the publication a "fraudulent base affair" and described John Ralston as well educated and "very much esteemed" wherever he was known in the state. This Antifederalist noted that "This is the first publication of any kind, either of intelligence or otherwise, that has ever appeared (in that *very impartial* paper) against the new constitution. And if the junto could in a *more honorable* way often procure and publish a similar letter (even though directed to a *countryman*) it would be of real service to the state" (Philadelphia *Independent Gazetteer*, 29 March, Mfm:Pa. 582). "X" attacked the publication of the letters as "a violation of that confidence without which society cannot exist. A seal in all civilized nations has ever been deemed sacred, but especially in mercantile Communities" (Philadelphia *Freeman's Journal*, 9 April, Mfm:Pa. 617). Writing for the *Pennsylvania Gazette*, "M" substantiated some of the "*solid facts*" found in the "Bryan letters," contradicting Federalist writers who questioned these facts. "M" concluded that "Having detected and exposed these fairy tales and stories of party, I shall take no notice of similar ones published on the same occasion" (16 April, Mfm:Pa. 629). Another Antifederalist, who also styled himself "M," asked the printer of the *New York Journal* to reprint the letters, which "contain a fund of real authenticated intelligence, and may be of use to the cause of liberty. Some may be surprised at the term conspirators being so familiarly used, but that is the general and accepted name by which the promoters of the new plan go in Pennsylvania. Do not omit the preface, as it will not injure the worthy character who is so much abused in it. Mr. Ralston was the unanimous choice of his county for a series of years as a representative, and his character established far above the reach of our modern patriots, especially such a one as that infamous wretch must be who could violate the sacredness of the seal by introducing to publication private correspondence" (*New York Journal*, 18 April). "A Friend to Law and Order," in an Antifederalist satirical preface in the *Freeman's Journal* of 2 April, submitted another intercepted letter for publication. The letter writer believed that the Constitution would not be ratified without amendments and charged that the Constitution was a conspiracy to establish a despotic government. "A Friend to Law and Order" asserted that the letter "was lately picked out of the pocket of a traveller in the stage, by a gentleman of great honour and love to his country, who hopes to be taken notice of according to his merits, as soon as matters are settled" (Mfm:Pa. 595). An acquaintance of "Honesty" found an alleged Federalist letter in which the writer thanked his correspondent for intercepting letters and promised him that he would be rewarded with "a good fat office." The writer encouraged his correspondent to open all letters suspected of containing Antifederalist material (*Independent Gazetteer*, 4 April, Mfm:Pa. 609).

Federalists accepted the authenticity of the "Bryan letters." In a private letter, Benjamin Rush wrote "I suppose you have seen Geo: Bryan's detected letters. They infallibly prove that he is the Author of the Centinel" (to [John Montgomery?], 9 April, Mfm:Pa. 614). "A Citizen" and "A Pennsylvanian" accused

Bryan of trying to promote anarchy, insurrection, and civil war, and attacked him for criticizing the commercial community of Philadelphia which was trying to improve the city's economy and the lot of all classes. They also charged that Bryan sought to gain fame at the expense of civil disorder and that he did not pay his debts. He was, in fact, a bankrupt trader before he became a Supreme Court judge (*Pennsylvania Gazette*, 2 April, Mfm:Pa. 599, 600). Several writers disputed the assertion in the "Bryan letters" that Federalists prevented the circulation of Antifederalist material and disagreed with his predictions about the chances of ratification in other states. Some writers also challenged the description in the letters of the Carlisle riot of 26 December 1787 and its aftermath. "Q" condemned the breaking of seals on the letters but asked that his readers "*not lose sight of the pernicious nature and tendency of the letters.*" The publication of the letters was justified, because the people had to know that a responsible officeholder had written such a reprehensible letter (*ibid.*, 16 April, Mfm:Pa. 630).

The "Bryan letter" of 7 March was reprinted in the New York *Daily Advertiser*, 29 March; *Pennsylvania Mercury*, 1 April; *Freeman's Journal*, 9 April; *New York Journal*, 18 April; Boston *American Herald*, 24 April; and *Carlisle Gazette*, 30 April. The *Freeman's Journal* did not print the preface by "X"; while the *Daily Advertiser* and the *American Herald* omitted the postscript. The *New York Packet*, 28 March, reprinted only the preface. The letter of 12 March was reprinted in the *Pennsylvania Mercury*, 1 April; *Freeman's Journal*, 9 April; and *Carlisle Gazette*, 30 April. The Winchester *Virginia Gazette*, 23 April, reprinted only the last paragraph.

Messrs. HALL & SELLERS, *The original Letters I send you for publication, and which will be left in your hands for inspection, afford one proof amongst a thousand, that the indefatigable Monster, the* CENTINEL, *is endued with a zeal and activity in every work of mischief always commensurate with its extent; for who but himself, to serve any cause whatever, would condescend to a correspondence with one of the sourest, narrowest, and most illiterate creatures in the state.*

                                                                                         X.

Philadelphia, 7th March, 1788.

DEAR SIR, Last Tuesday the post from New-England brought sad tidings for some folks here. The Convention of New-Hampshire, it seems, by 70 *against*, and 40 *for*,[1] have adjourned till 17th June. Had the final adjustment of the new system been put, it would have been rejected by a great majority. The friends of it, therefore, to let it fall easily, proposed the adjournment, and the others gave way. This disaster we consider as fatal to the business. So do its advocates here, and they are in the dumps, and some of the members of the General Convention are apologising for their conduct. Before this news came, the party was up in the skies, as their behaviour seemed to express. Yet their success at Boston was so moderated by the propositions for amendment, which, however superficial, broke the sanctity of the new Constitution. Besides, the president of the Boston Convention, *Hancock*, has written to our Assembly, sending their doings and the amendments, and desiring, that this state would adopt similar amendments.[2]–On the whole, as New-York is not likely to concur; nor Virginia, tho' General W. lives there; nor Rhode-Island; and as N. Carolina Convention meets not till 17th July, and will be much swayed by Virginia; as Maryland is much divided, if not on the whole against; I have no doubt there will be another General Convention. Georgia acceded to it, because pressed by an Indian war, and wanted aid immediately.

Failing, the conspirators against equal liberty will have much deceit and wicked conduct to answer for. They have seduced the post-officers to stop all news-papers from state to state, that contained investigations of their plan, so that the dissent of the minority of Pennsylvania did not get to Boston before their Convention rose.[3] Every little town furnished a flaming account, like those of Carlisle, Bethlehem,[4] &c. asserting how much the people of their place and neighbourhood approved the new plan. These were circulated and re-printed from Georgia to New-Hampshire, with parade. This deceived the people into a notion that there was a general approbation. In Virginia, at this moment, from the suppression of intelligence and by false letters, it is generally supposed that the opposition in Pennsylvania had vanished;[5] and at Boston, the news of the disturbances at *Carlisle* reaching Boston, before the Convention there rose, the whole was confidently denied.[6] As the Convention of Massachusetts was finishing, a vessel is made to arrive at a port 15 miles off, with account that N. Carolina had adopted, tho' that Convention sits not before July. Again, as the Convention of New-Hampshire was near finishing, this falshood is newly published at Newport in Rhode-Island, and another vessel pretended, to seduce another adoption.[7] These are but a specimen of these arts and inventions. But a lying tongue is but for a moment. The people every where will see and feel their frauds. Yet these are generally the doings of the first men in many of the states. I say nothing of the fraud of calling Conventions hastily in all the New-England states, save Rhode-Island, which has called none, in New-Jersey, in Pennsylvania and Delaware. In the southern states (all except Georgia) the calls of Conventions have been deliberate and distant; so in New-York. I am glad of the prospect we have, because it will prevent the danger of confusion and bloodshed. For if nine states had been nominally led into the plan, while the body of the people in many of them were still averse, civil war must have ensued, as the Conspirators would have endeavoured to set their scheme in motion, without funds to support the necessary standing army. This danger now seems to be over, for which we ought to be thankful.

In Cumberland county all are against it, except a small group in Carlisle, and a few, very few, scattered in the country. This small group, in October, met and censured their county representatives for attempting the breaking up of the late General Assembly, to prevent the calling of the people of every county east of Bedford to elect Convention in nine or ten days; with other matters favoring the new plan. These were paraded in the Carlisle Gazette as the sense of the people, and by the party published here and elsewhere.[8] The county resented it, and warned these men not to repeat the artifice. Yet on the 25th December the same people attempted to rejoice on occasion of the adoption by the Convention of Pennsylvania.

They were hindered: some blows ensued. Next day the same men, armed, made another essay; they were over-powered, and the effigies of two leading members of Convention were burned in contempt. Upon this, a letter with many affidavits was dispatched to Mr. M'Kean, pressing his warrants for 20 persons, charged with riots; among others Justice [John] Jordan. The business being irksome, Mr. M'Kean, alledging it was indelicate for him to act where he was ill-used, persuaded Mr. [William Augustus] Atlee, and laboured me to send up our warrant. I represented the danger of risquing insult to our precept, advising delay, and the rather, as no hasty steps had been taken to bring the city rioters to justice.[9] Mr. A. and Mr. [Jacob] Rush sent up their warrant. It lay some time in Carlisle, unexecuted, to bring the accused to submit and ask pardon. Nothing being done however, in this way, about 26th of February the sheriff was set to work. Eight or nine refusing to give bail, they were imprisoned. By the last accounts from Harrisburg, large numbers were assembled, from York and Dauphin, as well as Cumberland, to set the prisoners at large. This gives much uneasiness to the Conspirators here. Even the Chief Justice, 'tis said, had before the news came consented to drop the prosecution, as the members of Council feared the event. But he wrote to Mr. Atlee too late, if he has written. We hope no further mischief will ensue; tho' the Conspirators in Carlisle told Mr. M'Kean in their letter, they feared that their dwellings would be pulled down. Here, in October, we were forced to hold our tongues, lest well dressed ruffians should fall upon us. At this day the case is otherwise. Yet many are still silent, lest, the new plan being adopted, they might hereafter be ruined for opposing. Since it was commonly safe from immediate attack, some of us have been open and avowed, and risqued all the malice of these men. The common people are latterly too much of our opinions to hurt us. Indeed, none but *gentlemen mobs* have been active in Philadelphia.

In Montgomery, the current of the county is against the plan, the friends of it are silent; Berks very few, who favour it; the same in Dauphin. In the town of Lancaster there is a party, but few elsewhere in the county. In York, the opposers are very numerous. In Franklin they are the great body of the people. In Bedford and in the overhill counties very few are for it. Of Northumberland I can say little. Our friends in Bucks and Chester are much increased. The Quakers are changed generally. The solid Quakers here greatly dislike it; but they do not intermeddle.[10] Their young people favour it, and in this city, Baltimore, New-York, Boston, &c. there is a majority for it; most so in Boston. *Shays* insurrection has been made a great engine of terror to dispose people of that country to receive chains, if the western counties can be kept down. Shays and his adherents were roused to what they did by excessive taxes; perhaps contrived to dispose the New-England states to receive the new system, to which they would otherwise be averse.

Since writing the foregoing, we have accounts from Carlisle, that about 1000 armed men appeared there, and demanding of the sheriff to open the prison, set at liberty the persons charged as rioters, and burned the commitment.[11] The inhabitants of the town, in the mean while, kept close within their houses, and the armed men soon went away without doing any thing further. Mr. James Hanna, a constitutionalist, attorney at law at Newtown, was this day very unexpectedly chosen to succeed Colonel Hart, as recorder of deeds and register of wills of Bucks county. Mr. Dubois, nephew of Mr. Henry Wynkoop, was a competitor, yet, to the surprize of every body, and astonishment of Gerardus Wynkoop, Hanna had 36 votes, and Mr. Dubois but 26. Mr. Irwin, son of Arthur Irwin, of Tinicum, in Bucks county, had 5 votes.

The peculiar reason why the party for the new constitution is large here, is the supreme influence of the Bank,[12] the weight of Mr. Morris, the bankrupt and dependent state of the traders generally, the hopes that by giving large powers to Congress, no foreign ship will be allowed to carry off the rice, tobacco, flour, &c. but it shall be limitted to American bottoms. These, and a vain delusion, that present distress, caused by too large use and consumption of foreign goods, and the consequent shipping off of specie, would be relieved. At Boston all ranks have been taught to believe it would be a cure for every sore; so infatuated are the inhabitants.

The Assembly is not doing much. A short session is talked of.[13] A day has been spent on the subject of Wyoming, but to no purpose.[14] R. Morris is absent in Virginia.[15] He has been there some months. Our river is yet shut, but this cannot last above a day or two.

I am, Dear Sir, Your very humble Servant,
GEO. BRYAN.

To Mr. John Ralston,
　　Allen township, Northampton County.

P.S. We learn by Mr. Ellicot,[16] late a Commissioner for Pennsylvania in running the lines between us and Virginia, that beyond doubt Maryland will reject the new constitution of the general government. He is just come from Baltimore.

Philadelphia, 12th March, 1788.

DEAR SIR, I wrote a letter addressed to you on Saturday, the 8th instant. It contained a state of present intelligence as to the designed constitution of the United States. But there was a mistake in giving the vote of New-Hampshire adjournment till June. Instead of 70 to 40, it was 56 for and 51 against;[17] which shews its advocates nearly escaped a sudden rejection. The other numbers, 70 to 40, were the estimated size and strength of the parties, of the advocates and opposers. Those in favour of the plan cry out, that the others came fettered with instructions; yet this base practice was begun by their friends in Pennsylvania.[18] The place where the Convention of New-Hampshire sits on the 17th June is Concord, 100 miles farther inland, as I am told, than Exeter, where this body sat, which bodes no good to the *fœderal* party, as they falsely call themselves.

Saturday a person arrived by the stages from North-Carolina. He assures that there is no doubt that the new plan will be rejected by that state.

The Conspirators are fully detected in stopping the transmission of intelligence from state to state by tricks in the post-offices. Being charged with it early in February, they stifly denied it. It is at length become too palpable to all. Sure no business of a public nature has proceeded upon such base tricks of fraud and surprize!

I am, dear Sir, with compliments to all friends,

Your very obedient Servant,

GEO. BRYAN.

To Mr. John Ralston,

Allen Township, Northampton County.

[P.S.] Old Col. Hart is dead. Robert Whitehill has lately married a widow Montgomery, of Upper Octorara, Chester county.

1. This incorrect vote appeared in the *New York Journal* and *New York Morning Post* on 3 March (Appendix I) and was reprinted in the *Pennsylvania Packet* on the 5th, and in the *Pennsylvania Mercury* on the 6th. The correct vote–56 to 51 (CC:554)–was printed in Philadelphia for the first time in the *Federal Gazette* on 11 March. The 12 March letter contains the correct vote.

2. On 16 February Governor John Hancock, the president of the Massachusetts Convention, transmitted the Convention's proceedings and the form of ratification of the Constitution, which included recommendatory amendments to the Constitution, to the executives of the several states. Hancock's letter expressed the hope that the amendments might "meet with the concurrence" of the states. Twelve days later the Pennsylvania Supreme Executive Council turned these documents over to the state Assembly. On 29 March, the last day of the session, the Assembly read the amendments a second time and ordered that Hancock's letter and the amendments "be inserted on the minutes." For the amendments, see CC:508.

3. For the post office and the alleged suppression of Antifederalist newspapers, see Appendix II, and for the "Dissent of the Minority of the Pennsylvania Convention," see CC:353.

4. The proceedings of a meeting in Carlisle on 3 October were described briefly in the *Pennsylvania Gazette* on 10 October and printed in full in the *Pennsylvania Packet* on 15 October. The proceedings of a Northampton County meeting held in Bethlehem on 22 October were printed in the Philadelphia *Independent Gazetteer* on 26 October (RCS:Pa., 173–74, 229–30. For other meetings, see RCS:Pa., 228–29.).

5. See the Philadelphia *Freeman's Journal*, 30 January (CC:Vol. 3, Appendix I).

6. On 12 January the *Independent Gazetteer* published an extract of a Carlisle letter, dated 4 January, discussing the turbulent aftermath of the riot (Mfm:Pa. 328. For the riot, see *Independent Gazetteer*, 4 March, Appendix I.). On 28 January the Boston *American Herald* reprinted this extract. The next day a correspondent in the *Massachusetts Gazette* declared that the extract "is by no means founded in truth; the author of it being one of the mob who lately, in a riotous and hostile manner assembled together at that place, many of whom, without doubt, are now in custody for their misbehaviour. The citizens of Pennsylvania were never more united in any publick measure than they were in the adoption of the federal constitution." On 30 January the *Massachusetts Centinel* printed a letter, dated 14 January, from a "gentleman of eminence" from Philadelphia, who stated that "Under the mock appearance of extracts from a Carlisle paper, Judge

B. has given the publick a long account of the *distraction* which prevails in that place: But on the authority of a Rev. Clergyman from that country, I assure you, that it was a mere *fracas*, similar to which have happened there, ever since the Constitution of this State was adopted–between the Republicans and Constitutionalists–I do not know what to compare them to better than your Pope-mobs before the revolution" (Mfm:Pa. 392).

7. On 5 February, the day before the Massachusetts Convention ratified the Constitution, the *Massachusetts Gazette* announced the ratification of the Constitution by North Carolina. Nine days later the *Newport Herald* printed a similar report. The *Herald* item was reprinted in the *Pennsylvania Packet* on 4 March, and the next day the *Pennsylvania Gazette* challenged the validity of the report. (See "False Reports of North Carolina's Ratification of the Constitution," 5 February–5 March, Appendix I.)

8. See note 4 above.

9. A reference to two separate incidents in Philadelphia in 1787. On 29 September a mob forcibly returned two absent Antifederalist assemblymen in order to attain a quorum so that resolutions calling a state convention could be adopted. On the evening of 6 November, the day that delegates were elected to the state Convention, a mob attacked the houses of several prominent Antifederalists and a boarding house where other Antifederalists were staying. In neither case were the mob leaders tried and punished. (See CC:125; and RCS:Pa., 99–111, 235, 237–56.)

10. Federalists and Antifederalists held different positions with respect to the attitude of Quakers on the Constitution. (See CC:Vol. 2, p. 527n. See also *Independent Gazetteer*, 7 March, Appendix I.)

11. On 5 March the *Carlisle Gazette* reported that 1,500 militia had taken part in the effort to free the prisoners (RCS:Pa., 699–701). This report was reprinted in the *Independent Gazetteer* and *Pennsylvania Packet* on 14 and 15 March, respectively.

12. For the role of the Bank of North America in Pennsylvania politics, see RCS:Pa., *passim.*

13. The session began on 19 February and ended on 29 March.

14. For the dispute in the Wyoming Valley, see CC:364, note 2.

15. For Robert and Gouverneur Morris, who were in Virginia for business reasons, see CC:255, note 2; CC:Vol. 3, pp. 361, 561n; and CC:550, note 1.

16. Andrew Ellicott (1754–1820), a native of Pennsylvania, was a Baltimore mathematician and surveyor. In 1785 and 1786 he was a member of the Pennsylvania commissions for running the state's western and northern boundaries. Several newspaper reports contradicted the "Bryan letter's" statements about Ellicott. On 3 April the *Pennsylvania Mercury* reported that Ellicott had told Bryan "from present appearances he thought the Constitution would without doubt be adopted" (Mfm:Pa. 608). Six days later a correspondent in the *Pennsylvania Gazette* noted that Ellicott said he had not arrived in Philadelphia by 7 March, the date of "Bryan's letter." The correspondent asserted that Ellicott denied making any pessimistic predictions about the fate of the Constitution in Maryland and in fact had "always thought, that, even if certain characters opposed to the government should get into the Maryland Convention, they would not be able finally to prevent the adoption by that state" (Mfm:Pa. 620). Despite these denials, "M" maintained that "Many people can attest to the truth of what is in Mr. B—'s postscript" (*Pennsylvania Gazette*, 16 April, Mfm:Pa. 629). Finally, on 21 April Ellicott responded from Baltimore: "In consequence of finding my name mentioned in the postscript to the Honorable Judge Bryan's letter, dated the 7th of last month, and published in the Pennsylvania Gazette, I feel myself interested in stating the information I have constantly given with regard to the subject there alluded to.

"Immediately after I arrived in the city of Philadelphia, many of my acquaintance enquired about the probable fate of the new fœderal government in the state of Maryland. I informed them, that the opposition in that state was much more considerable than I at first imagined, or could reasonably have expected, and if certain well known political characters were sent to the convention, and interested themselves in opposition to the proposed general government, its fate would be very doubtful, and probably rejected. But I am very confident that I have never at any time expressed myself in the terms held out in the postscript to Mr. Bryan's letter. By this declaration I would not be understood to insinuate anything to the prejudice of Mr. Bryan, who must certainly have been misinformed on this occasion. Mr. Bryan's information was second-hand; his letter, as before observed, is dated the 7th, and the first time he conversed with me on that subject was on the 16th following. I have at all times given my opinion freely with regard to the adoption of the general government by the state of Maryland. That opinion I had taken up from attending to the disposition of the people, and not from either an attachment to party or prejudices for or against the proposed fœderal government. Every citizen of a free country has an unquestionable right to give his opinion on any political point, and when it is done with decency and candour, none but the base and narrow minded will reply or answer with abuse and scurrility. Such I hope may always meet with the contempt they justly merit.

"I have frequently heard the proposed fœderal government both condemned and applauded, without either condemning or applauding it myself. I have no doubt but it has both defects and excellencies. There may perhaps have been as good, and there has certainly been infinitely worse governments. I think I shall not be singular when I assert, that the advantages of any form of government can only be discovered when reduced to practice. Experiment will ever be found preferable to theory. The imperfections of any piece of mechanism are best discovered when the machine is put in motion, and from the same principle the necessary amendments or alterations will become obvious. From these, and other considerations, I am in favor of the adoption of the general government previous to any amendments; and more so, as it points out a mode to have the necessary alterations made at a future period. And that such alterations will be made, I have not the smallest doubt, as the proposed government is wholly by representation–and in all cases where the power proceeds from the people, and is lodged in a short periodical delegation, the wants and disposition of the people will always accompany the representation. I have now for the first time published my opinion on this great political question. I neither suspect the judgment or principle of those who think different from me, nor feel any particular attachment to those who correspond in sentiment" (*Pennsylvania Gazette*, 30 April, Mfm:Pa. 665).

17. See note 1 above.

18. On 22 October a Northampton County meeting of Federalists, held in the town of Bethlehem (note 4 above), resolved that each candidate nominated to the state convention "do make public declaration before this meeting, that, if it should be his lot, to be elected as Member of the said Convention, he will use his utmost endeavours, that the said constitution be ratified." The county's four candidates "severally made the said declaration before this meeting." On 3 November, three days before the election of state Convention delegates, a group of Federalists met in Philadelphia and appointed a committee "to wait upon the five persons fixed on as delegates to the state convention, and to demand, categorically 'whether they would support and adopt the proposed plan of government in all its parts, without alteration or amendment,' and unless they respectively declared in the affirmative, it was resolved to call another meeting to supply the place of such as hesitated or dissented" (*Pennsylvania Herald*, 7 November, RCS:Pa., 227).

648. Publicola: Address to the Freemen of North Carolina
State Gazette of North Carolina, 27 March[1]

(*Continued from our last.*)

There is an objection made to the new constitution, which I believe originated in this state, as I have never seen it in print.–It is I believe a very powerful reason with many among us, for opposing any alterations in the federal government; in some from mistaken zeal, in others from interested motives.–The objection is this–that if the new government takes place, the debts due to British subjects will be recoverable, and the argument to shew the injustice of this, is, "That our citizens bore the expences of the war, and had their property torn from them for the support of it, whilst the subjects of Britain remained entirely at their ease, or were employed in attempting to rob and enslave us. It would therefore, it is said, be manifest injustice that we should, out of the little pittance which we have left, or from the fruit of our labours, pay debts to those who have contributed to oppress, and reduce us to poverty." Perhaps in some instances, these reasons may be applicable; but we are to remember, that if any of us have been reduced to poverty by the war, nothing can be recovered of us, and the law will discharge us if we are insolvent.–The treaty of peace leaves the British subject open to recover his money, if the debtor is possessed of property; and it is shameless on our part, that it has not been executed with good faith.–This has given a plausible pretext for one breach on the part of the British, and for not making compensations for another.[2] These are the favourite reasons of a learned Judge, which as he has used them publicly, as well as privately, are no secrets. With what propriety they come from one in his station, the public will determine. If it should appear hereafter, that any one who uses these arguments against adopting the new constitution, should be found to be deeply indebted to British subjects, what shall we think of his patriotism? we shall be apt to conclude that private interest is at the bottom of his objections. But if we should be told that such a one acquired the most valuable part of his property, by contracting debts with British subjects, and that the same property remains at this day entire, and even considerably improved (the loss of a tame deer excepted) shall we not be convinced that his resentment against our late enemies is excited by the love of wealth, to the attainment of which he sacrifices the national faith. I have been thus particular in order to warn you against those who would endeavour to rekindle your resentment for their own particular purposes. You should never forget that the treaty of peace will one day be enforced; if not by ourselves, it certainly will by our enemies. Few of you owe debts to British subjects, and therefore I presume you will not readily consent to pay the debts of others. But if the courts are not speedily open for their recovery, you will either be taxed for the payment, or which is more probable they will be collected with much more certainty than federal taxes, and that too at the point of the bayonet.

Some of the most important considerations are yet to come. The states are now so feeble, that they are, by the confession of all, without any effective government–In case of attempts upon our independency, are Congress able to raise a regiment, or fit out a single ship of war? Can we in such an exigency, expect foreign assistance, while we are unwilling, or unable, to observe the treaties we have made, or to pay the monies we have borrowed? Six states have already adopted the new constitution, and there is every probability that three more, at the least, will come into the measure. What will become of North Carolina if we should refuse our assent? No man of the least knowledge in government will be so wild as to assert, that we can support ourselves. We shall unquestionably be deserted by South-Carolina, and most probably by Virginia; but if the latter should also refuse the new constitution, what would her strength avail us. Can we jointly repel a powerful enemy? Look back to the late war, and answer the question–Should we reject the new government we shall be the most contemptible state on the face of the earth–despised and ridiculed by all the nations in the world, and sunk even beneath the political character of Rhode-Island. The United States will treat us as foreigners, and will either preclude us from all commerce with them, or lay our trade under such severe restrictions, that the little we have now left will be totally annihilated; and in the end we shall be reduced to the mortification, of suing for admission into the union. Remember, my fellow citizens, it was by the strictest union we became independent. Our zeal during the war supplied the want of good government–Nothing but union can preserve us from destruction. Let every man make it his boast, that he continues a citizen of the United States–That was once a respectable appellation–Do not change it to be called a citizen of a single state however respectable. Whoever advises you to a measure so destructive, does not consider your honour, or your interest, but pursues his own selfish motives, and the gratification of a paltry and vicious ambition–The greatest part of you will, in such an event, remain obscure and unknown, whilst your advisers will exalt themselves upon the ruin of their country.

In some of the eastern states, those who oppose the new constitution, are branded as the emissaries of the British government; and accused of now endeavouring to bring about a reconciliation with our ancient masters. If the charge is just, a better scheme could not have been adopted, than to keep us divided and feeble. But the case appears to be different here. Those among us who are the most industrious to prevent a reform, have been some of the warmest opposers of the British government–Their zeal has been little short of persecution; but if we look around us, we shall discover, that a considerable number of them are such as were unknown or as persons of no consequence, previous to the war–They have arisen by accident into power, and influence, and now dread the loss of it. They make a merit of their uniform attachment to the American cause, though in fact many of them had nothing to lose, and consequently ran no risk in the contest; and since the peace has taken place, most of them have been equally uniform in opposing such measures as were best adapted to allay the animosities of parties, and restore the community to order and tranquillity–To this opposition, throughout all the states, it is owing, that a reform in government becomes necessary.

If we look on the other hand, to those who appear favourable to the new constitution, we can scarcely suppose the bulk of them to be actuated by any improper motives. Few, very few of them, indeed, can expect to be individually benefited. The honour of sitting in Congress, will be confined to seven at present–The number cannot be augmented until the population of the country is considerably encreased. The profits attending a seat in the national Councils, can be no temptation; for the allowance must necessarily be moderate. In all events it cannot be such as to be a compensation to those who must, in a great measure, abandon the care of their private affairs. The officers of Congress in the state will be very few. The Collectors of the imposts at the different ports, and such as may be necessary to the administration of justice in the federal courts, will be almost the whole that will be necessary. The great number of respectable persons who are in favour of the new government, and the impossibility that the greatest part of them can derive any partial benefit from it, are irrefragable proofs that they act from conviction.

The enemies of the new form of government endeavour to persuade others, what I can scarcely think they believe themselves; that the President of the United States is only another name for King, and that we shall be subject to all the evils of a monarchical government. How a magistrate, who is removeable at a short period, can be compared to an hereditary monarch, whose family, to all succeeding generations, as well as himself must be maintained in pomp and splendour, at an enormous expence to the nation; and whose power and influence will be proportionably great, these honest guardians of the rights of the people would do well to inform us–It needs no argument to prove that a government is the more forcible when the Executive department is in the hands of one, or a few. There can be no danger, where that one is liable to be removed every four years, and will be at all times responsible–It is a maxim in the British government that *the King can do no wrong*; that is, he is not amenable to the courts of justice, as the law has not provided any punishment for his misconduct; but the President of the United States will be liable to be impeached by the representatives of the people, and to be tried for his crimes–Yet we may remember that it was not the British form of government of which we complained; but the refusal on the part of the Legislature of that country, to let us participate of the rights which their other subjects enjoyed. Instead of the protectors of our privileges; King, Lords and Commons became our tyrants; and, animated by liberty, we spurned at their usurped authority, and threw off the yoke. Will our situation under the new government be similar? Can common sense, and common honesty view it in the same light? Exercise your own understandings, read and judge for yourselves; and you must necessarily be convinced, that those who would insidiously, under pretence of imaginary dangers, whisper you out of your senses, do not mean you well–The President, the Senators and Representatives in Congress, will be as much your own choice, and as much in your own power, as your Representatives in the General Assembly; with this difference, that they are not chosen so frequently. This became necessary to give stability to government–But they will be more in your power, if any of them abuse their trust,–you can impeach, and try them; but you cannot try a person impeached by your own Assembly. You have no constitutional provision for it; and your Judges have raised such a clamour about your ears, that no law can be obtained for the purpose. Yet I will do them justice. I verily believe that they would not object to a law for regulating trials upon impeachment, if the Assembly would graciously please to exempt their Honours from such trials.[3]

If after all you should be averse from receiving the new constitution, apprehending some danger to the liberties of the people, there is one certain rule, which cannot fail to point out the conduct which you ought to pursue. Attend to the conduct of the Judges on this great national question. If you find, as I am persuaded you will, that they are opposed to an alteration, your choice is made. All their maxims and all their actions, uniformly tend to encrease their own power. To avert the loss of that, they are now aiming at seats in the ensuing Convention–In opposing them, you can scarcely be wrong. If the present federal government remains, they will continue, as usual, to domineer over you. Should the new form be adopted, they will sink into their original insignificancy. They have nothing now to support them but that degree of respectability which people are apt to annex to their persons, though it properly belongs to their station. When that comes to be lessened, they will once more become, Tom, Dick and Harry.

If, in the course of these remarks, I have discovered any asperity, it should be considered, that it has arisen from facts within my own observation. I have not the most distant idea of censuring those who upon principle differ from me in opinion, whatever I may think of the futility of their reasons for so doing. I am sensible that while human beings exist, there must be various and contradictory sentiments upon every speculative subject; and even upon such as are in appearance purely practical. I am therefore ready to shew that indulgence to the errors, and mistakes of others, which I am sensible my own require.

1. For a general discussion of "Publicola" and the text of the first part of the essay, see CC:633.

2. Article IV of the Treaty of Peace provided that "Creditors on either Side shall meet no lawful Impediment to the Recovery of the full Value in Sterling Money, of all bona fide Debts heretofore contracted." Article V called on Congress to recommend to the states that confiscated property of British subjects and Loyalists be returned. Article VII provided that the British would withdraw from all their posts on American soil and would not carry away the slaves in their possession when they evacuated. After the war, British citizens and Loyalists often found it impossible to collect their debts or have their confiscated property returned. This served as a pretext for the British to retain

their western posts and to refuse to compensate Americans for the slaves that had been carried off when they evacuated.

3. Although Article XXIII of the North Carolina constitution provided for impeachment of state officeholders by the legislature (Thorpe, V, 2792), no procedures for impeachment had been enacted into law. In 1785 a bill was presented in the House of Commons to provide for "the trial of Judges of the Superior Courts of Law and Equity within this State for misdemeanor, or misbehaviour in office." Maclaine was a member of the committee to which the bill was sent. The committee reported a bill providing for impeachment of all officers including the Superior Court judges, but the bill was laid over to the next Assembly. In 1786 Maclaine reintroduced the bill, and once more it was not enacted (NCSR, XVII, 374, 389–91; XVIII, 340. See also CC:533, note 5.).

649. James Iredell: Address to the Freemen of Edenton, N.C., c. 28–29 March

On 28–29 March James Iredell was elected to represent the town of Edenton in the North Carolina Convention. Iredell had never before served in elective office.

The text of Iredell's address thanking the freemen of Edenton is taken from McRee, *Iredell*, II, 220. The first and last sentences of the address appeared in the Philadelphia *Federal Gazette*, 19 April, as excerpts from the no longer extant 2 April issue of the *Edenton Intelligencer*. The *Gazette's* excerpts were reprinted ten times by 29 May: N.H. (1), Mass. (3), R.I. (1), N.Y. (3), Pa. (2).

GENTLEMEN:–The distinguished honor of having been unanimously elected your Representative in the ensuing convention, without the least solicitation on my part, has made an impression on my heart which no time or circumstances can efface. My gratitude for it is inexpressible, but I am sensible will be shown in the most proper manner, by the zeal and fidelity with which it will be equally my duty and pleasure to execute this important trust. I shall have nothing to lament, but that my abilities will fall so far short of my ardent ambition to serve you. Under the conviction of my present sentiments, that the security of every thing dear to us depends on our adoption of the proposed constitution, I consider it one of the most awful subjects that was ever proposed for the consideration of a free people, and in giving it my utmost support (as I probably shall do), I shall have occasion for all the strength I can derive from the pleasing consciousness that in so doing I shall truly speak the respectable sense of my constituents. This will animate me beyond every thing in what I conceive the cause of Truth and Liberty. God forbid, indeed, that I should, by a blind admiration, imitate the conduct of those who indulge themselves in a blind rejection of it. The one would be as unworthy of the dignity of a free people, as the other is derogatory of those sentiments of respect and deference which we owe the great characters who formed it; and owe certainly as much for our own sakes, whose welfare they took so much pains to consult, as from the sentiments of gratitude with which every mind of sensibility must remember their former eminent services to their country. But I am convinced the more narrowly the constitution is examined by impartial minds, the more highly it must be approved; and from the consideration of our present critical situation, it will, perhaps, be deemed the only probable means of safety we have left.

650. Luther Martin: Address No. III
Maryland Journal, 28 March[1]

To the CITIZENS *of* MARYLAND.

There is, my fellow-citizens, scarcely an individual of common understanding, I believe, in this State, who is any ways acquainted with the proposed constitution, who doth not allow it to be, in many instances, extremely censurable, and that a variety of alterations and amendments are essentially requisite, to render it consistent with a reasonable security for the liberty of the respective states, and their citizens.

Aristides, it is true, is an exception from this observation; he declares, that "if the whole matter was left to his discretion, he would not change any part of the proposed constitution;"[2]–whether he meant this declaration as a proof of his *discretion*, I will not say; it will, however, readily be admitted, by most, as a proof of his enthusiastic zeal in favour of the system:–But it would be injustice to that writer not to observe, that if he is as much *mistaken* in the *other* parts of the constitution, as in that which relates to the judicial department,[3] the constitution which he is so earnestly recommending to his countrymen, and on which he is lavishing so liberally his commendation, is a *thing of his own creation*, and *totally different* from *that* which is offered for your acceptance.–He has given us an explanation of the original and appellate jurisdiction of the judiciary of the general government, and of the manner in which he supposes it is to operate, an explanation so *inconsistent* with the *intention* of its framers, and so *different* from its *true construction*, and from the effect which it will have, should the system be adopted, that I could scarce restrain my astonishment at the error, although I was, in some measure, prepared for it, by his previous acknowledgment, that he did not very well understand that part of the system;[4] a circumstance I apprehended he did not recollect at the time when he was bestowing upon it his dying benediction:–And if one of our judges, possessed of no common share of understanding, and of extensive acquired knowledge, who, as he informs us, has long made the science of government his peculiar study, so little understands the true import and construction of this constitution, and that too in a part more particularly within his own province, can it be wondered at that the people in general, whose knowledge in subjects of this nature is much more limited and circumscribed, should but imperfectly comprehend the extent, operation and consequences of so complex and intricate a system?–and is not this, of itself, a strong proof of the necessity that it should be corrected and amended, at least so as to render it more clear and comprehensible to those who are to decide upon it, or to be affected by it?

But although almost every one agrees the constitution, as it is, to be both defective and dangerous, we are not wanting in characters who earnestly advise us to adopt it, in its present form, with all its faults, and assure us we may safely rely on obtaining, hereafter, the amendments that are necessary:–But why, I pray you, my fellow-citizens, should we not insist upon the necessary amendments being made now, while we have the liberty of acting for ourselves, before the constitution becomes binding upon us by our assent, as every principle of reason, common sense and safety would dictate?–Because, say they, the sentiments of men are so different, and the interests of the different states are so jarring and dissonant, that there is no probability they would agree if alterations and amendments were attempted.–Thus, with one breath, they tell us that the obstacles to any alterations and amendments being agreed to by the states, are so insuperable, that it is vain to make the experiment, while in the next, they would persuade us it is so certain that states will accede to *those* which shall be necessary; and that *they may* be procured even after the system shall be ratified, that we need not hesitate swallowing the poison, from the ease and security of instantly obtaining the antidote; and they seem to think it astonishing that any person should find a difficulty in reconciling the absurdity and contradiction!

If it is easy to obtain proper amendments, do not let us sacrifice every thing that ought to be dear to freemen, for want of insisting upon its being done, while we have the power.

If the obtaining them will be difficult and improbable, for God's sake do not accept of such a form of government, as without amendments cannot fail of rendering you mere beasts of burthen, and reducing you to a level with your own slaves, with this aggravating distinction, that you *once* tasted the blessings of freedom.

Those who would wish you to believe that the faults in the system proposed are wholly or principally owing to the difference of state interests, and proceed from that cause, are either imposed upon themselves, or mean to impose upon you.–The principal question in which the state interests had any material effect, were those which related to representation, and the number in each branch of the legislature, whose concurrence should be necessary for passing navigation acts, or making commercial regulations.–But what state is there in the union whose interest would prompt it to give the general government the extensive and unlimited powers it possesses in the executive legislature and judicial departments, together with the powers over the militia, and the liberty of establishing a standing army without any restriction?–What state in the union considers it advantageous to its interest, that the President should be re-eligible–the members of both houses appointable to offices–the *judges* capable of holding *other offices* at the will and pleasure of the government, and that there should be no real responsibility either in the President, or in the members of either branch of the legislature?–or what state is there that would have been averse to a bill of rights, or that would have wished for the destruction of jury trial in a great variety of cases, and in a particular manner in *every case*, without exception, where the *government itself is interested?*–These parts of the system, so far from promoting the interest of any state, or states, have an immediate tendency to annihilate *all* the state governments indiscriminately, and to subvert their rights, and the rights of their citizens.–To oppose these, and to procure their alteration, is equally the interest of every state in the union.–The introduction of these parts of the system must not be attributed to the jarring interests of states, but to a very different source–the pride, the ambition and the interest of individuals:–This being the case, we may be enabled to form some judgment of the probability of obtaining a safe and proper system, should we have firmness and wisdom to reject that which is now offered; and also of the great improbability of procuring any amendments to the present system, if we should weakly and inconsiderately adopt it.

The *bold* and *daring* attempt that has been made to use, for the total annihilation of the states, that power that was delegated for their preservation, will put the different states on their guard. The votaries of ambition and interest being totally defeated in their attempt to establish themselves on the ruins of the states, which they *will be*, if this constitution is rejected, an attempt in which they had more probability of success from the total want of suspicion in their countrymen, than they can have hereafter; they will not hazard a second attempt of the same nature, in which they will have much less chance of success; besides, being once discovered, they will not be confided in. The true interest and happiness of the states and their citizens will, therefore, most probably, be the object, which will be principally sought for by a second convention, should a second be appointed, which, if *really aimed* at, I cannot think very difficult to accomplish, by giving to the federal government sufficient power for every salutary purpose, while the rights of the states and their citizens should be secure from any imminent danger.–But if the arts and influence of ambitious and interested men, even in their present situation, while more on a level with yourselves, and unarmed with any extraordinary powers, should procure you to adopt this system, dangerous as it is admitted to be to your rights, I will appeal to the understanding of every one of you, who will, on this occasion, give his reason fair-play, whether there is not every cause to believe they will, should this government be adopted, with that additional power, consequence and influence it will give them, most easily prevent the necessary alterations which might be wished for, the purpose of which would be directly opposite to their views, and defeat every attempt to procure them.–Be assured, whatever obstacles or difficulties may be at this time in the way of obtaining a proper system of government, they will be increased an hundred fold after this system is adopted.

Reflect also, I entreat you, my fellow-citizens, that the alterations and amendments which are wanted in the present system, are of such a nature as to *diminish* and *lessen*, to *check* and *restrain* the powers of the general government, not to *increase* and *enlarge* those powers:–If they were of the *last* kind, we might safely adopt it, and trust to giving greater powers hereafter, like a Physician who administers an emetick, *ex re nata*, giving a moderate dose at first, and increasing it afterwards as the constitution of the patient may require.–But I appeal to the history of mankind for this truth, *that when once power and authority are delegated to a government, it knows how to keep it, and is sufficiently and successfully fertile in expedients for that purpose:*–Nay more, the whole history of mankind proves, that so far from parting with the powers actually delegated to it, *government is constantly encroaching on the small pittance of rights reserved by the people to themselves, and gradually wresting them out of their hands, until it either terminates in their slavery, or forces them to arms, and brings about a revolution.*

From these observations it appears to me, my fellow-citizens, that nothing can be more weak and absurd, than to accept of a system that is admitted to stand in need of immediate amendments to render your rights secure; for remember, *if you fail in obtaining them, you cannot free yourselves from the yoke you will have placed on your necks, and servitude must, therefore, be your portion!*

Let me ask you, my fellow-citizens, what you would think of a Physician, who, because you were slightly indisposed, should bring you a dose, which properly corrected with other ingredients might be a salutary remedy, but, of itself was a deadly poison, and with great appearance of friendship and zeal, should advise you to swallow it immediately, and trust to accident for those requisites necessary to qualify its malignity, and prevent its destructive effects?–Would not you reject the advice, in however friendly a manner it might appear to be given, with indignation, and insist that he should first procure, and properly attemper, the necessary ingredients, since after the *fatal draught* was once received into your bowels, it would be too late, should the antidote prove unattainable, and death must ensue?–With the same indignation ought you, my fellow-citizens, to reject the advice of those *political quacks*, who, under pretence of healing the disorders of our present government, would urge you *rashly to gulp down* a constitution, which, in its present form, unaltered and unamended, would be as certain death to your liberty, as *arsenick* could be to your bodies.

Baltimore, March 25, 1788.

1. On 25 March the printer of the *Maryland Journal* indicated that the third number of Martin's address to the citizens of Maryland *"will be inserted in our next."* This third address by Martin was not reprinted.

2. See "Aristides" (Alexander Contee Hanson), *Remarks on the Proposed Plan of a Federal Government* . . ., 31 January (CC:490, p. 543).

3. See CC:490, pp. 519–20, 533–36.

4. See CC:490, p. 519.

651. Nicholas Collin to Matthias Hultgren
Philadelphia, 29 March (excerpt)[1]

. . . I have already told you about the New Form of Government which the grand Convention worked out here in Philadelphia last summer. Let Leufvenius,[2] in London, send for a copy of it. Now it has been adopted in this order: by Delaware, Pennsylvania, Jersey, Connecticut, Georgia, Massachusetts: the first and last of these with a small majority. In New Hampshire a convention indeed sat, but as the majority was found to be obstinate, it dissolved and is to meet again in June. Then the State-Conventions in Maryland, Virginia and the Carolinas will meet [also]. N York's meets in April[3]–there it is said to be difficult; likewise in Virginia. When 9 States have ratified, the first Congress will meet–but it cannot have any real power until at least all the large States have acceded. Party spirit is violent, and worst in this State. In Carlisle there has been a riot;[4] and many petitions have been presented to the Assembly against the Constitution.[5] Foederal and antifederal are now in America what hat and cap[6] were in Sweden. Even the better antif—l writers call the new Constitution a conspiracy, and show the public snares and chains in every section of it. It is, however, really good, and gives Congress the power to tax and defend the country, which is absolutely necessary. As has previously been related, I wrote a piece while the Convention was in Session–An essay on the means of promoting foederal Sentiments in the United States of America, by a foreign spectator, with the addition in the last number by a Native of Sweden. It circulated in 30 successive numbers for 2 months around the whole continent.[7] Just before the Convention published its work, I had gotten toward the end and proved that the power they had given Congress, and even some more was entirely necessary. To avoid all suspicion of any collusion, I visited none of its members beforehand, nor was I aware of the least of their proceedings. I wrote as my words were, unasked, unadvised, unbiased. This work pleased the Public and I may have some profit by it during my sojourn here. . . .

1. RC (Tr) (photostat), Amandus Johnson Papers, The Balch Institute for Ethnic Studies, Philadelphia. Printed: Amandus Johnson, *The Journal and Biography of Nicholas Collin, 1746-1831* (Philadelphia, 1936), 122–24. Matthias Hultgren (d. 1809) was rector of the Swedish churches in Pennsylvania from 1780 to 1786, at which time he was replaced by Collin. Hultgren left America in July 1786 and was perhaps in Sweden at the time that this letter was written.

2. Pastor of the Swedish Lutheran Church in London.

3. The election of delegates for the New York Convention was held from 29 April to 3 May. The Convention met on 17 June.

4. For the Carlisle riot, see Philadelphia *Independent Gazetteer*, 4 March (Appendix I).

5. For the petition campaign to overthrow Pennsylvania's ratification of the Constitution, see *Pennsylvania Gazette*, 26 March, note 2 (Appendix I).

6. In 1721 Russia and Sweden signed the Peace of Nystad by which Sweden gave up several Swedish provinces. After the peace Russia tried to intervene in Swedish domestic affairs. In 1738-39 the "Hat" Party, which wanted war with Russia and industrial growth, gained control of the government and called themselves *"hattar"* or "men of

boldness and action." The "hats" called their opponents "*nattmössor*" ("night-caps," or "ninnies"), hence "caps."

7. Between 6 August and 2 October 1787 the Philadelphia *Independent Gazetteer* published twenty-nine unnumbered essays written by Collin under the pseudonym "Foreign Spectator" (CC:124). In the twenty-ninth essay Collin identified himself as a "Native of Sweden." "A Supplement to the Essay on Federal Sentiments," which was unsigned, appeared in the *Gazetteer* on 23 October. In late 1788 Collin revived the series. Twenty-eight numbers were printed in the Philadelphia *Federal Gazette* between 21 October and 16 February 1789, in which Collin argued that the Constitution did not need amendments.

652. James Freeman to Theophilus Lindsey
Boston, 29 March (excerpt)[1]

. . . By this conveyance I send three copies of the debates of the Massachusetts convention,[2] one of which you will please to present to Dr Price, with my most respectful compliments, and another to my friend Mr Hazlitt.[3] The new constitution of government has been almost the sole object which has occupied the minds of the people of these states during several months past. It has kindled the flame of party zeal among us; but it has fortunately in its favour a large majority of the rich, the wise, and the virtuous. You will find the constitution less democratick, than might be expected from a people who are so fond of liberty. Various causes have conspired to render republican sentiments unfashionable; among which may be mentioned Mr J. Adams's publications,[4] a late insurrection in the state of Massachusetts,[5] and the corrupt proceedings of the legislature of Rhode-island.[6] Several states have not yet given their opinion; but the constitution will probably be adopted by eleven at least. It is supposed that New York and Rhode-island will be in the minority. A few of our old patriots fear that the government will terminate in aristocracy or monarchy. It is impossible to foresee what the event will be. I can only pray, that God will preserve us from the tyranny of kings, and the insolence of nobles. Amidst these apprehensions, it affords pleasure to reflect that though civil liberty may possibly lose, yet that religious liberty will certainly gain, by the new constitution. . . .

1. RC, Theophilus Lindsey Papers, Dr. Williams's Library, London, England. The Reverend James Freeman (1759–1835), a 1777 Harvard graduate, had been associated with King's Chapel in Boston since 1782. In 1785 this chapel, the oldest Episcopal church in New England, adopted a reformed liturgy that made it Unitarian. (This liturgy was similar to the one that had been used in the Reverend Theophilus Lindsey's Essex Street Church in London.) In 1786 and 1787 Freeman applied for ordination to the Episcopal bishops of Connecticut and New York but was denied because he refused to express a belief in the Trinity. In November 1787 Freeman was ordained by his own congregation, becoming the first Unitarian minister of King's Chapel. The Reverend Theophilus Lindsey (1723–1808) resigned his Episcopal living in 1773, and in 1774 he opened a chapel in London with the assistance of Joseph Priestley, Richard Price, and others. In 1774 he published a volume adapting *The Book of Common Prayer* to Unitarian doctrine and nine years later he published his *Historical View of the State of the Unitarian Doctrine and Worship from the Reformation to Our Own Time.* . . . Lindsey and Freeman had been corresponding since 1786.

2. On 18 March the *Massachusetts Gazette* announced the publication of a 220-page pamphlet containing the debates, resolutions, and proceedings of the Massachusetts Convention.

3. Richard Price (1723–1791) and William Hazlitt (1737–1820) were both Unitarian clergymen. Price wrote widely on theology, morals, finances, and politics. He supported American independence and the new Constitution (CC:22). Hazlitt, a former Presbyterian minister who studied at the University of Glasgow, lived in Philadelphia and then in Boston, from 1783 to about 1787.

4. For John Adams's *Defence of the Constitutions*, see CC:16, 557.

5. Shays's Rebellion.

6. For the Rhode Island legislature's paper money policies, which were widely criticized, see CC:263, note 7, and CC:269, note 4.

653. Paine Wingate to Timothy Pickering
New York, 29 March (excerpts)[1]

Mr. Hodgdon[2] who is now in this City, informs me that he can frequently transmit letters to you from Philadelphia, and by him I improve this opportunity of writing to you. The distance of your situation from New Hampshire & the difficulty of an intercourse between us has prevented my giving, and I suppose of receiving any direct intelligence from you for a long time. But this seperation has not obliterated my remembrance of or lessoned my affection for you. . . . I have been in New York since Feb. 10[3] & find my situation as agreeable as I could expect considering that I am very domestic & habituated to an active life.–I have nothing very important to communicate to you. The subject which ~~chiefly~~ engages the general attention at this time is the New Constitution. What will be the fate of it is yet uncertain, but those who are well wishers to their country & best know the situation we are in, are the most sensible of the necessity of its adoption; and great pains are taken to obtain the end. On the other hand there are powerful opposers to it, who avail themselves of some popular objections & they are too successful with the less knowing part of the country. In New Hampshire when the Convention met, there was a majority prejudiced against the plan. They were chiefly from the interior parts of the state & many of the delegates were instructed to vote against it. The most distinguished characters were in favor of it & after debating it for sometime there were a few converts made, who did not think themselves at liberty to go against their instructions & therefore obtained an adjournment. There is I think a probability that it will finally be adopted in New Hampshire altho' considerable danger that it will not. New York is very doubtful but it is not despaired of. Virginia & North Carolina are much in the same situation. Maryland & South Carolina are supposed to be fœderal. These two states will decide before the others & if they should agree to adopt, there will be but one of the doubtful ones necessary to make up the nine. The important decision upon the subject cannot be known before the last of July, & at any rate I do not see that the new Constitution can be got to go as early as Dec. next. Nothing but the

hope of a new can I fear keep the old Constitution from dissolution long.–
Sed nunquam de Republica desperandum.–The newspapers are so filled
with lyes that no dependance can be put on any accounts you receive in
them respecting the Constitution–I hope I shall soon have the pleasure of
hearing from you by letter, which direct to me in Congress at New York–
If you have any letters which you wish at any time to forward to Salem or
to any friends Eastward & if you will put them under cover to me, I will
take care of them & send them without hazard or expence to the place of
destination. If Congress should not adjourn which yet is uncertain, it is
likely that I shall remain in this place until Oct. next–

1. RC, Pickering Papers, MHi. Printed: Charles E.L. Wingate, *Life and Letters of
Paine Wingate: One of the Fathers of the Nation* (2 vols., Medford, Mass., 1930), I, 221–24.
Wingate (1739–1838)˙, a Stratham, N.H., farmer, had been a delegate to the state
constitutional convention in 1781 and was serving as a delegate to Congress. He was a
U.S. Senator, 1789–93; a U.S. Representative, 1793–95; and a judge of the New
Hampshire Superior Court, 1798–1809. Wingate was Pickering's brother-in-law, and
the two men had corresponded for many years. Pickering, a native of Salem, Mass.,
had moved to Pennsylvania in 1785.
2. Samuel Hodgdon (d. 1824), a Philadelphia merchant, was Pickering's close friend
and business associate.
3. Wingate was elected to Congress in September 1787 and took his seat on 11 February.

654. Jonathan Williams, Jr., to Alexander John Alexander
Philadelphia, 30 March (excerpt)[1]

. . . The new Constitution is going on well & I dare say will be adopted;
six states have already ratified it, & only six have determined at all. I shall
send you a number of newspapers when I have an Opportunity that will
occasion no expence.–The opposers to the new Government have done
reasoning on the subject, personal invective, ridiculous assertions and declamatory appeals to the Passions, make up the whole composition.[2] I
have frequently asked myself this Question, If this Government will not
secure the Liberties of the people consistent with a due exercise of legislative judicial & executive Powers, what Government can we make that will
do so? Then, after running over the whole field of opposition without finding a single Trait of a consistent plan; I am reduced to the alternative
which is vulgarly called Hobsons choice,[3] & this Government, or none in
Peace is the obvious conclusion. . . .

1. RC, Williams Mss, InU-Li. Alexander, a London merchant, was the uncle of
Williams' wife Mariamne.
2. At about this time, Williams' granduncle Benjamin Franklin drafted an essay
criticizing Philadelphia newspapers for "employing . . . personal accusation, detraction, and calumny." Franklin was upset that "the Spirit of Rancour, Malice, & *Hatred*
. . . breathes" in the city of "Brotherly Love." The essay was never published (Mfm:Pa.
588). For Williams' own newspaper writings, see CC:608.
3. To take what is offered, or nothing.

APPENDIX I

The documents printed in Appendix I are, for the most part, widely circulated squibs or fillers. Most of the squibs are either reports on the prospects of ratification in the various states or speculations about the attitudes of one or more persons on the Constitution. Others are reports of events, followed by some partisan commentary about them. Since Federalists controlled most newspapers, the majority of the squibs favor the Constitution or attack its opponents.

New York Packet, 1 February[1]

Extract of a letter from a gentleman in high office in Kentucky, to his friend in this city, dated Dec. 4, 1787.

"I am a great admirer of the Constitution, planned by the Convention for the United States. I think it will, if adopted, be the means of our salvation; and therefore, I most heartily and sincerely wish it may take place.–I honor in the highest degree the patriots who formed it, and think they deserve to be ranked amongst the greatest friends to mankind, that ever dignified human nature. Perhaps I maybe thought a little extravagant in my encomiums, but I cannot help thinking that every man who views our present state, almost approaching to anarchy, and big with danger to the existence of the Union, together with the situation in which the adoption of that Constitution will in all probability place us, with a judicious and impartial age, will join with me, and perhaps go beyond me."

1. Reprints by 18 February (8): Vt. (1), N.Y. (1), N.J. (1), Pa. (4), Md. (1). In addition the first two sentences were reprinted in the *Pennsylvania Mercury* on 7 February and reprinted five more times by 19 February: Mass. (2), N.Y. (1), Pa. (1), Md. (1).

New York Daily Advertiser, 2 February[1]

By advices from undoubted authority in Poughkeepsie, received last evening, we are informed it remains no longer a doubt, that in the Convention of Massachusetts there is a large majority in favor of the new Constitution; occasioned by a coalition of the Members from the province of Maine with the Federal party.

1. Reprints by 12 February (9): N.Y. (2), N.J. (2), Pa. (4), Md. (1).

False Reports of North Carolina's Ratification of the Constitution, 5 February–5 March

Massachusetts Gazette, 5 February[1]

It is with great satisfaction we announce to the publick the RATIFICATION of the New Constitution by the state of N. CAROLINA.–The intelligence of this happy event was received by capt. Kent, who arrived on Sunday last in ten days from Edenton, in that state. Capt. Kent says, that the ratification was unanimously agreed to on the 25th of Jan.–TWO only dissenting.–This is the SIXTH pillar.

Massachusetts Centinel, 6 February[2]

SIXTH PILLAR raised.

Capt. Kent, who arrived here on Sunday afternoon, in ten days, from Edenton, North-Carolina, brought the pleasing intelligence, that on the 25th of January, the Convention of that State ASSENTED TO, and RATIFIED the FEDERAL CONSTITUTION; with only *two* dissenting voices.

Newport Herald, 14 February[3]

By a vessel arrived here last Tuesday, in five days from North-Carolina, we have a confirmation of the pleasing intelligence of that State's adopting the New Constitution by a very large majority.

New York Journal, 14 February[4]

A last Wednesday's Boston paper announces "the ratification of the constitution by the convention of the state of North-Carolina, on the 25th Jan. with only two dissentients." This account was handed the printer by captain Kent, in ten days from Edenton to Boston.–As our last accounts from North-Carolina mentioned, that the convention was not to meet until July next, it is presumed, that captain Kent was misinformed, or perhaps mistook the house of assembly *appointing a convention*, for the convention *adopting the constitution*.[5]

New Hampshire Mercury, 20 February[6]

By the accession of North-Carolina, seven states have adopted the federal constitution; and shall New-Hampshire, who is so immediately interested, withhold her assent to so noble a structure?–*Forbid it Heaven!*

Pennsylvania Gazette, 5 March[7]

The account of the adoption of the new Fœderal Constitution by the Convention of North-Carolina, said to have been received by way of Rhode-Island, must be a mistake, as the election of a Convention for that state has not yet taken place. We trust, however, that though the paragraph in the Rhode-Island paper is not yet true, there is every reason to expect it will prove to be PROPHETIC.

1. Reprinted on 14 February in the Portland *Cumberland Gazette*, the *Newport Herald*, and the *New Haven Gazette*, and on 20 February in the *New Jersey Journal*.

2. Reprints by 25 February (11): Vt. (1), N.H. (3), Mass. (3), R.I. (1), Conn. (3).

3. Reprints by 7 March (17): N.H. (5), Mass. (9), R.I. (1), N.Y. (1), Pa. (1). The reprint in the *Massachusetts Centinel*, 20 February, was headed: "*SEVENTH PILLAR raised (if true).*" After the reprint, the *Centinel* stated "(*We wait with impatience for an official confirmation of this happy event.*)" Two New Hampshire reprints followed the *Centinel's* example, while the *Pennsylvania Packet*, 4 March, included only the postscript.

4. Reprinted: *Pennsylvania Packet*, 18 February; Poughkeepsie *Country Journal*, 19 February; *Pennsylvania Journal*, 20 February; *Albany Gazette*, 21 February (summary); Boston *American Herald*, 3 March; New Jersey *Brunswick Gazette*, 4 March.

5. On 6 December the North Carolina legislature called a state convention, which was to meet on 21 July. The *New York Journal*, 17 January, reported: "It is said, that North-Carolina convention are not to meet until July next." This report was reprinted five times by 20 February: N.H. (1), Mass. (2), Conn. (1), Pa. (1). The *Maryland Journal*, 29 February, stated that the Convention was scheduled to meet on 17 July. This account was reprinted in the March issue of the nationally circulated Philadelphia *American Museum* and the Philadelphia *Columbian Magazine* and in six newspapers by 27 March: R.I. (1), Conn. (1), Pa. (2), Va. (2). The Philadelphia *Freeman's Journal*, 12 March, printed a satirical Antifederalist letter from James de Caledonia (James Wilson) to James Bowdoin stating "Ha, ha! I find you have had our plan adopted (in your papers) by North-Carolina; when in fact their convention do not meet till July; and all that state is almost opposed to us" (Mfm:Pa. 512). See also CC:647.

6. Reprinted: Exeter, N.H., *Freeman's Oracle*, 22 February.

7. Reprinted: *Pennsylvania Mercury*, 6 March; *New Jersey Journal*, 12 March; *Providence Gazette*, 22 March.

New York Daily Advertiser, 5 February

The population figures printed below, though not so identified by the *Daily Advertiser*, were taken from a speech delivered by Charles Cotesworth Pinckney in the South Carolina House of Representatives on 17 January during a debate on a resolution calling for a state convention to consider the Constitution. Pinckney, a delegate to the Constitutional Convention, explained that the Convention had decided that one branch of Congress should be drawn "immediately from the people and that both wealth and numbers should be considered in the representation." The Convention believed that "the productive labour of the inhabitants was the best rule for ascertaining their wealth." Consequently, "we determined that representatives should be apportioned among the several states, by adding to the whole number of free persons three fifths of the slaves." (Pinckney's speech was printed in the Charleston *City Gazette* on 24 January. For the issue of "Population and Constitution-Making, 1774–1792," see CDR, 297–301.)

Postmaster General Ebenezer Hazard described the population figures in a postscript to his letter to Jedidiah Morse: " 'The Numbers' are copied from a News Paper.–A member of the Convention told me that *such* a Paper had been before that Body;–that it was not deemed *accurate*, but was thought to be as much so as could be expected in present Circumstances. It is curious, singular, & affecting, that the Slaves in the Southern States should be deemed equally numerous with *all* the Inhabitants of N. Hamp. Massa. & R. Island; & that they should make so great a Proportion as near ⅙ of all the Inhabitants of the Union" (14 February, Morse Papers, NHi).

By 3 May the *Daily Advertiser* item was reprinted in the February issue of the Philadelphia *Columbian Magazine* and in twenty-seven newspapers: N.H. (2), Mass. (6), R.I. (2), Conn. (5), N.Y. (3), N.J. (1), Pa. (4), Md. (1), Va. (2), Ga. (1).

The numbers in the different States, according to the most accurate accounts which could be obtained by the late Federal Convention, were as follow:

In New-Hampshire,	102,000
In Massachusetts,	360,000
In Rhode-Island,	58,000
In Connecticut,	202,000
In New York,	238,000
In New-Jersey,[1]	138,000
In Pennsylvania,	360,000
In Delaware,	37,000
In Maryland,	218,000
(including three-fifths of 80,000 Negroes)	
In Virginia,	420,000
(including 3–5ths of 280,000 Negroes)	
In North-Carolina,	200,000
(including three-fifths of 60,000 Negroes)	
In South Carolina,	150,000
(including three-fifths of 80,000 Negroes)	
In Georgia	90,000
(including three-fifths of 20,000 Negroes)	

1. The reprint in the *New York Packet*, 8 February, incorrectly listed New Jersey's population as 130,000. About half of the other reprints made the same mistake.

New York Journal, 5 February[1]

Extract of a letter from Charleston, Jan. 21.

"Saturday the house of representatives took up a report from a committee of the whole on the governer's message, accompanied by the federal constitution, which was unanimously agreed to.

"The house then took up some suplementary articles, when after debate, it was agreed, that an election for delegates should take place on the 11th and 12th days of April, to meet on the 12th of May in Charleston. Gen. Pinckney moved to meet in Charleston: no question in the house of representatives ever ran so close, the yeas being 76 the nays 75."

1. Reprinted: Providence *United States Chronicle*, 21 February; *Boston Gazette*, 25 February; *New Hampshire Mercury*, 27 February. Shorter reports of the calling of the South Carolina Convention appeared in the New York *Daily Advertiser* and *New York Journal* on 5 and 7 February, respectively. These reports were widely reprinted. See also "Reports of South Carolina's Call of a Convention," 21–25 February (Appendix I, below).

New York Packet, 5 February[1]

We are informed, from good authority, that the anti-fœderal interest is declining in the Massachusetts Convention; and, that that party finding this to be the case, moved for the general question; which motion was over-ruled by a majority of nearly two to one.[2] The Convention, therefore, continued debating upon the proposed constitution, by paragraphs, with much candor, information, judgment and ingenuity. Many mem-

bers, who came to the Convention, with prepossessions against the constitution, it is said, now candidly confess, that they have been deceived by
representations and arguments, calculated to inflame the mind, and pervert the judgment; and which, when impartially examined, vanish into air
before the scrutinizing eye of TRUTH. The best of men may be deceived by
specious reasonings, offered under the affected shew of patriotism: But
how worthy of a free man, in the exercise of his faculties, to relinquish
ERROR, when convinced–disdaining to persist in opposition, from a mere
spirit of contradiction, to the clearest dictates of propriety, common sense,
and the *public good.*

1. Reprints by 7 March (9): N.Y. (2), Pa. (4), Md. (2), Va. (1).
2. On 23 January Samuel Nasson, an Antifederalist delegate from Sanford, Maine,
moved "That this Convention, so far reconsider their former vote to discuss the Constitution by paragraphs, as to leave the subject at large open for consideration." After
some debate, Nasson withdrew his motion but promised to make it again the next day.
On the 24th Nasson renewed his motion which was defeated (*Massachusetts Centinel*, 9,
13 February).

Newburyport Essex Journal, 6 February[1]

*Extract of a letter from a gentleman in Charleston, South-Carolina to his friend in
this town, dated the 20th ult.*

"We are looking forward with great impatience for the adoption of the
Federal Constitution–it has lately been fully discussed in our House of
Assembly; and from the disposition of the people, we have not the smallest
doubt of its being adopted by this state–It will be of infinite advantage to
the Eastern states; for the policy of the federal government will doubtless
lead them to give a determined preference, if not an exclusive privilege, to
the vessels of America, to the carrying of its own produce; should that be
the case, we shall want annually, to export the produce of this state, from
20 to 25,000 tons of shipping, which, from the present situation of America, must be provided from the three Eastern states."

1. Reprinted: *New Hampshire Spy*, 8 February; *Newport Herald*, 21 February.

Boston Independent Chronicle, 7 February[1]

By a vessel which arrived at Salem on Sunday last, from South-Carolina, we hear that the New Constitution meets with general approbation
in that State, and that the Legislature thereof have issued writs for calling
a Convention, to meet on the 2d of March[2] next, at Charleston, to consider the proposed Federal Constitution.

1. Reprints by 16 February (12): N.H. (2), Mass. (4), R.I. (3), Conn. (3).
2. The South Carolina Senate had proposed that the state convention meet on 3
March. The House of Representatives, however, favored a later date, and the legislature scheduled the convention to convene on 12 May. None of the reprints corrected
the error.

Newport Herald, 7 February[1]

⟨A Correspondent observes, that no State in the Union hath such *interested motives* for adopting the NEW CONSTITUTION as this State. The chief dependance of our *Farmers, Merchants and Tradesmen, is the carrying trade, and a free entry of beef; barley, cheese, New-England rum, and our manufactured goods into our Sister States.* But these advantages we are unjustly deprived of for want of a Federal Power to control and equalize commerce. Most of the States have long had imposts on our exports to them, whether foreign or the growth and manufacture of this country.⟩[2] Virginia, by a late act,[3] have laid new duties, the particulars of which we are favored with, in a letter from a gentleman at Alexandria, dated the 8th of January, as follow:

⟨"Duties to take place in Virginia the 1st of March 1788.–
American articles.

New-England Rum 1*s*. per gal. Loaf and lump Sugar 3*d*. per lb. Dressed Leather 6*d*. lb. Tanned ditto 4*d*. lb. Cheese 2*d*. lb. Butter 4*d*. lb. Candles 4*d*. lb. Soap 4*d*. lb. Cordage 4*s*. cwt. Bar Iron 4*s*. cwt. Hollow Ware 4*s*. cwt. Nail Rods 6*s*. cwt. Axes 8*s*. per doz. Hoes 6*s*. doz. Mens and Womens Shoes 1*s*1 per pair. Salt Beef 20*s*. cwt. Pork 20*s*. cwt.

Foreign articles.

Brandy and other distilled Spirits 1*s*. per gal. Madeira Wine 1*s*6. gal. Other Wines 1*s*. gal. Porter 9*d*. gal. Pepper 6*d*. lb. Other Spices 4*d*. Bohea Tea 1*s*. Other Teas 2*s*."

These duties are so high as to amount almost to a prohibition–Not content with thus excluding us from a share in commerce, they suffer the British to outrival us in carrying their produce to market. Confederate States thus divided against themselves cannot stand.⟩[4] Our interest, our honor, and our liberty, all depend on our adopting the NEW CONSTITUTION–reject it and we fall.

1. Reprints by 22 March (6): N.H. (2), Mass. (1), Conn. (1), S.C. (1), Ga. (1). See also notes 2 and 4.
2. The text in angle brackets was reprinted eight times by 9 April: N.Y. (1), N.J. (1), Pa. (3), Md. (1), Va. (2).
3. This act, passed on 7 January 1788, was entitled "An act to amend the several acts of Assembly concerning naval officers and the collection of the Duties" (William Waller Hening, ed., *The Statutes at Large; Being a Collection of All the Laws of Virginia* . . . [13 vols., Richmond, 1809–1823], XII, 438–52).
4. The text in angle brackets was reprinted three times by 18 March: Mass. (1), Conn. (1), Md. (1).

New York Journal, 7 February[1]

The last intelligence from Boston, is, that the convention had made but little progress in their herculian task, having proceeded no farther than the first article of the constitution. Upon an arithmatical calculation, should each member, in that hon. body, be allowed *one hour* only to deliver his sentiments, reckoning six hours of speaking per day, the time thus spent would amount to SIXTY-ONE days.–It is said, that unless a seat be taken up early in the morning, in the house where the convention set (which will contain near 4000 persons) there is no possibility of crowding in.[2]

1. Reprinted: *Pennsylvania Packet*, 11 February; *Pennsylvania Mercury*, 12 February; Philadelphia *Freeman's Journal* and *Pennsylvania Journal*, 13 February; New Jersey *Brunswick Gazette* and Baltimore *Maryland Gazette*, 19 February; Winchester *Virginia Gazette*, 29 February (excerpt).

2. According to Henry Jackson of Boston, the gallery could hold 600–800 spectators (to Henry Knox, 20 January, Knox Papers, MHi).

New York Journal, 7 February[1]

Extract of a letter from Connecticut, Jan. 28.

"Notwithstanding the convention of this state have adopted the new constitution, you may rely upon it, that its adoption was not the voice of the people, by a great majority; neither would it have gone down in convention, had not some of its most artful members had recourse to every sophistical reason they were masters of, to deceive the less designing, and dragoon them into it."

1. Reprinted: New York *Daily Advertiser*, 8 February; Poughkeepsie *Country Journal*, 12 February; Philadelphia *Freeman's Journal*, 13 February; Annapolis *Maryland Gazette*, 21 February.

Pennsylvania Herald, 7 February[1]

Various letters from Virginia concur in declaring, that the example of the states which have already ratified the new constitution, has converted most of the disciples of mr. Mason, mr. Lee, mr. Gerry, &c.

1. Reprinted: *Pennsylvania Journal*, 9 February; *Maryland Journal*, 15 February; Newburyport *Essex Journal* and *Virginia Independent Chronicle*, 27 February; Exeter, N.H., *Freeman's Oracle*, 29 February.

New York Daily Advertiser, 8 February[1]

Extract of a letter from a gentleman in Boston, dated Jan. 30, to his friend in this city.

"The Convention has now proceeded as far as the 2d section of the 3d article, and by Tuesday next I suppose the business will be brought to a close. I am happy in informing you, that, from the most accurate calculation that has been made, there is a majority of *Thirty* in favor of the Constitution. Some of the Delegates, who were instructed by the towns they represented to vote against it at all events, have returned home and informed their constituents, that so much light had been thrown upon the subject, that they could not, as honest men, hold up their hands in opposition to the Constitution. The towns have sent them back, and directed them to vote as they thought best. The famous Bacon,[2] who has so often altered his mind, is now fully perswaded that we had better adopt it; so that, upon the whole, I have not the least doubt of its being ratified by a very considerable majority.

"The Governor made his appearance for the first time to-day; and as he is very popular, and has openly declared himself in favor of the Constitution, I make no doubt it will be the means of making many proselytes.[3] No new faces appear in the Convention against the plan of Government, and the opposers are daily diminishing. When this great and important business is determined, I shall duly advise you; and I am fully persuaded that I shall soon be able to inform you, that the honest yeomanry of Massachusetts have ratified and confirmed the Federal Constitution."

1. This letter was also printed in the *New York Packet* on 8 February. It was reprinted ten times by 7 March: N.Y. (1), N.J. (1), Pa. (5), Va. (3).

2. John Bacon (1738-1820), a farmer, was a justice of the peace and of the quorum. He represented Stockbridge in the Massachusetts House of Representatives and Senate intermittently from 1780 to 1806.

3. For Hancock's role in the state Convention, see CC:508.

Pennsylvania Mercury, 9 February[1]

The *antifederal junto*, in this city, hoped that they had found *one* convention, whose sentiments were congenial to their own–but alas! the latest accounts from Massachusetts have brought them *heavy* tidings; it appears that they have no *real* friends in that convention, except about *sixty*, who were, last winter, enrolled under the banners of SHAYS.[2]

1. Reprinted: Hartford *American Mercury*, 25 February; Newburyport *Essex Journal* and *Virginia Independent Chronicle*, 27 February; Exeter, N.H., *Freeman's Oracle* and Winchester *Virginia Gazette*, 29 February.

2. See also *Pennsylvania Gazette*, 12 March (Appendix I, below).

Connecticut Courant, 11 February[1]

Extract of a letter from a gentleman, of good observation and the best information, to his friend in this State, dated in England, 15th October 1787.

"I hope your internal commotions are at an end–Tumult at present extends her reign over the Eastern world. Turkey is threatened with a most formidable attack from the two empires–the war is begun–the other powers of Europe are interested in this quarrel, and must soon choose sides according to their interests–Great preparations are making for war in this country; France is doing the same–and amidst reiterated assurances of peaceable intentions, each party is straining every nerve, in the most rapid hostile preparations.–The storm must soon burst, and happy are ye if ye escape being hurried into its vortex. You may be assured that enmity to your country exists still in this quarter of the world, and opportunity is only wanting to display it. The hopes of your enemies are not unreasonably grounded, on your follies–your disunion–your disaffection to government, and a reverse of system is your only security; I hope this will take place, in consequence of the deliberations of your convention, and that whatever they recommend will be adopted. You can by no possible means procure more wisdom or integrity of counsel, and if ye neglect or cavil at this, your only remaining expectations of reform must be from necessity or accident, two hopeless sources. Of one thing be assured, the spirit of union, and the energy of good government never has been; perhaps on no future occasion will be, more necessary than at this hour–The country (France) which once protected you, is torn with dissentions, and un-nerved–that which hates you (England) is unanimous, and on tiptoe for war and revenge; your present conduct is eagerly watched–your future security depends on unanimity and energy."

1. Reprints by 20 March (9): N.H. (3), Mass. (1), R.I. (2), Conn. (2), Pa. (1).

New York Daily Advertiser, 11 February[1]

Extract of a letter from a gentleman in Boston, dated, Feb. 3, 1788

"Our Convention will pass the Federal Government by a considerable Majority. The more it is examined, the more Converts are made for its adoption.–This you may rely on."

1. Reprinted: *New York Packet*, 12 February; *Pennsylvania Packet*, 13 February; *Pennsylvania Mercury*, 14 February; Annapolis *Maryland Gazette*, 21 February.

Springfield Hampshire Chronicle, 13 February[1]

We have a right to assure the publick, from indisputable authority, that the Honourable ELBRIDGE GERRY openly declares, that notwithstanding he has uniformly opposed the adoption of the Constitution by this State, he now, since its ratification by a respectable Majority, considers it as his and the duty of every honest man in the community, to give it all the support in his power; and that he himself will certainly use his influence for this purpose.

1. Reprints by 27 March (10): Vt. (2), N.H. (1), Mass. (1), N.Y. (2), Pa. (3), N.C. (1). Similar reports of Gerry's conversion appeared in the *Pennsylvania Gazette*, 27 February, which was reprinted in the New York *Daily Advertiser*, 5 March, and the Richmond *Virginia Gazette and Weekly Advertiser*, 13 March. It was also paraphrased in the Winchester *Virginia Gazette*, 14 March.

Massachusetts Centinel, 13 February[1]

Extract of a letter from a gentleman in New-York, to his friend in this town, dated February 3, 1788.

"The Assembly of this State, carried the question last Thursday, for a Convention, to meet at Poughkeepsie, on the third Tuesday in June next–the resolution on this subject, recites the resolves of Congress of the 28th September[2]–The majority 27–minority 25. The senate will also be for it, by a small majority.–Some amendments to the resolve were attempted, with the view of subjecting the Constitution to amendments by the State Convention–but were frustrated–the majority 29–minority 23.

"By recent advices from Dutchess, Montgomery and Albany counties, the federal cause gains strength daily. It is said Mr. Samuel Chace, has withdrawn his opposition, in Maryland, and that the Constitution will be adopted there, without material opposition.

"Since closing my letter, I have been informed, that on Friday, the Senate concurred with the House, respecting the Convention to be held in June next."

1. Reprints by 28 February (10): N.H. (1), Mass. (6), R.I. (2), Conn. (1).
2. For the congressional resolution of 28 September submitting the Constitution to the states, see CC:95.

Philadelphia Freeman's Journal, 13 February[1]

Extract of a letter from Charleston (S.C.) *Jan.* 22.

"As to the New Constitution, I hope and think it will be adopted with amendments by this State; but the opposition is heavy and increasing. The Convention meets on the 12th of May–76 against 75 for meeting at Charleston. Our assembly, senate, &c. move up next January to Columbia, 150 miles back, where there is a State-house building. The country interest prevails over the mercantile in this State; this will operate strongly against the new constitution, as the farmers (who are rather contracted) entertain jealousies that it is a scheme to favor the mercantile interest; however, we will have most of the orators with us, and the influence of the town."

1. Reprints by 20 March (12): N.H. (1), Mass. (3), N.Y. (2), N.J. (1), Pa. (2), Md. (2), Va. (1). (See "Reports of South Carolina's Call of a Convention," 21–25 February, Appendix I, below.)

New Haven Gazette, 14 February[1]

On Monday last at 5 o'clock, P.M. arrived in this city authentic intelligence of the ratification of the Constitution by the convention of Massachusetts.–On this pleasing and important event the bells were rung and a salute of 13 rounds was fired, followed by three huzzas from a large concourse of people who had assembled on the occasion and testified their hearty approbation of the conduct of their good old friend and neighbour, who is so nearly allied to Connecticut in good sense and sound republican principles.–It was a pleasing circumstance that the hon. Rufus King Esq. arrived here on his way from Boston to New-York, while the salute was firing, and was a witness to the joy excited among us by the conduct of his native state.[2]

1. Reprints by 24 March (13): N.H. (2), Mass. (4), N.Y. (2), Pa. (4), S.C. (1).
2. King, a Federalist leader, had voted to ratify the Constitution in the Massachusetts Convention on 6 February.

Newport Herald, 14 February[1]

SEVEN STATES[2] have ratified the NEW CONSTITUTION.–New-Hampshire Convention are now in session, South-Carolina meets the 3d of March;[3] from authentic intelligence we are informed that both these States will adopt it by large majorities–Maryland meets the last of April–Virginia in June–New-York Assembly have 'ere this recommended a Convention.–From this state of the progress of the New Constitution, sound policy dictates to the leading members of our administration to recommend the appointment of a Convention as speedily as possible, and to exert their influence in the adoption of it.–Great good may they expect from this change of measures–for their systems are too much deranged to encourage *perseverance*, and their powers are too languid to be rendered efficient–this step of repentance will be a mantle to cover in oblivion many secret crimes, and a virtue which will obliterate many foul stains. Various are the opinions what will be the policy of our leading characters in government–Whatever it may be, this observation will ever be indisputable, that a perseverance in unfederalism will bring on this State the merited punishment for our national degeneracy, and establish us as a monumental example of the truth of that adage, *"Those whom* GOD *wills for destruction he first makes mad."*[4]

1. Reprints by 1 March (15): N.H. (3), Mass. (4), R.I. (1), N.Y. (2), N.J. (2), Pa. (3).

2. The editor of the *Herald* reported that North Carolina had ratified the Constitution, the sixth state to do so. Massachusetts was, therefore, the seventh. (See "False Reports of North Carolina's Ratification of the Constitution," 5 February–5 March, Appendix I, above.)

3. The South Carolina Convention was scheduled to convene on 12 May. See Boston *Independent Chronicle*, 7 February, note 2 (Appendix I, above).

4. Ascribed to Euripides and to Horace, although specific reference has not been located.

New York Packet, 15 February[1]

In consequence of the intelligence from Boston, of the ratification of the Fœderal Constitution by the State Convention of Massachusetts, the Fœderalists of New-York, yesterday testified their joy on the pleasing event. At sun rise a standard of the United States was hoisted on the Coffee-house, in which was inserted the following words–*"The Constitution, September 17th, 1787."* And at noon, another flag was displayed at the same place, in which was exhibited the figure of a pine tree, and these words–*"February 9, 88. Boston."* The standard of the Union was likewise displayed at the Fort, and the American vessels in the harbor hoisted their colours on the occasion.–At twelve o'clock, *six times thirteen guns* were discharged, in honor of the *six States* that have already ratified the Constitution, which were answered by *thirteen* guns from the ship Jenny, Capt. Thomson, bound for the East-Indies.

The joy and satisfaction exhibited by a *great majority* of the inhabitants of New-York, on this auspicious event, will certainly convince our brethren in the sister States, that this State cherishes in her bosom, many virtuous citizens, who most ardently wish for a government calculated *"to form a more perfect Union, establish justice, insure domestic tranquility, provide for the common defence, promote the general welfare, and secure the blessings of liberty to ourselves and our posterity."*

1. Reprints by 24 March (25): Vt. (2), N.H. (2), Mass. (8), R.I. (2), Conn. (6), N.Y. (2), Pa. (3). Five of the reprints omitted the second paragraph. For other accounts of New York City's celebration of Massachusetts' ratification, see the New York *Independent Journal*, 16 February (immediately below); New York *Daily Advertiser*, 15, 18 February; and *Massachusetts Centinel*, 27 February.

New York Independent Journal, 16 February[1]

We are happy in having it in our power to communicate to our readers the authentic and agreeable intelligence, of the adoption of the New Constitution by the State of Massachusetts.

The friends of America will no doubt consider this event as a most propitious omen of the rising prospect of American greatness, when they consider that a SIXTH State has already ratified a Constitution, which, in its formation, has employed the wisdom of the most distinguished patriots of the Thirteen States; and which, when candidly examined in all its parts, by the representatives of six of these States, has been found to be well calculated to promote unity, peace and harmony throughout the whole.

Upon the arrival of this agreeable intelligence in this City, the inhabitants in general discovered every appeerence of heartfelt joy.–At sun-rise on Thursday, an elegant flag was hoisted at the Coffee-house, in which the following words were inserted, *The Constitution, September* 17, 1787. At noon another flag representing a Pine Tree, appeared at the same place, with these words, *Boston, February* 9, 1788. At twelve o'clock six times thirteen guns were fired, in honour of the six States that had already adopted the Constitution. A Union Flag was displayed at the Fort, and the different vessels in the harbour discovered every appearance of rejoicing, by hoisting their flags.

When we consider that this constitution has in every State where it has been hitherto examined, been readily adopted, and that by a respectable majority, we have great reason to hope that the time is not far distant, when the Americans being represented by one general and permanent Government, will speedily rise to that dignity and consequence amongst the nations of the world, as must always attend a free, virtuous and powerful people.

1. Reprinted: *Pennsylvania Packet*, 22 February; Baltimore *Maryland Gazette*, 26 February; *Pennsylvania Gazette*, 27 February; *Norfolk and Portsmouth Journal*, 5 March; *State Gazette of North Carolina*, 27 March. The last paragraph alone was reprinted in the *Pennsylvania Mercury*, 11 March; *Maryland Journal*, 18 March, extra; *Virginia Centinel* and Winchester *Virginia Gazette*, 2 April. This paragraph was paraphrased and incorporated in an article in the *Massachusetts Centinel*, 8 March (Appendix I, below). The *Pennsylvania Journal*, 23 February, reprinted the first, second, and fourth paragraphs while substituting the *New York Packet's* account of the celebration (see 15 February, Appendix I, immediately above).

Accounts from England, 18 February–22 March

Pennsylvania Packet, 18 February[1]

Extract of a letter from an American Gentleman in London, dated Nov. 14, 1787.

"The federal constitution deserves that countenance and those exertions, which all cool and considerate men will, I hope, continue to give it. Mr. A—, after a thorough examination of the plan, although he wishes some parts of it had been built differently, and he thinks need a little amendment, approves, recommends, and hopes the same will be *unanimously adopted.*[2] Every *learned, good* and great man here, who is a well-wisher to our country, applauds the federal constitution, and only fears the people will be misled and not adopt it."

Philadelphia Freeman's Journal, 20 February[3]

Accounts from England by the last packet inform us, that they had received our newly proposed constitution, and that it was generally condemned by the real friends to mankind; that the old American whigs there, say, that from the extreme of liberty, we are rushing into the bonds of slavery; that our big men among us have taken advantage of our distresses to force on us a government which will enable them to lord it over us, at their pleasure, and riot on the spoils of our property; and that the Constitution is so plausibly, and at the same time so artfully framed as to require men of the first abilities and knowledge to unriddle and unravel *all* its latent and gilded evils.

Philadelphia Independent Gazetteer, 21 February[4]

The same accounts say, that the *British merchants* are very much pleased with this scheme of government; they are laughing in their sleeves, at the prospect of now having it in their power to collect all their *old American debts with interest*: for foreigners are by the 2d article of the new constitution, allowed to sue in the courts of Congress, and to drag the citizens of America from the remotest parts of the continent, *on an appeal* to the *supreme court* at the national seat of government, where jury trial in civil cases is abolished: hitherto juries have been favorable to fellow citizens, they have considered their distresses; but a court of law will not attend to *such trifles*. The British merchants like the tenth section of article the 1st, also, very much–which puts it out of the power of any of the states passing any instalment laws, or any laws to ease unfortunate debtors, or prevent the selling of our property (*these hard times*) for the benefit of British creditors.

Pennsylvania Gazette, 27 February[5]

We are authorised to assure the public, that the letter from London, of 4th December 1787, published in our last,[6] which speaks of the new Constitution as much approved by all our countrymen in England, and by every friendly Englishman there, is from an American gentleman in the employment of the United States, now in that capital. We are requested to insert this paragraph, because one of an opposite nature appeared lately in one of the public news papers of this city.

Massachusetts Centinel, 1 March[7]

It is with much pleasure we learn, that the opinion of that able statesman, his Excellency JOHN ADAMS, our late Ambassadour at the Court of London, on the federal Constitution, is decidedly in its favour: This information is the more pleasing, as we are now confirmed in a sentiment we have long entertained, that not one of those AMERICAN PATRIOTS, with whose names and actions the history of the eighteenth century will be embellished and enriched, are opposed to the Constitution now under the consideration of THE PEOPLE of America.

Charleston City Gazette, 22 March[8]

Mr. Adams, says an English paper, has given his sentiments in favor of the plan of government drawn up by the convention. He approves it because of its approach to the English constitution; and clearly proves, that in every republican state, the power has been vested in a something like king, lords and commons, though under different names. Every form of government has its imperfections, and the Americans now begin to think that they cannot make one which is perfect–because it must be composed of men who are not so.

1. Reprints by 31 March (16): N.H. (2), Mass. (4), R.I. (2), N.Y. (2), N.J. (1), Pa. (2), Md. (1), Va. (1), S.C. (1). The extract was taken from a letter from John Brown Cutting to Tench Coxe, 14 November, 4 December (CC:Vol. 2, Appendix II, and CC:531). Cutting had served briefly in 1787 as "ministerial amanuensis" to John Adams–minister plenipotentiary to Great Britain.

2. On 10 November, Adams wrote Thomas Jefferson that he had reservations about the Constitution, but concluded, "still I hope the Constitution will be adopted, and amendments be made at a more convenient opportunity" (CC:Vol. 2, Appendix II). For Adams's public statement concerning the Constitution and the need for amendments, see CC:557.

3. Reprints by 8 April (11): N.H. (1), Mass. (2), R.I. (2), N.Y. (2), Pa. (2), Md. (1), Va. (1). A paragraph was added in the Philadelphia Independent Gazetteer's reprint on 21 February (see immediately below).

4. This item was preceded by a reprint of the paragraph from the Freeman's Journal, 20 February (immediately above), and the combined paragraphs were reprinted in the New York Journal and the New York Morning Post, 25 February; the Boston American Herald, 6 March; the Providence Gazette, 15 March; and the Newport Mercury, 31 March.

5. Reprinted: New York Packet, 4 March; Richmond Virginia Gazette and Weekly Advertiser, 13 March; Providence Gazette, 15 March; State Gazette of South Carolina, 17 March; Winchester Virginia Gazette, 19 March.

6. The Pennsylvania Gazette had reprinted the extract from John Brown Cutting's letter on 20 February. No reference to the 4th of December had appeared in print, however. Perhaps the Gazette had access to the recipient's copy of the letter to Tench Coxe dated 14 November and 4 December since Coxe was a frequent contributor to the Gazette and other Philadelphia newspapers. (See note 1 above.)

7. Reprints by 2 April (13): Vt. (1), N.H. (1), Mass. (1), N.Y. (3), Pa. (3), Md. (1), Va. (3).

8. Reprinted: Charleston *Columbian Herald*, 24 March; Richmond *Virginia Gazette and Weekly Advertiser*, 24 April; Baltimore *Maryland Gazette*, 29 April. This item was first printed in a London newspaper at about the time that the last volume of Adams's *Defence of the Constitutions* was published. This volume contained Adams's comments on the new American Constitution (see CC:557. For a full discussion of the *Defence*, see CC:16.).

Massachusetts Gazette, 19 February[1]

The convention of New-York are to meet on the 17th of June–the anniversary of a period ever memorable to the citizens of America. May the members of the convention be actuated by motives equally noble and patriotick as those which stimulated the free born sons of Columbia, on the 17th of June, 1775,[2] to sacrifice their lives on the alter of freedom, in impeding the hostile encroachments of a despotick minion, and a band of British hirelings, upon the rights and properties of the inhabitants of this western world.

1. Reprints by 26 March (9): Mass. (1), N.Y. (3), N.J. (2), Pa. (3).
2. The reference is to the Battle of Bunker Hill.

Massachusetts Centinel, 20 February[1]
NEW-HAMPSHIRE CONVENTION.

By a gentleman who arrived in town yesterday from Exeter, we are informed, that the Convention of New-Hampshire, then in session in that place, had chosen for President, his Excellency JOHN SULLIVAN, Esq. and had proceeded to the discussion of the Constitution in the manner as in this Commonwealth; that from the complexion of the Convention, it was thought a considerable majority were in favour of the adoption of the Constitution, although a number of the towns had bound their delegates by instructions to vote against it–That the hon. Mr. Langdon, Judge Livermore, and a number of other able men, were warm advocates for it–and that Gen. Peabody, who had been supposed to be against it, had expressed himself in favour of its adoption, rather than to reject it.–On the whole, from the information we have been enabled to collect, and we have spared no pains to acquire it, we venture to predict, that the New-Hampshire Pillar will, in the course of a few days, be added as another supporter of the FEDERAL SUPERSTRUCTURE.

A gentleman from New-York assures us, that notwithstanding reports to the contrary, thirty-nine fortieths of the people of that city are in favour of the adoption of the federal Constitution: The opposers consisting only of a small group of salary-men.

All the States, except Rhode-Island, have called Conventions–and as the Assembly of that State is to meet next week, it is expected that she will not remain an exception to the measure–Should it be the case, it will be a very pleasureable event–for, saith the scripture, *there is more joy over one sinner that repenteth, than, &c.* [2]

1. The first paragraph was reprinted twenty-one times by 26 March: N.H. (1), Mass. (1), R.I. (2), Conn. (4), N.Y. (4), N.J. (2), Pa. (4), Md. (1), Va. (1), S.C. (1). The second paragraph was reprinted sixteen times by 29 March: N.H. (4), Mass. (2), R.I. (2), Conn. (2), N.Y. (1), Pa. (2), Md. (1), Va. (1), S.C. (1). The third paragraph was reprinted seventeen times by 17 March: Vt. (1), N.H. (3), Mass. (2), R.I. (1), Conn. (2), N.Y. (2), N.J. (2), Pa. (3), Md. (1). Eight newspapers reprinted all three paragraphs by 7 March: N.H. (1), Mass. (1), R.I. (1), Conn. (1), N.Y. (1), Pa. (2), Md. (1).

2. Luke 15:10.

Philadelphia Freeman's Journal, 20 February [1]

It appears that notwithstanding the province of Main was gained over by the promise of a separate state, yet there would have been a decided majority in the convention of Massachusetts against the new constitution, if it had not been for the *deceptive amendments* included in the ratification. The members for, were 187, against 168, majority 19–so that had ten of the majority voted against it, the constitution would have been rejected by that state; which it appears was the wish of above three-fourths of its inhabitants. The rejoicings of the town of Boston on this occasion, is similar to those of the people of Sweden, when (tired of the oppressions of an aristocratic senate) they made their king *absolute*.

1. Reprinted: Philadelphia *Independent Gazetteer*, 21 February; *New York Journal*, 23 February; *Maryland Journal*, 26 February; Boston *American Herald*, 6 March.

Pennsylvania Gazette, 20 February [1]

On Saturday last, upon the arrival of the news of the Ratification of the Fœderal Constitution by the powerful state of Massachusetts, the Bells of Christ-Church were rung, and Congratulations of Joy have appeared in every part of the City for several days past.

The conventions of Delaware, New-Jersey and Georgia, says a correspondent, adopted the new constitution unanimously.–There all was harmony. The minorities of the Connecticut and Massachusetts conventions acquiesced in the just authority of the majority, and all was harmony between the two sides of the question. Let us then in Pennsylvania support the honor of our state, by giving to each other the right hand of mutual regard, and making the kindest use of the time to come, which is yet dishonored by no dissentions.

The convention of New-Hampshire were to assemble the 13th instant. In that happy state, both parties, which formerly were warm, are most cordially united in favor of the new constitution.

The states which have already adopted the fœderal constitution contain a majority of *the free persons* of the United States, [2] and, what is a still more comfortable reflexion, are two thirds of the number which is necessary to render the government efficient. When we recollect that all but Rhode-Island have called a convention, and all the conventions, who have deter-mined, have given their fiat to the constitution, we cannot doubt that the next fœderal year[3] will commence with all the thirteen states united in the new confederacy.

Advices from Europe inform us, that the unfortunate Dutch patriots are miserably harrassed and insulted by the Orange party.[4] The new constitution of the United States, we think, will be found a blessing to many of the unfortunate friends to liberty in that distracted country.

The friends of the United States in England, whether Americans or Britons, are strong in their approbation of the new constitution.[5]

1. Reprints: 1st paragraph sixteen times by 31 March–Vt. (1), N.H. (3), Mass. (6), R.I. (2), Md. (2), Va. (1), N.C. (1); 2nd paragraph seven times by 3 May–N.Y. (1), N.J. (2), Pa. (4); 3rd paragraph three times by 27 February–N.Y. (1), N.J. (1), Md. (1); 4th paragraph five times by 3 March–R.I. (1), N.Y. (1), N.J. (1), Md. (2); 5th paragraph fourteen times by 25 March–N.H. (3), Mass. (5), N.Y. (1), N.J. (1), Pa. (1), Md. (2), Va. (1); and 6th paragraph eleven times by 25 March–N.H. (3), Mass. (1), R.I. (1), Conn. (1), N.Y. (1), N.J. (1), Md. (2), Va. (1).

2. See the population estimates printed in the New York *Daily Advertiser*, 5 February (Appendix I, above). The Census of 1790, however, counted 3,052,587 free persons in the United States and 1,417,354 in the six states that first ratified the Constitution. (See CDR, 297–301.)

3. The Articles of Confederation stipulated that Congress was to meet "on the first Monday in November in every year" (CDR, 87), which became the first day of the federal year.

4. For a discussion of Dutch politics, see CC:560, note 8.

5. At this point the reprint in the *Massachusetts Centinel*, 5 March, added: "This is true." Two of the three New Hampshire reprints followed the *Centinel's* example. (See "Accounts from England," 18 February–22 March, Appendix I, above.)

Newport Herald, 21 February[1]

The enemies of the New Constitution, says a Correspondent, consist of jealous, and uninformed characters, who oppose it for conscience sake.

Ambitious men, who aspire after unbounded popularity.–And last of all,

The indolent, the abandoned and the offscouring of the earth, who have no prospects but in a state of anarchy, where marauders, freebooters and knaves are licensed and encouraged.

1. Reprinted: *Boston Gazette*, 25 February; *New Hampshire Mercury*, 27 February; *Pennsylvania Packet*, 6 March; *Pennsylvania Journal*, 8 March; *Albany Gazette*, 13 March; *Virginia Independent Chronicle*, 19 March.

Reports of South Carolina's Call of a Convention
21–25 February

Newport Herald, 21 February[1]

By Capt. John Cahoone, who arrived here on Monday last, in seven days from Charlestown, we are favored with papers to the 11th Feb. instant, from which we have extracted the following intelligence.

The Assembly of South-Carolina, in taking up the proceedings of the Federal Convention, in order to recommend the appointment of Delegates to meet in Convention to consider of the New Constitution, entered into a lengthy and desultory conversation on its merits. A Mr. Lowndes appears the principal and only opponent to it: but the arguments he offered against it must operate strongly with these northern States to immediately ratify it.[2] The advantages these States would derive from becoming favored carriers of their produce, he conceived injurious to the southern interest, and this nursery of northern seamen would still add to the balance of power; but various members spoke with great liberality on those objections–On the union depended their existence. The northern States were able to protect, and certainly protection merited every advantages from commerce.

From the debates it appears that the question was not whether they should recommend the appointment of delegates to meet, &c. as it was granted on all sides, "that the Constitution must be submitted to a convention of the people;" but the question was in what place they should meet.–On the motion being put for the Convention to assemble in Charlestown on Monday the 12th of May next, it passed in the affirmative, by a majority of one. The reason of the division on this question, was, that the minority, who lived in other towns, wished it might assemble with them.

We are thus particular, as some persons, from not attending to the manner the question was put, supposed that there was so large a number against the assembling of a Convention, while it was only against the place of meeting.[3]

Massachusetts Centinel, 23 February[4]

By a vessel arrived here from Charlestown, South-Carolina, we have received papers to Jan. 26–By them it appears, that the Senate, Jan. 17, resolved, that the Convention of that State should meet on the *third* of March–In the same papers it appears, that the House of Representatives had resolved, that it should meet the 12th of May, nor does it appear, that either branch had concurred with the other–But if we may hazard a conjecture from the circumstance that all the representatives, save Mr. Lowndes, were in favour of the Constitution, we will venture to suppose, that a concurrence with the vote of the Senate took place–And we do it with some confidence, as a letter received by this vessel, dated two days later than the papers, mentions, that their Convention was to meet at

Charlestown on the third of March–and adds, "It must afford you satisfaction to be informed, that the merit of the proposed Constitution will bury all opposition in this State; for fortunately its adversaries are men of no influence. It is expected it will be ratified unanimously."[5]

Boston Gazette, 25 February[6]

Extract of a letter from Charlestown, South Carolina, dated February 11.

"On the motion being put, in the General Assembly,–For the Convention to assemble in Charlestown on the 12th of May next, it passed in the affirmative, by a majority of one. The reason of the division on this question was, that the minority who lived in other towns wished it might assemble with them. Some persons, from not attending to the manner the question was put, supposed that there was so large a number against the assembling of a Convention, while it was only against the *place* of meeting. It was granted on all sides, that the Constitution must be submitted to a Convention of the people."

1. Reprinted: *Massachusetts Gazette*, 26 February; *New Hampshire Spy*, 29 February. Both reprints omitted the last paragraph.

2. See *Pennsylvania Gazette*, 19 March, note 2 (Appendix I, below).

3. See the *New York Journal*, 5 February, and the Philadelphia *Freeman's Journal*, 13 February (Appendix I, above).

4. Reprinted: *New Hampshire Spy*, 26 February; Philadelphia *Federal Gazette* and *Pennsylvania Packet*, 13 March; *Philadelphische Correspondenz*, 18 March; *Virginia Independent Chronicle*, 26 March; Richmond *Virginia Gazette and Weekly Advertiser*, 3 April.

5. The Newburyport *Essex Journal*, 27 February, printed the following: "Another letter from the same place [Charleston], dated the 3d of March [*sic*], says, 'The adversaries of the constitution are men of no influence. The only antifederalist in the state legislature is Mr. Lowndes. It is expected the constitution will be ratified unanimously.' " This item was reprinted in the Exeter, N.H., *Freeman's Oracle*, 29 February.

6. Reprinted: *Worcester Magazine*, fourth week in February; *Newport Mercury*, 3 March; *Pennsylvania Packet*, 5 March; *Pennsylvania Mercury*, 6 March; *New York Morning Post*, 8 March; Baltimore *Maryland Gazette*, 14 March.

Pennsylvania Mercury, 21 February[1]

A correspondent wishes the public of Pennsylvania to compare the *generous manly conduct* of the *minority of Massachusetts*, with the *pitiful low indecency* of the *hated minority* of Pennsylvania. Even though at first inimical to the Constitution, when *convinced*, or *even* OUT-VOTED, THEY could eat the *bread* of *peace*, and drink the *glass* of *friendship* with their friends IN TOTO–and they could even declare with *transport*, they were beaten–they were out-voted– but at their return to *those* who *honoured them* with *their choice*, they would recommend *peace* and *harmony*, *union* and *submission*. But when the *incendiaries* of our own state even refused the *hand* of *friendship*, the *signature of consent*, and *the social feast, which bind* man and man together, they not only added neglect to their malicious refusal, but strove to spread dissention, and to raise rebellion *amongst* their constituents.

To you we cling as to a band of brothers–[2]
We thank you for your generous consent,
Respect you as the saviours of your country,
And *pray* the *head* of *all confederation*,
The author of the *sun*, the *moon*, the *stars*,
And all which feel his forcible command,
In one firm, fast-bound, mass of general union,
—TO BLESS YOU.

1. Reprints by 17 March (14): Mass. (8), R.I. (1), Conn. (1), N.Y. (1), N.J. (1), Va. (1), S.C. (1). The Connecticut and South Carolina reprints omitted the verse.
2. The phrase is taken from Shakespeare's *Henry V*, act 4, scene 3: "We few, we happy few, we band of brothers."

Middletown, Conn., Middlesex Gazette, 25 February[1]

Extract of a letter from a gentleman in Washington, (North-Carolina) to his friend in this city, dated January 13, 1788.

"I assure you all talk of War.–Constitution goes down here.–Convention meet in July next."

1. Reprints by 20 March (15): N.H. (2), Mass. (5), R.I. (3), Conn. (3), N.Y. (1), Pa. (1). The reprint in the *Massachusetts Centinel*, 8 March, added: "we make haste slowly." Four reprints added this statement: N.H. (1), Mass. (2), Conn. (1).

Salem Mercury, 26 February[1]

The purport of a letter received by the last Saturday's mail, from Providence, state of Rhodeisland, is–That a Protest was signing, to be presented to the Assembly of that state, which are to meet at Providence this week, impeaching the several states who have adopted the new constitution, with treason.

1. Reprints by 12 April (17): N.H. (4), Conn. (1), N.Y. (2), Pa. (4), Md. (1), Va. (3), S.C. (1), Ga. (1). This item is a paraphrase of a letter printed in the *Boston Gazette* on 25 February. For the text of the original, see CC:568, note 5.

Philadelphia Independent Gazetteer, 26 February[1]

Extract of a letter from Queen Ann's county, Maryland, February 18, 1788.

"Of all the arts practised by the advocates of the proposed system of arbitrary power, that of stopping all real information, and publishing a great deal of misinformation, they have been most successful in. At the time they dispaired of having even a respectable minority in the Massachusetts convention (as above three-fourths of the people of that state are in the opposition) these votaries of power were publishing that they would have three to one in the convention; in this manner have they deceived, and by this deception have they obtained considerable success. But they should remember the old proverb: *Whoso diggeth a pit shall fall therein, and he that rolleth a stone, it will return upon him.*

"In one of your papers is an extract of a letter, from this state, declaring that there will be a majority of two to one in favor of the proposed system in our convention; now this is absolutely a great falsehood, it will be quite the reverse; above three-fourths of the Western, and at least one-third of the Eastern Shores are warmly opposed to it. Mr. Martin, who has great influence here, *has let the cat out of the bag*; and none of *his colleagues* have dared to contradict any thing he has said, except a trifling circumstance concerning the New-York deputies; but Mr. Martin has since proved this fact, and *Mr. Jenifer is left in the lurch.*[2]

"By a letter I have from Charleston, it seems they *attempted* in the lower house what they accomplished in the senate, viz. to present an address of thanks to their federal deputies;[3] but in this they failed, as well as in endeavoring to get the convention called in March.[4] The noted Mr. *Lowndes* opposed it entirely; however, though there was a majority in that house in the opposition, yet they consented to call a convention, as their sister states had done it.

"Pray is not the people in your state generally opposed to it–Mr. — informs me this is the case; and he also tells me, that, except in the city of New-York, there are very few advocates of it in that state."

1. Reprinted: *New York Journal*, 3 March (excerpt); *Virginia Independent Chronicle*, 12 March.
2. See CC:414, note 7.
3. See CC:531, note 5.
4. See Boston *Independent Chronicle*, 7 February, note 2 (Appendix I, above).

Pennsylvania Mercury, 26 February[1]

Extract of a letter from a gentleman in Baltimore, to his friend in this city.

"The people are every day more enlightened, and numbers are continually adding strength to the federal party. The conclusion of Martin's information to the House of Assembly,[2] has convinced all his former friends, who have any sense, that he is an artful hypocrite. Even Mr. Goddard, hitherto against the new constitution, is now, by the force of the arguments published in his own paper,[3] become highly and truly federal.

"Having mentioned Mr. Goddard, I wish to do him the justice of saying, that throughout the whole of this important controversy, he conducted his paper with the utmost candor."

1. Reprints by 31 March (8): Mass. (3), R.I. (2), Conn. (1), N.Y (3).
2. See Luther Martin's *Genuine Information* XII (CC:516).
3. *Maryland Journal.*

Philadelphia Independent Gazetteer, 27 February[1]

A correspondent says, that the cause of despotism has met with no very brilliant success in the state of Massachusetts Bay. From among near four hundred members in convention, after all the unfair play that had been used, only a majority of nineteen could be found, for the ratification of the new constitution with amendments. There were 168 who would not adopt the constitution with the proposed amendments, which seems the strongest protest which can be made against it. If the other states therefore should proceed to the ratification of the new constitution we shall be troubled with eternal dissentions. ⟨Time and investigation (says our correspondent) will prove that there has been a deep laid scheme to enslave us. This scheme was probably invented in the society of the Cincinnati, who were to start up in every state in favor of the new constitution, and to give their voice as the voice of the people. We have been very neglectful of our interests in suffering this society to exist among us. That the honor is not hereditary does not make the society in any manner less mischievous for the present. Mr. *Rufus King*, in the convention of Massachusetts, had the audacity to confess that there was a secret design in the continental convention, which they wished to conceal till it was ripe for execution. He said to have divulged it would have been as foolish as if General Washington had divulged his scheme to attack the British in Boston, when he planted his cannon upon Dorchester hills.⟩

1. The *Maryland Journal*, 4 March, and the *Virginia Independent Chronicle*, 12 March, reprinted the entire article. The Winchester *Virginia Gazette*, 26 March, printed only that part of the item beginning "Mr. Rufus King. . . ." The text in angle brackets was reprinted five times by 18 April: N.H. (1), Mass. (3), R.I. (1). The *Massachusetts Centinel*, 9 April, printed the excerpt with an introduction: "We give the following, as a specimen of the dirty–dirty tricks of the antifederalists in the Southern States, to impose on the freemen of America–It is extracted from a Philadelphia paper." The *Centinel* version was reprinted in the *New Hampshire Spy*, 11 April, and the Springfield *Hampshire Chronicle*, 16 April.

Pennsylvania Gazette, 27 February[1]

It appears, by the proceedings of the South-Carolina legislature, that every man in both Houses (the Senate and the Assembly) were in favor of the new Constitution. As their legislature is much the most numerous in the union, in proportion to their number of free white inhabitants, this extraordinary unanimity affords an indubitable proof that we shall very soon reckon South-Carolina among the members of the *new confederacy*. Their legislature must consist of above 200 persons, for Charleston has 30 members. It may be justly said, South-Carolina is an opulent, enlightened, and yet a very rising state. Their Convention will meet on Monday next, the third day of March.[2]

1. Reprints by 20 March (17): Mass. (3), R.I. (1), Conn. (5), N.Y. (1), Pa. (3), Va. (3), S.C. (1).

2. See *Newport Herald*, 14 February, note 3 (Appendix I, above).

Pennsylvania Gazette, 27 February[1]

Extract of a letter from a gentleman in Wilmington, to his friend in this city, dated February 19, 1788.

"Be pleased to accept many thanks for thy very obliging letter of the 17th, and my hearty congratulations on the Ratification of the Fœderal Constitution by the state of Massachusetts. It is indeed an event that promises most happy consequences–that America will now enjoy peace, liberty and safety–be united at home, and respectable abroad. My hopes are enlivened. I look upon my children with an encreased satisfaction, because their lot in life seems to me to be rendered more favourable by the prospect of public felicity.

"May the gracious Providence, that has preserved us through so many dangers, difficulties and distresses, lead us into an establishment and conduct of beneficial influence to our fellow creatures in the other parts of the world."

1. Reprints, in whole or in part, by 26 March (10): N.H. (1), Mass. (3), R.I. (1), N.Y. (2), Pa. (2), Va. (1).

Pennsylvania Mercury, 28 February[1]

A correspondent cannot help remarking on the shuffling inconsistent conduct of the antifœderal politicians–One half of them decry the constitution, because men of education, great names, and the well-born, were the constructors of it.–The other half declaim against it, because men uneducated, men of common sense and mechanics, had a hand in erecting it. Many of their writers declare it is a constitution, which our rulers (the conspirators and demagogues) are going to rivet upon us: But Luther Martin, at the close of his information, complains heavily, that it is to be *forced* upon us through the medium of the people–that the state legislatures alone ought to decide upon it, and that the people have no right to judge for themselves, whether it is a government they will chuse to live under.[2]

1. Reprints by 27 March (7): Mass. (2), R.I. (1), N.Y. (3), Va. (1).
2. See Luther Martin's *Genuine Information* XII (CC:516).

New York Packet, 29 February[1]

Yesterday sailed from this Port for Canton, in China, the ship Jenny, Captain Thomson. As the ship passed the Battery, she fired a salute of thirteen guns, which was answered from the same place, by a detachment of artillery. The Jenny is the second ship, which has sailed this season from New-York, on so distant a voyage.

That Americans possess a spirit of commercial enterprize, is evinced by the many adventrous voyages which have been undertaken from several ports in the United States, since the conclusion of the late war.–Was America in possession of a firm national government, distant countries would not only behold, with veneration, the banners of Columbia; but the thunder of her cannon might victoriously resound to the most remote regions of the globe.

1. Reprints by 2 April (11): N.H. (2), Mass. (2), N.Y. (1), N.J. (1), Pa. (3), Md. (1), Va. (1).

Providence Gazette, 1 March[1]

The House Yesterday resumed the Consideration of appointing a State Convention, agreeably to the Mode proposed by the General Convention held at Philadelphia, and after a lengthy Discussion of the Subject resolved, that the fœderal Constitution proposed should be referred to the Consideration of the individual Freemen of the State, in their respective Town-Meetings.–On this Question, 15 Members voted for a Convention, and 42 for the above Reference.–Majority 27.

1. Reprints by 9 April (15): R.I. (1), Conn. (4), N.Y. (2), N.J. (1), Pa. (5), Md. (1), Va. (1).

New York Morning Post, 3 March[1]

By a letter from a gentleman at Boston, of the 23d February, who waited two days at Exeter, in New-Hampshire, to know the decision of the Convention, we are informed that it adjourned to June, that the adjournment was a measure of the friends to the Constitution, the Anti-Constitutionalists being 70 to 40, that if the adjournment had not been moved, the Constitution would have been instantly rejected, and that there was little hopes it would have a greater number of friends in June than it now has. The Aristocratics are quite in the dumps,[2] and are satisfied the plan cannot take without satisfactory amendments.

Extract of a letter from Boston, Feb. 24.

"The Convention of New-Hampshire have adjourned to June next. This measure was proposed by the Fœderalists, rather than to attempt to adopt the Constitution by a small majority. Upwards of forty towns have absurdly fettered their delegates with instructions against the Constitution. It is expected, upon more mature consideration that those instructions will be repealed, and the delegates suffered to act agreeable to their own judgments. In this case, there cannot be a doubt but the Convention will in their next session adopt a Constitution so replete with benefits to New Hampshire, as well as the Union in general."

1. The first letter was reprinted eight times by 12 April: N.J. (1), Pa. (4), Md. (1), Va. (1), S.C. (1). The second letter, which was also printed in the New York *Daily Advertiser* on 3 March, was reprinted thirteen times by 20 March: N.Y. (2), N.J. (1), Pa. (5), Md. (2), Va. (2), S.C. (1). Six of these newspapers reprinted both letters by 19 March: N.J. (1), Pa. (3), Md. (1), Va. (1). A paraphrase of the first letter appeared in the *New York Journal* on 3 March and was reprinted once each in Poughkeepsie, Philadelphia, Baltimore, and Winchester, Va., by 26 March.

2. The *New York Journal* paraphrase reads: "The aristocratical federalists, here, are quite stunn'd at this event. . . ."

New York Journal, 3 March[1]

Extract from a letter, dated Exeter, New-Hampshire, Feb. 22, 1788.

"After the repeated assurances I have given you of the favorable reception of the new constitution, and the fair prospect of its adoption, by a large majority of our convention, you will be greatly surprised when I inform you, that they have this day adjourned without taking the final question.–Unbounded confidence of success in any undertaking, as it rejects the necessary precaution and slackens exertion, always endangers the object. So confident were we of the prevailing voice in favor of the constitution, that no pains were taken to counteract the intrigues of a few notoriously vile characters, who were too successful in the dark and dirty business of seducing a great number of the interior towns, by false representation; to fetter their delegates with positive instructions to vote in all events against the constitution. After discussing the subject seven of eight days, and finding many of the members, who were instructed to the contrary convinced of the expediency and necessity of adopting the plan, and desirous to consult their constituents, the convention agreed to adjourn to June next, when I have no doubt the ratification will take place."

1. Reprints by 19 April (18): Conn. (3), N.Y. (3), Pa. (7), Md. (1), Va. (1), S.C. (1), Ga. (2).

Philadelphia Independent Gazetteer, 3 March[1]

Extract of a letter from York county, February 25, 1788.

"You may depend upon it, whatever you in the city may think of the business, we country people do not consider the new constitution adopted by this state. We look upon all yet done to be the work of the junto in the city, &c. We shall be very apt to make some *experiments* in the spring."[2]

1. Reprinted: *New York Journal*, 8 March; *Maryland Journal*, 14 March; Boston *American Herald*, 20 March; Winchester *Virginia Gazette*, 26 March.
2. John Clark (1751–1819), a York, Pa., lawyer, quoted and disputed this extract: "No People I beleive are better disposed than the Inhabitants of York County and will most Cordially receive the new plan of Government" (to John Nicholson, 11 March, Mfm:Pa. 506).

Philadelphia Independent Gazetteer, 4 March[1]

By two gentlemen just arrived from the westward, we are informed, that the people were marching with rapidity from all directions to the town of Carlisle, in Cumberland county, in order to set at liberty seven or eight gentlemen, who were confined in the gaol of that county for interrupting an attempt to hold a public rejoicing on the account of the new constitution having been adopted by the convention of this state. Our informants understood that about five thousand men were collecting; they actually met three hundred in one body on the ice, crossing from this side of Susquehanna, but were not informed of the event.

1. Reprints by 4 April (15): N.H. (3), Mass. (5), R.I. (1), N.Y. (2), Md. (1), Va. (3). The reprint in the *Massachusetts Centinel*, 19 March, was followed by another paragraph reprinted from the *Gazetteer* of 7 March that denied Quakers were Federalists (Appendix I, below). An editorial statement followed this second paragraph: "The above paragraphs are extracted from an antifederal paper, and are to be believed accordingly." The reprints in the *New Hampshire Spy*, 21 March, and the *New Hampshire Gazette*, 26 March, were followed by the same qualifier.

On 26 December a riot took place in Carlisle, Pa., as Antifederalists prevented Federalists from celebrating the state's ratification of the Constitution. Twenty-one men were arrested, seven of whom refused parole and wanted to stay in jail until their cases could be heard. Militiamen from several counties descended on Carlisle on 1 March to obtain forcibly the release of the seven imprisoned men. An "accommodation" was reached and the men were released without violence. Eventually all charges were dropped. (For the Carlisle riot and its aftermath, see CC:407, and RCS:Pa., 670–708.)

Providence United States Chronicle, 6 March[1]

We learn, from Maryland, by a Gentleman who is just returned from that State, That the Friends to the Federal Constitution there increase daily–That Governor Randolph's Letter to the Speaker of the Virginia Assembly[2] had been of infinite Service in that State and Virginia, in convincing the People of the absolute Necessity of an energetic Continental Government–and that the Constitution will certainly be adopted in Maryland, by a great Majority.

1. Reprints by 25 March (11): N.H. (3), Mass. (5), Conn. (1), Pa. (2). This item was excerpted and slightly paraphrased in the Charleston *City Gazette*, 1 April; the paraphrase was reprinted in the *Gazette of the State of Georgia*, 17 April.
2. See CC:385.

Philadelphia Independent Gazetteer, 7 March[1]

A correspondent says, it is an impudent falsehood to declare that the people called Quakers are generally attached to the new constitution. It is most certain that at their meetings of business they have determined not to support it. Every considerate person must know it to be against their principles, as one must suppose it to be against the principles of all the sincere professors of christianity, to raise a man to a throne,[2] in opposition to a lawful government, who notoriously holds negroes in slavery without any design of liberating them, and who sells them, when his necessities urge him to it, as if they were beasts.

1. Reprinted: Baltimore *Maryland Gazette*, 14 March; *Massachusetts Centinel*, 19 March; *New Hampshire Spy*, 21 March. See *Independent Gazetteer*, 4 March (Appendix I, above). For Pennsylvania Quakers and the Constitution, see CC:573.
2. George Washington.

Massachusetts Centinel, 8 March[1]
RHODE-ISLAND CONVENTIONS.

The General Assembly of the State of Rhode-Island, the 1st inst. passed an act, "*for submitting the consideration of the proposed Federal Constitution, to the freemen of that State"*–who are to meet in their respective towns, in town-Conventions, on the FOURTH MONDAY of March; (the 24th instant) when after discussing it, they are to give their assent, or disapprobation of it, by yeas and nays; which are to be sealed up by the Town-Clerk, and forwarded to the General Assembly, at their meeting on the last Monday in March:–Provision was sometime since made for the distribution of the Constitution.

We are happy in being able to assure the publick, that the above paragraph is authentick–and that the legislatures of ALL the States have now referred the proposed Constitution to the consideration of THE PEOPLE; and that the mode adopted in Rhode-Island is, as we are assured, most likely to insure the ratification of the Constitution there. When we consider that this system has been readily adopted in SIX STATES–unanimously, or by respectable majorities–and been rejected by none, we have abundant reason to hope, that the time is not far distant, when the citizens of America, represented by one general and permanent government, will rise to that dignity and importance among the nations of the world, as they are entitled to from their native genius–their extent of country–and from their being a free, united, and virtuous people.[2]

Extract of a letter from Providence, March 2.

"The General Assembly last night ordered the Hon. Peleg Arnold, and Jonathan J. Hazard, Esquires, two of our delegates to Congress, to proceed immediately to New-York, to take their seats in that Hon. Body. Our State is divided on the great question of the Constitution, as they were on the subject of paper-money, with scarcely an exception."

A gentleman of undoubted veracity assures a correspondent, that his Excellency JOHN COLLINS, Esq. Governour of Rhode-Island, is decidedly in favour of the adoption of the federal Constitution–he was therefore hurt at seeing in one of the late papers an attack upon him, as being in an opposite principle.

1. The first paragraph was reprinted eighteen times by 12 April: Vt. (1), N.H. (2), Mass. (5), N.Y. (1), N.J. (2), Pa. (4), Md. (2), S.C. (1). The second paragraph was reprinted twelve times by 10 April: N.H. (1), Mass. (2), Conn. (1), N.Y. (2), N.J. (1), Pa. (3), Md. (1), S.C. (1). Nine newspapers reprinted the first and second paragraphs as a unit by 10 April: N.H. (1), Mass. (2), N.Y. (1), N.J. (1), Pa. (2), Md. (1), S.C. (1).

The third paragraph was reprinted in the March issue of the New York *American Magazine* and in twenty-six newspapers by 9 April: Vt. (2), N.H. (4), Mass. (5), Conn. (2), N.Y. (4), N.J. (1), Pa. (4), Md. (1), Va. (3). The fourth paragraph was reprinted twenty times by 9 April (seven reprints excluded the last independent clause): N.H. (2), Mass. (3), Conn. (3), N.Y. (2), Pa. (4), Md. (1), Va. (5). Twelve newspapers reprinted both the third and fourth paragraphs by 9 April: N.H. (1), Mass. (3), Conn. (1), N.Y. (2), Pa. (2), Va. (3). Only three newspapers reprinted all four paragraphs: the *Salem Mercury*, 11 March; Portland *Cumberland Gazette*, 13 March; and *Pennsylvania Packet*, 19 March.

2. The last sentence in this paragraph was derived from a paragraph in the New York *Independent Journal*, 16 February (Appendix I, above).

Philadelphia Federal Gazette, 8 March[1]

Extract of a letter from a gentleman in Richmond, dated Feb. 28, to his friend in this city.

"We had great rejoicings here yesterday, by the federal men, on account of the ratification of the new constitution, by the state of Massachusetts. The citizens assembled at the Union tavern, about twelve o'clock, and hoisted up a flag on the top of the house, and kept it up till about 11 o'clock at night, when each repaired to his habitation pretty mellow with Madeira: a number of cannon were fired on this occasion–next Monday our election comes on for the Convention–I expect the governor and Mr. Marshall will be elected, as there seems to be little or no opposition.[2]

1. Reprinted: New York *Daily Advertiser*, 12 March; *Newport Mercury*, 24 March; *Massachusetts Spy*, 3 April; *Boston Gazette*, 7 April; *Vermont Journal*, 21 April.
2. Governor Edmund Randolph and John Marshall were elected to represent Henrico County in the Virginia Convention where they voted to ratify the Constitution in June 1788.

Poughkeepsie Country Journal, 11 March[1]

Extract of a letter from a gentleman in South Carolina, dated Jan. 30, 1788, to his friend in this place.

"The legislature of New York, I observe are to meet at Poughkeepsie.–The opposition of your G * * * * * * *,[2] and his party to the new constitution, has excited the curiosity as well as the indignation of America.–Should it be submitted to the people, and they reject it, he and his party must take the consequences to themselves; as it will involve not only your State, but the whole continent in a CIVIL WAR! Which may God in his goodness forbid. The convention of this State are to meet in May next–a Mr. Lowndes, is the only opponent I can hear of–but his influence is as feeble as his party is insignificant–being principally those men who were opposed to the Independence and the liberties of America.–I have not a doubt but we shall have a majority of at least 10 to 1."

1. Reprints by 10 April (8): N.H. (3), Mass. (2), Conn. (2), N.Y. (1).
2. Governor George Clinton.

Massachusetts Centinel, 12 March[1]

Accounts from Maryland acquaint us that there is not the least doubt of that State's adopting the proposed Constitution–by their Convention which is to meet next month.

1. Reprinted: *New Hampshire Spy*, 18 March; Northampton *Hampshire Gazette*, 19 March; Portland *Cumberland Gazette*, 20 March; *Worcester Magazine*, third week in March; *Vermont Journal*, 7 April.

Pennsylvania Gazette, 12 March[1]

A Correspondent remarks, that the present conduct of the most respectable persons in the opposition to the new government in Pennsylvania must be attended with the best effects. They seem disposed to acquiesce in the adoption of the Fœderal Constitution since the State Convention, the last and the present Legislature, and the Supreme Executive Council have all approved of it,[2] and they say that they now see that any amendments which may be found necessary can be provided for by the first Fœderal Legislature, who will be the representatives of the state governments in one branch, and of the people at large in the other.

We are informed from the best authority, that twenty of the Massachusetts minority were actually in arms in the year 1787, under DANIEL SHAYS, and that near eighty more of that minority were decided friends to his cause. It matters not to us whether that alarming disturbance was *ill* or *well* founded, but it must be very clear to every considerate man, that an attachment to an opposition against the government of Massachusetts is a very improper ground of opposition to the proposed Fœderal Constitution.–It is also very certain, that the remaining attachments to Great-Britain, in the northern parts of Massachusetts, and the influence of secret emissaries from the province of Canada, have had a very considerable effect. We wish however to do justice to the manly conduct of the members of the minority themselves, while we lament the effects of these baneful causes among their constituents.–Even they, we believe, are more deluded than dishonest. The adoption of the government will put an end to these pernicious practices of the enemies of our peace, liberty and safety.[3]

The case of the New-Hampshire Convention is very honorable to the American character. From want of opportunity to acquire due information, their constituents had instructed them to vote against the adoption; but on finding that the number, *bound up*, was so great that the question would be carried by a small majority, two thirds of the body determined to give their constituents an opportunity of forming a more just opinion, and of unraveling the deceptions that had been practised upon them.[4]

We hear that some of the zealous opposers of the constitution in this state have circulated copies of the reasons of dissent of our minority,[5] even into the western country of Georgia, where, it seems, however, no converts were made; for the Convention of that state adopted the constitution *unanimously*. This anti-fœderal committee of correspondence must have *raised* and *expended* the £2000 mentioned by Tom Peep.[6] Time, it seems, still continues to be the great discloser of facts.[7]

1. All four paragraphs were reprinted in only two newspapers–the *New York Morning Post*, 14 March, and the New York *Daily Advertiser*, 14 and 15 March. The first paragraph was reprinted nineteen times by 15 April: N.H. (3), Mass. (3), R.I. (2), Conn. (1), N.Y. (5), Pa. (2), Md. (1), Va. (2). For reprints of the remaining paragraphs, see notes 3, 4, and 7.
2. The 11th General Assembly called the state Convention and the 12th provided for the expenses of the Convention. On 21 February the Supreme Executive Council congratulated the Assembly on the state's ratification of the Constitution (Mfm:Pa. 442). For a similar argument, see the *Pennsylvania Gazette*, 19 March (Mfm:Pa. 546).

3. Reprinted: *New York Morning Post* and New York *Daily Advertiser*, 14 March; New York *Independent Journal*, 15 March; *Virginia Independent Chronicle*, 26 March; *State Gazette of South Carolina*, 31 March.

4. Reprinted: *New York Morning Post*, 14 March; New York *Daily Advertiser*, 15 March; *Virginia Independent Chronicle*, 26 March; *State Gazette of South Carolina*, 10 April; Winchester *Virginia Gazette*, 16 April.

5. "Dissent of the Minority of the Pennsylvania Convention," *Pennsylvania Packet*, 18 December (CC:353).

6. "Tom Peep" reported that a Federalist meeting was held in Philadelphia on 4 January at which James Wilson allegedly urged Federalists to fill the newspapers with items supporting the Constitution. Committees were supposedly appointed to raise money by subscriptions to defray the expenses of publication and distribution. The £2,000 figure was mentioned by "Peep Junior" who suggested that the money would be used for bribery (Philadelphia *Independent Gazetteer*, 10, 14 January, Mfm:Pa. 320, 330. See also "Centinel" X, *ibid.*, 12 January, CC:443.).

7. Reprints by 10 April (8): N.H. (1), Mass. (1), R.I. (1), Conn. (2), N.Y. (2), S.C. (1). The two Connecticut reprints omitted the last two sentences. The Massachusetts, New Hampshire, and Rhode Island reprints omitted the last sentence.

Philadelphia Independent Gazetteer, 14 March[1]

Extract of a letter from a gentleman in Maryland, to his friend in this city, dated March 4.

"The convention of Boston I find have agreed to the new constitution, but in such a manner, as will, in my opinion, considerably affect the system. New-York, Maryland, Virginia, North and South-Carolina, will, I am persuaded, in imitation, propose amendments, and this new government will not be established without paying a deference to the desire of so large a part of the confederation.

"If some amendments should be adopted, it will be all right, and the efforts of the minority have no other object than to secure, in *explicit terms*, some of the essential rights and privileges of freemen. It may be of dangerous consequence to refuse desires so reasonable. If the constitution should pass at all, I hope it will be in such a way as may encrease the unity of the states and the harmony of our citizens, and that we be not a house divided against itself."[2]

1. Reprinted: *New York Journal*, 18 March; *Albany Gazette*, 27 March; Boston *American Herald*, 7 April; Providence *United States Chronicle*, 17 April.

2. Mark 3:25.

Massachusetts Centinel, 15 March[1]

Thursday, April 10th, is appointed by his Excellency President Sullivan, as a day of Fasting and Prayer, in the State of New-Hampshire.– Among other objects, set forth in the proclamation,[2] for which the people are exhorted to assemble together is, that they may supplicate Almighty God, to graciously "grant to the members of the Convention, that wisdom, which is necessary to direct, and lead them into those measures which may promote the *interest* and *happiness* of the *United States*."

1. Reprints by 9 April (20): Vt. (1), Mass. (3), R.I. (3), Conn. (6), N.Y. (2), N.J. (1), Pa. (3), Md. (1).

2. For the proclamation of 29 February, see *New Hampshire Gazette*, 19 March.

Massachusetts Centinel, 19 March[1]
Of the CONSTITUTION–and of CONVENTIONS.

The States of *Massachusetts, Connecticut, New-Jersey, Pennsylvania, Delaware,* and *Georgia*, have ratified the Constitution. The Convention of *Maryland* meets about the 20th of April; of *South-Carolina*, the 12th of May; of *Virginia*, the last of May; of *New-York* and *New-Hampshire*, the 17th of June; and of *North-Carolina*, the 4th of July. *Rhode-Island*, we care but little about–she contains, indeed, a number of characters, who are pearls of price–and, could these be separated from the pebbles, which there abound, it would be more a matter of joy than lamen[ta]tion, to the honest and honourable part of mankind, was she sunk into one of our western water ponds. Her Legislature has submitted the Constitution to be discussed by the people, each in *propria personæ,*[2] the 24th inst.

1. Reprints, in whole or in part, by 24 April (9): Mass. (4), R.I. (1), Conn. (2), N.Y. (1), S.C. (1).

2. Instead of calling a state convention, the Rhode Island legislature submitted the Constitution to a statewide referendum where each freeman could vote in his town meeting.

Pennsylvania Gazette, 19 March[1]

The appointments of the State Conventions to meet the end of April, in May and in June, leaves a considerable interval before we can obtain additions to the present number; but, if we remember that six states have adopted, that none have yet refused, and that it was too reasonably feared that some might dissent, we shall confidently expect its adoption by nearly the whole number. All, we trust, will finally be included in one fold.

Though there is *very little* opposition to the proposed fœderal constitution in South-Carolina, it appears that a principal ground of objection with its opponents *there* is, that it will finally invest the fœderal legislature with a power *to regulate or prevent* the importation of slaves.[2] The Minority of Pennsylvania, who were always friends to the abolition of negro slavery, and the states of Rhode-Island and Massachusetts, who consider slaves as *freed* by coming into their jurisdiction, can never expect to agree with the gentlemen in Carolina, who oppose on such principles.

1. The first paragraph was reprinted eleven times by 10 April: Mass. (1), Conn. (1), N.Y. (2), N.J. (1), Pa. (3), Md. (1), Va. (1), S.C. (1). The second paragraph was reprinted eight times by 5 May: N.J. (1), Pa. (1), Md. (1), Va. (3), S.C. (2). Five of the newspapers reprinted both paragraphs by 9 April: N.J. (1), Pa. (1), Md. (1), Va. (1), S.C. (1). These two paragraphs were originally part of a series of five paragraphs in the *Pennsylvania Gazette*. Paragraphs 1, 2, and 5 deal primarily with the opposition to the Constitution within Pennsylvania and were reprinted fewer times than the two paragraphs printed here. For the texts of all five paragraphs, see Mfm:Pa. 546.

2. On 16 January, during the debate in the South Carolina House of Representatives over calling a state convention, Rawlins Lowndes defended slavery and the slave trade. He objected to the Northern States' "jealousy of our negro trade" and argued that the slave-trade provision of the Constitution was "*a stroke aimed at the prohibition of our negro trade* by an ungenerous limitation of twenty years, and this under the *specious pretext of humanity.* For his part, he thought *this sort of traffick justifiable* on the principles of RELIGION, HUMANITY and JUSTICE, for certainly to translate a *set* of human beings from a bad country to a better, was fulfilling every part of *those principles.*" Excerpts from Lowndes's speech were printed in the *Massachusetts Centinel,* 23 February, and reprinted in the *Worcester Magazine,* first week in March; *Connecticut Journal,* 12 March; *Pennsylvania Packet,* 17 March; *Pennsylvania Gazette,* 19 March; and the New Jersey *Brunswick Gazette,* 25 March. (The entire speech was first printed in the Charleston *City Gazette* on 21 January. None of the italics or capitalization for emphasis appeared in the *City Gazette.*) For the issue of slavery and the slave trade, see CC:Vol. 2, Appendix III.

New York Daily Advertiser, 25 March (excerpt)[1]
Extract of a letter from a Gentleman in Charleston, dated Feb. 26.
". . . This State feel their interest deeply concerned in adopting the new Constitution. This information you may depend on."

1. Reprints by 24 April (11): N.H. (1), Mass. (2), R.I. (2), Conn. (2), N.Y. (1), Pa. (2), S.C. (1).

Federalist
Massachusetts Centinel, 26 March[1]
FEDERAL ELECTIONEERING.
There is a man,[2] in the United States, who must present himself to the consideration of every freeman thereof, as a candidate for the important station of PRESIDENT of the UNITED STATES. He is known

As disinterested–and therefore it is certain that he will not fleece us.

As having voluntarily laid down his former power–and therefore that he will not abuse those he may receive hereafter.

As having no son–and therefore not exposing us to the danger of an hereditary successor.

As being of a most amiable temper–and therefore that he will not be vindictive or persecuting.

His character, in short, is A TISSUE OF VIRTUES, and as there are some of our countrymen who doubt the safety of the proposed government, it is happy for us that we have such an approved and faithful citizen to employ in the experiment.

1. Reprinted: *Pennsylvania Journal,* 9 April; *Maryland Journal* and Baltimore *Maryland Gazette,* 15 April; *Virginia Independent Chronicle,* 23 April, extra; *Virginia Centinel,* 30 April.
2. George Washington.

Pennsylvania Gazette, 26 March[1]
All the petitions against the new constitution have now been presented to the legislature. Taken together, the petitioners are much fewer than those in the city and county of Philadelphia only, who petitioned in favor

of it within a few days after it was published.[2] They can do the Constitution no injury, for they are not signed by one twentieth part of the people of the state.

How truly republican, says a correspondent, is the conduct of the minority of Connecticut. After a fair investigation and adoption of the Constitution, the most perfect harmony prevails between the gentlemen who formerly divided on the question. Equally honorable is the conduct of the minority of Massachusetts. We hope the same harmony will take place in Pennsylvania.

1. The first paragraph was reprinted seventeen times by 5 May: N.H. (1), Mass. (4), R.I. (1), Conn. (2), N.Y. (2), Pa. (3), Va. (2), S.C. (2). The second paragraph was reprinted in the Philadelphia *Federal Gazette*, 27 March; *Connecticut Courant*, 7 April; *Norwich Packet*, 10 April; *Salem Mercury*, 15 April; and *State Gazette of South Carolina*, 1 May. Only the *State Gazette of South Carolina* did not also reprint the first paragraph.

2. Pennsylvania Antifederalists mounted a petition campaign to the Assembly asking that the state's delegates to the Constitutional Convention "be brought to account for" exceeding their authority; that the ratification of the Constitution "not be confirmed by the legislature of this state"; and that the state's delegates in the Confederation Congress be so instructed. Petitions were circulating in western Pennsylvania by mid-January. The first newspaper version was printed in the *Carlisle Gazette* on 30 January (Mfm:Pa. 381) and was reprinted in Philadelphia, New York, and Boston. In March petitions with over 6,000 signatures were presented to the Assembly, where they were tabled. For "The Petition Campaign for Legislative Rejection of Ratification," 2 January–29 March, see RCS:Pa., 709–25. For the petitions of September 1787, which supported the Constitution and requested the state legislature to call a ratifying convention promptly, see RCS:Pa., 62, 64, 64–65, 65, 67, and Mfm:Pa. 61.

APPENDIX II

The Controversy over the Post Office
and the Circulation of Newspapers

Throughout the debate over the ratification of the Constitution, Antifederalists expressed concern that Federalists tampered with their mail. In October 1787 Richard Henry Lee, serving as a Virginia delegate to Congress, reported that letters written by him "and sent by the Post" had been stopped in their "passage" (to Samuel Adams, 27 October, CC:199). In mid-March 1788 Elbridge Gerry charged that "several letters from my friends in Newyork, & also to them have shared ye same fate . . . a species of robbery nearly allied to highway robbery . . . I am sorry to see it so frequent amongst us" (to J. Harley, 15 March, Sang Collection, Southern Illinois University, Carbondale). Antifederalists therefore tried to avoid the post office by entrusting their letters to couriers or by addressing their letters to third parties not politically suspect in the eyes of Federalists.

Beginning in January 1788, Antifederalists asserted that the post office itself was waylaying newspapers that contained Antifederalist material. They said that the writings of New York Antifederalists, such as "Brutus," "Cato," and "Cincinnatus," were not allowed to reach Philadelphia while the Pennsylvania Convention was sitting and that the "Dissent of the Minority of the Pennsylvania Convention" was prevented from getting to Boston while the Massachusetts Convention sat. Federalists denied these charges.

Antifederalists and Federalists were both concerned by the official changes in policy adopted by the post office. In November 1786 Postmaster General Ebenezer Hazard believed that stagecoach operators were charging the government too much for the delivery of the mail. He complained that some stagecoach operators would not alter their schedules so as to arrive in major commercial centers at times more convenient for postmasters. (Later Hazard charged that the stagecoach schedules also inconvenienced merchants.) Hazard recommended that stagecoaches continue to carry the mail from Philadelphia southward but that postriders on horseback carry the mail between Portland, Maine, and New York City. Between New York City and Philadelphia Hazard believed that "No Stages can do the Business so well on this Route as Post Riders" (JCC, XXXI, 922–23), claiming that postriders traveled "Night & Day," while stagecoach drivers were "careless, & inattentive to the Mail" (to Jeremy Belknap, 17 May, below).

On 14 February 1787 Congress read a draft ordinance for the operation of the post office which, among other things, would have formally authorized the continuation of the traditional practice of allowing printers to exchange single copies of their newspapers postage free. The ordinance, however, stipulated that newspapers would no longer be delivered to subscribers postage free (JCC, XXXII, 55–56). No further action was taken on the ordinance, but the alarm of many people was well expressed in a widely reprinted article first printed in the *Pennsylvania Herald* on 26 May: "there has hitherto been no charge for the conveyance of newspapers throughout the continent; but it has lately been said that a new arrangement is agitated by the post-masters, which will either deny to the printers the only eligible mode of supplying their subscribers, or impose so heavy a tax, that the remote circulation of their papers must be eventually discontinued. Besides the general arguments against this projected measure, something may be urged from the peculiar circumstances of the country. The strong and invidious distinction, which different habits, manners, and pursuits will naturally create between the eastern

540

and southern inhabitants of so extensive an empire, can only be counteracted by the freest communication of their opinions and politics, and, at this awful moment, when a council is convened [the Constitutional Convention], it may justly be said, to decide the fate of the Confederation, would it not be dangerous and impolitic to divert or destroy that great channel, which serves at once to gratify the curiosity, and to collect the voice of the people?''

On 15 October 1787 Congress, in response to another plea from Ebenezer Hazard, resolved that the Postmaster General be authorized to contract for the delivery of the mail during 1788 by stagecoaches or postriders, whichever "he may judge most expedient and beneficial; provided that preference is given to the transportation by stages to encourage this useful institution, when it can be done without material injury to the public" (JCC, XXXIII, 684). Soon after, the post office advertised in newspapers seeking bids for contracts to deliver the mail north of Philadelphia for the ensuing year. (See New York *Daily Advertiser*, 18 October.) Contracts were awarded to postriders whose bids were about forty percent lower than their stagecoach competitors (Hazard to Jeremy Belknap, 17 May, below). Hazard also abandoned tradition by disallowing the postage-free exchange of newspapers among printers–each printer was required to enter into an agreement with the postrider who carried his newspaper.

The "new arrangement" broke down almost immediately. Postriders, in general, were less reliable than stagecoaches in maintaining schedules and delivering mail. Postriders also often refused "to take papers for printers" (*New York Journal*, 23 January, below). When they did agree to carry newspapers, postriders sometimes found it either easier to throw them away or more profitable to sell them along the post roads. To obtain more reliable service, some printers reverted to stagecoach delivery; and, in an effort to counter the "new arrangement," some stagecoach operators even offered free delivery of letters and newspapers, the latter to both subscribers and printers (*New York Journal*, 10 March, below).

By March 1788 newspaper printers all over the country complained that beginning in January, they had not received their usual newspaper exchanges. Antifederalists believed that the "new arrangement" at the post office was intentionally designed to delay, if not totally stop, the free and widespread circulation of the few Antifederalist-oriented newspapers. The *New York Journal*, the Philadelphia *Independent Gazetteer*, and the Philadelphia *Freeman's Journal* were said to be most affected. (For descriptions of these newspapers, see CC:Vol. 1, pp. xxxiv-xxxviii.) Led by the printers of these newspapers–Thomas Greenleaf, Eleazer Oswald, and Francis Bailey, respectively–Antifederalists asserted that the Postmaster General through his chain of patronage–postmasters and postriders–had cut America's vital link of communications at a critical period in the debate over the Constitution. George Washington was disturbed that the post office's new policies had afforded Antifederalists "very plausible pretexts for dealing out their scandals, & exciting jealousies by inducing a belief that the suppression of intelligence at that critical juncture, was a wicked trick of policy, contrived by an Aristocratic Junto." Hazard had to be warned, continued Washington, "to wipe away the aspersion he has incautiously brought upon a good cause" (to John Jay, 18 July, below).

Hazard's new policies alienated all newspaper printers and stagecoach operators–two influential groups–as well as many politicians. The opposition to the Postmaster General was so strong that he was nearly dismissed from office by Congress in September 1788 (Belknap to Hazard, 23 September, LMCC, VIII, 793n). By the end of 1788, however, the post office issue had abated, but it remained in George Washington's memory. As president, Washington did not reappoint Hazard–one of only a handful of Confederation officers turned out of office. The right of printers to exchange their newspapers postage free remained an issue until 1792 when Congress provided by law "That every printer of newspapers may send one paper to each and every other printer of newspapers within the United States, free of postage, under such regulations, as the Postmaster General shall provide."

Centinel IX
Philadelphia Independent Gazetteer, 8 January (excerpt)[1]

. . . It is a fact that can be established, that during almost the whole of the time that the late convention of this state were assembled, the newspapers published in New-York, by Mr. Greenleaf, which contains the essays written there against the new government, such as the patriotic ones of Brutus, Cincinnatus,[2] Cato, &c. sent as usual by the printer of that place, to the printers of this city, miscarried in their conveyance, which prevented the republication in this state of many of these pieces, and since that period great irregularity prevails; and I stand informed that the printers in New-York complain that the free and independent newspapers of this city do not come to hand; whilst on the contrary, we find the devoted vehicles of despotism pass uninterrupted. I would ask what is the meaning of the new arrangement at the Post-Office, which abridges the circulation of newspapers at this momentous crisis, when our every concern is dependant upon a proper decision of the subject in discussion–No trivial excuse will be admitted; the Centinel will, as from the first approach of despotism, warn his countrymen of the insidious and base stratagems that are practising to hoodwink them out of their liberties. . . .

1. Reprinted: *Pennsylvania Herald*, and Philadelphia *Freeman's Journal*, 9 January; *New York Journal*, 14 January; *Carlisle Gazette*, 5 March, and in a New York Antifederalist pamphlet anthology (Evans 21344). For the complete text, see CC:427. "Centinel" repeated these charges in his 11th, 13th, and 14th essays printed in the *Gazetteer* on 16, 30 January, and 5 February (below).

2. On 30 January the Philadelphia *Freeman's Journal* reprinted "Cincinnatus" IV (*New York Journal*, 22 November, CC:287) with a preface by "L.M." addressed to the printer: "Inclosed is the Fourth Number of Cincinnatus which you did not receive, owing to some mishap; it is no matter of surprise to me, that it was stopped."

Thomas Greenleaf
New York Journal, 10 January (excerpt)[1]

Only two southern papers were received by yesterday's mail, which deprives us of the satisfaction we should otherwise have had of communicating what, peradventure, might have been handed. Notwithstanding this failure of intelligence through the channel of newspapers, by post (which failure, it is presumed, originates with the rider).[2] . . ."

1. Reprinted: *New Jersey Journal*, 16 January. For comments on this item, see "Centinel" XI, 16 January (below) and Thomas Greenleaf's statement in the *New York Journal*, 23 January (below).

2. The rest of this item, taken from a *"Private letter,"* described the Carlisle riot of 26 December (see Philadelphia *Independent Gazetteer*, 4 March, Appendix I).

Centinel XI
Philadelphia Independent Gazetteer, 16 January (excerpt)[1]

. . . In a former number[2] I stated a charge of a very heinous nature, and highly prejudicial to the public welfare, and at this great crisis peculiarly alarming and threatening to liberty; I mean the suppression of the circulation of the newspapers from state to state by the of–c–rs of the P–t–O—ce, who in violation of their duty and integrity have prostituted their of–ces to forward the nefarious design of enslaving their countrymen, by thus cutting off all communication by the usual vehicle between the patriots of America;–I find that notwithstanding that public appeal, they persevere in this villainous and daring practice. The newspapers of the other states that contain any useful information, are still withheld from the printers of this state, and I see by the annunciation of the Editor of Mr. Greenleaf's patriotic New-York paper, that the printers of that place are still treated in like manner; this informs his readers that but two southern papers have come to hand, and that they contain no information, which he affects to ascribe to the negligence of the p–t boy, not caring to quarrel with the p–t m–t–r g—l.[3] . . .

1. "Centinel" XI was also printed in the Philadelphia *Freeman's Journal* on 16 January and was reprinted in the *New York Journal* on 21 January. For the complete text, see CC:453.
2. See "Centinel" IX, 8 January (above).
3. See Thomas Greenleaf's statements in the *New York Journal*, 10 January (above).

Philadelphia Freeman's Journal, 16 January[1]

The conduct of Congress or the post master-general, in stopping the free circulation of the Newspapers at this critical juncture, is very alarming. From what this extraordinary measure has originated we do not pretend to say; but certainly the freemen of America will never suffer such a bare faced violation of their liberties to pass with impunity. This is a stretch of arbitrary power, that even Britain never attempted before the Revolution. By this manœuvre all communication is cut off between the States; so that the despots may assemble an *army* and subjugate the freemen in one state, before their friends in another hear of it.

1. This item was also printed in the Philadelphia *Independent Gazetteer* on 16 January. It was reprinted in the New Jersey *Brunswick Gazette*, 22 January; *New Jersey Journal*, 23 January; *New York Journal*, 25 January; and Charleston *City Gazette*, 22 February.

Providence Gazette, 19 January

☞ *Two Western and Southern Mails were due Yesterday–neither of them arrived at this Day's Publication.*

New Jersey Brunswick Gazette, 22 January

☞ No papers have been received from the eastward or southward by the last mails.

Delays in the Circulation of Luther Martin's Genuine Information, 22 January–8 April

Pennsylvania Packet, 22 January

Any person having the Maryland Gazette and Baltimore Advertiser, of Tuesday, January 8, 1788, containing the 4th continuation of Mr. Martin's Report to the House of Assembly of Maryland,–will much oblige the Printers of this paper by the loan of it, as they did not receive that publication through the usual channel.[1]

Pennsylvania Herald, 23 January[2]

The MARYLAND GAZETTE of the 8th inst. not having come to hand we are here obliged to omit the continuation of Mr. MARTIN'S SPEECH contained in that paper; but as soon as we receive it, shall take the earliest opportunity of presenting it to our readers.

Pennsylvania Packet, 1 February[3]

Not having, until yesterday, received the Maryland Gazette containing the following, we take the first opportunity of laying it before our readers.– This continuation should have been published between our papers of the 14th and 18th January.

Philadelphia Independent Gazetteer, 9 February[4]

The following continuation should have been inserted in our paper between the 22d and 24th January. The Maryland Gazette not having come regularly to hand, we were prevented from laying it before our readers at an earlier period.

New York Journal, 16 February[5]

The Printer hereof has taken great pains, and has been at some expence, to obtain the continuation of the hon. Mr. Martin's information to the legislature of Maryland, from Philadelphia; and he is happy to inform his readers, that he is now able (with a little omission) to re-continue it, on Monday, from his Register of the 18th ult.

Philadelphia Freeman's Journal, 27 February (excerpt)[6]

Extract of a letter from Worcester, (Massachusetts) *February* 11, 1788.

". . . I understand the deputies from the state of Maryland to the general Convention have been called before their Assembly, to give an account of the proceedings of that secret body; as the post office does not allow any newspapers to come this far, that contain any thing unfavourable to the New Constitution, I wish you would send me one of the papers in which Mr. Martin's information is.''

New York Journal, 8 April[7]

☞Yesterday the celebrated SPEECH of the Hon. LUTHER MARTIN, Esq. late a member of the gen. convention, from the state of Maryland, addressed to the house of assembly of that state, was completed in this paper. The several southern papers, which contained this speech, having been received very irregularly, and that chiefly by favor of correspondents, is the reason why this publication has been so long detained from the public, and finally so irregularly published as to render it difficult to have one collective view of it. That our readers may, notwithstanding, attain this collective view, the editor refers them to the following papers, viz., of January 15, 16, and 18; of February 18, 19, 20, 22, 25, 26, and 27; of March 1, 7, 12, 14, 15, 17, 18, and 19; and of April 7, 3, and 7, 1788.[8]

1. The *Packet* reprinted *Genuine Information* IV (Baltimore *Maryland Gazette*, 8 January, CC:425) on 1 February. The delay apparently occurred only with this number because installments I–III were reprinted between 5 and 14 January and V–VII between 18 and 25 January.

2. This item was printed as a preface to the *Herald's* and the *Independent Gazetteer's* (24 January) reprintings of the fifth installment of the *Genuine Information*. The *Gazetteer* finally reprinted *Genuine Information* IV on 9 February; the *Herald* ceased to exist after 14 February and never reprinted the fourth installment.

3. This item was printed as a preface to the reprinting of *Genuine Information* IV (see note 1, above).

4. This item was printed as a preface to the reprinting of *Genuine Information* IV (see note 2, above). The *Gazetteer* had reprinted the third and fifth installments on 22 and 24 January, respectively.

5. This item was printed two days before the *Journal's* reprinting of *Genuine Information* III (Baltimore *Maryland Gazette*, 4 January, CC:414). (See also *New York Journal*, 8 April, below.)

6. Three newspapers–*Maryland Journal*, 4 March, and the Winchester *Virginia Gazette* and the *Carlisle Gazette*, 26 March–reprinted parts of this letter, but none reprinted the material on the *Genuine Information*.

7. This item appeared the day after the *Journal* reprinted the last of the twelve installments of the *Genuine Information*.

8. The *Journal* reprinted the eleventh installment on 7 April and the twelfth on 3 and 7 April.

New York Journal, 23 January

Officers of the Post Office

MR. GREENLEAF, Respect for the public opinion induces the "Offi–c–rs of the P–st O—ce" to declare, that the allegations of the "Centinel" (re-published in your paper of this day)[1] respecting them, are *false*. They think this declaration due to the public and their own characters; but they will take no notice of the Centinel himself, as an anonimous political incendiary is below even contempt.

New-York, Jan. 21, 1788.

Thomas Greenleaf's Editorial Statement

☞As there has been a pointed reference to the editor of this paper, by the writer of the CENTINEL, and the above *Note*, upon the alarming subject of the *detention* of newspapers, he conceives himself under a peculiar obligation to make the following public avowal–that he has received none of the several papers, published at Philadelphia, by Col. Oswald, Mr. Bailey, or Messieurs Dunlap and Claypoole, or at Boston, by Messieurs Edes and Son, or Mr. Powers,[2] &c. &c. through the medium of the Post-Office, since the 1st inst–while others came to hand which contained none of those interesting essays upon the momentous topic, now in discussion, which the public have an indubitable right to the perusal of. (For which reason he has, by letters, requested them to forward regular files of their papers, by every private conveyance, as he has done, and shall do, of his to them; which request he here reiterates, thanking them for those already received by this means.)–The editor, however sensible he may be of the great utility of public Post-Offices, in all free countries, has not presumed to call in question the conduct of the "officers of the post-office," who have ever (within his *knowledge*) treated him impartially. He is credibly informed, that since January 1st, of the present year, the riders, in several instances, *have refused to take papers for printers, not being obliged* (as they say) *to carry them by contract.* If this be a political evil (which it is presumed no one will deny) a remedy for it *doubtless* will issue from a higher power than the Post-Master-General. Wherever the failure may originate, it will hold good, that "no evil can be remedied until known;" consequently, if this be an evil, the public will be obliged to the discoverer, who will doubtless pursue it so long as there exists no governmental edict to interdict the freeborn privilege of *publicly* complaining of *public* grievances.

1. "Centinel" XI, first printed in Philadelphia in the *Independent Gazetteer* and *Freeman's Journal* on 16 January (above), was reprinted in the *New York Journal* on 21 January.

2. Eleazer Oswald printed the *Independent Gazetteer*, Francis Bailey the *Freeman's Journal*, John Dunlap and David C. Claypoole the *Pennsylvania Packet*, Benjamin Edes, Sr., and Jr., the *Boston Gazette*, and Edward E. Powars the *American Herald*. The *Gazetteer, Journal,* and *Herald* were staunch Antifederalist newspapers. The *Boston Gazette* and the *Packet* reprinted significant amounts of Antifederalist material.

"M"
Philadelphia Independent Gazetteer, 26 January[1]

Mr. OSWALD, Every charge which the Centinel has brought against the O—c–rs of the P–st O—ce, is *false*, and shall be proved such, if he will dare to publish them with his *real name* subscribed; in which case he shall have the real name of his antagonist: If he refuses this, he must be considered as making *wanton* attacks upon the characters of men who act under the sanction of an oath. The public will be at no loss for the motives of his conduct, and the "O—c–rs of the P–st O—ce" will treat with deserved contempt the unmanly and cowardly assaults of such an unprincipled assassin.

1. Reprinted: Philadelphia *Freeman's Journal*, 30 January; *New York Journal*, 2 February; Boston *American Herald*, 10 March. For references to this item, see "Philo-Centinel," 31 January, and Ebenezer Hazard to Jeremy Belknap, 5 March (both below).

Boston Gazette, 28 January

We have received no Papers to the Southward of New-Haven for the Month past.

New Jersey Brunswick Gazette, 29 January

☞ *Solely on account of not receiving intelligence from our correspondents in the neighbouring states, we have been obliged to present our readers with but half a sheet this week.*

New Jersey Journal, 30 January

For some weeks past, we have scarcely received a paper from our numerous correspondents in the different states. The motive for this suppression of intelligence is best known to the post-master general! It has an oblique aspect of sinister views.–It is a disgrace to this enlightened age, and an harbinger of slavery, that when the press, under the most arbitrary governments, is daily growing more and more free, that the post-masters, or their jackalls, should essay to stop all communication between the states at this important crisis, by prohibiting that exchange of papers printers have enjoyed since the first establishment of a post-office in this continent. Such a most attrocious attack upon public freedom, demands the attention and resentment of every friend to the rights of his country; for if this mutual exchange cannot be accomplished without being subject to the caprice of a post-rider, besides satisfying his inordinate and unlimmitted demands, there will be few presses, and they will soon become entirely subservient to the influence of government. Instead of being the guardians of the public rights, they will be made the dangerous engines to gloss and colour over the most fatal designs against the common liberty and happiness.–Rouse, Printers! and oppose the hydra in embrio.

Centinel XIII
Philadelphia Independent Gazetteer, 30 January (excerpts)[1]

. . . The conspirators having been severely galled and checked in their career by the artillery of freedom, have made more vigorous and successful efforts to silence her batteries, while falsehood with all her delusions is making new and greater exertions in favor of ambition. On the one hand, every avenue to information is as far as possible cut off, the usual communication between the states through the medium of the press, is in a great measure destroyed by a new arrangement at the Post-Office, scarcely a newspaper is suffered to pass[a] by this conveyance. . . . In short, the conspirators have displayed so much ingenuity on this occasion, that if it had not been for the patriotism and firmness of some of the printers, which gave an opportunity to enlightened truth to come forward, and by her invincible powers to detect the sophistry, and expose the fallacy of such impositions, liberty must have been overcome by the wiles of ambition, and this land of freemen have become the miserable abode of slaves.

(a) *For the truth of this charge I appeal to the Printers.*

1. Reprinted: Philadelphia *Freeman's Journal*, 6 February; *New York Journal*, 12 February; Boston *American Herald*, 28 February. For the complete text, see CC:487.

Philo Centinel
Philadelphia Independent Gazetteer, 31 January[1]

Mr. OSWALD, A Person under the signature of M. has stood forth, asserting that the charge brought by Centinel against the Postmaster-General or some of his Officers, was false.[2] This writer must have a strange opinion of the citizens of Philadelphia, if he thinks his bare denial of the charge will satisfy them. Is it not well known, that for some weeks past, almost all the newspapers were stopped or destroyed, either by the post-rider, or by the officers of the post office? Certainly. I appeal to every printer in this city for the truth of this assertion. Nay, I would ask M. if he were not certain that his vindication was nothing but an unsupported assertion, and contradicted by the fact. I do not wish to criminate but I really declare that, I am afraid, M. is better acquainted with this secret affair than he ought to be. I wish the influence or b—y of the *well born of New-York* have not had their *proper* effect on this *understrapper.*

It is with pleasure I hear, that this scheme of stopping the free circulation of the newspapers never originated in Philadelphia; but on the contrary, the Deputy P. Master and the other Officers in the office of this city, were uniformly opposed to such an infernal violation of the liberties of the people;[3] and last week they forwarded the newspapers as usual: so that I hope the plot is discovered and frustrated.

1. Reprinted: Philadelphia *Freeman's Journal*, 6 February. On 31 January "Census" charged in the *Pennsylvania Mercury* that "the '*duncified*' author of Philadelphiensis, Philo-Centinel, &c. is known to be a certain *almanac maker* in the University" (Mfm:Pa. 396). This was an allusion to Benjamin Workman, a tutor in mathematics at the University of Pennsylvania and the publisher of *Father Tammany's Almanac.* "Census' " assertion touched off an exchange between him and "The Almanac-Maker" (*Pennsylvania Mercury*, 2, 9, 12 February, Mfm:Pa. 398, 416, 424).

2. See "M," *Independent Gazetteer*, 26 January (above).

3. For another defense of James Bryson, who was the assistant to the Postmaster General and the postmaster of Philadelphia, see Eleazer Oswald's statement in the *Independent Gazetteer*, 12 March (below).

Centinel XIV
Philadelphia Independent Gazetteer, 5 February (excerpt)[1]

. . . The O—rs of the P-t O—ce, fearful of the consequences of their conduct, are taking measures to invalidate the charge made against them.[2] As this is a matter of the highest importance to the public, it will be necessary to state the charge and the evidence. In two of my former numbers,[3] I asserted that the patriotic newspapers of this city and that of New-York miscarried in their passage, whilst the vehicles of despotism, meaning those newspapers in favor of the new constitution, passed as usual; and it was particularly asserted that the patriotic essays of Brutus, Cincinnatus, Cato, &c. published at New-York, were withheld during the greatest part of the time that our state convention sat; and in a late number,[4] I further asserted that since the late arrangement at the P-t O—ce, scarcely a newspaper was suffered to pass by the usual conveyance, and for the truth of this last charge I appealed to the printers; however I understand this last is not denied or controverted. When the dependence of the printers on the P-t O—ce is considered, the injury they may sustain by incurring the displeasure of these of—rs, and when to this is added that of the complexion of the printers in respect to the new constitution, that most of them are zealous in promoting its advancement, it can scarcely be expected that they would volunteer it against the P-t O—rs, or refuse their names to a certificate exculpating the of—rs; accordingly we find that most of the printers have signed a certificate that the newspapers arrived as usual prior to the first of January, when the new arrangement took place; however, the printer of the Freeman's Journal when applied to, had the spirit to refuse his name to the establishment of a falsehood, and upon being called upon to specify the missing papers, particularly during the sitting of the state convention, he pointed out and offered to give a list of a considerable number, instancing no less than seven successive Greenleaf's patriotic New-York papers, besides others occasionally with-held from him; Colonel Oswald was out of town when his family was applied to, or I have no doubt he would have observed a similar conduct. But there is a fact that will invalidate any certificate that can be procured on this occasion,[5] and is alone demonstrative of the suppression of the patriotic newspapers. The opponents to the new constitution in this state were anxious to avail themselves of the well-written essays of the New-York patriots, such as Brutus, Cincinnatus, Cato, &c. and with that view were attentive to have them republished here as soon as they came to hand, and especially during the sitting of our state convention, when they would have been the most useful to the cause of liberty by operating on the members of that convention; a recurrence to the free papers of this city at that period, well shew a great chasm in these republications, owing to the miscarriage of Greenleaf's New-York papers; agreeable to my assertions it will appear, that for the greatest part of the time that our state convention sat, scarcely any of the numbers of Brutus, Cincinnatus, Cato, &c. were republished in this city; the fifth number of Cincinnatus that contained very material information about the finances of the union, which strikes at some of the principal arguments in favor of the new constitution, which was published at New-York the 29th November, was not republished here until the 15th December following,[6] two or three days after the convention rose, and so of most of the other numbers of this and the other signatures; so great was the desire of the opponents here to republish them, that the fourth number of Cincinnatus was republished so lately as in Mr. Bailey's last paper,[7] which with other missing numbers were procured by private hands from New-York, and in two or three instances, irregular numbers were republished. The new arrangement at the P-t O—ce, novel in its nature, and peculiarly injurious by the suppression of information at this great crisis of public affairs, is a circumstance highly presumptive of the truth of the other charge.

1. Reprinted: Philadelphia *Freeman's Journal*, 6 February; *New York Journal*, 13, 15 February; Boston *American Herald*, 3, 6, 10 March. For the complete text, see CC:501.

2. See "Officers of the Post Office," *New York Journal*, 23 January (above), and Ebenezer Hazard to Jeremy Belknap, 10 May (below).

3. See "Centinel" IX and XI, 8 and 16 January (above).

4. See "Centinel" XIII, 30 January (above).

5. See Hazard to Belknap, 10 May (below).

6. See CC:501, note 13.

7. See CC:501, note 14.

Norfolk and Portsmouth Journal, 6 February

☞A disappointment in not receiving the Northern mail as usual (after waiting to the latest hour), renders an apology to our kind Subscribers necessary, in ushering to their presence a barren sheet for this week's Number. At the same time we hope, and can most assuredly inform our Readers that, as at all times, every requisite attention has, and will be paid, to afford the gratification which the earliest foreign or domestic intelligence can present. The Public will please to cast a favorable eye on this day's publication, and generously ascribe its *vacuum* to the real cause above assigned.[1]

1. On 30 January the Philadelphia *Freeman's Journal* reported: "By private accounts from Virginia, we learn . . . that the people to the southward were all kept in the dark by the stoppage of the newspapers in the Post Office" (CC:Vol. 3, Appendix I).

Albany Gazette, 7 February[1]

☞The Printer is unable to account for the failure of the New York papers–for several stages past he has received from only two of the Printers in that city, and by last evening's stage, none except the Daily Advertiser, from Mr. Childs.

1. On 16 February the editor of the *New York Journal* paraphrased the *Albany Gazette's* statement. Following the paraphrase the editor asked: "What comment can be made upon the above! that the paper printed at this office went from the Stage-Office in this city is certain."

Philadelphia Independent Gazetteer, 8 February (excerpt)[1]

Extract of a letter from the Eastern Shore of Maryland, to a gentleman in this city, dated Jan. 29, 1788.

. . . The *Post-Offices* are also under the influence of these sons of power, so much so that a paper printed at New-York cannot find its way to Philadelphia, Baltimore, or any of the other states; neither can the papers of the Southward proceed an inch farther than the office they are put in at, unless they should happen to contain the most fulsome elogiums, on Franky's *New Roof*,[2] which is to accommodate him and all the *Office-hunters* on the continent. . . .

1. Reprinted: *New York Morning Post*, 12 February; *New York Journal*, 22 February; Boston *American Herald*, 10 March. For the complete text, see CC:515.
2. Francis Hopkinson's "The New Roof," *Pennsylvania Packet*, 29 December (CC:395).

Massachusetts Centinel, 16 February[1]

The several Printers on the Continent are requested to notice in their papers, that since the commencement of the present year, the Printers in the northern States have received scarce a single paper, printed beyond the Hudson.–Notwithstanding the publick are exceedingly anxious, at the present all-important period, to be acquainted with the progress of political affairs, the Printers in Boston have not received any papers from New-York, for several weeks, though before January they were regularly received.–This calls loudly for remedy; and if, as it is said, it is owing to the design of some of the Mail-Carriers, it is hoped, that Congress, or the Post-Master General, will look into, and remedy it–as it must be of first importance, that the channels of information should be kept as free as possible.

1. Reprints by 26 March (21): N.H. (2), Mass. (4), R.I. (2), Conn. (1), N.Y. (3), N.J. (2), Pa. (5), Md. (1), Va. (1). The reprint in the *New York Journal*, 25 February, included the heading "(FACTS!!)." Ten of the reprints followed the *Journal's* example: N.Y. (2), N.J. (2), Pa. (4), Md. (1), Va. (1). For a comment by the *Journal's* editor on the reprinting of this item, see *New York Journal*, 10 March (below).
The *Centinel's* paragraph was reprinted in the Boston *Independent Chronicle* on Thursday, 21 February. The printers of the *Chronicle*, Adams and Nourse, wrote a letter, dated "Thursday Morning two oClock," to the secretary of Congress, Charles Thomson, complaining about the circulation of newspapers: "The Post refusing to bring on, or forward from hence, the public News Papers directed from one Printer to another, you will please to excuse our inclosing the within papers directed to our Delegates in Congress under cover of your Name, untill the several Stage drivers are brought to a sence of their duty–This insult offerred the *public* by these men at this important crisis, deprives the Union of every public information necessary for its well being." The letter

was docketed: "Note–from Printers in Boston to Mr Thomson Feby 1788" (PCC, Item 78, [Miscellaneous] Letters Addressed to Congress, 1775–89, Vol. 18, p. 651, DNA).

Centinel XV
Philadelphia Independent Gazetteer, 22 February (excerpt)[1]

. . . The magic of great names, the delusion of falsehood, the suppression of information, precipitation and fraud have been the instruments of this partial success, the pillars whereon the structure of tyranny has been so far raised. Those influential vehicles, the newspapers with few exceptions, have been devoted to the cause of despotism, and by the subserviency of the P— O—, the usefulness of the patriotic newspapers has been confined to the places of their publication, whilst falsehood and deception have had universal circulation, without the opportunity of refutation. The feigned unanimity of one part of America, has been represented to produce the acquiescence of another, and so mutually to impose upon the whole by the force of example. . . .

1. Reprinted: *New York Journal*, 26 February; Philadelphia *Freeman's Journal*, 27 February; *Albany Journal*, 3 March; *Carlisle Gazette*, 19 March. For the complete text, see CC:556.

Samuel A. Otis to James Warren
New York, 27 February (excerpt)[1]

. . . [P.S.] The Postmaster conducts poorly in shifting the Mail from Stages to Horses & I find your intelligence imperfect. The enclosed papers containing all the news, when you have read them please to hand to my other friends with my Compliments.

1. RC, Miscellaneous Legislative Documents, Senate Files, no. 843, M-Ar. A longer excerpt, concerned largely with the Western lands and the federal and state debts, is printed in LMCC, VIII, 702–3. Otis was a Massachusetts delegate to Congress and Warren was the speaker of the state House of Representatives. The docketing indicates that the letter was read in the House on 24 March and committed to a committee on the state's Western lands.

James Bowdoin to James de Caledonia
Philadelphia Independent Gazetteer, 27 February (excerpt)[1]

Boston, February 12, 1788.
. . . However as we have the P-t O—ce still at our service, you must prevent any of the newspapers which contain publications against us, getting out of your state. We have been remarkably successful in this hitherto; every newspaper against us has been stopped, even the reasons of dissent of your minority, and the information of Mr. Martin, has been scarcely heard of here; this was very fortunate, as it would certainly have

ruined us in this quarter. So great was the want of information here, that we made the people believe all to the southward of us, indeed that every state but our own were almost unanimous in favor of our plan. You would have laughed to have seen our newspapers on the day the final question was taken in our convention; there we published an account of the almost unanimous adoption of the constitution by the convention of North-Carolina; that the state of New-York had called a convention at a very early day, without any opposition; and the *trifling* opposition in your state had ceased; that Randolph, Mason, Lee, &c. had joined our party; and many other similar accounts. . . .

1. For the circulation, annotation, and complete text of this satirical Antifederalist letter, see CC:570. James de Caledonia was an Antifederalist name for James Wilson.

William Goddard to Mathew Carey
Baltimore, 28 February (excerpt)[1]

. . . All Intercourse between the several Printers of News-Papers on the Continent now appears to be stopt by the new & scandalous Regulations of the Post-Office–If Relief is not soon obtained, a new Post-Office & Riders will be established here, in Opposition to the present contemptible Establishment.[2]

1. RC, Lea and Febiger Collection, PHi. Goddard (1740–1817) was the printer of the *Maryland Journal* and served as an agent for the sale and distribution of Carey's Philadelphia *American Museum*.
2. Goddard was writing with some authority. He had been postmaster of Providence, R.I., from 1764 to 1769. From 1774 to 1775 he had established the "Constitutional" post office in opposition to the British system, with offices from Portsmouth, N.H., to Williamsburg, Va. In 1775 Goddard's postal system was absorbed into the post office created by the Continental Congress, and Goddard was appointed surveyor of post roads, a position he resigned from in 1776. Goddard's sister, Mary Katherine Goddard (1738–1816), was postmistress of Baltimore.

Maryland Journal, 29 February[1]

☞ The British January Packet is arrived at New-York from Falmouth. The Intelligence brought by her is not yet come to Hand, the News-Papers from our Correspondents being now prohibited coming in the Mails.–A similar Measure, previous to the American Revolution, was very severely reprobated and resented throughout the Continent, as having a manifest Tendency to endanger Public Liberty, (as well as greatly to injure Individuals) by shutting up the Channels of Public Information.–The present Post-Office Administration would do well to reflect on the Fate of their Predecessors.

> "*Learn to be Wise from others Harm,*
> "*And you shall do full well.*"

Extract of a Letter from a respectable Company of Printers in Massachusetts, to the Printer hereof, dated the 12th Instant.

"Your Paper has never come to Hand since the Commencement of the present Year, nor have we seen *one* during that Period. Whether the new Regulation in the Mails deprive us of it, do not know.–Are sorry it is so; wish for a Remedy[(a)] if one can be provided. We may very well complain of the like Evil southward of New-Haven, as to almost every Paper, all of which were heretofore very regularly received."

☞ (a) *The Remedy in contemplation is to establish* MAIL-COACHES *for the Carriage of* LETTERS, *on moderate Terms, and for maintaining a due Intercourse between the Publishers of News-Papers in the United States–*PRO BONO PUBLICO.

1. The first paragraph was reprinted ten times by 2 April: N.H. (2), Mass. (2), Conn. (2), N.Y. (1), N.J. (1), Va. (1), S.C. (1). Four reprints were immediately followed by another item criticizing the post office which was first printed in the *Massachusetts Gazette* on 21 March (below).

The extract of a letter from Massachusetts was reprinted nine times by 19 March: N.Y. (3), Pa. (4), N.J. (1), Va. (1). Five of the reprints included the footnote. Only the *New York Journal*, 11 March, 2 April; *New Jersey Journal*, 12 March; and Winchester *Virginia Gazette*, 14, 19 March, reprinted both paragraphs.

Ebenezer Hazard to Jeremy Belknap
New York, 5 March (excerpt)[1]

. . . Can it be possible that the Pennsa. Minority's Protest has but just reached you!–this surprizes me: it was published long before any hints were thrown out about *Delays*.[2] You ask, "has any Detention been purposely made?" I answer no:–an infamous Writer (antifl.) in Phila. under the Signature of *Centinel* asserted that "the of–c–rs of the P–t O—ce had prostituted their Offices & Integrity to the nefarious Purpose of enslaving their Countrymen"[3]–He made several Attacks before any notice was taken of him; when a piece appeared in a Phila. Paper, in which "the O—c–rs" &c. declared that every Charge brought against them by Centl. was *false*, & should be proved to be such, if he would dare to make them with his *real name* subscribed; in which Case he should know the real name of his Antagonist:–if he refused to do this, "he must be considered as making *wanton* Attacks upon the Characters of men who acted under the Sanction of an Oath,–the Public would be at no Loss for the Motives to his Conduct,–& the of–c–rs (&c) would treat with deserved Contempt the ungenerous & unmanly Assaults of so unprincipled an Assassin."[4]–He has never appeared yet, except *sub Clypeo*. The fact is, *the Office* has nothing to do with News Papers; it is a Matter merely between the Printers & the Riders who have the Carriage of them as a Perquisite. The two antifederal Printers in Phila. (Oswald & Bailey) & their Coadjutor, the brainless *Greenleaf* of New York, are the only ones who have published against the Office; & neither of them was a Printer before the War:–in short, the whole Noise appears to me to be an antifederal Manoeuvre, like the "Bribery & Corruption" at Boston.[5] . . .

1. RC, Belknap Papers, MHi. Printed: "Belknap-Hazard Correspondence," 23–25.
2. The "Dissent of the Minority of the Pennsylvania Convention" was reprinted in Boston as a pamphlet sometime before 11 February. For the debate over the circulation in Massachusetts, see CC:353, p. 11.
3. "Centinel" XI, Philadelphia *Independent Gazetteer*, 16 January (above and CC:453).
4. "M," *Independent Gazetteer*, 26 January (above).
5. A reference to a widely reprinted item entitled *"Bribery and Corruption*!!!" in the *Boston Gazette*, 21 January, charging that Massachusetts Convention delegates who opposed the Constitution were being paid to change their votes with money raised from wealthy individuals in a neighboring state. (See CC:547, note 6.)

Original Letters
Philadelphia Freeman's Journal, 5 March (excerpts)[1]

LETTER I. from Dr. R—, to Mr. H—l-n, New-York.

I return you thanks for your polite attention in sending the numbers of Publius so punctually; I am well pleased that our scheme of stopping the newspapers containing the Antifederal pieces, has succeeded; let Mr. — know, that 200 dollars will be forthwith transmitted as a small gratuity for his service. . . .

LETTER II. from Dr. R—, to Mr. H—l-n, New-York.

. . . I mentioned in my last, making a remittance of the 200 dollars for our friend in the P— O—; that matter cannot be accomplished for some time, until we receive some of the outstanding subscriptions;[2] in the mean time let the gentleman know, that he may make himself easy on the occasion, for he shall be honorably recompensed. . . .

1. These fictitious Antifederalist letters, allegedly from Benjamin Rush to Alexander Hamilton, were reprinted in the *Newport Mercury*, 24 March. For the complete texts, see Mfm:Pa. 487.
2. A reference to an alleged subscription fund of £2,000 that Philadelphia Federalists wanted to raise to pay for their publications and activities (*Pennsylvania Gazette*, 12 March, note 6, Appendix I).

Thomas Greenleaf's Editorial Statement
New York Journal, 10 March[1]

☞ The request of a DAILY READER, to insert a paragraph respecting the alarming delinquency of the post officers, from a Boston paper, is received, and would have been attended to this day, had it not been anticipated by the Editor so long ago as Monday the 25th ultimo, in the Register of which day it was inserted under the New-York head[2]–Since that date the Editor has received *nine* letters and notes from printers in the several states, informing of their not receiving the Register, and requesting that the Editor would, in future, find some other mode than the *post-office*, for conveyance, expressing a desire, that the other Printers might also alter their channel of conveyance if possible. ⟨The Editor receives the highest satisfaction in being authorised, by the proprietors of the stages both from the SOUTHARD and EASTWARD, to MAKE KNOWN, that they will, in future, carry all papers for PRINTERS and SUBSCRIBERS, as well as all LETTERS, GRATIS; from which circumstance it is to be hoped, that a channel of FREE COMMUNICATION of intelligence from state to state, will be again opened through the medium of the patriotism of the Eastern and Southern STAGE PROPRIETORS, who, when they formerly carried the MAILS, never GRUMBLED at rendering so essential a service to the community gratis.⟩

1. The text in angle brackets was reprinted in the Boston *American Herald* on 20 March and introduced with this statement: "Mr. GREENLEAF, Printer of the New-York Daily Patriotick Register, gives the following publick information (generous indeed on the part of the gentlemen stage-proprietors) viz."

2. See the *Massachusetts Centinel*, 16 February (above). The full title of the *Journal* was *The New-York Journal, and Daily Patriotic Register*.

Maryland Journal, 11 March[1]

☞ The Dearth of Public Intelligence observable in this Day's Journal, may be attributed to the total Stoppage of the usual Communication, thro' the Medium of News-Papers, not one having been *permitted* to come in the last Northern Mail, though, we are assured, they contain much Information interesting to the Public.

1. Reprinted: Philadelphia *Independent Gazetteer* and *Pennsylvania Packet*, 17 March; *New York Journal*, 19 March; Winchester *Virginia Gazette*, 26 March; Boston *American Herald*, 31 March. The *Herald's* reprint was prefaced: "A general, an *almost* universal complaint throughout the Confederated States of America."

James Bryson to James Madison
Philadelphia, 12 March[1]

Supposing that it might not be unacceptable; I have taken the liberty of enclosing you an extract from the Ordinance of Congress, for Regulating the Post Office &c concerning the powers given the Post Master General, respecting the carriage of News papers by the Posts–wishing at the same time (when you have leisure) that you would please to mention the circumstance to the other Gentlemen of the Committee, on Post Office business[2]– and that they would Urge the necessity of the Post Master General's puting the power given him, into execution.

I have to beg leave to mention, that if any *new Arangement* in the Depa[r]tment should take place during the time of your Attendance in Congress:[3] that I may be honoured with your friendship; as I have the sattisfaction of beleiving (and ~~also have~~ think that those who know me also beleive) that no man in America understand the Direction of the Post Office Department better than my self–and have always had the *labouring Oar*–and not the best reward–I only mention this, that in case Mr. H—d may have enemies[(a)] enough to displace him–I may not be forgot.–which friendship would ever be remembered.

> (a) I say Enemies, as I make no doubt but *even News paper* assertions may create him enemies

[Enclosure]

Extract from an Ordinance passed by the United States of America in Congress Assembled. October 18th. 1782, entituled: An ORDINANCE for Regulating the POST-OFFICE of the United States of America.–[4]

And be it ordained by the Authority Aforesaid, That it shall & may be lawful, for the Postmaster General, or any of his Deputies, to licence every Post Rider, to carry any News papers to and from any place or places within these United States, at such Moderate Rates as the Post Master General shall establish, he rendering the Post Riders Accountable to the Post Master General, or the respective Deputy Post Masters by whom they shall severally be employed, for such proportion of the Monies arising therefrom, as the Post Master General shall think proper, to be by him Credited to these United States in his General Account.–

1. RC, Madison Papers, DLC. Bryson (1744–1813) was postmaster of Philadelphia and the assistant to Postmaster General Ebenezer Hazard.

2. On 20 February Madison, Jonathan Dayton, and Jeremiah Wadsworth were appointed a committee "for preventing irregularities in the transportation of the mail" (JCC, XXXIV, 52n).

3. Madison left New York City around 4 March and did not return to Congress until 17 July.

4. JCC, XXIII, 677.

Eleazer Oswald's Statement
Philadelphia Independent Gazetteer, 12 March[1]

☞ The printer of this paper[2] earnestly solicits the attention of the public with regard to his situation–a situation in which he presumes not only all the *printers*, but every *freeman* in this country, will conceive themselves very deeply concerned.

He knows not on what ground the *Centinel* ventured to charge the *postmasters* with unfair deportment in the circulation of newspapers. Upon a liberal investigation of the subject, he cheerfully acquits Mr. *Bryson*, the gentleman who has the management of the post-office in this city. The Printers early represented to him that they did not receive an exchange of their newspapers as usual. He introduced their complaints to his principal, *Ebenezer Hazard*, Esq. post-master general. His answer,[3] far from affording the desired redress, contained a resolution, under his *new* arrangement, as he terms it, to persevere in the same line of conduct, to lord it over the printers, and thereby prevent the free communication of the sentiments of the people, in an impartial and unrestrained circulation of newspapers through the channel of the post-office. The eastern mails have arrived for several weeks past, and no papers have been received by the printers, except a few from some inconsiderable towns in the states of Connecticut and New-York, and now and then, by way of *grace* and *favor*, a single solitary paper from Boston or New-York.[4]

This is the situation of the printers here; a situation truly alarming, and deserving the immediate attention of the people themselves at large. When the vehicles of intelligence are closed at this alarming crisis, by the vile *edicts* of a despotic post-master: when the venerable usages of the country from time immemorial, are invaded to answer the dirty purposes of faction and party, or to gratify high-throned authority, and printers are debarred of their ancient privileges of interchanging their newspapers, let any man in his sober senses say whether *Americans* are not degraded from their rank as *freemen* into that of *slaves* and *vassals*. Such oppressions and atrocious exercises of power, were never expected in the morning of our peace and independency, when the great orb of freedom uplifted his beamy head "to chace the shades of night:" nor will they now bear the test of light.

The post-office, in its creation and establishment, was evidently intended for the good of the people, not for the emolument of a few of their servants and retainers. Hence arose the privileges now claimed by the printers of a mutual intercourse of newspapers through the channel of the post office: and until now never did a post-master, not even in the hot moments of *royal* zeal or *stamp-act* fury, assume a right to discontinue the communication of intelligence in this way. As old as the post-office itself, it has been customary for post-masters to despatch the papers of printers. This custom is therefore an established, uninterrupted custom of the country, that has antiquity, sterling antiquity, on its side; and as such is as obligatory as any positive law of the land. What right can the *post-master general* have to violate permanent laws and usages? Is he an officer of the public, and bound to adhere to such laws, or are the people the humble *captives* and *tenants* of his *will* and *pleasure?* Shall respectable rules and regulations fall a prey to his *flimsey* systems and *temporising* ARRANGEMENTS, or must his discretion submit to well concerted rules, sanctioned by experience, having a reference to the common welfare, and not accommodated to times or things, local or partisanning circumstances? A more oppressive engine could not be pointed at the press, nor levelled at the vitals of the printers. 'Tis to martyr freedom, and shake our privileges from the centre to the extremities.

Printing presses can never be better employed than in defending the birth-rights of the people; and the dignity of the post-office is not to be preserved by the arbitrary hand of power, and an overbearing disposition towards the printers, or in sowing the seeds of jealousy and discord. On the contrary, true dignity consists in looking after and supporting the general good, in which every citizen in a greater or lesser degree is equally interested. Tyrants and despots may flourish like a bay tree, and look green for a-while–But there is a time for all things, and monsters and oppressors are sure to wither.

Having offered these sentiments, which are purely from the printer's known attachment to the Freedom of the Press, he would willingly close. But as endeavors have been made to injure his paper, he would claim a moments more indulgence on the occasion.

Since the promulgation of the new scheme of government, several strictures appearing in this paper, under divers signatures, have given offence to some of its most zealous friends and advocates; and, in order to display the length of their revenge on the printer, have withdrawn their subscriptions,[5] and the most ungenerous means have been essayed to persuade others to pursue their path and follow the example. But let such persons now be told, that the only fault they could find with the printer, he flatters himself, was his love of integrity and impartiality. Freely has he published respective pieces relative to *federal* measures, both *for* and *against* the new constitution. No restrictions were on his paper–nor has partiality ever shewn her pallid face. What crime or offence has he committed in supporting an *impartial* line of conduct in his office? Is this the reason his paper should be treated as diffusing licentiousness, faction and rebellion? And is it for this the *pigmy* prophet DANIEL, the incessant trumpeter of the fugitive productions of *Galen* and his infamous *disciples*, attempts to dishonor the *Independent Gazetteer*, and to proclaim its approaching destiny:[6]

These base attempts to prejudice the printer and his family, he is happy to find, have, on trial, proved abortive–they could not be otherwise, as they sprung from *base born* minds and principles–For many of his fellow citizens, considering the procedures of his enemies as unworthy and illiberal, have repelled the premeditated injury, and generously contributed to the support of his paper, by enrolling their names as subscribers, and advancing their monies.

1. Reprinted: *New York Journal*, 21 March; *New Hampshire Spy*, 11 April. The copy of the *Independent Gazetteer* at the Library of Congress has three marginal notes. See notes 2, 4, and 5 below.

2. Marginal note: "See his Epitaph at the end of this Volume." This "Epitaph" has not been found.

3. See *New York Journal*, 23 January (above).

4. Marginal note: "See this paper March 24th. & Russel's vindication of the P.M.G. in that of April 10th." See Ebenezer Hazard's defense of himself in the *New York Journal*, 21 March (below) which was also printed in the *Independent Gazetteer* on 24 March. The reference to Russell's vindication of Hazard perhaps refers to "A Bostonian," *Independent Gazetteer*, 16 April (below).

5. Marginal note: "Hinc illæ lachrymæ!" (Hence those tears.)

6. References to Daniel Humphreys, printer of the *Pennsylvania Mercury*, and Dr. Benjamin Rush, who was believed to have contributed many essays to the *Mercury*. In February Eleazer Oswald charged that Rush, "in order to *save his bacon*," had become "the *humble* copyist" of Humphreys (*Independent Gazetteer*, 19 February, Mfm:Pa. 436). Between 21 February and 8 March, the *Pennsylvania Mercury* published several original

articles, by different writers, attacking the *Independent Gazetteer* and its publisher (Mfm:Pa.
443, 464, 474, 483, 501). And on 13 March "A Tiffany" wrote in the *Mercury* that
"Eleazer means to die hard, we find from his paper of this morning. . . . As to his
complaint that attempts have been made to injure his paper and thereby to distress his
family, I am sorry to say that the blame lies at his own door; let him ask his own
conscience who has attempted the ruin of his rising family? The answer must be–that
himself by his perverse conduct has done it" (Mfm:Pa. 521).

James de Caledonia to James Bowdoin
Philadelphia Freeman's Journal, 12 March (excerpt)[1]

. . . Every letter I open latterly brings black tidings; I tremble at the
cracking of every seal I break, as every piece of bad news seems to put my
commission as attorney-general (of the union) farther and farther out of
sight. About a month ago I had the *blank* form of it carefully drawn up by
a scrivener; but, my lord, a *blank* I am much afraid it will remain: and you
know how much I must spend if I live at all, and how I am reduced.

I said that accounts from every quarter were against us; but this truth,
my lord, none, but about ten of us in the state know any thing of; for we
publish both among our adherents and opponents that every thing is going
on favorably elsewhere: and I find our system of deception (which we laid
down in the beginning) is carried on with spirit all over the continent; it
has been of infinite service to us. And then our stopping all real intelligence, by preventing the newspapers going backwards and forwards thro'
the Post-Office, has been a very necessary precaution. . . .

1. Reprinted: Philadelphia *Independent Gazetteer*, 14 March. For the complete text of
this letter, dated Philadelphia, 10 March, see Mfm:Pa. 512. James de Caledonia was
an Antifederalist name for James Wilson.

New Hampshire Spy, 18 March[1]

For this three months past the printer of this paper has rarely received a
single paper from New-York or Philadelphia, by the mails which have
arrived during that period, notwithstanding he has been very careful in
forwarding his papers to the printers in the above cities, enclosed in small
packages, and directed to the "*Post-Office, New York,*" &c. He now calls
upon his brother Printers in the above cities, especially such as were, before this lapse, his steady correspondents, to oblige him so far as to inform,
whether they forward their papers or not. Need he suggest the very great
injury which this stoppage of the regular channels of intelligence may be
to these states?–no:–it must be obvious to every thinking person.–It is
much easier to obtain intelligence, and we have it more regular from,
Great-Britain, than from the Southern States, owing to the detention of
newspapers *somewhere!*

1. Reprinted: *New York Journal*, 31 March; Philadelphia *Independent Gazetteer*, 3 April;
Pennsylvania Packet, 4 April; *Pennsylvania Journal*, 5 April. Eleazer Oswald, the printer of
the *Gazetteer*, appended the following editorial comment to his reprint: "We can assure

our brother typo of New-Hampshire, that our papers have been deposited in the *post-office* as usual; and that if he has not received them, it is no fault of ours. But, should this acknowledgement ever reach him, he will probably be convinced that a certain *sublunary deity* of our own creation, who acts as *post-master-general* in New-York, has, in the plenitude of *his* power, thought proper to interdict the free circulation of newspapers since the 1st of January last. To him therefore the several printers in the United States must ascribe their disappointment; and by him only has the majesty of the people, in this respect, been abused and insulted. How long, oh *Americans*, are you tamely to submit to the daily indignities of one of your own servants!"

Manco
Maryland Journal, 18 March[1]

It is the established creed of America, that the Liberty of the Press is the *Palladium* of all the *civil, political* and *religious* rights of AMERICANS[2]–The News-Papers are the *best* vehicles of intelligence and information, respecting public affairs, to the people at large; and to stop their *free* circulation, is an act of injury and insult to the citizens of these United States. At no time can it be more necessary to keep open the channels of communication than at the present moment. The great motive for erecting the present Post-Office in America, was to promote the public good, by facilitating a constant and speedy conveyance of public despatches and private letters; and the *incidental revenue* arising from the latter, was but a *secondary* object. The mutual exchange of News-Papers by the Printers on this continent, in the mail, was always exercised under the British government, and continued since the revolution, until a few weeks ago, when Ebenezer Hazard, Esq; Post-Master-General, *prohibited* the sending any News-Papers in the mail.[3]–What must be the feelings of every Freeman in America, on the conduct of this *little despot in office?*–Take the alarm all ye Lovers of Freedom–it is a sample of what you may expect, if the NEW system of *national* government should be adopted.[4]–The first symptom of a design on the liberties of America is the shackling of the Press; the second is the cutting off the communication of sentiment in the News-Papers.–If the people submit to this conduct, nothing can rouse them from their lethargy, and their next sleep will be the sleep of Death–THE LOSS OF THEIR LIBERTIES.
Baltimore, March 17, 1788.

1. "Manco" was also printed, with slightly altered capitalization and punctuation, in the Baltimore *Maryland Gazette* on 18 March, and reprinted in the Winchester *Virginia Gazette* on 2 April. It was paraphrased and printed as "Watchman" in the Philadelphia *Independent Gazetteer*, 26 March (below). See also note 3 below.
2. "Manco" is paraphrasing *The Letters of Junius*: "Let it be impressed upon your minds, let it be instilled into your children, that the liberty of the press is the palladium of all civil, political and religious rights of freemen." (See "Philadelphiensis" VIII, Philadelphia *Freeman's Journal*, 23 January, CC:473.)
3. This sentence was quoted in "Mentor," Petersburg *Virginia Gazette*, 3 April (below).
4. "Tom Peep" responded to "Manco": "he tells us the news-papers are prohibited from being sent in the mail, and this he calls 'a sample of what may be expected, if the

new system of national government should be adopted.'–He seems to talk in prophetic language and to denounce the loss of our liberties–These are random flights, calculated for party purposes. It cannot be 'a sample of the new government,' which is as yet a non entity; but it plainly indicates the imbecility of the present system, when 'every little despot in office,' may act in his department as he pleases. Let us have done with the weak beggarly elements, under which we at present labour, and shew the world that Americans are capable of *self-government*, by making their servants responsible for their conduct" (Baltimore *Maryland Gazette*, 21 March).

Petition of the Philadelphia Newspaper Printers to the Pennsylvania Assembly, 20–29 March

On 20 March the printers of all eight Philadelphia newspapers signed a petition to the Pennsylvania Assembly about the new post office regulations. The printers requested that the Assembly instruct the state's delegates to Congress to investigate the matter and restore the privilege of a free exchange of newspapers among printers. Federalist Assemblyman William Lewis of Philadelphia presented the petition to the Assembly on 24 March at which time it was read. Three days later the petition was read a second time and was submitted to a three-man committee (Lewis, and Antifederalists James M'Lene and Joseph Hiester), which was ordered to draft instructions to the state's congressional delegates, if it deemed it necessary. On 29 March the committee reported. Federalist Assemblymen George Clymer and Thomas FitzSimons objected to the report because it implied a censure on the postmaster general. Despite these objections, James M'Lene and William Findley moved, and the Assembly agreed, that the instructions be accepted. No record of the instructions reaching the delegates in Congress has been found. Postmaster General Ebenezer Hazard wrote Jeremy Belknap on 15 May that one of the Pennsylvania delegates to Congress had told him "that no such thing had come on yet."

Printers' Petition, 20 March[1]

To the Honorable the Representatives of the Freemen of the Commonwealth of Pennsylvania, in General Assembly met.

The Petition of the Subscribers, Printers of Newspapers in the city of Philadelphia,

Humbly Sheweth, That, from the first establishment of a Post-Office in this country, the printers of newspapers have been accommodated, and the public greatly benefited, by the transmission of newspapers between the colonies and provinces (now states) in the mails.

That, this practice, so conducive to the preservation of liberty, and useful to the people, in maintaining harmony, removing prejudices and mistaken jealousies; and cultivating a good understanding between the distant colonies, was singularly beneficial on the approach of, and during the late glorious contest with Great Britain, as it afforded the means of regular and constant intercourse and intercommunication of sentiments between them.

That, in consequence of a regulation of the Post-Master-General of the United States, this ancient and highly advantageous practice has been discontinued since the beginning of the present year, for reasons unknown to your petitioners; and your petitioners are thereby prevented from affording that satisfaction to the public of the occurrences in other states, as formerly, which is so important to the safety, interest, and harmony of the United States.

That, your petitioners do not desire any newspapers should be conveyed with the mails, but such only as are sent to, and exchanged with, news printers.

Your petitioners therefore pray, that, your Honorable House will take the premises into consideration, and be pleased to instruct the delegates of this commonwealth in the Congress of the United States, to inquire into the premises, and to procure for your petitioners and their fellow printers throughout the United States of America, the restoration of this their necessary and long accustomed privilege, or such other relief in the premises as to your Honorable House may seem meet.

HALL and SELLERS,
THOMAS BRADFORD,
DUNLAP and CLAYPOOLE,
FRANCIS BAILEY,
Philadelphia, March 20, 1788.

ELEAZER OSWALD,
MELCHOR STEINER,
DANIEL HUMPHREYS,
JOHN M'CULLOCH.

Assembly Debates, Saturday, 29 March[2]

Mr. *Lewis*[3] also presented the report on the printers petition, which on motion was read a second time.–The following is the resolution offered by the committee, but it was prefaced with a train of observations and reasoning tending to shew the ground of complaint made by the printers, of the refusal of the postmaster to carry their news-papers free of expence.

Resolved, that a copy of the petition of divers printers of the city of Philadelphia, together with a copy of this resolution, be transmitted to the delegates of this state in congress, and that they be instructed to make with all due diligence, full enquiry into the truth of the facts therein contained, and that if the abuses therein complained of shall on such enquiry be found to exist, the said delegates shall use their best endeavors in congress to obtain redress of the same, in order that a knowledge of public events may have a free circulation throughout the United States of America.

Mr. *Clymer* was against adopting the report in that form, because he conceived it was not founded on that information which mr. Hazard had given in the public papers; from which it clearly appeared that the post-office had nothing to do with the carriage of news-papers, but that the mode of conducting that business was by the riders, who stipulated with the printers, for this purpose, at a price which was agreed between them, and allowed as a perquisite to the riders.[4] The committee perhaps had not viewed the business in this light, and therefore he moved to re-commit.

Mr. *Fitzsimons*. The preamble to the resolution seems in part to confirm the charges made by anonymous writers against that department, and it would be highly imprudent in this house to countenance such without we had an opportunity of informing ourselves fully on the subject. This part of the report in my opinion implies a censure which we shall hereafter learn is ungrounded, and what will then be our feelings? I think the prefatory part had better be left out; as for the resolution, it is well enough, for I think it right the matter should be left to congress, to do what they judge proper on this occasion, as they have the means of acquiring information, and it is a subject specially belonging to them.

Mr. *Clymer* thought it implied a censure that was calculated to inflame the public mind unnecessarily, and therefore wished it to be omitted.

Mr. *Lewis*. If the report, sir, is calculated to do those things with which it has been charged, I hope it will be rejected; but if it appears in a different point of view, the house will not object to the resolution.

The printers in this city have not thought proper to make an immediate application to congress, but have addressed the legislature to instruct their delegates to procure for them the privilege of transmitting their news-papers free of expence, which they alledge is a necessary and long accustomed privilege. The committee to whom their petition was referred, did not find that the house was disposed to enquire into the truth of the fact therein set forth, nor did they know of any authentic information. There were publications, sir, on each side of the question, but I look upon neither of them to be authentic information to the house, but as it is a subject of considerable importance, and the minds of some people seem to be agitated about it, the committee were led to offer a resolution which if adopted, puts it in a fair way of being decided. It is alledged that owing to some late regulation of the post-office the means of communicating public events is cut off, and that too at a very interesting period: this charge if well founded, is of a serious nature, and being of a serious nature, it is the duty of the house to take such steps as will lead to ascertain the truth of the fact; when if it should be found groundless, and I have no doubt but it will, the calumniator ought to be made known. But what can the house do more if the charge was true: they cannot displace the post-master, nor can they alter the regulation. The first of these belongs to congress, and the other is dependent upon it; there then is the proper place to have the business decided: the resolution offered you goes no further than to bring about such an examination. It conveys no censure on the post-master, nor was it intended so to do. I believe there has been no cause for the complaint and clamour which has been made, and I have a perfect reliance that it will turn out so.

The object of the report I have endeavored to state, and honorable gentlemen must see thro' a different medium from me, to imagine that the preamble has the least appearance of censure on the conduct of that officer. Nothing more is meant than to refer the case to the proper tribunal.

Mr. *Clymer* thought it would be giving pain to the post-master to see his official information neglected; for the publication, under his signature, appeared to be as authentic information as any that could be obtained.

Mr. *Fitzsimons* wished a full enquiry might be made, but he did not wish to convey a censure even by implication, for he was well satisfied that the case was placed in a true point of view by the post-master general, and that after the fullest enquiry nothing more would be discovered. He could not help thinking but that the publication of the post-master will be generally thought authentic information, for there was a wide difference between it and those of anonymous authors.

Mr. *Lewis.* There are charges by anonymous writers made against the post-master, and against a great many of the superior characters in the United States, most if not all of which I believe equally groundless: but do not force us to believe, sir, that what is offered in extenuation by the person charged is to be considered as authentic information;–I think gentlemen will not imagine, that the denial of a public officer that a charge is groundless is sufficient to acquit him; and therefore if I am not mistaken, the publication of the Postmaster ought not to prevent further investigation.

The question was now taken on the resolution and agreed to.

Philadelphia Freeman's Journal, 2 April[5]

Saturday last in the House of Assembly the Committee on the Petition of the Printers, reported instructions to the delegates from this state in Congress, to enquire into the cause of the stoppage of the Newspapers in the Post-Office for these several months past, when real intelligence and a free communication of sentiments is so necessary to be propagated; and to take such other steps as they may think proper to establish this most important right of the people on such a footing that it may not again be infringed: and the Legislature immediately adopted the report.

Ebenezer Hazard to Jeremy Belknap
   New York, 15 May (excerpt)[6]

. . . The Phila. Printers some Time since petitioned their Assembly about News Papers, wch. they alledged could not be Sent by Post, in Consequence of a regulation made by the P.M.G.–it was refered to a Committee–& the house finally (as appears by the *News Papers*) resolved that a Copy should be sent to their Delegates, with Instructions to make full Enquiry into the Truth of the facts; & if the abuse complained of shall, on such Enquiry, be found to exist, that the Delegates use their best endeavors in Congress to *obtain Redress of the same.*–One of the Delegates[7] told me today that no such thing had come on yet; & inter nos, he hinted a Doubt whether the Assembly had come to any Resolution about it–The Petition is said to have been presented on the 24th. & read a second Time on the 27th. *March,* so that there has been time enough to send it on. The Petition has got into the Papers, so that I suppose it will circulate & you will see it. My publication, I think, contains a full Answer to it,[8] & I suppose the Presidt. (Dr. Franklin) knowing the Petn. to mis-state facts, has paid no Attention to it. . . .

1. Philadelphia *Independent Gazetteer*, 10 May. Summaries and excerpts from the Assembly Minutes were published in the *Gazetteer* before and after the petition. The *Gazetteer's* account was reprinted in the *Pennsylvania Packet*, 13 May; Philadelphia *Freeman's Journal*, 14 May; New York *Daily Advertiser* and *New York Journal*, 17 May; Boston *American Herald*, 26 May; Charleston *City Gazette*, 20 June; and Charleston *Columbian Herald*, 23 June. The *Pennsylvania Packet*, 31 March, printed the Assembly Minutes of 24 March concerning the petition. The *Packet's* account was reprinted ten times by 8 May: N.H. (1), Mass. (3), R.I. (1), Conn. (3), N.Y. (1), Pa. (1).

2. *Proceedings and Debates of the General Assembly of Pennsylvania, as Taken in Short Hand by Thomas Lloyd* (4 vols., Philadelphia, 1787-1788), III (19 February-29 March 1788), 232-35 (Evans 21370).

3. William Lewis (1752-1819) of Philadelphia was a Quaker and a lawyer.

4. Clymer refers to Hazard's defense of himself, which was printed in the *New York Journal* on 21 March (below), and reprinted in six Philadelphia newspapers between 24 and 29 March.

5. Reprints by 7 May (10): N.H. (1), Mass. (1), N.J. (1), Pa. (1), Md. (2), Va. (3), S.C. (1).

6. RC, Belknap Papers, MHi. Printed: "Belknap-Hazard Correspondence," 38-39.

7. William Irvine and James R. Reid were the Pennsylvania delegates to Congress in attendance at this time.

8. For Hazard's defense of himself, see the *New York Journal*, 21 March (below).

New York Journal, 20 March

☞ The Editor acknowledges the Receipt of a Packet of late Papers from Philadelphia, *by a private conveyance*, with Thanks. A piece from the Chronicle of Freedom, of the 12th inst. Respecting the Post-Office, &c.[1] came too late for this Day's paper.

1. See the Philadelphia *Independent Gazetteer*, subtitled *the Chronicle of Freedom*, 12 March (above).

Massachusetts Gazette, 21 March[1]

It is a fact as lamentable as it is notorious, that the channel through which the publick are made acquainted with the events occouring in the different states is obstructed, and they are consequently deprived of ONE of those privileges which constitutes the blessing of being FREE! By what means, or by whose mismanagement this has been brought to pass, we cannot say–but so it is, that scarcely a news-paper has been received by the Printers in this town, southward of New-Haven, since the commencement of the present year. We do not attribute it to any evil design–we can only say, that it is a serious matter of publick notoriety, and wish that it lay in our power to remove this curse–for a CURSE it is. The publick, therefore, will cease to wonder at the barrenness of the publications in town since the commencement of the present year. The regular channel of information is stopped, and the evil is, or soon will be, most sensibly felt, if an effectual remedy is not speedily applied.–By the mail on Wednesday evening, the Printers in the metropolis received a single paper only, and that too printed in a country town.–How, then, can it be otherwise expected, than that our publications should be esteemed trifling, insignificant, and scarcely worth perusing, seeing that their natural food and only sustinance, which enliven and make them interesting, is denied them? This must surely awaken the people to a sense of the importance of this great privilege, and lead to an inquiry, why this thing is so.

1. Reprinted: *New Hampshire Gazette*, 26 March; Portland *Cumberland Gazette*, 27 March (excerpt); *New York Journal*, 2 April; Philadelphia *Independent Gazetteer*, 3 April; *Pennsylvania Packet*, 4 April; *Pennsylvania Journal*, 5 April. This paragraph from the *Massachusetts Gazette* was immediately preceded by another paragraph on the post office originally printed in the *Maryland Journal*, 29 February (above). (The New Hampshire, Maine, and New York reprints, listed above, followed the *Massachusetts Gazette's* example in reprinting the paragraph from the *Maryland Journal*.)

Ebenezer Hazard's Defense
New York Journal, 21 March[1]

Mr. GREENLEAF, I observe *in your paper of this date the following note, viz.* "A piece from the Chronicle of Freedom, of the 12th inst. respecting the Post-Office, &c. came too late for this day's paper:" *which leads me to suppose you intend to publish that "piece."*[2]*–if you do, I claim it as an act of justice due to the department, that you also publish the following, which has already been sent to the Printer of "the Chronicle of Freedom" for the same purpose.*

I am, Sir, Your humble Servant,
EBENEZER HAZARD.

General Post-Office, March 20, 1788.

GENERAL POST-OFFICE.

New-York, March 19, 1788.
Several paragraphs having lately appeared in some of the news-papers, reflecting upon the conduct of the officers of this department, on account of irregularity in the transportation of *news-papers*; and indecent attacks, of a more recent date, replete with illiberality and rancour, having been made upon the post-master-general, on the same account, he thinks it necessary to state the following facts, in order to prevent any undue impressions being made upon the public mind; viz.

That the post-office was established for the purpose of facilitating commercial correspondence; and has, properly speaking, no connection with news-papers, the carriage of which was an indulgence granted to the post-riders, prior to the revolution in America:

That the riders stipulated with the Printers for the carriage of their papers, at a price which was agreed upon between them; and this price was allowed as a *perquisite* to the riders:

That news-papers have never been considered as a part of the *mail*, nor (until a very few years) admitted into the same portmanteau with it; but were carried in saddle-bags, provided for that purpose, by the riders, at their own expence:

That, to promote general convenience, the post-masters (not officially) undertook to receive and distribute the news-papers brought by the riders, without any other compensation for their trouble than the compliment of a newspaper from each printer:

That, although the United States in Congress assembled, from an idea that beneficial improvements might be made in the transportation of the *mail*, have directed alterations as to the mode of carrying it; yet they have not directed any to be made in the custom respecting news-papers:

And, That the post-master-general has given no orders or directions about them, either to the post-masters, or to the riders.

From this succinct state of facts the post-master general apprehends it will clearly appear, that so far as the post-office is concerned, the carriage of news-papers rests exactly on its original foundation; and that the attempts to excite clamors against the department must have some other source than a failure in duty on the part of the officers.

1. This item was printed eighteen other times by 5 May: N.H. (1), Mass. (2), R.I. (2), Conn. (2), N.Y. (1), Pa. (6), Md. (2), Va. (1), S.C. (1). Like the *New York Journal* (above), four of the Philadelphia printings were prefaced by brief letters from Hazard to the printers. The letter to the *Independent Gazetteer*, 24 March, and the *Freeman's Journal*, 25 March, both Antifederalist newspapers, stated: "As the attacks lately made upon the Post-Office department have had a place in your paper, I have a claim upon both your impartiality and justice for the insertion of the enclosed, which I now make. . . ." The letter to the *Pennsylvania Packet*, 25 March, and the *Pennsylvania Journal*, 26 March, both Federalist newspapers, stated simply: "Your publishing the inclosed will much oblige. . . ." The letter to the *New York Journal* was reprinted once; that to the *Pennsylvania Packet* and *Pennsylvania Journal* twice; and that to the *Independent Gazetteer* and *Freeman's Journal* three times. Eight newspapers reprinted Hazard's defense without a prefatory letter.

2. See the *Independent Gazetteer*, 12 March, and the *New York Journal*, 20 March (both above). The *Journal* reprinted the *Gazetteer's* piece directly above Hazard's defense.

John Eager Howard to Jeremiah Wadsworth
Baltimore, c. 24 March (excerpt)[1]

. . . I have written to you several times about the Post office.–Great complaints are made and an opinion prevails that there is a combination to prevent a free communication of intelligence which injures our cause–I am informed that some papers respecting the office have been forwarded to me at N. York–If there are any please to open them and make what ever you think necessary of them

1. RC, Wadsworth Papers, CtHi. The letter has no place or date of writing. It is docketed "Colo Howard/Baltimore/March 1. 1788." A Baltimore postmark also appears on the address page but the exact date cannot be determined. From internal

evidence, it appears that the letter was written about 24 March. Howard (1752–1827), a Baltimore planter and land developer, had left Congress on 29 February, having served there for a little more than a month. In November 1788 he was elected governor of Maryland. On 20 February 1788 Wadsworth, a Hartford, Conn., merchant, had been appointed to a three-man committee "for preventing irregularities in the transportation of the mail." The other two members were Jonathan Dayton and James Madison. The committee was renewed on 27 March (JCC, XXXIV, 52n, 116n. For the membership of the later committee, see "Confederation Congress: Report of Committee on the Post Office," 7 May, below.).

A True Federalist
New York Journal, 25 March[1]

To Ebenezer Hazard, Esq.

SIR, You have at length deigned to reply to the many, many complaints, which the Printers from Boston to Virginia, have repeatedly exhibited against the department under your *sovereign* will and direction. How far you have exculpated yourself in Mr. *Greenleaf's* paper of Friday last, is not for me to decide. I may, however, venture to pronounce, that what you deem *"a succinct state of facts,"* will be considered as low subterfuges and mean evasions; and that your conduct in suppressing the free circulation of newspapers deserves the severest reprehension. The oppressions complained of, are generally known, felt, and acknowledged; you have, therefore, no chance to escape the just censures and execrations of the people: though you seek for refuge and protection under the wings of Congress, their resentment will even reach you there, and expose your *"dark deeds,"* to open day-light. But to the point and to your *succinct state of facts.*

You have either wilfully misrepresented the established rules and customs of the post-office before and since the revolution, or, you are totally ignorant of the subject. That the post-office was established for the benefit of the community at large, as well as "for the purpose of facilitating commercial correspondence," no one will presume to doubt. And here it would not be amiss to query how far have you, as post-master-general, facilitated *commercial* correspondence?–Let the candid merchants of Philadelphia and this place, declare in what manner they have been treated by the rigid adherence of post-masters and their assistants to *office* hours? Besides, newspapers are not infrequently of more service to merchants than letters from their most active and attentive correspondents.

But it is also a fact which cannot be denied or controverted, that the printers of newspapers have, time immemorial, enjoyed the privilege of exchanging their papers through the channel of the post-office; and that the carriage of the papers for their subscribers was a *perquisite* of the *post-rider,* with which the *postmaster* had no connection or concern. The riders "stipulated" with the printers *only* for the carriage of their papers directed to *subscribers*; but newspapers for the *printers* have ever been considered as a part of the mail, and, until your new arrangement, were admitted into the same portmanteau with it. The *opossum* or *false belly* of the mail was conceived in your own brain: it is a *monster* hitherto unknown among post-masters and printers; and future generations must confess themselves indebted for this *noble* production to your *enlarged* understanding.

These are stubborn facts which your piddling genius cannot invalidate or set aside. If it were necessary, I might, with great propriety, appeal, for additional support, to *John Laurance*, Esq. late a member of Congress, and now a senator of this state, who assisted near eight or ten years in the management of the post-office in this city, and to Mr. *Thomas Tillyer*, who was likewise an assistant in the post-office at Philadelphia, before the revolution: nay, I might refer you to Dr. *Franklin*, & *John Foxcroft*, Esq. the late post-masters general under the British administration.

And here it is worthy of remark, that so tenacious were the people of this privilege, that the British post-masters never attempted to preclude the printers' papers from the mail, not even after the battle of Lexington—And shall a *creature* who was *foisted* into the office by an *intriguing junto* of the *provincial Congress*, without the least claim or pretention thereto, now be permitted to exercise his interdictions? Can any man in his senses suppose that Congress ever meant or intended to place the post-office on a *worse* footing than before the revolution?–Be assured, sir, this antient and useful custom has long been fixed on too solid a foundation to be trampled under foot and destroyed by your fancied power and importance.

Since I have mentioned the subject of appeals, I appeal to Mr. Grummond, who has contracted with you for the transportation of the mail on *horseback* from this city to Philadelphia, whether you did not absolutely declare to him that he had nothing to do with the printers' newspapers, though you have positively asserted, in your *succinct* state of facts, that you had given *no* orders or directions about them either to the *post-masters*, or to the riders? Here the eye of suspicion looks shrewdly on you, and seems to call your veracity in question. Did not the post-master in Philadelphia receive your instructions on this subject? or was your lengthy epistle to Mr. Bryson, couched in such ambiguous terms as to admit a double construction?

I appeal to the post-master at Bristol,[2] whether, under the idea of his acting agreeably to your orders and opinion; the rider employed by Mr. Grummond, has not recently thrown out the printers' papers, which you were so condescending as to admit into the *false-belly* of the mail, declaring that he would not carry them; and whether he did not scatter them along the road near Bristol? and I appeal to Mr. Thompson, secretary of Congress, whether, since the new arrangement, he has not complained to a certain printer, in Philadelphia, that the papers for Congress did not come forward as usual? How ridiculous and absurd then must this *excellent* arrangement appear, when the papers for the Congress themselves have been, and perhaps now are, at the mercy and under the controul of the *post-riders*, who derive their consequence and insolence from the post-master general?

As you have availed yourself of a resolution of Congress in the year *1782*, by giving us a *partial* quotation relative to the *post-office*, I have taken the trouble to transcribe their late resolutions *in toto*, on the same subject, for your consideration, as well as to satisfy more fully the public mind with regard to your contumely, insolence of office, and unwarrantable stretch of authority.

IN CONGRESS, July 26, 1787.

On the report of a committee, consisting of Mr. Dane, Mr. Hawkins, and Mr. Pierce, to whom was referred a letter from the post-master general,

RESOLVED, That the post-master-general be, and he is hereby author-ised and instructed to enter into contracts with sufficient security for the conveyance of the mails for one year, commencing on the first day of January next, from Portland in Massachusetts, to Savannah, in Georgia, by stage carriages, if practicable,[a] and that the same be done by four or more separate contracts, and in case of only four contracts, the first to extend from Portland to New-York; the second from New-York to Phila-delphia; the third from Philadelphia to Suffolk in Virginia; and the fourth from Suffolk to Savannah, by such route as the post-master-general may find most convenient.

Monday, October 15, 1787.

On motion of Mr. H. Lee, seconded by Mr. Carrington,

Resolved, That the post-master-general be, and he is hereby authorised to contract for the transportation of the mail for the year 1788, by stage carriages or horses, as he may judge most expedient and beneficial; pro-vided that preference be given to the transportation by stages to encourage this useful institution when it can be done without material injury to the public,[b] and that the mail be conveyed three times per week, from the first of May to the first of November, and twice a week from the first of November to the first of May, from Portland in Massachusetts, to Suffolk in Virginia, and twice a week from the first of May to the first of Novem-ber, and once a week from the first of November to the first of May, from Suffolk to Savannah in Georgia.

On motion,

Resolved, That the post-master-general be, and he is hereby authorised to alter the route from Petersburgh in Virginia, to Savannah in Georgia, to Augusta in Georgia; provided he may judge it beneficial and expedient, and that in case of such alteration he establish cross-posts, agreeably to the principles provided in the resolve of the 15th of February, 1787, to the commercial towns on the sea coast.

From this plain state of facts, there can be no doubt but you have acted not *officially*, but officiously and tyrannically, and that the exchange of the printers newspapers does *not* rest on its original foundation. This has been the sole cause of all the complaints and objections which have been raised against the department, and which have involved you in your present disagreeable dilemma.

The interest and welfare of society require and demand, that the postmaster general should, at all times, "promote the general convenience," and that he should not impede or obstruct the free communication of sentiments, through the regular channels of intelligence, especially at this important and interesting period, when the liberties of America are, as it were, suspended by a single thread.

Rotation of office is allowed, on all hands, to be one of the greatest excellencies of a republican government: it is high time then for a change in the administration of the post-office; if the late arbitrary and unjustifiable procedures of the head of the department, with respect to the circulation of newspapers, did not loudly call for the measure.

For the present I shall take my leave, and resign you up to the merited correction of your superiors.

New-York, March 23, 1788.

> (a) Query–Whether it was not *practicable* to contract with the stage owners from Portsmouth, in New-Hampshire, to Suffolk, in Virginia?
> (b) Quere–What material injury could the public have sustained, had the contract, for the transportation of the mails, been made with the proprietors of the stages?

1. On 24 March the *New York Journal* announced that "A True Federalist" "came too late for Publication but will appear in our next." According to Ebenezer Hazard, "A True Federalist" was written by Eleazer Oswald, who was in New York City at this time (Hazard to Jeremy Belknap, 10 May, below). "A True Federalist" was reprinted in the Philadelphia *Independent Gazetteer*, 31 March; *New Hampshire Spy*, 15 April; and Boston *American Herald*, 21 April. The reprint in the *Spy* was prefaced: "In our last we presented our readers with some strictures upon the conduct of Mr. HAZARD, Post Master-General [see Eleazer Oswald's Statement, 12 March, above]; together with his reply thereto. The following piece, addressed to *that gentleman*, affording much information, we deem it our duty to lay the same before the public."

For Hazard's defense of himself, to which "A True Federalist" is a reply, see the *New York Journal*, 21 March (above).

2. Charles Bessonett was postmaster at Bristol, Pa. Bristol, twenty miles northeast of Philadelphia, is on the Delaware River opposite Burlington, N.J.

Watchman
Philadelphia Independent Gazetteer, 26 March[1]

MR. OSWALD, In yesterday's paper I observed a publication from Ebenezer Hazard, Esquire, Post Master-General,[2] in which he endeavors to exculpate himself from the heavy charges made against him from all parts of the continent of stopping every *free* paper in the post office, thereby preventing due intelligence getting to the people in the different states at this most important crisis. A heavy charge indeed, an ESTABLISHED USAGE older than our governments, to be broken by a petty officer, and so much against the voice of the people. It is the established creed of America, that the liberty of the press is the *palladium* of all the *civil, political* and *religious* rights of AMERICANS. The newspapers are the best vehicles of intelligence and information, respecting public affairs to the people at large; and to stop their *free* circulation, is an act of injury and insult to these United States. At no time can it be more necessary to keep open the channels of communication, than the present moment. The great motive for erecting the present post-office in America, was to promote the public good, by facilitating a constant and speedy conveyance of public dispatches and private letters; and the *incidental revenue arising* from the latter, was but a secondary object. The mutual exchange of newspapers by the printers on this continent, in the mail, was always exercised under the British government, and continued since the revolution, until a few months ago, when the said Ebenezer Hazard, Esquire, *prohibited* sending any papers in the mail. What must be the feelings of every freeman in America, on the conduct of this *little despot in office?* And what does he say in his defence? Nothing! A few paltry low evasions, and unsupported assertions make up his performance. Take the alarm all ye lovers of freedom–it is a sample of what you may expect, if the NEW system of national government should be adopted.–The first symptom of a design on the liberties of America, is the shackling of the press; the second is the cutting off the communication of sentiments in the newspapers.–If the people of America submit to this conduct, nothing can rouse them from their lethargy, and their next sleep will be the sleep of death–THE LOSS OF THEIR LIBERTIES.

N.B. The printers at *Baltimore* announce, that within this some weeks past, they have not received a *single* paper through the post-office.[3] The *campaign* coming on there soon, doubtless is the cause of this *total* stoppage.[4]

1. Reprinted: *New York Journal*, 31 March; Boston *American Herald*, 10 April; *Massachusetts Gazette*, 11 April. "Watchman" is a paraphrase of "Manco," *Maryland Journal*, 18 March (above).

2. Hazard's defense, printed in the *New York Journal*, 21 March (above), was reprinted in the *Independent Gazetteer* on the 24th and in the Philadelphia *Federal Gazette* and the *Pennsylvania Packet* the next day.

3. See William Goddard to Mathew Carey, 28 February, and *Maryland Journal*, 29 February, 11 March (all above).

4. The election of delegates to the Maryland Convention was scheduled to take place on 7 April and the convention was to meet two weeks later.

Purported Letters from George Bryan to John Ralston
Pennsylvania Gazette, 26 March (excerpts)

The two excerpts printed below are from letters allegedly written by George Bryan, a Philadelphia Antifederalist leader, to John Ralston of Northampton County, Pa., on 7 and 12 March, respectively. The letters were submitted to the *Pennsylvania Gazette* by "X" who wanted to demonstrate to the public the mischief that Bryan was creating. For the complete texts, circulation, and impact of these letters, see CC:647; and for an Antifederalist response, see "A Friend to Law and Order," Philadelphia *Freeman's Journal*, 2 April (below).

[7 March] . . . Failing, the conspirators against equal liberty will have much deceit and wicked conduct to answer for. They have seduced the post-officers to stop all news-papers from state to state, that contained investigations of their plan, so that the dissent of the minority of Pennsylvania did not get to Boston before their Convention rose.[1] . . .

[12 March] . . . The Conspirators are fully detected in stopping the transmission of intelligence from state to state by tricks in the post-offices. Being charged with it early in February, they stifly denied it. It is at length become too palpable to all. Sure no business of a public nature has proceeded upon such base tricks of fraud and surprize! . . .

1. "A Pennsylvanian" responded: "Do you really believe the friends of the federal government have seduced the Post-Office to stop all news-papers from state to state? Do you really believe that the dissent of the Pennsylvania minority did not reach Boston till after their Convention arose?" (*Pennsylvania Gazette*, 2 April, Mfm:Pa. 600). "A Pennsylvanian" was a pseudonym used by Tench Coxe in four newspaper essays printed in the *Pennsylvania Gazette* between 6 and 27 February (Mfm:Pa. 408, 430, 439, 459).

Winchester Virginia Gazette, 26 March–9 April

Matthias Bartgis and Nathaniel Willis, the printers of the Winchester *Virginia Gazette*, took a decided stand on the controversy over the circulation of newspapers among printers. From 14 March to 21 May almost every issue of the *Gazette* contained at least one item (either an original piece or a reprinting) decrying the post office's new policies. The publication of these and other Antifederalist items provoked "*a gentleman in the country*" to accuse the printers of being "strong antifederalists." (The *Gazette* was the only Virginia newspaper to reprint the "Dissent of the Minority of the Pennsylvania Convention." The "Dissent" took up virtually the entire first page of six of the seven issues of the *Gazette* between 1 February and 14 March.) The printers defended their conduct by stating that, whatever their "*private sentiments . . .* may be, on political subjects, they ever have endeavoured to demonstrate a *strict equality* of publications on the new government: *unbiassed by party, and unawed by frowns, they are determined to be free.*"

The Editors, 26 March[1]

The Editors of this Paper, feel with their brother Printers throughout the United States,[2] the ill-consequences of a *late* regulation at the general Post-Office, for stopping the circulation of the news-papers through the medium of the mails, they not having received any Northern papers, except by transcient conveyance, for several months past.[3] Whatever *secret views* the promoters of this diabolical plan may have, we hope the guardians of our liberty and future safety, will be vigilant in frustrating so dangerous a measure, which may eventually lead us blind-fold to the rivets of slavery. If this is a *sample* of what we *may expect* from the establishment of the Federal Constitution, may we not with propriety say, from *such a government*, "*Good Lord, deliver us.*"

A Federalist: To the Editors, 2 April

Of all the anti-federal productions which have yet appeared, the paragraph in your last paper, respecting the stoppage of the circulation of newspapers is the most extraordinary. If the fact be as there stated, it is a grievance which ought to be redressed, but it is inconsistency in the extreme to charge a government which is not in existence, with the maladministration of the present government. If Congress authorise the abuse, it affords an additional reason for their dissolution, and for the establishment of a government on more liberal principles, in which our rulers will be chosen by the people at large, and consequently we may expect them to be more attentive to our interests, and more vigilant guardians of our liberties, than the members of the present Congress.

The Editors, 2 April[4]

☞ The Editors sincerely wish that the new Constitution had been so framed, that *every paragraph* published on that important subject, could have been truly federal, but when opinions vary, and it is submitted to the People for free discussion, to see *men in public office* taking undue measures to establish it, without a thorough investigation, and by means which not only grossly infringes on the liberties of the people, but strikes a fatal blow at their very political existence, the Editors think it a duty incumbent on them as Printers of a public paper, to give the alarm. It ever has been, (even under the tyrannical government of Britain) an invariable privilege to suffer, for the public good, a free passage for news-papers in the mails, but of late, for reasons which the Editors wish not to suggest, they are prohibited. Whatever may be the views of *public men* at the present day, if they should be continued in office (which it is more than probable they will, unless from their present conduct they are well guarded against) may we not expect the same measures? which, if practised, we may bid adieu to that *scourge to tyrants, an unrestrained Press*.

The most distant view of injuring the Constitution did not exist by publishing the paragraph above referred to, but, that due notice might be taken of so daring a breach of public confidence.

One of the People, 9 April

Extract of a letter from a gentleman in the country, to his friend in town.

"From Messi'rs Bartgis & Company's addresses to the public, in their papers of the 7th and 14th instant, I was led to believe, that they were no party men.[5] But from their piece in the last *Winchester Gazette*, I take them to be strong anti-federalists: be that as it may, I am clear of opinion, every man has a right to enjoy his own opinion. But I am also of opinion that they, nor no other man can, with propriety, lay the blame of their not receiving the northern papers, to the Federal Constitution, when every body knows, that Constitution has not taken place, and of course can have no effect. If the Post-Master-General, his deputy, his deputy's deputy, or any other, has stop'd the circulation of news, as they have set forth in their piece, the Post-Master-General, his deputy, &c. are liable to public censure, and ought to be exposed, then their prayer would [have] been with more propriety thus: From our present, or any other government, which will suffer the Post-Master-General, his deputy, his deputy's deputy, or any other person whatever to stop the[6]

Winchester, 31st March, 1788.

The Editors, 9 April

☞ The Editors with the greatest reluctance again trouble their readers with a defence of their public conduct, as Printers:–they have before asserted, that no intention existed with them of injuring the constitution:–they wish to expose every *secret* attempted to effect a *partial* circulation of observations wrote on the subject, *by men who are looking for continuations of lucrative offices.* Had an effort been made by those *opposed* to the constitution, to wrest from the public eye, *the means of information,* they would as readily have exposed them. They conceive it *their duty* to be watchful of every attempt to destroy our dear-earn'd freedom, let the design come from what man, or set of men, it may.

Whatever the *private sentiments* of the Editors may be, on political subjects, they ever have endeavoured to demonstrate a *strict equality* of publications on the new government: *unbiassed by party, and unawed by frowns, they are determined to be free.*

1. Reprinted: Philadelphia *Independent Gazetteer,* 8 April; *New York Journal,* 12 April; Boston *American Herald,* 28 April.

2. Reprints of the *Massachusetts Centinel,* 16 February, and the *Maryland Journal,* 11 March (both above), also appeared on the same page of the *Virginia Gazette.* On the 14th and 19th the *Gazette* had reprinted similar items from the *Maryland Journal* of 29 February (above).

3. The first page of this issue of the *Virginia Gazette* was introduced with an editorial: "Through the *attention* of our worthy Correspondent at Baltimore, in forwarding us several of his late papers, by a private hand, we are enabled to communicate the following *interesting intelligence,* viz."

4. "Manco," *Maryland Journal,* 18 March (above) appeared in the same issue as this editorial.

5. Matthias Bartgis, proprietor and editor of the Winchester *Virginia Gazette,* announced on 7 March that he was "unalterably determined to persevere in his professional character, an *unbiassed, impartial Printer*" despite the efforts of the "secret views of an ungrateful party" in Winchester. Nathaniel Willis, Bartgis' new partner, introduced himself to his readers in the *Gazette* on 14 March, and stated that he intended to keep the *Gazette "open* for a full discussion of all momentous subjects & unbiassed by party, he will aim to be *just."*

6. The remainder of this item, except for the place and date of writing, has been clipped out of the only extant copy of this issue of the *Gazette.*

New Hampshire Spy, 28 March[1]

On stopping public Newspapers.

A Correspondent has favoured us with the following observations on the late *alarming* and *iniquitous* practice of interrupting the regular channels of intelligence:–

–"The stopping of public newspapers, in a free country, is an outrage upon all mankind, because it interrupts business, and foils the public in general of the only easy and expeditious mode of communicating important events and sentiments.–In them we find many interesting thoughts in religion, morals, politics, law, physic, agriculture, and commerce–by them we learn the state of foreign nations and foreign affairs–the various things that concern domestic œconomicks, as well as the casualties of neighbourhoods. The merchant learns the general state of trade, hears the prices current, knows his losses in every quarter of the globe–thus he and the insurer are mutually advantaged and do mutual benefit to the community. The artist hears of employ or presents an advertisement of the various things he has for sale. The learned hears of new publications–their vent is increased–and innumerable advantages are extended to all.

"I wish our Members of Congress, Rulers or influential men in the states, would use their influence to check this *growing injury* to the community, and that a proper complaint be made to the Post-Master-General. I fear the evil does not lay in any particular place, but in the —— in general."

1. Reprinted: *New York Journal*, 10 April; Exeter, N.H., *Freeman's Oracle*, 11 April; Philadelphia *Independent Gazetteer*, 14 April; New Jersey *Brunswick Gazette*, 15 April.

A Friend to Law and Order
Philadelphia Freeman's Journal, 2 April (excerpt)[1]

Mr. PRINTER, Mr. Bryan's letters, which were published last week,[2] are not the only ones, that have been intercepted by the friends of good government; and it is to be hoped, that a number of other letters will speedily be laid before the Public.–The following was lately picked out of the pocket of a traveller in the stage, by a gentleman of great honour and love to his country, who hopes to be taken notice of according to his merits, as soon as matters are settled. Unfortunately the caitiff, who wrote it, has used only initials, instead of names at length, both in the signature and superscription, in hopes of escaping detection; but means are in use which, it is expected, will speedily drag the villain forth into open day-light. The little judge is watching under the eaves of the school-houses every night; the post-offices and the houses where letters are deposited, to go into the country, are all examined, to discover the hand writing; and we are dealing with a servant, whose master is believed to know something about it; so that we can hardly fail of success.

[Fictitious Letter from B.Y. to L.X., Philadelphia, 13 March.]

. . . It is near a twelvemonth, since I was told, very seriously, that there was a communication between people in the different parts of the continent, to bring about a new revolution, at the expence of our liberties; and a number of circumstances were told to confirm it.–I confess, at that time, I disbelieved it; but, from what has since happened, I have altered my opinion. The precipitancy and violence which was used and attempted, in different parts of the continent, to fasten the new Constitution about our necks, before the people at large could know what was doing; the similarity of language and conduct, in different places at the same time, with the new and extraordinary appearance of *Mobs with powdered hair*, made me think seriously of what I had heard before. But, above all, when I reflect upon the attempts which are continually made, to prevent the communication of intelligence, between those who are not friends to the proposed Constitution *in toto*; or who wish for amendments; the stopping of newspapers, the breaking open of packets and destroying them, on the roads; the continual miscarriages of letters by every species of conveyance, if written by the friends of liberty, and which, I have no doubt, are intercepted by the conspirators and their tools:–in short, when I observe the same system of fraud, circumvention and violence, pervading most parts of the continent at once, I cannot ascribe it to accident; but to a preconcerted design amongst the chosen members of a conspiracy. . . .

1. For the complete text, see Mfm:Pa. 595.
2. See the *Pennsylvania Gazette*, 26 March (above).

Mentor
Petersburg Virginia Gazette, 3 April[1]

Messrs. HUNTER and PRENTIS, When we consider the peculiar advantages arising from a free, expeditious, and general communication of sentiments upon all subjects which concern the public weal, through the channel of newspapers–a channel through which the precious stream of political instruction is diffused, in governments like ours, more extensively than by any other method the wisdom and ingenuity of man hath as yet suggested; have we not reason to be grateful to the God of humanity and liberty, who hath placed us, after a long and painful struggle, in so eligible a situation, as to enable us to receive instruction from the ingenious and benevolent disquisitions of many of our fellow-citizens; which through the channel of a newspaper, and under the auspices of a free press, have gone forth as political missionaries, to inform the minds and enlarge the understandings of the bulk of the people, as to those leading and essential points which contain every thing dear to them as men and members of society? If these advantages are to be derived from a free circulation of knowledge among that class of men who most require it, what evil consequences may we not apprehend from a contrary conduct being persued? What have we not a right to expect will be the fate of our natural rights–and what new species of tyranny may we not experience, when any one individual, by virtue of, and under the authority of office, shall dare, under the eye too of our rulers, to check or suppress an institution so highly necessary and beneficial as that established even in the bondage of monarchy, for the conveyance of letters, newspapers, &c.? What must be our opinion of the merits of that system (if it be done to promote any particular one) which should require the adoption and exertion of such unwarrantable and injurious powers to support and establish it? What must we think of the regard of those in authority, who either encourage this unfriendly measure, or connive at its continuance, by not suppressing it? In short, are we not to think that our rights and liberties, our instruction and welfare, are no longer leading objects in the eyes of those we have set over us; and that they are sighing after the loaves and fishes of monarchy, when they shall permit any measure to be adopted and continued, which shall be pregnant with mischief to their constituents; or when they shall be so unmindful of their trust, as to suffer any man to exercise the powers of office, who shall have shewn himself the pliant agent for the basest of purposes?

I am led into this train of thought, Gentlemen, by having noticed for some time past, and in this most important of all periods to the citizens of America, the great difficulty of procuring intelligence from the northern and eastern states, respecting their debates and proceedings on that grand question which hath now become the object of anxious attention to every well-wisher of his country; and was not able to account for so unfortunate a circumstance as I then conceived it, until I observed the iniquitous mystery, in some degree, developed by a writer in a late Baltimore paper.[a]

In order that the suggestions of that writer may be corroborated or confuted by concurrent testimony, and as the present is a period too big with important consequences, to prevent any man from making every inquiry necessary to his welfare and happiness, I must request you to inform the public, through your very useful paper, in what manner the newspapers have been transmitted to you from that quarter of the United States–whether you have received them as regularly as the late rigorous season would permit?[2] If not, at what period did the regular conveyance of them cease? Happy shall I be to find that my apprehensions have been without foundation–but should they appear to be supported by melancholy fact, I shall lament the early departure of that noble, disinterested, independent spirit of republican virtue, which was once so dear to, and idolized by, the patriotic sons of Columbia!

(a) The mutual exchange of newspapers by the Printers on this continent, in the mail, was always exercised under the British government, and continued since the revolution, until a few weeks ago, when Ebenezer Hazard, Esq. Post-Master-General, *prohibited* the sending any newspapers in the mail. *See Maryland Journal, March* 18.[3]

⟨In compliance with the request of the author of the above, the Printers beg leave to inform the public, that since the beginning of January last, no newspapers have arrived to them from any of the Printers to the northward and eastward of Philadelphia; though previous to that time they came regularly to hand. The PETERSBURG INTELLIGENCER, is forwarded from this office to most of the Printers on the continent; but if the mode of conveyance by the mail is stopped, it is highly probable they are detained in some of the Post-Offices.⟩

1. "Mentor" was reprinted in the Philadelphia *Independent Gazetteer*, 18 April, and the Winchester *Virginia Gazette*, 23 April, under the dateline "From the Petersburgh Intelligencer." The *Gazette's* dateline also indicated that "Mentor" first appeared on 3 April. Since the *Virginia Gazette, and Petersburg Intelligencer* for 3 April is no longer extant, "Mentor" is transcribed from the *Independent Gazetteer*.

The editorial response to "Mentor" and the excerpt quoted from "Manco," *Maryland Journal*, 18 March, were reprinted only in the *Independent Gazetteer*. The Winchester *Virginia Gazette* had reprinted "Manco" on 2 April.

2. The winter of 1787–1788 was particularly severe. Arthur Lee, in Alexandria, Va., on his way to New York City, wrote on 19 February: "After waiting four days at Col. Masons, in hopes of a passage there over the [Potomac] river, I set forward for Georgetown & learn here that the passage is impracticable there. There is such an aggregation of Ice both there & here that nothing but a general thaw will enable me to cross, & the same thaw will render the roads almost impassable. . . . The ice keeps the northern Mail at Georgetown, so that there are no late Advices from the northward" (to Richard Henry Lee, Lee Family Papers, ViU).

3. See "Manco," *Maryland Journal*, 18 March (above).

Centinel XVIII
Philadelphia Independent Gazetteer, 9 April (excerpt)[1]

. . . Notwithstanding many thousand copies of the Reasons of Dissent of the minority of the late convention of this state were printed and forwarded in every direction, and by various conveyances, scarcely any of these got beyond the limits of this state, and most of them not until a long time after their publication. The printer of these Reasons, by particular desire, addressed a copy of them to every printer in the union, which he sent to the Post-office to be conveyed in the mail as usual, long before the *new arrangement*, as it is called, took place; and yet we since find that none of them reached the place of their destination. This is a full demonstration of the subserviency of the Post Office, and a striking evidence of the vigilance that has been exerted to suppress information. It is greatly to be regretted that the opposition in Massachusetts were denied the benefits of our discussion, that the unanswerable dissent of our minority did not reach Boston in time to influence the decision of the great question by their convention, as it would in all probability have enabled patriotism to triumph; not that I would derogate from the good sense and public spirit of that state, which I have no doubt would in common circumstances have shone with equal splendor, but this was far from being the case; the new constitution was viewed in Massachusetts through the medium of a SHAYS, the terrors of HIS insurrection had not subsided; a government that would have been execrated at another time was embraced by many as a refuge from anarchy, and thus liberty deformed by mad riot and dissention, lost her ablest advocates.

As the liberties of all the states in the union are struck at in common with those of Pennsylvania, by the conduct of the Post-Master General and deputies, I trust that the example which her Legislature[a] has set by instructing her delegates in Congress on this subject,[2] will be followed by the others, that with one accord they will hurl their vengeance on the venal instruments of ambition, who have presumed to prostrate one of the principal bulwarks of liberty. In a confederated government of such extent as the United States, the freest communication of sentiment and information should be maintained, as the liberties, happiness and welfare of the union depend upon a concert of counsels; the signals of alarm whenever ambition should rear its baneful head, ought to be uniform: without this communication between the members of the confederacy the freedom of the press, if it could be maintained in so severed a situation, would cease to be a security against the encroachments of tyranny. The truth of the foregoing position is strikingly illustrated on the present occasion; for want of this intercommunity of sentiment and information, the liberties of this country are brought to an awful crisis; ambition has made a great stride towards dominion; has succeeded thro' the medium of muzzled presses to delude a great body of the people in the other states, and threatens to overwhelm the enlightened opposition in this by *external* force. Here, indeed, notwithstanding every nerve was strained, by the conspirators, to muzzle or demolish every newspaper that allowed free discussion, two printers have asserted the independency of the press, whereby the arts of ambition have been detected, and the new system has been pourtrayed in its native villainy; its advocates have long since abandoned the field of argument, relinquished the unequal contest, and truth and patriotism reigns triumphant in this state; but the conspirators trust to their success in the other states for the attainment of their darling object, and therefore all their vigilance is exerted to prevent the infectious spirit of freedom and enlightened patriotism communicating to the rest of the union—all intercourse is as far as possible cut off. . . .

(a) *The application to Congress from our Legislature, was made upon the complaint of all the printers of newspapers in the city of Philadelphia.*

1. "Centinel" XVIII was also printed in the Philadelphia *Freeman's Journal* on 9 April and was reprinted in the *New York Journal*, 12 April. For the complete text, see CC:671. For the controversy over the circulation of the "Dissent of the Minority of the Pennsylvania Convention," see CC:353, pp. 10–11.

2. See "Petition of the Philadelphia Newspaper Printers to the Pennsylvania Assembly," 20–29 March (above).

Algernon
Philadelphia Independent Gazetteer, 10 April[1]

To Ebenezer Hazard, Esquire, Post-Master-General.

SIR, The important advantages resulting from the freedom of the press, and the unrestrained circulation of its papers, are known, felt, and admired in every free government: You are not, therefore, to be told, that to shackle the press is to enslave the people.

You, a servant of the people, have dared to curtail their rights, by stopping the ancient channel of communication–at a time too, when information is of the last importance; when the mind is to be exercised on a subject, the greatest that ever engrossed the public attention. In this you have violated the duties of your office, and arraigned the understanding of those gentlemen in Congress whose *misplaced* confidence drew you from *obscurity*, and gave you undeserved bread. How infatuated are some men! Had you suffered the *counter* to bound your ambition, and confined your pursuits to the *selling of books*,[2] you might have continued to this day unnoticed;–you might have shunned the scorn, and the execration of your fellow-citizens. It was a kind of *suicide* committed on your character (and a sad reflexion on the mistaken zeal of your friends!) to bolt into an office so unsuitable to your talents,–so foreign to your *visible* pretensions. A stranger to the education and manners of a gentleman, the candor of an ingenious mind, and the philanthropy of an honest heart, you stand a living monument (tho' not a single one) of the culpability of those we sometimes intrust. If you have virtues, they are of the negative kind only, and cannot recommend you.

Your conduct has roused my indignation–but, mark!–it is the indignation of thousands. The freemen of the United States are alarmed at the audacity of your attempt; and the offended dignity of the people cannot be appeased, but by your dismission from the trust you have so flagrantly abused. The public monies ought not to be lavished on the *worthless* and *undeserving.* America has many sons–many alas! too much neglected!–who deserve better of their country than either the present Post-Master-General, or a late Comptroller of Accounts,[3] whose ungracious demeanor in office became proverbial–and could only be palliated by a recurrence to his early *walks* in life, and the known propensity of his countrymen to *lord it, when in luck.*

But, softly,–my present business is with YOU. You have unkenneled yourself, and become *fair game*; do not blame me, then, for joining in the chace.

Your *justification* (pardon, Sir, a *misnomer*) now at the bar of the public,[4] far from acquitting only serves to *condemn* you. It is a pitiful evasion, yet a bold attempt: But, as it was, doubtless, intended to answer a better purpose, we are left to reflect on that matchless effrontery which betrayed you to *hazard* another imposition on a whole people. Though no man will ac-

cuse you of rashness in the field; all must applaud your spirit and enterprise out of it. Few–very few, besides yourself, would have ventured the
most unqualified assertions to establish *notorious falsehoods* as truth–Allow
me a question, or two–

Q. 1. How came you to exercise your discretion (or, rather, *indiscretion*)
upon an obsolete resolution of Congress, at this *peculiarly interesting crisis?*

Q. 2. Has not your assistant here,[5] *conformably to your instructions*, declared to several printers, That no newspapers would, in future, be forwarded by post, *unless paid for?*

Q. 3. By what evil genius, then, were you seduced to declare in the face
of the world, "That the Post-Master-General has given NO ORDERS OR
DIRECTIONS about them, either to the Post-Masters, or to the Riders?"

Oh shame! where is thy sting!

Philadelphia, April 7th, 1788.

1. Reprinted: *Newport Mercury*, 28 April; Hartford *American Mercury*, 28 April.
2. Before the Revolution, Hazard was first an employee of and then a partner with
Garrat Noel, a New York City bookseller.
3. James Milligan served as comptroller of the treasury from 13 October 1781 until 1
November 1787 when the office was abolished. On 12 March "A Friend to the People"
referred to Milligan as one of Robert Morris' "creatures" (Philadelphia *Freeman's Journal*, Mfm:Pa. 511). Three days later, "Z" asserted that Milligan "was always unbiassed
in his office by any motives, but those of duty and of justice" and was "of irreproacha-
ble character" (*Independent Gazetteer*, Mfm:Pa. 529).
4. For Hazard's defense of himself, see *New York Journal*, 21 March (above).
5. James Bryson, postmaster of Philadelphia.

New Hampshire Spy, 11 April

Received by this day's mail *one Philadelphia paper!–When will miracles
cease?*

Ebenezer Hazard to Jeremy Belknap
New York, 12 April[1]

The enclosed is just recd. from Philadelphia; & that it may not be delayed I write though it is Saturday Night & I am wearied by the Labors of
the Week.–

Have you seen any of the Attacks upon me about News Papers?–Oswald & Bailey (the antifederal Printers in Phila.) & Oswald's Echo
(Greenleaf) in this City have been pelting me at a most unmerciful Rate.
I have not condescended to reply to any of them, except in one Instance,
when I was *first* attacked *by name*, & Oswald avowed himself to be the
Writer:[2] a Copy of what I then published you have enclosed, & may make
what use you please of it. Their subsequent Publications have been little
more than Repetitions of their former Assertions (which are fully replied
to in the enclosed) with a tolerable Addition of Scurrility–The whole arises
from a Design in the Antifederalists in Phila. to prevent the Adoption of

the new Constitution by the States which have not yet met in Convention:
at least, this is my Opinion:–to effect this they pretend that News Papers
containing antifederal Pieces have not been allowed to circulate, while others have been forwarded with Eagerness, & by this they design to raise
Tumults among the People. But they will find all their Art insufficient to
prevent the Adoption of the new Constitution, or I am much mistaken.–
However, they will stop at nothing:–though their Champion, the Centinel, has been more than once detected in Falsehoods, he writes on without
a Blush.–I have given you these hints that if you hear the Matter talked
of, you may be able to talk about it: but don't let it be known that you
have any thing upon the Subject *from me.*–

1. RC, Belknap Papers, MHi.
2. For Oswald's attack on Hazard, see Philadelphia *Independent Gazetteer,* 12 March,
and for Hazard's defense, see *New York Journal,* 21 March (both above).

The Circulation of the Massachusetts Legislature's Answer to Governor John Hancock's Speech Philadelphia Independent Gazetteer, 15–28 April[1]

A Correspondent, 15 April[2]

Mr. Hazard, the Post-Master-General, observes a correspondent, still
continues the practice of suppressing all useful information, and spreading
delusion and falsehood. Not a single newspaper that contains essays or
intelligence against the new system of slavery, but what is quashed or
purloined in the Post-office at New-York, while those papers which may
with the strictest truth be called the vehicles of despotism, pass from place
to place unmolested. A gentleman from New-York, continues our correspondent, saw in the newspapers of that place, the answer of the General
Court (or House of Representatives) of the Commonwealth of Massachusetts, to Governor *Hancock's* speech, in which they absolutely, in the most
pointed terms, disapprove, and reprobate the proceedings of the Convention (general as well as state). This intelligence reached New-York; but,
altho' Mr. Hazard, in the fulness of his majesty, took care to allow us the
perusal of Mr. Hancock's fine speech, to which the other was an answer,
determined it should travel no farther southward. The conduct of the Post-
Masters under the British government, when they attempted to enslave
us, was sometimes arbitrary and oppressive, but they never exercised the
horrid tyranny which Mr. Hazard has attempted to set up. May Mr. Hazard, his abettors, tools, and retainers, experience, at least, a similar fate to
that of their predecessors, though their enormities demand a much severer
expiation!

A Bostonian, 16 April[3]

Mr. OSWALD, I have this moment seen a paragraph in your paper of
this day, asserting that "A gentleman from New-York, saw in the newspapers of *that* place, the answer of the General Court (or House of Repre-

sentatives) of the Commonwealth of Massachusetts, to Governor *Hancock's* speech, in which they absolutely, in the most pointed terms, disapprove, and reprobate the proceedings of the Convention (general as well as state).

That this gentleman may have seen this, or any other erroneous information in a New-York paper, I can very easily believe. But that the legislature of Massachusetts, ever did as a body reprobate the proceedings of the *general and state convention*; I certainly never can believe, unless it be produced by authority from their own journals.

I am well acquainted with the political sentiments of my native state, and from this knowledge I am persuaded that there is a respectable majority in favor of the new federal constitution in point of *number*, that the majority is far more respectable in point of *independent men*, and that men of large landed property are almost unanimous in the question. That there are some respectable and independent men of great abilities and integrity opposed to it, I am free to allow; but where on earth is a political institution to be found that has not been theoretically disapproved, before the practice had pointed out theoretical errors? In this instance, it is remarkable, that what the general convention have produced as *a system of practice*, formed by four months consideration of the various passions, interests and situations of the people to be governed, is opposed upon general theoretical principles which would as well apply to the old eastern world, as they do to this new western hemisphere.

But to return to the point. I shall consider it a favor personally rendered to me, if you will write to your correspondent printer in New-York (who no doubt keeps a file of papers) for the very paper alluded to, and give us in your Gazetteer the full amount of this reprobation, cloathed with all the authority that it is capable of. If this does not appear in course, you will permit me to suppose that you are misinformed, and in the mean time I presume that the public will suspend their opinion.

I am your most obedient servant,

P.S. I do not pretend to judge of the charges against the Post Master General; but if you apprehend the desired paper cannot be obtained by that conveyance, please to order it by the stage.

Philadelphia, April 15, 1788.

Eleazer Oswald's Editorial Statement, 16 April[4]

Under the fullest conviction that no reliance or dependence can be placed on the present capricious and despotic *Post-Master-General*, the author of the above may rest assured that the printer of the Gazetteer hath already sent to New-York for the paper in question, by the very mode pointed out; and that as soon as he shall be able to obtain it, the answer of the legislature of Massachusetts to governor Hancock, shall be faithfully inserted in this paper.

Eleazer Oswald's Editorial Statement, 28 April

We have at length procured the New-York Journal of the 24th March last (but not through the medium of Mr. Post-Master's *opposum-*) to which one of our correspondents had reference in our paper of the 16th instant, and now take the earliest opportunity of laying before our readers,[5] all that have reached us on the subject of the reply of the General Court of Massachusetts to Governor Hancock's late spech. The irregularity of our communications must be solely ascribed to the Post-Master General, who is still permitted to exercise the most execrable tyranny over the Printers, and to sport with the sacred liberties of the people.

1. For Governor Hancock's speech and the reply of the Massachusetts House of Representatives, see CC:566.

2. Reprinted: Philadelphia *Freeman's Journal*, 16 April; Baltimore *Maryland Gazette*, 22 April; Winchester *Virginia Gazette*, 14 May. The copy of the *Independent Gazetteer* at the Library of Congress contains this marginal note: "See the *Bostonian* in next Paper."

3. "A Bostonian" was perhaps Jonathan Williams, Jr. (CC:566, 608).

4. This editorial comment was printed in brackets immediately below "A Bostonian."

5. See CC:566-C. For the meaning of the term "Mr. Postmaster's *opposum*," see "A True Federalist," *New York Journal*, 26 March (above).

A Friend to the People
Philadelphia Freeman's Journal, 16 April[1]

When the advocates of despotic power found their efforts to shackle the press unsuccessful in many of the States, their next step was as much as possible to cut off all communication of sentiment, and to prevent any publications developing the mysteries and dangers of their plan from going out of one State into another, and also to cut off all real intelligence; all this was effectually performed by means of the Post-Office, which for several months past has stopped and destroyed every newspaper which contained any real intelligence or patriotic publications, while those papers containing sophistical delusion, deception and falsehood were propagated through the continent with industry. It is remarkable that the same conduct was observed by Post Officers under the British government, when *foreign* tyrants endeavoured to enslave America.

The groundless assertions and paltry evasions which make up the *publication* of Ebenezer Hazard (that appeared last week)[2] can only be equalled by the enormity of the crime of which he stands charged:–And as the Legislature of this State has taken the subject up so warmly, and have instructed our delegates in Congress to enquire into the business,[3] it is to be hoped that Congress will take such measures, that in the event Mr. E. Hazard will meet with his deserts, for rendering an office established for the general welfare of the people an instrument of tyranny.

2d *April.*

1. Reprinted: Philadelphia *Independent Gazetteer*, 17 April.
2. For Hazard's defense of himself, see the *New York Journal*, 21 March (above).
3. See "Petition of the Philadelphia Newspaper Printers to the Pennsylvania Assembly," 20–29 March (above).

Samuel A. Otis to George Thatcher
New York, 19 April (excerpt)[1]

. . . I think Hazzard is in a bad box. The fœderalists frown upon him for being anti. The opposers of fœderalism charge him hard with stoping the papers, & "muzzling the press" to facilitate the purposes of despotism–I hope they will not oust him, but a little shaking will put him right: The offircers of Congress will receive no injury by *shaking*. . . .

1. RC, Dreer Collection, PHi. A longer excerpt is published in LMCC, VIII, 716–17.

Philadelphia Independent Gazetteer, 21 April[1]

The *Post-Office*, observes a correspondent, is considered of manifest and universal advantage. It has not merely commercial intercourses in view, but at the same time comprehends the free and unreserved communication of every kind of foreign and domestic intelligence.

Of very extensive importance indeed is the circulation of *newspapers*, whereby we are made acquainted with the particular transactions and measures of the different states in the union; and, not like men duped or hoodwinked, we are enabled to form our own sentiments, and regulate our conduct accordingly.

Every attempt to impede the communication of intelligence is highly injurious to the common welfare, and should be reprobated by every lover of his country, as an invasion of his most capital privileges. And the complaints with which almost every paper in America is impregnated, respecting the Post-Master General having suspended the newspapers in their circulation through his office, loudly call for general and earnest attention.

It is a pleasing consolation however, that the several Printers here, with an animation and spirit which does them honor, have formally represented to the assembly their grievous situation, in order that the same may be redressed upon application to congress, under whose direct controul *Master Post-man* is most unquestionably.[2]

Yet it seems extraordinary, that the Printers should be reduced to this disagreeable situation, or allow themselves to be the tame, passive subjects of the Post-Master's caprice and oppression. It would appear almost incredible, did not the truth stand uncontroverted, that any American, holding so advantageous a station as the Post-Office, should conceive himself such an unlimited sovereign and demi-god in office, that he would of his own accord, abrogate the former customs of the country, and prevent the Printers from receiving their papers as heretofore. No matter what motives have contributed to this execrable event; whether motives of faction, motives of selfishness, or motives of lordly tyranny, the Post-Master-General stands alike under every view of things, and deserves general detestation for his arbitrary, overbearing conduct.

Circumstances frequently alter the consideration and aspect of cases–and there are seasons when the audacious steps taken by the present Post-Master *Hazard*, would be less excuseable than at this highly interesting period, when popular curiosity, and popular anxiety, are so equally awakened, and all that is dear to our country seems brought to the very stake. Such unbridled insolence was never exercised in *England* from the time of *Edmund Prideaux*, the first Post-Master, downwards–And lamentable it confessedly is, that it was reserved for Mr. *Hazard* alone to introduce the first scenery in *America*.

In England the Post-Office was originally conducted by some individuals, who confined themselves to the furnishing Post-Horses to persons who were desirous to travel expeditiously, and to the dispatching of extraordinary pacquets upon special occasions. But many inconveniencies flowed for want of a regular establishment, as many rival, independent offices only serve to ruin one another; and Mr. Prideaux, the Attorney-General to the Commonwealth, after the death of Charles the first, it is said planned the outlines of the first Post-Office, and both Houses of Parliament in due form established the office upon his system. A variety of statutes subsequent to the revolution added further regulations to the plan, which prove it was viewed by the Grand Council of the nation as their favorite offspring. Among other regulations and amendments, letters to Members of Parliament, &c. are acquitted of postage, and newspapers in particular are expressly directed to be carried free.

If the Post-Office in England is under this happy tutelage, what anxiety ought not Congress to display upon the representation of our own legislature in favor of the free carriage of newspapers in the mail? They ought to interpose with maternal feelings, and as soon as possible dismiss the Post-Master-General, or convince him that he has no manner of right to trample upon our old privileges, which time and ancient usage have dignified beyond expression.

1. Reprinted: Boston *American Herald*, 19 May.
2. See "Petition of the Philadelphia Newspaper Printers to the Pennsylvania Assembly," 20–29 March (above).

Philadelphia Independent Gazetteer, 6 May[1]

Extract of a letter from Boston, of a late date, to the Printer.

"Certainly it is a melancholly consideration, that a general stagnation of public information, southward of us, has, for some months past, taken place. Were our country invested with a military enemy, spiritedly engaged in intercepting all communications, perhaps, it could not be more so. European intelligence we receive of a later date than American occurrences, not 200 miles from us, or from some parts of the United States. The error here is of so singular a nature, as to excite the astonishment of the most considerable characters among us, and sufficiently produces a general alarm. A remedy we have been informed was in contemplation; if effected, you will be so obliging as to favor us with your paper as heretofore."

1. Reprinted: Philadelphia *Freeman's Journal*, 7 May; *New York Journal*, 12 May; Winchester *Virginia Gazette*, 21 May (excerpt). The *Virginia Gazette* omitted the last sentence.

Confederation Congress: Report of Committee on the Post Office, 7 May[1]

Whereas difficulties have been lately experienced by the several printers in the exchange of their papers by post and doubts have arisen how far they have the right of making such exchange free from postage, therefore Resolved,

That, in order to promote the circulation of useful intelligence the printers of newspapers throughout these states, be allowed to exchange their papers with each other by means of the public mail without any charge of postage–Provided always that no newspaper shall be suffered to pass in the mail unless it shall be thoroughly dry & the wrapper left open at one end so that it may be clearly seen how many newspapers & other publications & whether any letters, are contained therein; and if it shall appear upon examination that any letters are concealed under such wrapper, the full rate of postage shall be charged not only on such letter, but also on the other contents of the wrapper–

1. MS, PCC, Item 61, Letters and Papers of Richard Bache and Ebenezer Hazard, Postmasters General, 1777–88, and Reports of Committees of Congress on the Post Office, 1776–88, pp. 567–68, DNA. This report was docketed: "No. 36–/Report of Comte on post Office/for printers exchanging/their papers with each other/by the mail.–/Entd. read May 7. 1788." Congress read the report on 7 May, but apparently took no further action. The report was probably drafted by a committee that was appointed on 20 February and reappointed on 27 March. The latter committee consisted of Jonathan Dayton, Jeremiah Wadsworth, Nathan Dane, John Brown, and Thomas Tudor Tucker (JCC, XXXIV, 52n, 116n, 144n. For the membership of the earlier committee, see John Eager Howard to Jeremiah Wadsworth, c. 24 March, above.).

Massachusetts Centinel, 7 May[1]

STOPPAGE *of* NEWSPAPERS.

The torrent of abuse which hath been poured fourth in the antifederal papers, published in New-York and Philadelphia–and in some others, whose Editors were misinformed, intended to injure the reputation of Mr. Hazard, as Post-Master-General, and as a man, is as undeservedly bestowed, as it is without measure.

We were *the first* to mention, and to deplore, the frequent *miscarriages* of the *newspapers*, which we supposed were directed to us from the other States[2]–We made *inquiry* into the *cause* of this miscarriage; and the result has convinced us, that it was *not* owing to any mal-conduct in the Post-Master-General; but might be imputed partly to the neglect of the Print-ers–and more to the peculation of the persons who carry the mails on horseback, between Hartford and New-York–who, we are confidently told, do not scruple to break the bundles, and take from, and sell, the newspa-pers directed to Printers. These Mail-Carriers, therefore, and the Printers, are alone blameable.–The former, we are told, will not long be continued in employ–the latter, we trust, will remedy their part of the evil. However a radical cure will not be effected until the mails are again carried in the Stages, as during the time they carried them, no cause of complaint ex-isted.

What then, it will be inquired, has occasioned the invective against the Post-Master-General, in the papers? It may be replied–to answer a politi-cal purpose. Drowning men catch at *any thing* to keep their heads above water–So when argument has failed, those who experience the failure, will also catch at any thing to keep contention alive:–We have, therefore, seen in the antifederal papers, the most unfounded charges against the Post-Master-General, (who is esteemed a federalist) of *intentionally stopping* the circulation of *"antifederal papers"*–while the writers in those papers, which are conducted on the broad plan of impartiality, have patiently waited for *evidence* of the culpability of the persons suspected.

Among the instances of mal-conduct in the officers of the Post-office, set forth by the antifederal writers–the stoppage of the papers, containing the *"Reasons of Dissent of the Minority of the Convention of Pennsylvania,"* has been the principal: These writers have not scrupled to assert, that the said *"Rea-sons, &c."* were not, in consequence of this malversation, received in this town, until after the adoption of the Constitution by our Convention–and that after they were received, they had *a most wonderful effect*, in turning people against the federal plan.–The Printers in this town know this to be a falshood–and it is their duty to undeceive the publick (if, in fact, any were deceived) respecting it. The Printer of this paper, assures his readers that he received *three* copies of these "Reasons," by one mail, and within *ten* days after they were signed at Philadelphia–one in Messrs. *Dunlap* & *Claypoole*'s paper; another in Mr. *Bailey*'s, and a third printed separately by Col. *Oswald*: Other Printers, we suppose, received as many.[3]

The other charges of *partial stoppages*, made by these writers (which, by the by, are all laid at Mr. Hazard's door) are alike ill-founded–and they will answer no other purpose, than serving to convince the unconvinced part of the world, of the baseness of that cause, to support which its advo-cates are obliged to resort to misrepresentations, and to falshoods.

1. Reprinted: *Newport Mercury*, 19 May (only first two paragraphs); New York *Daily Advertiser*, 20 May; New York *Independent Journal*, 21 May; Philadelphia *Freeman's Jour-nal*, 28 May; *Pennsylvania Mercury*, 29 May.

2. See *Massachusetts Centinel*, 16 February (above).
3. For the debate over the reprinting of the "Dissent of the Minority of the Pennsylvania Convention" in Boston, see CC:353, p. 11.

Ebenezer Hazard to Jeremy Belknap
New York, 10 May (excerpt)[1]

. . . The virulent Pieces against me were generally written by Oswald the Printer of the Independent Gazetteer published at Phila.–*he* wrote that in which my *deigning* was mentioned:[2]–he was then in this City. I do not think R.H.L.[3] had any thing to do with them. I suppose you are no Stranger to Oswald's Character: if you are, you may get some accurate Information from the enclosed Pamphlet, which I wish you to return when you have done with it.[4] The enclosed Part of an original Letter, which I have lately recd. relates to him: I wish you to have it printed in one of your Papers if you can have it done without the Printer's knowing any Person concerned in it. So far as I learn from different Quarters Oswald's publications against the Department have had no Effect:–they are *generally* "regarded as the overflowings of antifederal" Gall, and as Attempts to injure the new Constitution:–as the hopes of the Party fail, the Attacks upon me become less frequent:–they have had so little effect upon C— that they have not directed any Enquiry to be made:–two or three individual members have called merely for their own Satisfaction, & received it compleatly; for I shewed them a Certificate from the Contractor for carrying the Mail between this Place & Phila. that he called upon the Printers in both Cities (before he began to ride) & offered to carry their Exchange Papers *gratis*:–another from a man he employs, certifying that he did it in *his* Presence; & another from the Philada. Printers themselves (Oswald was out of town then, but his Foreman's Name is among them) certifying that during the Time the *Centinel* said the Papers were withheld (while the Pennsa. Convention were sitting) they were recd. as regularly as at other Times.[5]–I shewed them too from the Acts of the British Parliament that, even in England, News Papers are not considered as a Part of the Mail, but that the Privilege of *franking* them is expressly reserved to the Clerks in the Post-Office as their Perquisite:–All this might have appeared in the *News Papers* for my Vindication, but I thought any thing more than the Piece I sent you was unnecessary.[6]–It is a just Remark I have heard made by Dr. Witherspoon, that "false Reports will *die* much sooner than they can *be killed*"; & this too had weight with me.–I felt too that my Character was too well established to be injured by such Attacks made by such Adversaries, & I knew that the Attacks could not be directed against any Point in which I was less vulnerable. For these Reasons I have not published any thing except the "succinct state of facts," nor shall I "deign" to publish any thing more upon the same Subject, unless new Reasons may occur, of which I am at present ignorant.–I had it in Contemplation to *prosecute* Oswald in Pennsa. but friends, whom I consulted, dissuaded me from it, alledging that he was going down hill very fast, & that a prosecution would support him.–The Veracity of (I suppose *himself*) one of his Correspondents has lately been disproved by "a Bostonian."[7] It was asserted that a Gentn. from New York had seen in the Papers of that Place *an answer from the Genl Court* of Massa. to the Govrs. Speech, in which they pointedly & in express terms reprobated the Proceedings of the Convention, "both general & state."–The "Bostonian" disbelieved it & called upon Oswald to write to his correspondent Printer in N. York for the Paper, & then to publish *the Answer*;–which he did;–& it turns out to be nothing more than an Extract of *a Letter from Boston* dated March *19*th. & published in Greenleaf's Paper in this City the *24*th.–which the Bostonian has taken proper notice of.–March 19th. was *Wednesday*, & the 24th. *Monday*:–qus. how did that Letter reach N. York so as to appear there in Print by 8 O Clock A.M. on Monday 24th.–It could not have arrived by *Post* before the 26th.–The *Stage* left Boston on Thursday the 20th.–arrived at Hartford in the Evg. of Saturday 22d. & does not travel on Sunday, & the Letter could not have come from Hartford hither (130 miles) on *Monday* before 8 O Clock A.M.–There was no Arrival from *Rhode Island*, except one Vessel which left *Newport* the *19*th.–the Day the Letter is dated at Boston.– So much for Antifederal Veracity! I believe the Letter was wrote here.–

I have mentioned Greenleaf:–he is *our* antifederal Printer;–a poor thick-sculled Creature, & so much in debt to Oswald for his printing Office, as not to dare to offend him:[8] I suspect this made him antifederal:–*he* has got into a Scrape too; but as the Story is too long for me to tell I will *lend* you the Papers:–return them when you have read them:[9]–in short, the poor Antifeds. seem to have got almost to "the length of their Tether," as Govr. Hutchinson said.–The Maryland Majority has staggered them very much:–So. Carolina will repeat the Blow, & I think Virginia will give them the *Coup de Grace*. We cannot tell how our Election has gone in this State, as the Ballots will not be opened & counted before the latter end of this month:[10]–I think it doubtful whether Feds. or Antis. will be most numerous in Convention, though I have little doubt that they will adopt the Constitution:–it is probable that some may propose to have the Breeches altered before they try them on; but I fancy the majority will be for wearing them as they are. I believe F.H. wrote the Piece about the Breeches.[11] . . .

1. RC, Belknap Papers, MHi. Printed: "Belknap-Hazard Correspondence," 35–38.

2. "A True Federalist," *New York Journal*, 25 March (above).

3. Richard Henry Lee.

4. Probably Mathew Carey's *The Plagi-Scurriliad: A Hudibrastic Poem. Dedicated to Col. Eleazer Oswald* (Philadelphia, 1786) (Evans 19540). On 7 April Hazard wrote Carey that "I have never had an Opportunity of seeing the Plagi-Scurrilliad til very lately, when a typographical friend, finding that the Hero of that Poem had *bejuniused* me, put it into my hands. Whether the Introductory Remarks of Gulliverus, the Recommendations of Scribblerus Quartus, the Approbation of the Secretaries, or my own ~~Opinion~~ Feelings

prejudiced me in its Favor, I will not pretend to say, but I wish to own the Poem, & to add it to my Farrago of Pamphlets. Can you favor me with a Copy, under an Assurance that I will never let it be known from whence I recd. it; if you can you will much oblige" (Lea and Febiger Papers, PHi).

5. See "Centinel" IX and XIV, Philadelphia *Independent Gazetteer*, 8 January, 5 February (above).

6. For Hazard's defense of himself, see the *New York Journal*, 21 March (above). Hazard had sent a copy of his defense to Belknap on 12 April (above).

7. See "The Circulation of the Massachusetts Legislature's Answer to Governor John Hancock's Speech," Philadelphia *Independent Gazetteer*, 15–28 April (above) and CC:566.

8. Beginning in 1785 Greenleaf managed the *New York Journal* under Oswald's direction, and in January 1787 he purchased the newspaper from its owner, Elizabeth Holt (CC:Vol. 1, xxxv, xxxvii).

9. On 29 April Greenleaf printed twenty special copies of his *Journal* that differed in one respect from his regular issue of the day. At the request of Thomas Wooldridge, a former British merchant now living in New York City, Greenleaf inserted an announcement that Wooldridge had been appointed British vice consul for New England. All twenty special copies of the *Journal* were sold to Wooldridge, who had been recently released from debtors' prison. Suspicions arose almost immediately about the authenticity of the announcement, and on 2 May Greenleaf explained his action in the *Journal*. The next day two items in the New York *Daily Advertiser* challenged Greenleaf's explanation and denounced him for his complicity with Wooldridge in printing a fraudulent announcement. Greenleaf defended his actions and attacked the printer of the *Advertiser* for trying to destroy his "credit and reputation" (*New York Journal*, 5 May). On 6 May the *Advertiser* printed a deposition given by George Knox before state Supreme Court Chief Justice Richard Morris that challenged much of Greenleaf's defense. Knox confronted Greenleaf about the announcement on 30 April, the day after it was printed. All in all, the incident was "the town-talk for several days" and, according to the *Advertiser*, Greenleaf's actions "excited general indignation."

10. The election of New York Convention delegates took place between 29 April and 3 May. The election law of February 1787 and the resolutions calling the state convention provided, however, that the ballot boxes were not to be opened until the last Tuesday in May, i.e., the 27th. The results then had to be officially reported within two weeks.

11. A reference to a widely reprinted allegorical essay by "Peter Prejudice" that was first printed in the Philadelphia *Federal Gazette* on 15 April (CC:685). Hazard believed that the author was Francis Hopkinson, but the reprint in the June issue of the Philadelphia *American Museum* identified the author as John Mifflin, Esquire.

Ebenezer Hazard to Jeremy Belknap
New York, 17 May (excerpts)[1]

I thank you for the Centinel enclosed in yours of 11th. Inst.–Russel has acted like a candid man, and you will oblige me by thanking him for doing *me* so much Justice.[2] He has rightly accounted for all the *Philadelphian* Abuse of me, & *that* gave Rise to all which issued from more distant Presses.–It was natural enough for Printers in distant Parts of the Union to suppose, if their Papers came irregularly, that it was owing to some unfriendly Regulation in the Post Office, especially when it was asserted by a brother Printer near the *Head Quarters* of the Union; but what surprizes me is that the Printers did not see the *Improbability* of the Charge brought against the P.M.G. which was that he prohibited the Circulation of News Papers containing *antifederal* Pieces while he promoted that of those which contained *federal*.-to do this he must of Course examine *all the Papers* that were published, which would fully occupy all his Time, & put it out of his Power to do any part of his proper Business:-a moment's Reflection must have shewn them that the Charge was false:-& had they attended to this Circumstance, that General Washington, Dr. Franklin, & others of our most respectable Characters, to whom the Union is under the greatest Obligations, were abused by the same Writers, at the same Time, & for the same Cause (i.e. being Federalists) they could have had no doubt about the *Reason* why the Charge was made.-To blackguard *me* in such Company was really doing me honor, though it was done unintentionally. I suspect Mr. Russel has been misinformed about the Mail Carriers between this City & Hartford:-from the Character of the Contractor, as well as some personal Knowledge of him, I do not believe he would be concerned in, or permit, such Conduct as is alledged; however, though this is a matter with which I have no Business, properly speaking, yet as Mr Russel has behaved so much like a Gentleman with Respect to me, I will enquire of the Contractor about it when I can see him. But I believe the most of the News Papers are sent by Stage, as Greenleaf (one of our Printers) informed the Public some time ago that his were sent in that way.[3] Russel is wrong if he supposes the Stages, *generally* will do to carry the Mail:-in Point of Case they might do to the Eastward of this City, & had the Proprietors asked a reasonable Price they would have got it; but they demanded 3014^{66}%$_9$ Dolls. & I have it done now for 1790 by men who are at every Expence on Accot. of the Mail, whereas the Proprietors of the Stages would be at no extra Expence on that Account. For this Reason the *Eastern* Stages lost the Mail. Between this City & Phila. Stages *cannot* carry the Mail so expeditiously as Riders, for these travel Night & Day:-besides, the Drivers were so careless, & inattentive to the Mail that I had a vast many Complaints from Passengers among whom were some members of Congs.-indeed even the Passengers & Baggage were so much neglected, that the Proprietors lost Custom by it, & have since acknowledged it in the News Papers, & promised Amendment. But enough of this-I give you the Information merely that you may be able to *talk* upon these Subjects, should you hear them mentioned in Conversation.-I must add, that it was while the *Stages* carried the Mail that the "Centinel" complained in the Phila. Papers that "the Conspirators" prevented the circulation of antifedl. Papers by means of the Post Office.[4] . . .

Well, as I told you, the Phila. Printers Petition is circulating:-it was published here today:[5]-Russel's Publication will be a good Reply to it, & I suppose *some* of our Printers will have Grace enough to give it a Place. His so plumply denying the Assertion that "the Reasons &c." did not reach Boston til your Convention had determined upon the Constitution, will mortify the Antifeds. in Phila. not a little; & I think the Feds. will crow upon it. . . .

1. RC, Belknap Papers, MHi. Printed: "Belknap-Hazard Correspondence," 43–45.

2. See *Massachusetts Centinel*, 7 May (above). This item was reprinted in the New York *Daily Advertiser* on 20 May and the New York *Independent Journal* on 21 May.

3. See *New York Journal*, 10 March (above).

4. See "Centinel" IX and XIV, Philadelphia *Independent Gazetteer*, 8 January and 5 February (above).

5. See "Petition of the Philadelphia Newspaper Printers to the Pennsylvania Assembly," 20–29 March (above). The petition and excerpts from the Assembly's Minutes were reprinted in the *New York Journal* and the New York *Daily Advertiser* on 17 May.

Salem Mercury, 27 May[1]

The PUBLISHERS hereof to their BRETHREN at the Southward.

☞ *Strange* as it may appear, nevertheless it is *true*, that the Printers of the *Salem Mercury* receive *few*–VERY FEW–publick newspapers from the Southward, except those obtained through private channels–NONE from Baltimore, NONE from Philadelphia, the *Independent Gazetteer* excepted, NONE AT ALL from New-York, notwithstanding the papers from this Office are invariably sent on, and known to be received. The evil complained of, is not a contracted one, its influence extends to our brethren, in general, in New-England; and is of so *dark* a complexion as may well give birth to alarming apprehensions. A respectable character, however, in office, in the city of New-York, in a letter to the Printers hereof, observes, "Every newspaper sent to this office, to be forwarded, I have sent off with the mails.–What I have received have been generally done up in so wretched a manner, that I am sure they never can go any distance in the mail, without being all loose, so as not to know what place they are for. I think if the newspapers were done up, well dryed, with a good cover, and tyed, they would not miscarry, as the complaint now is." Where then, think ye, lurks the evil? Devoutly is it wished, that our Southern brethren would probe the affair, and find it–anxiously investigate the cause of so *dangerous* an impediment.

1. Reprinted: *New York Journal*, 5 June; *Pennsylvania Packet*, 11 June.

George Washington to John Jay
Mount Vernon, 18 July (excerpt)[1]

. . . While we are awaiting the result [of the New York Convention] with the greatest anxiety our Printers are not so fortunate as to obtain any Papers from the Eastward.–Mine, which have generally been more regular, have, however, frequently been interrupted for sometime past.–

It is extremely to be lamented that a new arrangement in the Post Office, unfavorable to the circulation of intelligence, should have taken place at the instant when the momentous question of a general government was to come before the People.–I have seen no good apology, not even in Mr. Hazard's publication,[2] for deviating from the old custom of permitting Printers to exchange their Papers by the Mail.–That practice was a great public convenience & gratification.–If the priviledge was not from convention an original right, it had from prescription strong pretensions for continuance; especially at so interesting a period.–The interruption in that mode of conveyance, has not only given great concern to the friends of the Constitution, who wished the public to be possessed of every thing that might be printed on both sides of the question: but it has afforded its enemies very plausible pretexts for dealing out their scandals, & exciting jealousies by inducing a belief that the suppression of intelligence at that critical juncture, was a wicked trick of policy, contrived by an Aristocratic Junto.–Now, if the Postmaster General (with whose character I am unacquainted & therefore would not be understood to form an unfavorable opinion of his motives) has any candid advisers who conceive that he merits the public employment they ought to counsel him to wipe away the aspersion he has incautiously brought upon a good cause–if he is unworthy of the Office he holds, it would be well that the ground of a complaint, apparently so general, should be enquired into, and, if founded, redressed through the medium of a better appointment.–It is a matter, in my judgment, of primary importance that the public mind should be relieved from inquietude on this subject.–I know it is said that the irregularity or defect has happened accidentally, in consequence of the contract for transporting the Mail on horseback, instead of having it carried in the *Stages*–but I must confess, I could never account, upon any satisfactory principles, for the inveterate enmity with which the Post Master General is asserted to be actuated against that valuable institution.–It has often been understood by wise politicians and enlightened patriots that giving a facility to the means of travelling for Strangers and of intercourse for Citizens, was an object of Legislative concern & a circumstance highly beneficial to any Country.–In England, I am told, they consider the Mail Coaches as a great modern improvement in their Post-Office regulations.–I trust we are not too old, or too proud to profit by the experience of others.–In this article the Materials are amply within our reach.–I am taught to imagine that the horses, the vehicles, and the accomodations in America (with very little encouragement) might in a short period become as good as the same articles are to be found in any Country of Europe–and, at the same time, I am sorry to learn that the line of Stages is at present interrupted in some parts of New England and totally discontinued at the Southward.–

I mention these suggestions only as my particular thoughts on an Establishment, which I had conceived to be of great importance–Your proximity to the person in question & connection with the characters in power, will enable you to decide better than I can on the validity of the allegations; and in that case, to weigh the expediency of dropping such hints as may serve to give satisfaction to the Public. . . .

1. RC, John Jay-Iselin Collection, NNC. Printed: Henry P. Johnston, ed., *The Correspondence and Public Papers of John Jay* . . . (New York and London, 1890–1893), III, 349–51.

2. For Hazard's defense, see the *New York Journal*, 21 March (above).

APPENDIX III

This table illustrates the circulation of all items in Volume 4 of *Commentaries on the Constitution* that were published in newspapers or as broadsides or pamphlets. The total figure for each item includes the original publication and all reprints, including the reprints of significant excerpts. An asterisk (*) indicates publication in the Philadelphia *American Museum*, which had a national circulation. A plus sign (+) indicates publication as a broadside, pamphlet, or book.

This table is included in *Commentaries* as an aid in comparing reprint data. Headnotes and footnotes of documents often contain additional information about circulation and should also be consulted.

		New Hampshire	Massachusetts	Rhode Island	Connecticut	New York	New Jersey	Pennsylvania	Delaware	Maryland	Virginia	North Carolina	South Carolina	Georgia	Vermont	Total
492.	Publius															
	The Federalist 48					4+										4
493.	Genuine Information X		1			1		3+	1							6
495.	Publius															
	The Federalist 49					4+										4
498.	Civis					1		2*		1	2		2+			8
500.	Publius															
	The Federalist 50					4+										4
501.	Centinel XIV		1			1		2								4
502.	Genuine Information XI					1		3+	1							5
503.	Publius															
	The Federalist 51					4+										4
504.	"A.B."	2	3	1	2	2		4*		1	2		1	1		19
505.	A Freeman III							4*	1							5
506.	An Old Whig VIII							1								1
507.	Philadelphiensis IX							2								2
508.	Mass. Amendments															
	Mass. Centinel	1	9	3	5	5	1	6		1	2					33
	Mass. Gazette	1	7	4	1	3		6*		3			1		1	27
510.	Brutus XII					1										1
511.	Lloyd's Debates+							1+								1
514.	Publius															
	The Federalist 52					3+										3

No.	Title	New Hampshire	Massachusetts	Rhode Island	Connecticut	New York	New Jersey	Pennsylvania	Delaware	Maryland	Virginia	North Carolina	South Carolina	Georgia	Vermont	Total
515.	Philadelphia Independent Gazetteer		1			2	1									4
516.	Genuine Information XII		1			1		3+		1						6
519.	Publius The Federalist 53					3+										3
523.	Charleston City Gazette				4	2	1	2		1			1			11
524.	Publius The Federalist 54					3+										3
525.	Publius The Federalist 55					3+										3
526.	A Citizen of the United States	1	3		1	3		1		1						10
529A.	New Haven Gazette	2	9	2	3	6	2	7		1	2			1		35
529B.	A Real Patriot		1	1		1	1									4
530.	Brutus XII (con't.)					1										1
533.	Publius The Federalist 56					3+										3
534.	Spurious Centinel XV	1	3	2	4	1		2		1	2			1		17
542.	Publius The Federalist 57					3+										3
546.	Publius The Federalist 58					3+										3
547.	Philadelphiensis X							2								2
548.	Marcus I											1	2+			3
551.	Brutus XIII					1										1
552.	A Yankee	2	6	3	5	2	1	2			1	4	2	2	2	32
553.	The New Litany	1	2		2	1		2			3	1	2	1	2	17
554B.	Mass. Centinel		4		5	3	1	4			1					18
555.	Publius The Federalist 59					3+										3
556.	Centinel XV					2		3								5
557.	Adams, *Defence*	1	7	1	2	1	1	2			2			1		18
558.	Publius The Federalist 60					3+										3
559.	Albany Federal Herald					5	1	1		1						8
560.	Hugh Williamson's Speech					1		2*						1		4
564.	Publius The Federalist 61					3+										3
565.	Centinel XVI					1		2								3

	New Hampshire	Massachusetts	Rhode Island	Connecticut	New York	New Jersey	Pennsylvania	Delaware	Maryland	Virginia	North Carolina	South Carolina	Georgia	Vermont	Total
566A. John Hancock's Speech	2	11	2	4	5		6*		1	3	1	1			36
566C. New York Journal		1			1		2		2	1					7
569. Publius The Federalist 62					3+										3
570. Bowdoin to de Caledonia		2			1		1								4
571. Marcus II										1	2+				3
576. Brutus XIV		1			1										2
577. Arraignment of Centinel					1		1								2
580. Md. Landholder X		1	1				2		1						5
581. A Columbian Patriot+		1+			1+		2								4
582. Publius The Federalist 63					3+										3
588. Landholder X	4	6		4	1							1			16
592A. Publius The Federalist 64					3+										3
593. Philadelphia Freeman's Journal		1	2		3		2								8
594. Pa. Gazette	1	1			2	1	2			1					8
595. "A.B.C."	1	2					1								4
596. Marcus III										1	2+				3
598. Brutus XIV (con't.)					1										1
601. Publius The Federalist 65					3+										3
602. Philadelphia Independent Gazetteer					4	1	2		2	2					11
603. Philadelphia Independent Gazetteer			1	1	2		1								5
604. Luther Martin						1	1		1						3
607. Publius The Federalist 66					3+										3
608A. Fabrick of Freedom (verse)						1	1			1		1	1		5
608B. Fabrick of Freedom (music)							1								1
609. Philadelphiensis XI							1								1
611. Landholder XI	3	3	3												9
612. Publius The Federalist 67					3+										3
614. Philadelphia Freeman's Journal		1			1		1								3

	New Hampshire	Massachusetts	Rhode Island	Connecticut	New York	New Jersey	Pennsylvania	Delaware	Maryland	Virginia	North Carolina	South Carolina	Georgia	Vermont	Total
615. Publius The Federalist 68					3+										3
616. Marcus IV										1	2+				3
617. Publius The Federalist 69					3+										3
619. Publius The Federalist 70					3+										3
622. Landholder XII	2	5	3	3	2	1	5*								21
624. Poughkeepsie Country Journal		1		1	2		1					1			6
625. Publius The Federalist 71					3+										3
626. Luther Martin Address No. I		2				1	2	1							6
627. Mass. Centinel	1	5	2	3	3	2	5		1	2		2			26
628. Publius The Federalist 72					3+										3
629. Va. Independent Chronicle (all)		3		3	3	1	4			1		1			16
(1st paragraph)	4	6	3	4	3	1	4			1		1			27
(2nd paragraph)	4	5	3	3	3	1	4			1		1			25
(3rd paragraph)	3	6	3	4	3	1	4			1		1			26
(4th paragraph)	1	3		3	3	1	4			1		1			17
630. Marcus V										1	2+				3
632. Brutus XV		1	1		1										3
633. Publicola											2+				2
634. Gazette of the State of Ga.		1											1		2
635. Publius The Federalist 73					3+										3
636. Luther Martin Address No. II							3	1							4
638A. Mass. Centinel	3	8	3	9	6	2	10		1	3		1	2	2	50
639A. N.Y. Independent Journal					2					2					4
639B. Publius The Federalist Preface+					1+										1
641. Landholder XIII	3	2	1	5											11
642. Centinel XVII									2						2
643. Salem Mercury	3	3	2	2	1		3			1		1			16
644. Publius The Federalist 74					3+										3
646. Publius The Federalist 75					3+										3

	New Hampshire	Massachusetts	Rhode Island	Connecticut	New York	New Jersey	Pennsylvania	Delaware	Maryland	Virginia	North Carolina	South Carolina	Georgia	Vermont	Total
647. Pa. Gazette															
(7 March letter)		1			2		4								7
(12 March letter)							4			1					5
648. Publicola (con't.)											2+				2
649. James Iredell															
Address	1	3	1		3		3					1			12
650. Luther Martin															
Address No. III									1						1
APPENDIX I: SQUIBS															
N.Y. Packet															
1 February					2	1	4		1					1	9
N.Y. Daily Advertiser															
2 February					3	2	4		1						10
False Reports on N.C.															
Mass. Gazette															
5 February		2	1	1		1									5
Mass. Centinel															
6 February	3	4	1	3										1	12
Newport Herald															
14 February	5	9	2		1		1								18
N.Y. Journal															
14 February		1			3	1	2								7
N.H. Mercury															
20 February	2														2
Pa. Gazette															
5 March			1			1	2								4
N.Y. Daily Advertiser															
5 February	2	6	2	5	4	1	5		1	2			1		29
N.Y. Journal															
5 February	1	1	1		1										4
N.Y. Packet															
5 February					3		4		2	1					10
Essex Journal															
6 February	1	1	1												3
Independent Chronicle															
7 February	2	5	3	3											13
Newport Herald															
7 February	2	2	1	2	1	1	3		2	2			1	1	18
N.Y. Journal															
7 February					1	1	4		1	1					8
N.Y. Journal															
7 February					3	1	1								5
Pa. Herald															
7 February	1	1					2		1	1					6

	New Hampshire	Massachusetts	Rhode Island	Connecticut	New York	New Jersey	Pennsylvania	Delaware	Maryland	Virginia	North Carolina	South Carolina	Georgia	Vermont	Total
N.Y. Daily Advertiser															
8 February					3	1	5			3					12
Pa. Mercury															
9 February	1	1		1			1			2					6
Conn. Courant															
11 February	3	1	2	3			1								10
N.Y. Daily Advertiser															
11 February					2		2	1							5
Hampshire Chronicle															
13 February	1	2			2		3					1		2	11
Mass. Centinel															
13 February	1	7	2	1											11
Freeman's Journal															
13 February	1	3			2	1	3		2	1					13
New Haven Gazette															
14 February	2	4		1	2		4					1			14
Newport Herald															
14 February	3	4	2		2	2	3								16
N.Y. Packet															
15 February	2	8	2	6	3		3							2	26
Independent Journal															
16 February					1		2		1	1	1				6
(last paragraph alone)							1		1	2					4
Accounts from England															
Pa. Packet															
18 February	2	4	2		2	1	3		1	1			1		17
Freeman's Journal															
20 February	1	2	2		2		3		1	1					12
Independent Gazetteer															
21 February		1	2		2		1								6
Pa. Gazette															
27 February			1		1		1			2			1		6
Mass. Centinel															
1 March	1	2			3		3		1	3				1	14
City Gazette															
22 March									1	1			2		4
Mass. Gazette															
19 February		2			3	2	3								10
Mass. Centinel															
20 February (all)	1	2	1	1	1		2		1						9
(1st paragraph)	1	2	2	4	4	2	4		1	1			1		22
(2nd paragraph)	4	3	2	2	1		2		1	1			1		17
(3rd paragraph)	3	3	1	2	2	2	3		1					1	18
Freeman's Journal															
20 February		1			1		2		1						5

	New Hampshire	Massachusetts	Rhode Island	Connecticut	New York	New Jersey	Pennsylvania	Delaware	Maryland	Virginia	North Carolina	South Carolina	Georgia	Vermont	Total
Pa. Gazette															
20 February (all)							1								1
(1st paragraph)	3	6	2				1		2	1	1			1	17
(2nd paragraph)					1	2	5								8
(3rd paragraph)					1	1	1		1						4
(4th paragraph)			1		1	1	1		2						6
(5th paragraph)	3	5			1	1	2		2	1					15
(6th paragraph)	3	1	1	1	1	1	1		2	1					12
Newport Herald															
21 February	1	1	1		1		2			1					7
Reports of S.C.															
Newport Herald															
21 February	1	1	1												3
Mass. Centinel															
23 February	1	1					3			2					7
Boston Gazette															
25 February		2	1		1		2		1						7
Pa. Mercury															
21 February		8	1	1	1	1	1			1		1			15
Middlesex Gazette															
25 February	2	5	3	4	1		1								16
Salem Mercury															
26 February	4	1		1	2		4		1	3		1	1		18
Independent Gazetteer															
26 February					1		1			1					3
Pa. Mercury															
26 February		3	2	1	3		1								10
Independent Gazetteer															
27 February	1	3	1				1		1	1					8
Pa. Gazette															
27 February		3	1	5	1		4			3		1			18
Pa. Gazette															
27 February	1	3	1		2		3			1					11
Pa. Mercury															
28 February		2	1		3		1			1					8
N.Y. Packet															
29 February	2	2			2	1	3		1	1					12
Providence Gazette															
1 March			2	4	2	1	5		1	1					16
N.Y. Morning Post															
3 March (both)					1	1	3		1	1					7
(1st letter)					1	1	4		1	1			1		9
(2nd letter)					4	1	5		2	2			1		15
N.Y. Journal															
3 March			3	4			7		1	1			1	2	19

	New Hampshire	Massachusetts	Rhode Island	Connecticut	New York	New Jersey	Pennsylvania	Delaware	Maryland	Virginia	North Carolina	South Carolina	Georgia	Vermont	Total
Independent Gazetteer 3 March		1			1		1		1	1					5
Independent Gazetteer 4 March	3	5	1		2		1		1	3					16
U.S. Chronicle 6 March	3	5	1	1			2								12
Independent Gazetteer 7 March	1	1					1		1						4
Mass. Centinel 8 March (all)		3					1								4
(1st paragraph)	2	6			1	2	4		2			1		1	19
(2nd paragraph)	1	3		1	2	1	3		1			1			13
(3rd paragraph)	4	6		2	5	1	4		1	3				2	28
(4th paragraph)	2	4		3	2		4		1	5					21
Federal Gazette 8 March		2	1		1		1							1	6
Country Journal 11 March	3	2			2	2									9
Mass. Centinel 12 March	1	4												1	6
Pa. Gazette 12 March (all)					2		1								3
(1st paragraph)	3	3	2	1	5		3		1	2					20
(2nd paragraph)					3		1			1		1			6
(3rd paragraph)					2		1			2		1			6
(4th paragraph)	1	1	1	2	2		1					1			9
Independent Gazetteer 14 March		1	1		2		1								5
Mass. Centinel 15 March		4	3	6	2	1	3		1					1	21
Mass. Centinel 19 March		5	1	2	1							1			10
Pa. Gazette 19 March (both)						1	2		1	1		1			6
(1st paragraph)		1		1	2	1	4		1	1		1			12
(2nd paragraph)					1		2		1	3		2			9
N.Y. Daily Advertiser 25 March	1	2	2	2	2		2						1		12
Mass. Centinel 26 March		1					1		2	2					6
Pa. Gazette 26 March (both)		1		2			2								5
(1st paragraph)	1	4	1	2	2		4			2			2		18
(2nd paragraph)		1		2			2						1		6

APPENDIX II: MAILS

	New Hampshire	Massachusetts	Rhode Island	Connecticut	New York	New Jersey	Pennsylvania	Delaware	Maryland	Virginia	North Carolina	South Carolina	Georgia	Vermont	Total
Centinel IX															
8 January					2+		3								5
N.Y. Journal															
10 January					1	1									2
Centinel XI															
16 January					1		2								3
Freeman's Journal															
16 January					1	2	2					1			6
Providence Gazette															
19 January			1												1
Brunswick Gazette															
22 January						1									1
Genuine Information															
Pa. Packet															
22 January							1								1
Pa. Herald															
23 January							1								1
Pa. Packet															
1 February							1								1
Independent Gazetteer															
9 February							1								1
N.Y. Journal															
18 February					1										1
Freeman's Journal															
27 February							1								1
N.Y. Journal															
8 April					1										1
N.Y. Journal															
23 January					1										1
"M"															
26 January	1				1		2								4
Boston Gazette															
28 January	1														1
Brunswick Gazette															
29 January						1									1
N.J. Journal															
30 January						1									1
Centinel XIII															
30 January	1				1		2								4
Philo Centinel															
31 January							2								2
Centinel XIV															
5 February	1				1		2								4

	New Hampshire	Massachusetts	Rhode Island	Connecticut	New York	New Jersey	Pennsylvania	Delaware	Maryland	Virginia	North Carolina	South Carolina	Georgia	Vermont	Total
Norfolk and Portsmouth Journal 6 February										1					1
Albany Gazette 7 February					1										1
Independent Gazetteer 8 February		1			2		1								4
Mass. Centinel 16 February	2	5	2	1	3	2	5		1	1					22
Centinel XV 22 February					2		3								5
Bowdoin to de Caledonia 27 February		2			1		1								4
Md. Journal 29 February (both)					1	1			1	1					4
(1st paragraph)	2	2		2	1	1			1	1		1			11
(2nd paragraph)					3	1	4		1	1					10
Original letters 5 March			1				1								2
Greenleaf's Statement 10 March		1			1										2
Md. Journal 11 March		1			1		2		1	1					6
Eleazer Oswald 12 March	1				1		1								3
de Caledonia to Bowdoin 12 March							2								2
Manco 18 March										2	1				3
N.H. Spy 18 March	1				1		3								5
Philadelphia Newspaper Petition Petition – Gazetteer		1			2		3						2		8
Petition – Pa. Packet	1	3	1	3	1		2								11
Freeman's Journal 2 April	1	1				1	2			2	3		1		11
N.Y. Journal 20 March					1										1
Mass. Gazette 21 March	1	2			1		3								7
Ebenezer Hazard's Defense, 21 March	1	2	2	2	2		6			2	1		1		19
A True Federalist 25 March	1	1			1		1								4

	New Hampshire	Massachusetts	Rhode Island	Connecticut	New York	New Jersey	Pennsylvania	Delaware	Maryland	Virginia	North Carolina	South Carolina	Georgia	Vermont	Total
Watchman															
26 March		2			1		1								4
Bryan Letters															
26 March		1			3		4								8
Winchester Va. Gazette															
The Editors, 26 March		1			1		1			1					4
A Federalist, 2 April										1					1
The Editors, 2 April										1					1
One of the People, 9 April										1					1
The Editors, 9 April										1					1
N.H. Spy															
28 March	2				1	1	1								5
A Friend to Law															
and Order, 2 April							1								1
Centinel XVIII															
9 April					1		2								3
Algernon															
10 April			1	1			1								3
N.H. Spy															
11 April	1														1
Mass. Legislature's															
Answer to Governor															
A Correspondent															
15 April							2			1	1				4
A Bostonian															
16 April							1								1
Eleazer Oswald															
16 April							1								1
Eleazer Oswald															
28 April							1								1
A Friend to the People															
16 April							2								2
Independent Gazetteer															
21 April		1					1								2
Independent Gazetteer															
6 May					1		2				1				4
Mass. Centinel															
7 May		1	1		2		2								6
Salem Mercury															
27 May		1			1		1								3

Index

An asterisk denotes a signer of the Constitution. Several main entries are compilations of similar items: Biblical References; Broadsides, Pamphlets, and Books; Classical Antiquity; Governments, Ancient and Modern; Newspapers; Political and Legal Writers and Writings; Printers and Booksellers; and Pseudonyms. The pseudonymous items printed in this volume and in earlier volumes of *Commentaries on the Constitution* are also indexed separately. When a pseudonym has been identified, the name of the author has been placed in parentheses. Biographical information in earlier volumes of *Commentaries* is indicated by a volume and page reference placed in parentheses immediately after the name of the person. Sketches of newspapers printed in Volume 1 of *Commentaries* have been placed in parentheses immediately following the name of the newspaper.

"A.B." (Francis Hopkinson), 47–48

ADAMS, ABIGAIL (Mass.; CC:Vol. 2, 462n)
—letter from: quoted, 191n

ADAMS, JOHN (Mass.; CC:Vol. 1, 81n), 239, 242n; supports Constitution, 519, 520
—letters from, 481; quoted, 191n, 520n; cited, 255
—letters to, 255; cited, 255, 255n
—*Defence of the Constitutions*, 191n–92n, 192, 213, 239, 255, 504, 521n; text of, 192–95

ADAMS, JOHN QUINCY (Mass.; CC:Vol. 2, 220n)
—letter to: quoted, 62n
—diary of: quoted, 179n–80n, 192n

ADAMS, SAMUEL (Mass.; CC:Vol. 1, 325n): and Mass. amendments to Constitution, 67n; and opposition to Constitution, 116, 150, 289n; as president of Mass. Senate, 228n
—letters to: quoted, 64n, 66n, 540n
—speech in Mass. Convention: quoted, 63n

ADAMS AND NOURSE (Mass.)
—letter from, 551n–52n
See also Newspapers, Massachusetts *Independent Chronicle*

ADMIRALTY JURISDICTION: *See* Judiciary, U.S.

AGRICULTURE, 197–98, 278, 473, 473–74; importance of, 131, 197; Constitution will prohibit agrarian laws, 190, 361. *See also* Farmers

ALBANY, N.Y.: Federalists and Federalist literature in, 65n, 308, 467n, 468n, 515; Antifederalist literature in, 66n, 274n, 550, 551n; Assembly representation of, 148–49
—Antifederal committee letter from: quoted, 274n

ALEXANDER, ALEXANDER JOHN (England): id., 506n
—letter to, 506

ALEXANDRIA, VA., 300n

"ALGERNON," 582–83

ALIENS, 301n

ALLEN, ANDREW (England; CC:Vol. 1, 360n)
—letters from: quoted, 123; cited, 122

ALLIN, THOMAS (Va.): id., 262n; 263

ALSOP, JOHN (N.Y.)
—letters to: quoted, 273n, 274n

AMBASSADORS, 255–56, 391

AMENDMENTS TO ARTICLES OF CONFEDERATION, 373–74, 374n; population amendment of 1783, 15n, 110n–11n; unanimity of states needed to obtain, 89–90; need for, 105; states refuse to pass out of jealousy, 272n. *See also* Articles of Confederation; Constitutional Convention; Impost; Ratification, procedure for

AMENDMENTS TO CONSTITUTION, 472; praise of Constitution's provision for, 27, 71, 117, 128, 195, 301, 438, 493n; should be adopted before Constitution is ratified, 52–56, 61n–62n, 65n–66n, 96, 102, 116, 212, 283–84, 331, 365–66, 434, 438, 486n, 499–500, 501, 501–2, 530; criticism of Constitution's provision for, 53, 55–56, 320; opposition to, 61n–62n, 287, 504n; should be adopted after establishment of new

vored, 352; congressional resolution of 28 Sept. 1787, 438–39; dangerous if nine states with less than a majority of the people should ratify, 488; debate over sanctions against non-ratifying states after establishment of new government, 495. *See also* Amendments to Constitution; Convention, second constitutional; Conventions, state

RATIFICATION, PROSPECTS FOR: favorable, 20n, 71, 82, 83n, 104, 105, 117, 136, 138, 139–40, 142, 143–44, 149, 151–52, 171, 185, 192n, 209–10, 229, 231, 264, 300, 302, 308, 335n, 395, 465, 481, 487n, 495, 504, 506, 518, 533, 537, 583–84, 592; doubtful, 64n, 180n–81n, 182n, 190–91, 223n, 304, 375, 394–95, 471, 478, 486n, 487–88, 530; harm done by closeness of Mass. Convention ratification vote, 160; uncertainty of, 403. *See also* Amendments to Constitution; Entries for individual states

READ, JAMES (N.C.): id., 309n; 308
READ, JAMES (Pa.), 31n
"A REAL PATRIOT," 118–19
RECALL, 114
REID, JAMES R. (Pa.; CC:Vol. 3, 374n), 566n
REID, JOHN (N.Y.), 175n
RELIGION, 225–26, 392, 473, 517; debate over Constitution's prohibition of a religious test for officeholding, 84, 89, 93n, 145, 260; debate over role of God in writing and ratifying Constitution, 94–95, 171, 350; God calls George Washington to be first President of U.S., 149; debate over Constitution's lack of provision protecting freedom of, 211, 240, 252, 254, 254n, 279, 419, 456, 504; Constitution will support, 409, 410; diminished influence of under Confederation, 410; importance of free press to, 561n, 573, 578–79. *See also* Baptists; Biblical references; Bill of rights; Clergy; Mohammed; Quakers

REPRESENTATION, 86; differs in two houses of Congress, 12; argument that geographic sections are represented equitably under Constitution, 23–24, 67n; debate over adequacy of in Congress under Constitution, 66n, 160–61; in House of Representatives, 68,

107–10, 120n, 131, 147–48, 164, 166, 168, 272n, 281; equality of is basis of free government, 278, 295–96; debate in Constitutional Convention over, 415–16, 418–19, 420n, 500, 509n, 509–10. *See also* House of Representatives, U.S.; Population; Senate, U.S.; Taxation; Three-fifths clause

REPRIEVES: *See* Pardons and reprieves
REPUBLICAN FORM OF GOVERNMENT, 83, 106, 138, 145, 147, 193, 222n, 276, 288, 321, 322, 377, 412–13, 504; debate over danger of despotism under, 4–5, 26; people are source of power in, 16–17; tends to aggrandize legislative branch of government, 18, 44–45, 413, 448; cannot exist over a vast territory, 35–36, 40, 282, 373, 481; can exist over a vast territory, 46–47, 49, 294; presupposes good qualities in human nature, 114–15, 194, 234; debate over Constitution's guarantee of to states, 253, 280; Constitutional Convention creates only image of, 277–78, 284; need for strong executive in, 396–402; need for balanced government under, 520

REQUISITIONS, 395; system of should be used under Constitution, 34, 50–51, 66n, 68, 137–38, 267, 271n; failure of states to pay under Confederation, 67n, 127, 137–38, 205, 206–7, 220, 221, 364, 375, 441, 475, 476; argument that it is not an effective system for raising revenue, 67n, 206–7; amounts paid by states under Confederation, 206–7, 209n, 220, 364, 366n, 375n, 395n; debate in Constitutional Convention over use of coercion to collect, 419, 420

RESERVED POWERS: debate over need for amendment to Constitution guaranteeing to states, 65n, 66n, 66n–67n, 67n, 68, 137–38, 202–3, 204, 290n, 443. *See also* Necessary and proper clause; States, impact of Constitution upon

REVOLUTION, RIGHT OF, 196, 199, 420. *See also* Social compact

RHODE ISLAND, 25, 287, 495, 537; influence of Mass. on, 20, 82; prospects for ratification in, 72n, 180n–81n, 341, 367, 408, 462, 471, 487, 504, 533; delegates to Congress from, 81, 533; leg-